The Great Vedic Tales

The Great Vedic Tales

P. Narahari, IAS & Prathviraj Singh

Published by
PRABHAT PAPERBACKS
An imprint of Prabhat Prakashan Pvt. Ltd.
4/19 Asaf Ali Road,
New Delhi-110002 (INDIA)
e-mail: prabhatbooks@gmail.com

ISBN 978-93-5521-361-7
THE GREAT VEDIC TALES
by P. Narahari, IAS & Prathviraj Singh

Edition
First, 2022

Price
₹ 250.00 (Rupees Two Hundred Fifty only)

Printed at
R-Tech Offset Printers, Delhi

This book is dedicated to all the Raag-Yogis, sung & unsung who devoted their life to serve Naad-Brahma (God in form of music) without any greed of glory or fame.

—P. Narahari IAS & Prathviraj Singh

Blessings Letter

6th March, 2022

Swami Avdheshanand Giri
Junapithadheeshwar Acharya Mahamandaleshwar

Dear P. Narahari Ji & Prathviraj Singh Ji,

Delighted and thrilled to read your book 'The Great Vedic Tales'.

The eternal Vedic culture of India is eternally integrated with nature and is constantly evolving. It is contemporary in every context. But in the world where material pleasure is paramount society remains unfamiliar with the cultural divinity of Vedic values. However attempts have been made but the western approach to see and understand Vedic values is inadequate, the priorities of western philosophers, historians or scientists are focused only on materialistic or sense-borne pleasures, while the fundamental basis of Indian thought is spiritual happiness or transcendental thinking.

I am very happy to know that just like their first book 'The Great Tale of Hinduism' in this book too, the authors have diminished the difference between religion and science and a Vedic yogi and scientist. And definitely to do so they have presented the Vedic concepts of reality and existence in a most reasonable and ascertainable manner. Like its first part this book too not only resolves the misinformation or misconceptions related to Indian history, tradition, culture, science but at the same time it also advocates for their continuance and universality.

While being specific to the topics propounded in the book, the section about *Naadbrahma* that discusses the divinity of music is the most impressive one. Where the authors have expounded the Vedic conception of the supreme creator in the form of sound the eternal hum also called *Anhad-naad*. Further this section dwells on the evolution of music from the eternal hum to music and music into meditation.

The second section talks about the relevance of Sanskrit even in modern times. Here to establish their point the authors have presented some of the most exquisite poetries of Sanskrit to demonstrate the poetic prowess of Sanskrit scholars of ancient India. The later part of the section about Sanskrit introduces its readers to ancient Sanskrit scholars and grammarians, who are not known to many otherwise.

The chapter about the Vedic conception of time will definitely wonderstruck the reader who is fascinated by this concept of relativity of time. Reading of this section also makes us realize that our very own scriptures are the storehouse of wisdom that we are searching outward.

The chapters about Vedic astrology and astronomy is a must read section for those who are yet to discover science in these two streams of Vedic knowledge or who think that it is nothing but science of mumbo jumbo. Through the illustration of Ramayana authors have shown the pervasiveness of astrology through all the sections of ancient Indian society. And other illustrations show how much information is coded in the Puranic tales.

The last chapter about truth and its significance in Sanatan Dharma was the best way to wrap up this beautiful document. This book not only gives an epoch-making discussion of Vedic wisdom but also seems to be successful in resolving the confusion spread in the context of Sanatan-Vedic Hinduism and Indian way of life. I extend my best wishes to both of you on the publication of this wonderful book.

(Swami Avdheshanand Giri Ji Maharaj)

Authors' Guide to Read this Book

Dear reader,

Namaste! 

"I bow to the divine in you"

Every writer is the creator of his own universe that he draws on paper through words and imagination. Which justifies some of his deviations from the conventional rules of writing. Likewise there are some rules of reading too and the first of which says that you must read any book sequentially, chapter by chapter, cover to cover. However in this book you can take some liberty to and pick up some random chapters as long as you adhere to the order of sections. This book is divided into 5 sections and 9 chapters, where the first 3 chapters are about *Naadbrahma* or classical Indian music. Chapter number 4&5 talks about the relevance of Sanskrit in modern times. Chapter 6 is about the Vedic concept of 'Kaala' (time). Chapter 7&8 deals with Vedic astronomy and astrology respectively.

The 9th chapter is the conclusion of all the ideas presented in this book. Hence however there is no compulsion of going sequentially but in order to enjoy the book to its fullest you need to read it section by section.

In this book there are some terminologies which also require some explanation so that the percept of authors' and reader synchronize to its best. For example the reader must be able to distinguish between the terms *Vedic-kaal* or Vedic traditions and *Puranic-kaal* or Puranic traditions. Where *Vedic-kaal* is the time when all four Vedas were prevailing and Puranas are yet manifest in Hindu Society. Primarily in *Vedic-kaal* the transmission of knowledge was happening through direct sermons or sometimes a debate or simple conversation between two *rishis*.

Whereas in Puranic tradition the transmission of religious ideas and ethos are happening through the stories and tales. For better clarity you also can see the *Satyug* and early Kretayug as *Vedic-kaal* and the later part of *Kretayug* till present as *Puranic-kaal*.

A similar concept stands for Vedic *rishis* and Vedic music, where the *rishi* are who either have contributed directly in Vedas and mentioned in any of four Vedas; or the *rishis* who spent their life endorsing Vedas are Vedic *rishi* and the *rishis* of *Puranic-kaal* are mentioned as maharishi or *rishi*. At the same time music in *Vedic-kaal* was very crude where chanting Vedic hymns or chanting of Aum was considered as practicing music.

One more concept our reader should know before embarking this trail of Vedic description of music, language, time and the universe. As we know that in the last couple of decades some authentic research and discoveries like Sinauli busted the myths of Aryan Invasion Theory and history of India shifted back a few more thousand years. Which means the conventional division of Indian history doesn't fit in the timeline anymore. The conventional division done by Indologists or the Western historians describes 80% of ancient history of India as the history of uncivilized hunters and gatherers and only the last part that begins with Alexander's advance towards India recognised the beginning of kingdom and civilisation in India; around Maurya Empire. Similarly the Medieval age is the age of Muslim rulers and the modern history is the age English colonization and dominance.

But now with some recent discoveries that pushes back the history of civilization and kingdoms in India thousands of years ago and therefore a new demarcation should be introduced for better understanding. However we leave this task for trained historians and for our convenience we divided Hindu history in *Vedic-kaal*, *Puranic-kaal*, pre-medieval (the age of Maurya's and Gupta's), Medieval and Modern.

One more thing that might catch your attention is the use of italics for some names and terms and not for some others should also be clarified. We believe that though not English terms still anyone who has Interest in India traditions will be having enough acquaintance with terms like Ram, Krishna Vedas, Vedic, Yoga, Buddha, Dharma, Karma, Ayurveda, Ramayana, Mahabharata and few more in the book. Hence we never bother to use italic font for these terms, however all other Sanskrit or Hindi names of *rishis* are mentioned in italics.

Lastly, to eliminate confusion between Brahma and *Brahman* we must clarify that Brahma is the creator god of the well known Hindu trinity of Brahma, Vishnu and Shiva. Whereas *Brahman* in italics is the supreme soul, the formless, omnipresent supreme energy from whom even the trinity draws their authority and power.

With all aforementioned expositions we hope you enjoy reading this book!

Contents

Naad Brahma

कामस्तदग्रे समवर्तताधि मनसो रेत:प्रथमं यदासीत्।
सतो बन्धुमसति निरविन्दन्हृदि प्रतीष्या कवयो मनीषा॥ ४॥

In the beginning desire descended on it that was the primal seed, born of the mind. The sages who have searched their hearts with wisdom
Know that which is, is kin to that which is not.

(The Nāsadīya Sūkta also known as the Hymn of Creation is the 129th hymn of the 10th mandala of the Rigveda (10:129).

Let there be light

Genesis 1:3, Bible

Kun Faya Kun
'Be! And it has occurred!

(In several verses of the Qur'an)

Any thoughtful mind that can think beyond survival,

if he takes a look at the magical wonders of creation around him, the huge oceans, lofty mountains, waterfalls, twinkling stars, the cycle of giant spheres that appears and disappears systematically to heat up and cool down the world; he must have thought or became curious to know, who has created this wonder. Who made creatures breathe on oxygen and who made oxygen heavier than other gases of the atmosphere, to be near the surface, where actually life happens? How come every essentials of life are readily available and everything harmful is beyond reach in nature. All these wonders signify that life on this planet or may be on other planets is not just an accident; there is some divine will behind this magic because a series of so many beautiful accidents or coincidences are also no less than a magic. But why did this magic happen? What was his/her purpose with this creation? Why did the cosmic force give this extraordinary intelligence to humans? Is it just for better survival? No way! Or is there any purpose God wants to fulfil through human lives? All these inexorable questions certainly have boggled the human mind for a long period of time, until they got some satisfactory answers to these riddles. And definitely whichever set of wisdom has answered these complex yet unpreventable questions, it must have become their religion.

Every great religion of the world has described the very beginning of the creation in its own way and so has the Sanatana Dharma. But there are few elements that distinguish the envisioning of creation in Sanatana Dharma from other religions. Many Vedic hymns and rishis see the creation and the destruction as a cyclic and unending process. At the same time, where other religions see the very beginning with manifestation of matter and light at the wish of the Supreme God, Sanatana Dharma not only sees a third mandatory element i.e. sound or the eternal music but it went on to describes the form of the Supreme Creator not in any other matter or element but in the form of music and revered him as *Naad Brahma*.

Today, we have many versions of the theory of creation; some are religious and some non-religious. Most of them describe the beginning of this universe with an explosion. In scientific terms, we call it 'Big Bang'. In many religious books like in the Bible or Quran, the beginning of the creation is described as the will or when the almighty wished it to happen. The wish of almighty manifested with the manifestation of light or fire at the very beginning. It can be seen related to the most accepted scientific theory of modern times, 'The Big Bang Theory' where everything began with an explosion in an infinitely dense particle. And very reasonably no one can imagine any explosion without a bang sound. In Sanatana Dharma, this sound gradually evolves to become music and the basis of creation. However, deference for music is there in every religion but in Sanatana Dharma, music has a very special place which is no less than God itself. In many Vedic hymns, Vedic rishis described the form of God as the eternal 'humm' that permeates in the entire creation. In the Vedas, it is called AUM, *Pranav* or *Anhad Naad*. Eventually the *Anhad Naad*, the eternal music,

AUM, is accepted as the form of God not just in Sanatana Dharma but in all religions originated on the Indian land.

ओमित्येतदक्षरमिदँ सर्वं तस्योपव्याख्यानं भूतं भवद्भविष्यदिति सर्वमोङ्कार एव।
यच्चान्यत्त्रिकालातीतं तदप्योङ्कार एव॥

"OM is this imperishable Word, OM is the Universe, and this is the exposition of OM. The past, the present and the future, all that was, all that is, all that will be, is OM. Likewise all else that may exist beyond the bounds of Time, that too is OM[1]*"*

When Vedic rishis discovered the presence of God in music, they had to find ways to align human consciousness with God through music. The musical rituals they developed to worship god is distinctly mentioned in the Samaveda, one of the four the Vedas which is dedicated to music and dance. The Samaveda, popularly known as the storehouse of knowledge of chants, is also the oldest surviving book in the world that contains melodies with musical notations.

Vedic rishis found the way to worship the God, who they saw in the form of music and called it *Naad-Brahma*. They immersed themselves into nature with utmost concentration of mind and came up with the most blissful way of devotion and called it *Raga-yoga*. Every *Raga* is derived from the rhythmic dance of nature; flowing of wind, chirping of birds, rustle of leaves and

---

1. (Web credits: https://satyameva.org/om-the-imperishable-word-2/)

in every movement of nature. In this process of finding music in every subtle act of nature, perhaps they could hear something that is inaudible to human ears otherwise. Vedic rishis described one such music of the cyclical rise and setting of the Sun and Moon as 'the music of spheres'. Isn't it astonishing that they derived music out of many natural phenomena that can sensitise or enlighten the soul and spirit of the person who immersed him/herself into it. For any person with ordinary consciousness, it is hard to hear or even believe that there is sound or music involved in growing or setting of plants, burning of fire, in eclipse or we can say in every movement of nature where production, destruction or transmission of energy is taking place. However only an utterly conscious mind can discover music in all of these subtle acts of nature. And that being the reason, the Vedic music has all the cycles and rhythms of the physiology. Anyone can by aligning his/her consciousness with the supreme consciousness, can find resemblance between Vedic music and biological functioning of the human body. There is a subtle connection between the biological functions like hormonal secretion, metabolism, cardiac rhythms and Vedic music. In fact, there is evidence to prove that if used consciously, music can keep the mind and body in tune with the rhythms of nature. Perhaps that being the reason in Vedic tradition, they conceived the form of God in sound or music and defined *Naad-Brahma* as the supreme creator and preserver of the universe.

Of course, in Vedic tradition, they not just

philosophically define God in the form of music but there are tales to tell how the *Naad* is sustaining the creation.

The legend of *Rishi Panini* is one such amazing tale that explains how *Naad-Brahma* is the basis of life and creativity around us. I can write, you can read and everyone can express their ideas and thoughts perfectly just because we have a sophisticated common language and script. Language is, of course, something that distinguishes us from other species on the earth; not many of them have the luxury to communicate their thoughts the way humans can. The development and passing on of knowledge is also possible because of the development of comprehensive language and writing techniques, which clearly means that evolution of today's modern world is indebted to development of language. But to whom are the languages indebted to? We all know that Sanskrit is the mother of many modern languages of the world including English. But do you know who is the father of Sanskrit, that is mother to the majority of the languages of the world? *Rishi Panini* is popularly known as the father of Sanskrit grammar. He was the one who defined the rules on linguistics, syntax and semantics of Sanskrit language in his iconic text *Astadhyayi* which means 'eight chapters'. This text directly became the foundation for grammatical rules of many modern languages of today's world. The most startling thing about *Astadhyayi* is that it has its origin in music. That being so, music is also the foundation of languages and subsequently, the foundation of all the inventions and discoveries that humans can be proud about. As we know that without a sophisticated writing technique, transmission of knowledge between generations would not be possible and many wonders that humans have created would not have happened.

The epic of *Panini* says that he was born to a great scholar and astrologer *Pani*, who lived on the banks of river Indus. When *Panini* was a small kid, some great sanyasi visited his house. *Panini's* parents treated him with humility and respect. After serving them with the best of their service, *Pani* requested the sanyasi to bless his son to become a great scholar. But after observing *Panini's* astrological characteristics, the sanyasi became quite sad. On being asked eagerly by *Pani* the cause of his concern, the sanyasi replied "Ohh *Pani*! you are a wise, humble and a righteous man but the fate of your son says that he will be thick-headed and sans education. He does not have *vidya* (knowledge) in his fate". Listening to this, both the parents of *Panini* plunged into gloom for a time. But as the legend says, *Panini's* father dedicated his son's life in devotion to Lord Shiva who is the ultimate source of wisdom. And one day, at the zenith of this concentration, *Panini* was meditating Lord Shiva to know the root of all knowledge in the universe, Shiva appeared before him and to wake *Panini* from his penance, Shiva sounded his *damru* (a percussion instrument always seen attached to Shiva's trident). When *Panini* woke up, the beats of the *damru* were reverberating in *Panini's* ears. He prostrated himself before Lord Shiva. Shiva blessed him with *vidya* and disappeared. The legend says that *Panini* derived the

rules of phonetics and semantics of Sanskrit language from the beats of the *damru* that were reverberating in his ears for days. The first fourteen verses are the alphabetical representation of *damru* beats as revealed to *Panini* and became the recitation of the Sanskrit *Varna-mala* (Sanskrit alphabet) i.e. 47 letters; 14 vowels and 33 consonants also called *Akshara Samamnaya*, 'recitation of phonemes'. As they are revealed to *Panini* by Lord Shiva, he named it Shiva-Sutra.

This legend not only tells us about the origin of Sanskrit grammar or the enlightenment of *Panini* through music or the importance of music (which is actually an organised and rhythmic form of sound) but also answers the curiosity why all the Hindu deities are always depicted with musical instruments. Vedic religion did not grow based on the anthropocentric view of the cosmos; instead, it is knitted around the philosophy of the living consciousness of the universe that guides humankind with the ways to be one with it. The Indian scriptures define music as vibrations that are actually the root of creation. They say the entire being of this universe is nothing but extension of music and this is why yogis and rishis of Vedic tradition reverently called it *Naad-Brahma*. The Samaveda describes music as one of the easiest and joyful ways to find God within.

Who else better than Krishna, the *Purna-avatar*, the giver of Gita can substantiate the importance of *Sangeet Sadhna* (devotion through music). Krishna in Bhagavad Gita announced *Sangeet Sadhna* as his personal favourite. The melodious and musical nature of Samaveda, made

Krishna identify himself with Samaveda out of all the four Vedas, the Veda which has the secrets of experience of divination through music and melodies or *Raga-yoga*.

वेदनां सामवेदोऽस्मि

[Bhagavad Gita; 109:22]

"*Vedanaam Sama-vedo'smi*"—Amongst the Vedas, I am the Samaveda.

तत्र स्वरा:

षड्जश्च ऋषभश्चैव गान्धारो मध्यमस्तथा।

पञ्चमो धैवतश्चैव सप्तमोऽथ निषादवान्॥ २१॥

With this verse, Samaveda lays the foundation of Classical Indian Music. Its seven musical notes: *shadja* (षड्ज), *rishabh* (ऋषभ), *gandhar* (गान्धार), *madhyam* (मध्यम), *pancham* (पञ्चम), *dhaivat* (धैवत) and *nishad* (निषाद). These seven swaras are shortened to Sa, Ri (Carnatic) or Re (Hindustani), Ga, Ma, Pa, Dha, and Ni.

We are trying to take you through the journey in which the first sound became the 'eternal humm' of the cosmos and called *Anhad-Naad* and gradually grew to become the finest form of meditation to synchronise your consciousness with the universal consciousness. That journey goes on and the discipline of music becomes the companion of mankind in their journey of evolution and growth. To see the first ever application of music by Vedic rishis to make humans more evolved and wise, let's take a look at the compilation of the Vedas, the finest and the original wisdom bestowed upon humans by the cosmos. The cosmos also chose some brilliant minds to be the first recipients of this wisdom with the responsibility of passing it on to the coming generations, of course, without any adulteration or corruption. And through these Vedic rishis, the Vedas took the tangible form so that any human can become a part of this universal wisdom. However, because many brilliant minds across the world have been admirers of Vedic wisdom and due to them very candidly praised the Vedic approach towards life and spirituality many of us accept the supremacy of the Vedas as spiritual text. But we certainly doubt that the blessing or blissfulness will be the first experience of the reader of the Vedas from our generation who is not trained to read Vedic Sanskrit. The free spirited youth of this generation who are trained to think rationally and question everything that seems weird or unconventional to them. Of course, will this raises the question that why our rishis compiled the Vedas in the form of this complex and elusive poetry. Why didn't they write down the Vedas in the didactic formats similar to our academic books, where everything is written in a straightforward way, in the form of prose or commentary? Although there is not a simple explanation for this but one thing for sure is that after learning the reason behind conversion of the most exquisite knowledge of the universe into complex poetry, you will become a fan of the foreknowledge and vision of our Vedic rishis.

To solve this riddle, you need to put yourself in the place of those rishis, who were in charge of preserving Vedic knowledge for the coming generations from any interpolation or corruption. And mind you, their vision was way farther than 1000 or 2000 years. Any securing it in a digital format into some super secure hard drive or supercomputer or any other idea like making multiple copies on paper cannot guarantee securing your data beyond 1000 years. But the Vedic knowledge you read today is at least 4000-5000 years old and that too without any interpolation. Another thing we want to remind you that it was the time of oral transmission of knowledge, which is generally bound to mix up with personal interpretations and opinions. But all thanks to our genius Vedic rishis, who by their matchless intellect found a super-secure way to encode this cosmic wisdom and institutionalised Vedic *Gurukul-parampara* (Ancient Indian education system) for its smooth transition from one generation to another.

No wonder, Vedic rishis too, when pondering solutions for this riddle found their refuge in music and melodies. A prosody intoned under the rules of mathematics, becomes a 'goof-proof ' algorithm to tamper with. The *mantras*, *chanda* or prayers of the Vedas that one finds difficult to read or understand is actually a highly sophisticated algorithm of poetry which, if recited with a specific rhythm of music or tala becomes an embedded structure of musical metres which prevent any errors of memory or oral transmission from one generation to another.

To understand it better, you can do a practical yourself. Write down any poem you remember and then sing it with its rhythm. Now try to replace any of its words without breaking its metre and rhythm. And if you find it difficult, we are pretty sure you won't even try to mess up with Vedic poetry which is way more complex and sophisticated to be adulterated.

Till now, we know, music was the original source of the creation, begetter of the languages. It is the preserver of the Vedas and of course, in its form of the ultimate creator, it is the ultimate goal to be achieved through Vedic knowledge. Music is one of the most joyful ways of devotion prescribed by the Vedas and perhaps the easiest one too because God in the form of music can be experienced straight away, with no future hopes, no promise of afterlife. Just align yourself with the cosmic music or music of this creation and you will be in a state of *samadhi*, often called trance nowadays. The master of classical music or *rag-yogis* often talks about the music floating around you in the form of vibration, in the form of energy and that helps *rag-yogis* to ascertain the appropriate raga of the pahar (time of the day). The one who has mastered this art can synchronise his consciousness with surroundings and can listen or feel the raga flowing in the wind at a particular time of the day. But of course, firstly, one needs to develop his or her faculties to attain that purity of mind that can align with the cosmic music, through meditation and training. *Sangeet sadhna* or training of classical music has the power to uplift the consciousness of a person who is ready to dissolve his identity into the vast ocean of music, which our Vedic rishis call the *Naad-Brahma.*

Sanatana Dharma which describes the beginning of this creation with a bang and subtle music (*Anhad-Naad*) also depicts the destruction of it with music; actually with the ultimate expression of music i.e. dance. *Nataraja*, a form of Shiva who is the God of dance and drama in Hindu tradition surprisingly also venerated as god of destruction. Iconography of *Nataraja* says that this universe is nothing but a dance of energies and hence nothing is static. Even the objects that seem to be static are actually in motion at atomic and subatomic level. Which in Hindu legends is represented by *Lasya* or *Anand-Tandava*, a joyful dance of Shiva and Shakti. This dance is personification of eternal dynamism of the universe since the creation to the present state of blissful existence. The legends of *Nataraja* says that when the universe is full of excess negative energy; to make way for a new beginning, the *Ananda-Tandava* turns into *Rudra-Tandava* or *Pralay-Tandava* which depicts Shiva in the form of the destroyer of the creation. When the *Ananda-Tandava* of *Nataraja* turns into *Pralay-Tandava* the dance of electrons, protons and neutrons inside atoms, which was happening to sustain the world, now starts to collapse in its nucleus. Similarly, the planets into stars and stars into bigger stars. With the chain of supernova explosions, the universe ceases to be. And again, the only thing remaining is the *Naad* or *Anhad-Naad*, the eternal music.

As Shruti says the music is the *Aadi* (the beginning), *Madhya* (the middle) and *Anta* (the end) of everything. The story that begins with the *Naad* (music), sustained by the *Naad*, will end with nothing but a reverberation of the *Naad*.

Trancition of Sangeet

Trancition is the fusion of two words, trance and transition. And we will discuss *Sangeet* (music) in the context of both. In the previous chapter we have learned the cosmic nature of music or we should better call it the musical nature of the cosmos. Music as the original form of the supreme creator, Music as the energy that runs the existence and also the precursor of ultimate destruction. Sanatan dharma, in which fathoming out the truth, the real nature of existence and to know the real purpose of human existence is the only religion of mankind. And when the Vedic rishis made *Sangeet* (music) the axis of their religious philosophy the music actually descended in the lives of mankind. Since then music has travelled a long journey in order to evolve to the form we know it today.

In the land where the life of people was being governed by the Vedas and the Vedas itself in a way governed by music, transition in music was inevitable to happen.

People who found God in music tend to see music in every beat of nature surrounding them. And how can they not develop it further to make it an intimate part of their life? Eventually, we have a very refined discipline of classical music in India. Which with time got divided into two streams of Hindustani and Carnatic music. Which was actually the transition of music from the Vedic times to the present.

Now let's discuss the trance part of *Sangeet* (music).

Trance is a word we get to hear very often primarily because of two things - when we listen to druggies talking about their 'out of the world experience' under the influence of drugs. In which they very mistakenly compare the state of mental blackout or the state of neglect of their body and world, with the ecstasy of *yogic-samadhi*. The second reason for the popularity of this word amongst the youngsters is due to the genre of electronic music which is supposed to take you to another realm of existence through its hypnotic rhythms and beats. Another important reason why this word trance sounds so enigmatic to us is because many great actors like Jim Carrey, Bruce Lee or artists like late Pt. Ravi Shankar or Pt. Jasraj and even scientists as great as Einstein, while sharing the moment of their greatest accomplishment said, it actually occurred when they were lost. Elements of surprise and humility are very much evident in their statement, especially when they talk about achievement and say that they did not do it; it just happened to them. They often try to explain that the cosmic just allowed them to align their genius with the fathomless wisdom of the universe. And when they were lost into a mysterious mental state, they suddenly started working beyond the limitation of their knowledge, ideas or their mind itself. They also described this mystical state as trance. Hence so much magic locked in this one word 'trance', but no cognitive psychologists till date have been able to unlock this magic successfully. No technique has been developed till date to recreate that real moment of ecstasy even with the help of people who have been in this mystical realm before.

After making a failed attempt of decoding the mystery of trance through sincere research in science journals, books of modern medical science and books of human psychology, when we left with nothing, we took refuge in the ultimate powerhouse of traditional Hindu knowledge, the Vedas.

The Vedas not just explained it thousands of years ago as why it is impossible to enter the realm of bliss with your mind in play but they have also gracefully unveiled the ways to understand and achieve it by surrendering yourself to that moment of cosmic blessing.

The Vedas speak about different layers of identity and after shedding all of them, the remainder is God or *Brahman*, as it is called in the Vedas. The uppermost layer of the identity is 'body' which is considered 'self' by utter ignorance. The second layer is the life breath, generally not much discussed in modern psychology or medical science. The third layer is the mind or *Manomaya-kosha*, which is considered the real identity of a man by modern psychologists or philosophers. But of course, Vedic science went more deeper in its approach in dissecting or peeling off the layers of real identity of a man. They define the human mind as a heap of experiences, impressions and learning, gathered through his/her lifetime and hence, it is constantly changing with time. A person in coma or in a vegetative state is an example of the first two layers working without *Manomaya-kosha* in play. And it signifies that you are not your mind or body or breath.

Then the Vedas take you a little more deeper and the next layer they define is called *Vijnanamaya-kosha*. *Vijnanamaya-kosha* is the form of intellect which is free of memory of your brain. When you were yet to learn anything about the world, your *Vijnanamaya-kosha* was very much there to govern you. Many small kids sometimes don't like to be friendly with some specific person; perhaps they can sense the immoral vibes which grown-ups fail to sense due to the dominance of their mind (analytical judgement about the person or situation) over their heart (*Vijnanamaya-kosha*). Modern science describes *Vijnanamaya-kosha* as intuitive wisdom which works beyond the analytical capabilities of your brain. Where your *Manomaya-kosha* or mind can act only by using previous knowledge, experiences and insights. The intuitive wisdom works beyond the criterions of past knowledge, and somewhat involves the conscience of a person.

In many difficult situations of your life, you were

definitely being told to listen to your heart over mind. Sometimes you make a decision that doesn't match your demeanour but make it because you 'feel it in your gut'. Or when you meet a new person with a lucrative business proposal, which seems viable by all your business ken but unexplainably you decline this proposal, saying you are not getting positive vibes. Or sometimes some of your family members feel jittery or anxious for no apparent reason but suddenly some adverse event takes place in the family. All these are the examples of intuitive wisdom commonly known as hunch, gut or sixth sense. Psychologists are still not able to define this layer of wisdom whereas the Vedas not just deeply crystallised *Vijnanamaya-kosha* but also provided meditation techniques to optimise this omniscient nature of your intellect. The Vedas also describe why intuitive wisdom is more accurate or reliable than analytical wisdom or how some rishis could caution someone beforehand about the forthcoming danger. The reason why the Vedas adulate the wisdom of *Vijnanamaya-kosha* more than *Manomaya-kosha* is because it is closer to your true self, the *Atman*. Of course, the yogic techniques and meditation we do is to optimise *Vijnanamaya-kosha*.

The reason for our entire focus just on the enhancement of *Vijnanamaya-kosha* or *Manomaya-kosha* is because we want to become more intelligent, richer and more successful in this material world. But you might like to change your preference after learning the view of the Vedas on your mundane successes and achievements. The Vedas describe all the joy of your success as temporary and negligible when compared with the bliss of *yogic-samadhi*. This state of blissfulness lies in one more deeper layer or should we say a more closer layer to God, the God within you, the layer named *Anandamaya-kosha*. The state of blissfulness is described as closest to God, more so in the Hindu scriptures at many places. God is described as *Anand-Swaroopa*, who can be experienced in pure bliss. But before we proceed further, we want to clarify one more time that your higher degree of happiness, which you casually call bliss, is different from the bliss we are referring to.

This bliss of the spiritual realm can be experienced only when you rise above your feelings, emotions, biases or prejudices; in short, when you forget yourself, leave all your false identities behind. *Anandamaya-kosha* is the source of the highest degree of joy, peace, contentment and love. Only the attainment of that can let you feel the absolute fulfilment; let you experience the entirety in your own self. The Vedas claim that anyone who has tasted the nectar of bliss of *Anandamaya-kosha* will no more value any other material achievement over the eternal joy of this state.

When the Vedas eulogised something so much, they must have prescribed some ways to reach there. It must be difficult to attain something that requires you to rise above your mind, body, senses, intellect, everything that binds you in 'you'. However, this spiritual quote of rising above your actions and desires sounds very tempting but we all know that this is one of the most convoluted practises of *yog-sadhna*. And once again *Sangeet* (music) became the saviour of mankind to help them retreat to their true identity. The Vedas say, and many of us will substantiate with their personal experience that immersing yourself completely into music can take you to the realm of spirituality, which is unreachable otherwise. The degree of divinity or wholeness that we can feel in the moment when we are lost in music is higher than hours' long practice of meditation, provided you know the trick of surrendering yourself to music.

We all have seen musicians who sometimes immersed themselves into their performances knowingly or unknowingly. These tantalising moments of trance happen when they forget what they are performing or where or for whom they are performing, a state of ecstasy, a state from which they didn't want to descend, for anything of this world. And these are the performances a connoisseur of music yearns for.

Ragas do gratify the soul of the listeners and not just the senses. They create a consoling and transcending attitude of the mind, elevate the listener to an ethereal plane and purify the knots of the mind.

This distinction of music as the highest form of meditation is actually one more way showing us the generosity of the creator, who made sure that every essential thing for growth and survival is readily available around us in abundance. We learnt about music as a form of creator, God; we discussed music as the original source of wisdom and the form of the energy sustaining the world. Now let us learn about music as the most celebrated and revered form of art.

As per the legends, three asura brothers namely, *Tarakaksha*, *Vidhyunmali* and *Kamalaksha* after severe penance towards Brahma got the boon and became unconquerable and unslayable. After they became invincible they built three flying fortified cities of gold, silver and iron respectively for each of them, which provided them further protection from any attack by the Devas. With this boon of invincibility, they started harassing the Devas, who eventually came to Shiva to seek protection. Convinced with their request and agony, Shiva marches to slay these *asuras*. Using the earth as his chariot, sun and moon as the wheels of the chariot and Brahma as the Charioteer, Shiva holds the bow made of Mount *Meru* using the serpent king *Vasuki* as the bow string and arrows of *Agni*. This is how Shiva accompanied by all Devas charged on all the three asuras.

But before the attacks, Shiva smells the pride of the Devas who offered help to him in the form of his weapons and only because of their help Shiva will be able to defeat the enemy undefeatable otherwise. Realising the arrogance of the Devas, Shiva on reaching Tripuram, the three citadels, just let out a fine smile at Tripuram. A huge fireball broke out of his smile which reduced the three citadels into ashes. With this one move, Shiva destroyed the arrogance of both the *suras* (Devas) and *asuras* (Demons) simultaneously. They all bowed down to the lord to seek his gracious kindness and forgiveness for their folly.

Shiva forgave the three demons and made *Tarakaksha* and *Kamalaksha* as his gatekeepers and kept *Vidhyunmali* to play *Kudamuzha* (a pot like percussion instrument, mentioned in many Dravidian Legends[2].

Since Shiva destroyed the three citadels, he was called *Tripura-Samhara-Murthy* and in short as *Tripurari*. A temple dedicated to *Tripura-Samhara-Murthy* is located in the Cuddalore district of Tamil Nadu. The temple itself is in the form of a chariot depicting the legend and one of the *Ashta Veeratana Sthalams* (8 places where Shiva performed his heroic activity).

To celebrate this victory over *asuras* and especially over *ahamkara* (false pride or arrogance) of Devas, Shiva introduced many new *ragas* derived from cosmic music based on which Brahma, the creator made many *raginis* (the feminine counterpart of *raga*) and appointed *Bharatmuni* as preserver and broadcaster of this sacred knowledge. And in order to uphold the responsibility shouldered by Brahma, *Bharatmuni* created *Natyashastra*, an ancient treatise that codifies the principles of *gaan* (melos), *nritya* (dance) and *vaad* (syllabic recital). A combined performance of all to present some legends like Victory of *Tripurari* or *Tripura-Samhara-Murthy* became the earliest form of drama. Besides defining the rules of art and drama, *Natyashastra* also set the standards for aesthetics and decorum of a performance. One thing we need to keep in mind about *Natyashastra* is that the period we are discussing here is the time when music was yet to evolve as a source of entertainment. In the classical Vedic period, music was a sacred tool to

---

2. Web Credits (https://www.thehindu.com/entertainment/music/rhythm-of-the-celestial-sphere/article27546789.ece)

experience the essence of a man's own consciousness. Natyashastra is the oldest document which has presented the elaborate rules of music and dance as a balanced source of entertainment and spiritual practice (*Sadhna*).

One more such revered document that draws a parallel between the law of creation and music is *Sangeet Ratnakar* of *Pt. Sharngadev*. In the document, *Pt. Sharngadev* gave mathematical formulations to create new ragas using various permutations and combinations. Interestingly, the algorithms he gave to define the natural order of *swara* are now being used in computer programming. *Sharngadev* describes a method of singing called *Merukhand* which consists of various combinations and permutations of *swara* patterns. Due to *Sharngadev's* musical brilliance and his mathematical interpretation of music today, *Sangeet Ratnakar* is recognised as the basis for both the Hindustani and Carnatic systems of music which makes *Sangeet Ratnakar* a significant treatise of classical Indian music tradition. Written in the thirteenth century, *Sangeet Ratnakar* is also called '*Saptadhyayi*' as it consists of seven chapters. The second chapter of *Sangeet Ratnakar* called '*Ragavivekadhyaya*', where *Sharngadev* discusses the tenfold classification of *ragas* and a total of 264 *ragas* mentioned with relative comparison of old tradition with the contemporary tradition. *Sharngadev* had re-established concepts of music in such a comprehensive manner that to this day, definitions of basic terminology are quoted from his treatise.

Because of the contribution of *Bharatmuni*, *Sharngadev*, *Dattil*, *Matang Rishi*, and many other geniuses, the tradition of music can travel that far without losing its sanctity.

Gradually with passage of time, a different discipline of music for the stage evolved from the music of *sadhna* (devotion). For millennia music, dance and drama evolved in temples of India. We ought to know that temples were not just places of worship in Hindu tradition but besides devotion they were also serving the purpose of an educational institute, *Ayurvedic Chikitsalaya*, a bank, a storehouse of food grains (as a contingency reserve), they were also shelter houses for the art and culture of the country. The temple economy used to play an important role in many ways for civil society which was funding them. Remnants of exquisite architecture, engineering and sculpture can be seen in temples of classical or mediaeval India. These sculptures were not made just to showcase their sculpting skills but on a close observation, you will find that every piece of sculpture is an attempt to preserve some traditional knowledge or art. One such example is *Chidambaram Nataraja* temple of Tamil Nadu (We read about the same temple in reference of *Apasmara* and Shiva's tale), the gateways or *Gopurams* of this temple is embellished with sculptural representations of the 108 *karanas* (dance poses) of *Bharatanatyam*, intricately carved in small rectangular panels. We came to know about the usage of many musical instruments in classical time by their physical representations on temple walls. *Shri Chennakesava* temple of Belur which is a marvel of architecture and Vedic science has 650 carvings of elephants in different moods and every figure is different from another. On the wall of the temple, one can see the legend of *Ravana* lifting Mount *Kailash* besides a lady depicted playing the *Rudra-Veena* on the temple walls which made us aware of the forgotten instrument, we had heard about only in legends otherwise[3].

As per the legends, Shiva is said to have taken inspiration from Parvati's form and created this instrument. Thus known after the other name of Lord Shiva (*Rudra*), Shiva was the first to play this instrument and he taught it to Parvati who in turn taught it to Saraswati. The credit to bring this sacred instrument to *prithvi-lok* goes to *Narada*, who learnt it from Saraswati and brought it down to earth. In the Vedic times, when music was yet to evolve as a form of art and only revered as the highest form of devotion, *Rudra-Veena* was used as an accompaniment for *Veda-mantra pathan* (vedic recital) by Vedic-rishis. It held a place of reverence equivalent to that of the *shank* (conch) or *jagate* (circular plate/gong used in temples) that produces sounds during worship rituals but are not specifically used for producing music. It was treated with the same sanctity accorded to the sacred idol. Only selected people were allowed to touch it and that too only after purifying themselves.

The unique design of the instrument enhances the respectability of the person playing the instrument. The centre of *Rudra-Veena* falls between the navel and the heart and vibration created by the instrument flows through the

3. (https://www.inditales.com/chennakesava-temple-belur-karnataka/)

body of the musician playing it. The vibrations circulate in the inner body with the sound of 'Om' entering the left ear from the left *tumba*. The right *tumba's* vibrations go through the lower body through the right thigh. These vibrations produce inner well-being and tune the player of this instrument to the universal *Nada* (sound). The instrument is itself a tool of *pranayam* and yoga. Mastering breathing is the primary prerequisite to learn this sacred instrument. Perhaps this is the reason that only few artists in the world have kept the tradition of playing *Rudra-Veena* alive. Among these few people, one is the name of former President of India late Shri APJ Abdul Kalam, who used to take refuge from his hectic schedule in the lap of music through *Rudra-Veena*. Recently, *Rudra-Veena* was adopted as a world heritage instrument and is being protected and promoted by UNESCO[4].

Modern physics has shown that the rhythm of creation and destruction is not just manifest to turn off season and the living and death of creatures but is also the very essence of inorganic matter. We all have learnt the classic textbook example that the rhythm of footsteps can break bridges. An incident happened in April 1831 where a troop of British soldiers were marching across a bridge in Broughton in England and suddenly the bridge broke apart and many soldiers fell into the river underneath. Post the incident, the British Army issued general orders

4. Web credits: https://www.google.com/amp/s/www.thehindu.com/features/friday-review/music/jyoti-hegde-the-first-female-rudrav eena-artist/article7919310.ece/amp/

that soldiers crossing a long bridge must break strides or not march in unison, to stop such a situation of resonance from occurring again.

Many modern researchers confirmed recently what the Vedas proclaimed in the beginning, that every living or non-living body in this universe including the creator himself/herself is actually in the form of musical vibrations or energy. However rigid or huge or solid a structure looks, it has an intrinsic frequency of vibrations. Any sound or music that can amplify the vibrations of that object or body can bring some changes to its original state. In the tradition of classical music, there are many popular tales which describe the power of music in terms of modern physics. Lighting of diyas (oil lamps) and melting of rocks or precipitation of clouds are some popular legends about famous mediaeval singer *Tansen* who was one of the gems in Emperor Akbar's court. Even in recent times, some incidents were reported where the dome of a huge structure under which this musical performance was taking place suddenly got a crack because of the intensity of the singer's performance or in scientific terms, the frequency of that dome and pitch of the singer matches accidentally. Exactly the way glasses break when the pitch of an Opera singer matches the frequency of the glass objects.

The entire point of describing the perceptible power of music in this material world is to make our readers aware about the sacred as well as the therapeutic properties of music. The ancient rishis worked close to Nature and formulated musical syllables by paying close attention to the cries of birds, flow of wind, rhythm of river flow over a period of time. And this is the reason that Vedic music has all the cycles and rhythms of human physiology - hormonal secretion, metabolism and cardiac rhythms, which keeps the mind and body in tune with the rhythms of Nature. The therapeutic properties of ancient Indian music like *Naada-yoga*, Vedic chanting and *raga chikitsa* (music therapy or therapy by *ragas*) have been recognised by medical professionals, psychologists and music therapists. That means when you immerse yourself into classical music, you are not just benefiting from the intrinsic joy of it or not that it is affecting the inner layers of your identity but also heals and treats your body.

Every human society across the world has developed their kind of music discipline to celebrate their joy, express their grief or invoke their vigour. In a matured discipline of music, it has a set of melodies (*ragas* in Indian terms), instruments and some dance-form that goes well with their melody and beats. In India, the roots of music are found in many ancient literatures and the way they have described and classified it shows their deep understanding and research of music. *Natyashastra* categorised musical instruments into four groups based on their acoustic principle (through the way they create sound and not on the material they are made up of). Like there is a separate category for the instrument that works on the principles of strings (chordophones) *veena* or *tanpura* and the instrument that works on the principles of inflow and outflow of air or breath (aerophones) like flute has a separate chapter in

Natyashastra. The extensive study and description of *ragas*, tala, instrument and various dance poses makes the Hindu musical tradition richest and oldest in the entire world. The diversity presents Hindu traditions about various Gods and their nature or the different ways to worship them; even the architecture of their temples is different from others. By taking a closer look, anyone can find the apparent difference in the architecture of Shiva temple from Vaishnav temples. This diversity also reflects in the musical tradition that developed as a devotional practice to please their favourite God. Although there are many nuances and subtleties in music in India but the major classification is based on their geographical locations, that is, Hindustani music, which is a prevalent musical tradition of Northern India and Carnatic music that belongs to the southern part of India. Although this divide is not very old and these two streams of classical Indian music got two separate identities just a few centuries ago. And perhaps that being the reason there are more similarities than differences in these two traditions of Indian classical music.

There are so many streaks, so many differences, so many similarities, so much science, so much devotion and many more so many that are still remaining to be discussed about music with reference to the vast ocean of music in Hindu tradition.

Resonance of Royalty

The contribution of Hinduism in the growth and development of humanity is undepartable and preordained. After observing the human history on this planet through the perspective of Hinduism we are completely convinced that humanity wouldn't be the same without the guiding light of the Vedas and Vedic rishis. We sincerely doubt that without the receptive consciousness of Vedic rishis, humans will ever be able to discover *ragas* in blowing of winds, in setting and rising of the Sun and the moon. Humanity might be deprived of the therapeutic uses of music forever. Very likely that for humanity, music would have been restricted to just as a mood enhancer. Among so many religions and so many philosophies of the world only in Hinduism the supreme energy, the supreme creator is explained in the form of music as a fundamental energy that is sustaining the creation. We already read that in Hindu tradition music has descended from *devloka* to *mrityu-loka* as a tool of devotion. However from vedic scriptures and temples gradually music traverse to royal courts and then became the part of life of every common being. Undoubtedly this journey has not taken place in isolation and so was not very smooth and simple. Many alien factors including the consistent flux of foregin cultures played a part in this journey of music from *devloka* to royal courts of *mrityu-loka*. Apparently this flux of cultures posed a huge challenge to everything original about this land. But the beauty of this land lies in its unique art of adaptation by retaining the original essence of something. This time again the strike of outlandish outlooks made Hindus to think beyond their existing limits of imagination, with a new perspective. Eventually the Hindu civilisation in order to cope with change absorbed many new things, however by retaining the soul and essence of hinduism in it. And today, in the process of retro-analysis we can tell you that no other civilisation or country in the world could sustain it so nicely as the Indian society has done.

Music which was Initially used to give incantation to Vedic mantras adapted to accompany dance and drama on stage for storytelling and entertainment. Where in pre-medieval and mediaeval era the *ragas* and poetries were only being used to invoke vigour in warriors or devotion in devotees, now in the royal courts is being used to invoke sensuality and romance. And again when Persian, Turkish and Mongol influence fell upon the court music through muslim muscians, who were primarily romantic poets; apprently because in Islam there is no room for music and poetry for religious purpose. Perhaps that being the reason *Sufi fakirs* even in their religious poetaries used romantic metaphors like *mehboob*, *rangrez* and *Jaan e Jigar* for God. The first such prominent musician of Delhi Sultanate who fused the Arabic and Persian style of singing with classical Indian music was *Amir Khusro*. The poetries of *Amir Khusro* that were written for his spiritual master *Sheik Nizzamuddin Auliya* are the most popular *Sufi Qawwalis* and most liked *sufi* music in the Indian subcontinent.

Gradually music from Vedic scriptures & temples traversed to royal courts. However this journey was quite complex & didn't happen in isolation. It was the time of India where the entire culture was in flux due to various foreign rulers of Delhi from different lands and different cultures. Whereas many cultures, religions or empires that were ruling the world in their times have been wiped out when the waves of revolutionary ideas hit them. The existing Indian society with the ingrained dynamism not sustained and survived but emerged triumphant from these constant threats. However Indian society in order to cope with change had to absorb many new things but it could successfully retain the soul of Hinduism in it. The same has happened with Indian music; we saw how music began with the beginning of this creation and it grew into various forms inside nature and especially in human society.

Where on the one hand, Indian music in the North was going through lots of changes due to the fusion of foreign styles, the Southern music distanced itself in order to retain the originality of Indian classical music. Later, the separated stream was distinctly known as Carnatic music. Whereas the Northern stream that absorbed the Persian and Arabic style of music became Hindustani music. However, it is impossible to completely divorce the identities of these two streams of music as they had the same origin, background and rules. Hence, in order to differentiate them, we first need to delve into the fundamental factors that give any music a separate identity. Although technically, there are many things that define the type of music like language of poetry, instruments, intonations but the most intrinsic distinction that is paramount to all is its philosophy. For instance, in renditions of Hindustani music, use of dialects of northern India like Brij and Awadhi is very common whereas instruments like tabla, harmonium and dholak play an important part. While the renditions of Carnatic music is mostly in Tamil or Telugu, Kannada, Sanskrit and Malayalam, the instruments that mark the distinction in Carnatic music are mridangam, violin, kanjira and venu. Besides the many differences that separate one stream from another, the real distinction is in their philosophy of music. Since Hindustani music is primarily developed in royal courts of Muslim emperors, the philosophy was to impress the king and royal guests. Hence, it involves long cadence and trials in incantation to show their hold and strength of breath. Many legends of great singers like *Tansen* (one of the nine gems of Akbar's court), where he demonstrated the magical power of music through his singing; legends like lighting of lamps or attracting rain using specific *ragas* are few of many popular ones from Akbar's court only. We have already read in the last chapter about the effects of music on all living and nonliving things. But definitely besides breaking bridges and domes, music can also create magic by its ubiquitous presence. One such legend of *Tansen* will tell what the expertise over the ragas can do in the physical and metaphysical world around you. This favourite singer of Akbar, by invoking certain raga, can diminish sunlight and create a dusky effect that can turn the day into night.

Just like the folklore of Akbar-Birbal where Akbar often tasked *Birbal* with some weird challenges and through his extraordinary intellect, *Birbal* always overcame the challenge. Similar tales of Akbar and *Tansen* where Akbar demands *Tansen* to create magic using his command over various *ragas* are also very common. In one such legend, the courtiers of Akbar who were jealous of the overwhelmed affection of the emperor for *Tansen* think of a ruse to trouble him. They spread the word in the court that *Tansen* can light up lamps with his performance which evidently made Akbar curious to see him doing the same in his court. Without knowing the repercussions, Akbar asked *Tansen* to perform the feat. Certainly, *Tansen* did not want to disobey the king but he was worried as *raga-Deepak* not only lit up the lamps, but it heats up the environment so much that it also can cause some fire accidents. He requested the emperor for some time to prepare and in this duration, he ensured that his daughter gained command over *raga-Malhar* so in case of any undesirable situation, she can bring the rain. On the decided day of the performance, *Tansen* started singing *raga-Deepak* due to which the temperature of the court rose so much that everybody started sweating. Only when *Tansen's* daughter sang *Megh-Malhar* that caused rain, everybody found some relief. The story says that it took *Tansen* a few months to recover from the after effects of the overheating of *raga-Deepak* produced in his body.

However, due to *Tansen's* presence in the royal court of Emperor Akbar, he became the epitome of classical Hindustani singing that can create magical effects but certainly India had many such unsung legends. One more such legend was *Baiju* who challenged *Tansen*. As per the condition of this battle, one who cracked the marble stone through his singing would be declared victorious. Both were the votaries of a great saint and devotees of *Naad-brahma*, *Swami Haridas* who himself was the singer of par excellence. The legend says that both *Tansen* and *Baiju* sang so intensely that the marble stone not just cracked but started melting.

These legends and along with many others depict the scenario of a new India which is being ruled by foreign kings, who were naturally unaware of the Vedic wisdom. And because of their sceptical nature towards the genius of Hindu traditions and wisdom, we were re-exploring our indigenous wisdom. Of course they were ignorant of the fact that centuries ago Vedic rishis had described the immense possibility of healing, mind and body by the use of music. Since ancient times till recently, no other country or civilisation in the world explored music so exhaustively the way Indians have done. The development of Hindustani music had happened to pacify or invoke certain emotions, mainly sensual, romantic or sad moods of the audience. Hence, many new experiments were done with language, lyrics, poetry and presentation of the performance by the singers and the musicians to create the magic, to enhance the mood or to indulge the listener in a particular way. And with the unique tradition of songs for every mood and occasion that started in the royal courts of mediaeval India, continue till date through the songs in Indian films. And with the advance of technology, the art-form that was restricted to royal courts for some centuries in mediaeval India again became a part of everybody's life.

We have already learnt that initially music grew only in gurukuls and ashrams among the rishis and their votaries, but gradually it dissipated to common people through temple culture in the form of devotional songs and plays. And for almost two millennia, a huge group of intellectuals kept music devoted only to God, especially in the southern part of India which still more or less remained untouched by any foreign influences. People and kings of southern India, for a long time tried to maintain the sanctity of devotional nature of music and that was the primary reason behind the separation between Hindustani (Northern) and Carnatic (Southern) music.

In Carnatic music, the period of the latter half of 18th and first half of the 19th centuries is considered the most glorious period. It was the time when masters like

Thyagaraja, Muthuswamy Dikshitar, Shyama Sastri (the Musical Trinity of Carnatic music) and other legends lived. This period is popularly called the golden age of Carnatic music. There is no doubt that *Thyagaraja* was like an ocean of the noblest traditions of Carnatic music, devotion and renunciation. *Thyagaraja* grew up in a family devoted to lord Rama and so was *Thyagaraja*. But from childhood, the influence of the celestial sage *Narada* on *Thyagaraja* was huge. Eventually pleased by his purity and devotion towards music, a hermit gave him a mantra to invoke *Narada*. Legends say that one day, when *Thyagaraja* was meditating on the mantra, miraculously, *Narada* appeared before him first disguised as an old man then as *Narada* himself. *Narada* vouchsafed *Thyagaraja* with the long lost treatises on music. As we know from the last chapter, sage *Narada* was the one who was given the responsibility to preserve music for mankind by Lord Brahma alongside *Bharatmuni*. The treatise of music bequeathed to *Thyagaraja* by *Narada* became the foundation stone of Carnatic music and based on that *Thyagaraja* reviewed the entire music tradition of South India. Due to his exemplary composition in devotion to Lord Rama, he is called *Valmiki* of *Madhyakalam* (*Valmiki* of mediaeval age) by his disciples.

Similarly *Muthuswamy Dikshitar*, who was a rare combination of a scholar, musician and a saint, took Carnatic music to the heights of multidimensional beauty by his matchless proficiency over harmony and ken of poetry. The last member of this mythical trio, *Shri Shyama*

Sastri through his permutative genius introduced various new rhythmical frameworks in southern music. His contribution in developing many *Thala Prastharam* is not just significant but exemplary in many ways. The kind of great creative artist that he was, he originated the musical form of *swarajathi* and converted it into an attractive musical form, as it was originally a dance framework. Only a man of his genius could so masterfully eliminate the passages of *jathis* that stood unparalleled, both in terms of delineation of *raga-Bhava* (mood of raga) and fecundity of musical ideas. Undoubtedly, Carnatic music owes a lot to this musical trinity, through whose unparalleled devotion to their craft southern music reached the acme of perfection.

Apparently, due to this unbroken chain of countless geniuses in the tradition of Indian classical music, India has the richest legacy of music. And though it separated into different streams, they have more similarities than differences in their fundamentals. However, we can rest our efforts of differentiating Hindustani and Carnatic music by stating the most intrinsic difference between these two streams that in Carnatic music, bliss of the singer is more important. Whereas in Hindustani music, the joy of a singer is often a derivative of the admiration that comes from the royal guests.

We have seen the journey of music that descended from the assembly of gods and reached the royal courts and how it became the reflection of the society of its origin and defines the underlying culture. And not just music but any form of art reflects the social and political condition of the society which means through a close study of poetry, paintings, dance, plays and music you also can study the economic, social and political conditions of that particular time period in which the art forms have developed. Hence besides spiritual upliftment, entertainment and an effective therapy art, dance, drama and music has also served humankind by passing down the essence of history and traditional values.

The same is true for our next art form that is dance, which is depicted with equal respect as music in Hindu mythology. In fact, the Vedic idea of creation sees the entire universe from beginning to end in between the two dances of Shiva - *Tandav* and *Lasya*. *Tandav* or *Pralay Tandava* is considered as the dance of destruction and Lasya or *Anand Tantava* is a playful dance of Shiva-Parvati that depicts the harmony, fertility and creativity of nature. Dance in the Vedic period is used as an expression of universal energies, which is expressed through specific *mudras* or gestures. These gestures too are considered *yogic* in nature in Hinduism, Buddhism and Jainism. To define the relation between dance and music, all we can say is that dance is the only way to see the music through the physical expressions of the rhythm and beats. Dance is also the ultimate expression of the joy generated in the body through music. Although just like music, initially dance too was just a format of yoga where sacred poses were performed in a rhythm to be coherent with cosmic energy.

"Whosoever knoweth the power of the dance, dwelleth in God."

Rumi, a Sufi poet and mystic who is credited with having found *Mevlevi* order in *Sufism*, an offshoot of Islam, emerged in fusion with philosophies of Hinduism, philoshopies of meditation, music and dance. Rumi was the first *Sufi* mystic to define dance as a way to unite the body, mind, heart and soul also known as the Order of the Whirling Dervishes. It is a famous Sufi dance in which the dancer immerses the soul into the divine, the experience famously called *Fana* in *Sufism*. Not just in *Sufi* tradition but in many cultural traditions of Central Asia, Egypt and Persia, the people of higher wisdom and mystic element saw dance and music as a way to connect their soul to higher consciousness. In fact, due to the spread of *Sufism* in the middle-east and Central Asia, the divine nature of dance popularised the ecstatic *Sufi* whirling or Egyptian ritual dance in the entire region.

Natyashastra defines dance as a way to experience a different dimension and merge into the greater dance of the universe. In *Natyashastra*, *Natya Sadhana* is a feeling of being one with the cosmos by simultaneously expressing your individuality; which means the highest realisation of truth can be observed repeatedly when the dancer is completely immersed in dance. For instance, in *Bharatanatyam*, a dancer depicts the polarities like soft and fierce, mighty and meek, beautiful and ugly, man and woman in order to serve the purpose of craft. And that becomes his/her *sadhna* (worship) through which the artist reaches far and wide and is open to mystical secrets of the cosmos by accessing his subtle senses and the unlocked mind. Many Hindu scriptures describe the sacred symbology of movements by linking its undulations, waves, spirals, circles and infinity loops with the beginning point: the '*bindu-navel*' of the universe.

In Hindu tradition, everything that can lead mankind on the true journey of life is not just introduced but also endorsed by some *rishi*, some incarnation or some divine being. But for a few special treasures, God himself descends to *Mrityuloka* to vouchsafe his dearest creation to mankind. Likewise, the divinity of dance in *Bharatvarsh* was expounded by Shri Krishna himself, the most heroic God and choreographer of Mahabharata who wielded flute and chakra with equal perfection.

However Gita, the principal book of Sanatana Dharma is considered the biggest gift of Krishna to mankind but for the devotees of *bhakti* tradition, who seek God in love, for them *raas-leela* of Krishna is way more sacred and a greater treasure than anything else. *Raas-leela* is the divine night of eternal dance that symbolises the soul's unceasing struggle to break the constraints of the body and merge with the supra-reality. It is the full moon night when the enchanting melody of Krishna's flute draws all *gopis* (milkmaid) in *Nidhivan*. Gopis represent the human nature that tends to set boundaries which restricts them to explore their full potential and through *raas-leela*, Krishna breaks all the social compulsions, mental boundaries for his devotees. The magical night of ecstasy where the cosmic dance of the universe was replicated by Krishna and the *gopis*. The temptation of this blissful night was so high that even the Gods from heaven craved to have glimpses of it. The legend says that when Shiva, the ultimate God of dance and music decided to join the *raas-leela*, he was stopped by *Yogmaya* (the goddess of divine illusion) saying that except Krishna no man was allowed to be part of this raas. The story says that Shiva who wanted to join this play at any cost decked in woman's attire with ornaments and took the form of *Vraja* gopi and became the part of divine celebration. In Vrindavan to this day, Shiva is worshipped in his feminine form. Ultimately, this divine act of Krishna and the participation of Shiva in it in a feminine form carries the message that an ideal human character is a blend of masculinity and femininity. *Nritya-Sadhana* manifests this ideal blend of a woman with a tinge of masculinity and a man with a tinge of femininity. Contrary to this, an alpha or the all masculine man is, of course, the character of beasts or animals. Some degree of femininity is required to make a man out of an animal and this was the essence of Krishna's life. Shiva, the most athletic God, the God of destruction validated Krishna's message by accepting the feminine form when he joined Krishna's *raas-leela* taking the form of a *gopi*.

The significance of *raas-leela* in the Hindu culture is such that in all formats of classical dance, the artists celebrate the *raas-leela* in their act. To replicate that moment of bliss by their performance is the ultimate goal of every classical dancer by showing traits of masculinity and femininity both. In *yogic* cult, *yogis* relate the geometry of dance poses with the energies of earth, air, fire and water in our own beings. The breath work, poetry, whirling and chanting in dance has the validation of highest order as a form of meditation by *Yogeshwar* Krishna himself. Bhagvatam also has a story of *Pradyumna*, the great grandson of Krishna and reincarnation of Kama (god of pleasure). *Pradyumna* learnt '*Lasya*' style of dancing with his wife Usha from Goddess Parvati to further popularised it in *Mrityuloka*. Similarly, the closest companion of Krishna, the finest archer and bravest warrior Arjuna too, was the adherent of *Nritya Sadhana*. He learnt the art of dancing from *Urvashi*, a nymph from heaven, the *Nritya Sadhana* also helped him during the period of his banishment when *Pandavas* were required to live incognito. In the form of eunuch *Brihannala*, Arjuna taught the art of dancing to Princess *Uttara* who later also became his daughter-in-law. Interestingly, not just Mahabharata but Ramayana also is full of characters who endorsed *Nritya Sadhana*. Ravana, the fiercest warrior and the alpha character of Ramayana, was a master of music and dance. As per some legends, Ravana has the credit of having introduced *Rudra veena* (the most sacred musical instrument of heaven) to mankind.

A votary of *Nritya Sadhana* experiences mother nature and the direct expression of this divine creation through the sacred geometry that can be found in the vastness of nature and the perfect patterns of the universe. A *Nritya Sadhak* (votary of dance) moves in synchronisation with lunar rhythms to connect with naturally arising instinctual wisdom, insight, vitality and joy. Many deities, rishis and gods have proclaimed that *nritya sadhana* is the most powerful way to taste the supreme joy of ultimate consciousness, which is actually the goal of all devotion, worship, meditation and rituals.

Surprisingly, not just rishis, incarnations and gods but *Nritya Sadhana* was endorsed by the architecture of many sacred monuments. The architecture of Chidambaram temple is said to be inspired by the dance poses so that it can transmit more cosmic energy to visitors. Perhaps that being the reason, these dance poses are also depicted on the walls or the entrance of these temples in order to communicate the importance of dance further. Along with time, just like in the case with music, dance also evolved in temple tradition. And this tradition played an important role in the process of evolution of dance. Through the unique visual ability, dance was used to communicate the mythological legends with the proper expression, feeling and mood of the storyline. It was aimed to leave a deeper impression on the viewer's mind by engaging his emotions and mind.

Gradually with time as a companion of music, dance also reached into the royal courts to entice the attention and interest of the ruling class. Now with the change in philosophy, many new experiments in this art-form began to happen. Dance evolved aesthetically to impress the viewer rather than just communication. More sharp and technical moves were added, beauty and speed in the motion became more important. The acrobatic moves which need a physically fit body of a performer made the classical dance a rare skill, learnt by thorough dedication.

Besides the court dance, many adaptations of classical dance emerged with time, which includes many aspects of local culture and folklore. These regional dances have many elements that also communicate the underlying theme or the story and not just demonstrate the acrobatic ability of the performer. Through *Angika abhinaya*, the performer uses all major, minor and auxiliary limbs like the poses of legs, waist and gestures of hands, fingers, eyeballs etc. to communicate. *Bharatnatyam*, the oldest and the most prominent among Indian classical dances is known for its mastery in *Angika abhinaya*.

Vachika abhinaya constitutes poetry accompanied by dance and narrates the story verbally to fill the gaps in communication. *Manipuri* is the dance form that uses *Vachika* as a major part of performance. *Aharya abhinaya* means the costume, stage decoration and makeup of the performer which also plays an important role. *Kathakali*, the classical dance of Kerala is famous for its exuberant makeup and costume. Last and the most difficult one is *Satvika abhinaya* through which the performer has to express the emotion and story through acting, using his/her mental disposition and emotional connection with the story.

Although too much science and technicality is involved in the description given in this chapter, yet we want to conclude by saying that dance is nothing more than an overflow of energy and emotion through bodily movements. Exactly the way Shiva does it, anger and destruction through *Tandav* whereas joy and liveliness through *Lasya*.

Words of Divine: Samskrutam

वन्देऽहं देवं तं श्रीतं रन्तारं कालं भासा यः।
रामो रामाधीराप्यागो लीलामारायोध्ये वासे॥

"I pay my obeisance to Lord Shri Rama, who with his heart pining for Sita travelled across the Sahyadri Hills and returned to Ayodhya after killing Ravana and lived with his consort Sita, in Ayodhya for a long time"

In our books about Hinduism, we have presented many Sanskrit shlokas to show the wisdom of ancient Hindus or the rich philosophy of Vedas. But this *shloka* here is just to demonstrate the magic and beauty of Sanskrit. The aforementioned *shloka* is a type of *Anulom-Pratilom* poetry of Sanskrit, in which the reverse order of the sentence also has some meaning. Although we have read many such sentences in English too which are called Palindrome poetry. However the basic difference in Palindrome poetry of English and *Anulom-Pratilom*

poetry of Sanskrit is that in English, palindrome sentences mean the same in reverse order too, whereas in Sanskrit words are very intelligently used for multiple meanings. For example, the *shloka* given above describes the story of Lord Rama, now read the same *shloka* in reverse order,

सेवा ध्येयो रामालालीगोप्याराधीमारामोरा।
यस्साभालंकारंतारंतंश्रीतंवन्देहंदेव ॥

I bow to Lord Shri Krishna, whose chest is the sporting resort of Shri Lakshmi; who is fit to be contemplated through penance and sacrifice, who fondles Rukmani and his other consorts and who is worshipped by the gopis, and who is decked with jewels radiating splendour[5].

The same shloka now depicts the life story of Lord Krishna. This is a piece of wisdom of a 17th century Tamil sage of *Kanchipuram*, *Sri Venkateswara*. The supremacy of Sanskrit is no more a matter of discussion or debate; rather, it is a matter of research and rediscovery of its hidden greatness. Many countries and educational institutes are exploring the possibilities of its advancement by reviewing the ancient wisdom. Of course, the primary requisite to explore the ancient Indian wisdom is the deep study of Sanskrit. Naturally, without the understanding of Sanskrit, the treasure house of wisdom, The Vedas, the Puranas and many other ancient literature will remain

5. Web credits: for Sanskrit shloka and translation http://www.sanskritebooks.org/2009/09/raghava-yadaviyam-with-english-translation/

closed like a door to India and the world. Certainly, Sanskrit can unlock many mysteries of universal consciousness and take you to the higher realm of understanding of this cosmos.

Yet one should not reduce the significance of Sanskrit to a historical language that enables us to understand the ancient literature and the ways Vedic rishis used to perceive this universe and human life. Sanskrit is way more than a language; it holds all the potentials of cosmic sounds. Undoubtedly, Sanskrit holds so much science in itself that in the last two centuries, it has attracted almost every genius, every analytical mind of the world.

Unfortunately, this treasure of wisdom is most neglected in the country of its own origin. To the surprise of many Indians, It is not India but Germany that is the storehouse of Sanskrit researchers of the world. The most number of PHDs in Sanskrit are produced by Germany and England.

We all have read many theories and trivia about Sanskrit in the last four decades and the most popular one is its utility as the most efficient computing language. Which is of course true to some extent but the Hindu way of learning says or exactly what we are trying to endorse through our books that a learner should touch the fathom of everything that interests his/her curiosity. Because complacently believing any superficial statements given by a well dressed gentleman is of course not what Hinduism promotes and definitely against the Hindu way of learning. Hence, here too, let us start from the beginning and go back to the origin of speech, origin of communication, today simply known as language.

The most significant aspect of any language is the subjectivity of it; anything that can communicate something to someone can be called a language. Almost all living creatures communicate with their fellow creatures using the most common medium i.e. sound. And the richness of their language is dependent on the development of their faculties of listening and producing sound. Only the capability of producing a variety of sounds and listing all of them enabled humans to develop the sophisticated languages that we have today. The articulatory system of humans, that is, the lungs, vocal folds, tongue, teeth, lips, nose, all enable us to produce a huge variety of sounds. And to complement that, the auditory system of only humans can match the range of acoustic characteristics and frequencies that are most common in human speech.

Sanskrit is the only language that uses the entire articulatory system in the most efficient manner. It has way more science hidden in it than a language can contain. Perhaps this is the reason *Ashtadhyayi*, the grammar of Sanskrit developed by *Maharishi Panini*, which is also the oldest and the most scientific one, requires no changes even after so many millennia. Of course, the sagacity of the people who developed it made it eternal.

We have already read the story of the origin of Ashtadhyayi from the beats of damru of Shiva, from which *Maharshi Panini* derived *Shiva-sutra* or *Mahesvara Sutrani*, the fourteen verses that organise the phonemes of Sanskrit as referred to in the *Ashtadhyayi*. The greatness of *Panini's* grammar is substantiated by many western scholars by declaring it one of the greatest innovations of mankind. This treatise consists of about 3959 sutras which can handle the nuances and intricacies of any language in the universe, empirically and anatomically. Panini arranged the Sanskrit phonemes in such a manner that it uses the entire articulatory system of human speech in the most efficient way.

One more interesting fact about Sanskrit is that it is the language that helped us to communicate with animals in our farms for thousands of years and in this age too in its original form is equally compatible to communicate with highly smart computers with the same efficacy. We cannot take the fact for granted how difficult it is to keep up the pace with ever growing human intelligence and its needs in this age of robust advancement. Only the conscientiously and meticulously crafted rules of grammar and phonetics can enable a language to be relevant for the complex needs of the present generation. Exactly the way Sanskrit is keeping pace with the changing needs of time from thousands of generations.

नृत्तावसाने नटराजराजो ननाद ढक्कां नवपञ्चवारम्।
उद्धर्त्तुकामो सनकादिसिद्धादिनेतद्विमर्शे शिवसूत्रजालम्॥

"At the end of his cosmic dance, Shiva, the Lord of dance, with a view to bless the sages Sanaka and others, played on his damru fourteen times, from which emerged the

following fourteen sutras, popularly known as Shiva Sutras or Maheshwara Sutras"

How can something that descended on earth for humans by God, can be ordinary? How can Sanskrit just be a language? It has to contain the essence of the magic of the cosmos, it was derived from. But as it is mentioned by *Dirgh Jeevi Maharishi Kakbhushundi* (this conversation is there in the first vol. of 'The Great Tale of Hinduism') that the Vedas are eternal and revealed to mankind in every creation but their understanding of the Vedas is subjected to the development of *pragya* (sapience) of humans of that age. The same can be said about Sanskrit in which some of our rishis found complex mathematical principles that later came to be known as the Fibonacci series and Pascal triangle. Some other rishis discovered profound basics of physics in Sanskrit grammar, some found poetry and some the philosophy and purpose of human life. Evidently, in the present time where Hindus, who are living under the shadows of ignorance of their own identity, could only see Sanskrit as a language of religious ceremonies. But if anyone with determination and faith set on to delve deep into this quantum of cosmic knowledge would start to see the magic of Sanskrit at the very elementary level. You don't need to wait long or become a research scholar to observe the magic hidden in Sanskrit. Just by looking at the elementary alphabet chart of Sanskrit prepared by *Maharishi Panini* millennia ago you can experience the acoustic science of Sanskrit. You can Google it now and start pronouncing the alphabets arranged in this chart row by row. You will find that every row has the arrangement of alphabets that uses a particular part of your vocal faculty. For example, when you pronounce क (Ka) ख (Kha) ग (Ga) घ (Gha) ङ (na) which are also referred as Guttural, your tongue will slightly touch the soft palate and obstruct the airflow. Astonishingly, human oral systems cannot obstruct the airflow below this position and therefore, no wonder that क (Ka) is not only the first consonantal sound in Sanskrit but in all other languages too that have been born from Sanskrit.

Unfortunately, Sanskrit in India is facing the same fate as of the other ancient Hindu traditions, due to the lackadaisical attitude of its inheritor. The present generation of Indians who are actually the inheritors of the ancient Indian wisdom either lack the temperament of research and innovation or wait for some western scholar to validate it. The bigger damage to the credibility of Vedic wisdom is caused in recent years by the attitude of work-shy Hindus, who try to make mountains out of molehills in the form of appreciation by some Western scholars. And when any curious mind with the real zeal of learning and studying about the ancient Indian wisdom tries to climb these made up mountains, finds more myths than facts. And eventually, ends up rejecting the complete idea and tags the entire ancient Indian wisdom as baseless fiction work of over-enthusiast. The same is the case with Sanskrit where the greatness of it is defined through more myths than facts which can be seen in the following example.

A considerable excitement was triggered in India when a NASA scientist Rick Briggs in 1985 expressed his observation under the title 'Knowledge Representation in Sanskrit and Artificial Intelligence'. In this article, Briggs states Sanskrit as a language that has the oldest grammatical tradition that has continued to exist with undiminished vigour until the present. This statement of Briggs suggested that Sanskrit is the most apt language to be used to communicate to computers or machines designed for learning Artificial Intelligence. But while quoting this, we forget that now anybody can draw correct results of spoken words in broken English or a regional dialect using mobile phones.

That means the present generation of scientists have successfully found alternate solutions to the idea suggested by Briggs in 1985. Yet this nowhere undermines the latent genius of Sanskrit and supremacy of this perfectly sculpted language. However, when Indian scholars endorse a forty year- old theory of a Western scholar that holds no significance now evinces the unenthusiastic attitude of them towards Sanskrit. Because had they had any true admiration or respect for their heritage would definitely have led them to delve into the sea of immense possibilities of Sanskrit.

To get a glimpse of the magic and the possibilities that we have claimed to be hidden in Sanskrit, let us look at its characteristics. First of all, you need to know that Sanskrit has a unique way of defining things using its property, root-sound and therefore, it has the biggest vocabulary bank, way bigger than any other language. Where English has only one word each for love and water, Sanskrit has 96 ways to say love, around 70 words for water and over 122 words to describe 'to go', all of it precisely and specifically. Just because of the richness of the words in Sanskrit, the world's most complex and beautiful poetry was created in it. *Shishupala Vadha*, the *Mahakavya* of *Maharishi Magha* who lived between the 7th and 8th century, is one of the most legendary works done in the field of poetry by human kind in terms of linguistics and aesthetics of a language. This *Mahakavya* is the wonderland of Sanskrit where the poet most aptly used the strength of Sanskrit to demonstrate its magic. For example, we are presenting one shloka from his seminal work where he wrote the whole shloka with only one consonant.

दाददो दुद्ददुद्दादी दाददो दूददीददोः ।
दुद्दादं दददे दुद्दे दादाददददोऽददः ॥

"Sri Krishna, the giver of every boon, the scourge of the evil-minded, the purifier, the one whose arms can annihilate the wicked who cause suffering to others, shot his pain-causing arrow at the enemy"

One more such example can be seen in the most sacred work of Shri Adi Shankaracharya in *Mahishasura-Mardini Stotram* where the entire line is written using the same word but for different meaning using different context, which is obviously impossible with any other language.

अयि सुमनः सुमनः सुमनः सुमनोहर कान्तियुते
श्रितरजनीरज-नीरज-नीरजनी-रजनीकर-वक्त्रवृते।
सुनयनविभ्रम-रभ्र-मर-भ्रमर-भ्रमर-भ्रमराधिपते
जय जय हे महिषासुर-मर्दिनि रम्यकपर्दिनि शैलसुते॥

O the Goddess who is beautiful and with a delicate heart like that of the flowers of devas, who is bright and shining.

Whose face is like the moon which is cool and blossoms the lotuses by your shine,

Who has good looking eyes and by the movements of your eyes, you had attracted several bees and destroyed the demons like the queen of bees (Bramaradhipathe),

Victory to you, victory to you, the destroyer of Mahishasura, the one with beautiful-braided hair, the daughter of the mountain.

These shlokas may also demonstrate the complexity of Sanskrit language but nobody can deny the brilliance of the votaries of this language and the strength of Sanskrit grammar and its vocabulary. Sanskrit has 48 alphabets (13 vowels, 33 consonants, one Anusvara, one Visarga); Russian has 35 alphabets, Arabic and Turkish 22 each, Persian has 31 alphabets, Spanish 35, French 25, English 26, and Tamil 30 + 1. And the most amazing thing about Sanskrit is that it has more mathematics in it than language. The meticulously defined rules of Sanskrit grammar have the resemblance with fundamental theories of physics and mathematics. To establish our point, let us present one more shloka from *Shishupala Vadha* of *Maharishi Magha.*

सकारनानारकास-	Sakāranānārakāsa
कायसाददसायका।	Kāyasādadasāyakā
रसाहवावाहसार-	Rasāhavā vāhasāra
नादवाददवादना॥	Nādavādadavādanā

(And the lines reversed)

Sa Kā Ra Nā Nā Ra Kā Sa	Nā Da Vā Da Da Vā Da Nā
Kā Ya Sā Da Da Sā Ya Kā	Ra Sā Ha Vā Vā Ha Sā Ra
Ra Sā Ha Vā Vā Ha Sā Ra	Kā Ya Sā Da Da Sā Ya Kā
Nā Da Vā Da Da Vā Da Nā	Sa Kā Ra Nā Nā Ra Kā Sa

"[That army], which relished battle (rasāhavā) contained allies who brought low the bodes and gaits of their various striving enemies (sakāranānārakāsakāyasādadasāyakā), and in it the cries of the best of mounts contended with musical instruments (vāhasāranādavādadavādanā)[6]."

This metrics table like equation is another show of proficiency of a linguistic scholar of Sanskrit. This is the example of *sarvatobhadra*, 'perfect in every direction' means it yields the same text if read forwards, backwards, down, or up but with a beautiful meaning. Now we can imagine what in Sanskrit is gravitating to the research scholars of the world including computer scientists. The

6. Web credits: https://en.wikipedia.org/wiki/Shishupala_Vadha

positional notation is a primary contribution of Sanskrit to the development of modern mathematics and Sanskrit was the main element in ancient India to bridge mathematics to linguistics. Another example in which we can see resemblance to the structures used in computer science is in the rules of *Aksharaganah* defined by *Pingalacharya*. The Rules defined by *Pingalacharya* somewhere around 200-300 BCE for Chhandas or poetry metre look similar to binary combinations. His famous text *Chandahsastra* is the first known description of a binary numeral system in connection with the systematic enumeration of metres with fixed patterns of short and long syllables. Here 3, 4, 6 or 8 lettered *ganas aksharaganah* generate the same sequence of *laghu* (0) and *guru* (1) combinations as in modern digital computers. Sanskrit script (*Devanagari*) is phonetic, not spelling based like English. This phonetic transcription property of Sanskrit is useful if phonetic instructions are fed to a computer or robot. Since we know that ancient Indians had an aversion for writing and every form of knowledge was passed down to the next generation orally, they also had developed methods to communicate mathematical rules orally. In ancient India, algebra was differentiated from modern arithmetic by its use of symbols to represent numbers. One prominent method was *Bhuta Sankhya* (भूतसङ्खया) where *Bhuta* means body and *Sankhya* means number. In the *Bhuta Sankhya* system, unlike now where we have given a number a name, the names of objects representing their values were used.

Bhutasankhya name			Meaning
0	shunya	Kha, aakasha, gagana, bindu, megha	Sky, sky, sky, dot, cloud
1	Eka	Chandra, indu, bhumi, prithvi, roopa	Moon, moon, earth, earth, form
2	dvi	Akshi, netra, hasta, ashvini, oshta	Eyes, eyes, hands, twins, lips
3	threeNi	Loka, agni, raama, guNa, haranetra	Worlds, fire, Rama, guNa, Siva's eyes
4	chatur	Veda, yuga, samudra, saagara	Veda, epochs, oceans, oceans
5	pancha	Bhuta, bhaava, paandava, indriya	Elements, expressions, Pandavas, senses
6	shad	Krittika, anga, rtu, rasa, shanmukha	Pleiades, Vedangas, seasons, tastes, Skanda
7	sapta	Svara, giri, achala, rshi, vaara	Musical notes, mountains, seers, weekdays
8	ashTa	Vasu, dik, diggaja, anushtubh	Vasus, directions, elephants, vedic metre
9	nava	Graha, ratna, nanda, yantra	Planets, gems, Nandas, devices

Bhaskara-II around 1150 described algebra as analysis (*bija*) assisted by letters or symbols (*varna*), whose properties are discovered through considerable intellectual effort. As all our Sanskrit texts including *siddhantas* on astronomy and mathematics were composed in verse, they only had to fit the syllabic rules of *chhandas*. This system has the advantage of writing long numbers without mentioning all the place names like. For example, 1,44,63,895 could be written as eka-yuga-yuga-rasa-guna-vasu-graha-paandava without all the mentions of crores, lakhs, thousands, hundreds etc., as compact as possible using words alone.

The other system was *Katapayadi Samkhya* where numbers were written using a defined set of consonants (*vyanjana*). The following verse found in *Sankara Varman's Sadratnamala* explains the mechanism of the *Katapayadi* system.

नञावचश्य शून्यानि संख्याः कटपयादयः।
मिश्रे तूपान्त्यहल संख्यान च चिन्त्यो हलस्वरः॥

na (न), nya (ञ) and a (अ)-s, i.e., vowels represent zero. The nine integers are represented by consonant group beginning with ka, ṭa, pa, ya. In a conjunct consonant, the last of the consonants alone will count. A consonant without a vowel is to be ignored.

This verse encrypts the value of pi (π) up to 31 decimal places

गोपीभाग्यमधुव्रात-शृङ्गिशोदधिसन्धिग।
खलजीवितखाताव गलहालारसंधर॥

If the above given verse is decoded according to Katapayadi system, it directly yields the decimal equivalent of pi divided by 10: pi/10 = 0.31415926535897932384626 433832792[7]

Even the glimpses of these seminal works explain the reason why Sanskrit is gravitating to researchers and scholars worldwide including the votaries of science and logic. It also advocates our point that these traditional languages hold a sea of wisdom in them and a proper exploration will certainly contribute to the inclusive advancement of humanity. This is exactly why Germany, one of the most research-oriented and technology-driven nations, has 14 universities that run elite courses of Sanskrit. Not just Germany but the entire Europe and many developed nations like Australia and Japan have an inclination for Sanskrit. Courses in Sanskrit are among the most popular courses in the most reputed universities of the West including Harvard. Their inclination is adequately complemented by the Sanskrit literatures that ascertain the fact that Sanskrit has way more hidden knowledge in it than one can imagine. Perhaps this is the reason, countless Western scholars and scientists of the 18th and 19th century overwhelmingly acknowledged the greatness of Sanskrit. Of course in Sanskrit literature, they found immense scope for development in almost any area of studies. Voltaire,

7. Web Credits: https://en.wikipedia.org/wiki/Katapayadi_system #:~:text=For%20example%2C%20ba%20(%E0%A4%AC),)%20 %2B%20a%20(%E0%A4%85).

Hegel, Leo Tolstoy, Schopenhauer, Emerson, T.S. Eliot, Niels Bohr, Schrodinger, Heisenberg, Oppenheimer, Mark Twain, Henry Thoreau, Car Jung, J.D. Salinger and many other scholars learnt Sanskrit or studied Sanskrit literature to strengthen their intellectual prowess. Not just the hidden knowledge of science and mathematics stirred the hearts and minds around the world but Sanskrit plays and poems have also left an indelible mark on a global level. The early 19th century was the time of obsession of *Kalidas's Abhigyan-Shakuntalam* for almost every European poet and play-writer. In the little span of three decades, around 46 translations into 14 European languages have happened of this master-piece of Sanskrit literature. *Shakuntalam* had created such a sensation in Germany that its translation had gained a 'rock star' status in a few months of its launch. Due to the popularity of this Sanskrit play Otto von Böhtlingk, a Russian-German indologist, published a Sanskrit dictionary in a short version. Ultimately, along with the perseverance of Vedic wisdom and transmission of exquisite knowledge to many generations, Sanskrit has also introduced the real India to the world.

From the all aforementioned examples that establish the omnipresent wisdom of Sanskrit, we can easily ascertain that all these mathematical wonders are actually the primary goal and not an incidental by-product of these ancient Indian Sanskrit scholars. The well-knitted syntactic and semantic structure of Sanskrit and well-defined rules of its grammar for phrasing and synthesising makes Sanskrit a language of past, present and future.

Chiselled to Perfection: Samskrutam

Language is one of the earliest and greatest innovations of humans which certainly manifested them as the wisest species of this planet. But have you ever wondered, despite having the same acoustic and articulatory system, why the evolution of languages in different human societies happened differently. Whereas in the case of other species/animals, for example, dogs or cats communicate with similar sounds across the world. The distinction in languages for different human societies signifies that evolution of a language is subject to sapience and the perception of its speaker. A sophisticated society tends to develop a more sophisticated language and eventually, a sophisticated language helps them in further development. We can say that sophistication in a language is actually a reflection of the intelligence of the society it has developed within. Perhaps this is the reason that in the long history of human civilisation, only few languages have passed the test of time to thrive till the present. And as we know that in the age of homogenisation, only the thing that promises some value in the present or sometime in near future can sustain and survive.

Sanskrit, Latin, Iranian, Greek, Chinese (Mandarin), Arabic and Hebrew are few of those traditional languages which have been the witness of growth of human civilisation. The use of the term "witness of growth" for language, is to make you realise that any ancient language that has travelled through thousands of generations, is not merely a tool of communication. Naturally, with the maturity of thousands of years, these languages have also become a storehouse of the ancestral wisdom possessed by their speakers. Not just the literature developed to a high degree of complexity, but even regular proverbs are equally carrying the glimpse of the ancestral wisdom of concerned society. We barely realise the fact that had these languages not played the role of a bridge of wisdom between our ancestors and us, indistinctly, we would not have been as advanced as we are now. The lost treasure of Harappan wisdom is still unrevealed to us in the absence of understanding of their script or the underlying language. On the other hand the discovery of wisdom with the decipherment of Rock Edicts of Ashoka by the British archaeologist and historian, James Prinsep opened the window to a lost treasure of wisdom of ancient India. These are two such historical events that exemplify the role of a language between the modern age and the ancient wisdom gained through ages. Imagine if the Rock Edicts of Ashoka would not have been deciphered successfully, one of the greatest kings of history would have been restricted to footnotes, as a mythological figure of Buddhist literature. All thanks to this discovery, India as an independent nation could take its inspiration from the holistic approach of king Ashoka the Great, for its *Panchsheel* principles - the fundamentals of Indian diplomacy with a holistic world view. This further gives credence to our point that the ancient languages should not be judged merely as a tool of communication but they should be seen as what they actually are, the greatest wealth of a society that it accumulated through generations.

ॐ भूर्भुवः स्वः तत्सवितुर्वरेण्यं।
भर्गो देवस्यधीमहि धियोयोनः प्रचोदयात्॥

"OM. Here's meditating upon the one who governs the universe, to illuminate our minds by eliminating ignorance. We meditate upon Ishwar, the one who sustains life. Enlighten us"

Aforementioned is one of the most popular Vedic *Mantras* of *Anushtubh Chhanda* (metre) known as the *Gayatri-mantra*. This and many other such Vedic *Mantras* and *shlokas* in Sanskrit, are prayers to God to increase the intuitive wisdom of the enchanter. The Vedas means wisdom and anyone who gains knowledge of the Vedas, gains wisdom, not just the literary knowledge written in the Vedas but our scripture claims that enchanting Vedic hymns also increases memory, ability to think and perceive. At the same time it also increases the intuitive wisdom of the learner.

In every Hindu family parents tell their children to say *Gayatri-mantra* every day 108 times, and they will never fail in exams. Which implies that the knowledge of the effect of Sanskrit shlokas on human intelligence in right metre and intonation was with us forever. But again like many other things, this too got validation when an American scientist Dr. James Hartzell published his research in the journal, Scientific American in January 2018. His research shows the effect of enchanting Sanskrit verses. The research paper reads the observation of his research to prove that recitation and memorising Sanskrit verses caused the development of certain parts of the brain that enhance the ability to think, memorise and make decisions. Although this research found similar results for many ancient languages but in India, this Western discovery caused a buzz as always. This phenomenon was called the 'Sanskrit effect'. This is one of the discoveries that only triggered pride and excitement in Indians but not the curiosity and temperament to explore further possibilities themselves.

There is a lot of buzz about the hidden treasure of Sanskrit but paradoxically all of these debates, discussions and admiration are in English by the people who barely can read or understand Sanskrit. And the most disheartening is the neglect of Sanskrit on the land which has thrived on it for hundreds of generations. We certainly do not promote being jingoistic or to unnecessarily glorify a past that cannot secure your development in the present. Hence by all means, we are trying to present here some authentic glimpse of the wisdom locked in the Hindu scriptures that can only be unlocked by the proper understanding of Sanskrit. The age of English, Hindi or any other regional Indian language that was born of Sanskrit is not older than 2,000 years, which is just 30 percent of the known history of this land. Moreover, all scriptures and literature that Indians cherish and are proud of was written originally in Sanskrit. And the most important fact we need to consider is that the Sanskrit speaking Hindus were the people who compiled the Vedas and the Upanishads. In the age of Sanskrit only the Vedic sciences of astronomy, chemistry, architecture, medicine, mathematics and philosophy were developed. Besides the literary treasures of that golden age, we have the evidence that substantiates the presence of a well-organised structure of governance at multiple levels, justice delivery system and of course, a well flourishing economy.

However, unlike the present, material gain was not the only pursuit of Hindus/Indians and perhaps more than any other discovery or innovation, this is the point which proves that the Sanskrit speaking Hindus were more contained and wiser than than the later generations that actually ignored Sanskrit. After all, every stream of science developed then was the product of some spiritual pursuit and a disciplined life of Vedic rishis. That also justifies the case that why our rishis or the ancient scientists never extended their research to add luxury into human life through mass production of gadgets. Don't forget that besides the exquisite knowledge of science and language, they also had the most exquisite philosophy to guide their endeavours.

This means learning Sanskrit will not only connect to ancient wisdom and storehouse of knowledge of the Vedic age but it will also help us to understand the way Vedic rishis, the writers of the Vedas and the Puranas used to think. Possibly, knowing the approach of the ancient geniuses towards life can open a new dimension of knowledge to us. As it is very much evident that the present state of knowledge, education and aspirations are not leading humanity in the sustainable direction.

Hence a holistic course correction is highly needed which can lead us to a new approach of science and rationality with the Vedic philosophy of *sarve bhavantu sukhinah* (may all living creatures be happy). That gives us ample reasons to revive Sanskrit.

Certainly besides the holistic approach, learning Sanskrit will not deviate us from the path of progress and development. The point where you embark on the journey of mastering Sanskrit, you will read the finest treatise of grammar ever written as the study of phonetics, rhythms, etymology, astronomy and science behind Vedic rituals makes the complete structure of Sanskrit language. The course of Sanskrit will also acquaint the learner with literature of the most exquisite standard. The ancient scriptures which are the part of Sanskrit learning makes the disciple master of so many disciplines of science. Perhaps that was the reason the Sanskrit poets like *Valmiki* or *Kalidasa* at some points in their respective literature demonstrated the exquisite knowledge of astrology, geography and many more disciplines of sciences.

Sanskrit played an important role in development of Indian society at the same time some ancient Indian geniuses through their remarkable contribution made Sanskrit grow and mature on this land. We have already learnt the story of the descent of Sanskrit grammar in this world by lord Shiva to *Panini*. Now let's take a look at the work of some other geniuses who sculpted Sanskrit to its impeccable perfection.

One such genius was *Pingalacharya*, whose valuable contribution to Sanskrit made this language impeccable. He is less known as a grammarian and more popular as an ancient mathematician perhaps because of the resemblance of his work with salient mathematical principles like Fibonacci series, Binary system and Pascal's triangle. *Pingalacharya*, the second-century BCE grammarian, dedicated his life to codifying the rule of poetic metres of Sanskrit. Although his intention was to enrich the 'language of the universe' but the empirical nature of Sanskrit made him intentionally or unintentionally develop 'the only universal language' of the world i.e. mathematics. Although *Pingalacharya's* magnum opus, *Chhandashaastra* (छदः:शास्त्र) is a seminal compendious treatise on Sanskrit prosody, he never intended to directly pursue the discovery of the mathematical formulations.

Instead he was in pursuit to arrange the syllables in the best possible way in a Sanskrit verse so that the verse sounds pleasant to the listener. And in this process, he found the solution in the form of *Lagakriya*, a set of rules to arrange syllables in Sanskrit poetry with a rhythm that resembles mathematical formulation. Besides making the verses sound pleasant, the principle laid down by *Pingalacharya* also helped to keep the originality of Vedic literature intact and incorruptibles. At the same time these musical and rhythmic verses were also the easiest way to infuse the lengthy Sanskrit poetries into memory.

However *Lagakriya*, these days, is not celebrated as a work that sets rules for Sanskrit poetry; instead today, we know *Chandashaastra* for providing the detailed algorithm that has the potential to create a Binary code, which is the fundamental language of modern-day computing. But one thing is clear that *Pingalacharya's* profound devotion for Sanskrit gifted humanity with something that carved several generations of scholars, poets and mathematicians. Unlike *Panini*, very little is known about the early life of *Pingalacharya*. It was only through his remarkable and brilliant work, he marked his name in the annals of ancient geniuses. The *Chandashaastra* is a work of eight chapters in sutra style and due to its complex nature of poetry it became inaccessible to later generations. Perhaps because their knowledge and comprehension of Sanskrit is also diluted with time. *Pingala's* writing was in sutra style where the radical contractions of rules were accomplished by enciphering entire words and sets into single alphabets, characters or syllables. The understanding of his work is dependent on the reader's knowledge of the subject and his keenness to learn more. Evidently in the present context, it is even beyond the ability of any ordinary graduate in Sanskrit to eliminate the error of ambiguity to decode and comprehend the original sutra without commentary.

Only through the elaborated commentary of *Chhandashaastra* written by 10th century mathematician *Halayudha* with the name *Mrita-Sanjivani* today, we understand the coded knowledge of it. *Mrita-Sanjivani* contains the clear description of Pascal's triangle and Fibonacci numbers explain it as the staircase of Mount *Meru* or *Meru Prastara* and *Matrameru* as it is called by *Halayudha*. It is based on *Pingalacharya's* work and *Halayudha's Mrita-Sanjivani*. The Jain scholar, *Hemachandra* in the 12th Century C.E., wrote a detailed commentary on the Fibonacci numbers half a century before Fibonacci's derivation.

Rishi Katyayana is another name in this list of Sanskrit grammarian cum mathematicians. And just like *Pingala*, the early life of *Katyayana* too is very less known, although some legends related to his birth described him as a reincarnation of lord Shiva's Gana, *Pushpadanta* who was cursed by Shiva to live as a human for the sin he had committed by breaching the privacy of Shiva and his consort Parvati. But in his human form, by attaining perfection in various streams of knowledge and science and by his hard penance, he again earned the affection of Shiva and Parvati. *Garuda Purana* mentions him as someone who learnt the rules of Sanskrit grammar from Kartikeya, son of Lord Shiva.

कुमार उवाच।
अथ व्याकरणं वक्ष्ये कात्यायन समासत: ।
सिद्धशब्दविवेकाय बालव्युत्पत्तिहेतवे ॥ GP 1,205.1 ॥

Kumara said: O Katyayana, I shall briefly expound the rules of grammar which will enable infants to easily comprehend that subject and to understand the formation of words and their derivatives.

Kartikeya taught him the grammar in a way that it would be understood even by a child. His two noted works are *Vartika*, an elaborated commentary on *Panini's* grammar and *Sulbasutra* that is one of the three *Sulbasutras* popular today. *Katyayana's Sulbasutra* explains the methods of construction, dealing with rectangles and other geometric figures useful for making fire altar. Undoubtedly, he wrote *Sulbasutra* to provide rules for religious rites and to improve and expand on the rules which had been given by his predecessors. That again means *Katyayana's* contribution to mathematics or geometry was incidental or we can say it was the outcome of spiritual pursuit. Or perhaps, we are undermining the fact that it was the time when transmission of knowledge was oral and not in a written format and hence, it restricted the use of numerals for calculation. Evidently, the mathematical principles, problems and their solutions were explained

orally in the form of poetry or prose. Hence, impeccable rules of grammar and pronunciation are the only ways to eliminate ambiguity and errors from typical mathematical communications. And most convincingly, this was the reason that every great mathematician was also a grammarian or perhaps vice-versa.

The last genius in our list whose contribution to Sanskrit is matchless again is not commemorated for his work for Sanskrit. Similar to the other grammarians of our list, Maharishi *Patanjali* is also celebrated in the world for his contribution to ayurveda but his identity as one of the greatest grammarians is least known. And again, we want to reiterate our point that Sanskrit is not just a tool of communication but it is a window that opens into the storehouse of ancient Hindu knowledge. This clearly means learning Sanskrit not just to enrich a person by one more language; rather, it simultaneously introduces the learner to numerous empirical streams of ancient Hindu science, which is evidently reclaiming its significance in the modern world with lots of untapped potential. Life of Maharishi *Patanjali* also corroborates the aforementioned statement as this genius was an expert of at least three branches of Sanskrit studies namely *yoga*, *vyakarana*, and *ayurveda*. According to a legend, he is considered to be an incarnation of *Sheshanaga*. *Patanjali* had a miraculous childhood; the legend says that from the moment he was born, he could communicate fully and discuss many topics with the intellect and understanding of a sage. The intensity of his eye, mind and mouth were such that on one occasion, when the inhabitants of *Bhotabhandra* disturbed him in the middle of his religious austerities and ridiculed him. *Patanjali* reduced them to ashes with nothing but with the fire of his mouth and speech.

योगेन चित्तस्य पदेन वाचां मलं शरीरस्य च वैद्यकेन।
योऽपाकरोत्तं प्रवरं मुनीनां पतञ्जलिं प्राञ्जलिरानतोऽस्मि॥

I bow down with folded palms to Sage Patanjali, the most exalted among the contemplative sages, who removes the impurity of the mind-content through yoga, of speech through grammar and of the body through Ayurveda.

This verse regards him as a sage who cleansed dirtiness of mind with yoga, impurity of speech (Sanskrit) by grammar and toxins of body with *ayurveda*. *Patanjali's* prolific contributions in the science of meditation, science of language and science of medicines is benefitting the entire humanity even today, directly or indirectly.

Patanjali's Yoga sutra and tenets of *Ashtanga-Yoga* given by him are being cherished and practised worldwide in order to take refuge in your true self. The eight angas of *Ashtanga-Yoga* are *yama, niyama, asana, pranayama, pratyahara, dharana, dhyana* and *samadhi*, through which anyone can take control over his senses and make his mind clear or without disturbances that leads to the state of ecstasy.

As a grammarian, Maharishi *Patanajali* gave this world *Mahabhasya*, a commentary on *Panini's* sutras, in a form that quoted the commentary of *Katyayana's Vartika*. It is the first and oldest existing commentary on the *Ashtadhyayi* of *Panini*. *Katyayana* wrote a number of *vartikas* to supplement *Paninian* rules but in *Mahabhasya*, *Patanjali* discussed *Katyayana's* comments, sometimes supporting it or sometimes rejecting it.

Dealing with 1228 rules of *Panini*, it has remained supremely authoritative and furnishes the last and final word in all cases of serious doubts ever raised over grammatical issues. Thus this trio (*trimurti*) of *panini*, *Katyayana* and *Patanjali* are revered as the three sages or *Muni-Traya* of Sanskrit *Vyakarana Shastra*. It means this trio has the credit to sculpt the grammar of Sanskrit to the level of perfection. And only the level of perfection in learning enables a seeker to benefit from the most exquisite knowledge of the universe locked into the Vedas and Upanishads. A person should be well-versed in all components of Sanskrit like the proper knowledge of letters (*varnas*), accent (*swara*), time consumed in articulating vowel (*matra*), effort (*bala*) melodious chanting of mantras (*sama*) and conjugation of letters (*sandhi*). If some mistake is committed in any of the above six components, instead of giving it the desired result, it can lead to severe misinterpretation.

Today, we fail to see how much of our advancement and comfortable lifestyle owes to the brilliance of these unsung and forgotten geniuses. Of course, the negligence of Sanskrit is the primary reason for this disconnect. The essence of the work of these rishis lives in a few surviving texts, reserved to a quiet corner of our collective conscience.

But undoubtedly, it affects us from the very fundamental beliefs of our life to the great pinnacles of scientific thought and reasoning. Hence, whatever knowledge you acquire today be called wise or to take humanity forward, it has its origin somewhere in the past when the unceasing quest for knowledge and burning curiosity of our ancestors developed the profound base of it. And in order to ensure that we lose nothing of the precious heritage left for us, we must revisit our past. Certainly, Sanskrit serves as a visa to visit this wonderland of our ancestral wisdom.

This designates Sanskrit as the only key to unlock the Vedic literature as it is impossible to analyse and determine the correct meaning of the words of the Vedic literature without knowing its language. And not doing so, we will equally be the culprits for vandalising the invaluable heritage of rishis and maharishis, the way the ignorant invaders who destroyed Nalanda and Takshashila were, due to negligence of knowledge and learning.

Kaala—The Fourth Dimension

न पर्यदेवन्विधवा न च व्यालकृतं भयम्।
न व्याधिजं भयन् वापि रामे राज्यं प्रशासति॥ ६-१२८-९९

"While Rama was ruling the kingdom, there were no widows to lament, nor was there danger from wild animals, nor any fear born of diseases"

The above mentioned is the *shloka* of *Valmiki Ramayana* that describes the state of convenience and painlessness of people in *Ram-rajya* (Rule of King Ram). *Valmiki* is called *AdiKavi* in Vedic tradition because it is he who created the first ever poetry to curse a hunter who killed a love-lorn male *Krauncha* bird (crane). The Ramayana was *Valmiki's* epic creation that depicts the life story of Lord Rama. But the most special thing about this epic is that unlike other epics written based on the memories of the events that took place in the past, *Valmiki Ramayan* was Ramayana written years before Rama was even born. We know it is quite hard to accept this for many who don't accept superficial things without knowing the underlying logic or science of something. And on a pleasant note, it needs to be said that the Vedic tradition of learning promotes this inquisitiveness of learners and discourages the nature of accepting things due to their sacrosanct nature. So allow us to take you on a trail of time as per the Vedic perspective of it.

But before we visit anything from the Vedic age, let's take a look at some theories of modern times. As it is already mentioned in this book that it is not the people with higher scientific temperament or scientific ken who reject the Vedic ideas outright but it is actually the people for whom both science and the Vedas are equally mysterious do ridicule any such parallel between science and the Vedas. Hence, whenever anyone draws any such connection between modern science and Vedic knowledge, it is recommended to validate it by some modern experiment or established theory. In support of our statement with regards to Rishi Valmiki and his foresight or the exact prediction of Rama's life years before Rama was actually born, we would like to quote Laplace's theory of determinism or 'Laplace's Demon'.

"We may regard the present state of the universe as the effect of its past and the cause of its future. An intellect which at any given moment knew all of the forces that animate nature and the mutual positions of the beings that compose it, if this intellect were vast enough to submit the data to analysis, could

condense into a single formula the movement of the greatest bodies of the universe and that of the lightest atom; for such an intellect nothing could be uncertain and the future just like the past would be present before its eyes."

—Marquis Pierre Simon de Laplace

It means for the higher intellect which is called a Demon by Laplace, nothing is future or past; everything there before his/her eyes is like in the present. The same thing is said in the Vedic scriptures about *yogis* who unlocked the potential of their brain by *yog-sadhna*. They say that time will be a delusion for the yogi who is living in a higher realm of mind; all past, present and future are alike for him/her.

If you are a fan of Sci-fi movies, you must have seen 'Lucy' 2014, a movie based on an accident of protagonist Lucy who unlocks 100% of her cerebral capabilities gradually throughout the movie. At the end of the movie, when Lucy unlocks 90% of her brain, she surpasses the boundaries of time and space and is able to travel through time and space. In an amazing scene, she goes to the point of the beginning of human life on this planet to the present time. Besides the picturisation of the scene, even more amazing is the concept which shows a connection between higher brain capacity and opening of new dimensions of reality. The only connection we see otherwise is that some human of high intellect might be able to develop a device that makes time travel possible. However as a race, we are not sure that we will be able to handle any such innovation yet or not. But what if we tell you that this concept is not new for humans and Vedic rishis were very well-versed in the science of time travel. Exactly like the movie where they did not bother to develop any device for time travel, Vedic rishis too were traversing through time and space by their enhanced wisdom and *yogic* power. However it is unclear if the writers or creators of this movie have taken their inspiration for the story from the Vedas but their depiction of the concepts of human perfection resembles the concept of four stages of yogic perfection (an ascending state of the mind of *yogis*). The culmination point or the last state 'Turiya' is defined as a state when a yogi is free of every limitation of matter, time, space, life and death. Many puranic stories talk about the reappearance of rishis or avatars to guide or help their devotees even after thousands of years of their physical demise. There are so many stories where Krishna appeared before his devotees like *Meera-Bai* or Ram appeared before *Tulsidas* or great rishis who came to the rescue of their devotees in their difficult time or provided them with the right guidance. *Tulsidas, Meera, Danna Jat* and other devotees had the divine experience of meeting their respective form of God who lived thousands of years ago. Many disciples have received guidance from their holy-master even after their demise. We can deduce that all these great yogis had surpassed the limits of birth and death, time and space through their higher level of yogic wisdom or in 'scientific' terms, by the unlocked brain. In fact, the other abilities too that are shown in the movie with the unlocking of the brain, coincidently or perhaps inspired; shows similarity with the traits of *yogis* described in Puranic stories. Quite often in Puranic tales, we read about *yogis* who sit in *samadhi* for years and wake up only when they are required to play some essential role in the on-going event designed by the cosmos for them. The story of *Rishi Shringi* who performed the *yajna* that causes lord Rama and his brothers to be born was one such story. Sitting in samadhi for years without eating anything is possible only when you win your hunger and are able to control the metabolism of your body, just as the protagonist Lucy is shown to be doing in the movie when she unlocks 25% of her brain. The most recent evidence of yogic samadhi is found in an excavation site of Balathal Rajasthan where a 2,700 years old skeleton of a yogi sitting in padmasana and gyan mudra is found. The age of the skeleton is determined by carbon dating technique but after learning about so many yogic capabilities, we have a strong reason to see the skeleton much older than it is determined.

But neither the movie nor the other states of yogic perfection is our topic for this section. Hence, we must come back to the subject matter of this section and the most important element of this cosmic, time.

कालो अश्वों वहति सप्तरश्मि : सहस्राक्षो अजरो भुरिरेता: ।
तमारोहन्ति कवयो विपश्चितस्तस्य चक्रा भुवनानि विश्वा ॥

—Atharvaveda; अथर्ववेद : 19/53/1

This *shloka* of Atharvaveda's *Kaal-Suktam* defines time

as a horse which is the driving force behind the ceaseless motion of the entire cosmos, *sapt-rashmi* (can be interpreted as the 7 rays of sun), has thousands of eyes, which means that it sees everything that happened, is eternally young and the most powerful. The second line of the *shloka* that we are trying to establish through this chapter says, "The seers of high wisdom will mount this horse", meaning the man who has developed the high level of cosmic wisdom through yoga can traverse through *kaala* (time). The last part of this shloka states *kaala* as the most powerful element of the universe which reigns over the entire existence and never ceases or amends its motion for anyone. However, both modern science and the Vedic tradition talk about one ultimate force before which even the time bends. The Vedic tradition states Shiva as *Mahakaala*, god of time and death, the only entity in the entire universe that can command the motion of time if he desires so. Similarly, scientists of the modern age talk about extremely dense objects called black holes, with the extremely strong gravitational pull that can even bend the motion of time. Despite tremendous similarities between Shiva and black holes, due to lack of Vedic affiliation, we will not draw any parallel between Shiva and these highly dense objects. Black holes are highly dense points in the universe which can devour many solar systems and be the cause of *pralay* (*pralay* is different from *Mahapralaya* in which the entire universe will be dissolved). The Puranas describe shiva, the god of destruction too with similar characteristics, the replica or original fragment of the Supreme God, *Brahman* and that is why he is called *ajanma* (never born), *avinashi* (indestructible) and someone in whom this entire creation will dissolve one day. The rule of creation says anyone who is born has to die one day including the gods. Just like humans, their life too is limited by time/age; the age of Brahma is discussed in later part of this chapter. Vishnu at the beginning of creation and with ultimate destruction (*Mahapralaya*) ceases to exist. But Shiva who was never born is beyond the limits of death and time. Shiva Puran praises Shiva as the originator of the energy which made this creation to happen; this very energy initiated the ceaseless motion of time. And due to this reason, worship of Shiva has been associated with worship of time and death in many puranic tales. Not just in the purana, but there is also some archaeological evidence of the relation between the worship of Shiva and worship of time. You all have heard about *Mahakaala Jyotirlinga* temple in Ujjain, Madhya Pradesh. As the name suggests, this temple has been associated with both death and time. The site of the temple was originally a crematorium till the temple was built there by the great king *Vikramaditya*, which signifies that Shiva is the ultimate resort of human life. In the end, nothing but Shiva will be the final truth of everybody's life. And as the Hindu concept of life says, it is nothing but play of time and karma of a soul in this *Mrityuloka*. The end of time of a soul on this planet is actually known as death and hence, it is all about time.

Therefore, our ancestors used to see some geographical connection between *Mahakaal* and time calculation.

Vikram Samvat, a calendar system ascribed to King *Vikramaditya* used to consider Ujjain as the centre of the universe. In fact, in 1884, Greenwich became universally accepted as the prime meridian, the international standard for 0° longitude from which time is calculated for the entire world. Ujjain was considered the central meridian for time in India to prepare Hindu *Panchang* (almanack). The famous astronomical treatise *Surya Siddhanta* also recognises Ujjain as the naval point of earth and situated geographically at the precise spot where the zero meridian of longitude and the Tropic of Cancer intersects.

However, the calculation of time from a precise single point is just a tool of human convenience. Otherwise, the best time keeping machine in the world is your own body. Nothing can keep the time more accurate for you than your biological cycles/clock. The rate by which the tissues of a body decay can also be a subjective unit of time for a man. Just like *Rishi Lomesh* who had the boon of long life; he had the boon to live till the time all the tissues of his body dies, which of course, sounds like simple biology of every human body and not a boon. But the catch was that each tissue of *Rishi Lomesh* dies in thousands of years and just like any other human being, he has millions and trillions of tissues to shed before he dies. Therefore, his age is to be calculated in *yugas* and *maha-yugas* and not in years. The curious case of *Rishi Lomesh* substantiates our definition of life as per Hindu tradition that life is nothing but the lapse of time of a body. Although *Rishi Lomesh* has time in abundance, still his time too will lapse one day and that makes him the subject of time. But if you are not *Rishi Lomesh* and your biology works as usual as any other human being, you must keep the time as the most precious commodity because it is running incessantly and never coming back.

Wise men say that to understand the value of time, you should track time in seconds and not in days or hours. And if every second is so valuable for us, let's try to understand how every second is defined. Of course, there would be a standard for it too just like we have for other units of weight and length; or the way the ancient Hindus had the set standard for their smallest standard unit of time, *nimisha*.

A *nimisha* is the time taken in a blink of your eyes and unlike other biological activities like breathing or pulse which varies with condition of a body, it is the most standard activity for all types and conditions of the human body. In classical India, *nimisha* used the reference unit of time to calculate the higher and lower units of time,where 3 *nimishas* is 1 *kshana*, 5 *kshanas* is 1 *kashtha* and so on. Likewise, the modern standard of time is defined by hours, minutes and seconds where 1 minute is 60 sec and 60 minutes is 1 hour. But what is 1 second?

The journey of humans keeping time is a long one and in this process of comprehending and defining the value of time, we tried many things to eliminate every slightest discrepancy possible. In the olden days, techniques like water clocks or sundials were being used. Then we divided a calendar year or a day by the fraction of 60 which is called sexagesimal divisions. Standard movement of pendulum of 1 metre was also a parameter to define 1 second till the time we found the most reliable and accurate method through atomic reaction in which one second is exactly "the duration of 9,192,631,770 periods of the radiation corresponding to the transition between the two hyperfine levels of the fundamental unperturbed ground-state of the caesium-133 atom" (at a temperature of 0 K).

Accurate or less accurate but all these biological, mechanical or atomic methods can tell you the passing of time in the same interval. But if you want to go beyond time, which has been an age-old urge of humans, we need to rise way above ordinary human intelligence. In fact, this idea of stopping time itself sounds very impractical and impossible. Many great scientists have given their viewpoint on the possibility of making time-machines. Einstein's theory of relativity was the point in modern history that stirred the debate about the possibility of making a time machine.

The machine, if made successfully, can allow the user to play around with the past, present and future. However Stephen Hawking in his renowned work 'A Brief History of Time' defined theoretically why time travel is not possible and his objection holds many validations. Undoubtedly, no one in the modern times knows 'Time' the way Stephen Hawking or Einstein did. Yet, the degree of understanding of *kaala* (time) in the Vedas or in other Hindu scripture puts Vedic rishis on a higher reverence point.

However, the urge of the Vedic people to ride over

time is quite surprising because they had tremendous respect for the laws of nature and their philosophy teaches to accept the will of the cosmos without interfering with it, even if they can. With respect to time and death, their philosophy is quite unusual and their efforts to dodge them are startling, especially for the *yogis* who renounced the material pleasure to live a life of austerity and were always busy in the pursuit of knowledge. Why did they want to live for thousands of years even when they had renounced every other thing in the world? With a life with no worldly desires, why did they have so much obsession for a long life? To understand this clearly, we need to look at some Puranic tales of some such yogis who were in the pursuit of life beyond time. And undoubtedly in their pursuit, Mahadev Shiva, the God of time was their muse and impulse.

The epic of *Rishi Markandey* is one such tale where gati (speed) of *kaala* (time) made an exception on the command of God Shiva. Once there was a sage *Mrikandu* who was childless for a long time. He and his wife *Marudmati* worshipped Shiva to seek boon for begetting a son. Pleased by their devotion, Shiva offered them two choices, either to have a righteous and wise son, but with a short age of 16 years or a stupid, thick headed child of low intellect but with a long life. *Mrikandu* chose to have a short lived but intelligent son and he was blessed with *Markandeya*, an exceptionally wise son who was destined to live just for 16 years of age. *Markandeya* grew up to be a great scholar; he mastered all the Vedas at an early age. When he turned

16, he devoted himself in the worship of lord Shiva and on the day of his destined death, he continued his worship of Shiva in his aniconic form of *Shivalingam*. When *Yama*, the god of death came to take his soul out of his body, *Markandeya* embraced the *Shivalingam*. When *Yama* sprung his noose over *Markandeya*, it accidently landed around the *Shivalingam*. Looking at the state of complete surrender of *Markandeya*, Shiva emerged to his rescue and killed the god of death himself, whom he revived later. In his explanation, *Yama* said to Shiva that *Markandeya* had finished his time on earth and it was his duty to take him to *Yamalok*. To relieve both *Yama* and *Markandeya* of their difficulty, Shiva ordered kaala to make an exception for *Markandeya*. This is how Rishi *Markandeya* got the boon to never grow old and be 16 year old eternally. Therefore, besides the profound message given through the choice made by the parents of Rishi *Markandeya* that a short life but lived wisely is way greater than a long but unwise life; this story also tells how Shiva stopped the motion of time.

This actually means that time had made an exception for *Markandeya* and ceased his motion for him and eventually, he remained the same age of 16 years till the end of this world. To this day, *Rishi Markandeya* is reckoned as the great *Chiranjivi* of Puranic tradition with his eternal youth.

Not only *Rishi Markandeya* but there are several *rishis* in Hindu tradition who are revered as *Chiranjivi*, the long lived. All the rishis who were long lived can also travel to different *loka* with their physical body, which substantiates that a yogic accomplishment which enables a *yogi* to traverse through time also enables him to traverse through space. Possibly, this *yogic* accomplishment opens up a different dimension for a *yogi*, which otherwise remains unknown to others. Very logically so because till the time a *yogi* is bound by the time limit of his human body, his travel to a *loka*, where time runs differently makes his travel chaotic for his life back on this planet. In fact, there is a puranic tale that explains the consequences of playing with time without mastery over this quintessential element of creation. *King Kakudmi*, a very wise and benevolent king who ruled in the later part of *Satyuga* had a virtuous daughter named *Revati*. Though they were humans, both King *Kakudmi* and *Revati* were well-versed in *yogic vidyas* and Vedic knowledge. Looking at the superior attributes of his daughter, the king wanted a groom, who would be the best among men for *Revati*. And hence he thought no one less than the Creator himself, Lord Brahma can help him to find an equivalent match for *Revati*. Using their yogic powers, they both reached *Brahma-loka*. When they arrived, Brahma was listening to a musical performance by the *Gandharvas*, and as a courteous call, they did not interject in the middle and waited a few minutes until the performance was finished. After both *Revati* and *Kakudmi* greeted Brahma with humility and respect, *Kakudmi* explained the reason for his visit and presented the list of shortlisted prospects for her daughter. The creator god after listening to the king's concerns explained to him some startling facts about the passing of time at different lokas which he had ignored during his visit. Brahma said the few minutes that he had spent along with his daughter in *Brahma-loka* was equivalent to a *Chaturyuga* in *Mrityu-loka* (earth); which means when he goes back, all the prospect males, their grandsons, and their grand-grandsons would have gone. Whatever he had left behind in *Mrityu-loka* would vanish and till the time he reached there, the earth would be about to enter into *Kali-yuga*. Brahma said, "Still to your consolation O great king! I tell you the groom you are looking for, *Balarama*, incarnation of *Sesh-naag* and the elder brother of Krishna will be in the marriageable age and will be the most suitable partner for your virtuous daughter." On Brahma's advice, both *Kakudmi* and *Revati* descended to *Mrityu-loka* and met Krishna and his elder brother Balarama and narrated the entire story. The match made by Brahma himself was well accepted by everybody. Yet the difference in the makeup of people of two different *yugas* was a big hurdle. *Revati* was way much taller than *Balarama*. The story says *Balrama* with his plough tapped *Revati* on the shoulder that shrunk her to his size.

However, the story ends with a happy ending but the subtle message that it carries, tells us that laws of creation are not the things to play around for fun. Possibly due to his proximity with gods, *King Kakudmi* learnt the trick to travel through different *lokas*, which meant that he got mastery over the dimensions of space but certainly he was ignorant of the aspects of time. Although Hindu Puranas are full of characters who used to travel to different *lokas* very frequently, no such issue of time arose with them in any other story, which clearly demonstrates that Vedic scriptures define every phenomenon related to travel through time and space through a sequence of events.

A *yogi* who is graduating in his pursuit of perfection attains many *yogic* powers and the one who reaches to fourth stage of *yogic* perfection (*Samadhi Avastha*) is able to rise above the limits of time and space as mentioned in the *shloka* of *Atharva-Veda*. It means for a *yogi* in this stage, time and space is just a delusion. That means they cease to happen for a *yogi* of that perfection and adhering to the limits of time and space is just a choice for him/her. *Rishi Narad* is the perfect example of the *yogi* who knows how to wield the *yogic* powers of time travel without creating any disturbance into it. *Narada* is the quintessential character of almost every Puranic epic and his primary role was to guide and make the main characters of the epic aware about the ongoing events of *Triloka*. His power to travel with the speed of mind and knowledge of the past, present and the future makes *Rishi Narad Trikaal-darshi* or *Trikaal-jnani* (knower of everything).

Don't you think if we superimpose the state of mind which is called *Trikaal-jnani* or *Trikaal-darshi* in Hindu Puranas, it will match the cosmic phenomenon Einstein had explained in his theory of relativity; a point where present, past and future exist simultaneously, a bend in space, time fabric? This is exactly the concept shown in Christopher Nolan's epic science-fiction movie Interstellar. The thought itself is very exciting and amusing that 'primitive' Vedic Rishis had mastery over the cosmic phenomenon that still is a big, big mystery for scientists equipped with space stations, supercomputers, the Hubble telescope and what not. Isn't it?

Unlike the scientists or physicists of today, the Vedic rishis did not leave behind high-tech infrastructure, tools and gadgets to replicate their success. What they left was some scriptures and some techniques to delve deep into yourself, your true self. And the biggest catch you find after exploring the Vedic scriptures was that the most ambitious achievement for the finest brain of today was just a by-product of *yogic-sadhna* aimed to discover the ubiquitous soul, the true you, the self actualization. No wonder, if we can change our approach towards Vedic knowledge, we will be able to unlock our inside what we are trying to search going outwards. We all have read or heard these tales of Puranas where yogis warn about some catastrophe of the future, exactly the way Ved-Vyasa did in the Mahabharata. But, of course, none of us took these 'folktales' seriously enough to ponder upon with a scientific perspective. Einstein's theory of relativity and Stephen Hawking's 'A Brief History of Time' unveils many facts about the concept of time which definitely allow a brain burning with curiosity to see 'time' differently. The well accepted theory of relativity says just like the weight of an object, time too is subjected to the gravitational force of space. If you measure your weight of 100 pounds on earth, you will measure it much lighter on the moon and likewise, time will also pass faster for you there. Of course, these are the observations of the greatest minds of modern age and astonishingly somewhat similar concepts were given by 'primitive' rishis in the Puranas. The Puranic concepts of time are divided between different *lokas* (Hindu realm of existence). They say time passes slower in *Pitra-loka* (realm where our forefathers live), 30 solar years (a human year in Hindu tradition is measured by a complete cycle of the sun between the northern point (*uttarayana*) and the southern point (*dakshinayana*) in the sky. A new year commences only when the sun returns to the same starting point) are equivalent to one year of *Pitra-loka*. Similarly one year of *Deva-loka* is equal to 360 solar years. By the same reference of calculation, one *Manvantara* (lifespan of a *Manu*, the progenitor of mankind) is made up of 3,067,200 solar years. And in a single day of Brahma, 14 such *Manvantaras* passed by and that's called a *Kalpa*. All these references of time for different realms of existence are wonders of Hindu scripture. Yet, there is a possibility that any of our readers clouded by doubts might consider it a coincidentally drawn parallel between a well accepted theory and fictitious information given in 'outdated religious scriptures'. On that account, it becomes our duty to present our readers with some more palpable evidence before we proceed to some other point. Hence, let's take a look at something that can be verified by any seeker. An exercise prevalent even to this day, which holds a lot of scientific weighting, however just like every other Vedic treasure we are surrounded by, we overlooked the practicality of it as well. While attending a *Yajna* for yourself or your kith and kin, you might have noticed that before the *Yajna* begins, *Pandits* announce some details that contain information of the *Yajmana* (doer). In these details, the Vedic scholar locates the doer in this universe (not just in your city or country) perfectly with reference to time and space. This is a kind of vow or *sankalpa* as it is said in which a doer announces before the *Purohit* to complete the *Yajna*, come what may happen. We have seen in the second chapter of this book about the value of spoken words or mantra or sound all together in Vedic tradition. Certainly they believe that sounds, in the form of vibrations never lapse; instead it lives forever in space. Keeping this in mind and in order to avoid any confusion, they invented a way to address and distinguish their *Yajmana*, the doer with highest order of precision.

ऊँविष्णुर्विष्णुर्विष्णुः श्रीमद्भगवतो महापुरुषस्य विष्णोराज्ञया प्रवर्त्तमानस्य अद्य श्री ब्रह्मणोऽह्नि द्वितीय परार्धे श्री श्वेत वाराह कल्पै ववैस्वत मन्वन्तरे अष्टाविंशतितमे युगे कलियुगे कलि प्रथमचरणे भूर्लोके जम्बूद्वीपे भारत वर्षे भरत खंडे आर्यावर्तान्तर्गतैकदेशे---*--- नगरे ---**--- ग्रामे वा बौद्धावतारे विजय नाम संवत्सरे श्री सूर्ये दक्षिणायने वर्षा ऋतौ महामाँगल्यप्रद मासोत्तमे शुभ भाद्रप्रद मासे शुक्लपक्षे चतुर्थ्याम् तिथौ भृगुवासरे हस्त नक्षत्रे शुभ योगे गर करणे तुला राशि स्थिते चन्द्रे सिंह राशि स्थिते सूर्य वृष राशि स्थिते देवगुरौ शेषेषु ग्रहेषु च यथा यथा राशि स्थान स्थितेषु सत्सु एवं ग्रह गुणगण विशेषण विशिष्टायाँ चतुर्थ्याम् शुभ पुण्य तिथौ -- +-- गौत्रः --++-- अमुक शर्मा, वर्मा, गुप्ता, दासोऽहं मम आत्मनः श्रीमन् महागणपति प्रीत्यर्थम् यथालब्धोपचारैस्तदीयं पूजनं करिष्ये।

The above given is the *sankalp* (vow) by *Yajamana* (doer) with the highest order of precision with reference to time and space, holds way more information about a man than his Unique Identity Number or social security number or PIN code of your area or any set of identity we use these days to distinguish ourselves with others. Beside the name of your planet, country, region, city, village and address of biological lineage (gotra), it actually tells the precise time of exercise; *Shveta-Varaha Kalpa*, *Saptam* (seventh) *Manvantara* or *Vaivaswatha Manvantara*, *Kaliyuga*, first part of *Kaliyuga* (Our Vedic calculation marks the beginning of *Kaliyuga* at 3102 BCE, the point of departure of Lord Krishna from earth). The month of *Yajna*, *Paksh* (*shukla* or *Krishna*, refers to lunar orientation) is part of the month, day of week, position of planets (which is considered to be the most accurate determination of time in Vedic tradition).

This ages-old Vedic ritual not just demonstrates clarity and precision with reference to time and space but it also signifies their scholarship over the subject. The spread of units of time from 10-7 *Truti* to *Maha-Kalpa* 1022 is another attestation of the knowledge of time of the Vedic people. And mind you, when we talk of the Vedic age, it is considered by a modern human being as the age where they had nothing but time. This was the age without mobile, Internet, office, aeroplanes or anything that can connect you to the outside world and eventually can keep you busy in the things beyond your physical reach. Of course, the reach of a Vedic person is not supposed to be more than a few yards or utmost some kilometres. If that was so, why did Vedic rishis want to live eternal or why living for thousands of years was considered to be the biggest boon even when they had overcome their mundane desires and were living a life of austerity?

Answers to this might help us to know the approach of the Vedic people towards their life. The way they were using their discoveries, their wisdom acquired from the Vedas might help us with their philosophy of using science. Although we believe the line of approach of humans towards the utility of science has been the same till today be it medical science, war and weaponry techniques, economy, agriculture, astronomy, mathematics, literature or jurisprudence; all the branches of science have been the same since classical time. The only point we are missing or the only difference in the modern approach of science is that we are undermining the peace of mind or the spiritual satisfaction of the soul a lot. Modern science has almost ignored the primary requirement of mind and soul and outsourced this department to religious teachers. Whereas spiritual satisfaction and the enlightenment and fulfilment of soul had been the primary focus of Vedic scientists. The degree of their dedication can be imagined by the fact that they kept the pursuit of real wisdom above all human desires. And perhaps the mystery of creation, the truth of human life they wanted to unlock, required the penance of beyond a lifetime, which enabled them to find the way to conquer time and accomplish the most precious thing a human can ever accomplish. We have learnt the epics of *yogis* who through the power of their *yogic* wisdom lived for thousands of years and in their pursuit of knowledge travelled to and fro to various *lokas*. In the same order, we have tales of yogis who acquired someone else's body, some dead-body relatively young so that they can continue their penance and achieve the desired level of yogic perfection.

The act of acquiring a body is called '*par-kaya pravesh*' in tantra tradition and there is an epic of *Adi Shankaracharya* who used this technique to obtain knowledge. In the very famous *Vada* or *Shastrarth* (practice of religious debate) between *Mandan Mishra* and *Shankaracharya* which spanned for days in which both the competitors exhausted their bank of knowledge about all the acknowledged fields of philosophies. Finally, *Shankaracharya* emerged victorious and was to be declared winner by *Ubhaya Bharati*, wife of *Mandan Mishra*, who also was the arbiter of the debate. But being noted scholar herself, *Ubhaya Bharati* took over the debate from her husband's side on the excuse that if her husband loses the debate, as per the condition of debate, she also has to accept *Shankaracharya* as her master. Therefore, it was her right to participate in the debate as her life-choices were also on stake. Being aware of the supremacy of knowledge of *Shankaracharya* in religious and spiritual philosophies, *Ubhaya Bharati* directed the debate into something any *Sanyasi* would be unfamiliar with. Knowing about *Shankaracharya's* oath of celibacy, *Ubhaya Bharati* very cleverly put questions to *Shankaracharya* about *Kama-Shastra* (science of eroticism). Clueless about this discipline, *Shankaracharya* asked for a period of six months. And in order to simultaneously keep his oath of celibacy and learn about erotic pleasure, *Shankaracharya* acquired the body of a dead king and through his body, *Shankaracharya* learnt everything about the science of marital life and resumed the debate with *Ubhaya Bharati*. Under the rich tradition of *Vada* when *Shankaracharya* satisfied the scholarly couple *Ubhaya Bharati* and *Mandana Misra*, they accepted defeat and bowed their heads in humility to become the followers of *Adi Shankaracharya* as per the condition of debate.

This legend shows that *yogis* were using the human body as a tool to experience the ultimate truth of this existence, which most apparently cannot be experienced without a physical body. And a prolonged life is just a way to break the cycle of death and rebirth so that they can preserve their first hand experience earned through *Samadhi* in this birth. Hence their race against time too was just a way to unlock the secret of this fourth dimension or perhaps all the dimensions still unknown to us. And this is how the worship of 'Time' just like any other force of nature began. As per the Vedic tradition, they would worship everything, aid of what they required in their spiritual pursuit and of course, the element of time was most important and the most powerful of those.

The Celestial Gods

ततो यज्ञे समाप्ते तु ऋतूनां षट् समत्ययुः।
तत च द्वादशे मासे चैत्रे नावमिके तिथौ॥ १-१८-८
नक्क्षत्रे अदिति दैवत्ये स्व उच्छ संस्थेषु पंचसु।
ग्रहेषु कर्कटे लग्ने वाक्पता इंदुना सह॥ १-१८-९
प्रोद्यमाने जगन्नाथं सर्वलोक नमस्कृतम्।
कौसल्या अजनयत् रामम् सर्व लक्षण संयुतम॥ १-१८-१०

These *shlokas* of *Valmiki Ramayana* was to break the auspicious news of Lord Rama's birth but as we have seen so far in this book, there was no division between science and religion in the Vedic times, primarily because Vedic rishis were actually scholars and scientists at the same time. In concurrence with this fact, none of the Hindu religious scriptures were written without astronomical, mathematical or geographical details. You will see glimpses of the scientific temperament and knowledge of astrology, mathematics and physiology of Vedic rishis in all the Puranas or classical literatures.

These *shlokas* tell about the precise time of Rama's birth with astounding astrological details. Rendering such details is still very difficult (without Hindu almanack/panchang) for any layman (non-specialist of astronomy) even in the age of software, computers and all advanced gadgets. And in classical India, a poet rishi mentioning all such details shows the omniscient nature of Vedic rishis. Instead of simply mentioning that the lord of all worlds was born with all desired qualities, *Valmiki* says Sri Rama was born on the 9th day also known as *navami*, of the waxing moon fortnight, otherwise known as *Shukla Paksha*, in the month of *Chaitra*. When the presiding deity of the ruling star of the day is *Aditi*, where the ruling star of day is *punarvasu*, the asterism is in the ascendant, and when five of the nine planets viz. Sun, Mars, Jupiter, Saturn, and Venus are at their highest position. Queen *Kausalya* gave birth to a son with all the divine attributes like lotus-red eyes, lengthy arms, roseate lips, voice like drumbeat, and who took birth to delight the *Ikshvaku* Dynasty, who is adored by all the worlds, and who is the greatly blessed epitome of Vishnu, namely Rama.

By deduction we also know that the Sun was in Aries, Mars in Capricorn, Jupiter in Cancer, Venus in Pisces and Saturn in Libra. Sun and Venus are always within 47 degrees of each other and that condition is fulfilled if Sun is in Aries and Venus is in Pisces. If Sun and Venus are exalted, Mercury cannot be exalted because Mercury is always within 28 degrees of the Sun. If the Sun is in Aries, Mercury cannot be in its exaltation sign Virgo. Aries and Virgo are too far apart. Since Moon and Jupiter are together in Cancer in the first house or ascendant, it caused one of the best forms of *Gajakesari Yoga*, a rare astrological combination that is considered to be very auspicious and harbinger of good fortune.

According to *Valmiki*, the entire solar system was celebrating the birth of Rama and as a sign of honour, they aligned themselves in the most auspicious combination; a horoscope of unmatched glory that will last forever. The reason *Valmiki* mentions so many astronomical details of the time of Lord Rama's birth is just to describe the degree of auspiciousness at the time of Rama's birth. Certainly his intention was not to leave a clue so that future generations could find out the exact date and time of Rama's birth. If that had been his intention, Valmiki could have used the more precise time detailing method known to ancient Indians since time immemorial. To add a high level of precision, ancient Indians use the five dimensional description of time that imparts *Nakshatra, tithi* (day of month), *Vara* (day of week), *Yoga* (angle of sun and moon) and *Karana* of the event that occurred.

We believe that traditional Indian knowledge of astrology (the science of rendering auspicious muhurats) was actually the precursor of astronomy (the science of calculating planetary positions) and trigonometry in the puranic time. Hence unlike the common belief of the West, astronomy in Indian tradition is not the science developed by shepherds and sailors. Instead in India, conception of the universe, observation of relative motion of other planets and of course, their significance was among the primaeval knowledge Indians possessed. Towards the end of last millennium, modern historians were writing history with a Eurocentric view that glorified only Western thinkers, philosophers and astronomers as if only the West had a monopoly over science and advancement. Their generosity in giving credits to India is restricted to ayurveda, meditation and other spiritual techniques. Inevitably, they don't want to share the credit of making humanity scientifically advanced with anyone else. And that is why they rigorously undermined the wisdom of some oldest civilisations, especially Indian. However, they give some credit to Egyptians, Babylonians and Sumerians without any hesitation. As the civilisations of Babylonians and Egyptians were not in continuity to pose any challenge to Western monopoly over science, the only fellows remaining without credits were the Indians who could have ancestral claims over many discoveries that changed the world. In the Eurocentric theory the classical Indian wisdom or the knowledge imparted in scripture is attributed to transboundary transmission of knowledge, from west to east, especially from Europe to India. They see two major events that brought some of the science into India, the 'land of mumbo jumbo'. One is, of course, Alexander's advance to India and the second era of science and development began after Muslim invasion that brought all the wisdom of middle-east with them. However prejudiced one becomes in his approach, it is nearly impossible for anyone to ignore the scientific wisdom of ancient Indians after taking a closer look at scriptures and temples, which are the most exquisite wonders of science and architecture in itself. All these Eurocentric theories are the product of colonisation where the imperial power was using these propagandas to tame the discontent of the people in their colonies. But like radioactive radiation, the harmful effects of these maliciously spread theories also haunt and affect the future generation negatively. It therefore becomes very necessary to expose the reality of such false propagandas.

To debunk this theory about 'ignorant India' here we are presenting the Indian knowledge system of astronomy of two different classifications: the *Vedanga-Jyotisha* and *Siddhanta-Jyotisha*. *Vedanga-Jyotisha* represents the Vedic knowledge tradition of India, definitely way before Alexander or Plato or Ptolemy. And the *Siddhanta-Jyotisha* represents the age of Great-Indian Mathematicians like Bhaskara, Brahmagupta, Varahmihira and many more who lived in the time when the West was going through dark ages. To take a glance at what Indians were doing with the formulas handed over to them by their *siddhantika purvacharya* (predecessors), take a look at this verse of *Sayanacharya's* brilliant work.

तथा च स्मर्यते योजनानां सहस्त्रं द्वे द्वे शते द्वे च
योजने एकेन निमिषार्धेन क्रममाण नमोऽस्तुते ॥

Sayanacharya was a minister in the court of Bukka Raya l of Vijayanagar Empire, who wrote a very popular commentary of Rig Veda and it is his commentary that was translated by Max Muller in English. He has written hundreds of commentary on Vedic scriptures and definitely was a gem of the king Bukka's court. In his commentary on a Rig Vedic verse about sun god, he wrote the aforementioned verse which praises the sun god by saying "*bow to the god whose light traverses 2202 yojanas in half a nimisha.*" *Nimisha* is of course a unit of time in Hindu *Kaal-Ganana* system (System of time Calculation) and 1 *nimisha* is equivalent to 16/75 sec. *Yojana* is a unit of length representing 12 kilometres or 8 miles. By putting these values in *Sayanacharya's* verse, you will get the speed of light 280,094 km/sec, of course, with a deviation with modern value i.e. 299792 km/sec. Yet when *Sayanacharya* was writing these verses, half of the world was debating whether the earth is round or flat. Probably, these poetries of ancient and mediaeval ages might vindicate Indians who were considered to be utterly ignorant till the time the British colonised them or some foreign culture taught them science.

Although Rama's birth chart with precise locations of planets and *Sayanacharya's* work in the field of astronomy is remarkable in their own way, yet, we are in no way trying to glorify Vedic knowledge of astrology by these incidentally mentioned snippets. The Vedic science of astrology is deep like a sea and fathomless like the universe that we have divided into two periods: the *Kaala* of *Vedanga Jyotisha* and *Siddhantik Kaala* (period) of astronomy. *Vedanga Jyotisha* deals with ascertaining time, particularly forecasting auspicious day and time for Vedic rituals and preparing calendars with accurate prediction of eclipse and occultation. The ancient Vedic texts describe five measures of time– *savana*, solar, lunar and sidereal, and *nakshatra* (lunar position in twenty seven constellations with a prominent star, taras it is named after). Astronomy of Vedic period was centric to events and people on the earth. Moreover, the mention of astronomy in Vedic hymns due to its poetic format of story-telling is quite alluding. For instance, try to figure out what this verse of Rig-Veda says:

Twelve spoke boards, one wheel, three navels. Who understands these? In these are 360 Shankus (rods) put in like pegs which do not get loosened.

—Rig Veda Samhita 1.164.48

This riddle-like verse mentions how a year looks like in Vedic India with 12 months and 360 days (lunar month of 30 days each with an *adhika maasa* (extra month) to align it with solar calendar). In fact in Puranic scriptures many mythological tales allude to the astronomical details of high significance. One such mythological tale that contains the essence of astronomical knowledge of ancient India was the epic of Moon and his 27 wives, who all were daughters of *Daksha-Prajapati*. Moon, among all his wives was a little extra fond of his fourth wife *Rohini*, whom he also paid more frequent visits to. This biassed attitude of Moon naturally invoked resentment from his other wives and as a protest, they leave Moon and complain to their father, *Daksha* about this prejudice. Outraged by the sorrow of his daughters, *Daksha* immediately curses Moon to lose all his radiance and charm. Distressed by the curse, Moon takes shelter in Shiva's refuge and pleads for relaxation. Shiva, instead of removing the curse completely, mellows it down. Now Moon will not be without radiance; rather, he will get his charm back gradually in a cycle of 15 days. And that explains the cause of the waning and waxing cycle of the Moon. Similarly, the 27 wives of the moon are the 27 *nakshatras*, the celestial division of the sky subtended 360° into 27 equal portions of 13°20 mins each. Every *nakshatra* is named after a prominent star of it. *Rohini*, which is also a *nakshatra* or the prominent star of *Rohini nakshatra* is depicted as the favourite wife of the moon. And it might surprise you that it is the star that observes very frequent lunar occultation as it is told in the story. Whereas the other stars, exactly as it is said in the story about other wives (stars of *nakshatra*), observe lunar occultation as a rare phenomenon.

Many puranic stories and Vedic hymns have a lot of science and astronomy encoded in them. In fact, almost every puranic scripture contains some astronomical or astrological references that give an idea about the period and time of the event. Very similar to the *shloka* of Valmiki Ramayana given at the beginning of this section, more than 250 astrological references are given in the Mahabharata, which not only helps us to determine the date of the event but also tells us the spread of knowledge of mathematics and astronomy in classical India. Astronomical references will not surprise anyone who is aware of the fact that many of the prominent characters were the master astronomers. Krishna and *Balarama* who resided in *Avantika* (Ujjaini) at *Guru Sandipani's ashram* for their studies was the centre for mathematical and astronomical studies from a long time in history. Likewise *Bhishma* was a noted mathematician and an astrologer who also trained all three of his disciples *Vidura, Pandu* and *Dhritarashtra* in various disciplines including astronomy. It is no surprise that *Dhritarashtra* mentioned many peculiar astronomical events that might have taken place during the Mahabharata period.

It is very likely though that the mention of eclipse or some planetary positions with precise location will not entice a reader of modern time, especially for whom all this information is just a click away. But definitely possessing the level of wisdom before 1200 BCE that required calculating the positions of planets, upcoming astronomical events, eclipse and its factor to precision (which was exclusive to Indian astronomy) was definitely a big deal. In the present time, when a calendar of hundreds of years ahead is handy to even a 14 year old, all these details might become so elementary that it cannot excite you anymore. But allow us to take you on a tour of the time when most of the civilisations were unaware of the science behind these astronomical events. Would you believe if we said that even a tiny piece of information could have changed the course of the history of the world?

In October 2134 BC, the Chinese emperor *Chun* got two of his men *Ho* and *Hi* executed because they failed to alert the emperor when a dragon was swallowing the sun.

They could beat the drums and shoot fire arrows to frighten away the dragon. Although they saved the sun eventually, but the emperor had *Ho* and *Hi* executed for the neglect of their duty. But yes, that was 2134 BC and ignorance of a complex astronomical event can be ignored for that age. What if we tell you that the history of England could have been different if the astronomers of Europe could predict the solar eclipse of 5 May, 840 CE? King Louis of Bavaria was ruling a great part of Europe. But he was so frightened by the eclipse that he died shortly thereafter. The sudden death of the King left the vast empire unattended, sparked a dispute among his sons for the throne. And this dispute of succession eventually had Europe divided into three large areas corresponding to France, Germany and Italy.

Coming back to our point, what purpose do these mythological tales serve; a long tale that alludes to a little scientific or astronomical detail. We believe that these perfectly knitted tales not only explain the understanding of the universe in an illustrative way but also give direction to the scattered thoughts of thinkers and philosophers. As we have been saying this throughout in our book that in ancient India, there was not any divide between religion and science. Even the rishis who were also part of mythological tales have also given the wonderful treatise on ayurveda, astronomy and many other things that later developed to become many reputed disciplines of science. As we already have mentioned, Indian science of astronomy is divided between *Vedanga-Jyotisha* and *Siddhanta-Jyotisha*. *Vedanga-Jyotisha* is more allusive and indirect whereas *Siddhanta*

Jyotisha is treatises specially developed to educate the mind, entirely dedicated to learn the science behind the complex astronomical phenomenon. One such *Siddhanta* was given by *Maharishi Vashisht* who is also one of the *Saptarishis* and therefore a prominent star of the Ursa Major (*Saptarishi*) constellation. *Vashisht Siddhant* is one of the oldest treatises of Indian astronomy which besides telling the speed of the sun, the moon, planets like mars, Jupiter and Saturn, it also describes the increase and decrease in the length of the day in various seasons. And like a great teacher, *Maharishi Vashisht* not only educates his pupils through the discoveries he made and calculated but also prescribes the future generations of astronomers not to rely only on mathematical calculations to predict astronomical phenomena. *Maharishi Vashisht* very categorically stated that in the long run, the movement of celestial bodies may differ that will cause an error in calculation. Hence in order to maintain precision in astronomy, an astronomer should practice both observation and calculation side by side.

Unfortunately, the original text of many *Siddhantas* given by Vedic Rishis like *Parashar*, *Vyasa*, *Pitamaha*, *Lomas*, *Angira* are now lost. Yet some phenomenal work is preserved in the form of commentaries or fragments of original text. For instance, *Surya-Siddhanta*, the most famous of all the *siddhantika* works, was originally created by *Mayasura*, father-in-law of Ravana. *Mayasura*, besides being a great mathematician and astronomer, was also an exquisite engineer and architect. According to the Mahabharata, on the insistence of Krishna, *Mayasura* constructed the grand palace for *Pandavas*, full of wonders and illusions in Indraprastha. He also gifted *Bheema* his mace. It is said that the sun god himself revealed to *Mayasura* the exquisite knowledge of the universe and planetary motions. *Surya-Siddhanta* asserts that earth and all planets orbit around the sun which is treated as a stationary globe. It calculates the earth's diameter to be 8000 miles (7928 miles, modern value), and the diameter of the moon as 2400 miles (2160 miles, modern value). This was the earliest text to discuss trigonometric functions and sexagesimal fractions. And as asserted by many modern scholars, *Surya Siddhanta* is the most reasonably accurate text among all ancient astronomical texts from Babylon, Sumer and Greece.

Very similar to other classic literature, *Surya Siddhanta* too is written in poetic-rhyming metre that explains complex mathematical theorems using *Bhutasankhya* system (refer chapter 6) to represent numerical values. Almost all *Siddhantika* treatises used a typical cryptic style that is easier to remember and transmit without any errors of human memory. Evidently, the rich and impeccable Sanskrit tradition made it possible for mathematicians and astrologers to pass on their knowledge to the next generations. These rhythmic-poetries offer encoded firsthand knowledge in terms of formulas to calculate the orbits and diameters of celestial bodies. Equations presented in *Surya Siddhanta* also offers the formulas to predict the current locations, time of orbit and diameter of the planets of our solar system which helped us to calculate the solar year up to accuracy of second; that is, a solar year consists

of 365 days 6 hours 12 minutes and 36.56 seconds. It also gave methods to factor the lunar month that consists of 27 days 7 hours 39 minutes 12.63 seconds, which eventually allowed us to develop the Luni-Solar calendar by adding an *adhika maasa* (extra month) in a cycle of approx 33 month. In the table below, you can see the level of accuracy offered by *Suryaa-Siddhanta* in terms of calculating orbit time of different planets vis-á-vis their modern value.

Surya Siddhanta		**Modern Values**
Moon	27.322 days	27.32166 days
Mercury	87.97 days	87.969 days
Mars	687 days	686.98 days
Venus	224.7 days	224.701 days
Jupiter	4,332.3 days	4,332.587 days
Saturn	10,765.77 days	10,759.202 days

Surya Siddhanta was such a significant book on astronomy that it changed the course of perceiving cosmos not just in India but around the world. In the 750's CE, *Surya Siddhanta* was translated into Arabic during the reign of Abbasid Caliph *Al-Mansur*. With this light of knowledge of mathematics, astronomy and ayurveda, Arabia entered the golden age of knowledge. And it is from Arabia, the Vedic knowledge disseminated to Europe during crusade wars, without giving much credit to the source of origin of that wisdom, which certainly was India.

The Extra-Terrestrial Gods

In the previous chapter, we discussed astronomy in detail; which of course, is a branch of astrology. Astrology is a rough translation of the Sanskrit word *jyotisha*; originally used in India to describe the science of prediction. Here *jyoti* means light—the light of heavenly bodies that illuminate in the dark or at night. In Indian terms, therefore, astrology can also be called the science of light. In the previous chapter, we saw the stretch of knowledge classical Indians possessed about their observational universe. In most of the world's religions, the three worlds are mentioned as Heaven, Hell and Earth. However, in Hinduism the entire cosmos is divided into fourteen *lokas*. These fourteen *lokas* together are called the *Brahmanda* (Universe). Out of these, the part of the universe that can affect humans on earth or that can be seen by naked eyes is divided into three *lokas* namely *Bhu*, *Bhuva* and *Swaha loka*. Where *Bhu loka* is the earth, the *Bhuva loka* is located between earth

and sun and abode of *munis* and *siddhas*. It is identified with the Earth's atmosphere and the space, which is in the immediate vicinity of the Earth. *Swaha loka* is between the sun and polar star and it is the abode of Indra and other demi-gods, the devas. If this sound of *Bhu, Bhuva, Swaha* sounds familiar to you, let us help remind you where you heard it before, perhaps multiple times. The most popular of Vedic chants, the *Gayatri mantra* begins with bowing to the universal force called *Om* that is omnipresent in the entire universe and the lord of *Bhu, Bhuva, Swaha loka*.

Let us get back to our primary business to explore the extent of knowledge of ancient Indians of their observational universe which they have divided into three *loka* and often referred to as the *Loka-aloka* Mountain, which means a border between 'a world and no world'. Where the *loka* means the world in *Bhu, Bhuva, Swaha* and *Aloka* or no world are the other Lokas beyond this point of observational universe. As we can figure out in puranic cosmology, the border between the known universe and the universe beyond that point is divided by a point described as a mountain range and referred to as *Lokaloka* mountain.

Undoubtedly India was one of those ancient civilisations who got fascinated by the illuminating sky and discovered the hidden secrets of it. Here we are going to take a look at why ancient Indians were keeping track of those celestial bodies so diligently. Did they believe that the positions of these planets have actually had some impact on their lives or extra-terrestrial events? And how right they were in believing so?

"Believing nothing, the skeptic is blind; believing everything, the naif is lame"

Before anything else we need to know that predicting the future was not exclusive in ancient India. People across all the ancient civilisations were reading omens to portent future events. In fact many civilisations, Egypt, Greece and Sumeria had believed that celestial bodies and their positions affected natural events and people on earth. People in Egypt used to see the connection between the heliacal rising of the Sirius star in mid-August with heavy flooding in the Nile river till recently. People in Greece developed their own science of prediction dependent on the positions of stars and planets. Although it's quite similar to Indian astrology in many ways, the fundamental difference was in the nature of prediction. Western astrology is more into predicting the psychology of a person by analysing his Zodiac sign and planetary positions. Whereas Indian astrology predicts all major future events of life as well, which includes the prediction of health issues, career, marriage, children, and change in demeanour or hobbies with change in position of planets in horoscopes. Which implies that the mind, body and life energies of every human is affected by the positions of planets and stars of his/her horoscope. Millions of people across the world have got their horoscope read and got predictions about their life and future to a certain degree. Yet the people who consider themselves the flag bearers of rational and scientific thinking, outright reject any such idea which is based on a primitive concept that sees a connection between life on earth and heavenly bodies in sky. And perhaps due this preconceived prejudice for their own ancient tradition Indians are not able to claim the treasure of their rich past.

A social phenomenon of the Indian education system where all analytical, rational and brilliant minds are routed into the disciplines of maths and science with a derogatory viewpoint for Vedic traditions. Whereas Vedic schools have become the centre for religious studies, where disciples gain Vedic knowledge just to secure their livelihood as per their family traditions. Means scientific temperament or analytical thinking is not at all a criterion for votaries of Vedic studies in these Vedic schools. This has created a hiatus between science and religion where all analytical and aspirational minds are routed towards science and all religious bent of mind votaries join Vedic studies. This divorce between the Vedas and analytical thinking is itself paradoxical in nature. Rarely, a few scientific minds after claiming success in some stream of modern science look back to foraging through the written treasure of Hindu scriptures.

The most amusing fact about the clash between science and Vedic approach of life is that generally the people who proclaim themselves staunch proponents of science are actually the ones who barely know science. Whereas, the real custodians of science from Newton to Einstein to Stephen Hawking have all admitted that there is something magical about this creation, which can be explained very well by religious philosophies. To further crystallise our point about this debate between religion and science, let's take a look at the famous quotes of world famous scientists.

"Science without religion is lame, religion without science is blind."—Albert Einstein.

"All matter originates and exists only by virtue of a force which brings the particle of an atom to vibration and holds this most minute solar system of the atom together. We must assume behind this force the existence of a conscious and intelligent mind. This mind is the matrix of all matter."—Max Planck

Such sharp contrast is there between the statements of the people who actually lived science and the people who just like to promote science so that they can demean everything related to religion. Even if religion (specifically Hinduism) says to question, analyse and verify before you accept anything as truth. People with prejudice find it ludicrous to predict the future of an individual just by analysing some charts and doing some calculations. Possibly, they fail to see the same thing is being done with them in the name of science. 50 percent of our decisions are being governed or influenced by algorithms or patterns of past behaviour. Today our choices of food, clothes and places to visit are governed by these algorithms. An algorithm can tell you the effects of a drug on your body, an alternate route with less traffic, or customer foot-falls in a restaurant or in a market at a particular time. This is exactly the way astrology helps you to make the right choices. That also means the science of predicting the future has been an eternal quest of human beings. However, when it is done involving some past data, a well developed algorithm and a lot of calculation, it qualifies to become a reputed branch of science.

We assume till this point in our book we have presented enough references and examples that establishes the scientific temperament of ancient Indians and their application of mathematics and physics in everyday life. This also means that the charts of astrology too can be seen as a kind of algorithm based on the previous data by highly skilled mathematicians, physicists and cosmologists of Vedic India. The only distinction is that the phenomenons Vedic astrologers were reading to develop a data-bank, upon which the science of prediction is based, have a way bigger than the modern scientist are collecting and interpreting today. To simplify this, let us take an example from the lives around us. We are surrounded by many such species who lived on this planet for millennia, even before homo-sapiens came into the scene. The clue of the higher genetic wisdom of these creatures can be seen, when they by their weird behaviour, indicated an envisioned catastrophe like earthquake, tsunami, flood, etc., which again brings us to our point that science is not only what we understand by our limited logic and little wisdom. An entire new world of magic remains to be explored and learned. Along the similar lines of this idea, a new stream of science is trying to develop the Swarm Intelligence (SI), a technique of computational intelligence based upon the iteration of an intelligent behaviour by a colony of ants, or swarm of locusts or bees; otherwise absent in the individual agents of these groups. This clearly implies that nature has not limited the extent of imparting intelligence only to humans. And humans need to develop some more respect for all the wonders of nature; whether we understand it or not, for the time being.

Coming back to astrology, which has an ancient set of data based upon the things millenniums older than the existence of humans on this planet. At the same time, the rich data is used under the standard set of rules based on sheer mathematics, just like any other algorithmic model used today to get desired results. In fact, in India, astrology was the precursor of mathematical theories. The pursuit of gaining higher precision in astrology became the reason for ancient Indians to grow in the disciplines of astronomy and mathematics, all driven by curiosity about the effects of celestial bodies and their movement on human life on this planet.

However, the effects of giant bodies like Jupiter, the moon and sun on humans is well established. The gravitational pull of a full moon not only affects the tides of the sea but also exert influence on the body fluids of humans and other living creatures. Biological studies are there to prove that the secretion of certain hormones rises near the full moon and decreases during the new moon. Similarly, the change not just in seasons but in the behaviour of living beings on earth too can be noticed at summer and winter solstices. There are enough scientific studies to prove the effects of season on the physiology of a person born in that particular season. Your month of birth does influence your personality throughout life. For instance, schizophrenia is more common in people born in January, February and March. A majority of people suffering from autism are born in April, May, June and July. Not only disorder, but statistical evidence too suggests that the month of birth can also indicate the future inclination of a newborn. In fact Hippocrates, the father of Western medicine, observed a connection between the movements of stars and disease. Hippocrates wrote "The contribution of astrology to medicine is not a small one but a very great one indeed." Many researchers have been suggesting that astronomical information could be a great tool of diagnosis and preventive care[8].

In fact, many streams of modern physics started seeing an interrelated connection on a subtle level between life on earth and cosmos. The link between astrology and Ayurveda are millennia old and work best when used together. The fundamentals of Ayurveda are guided by tridosha (biological humors) Vata, Pitta and Kapha. All nine heavenly bodies of astrology relate to some dosha in a specific position. The Sun, Mars and Ketu are pitta or fiery planets. Jupiter, Moon, and Venus are kapha or watery in nature. Mercury, Saturn and Rahu are vata or airy in nature. Similarly, the twelve signs of the zodiac (*rashis*) follow the scheme of the elements as earth, water, fire

8. (Web credits https://www.washingtonpost.com/news/wonk/wp/2015/06/15/what-your-birth-month-means-for-your-risk-of-diseas e/)

or air signs, starting with Aries and the fire element. The twelve houses (*bhavas*) relate to different parts of the body, functions of the mind and factors of health and disease, starting with the first house as the head and relating to our overall health. Combined with yoga, astrology can heal, treat or prevent the foreseen sickness.

Specifically *Jyotish* (astrology) is a way to understand the natural connection between humans and the cosmos. Astrology, which includes astronomy, meteorology, palmistry, *swara* (reading of breath), *shagun* (reading of omens) is not to fill your life with superstitions and self doubts. If used carefully, it can guide you through the upcoming difficult patch of life or can help you make decisions. Exactly the way a counsellor provides you a more practical career guidance by observing your demeanour, inclinations and temper. Similarly your *grahas* (planets) can guide you at the junctures of dilemmas of life. Based on the ages-old data processed through charts and calculation, astrology can predict your areas of interests in the present and the changes in your inclinations with time, which of course, can help to make better career choices. Besides career and health, *Jyotish* also helps you to find a partner with better compatibility, timings of children, domestic happiness and of course the spiritual guidance on the path of self-knowledge.

By now, we all know that the entire cosmos has the same beginning. In fact, whatever you can see around, including the fellow humans consisting of the elements, spread out during the Big Bang. Isn't it amazing that man and a star born billions of years apart contain the same elements at its core? Empirically, the elements at the core of a man which defines his demeanour and also influences his actions and decisions are affected by a huge mass of the same elements aligned in a special celestial position. Exactly the way full moon and new moon affect the hormone level of a human body and tides in the ocean. Deciphering these effects of planetary motions and their positions on events and individuals on the earth is astrology. Every planet in different positions and different combinations leaves different impacts on every individual or a group of individuals.

For better clarity, let us understand the dominant effect of all nine planets of Vedic astrology. But the *Navagrahas* (nine planets) of astrology are different from the nine planets of the solar system; rather, they are the celestial bodies chosen by Vedic astrologers according to their capacity of impacting human life and on the earth. Here are the nine celestial bodies of Vedic astrology.

In astrology, the *Navagraha* are the forces that influence the decision making of human beings. In fact when the *grahas* are active in a particular *dashas* or periodicities they are said to be particularly empowered to direct the affairs of people and events on earth.

Here, *Rahu* and *Ketu* are the points where the moon crosses the ecliptic plane (known as the ascending and descending nodes of the moon). They are primarily used to calculate the dates of eclipses. They are described as "shadow planets" because they are not visible in the night sky. *Rahu* has an orbital cycle of 18 years, *Ketu* an orbital cycle of 7 years and they are always retrograde in motion and 180 degrees from each other.

Rahu makes you constantly dissatisfied with your ambitions, gains, success, money, and lifestyle. There is an insatiable hunger for more. It drowns the native into unconscious desires, which he is unable to comprehend but relentlessly pursues. This leads to addictions, obsessive behaviour, overly ambitious nature, unrealistic expectations, and fantasies. On one hand, *Ketu* relates to karma, gives the results of the deeds you performed in past life and, it relates to spirituality, liberation, and mysteries of life.

Mars (*Mangal*): With fire as its element, Mars in Vedic astrology is a masculine planet, signifying strength and supremacy. The positive influence of this fiery planet is associated with courage, enthusiasm, activity, youth, vitality, dynamism, confidence, initiation, innovation, and originality. Its negative influence connotes arrogance, ego, anger, stubbornness, selfish temperament, and recklessness.

Mars in horoscope can be both positive and malefic depending upon its placement. It can help overcome challenges, topple competition, and win over enemies. On the other hand, its energy can be self-destructive too, causing harm, injury, wounds, accidents, and excessive sexual urge to the native. A well-placed Mars in horoscope can be very positive as it makes the person a saintly fighter. Such a person usually has high values and is a justice-loving soul backed by ambition and fearlessness. They have good control over their aggressive instincts and use them wisely.

People having Mars in ascendance are usually attractive and look younger than their age. Such a person usually has effective administration and leadership skills. On the other hand, an afflicted Mars can make the person timid and fearful and if Mars is too strong in the chart, it can make the person violent and prone to self-destructive aggression.

Sun (*Surya*): In Vedic astrology Sun occupies the position of king and being a natural father of the solar system, it stands for all the masculine influences in one's life including father, husband, and male children. While the Sun represents our innermost self, the soul, we as individuals tend to only manifest the outer self or ego. It gives the natives the ability to lead, desire to earn name and fame, an ambitious attitude, optimism, and a strong will to tackle challenges effectively.

Sun is also responsible for good health, vitality and wellbeing. A strong Sun in horoscope indicates a person with leadership qualities. Such a person usually enjoys a higher position in society and shares a cordial relationship with father. A weak Sun in horoscopes can also affect one's relation with father or cause problems to the father. Natives with weak Sun usually suffer from low stamina, self-esteem, and indecisiveness.

The Moon (*Chandra*) is the closest celestial body to Earth, and has the deepest impact upon human life. In fact, depth is what the Moon is all about when it comes to its astrological interpretation. It is the representation of our inner profundity, our emotions, instincts, mood swings, behaviour, and how we feel about things and people. The way the Sun governs our soul and spirit, the Moon is what governs our mind and inner self. Moon in Vedic astrology is the silver goddess that caresses us from the very beginning in the form of our mother. It is the representation of femininity, motherhood, care, compassion, love, and sensitivity. People having a prominent Moon in the horoscope are often emotional beings with a nurturing attitude. Natives with Moon in Cancer often turn out to be the best parents in the world.

Jupiter (*Bṛhaspati*) is the biggest planet in the solar system. The closest it has ever been to Earth is 588 million kilometres. Jupiter has 63 natural satellites as Earth has the Moon as its own. Jupiter in Vedic astrology is considered to be the most benevolent of all planets, thus naturally associated with luck, fortune, and wealth. Its benefic presence can turn rags into riches. Jupiter planet is the guardian of the thinking person, the ruler of higher intellect, the embodiment of lady luck, and signifies spiritual wisdom. Jupiter represents your ideology in life. And in spiritual terms, it rules over faith, religion, philosophy, and the search for the ultimate truth of life. Jupiter governs your intrinsic curiosity to find the answers, and explore the world in the process; thus, foreign travel comes under the domain of this planet.

Saturn (*Shani*) is the second biggest planet of the celestial sphere after Jupiter. This ringed planet is 1.35 billion km in circumference. Saturn takes around 30 years to revolve around the zodiacal circle and stays in each sign for about 2.5 years. Saturn in astrology is about being disciplined, managing your time and meeting deadlines, all while keeping the restrictions in mind. There are times when you feel why your life is so difficult when you are doing everything right. It wants you to work hard, put in your best efforts, learn from your mistakes so when you get a taste of success, it still keeps you humble and grounded, despite having a wealth of knowledge. Saturn is thus a strict teacher, who is austere, but only for the benefit of the student.

Mercury (*Budha*) planet is the closest to the Sun in the celestial sphere. Mercury stays in one sign for around 25 days and takes about 10 months roughly to transit through the whole zodiacal belt. In Vedic astrology, Mercury is a neutral planet, rules over your rationality, perception and opinions, which determines your ability to negotiate, coordinate, think, understand and process information. If Mercury is strong in a horoscope, the person is likely to be a good communicator having the power to persuade. This winged marshal of the celestial sphere asks you to put logic into things, speak to your advantage, and bestows us with intellect and rationality to do it all.

Venus (*Shukra*) is the third brightest celestial body and is second closest to the Sun after Mercury. Also, it is the closest planet to Earth with the shortest distance ever being 40 million km. Venus in Vedic astrology takes around 12 months to complete one circle around the zodiac belt and stays in one sign for about 28 days. And as per Vedic astrology, Venus is love personified, it is about emotional attachment, physical attraction, marriage, union, partnership, art, culture, creativity, happiness, passion, and all that is beautiful. Venus teaches us to appreciate what is best in others; it also gives a push towards material comforts. It rules over how you socialise and indulge. Venus is all about desires, the desire for wealth and riches, the desire for sensual pleasures, the desire to see the world from rose-tinted glasses, the desire to be surrounded by beauty and creativity[9].

The way *Jyotish* sees a connection between human life on this planet and the celestial bodies is undoubtedly amazing. Like yoga, *Jyotisha* is a super science that links us with the cosmic intelligence behind nature. The principles of Vedic astrology hold the message that we humans have the same component the entire universe is made up of. New discoveries in quantum physics demonstrate the interrelatedness of the universe, showing subtle levels of immediate interaction even at great distances of time and space. *Jyotisha* is an integral aspect of the traditional Vedic sciences, along with Ayurveda, *Vastu* and yoga, all of which are usually used together.

By advocating astrology we don't want you to become a lifeless superstitious person. On the contrary, by presenting the affiliation of renowned scientists we want to encourage our young readers to explore a new dimension of science and logic that has mostly remained untouched by brilliant minds of this century.

---

9. Web credits for Navgraha astrological description: https://www.indastro.com/planets/

The Quest of Truth

The world we live in is divided in two particular categories. Here, people either subscribe to traditional religious worldviews in which they like to live their life with popular beliefs of the religion they have already subscribed to or they are born into. Or the second way is one in which they prefer to live according to a rational and science-oriented outlook. The second way nowadays is more close to atheism, where in order to keep their rationality free and objective, people tend to defy all religions. Of course, the idea of living with nothing but rationality sounds perfect, and this was the reason that the archetypal idea of discarding all religions and leading human life with a particular outlook emerged many times in recent history. Whether in the form of Neoplatonism or Marxism, any many other philosophies that emerged and revolutionised the world for a brief time. However, any such idea or philosophy could not sustain long nor could it replace the idea of living life in the shelter of some religion. Most probably because it does not function in reality the way it sounds. Because the parameters of defining rationality vary for every person and the faculties, including the brain of any person, judges reality differently and it may be deceiving sometimes and reveal different realities under different circumstances.

Today, with all the scientific advancement we can see inside a human body and dissect it up to the level of a chromosome. Yet there are many apparent things and natural phenomena we fail to describe or understand. At this juncture, the journey of rationality offers two routes, one where some relentlessly determined minds like Sir Stephen Hawking, Galileo, Buddha or Mahavir dedicate their entire lives to know the fundamentals of human life and realities of this cosmos. Just like the Vedic rishis we read about in this book, who committed themselves to break the illusion of this mundane life and decoded the reality beyond. And in their journey of unveiling the truth, they also made remarkable discoveries about the physical reality of the cosmos and human body; glimpses of which we have seen in this book.

The alternate route is where people start taking a shortcut and become dependent upon some ready-made truth. Most of the second kind of people, gradually start living their life based on some popular theories, sometimes distorted and manipulated, perhaps because anything in the name of science and rationality will be accepted by this group easily. And just like the religiously orthodox people they too become equally susceptible of being befooled in the name of rationality. However, we are in no way trying to demean either religion or science as in the very first place, any follower of the Vedas does not see any difference between science and religion. But the message we are trying to convey through this book is that the orthodoxy of non-religious and self proclaimed free-thinkers is no less than the orthodoxy of religious people. And the only way to get rid of orthodoxy and find the truth is by exploring it yourself. As it is already mentioned in this book, befooling of people in the name of religion started only when people became slaves of somebody else's religious experience. This means, whether religious or atheist you will be manipulated for some somebody else's good; if yourself is not a pursuer of truth.

Through this book we strive to present a glimpse of the first hand wisdom encoded in the Vedas. All the eight previous chapters present the cosmic outlook of the Vedas, which involves all the fundamentals of this physical reality. It might be surprising for many of those who thought of the Vedas as mere books of prayers and rituals that in Vedic dharma, mathematics has a spiritual aspect. In Sanatan Dharma, mathematics is a doorway of its other four branches which are arithmetic, geometry, astronomy and music. The Vedas do not endorse scientific temperament and learning mathematics only for practical utility in this material world. The Vedas have authenticated the belief that numbers are the sacred language of the universe. In the repeated patterns of algebraic formulas and geographical shapes, the orbits of the planets and harmonious intervals of musical tones, the Vedic rishis saw a rational cosmic force at work, which they called *Brahman*, the Supreme Creator of the universe.

With this outlook, those superior minds delved into the Vedas with the spirit of inquiry to find the ways to synchronise with the omnipresent universal force, *Brahman*. This means that even the religious tenets of Sanatan Dharma have been born out of logic and science. Every belief has to go through a long journey of time and tests to become part of the Sanatan system of beliefs.

A spiritual experience of some wise soul might have lived with him as a percept for a long time before it could become his philosophy. Over a sweet period of time, if that philosophy could guide a large group of people through their time of distress it could become a tenet. Again, a successful application of that tenet by many successive generations may make them accept it as religious principle. Thus, the tradition of worshipping time, getting yourself focused using the bliss of music or enhancing your knowledge through learning the Vedas has grown into Vedic society only after the verification by many minds in concert with cosmic wisdom. No religious idea was imposed on them, not even by God. God just directed them towards the truth. Just as in the Gita, where Shri Krishna reveals to Arjuna the fundamentals of existence but in the end asks him to choose his own course. Your actions should be guided by your own thoughts. And this unique journey towards the truth of an individual, based on his own experiences is called spirituality.

If you are thinking why we seem so much obsessed with the word 'truth', let us clarify what we actually mean by truth and what connection it has with spirituality and why it holds so much significance in Vedic tradition. But before we proceed we need to crystallise the definition of truth according to Sanatan Dharma. In Sanatan Dharma, truth is not just the opposite of falsehood, it is also the best philosophy to live by. Interestingly, it should not be religious. Instead once you find it, it should become your religion. Finding the truth in Sanatan Dharma never means to immerse yourself into the devotion of some supreme being so that you can ensure a better life after death. But it is to ensure a life without duplicity and ignorance. It is not any intangible, superficial term that takes you away from this material world and makes you live in some dreamlike mental state, detached from the realities of the world around you. Instead, truth is something that allows you to live a successful life in this world and beyond; if you find a 'world beyond' in your journey of truth. Truth is always liberating and anything that binds you is surely a delusion. It means nothing is binding on you, not even the Vedas; they are just like an instruction manual which you may refer through your journey, like many Vedic rishis did. Or you also can choose to defy everything and find your own way just the way the Buddha did. The only mandatory prescription the Vedas give to all who set out on this journey is to seek it beyond your present state of education, intelligence and limits of perception about reality. This is because your existing cognizance may deceive you into accepting your subjective reality as the universal truth. To crystallise the convoluted nature of truth you can refer to this statement of Mark Twain, which is very much in concert with the idea of truth in the Vedas:

"Truth is stranger than fiction, but it is because Fiction is obliged to stick to possibilities; Truth isn't."

Ultimately, a life lived in the shadow of ignorance and vanity is felony and a life in pursuit of truth is actual religion in Vedic tradition. That is the reason seekers are the most respected here. And it is only due to this reason this book tries to inspire its readers to be free of all biases and prejudice and find their own religion and set their own course of spirituality. As the great Indian philosopher and spiritual teacher Swami Vivekananda said:

"Every civilisation or culture has a particular life-centre, a dominant characteristic or trend and the life-centre of Indian culture is spirituality."

Of course, here spirituality means a way of life oriented towards the ultimate purpose of life, which every man should strive to achieve. This is the message that has reverberated throughout many Vedic scriptures and eulogised by many thinkers and philosophers of the world. Apollonius Tyaneus, a Greek thinker and traveller of the 1st century AD appreciated this spirit of ancient Indians, saying,

"In India, I found a race of mortals living upon the Earth but not adhering to it; inhabiting cities but not being fixed to them; possessing everything but possessed by nothing".

Ancient Indians developed and discovered many techniques that made human life simpler and advanced materially but never struck to this kind of advancement. They certainly believe that human excellence depends on the development of art. That being the reason, ancient India was the first civilisation to inculcate art, drama, dance, music and poetry into human life with the spiritual aspect of it. It also developed the finest language that helped them to express their experiences artistically and efficiently. This rich heritage of ancient India earned many admirers across the boundaries of regions and religions. Mark Twain being an aficionado of Indian heritage spoke many things to appreciate Indian traditions and culture:

"India is the cradle of the human race, the birthplace of human speech, the mother of history, the grandmother of legends and the great grandmother of tradition. Our most valuable and the most constructive materials in the history of man are treasured up in India only".

In this book, we have tried to present some glimpse of the greatness earned by Vedic rishis with a liberated and objective outlook towards the world and reality. Hence this document might help to bridge between science and spirituality. We believe the fragments of knowledge we have gleaned from the Vedas and presented here in this book will help any seeker to see the world around him/her with a broader perspective. And the Vedic outlook of the cosmos might align your consciousness with the universe or at least help to direct in this direction. To sum up, this intricate distinction between reality and fiction or truth and pretence, we quote the great Buddhist monk and philosopher Bodhidharma:

"When you don't understand, you depend on reality. When you do understand, reality depends on you."

It means when you don't understand, you rely on a belief system that is made up of things you have heard and believed before, based on your subjective knowledge and experience and thus depend on a fabricated reality, created by your own mind, which will be different from the universal reality. Whereas, in order to decode the universal reality or the ultimate truth you need to become free of the limitations of mind and experiences. Only then you will be able to synchronise with the cosmic intelligence that allows you to see through all pretences and illusions.

शादी का लड्डू

शादी का लड्डू

चैताली हातीसकर

प्रकाशक

प्रभात पेपरबैक्स

प्रभात प्रकाशन प्रा. लि. का उपक्रम

4/19 आसफ अली रोड, नई दिल्ली–110002

फोन : 23289777 • हेल्पलाइन नं. : 7827007777

इ–मेल : prabhatbooks@gmail.com ❖ वेब ठिकाना : www.prabhatbooks.com

संस्करण

प्रथम, 2022

सर्वाधिकार

सुरक्षित

अनुवाद

नीलिमा तांबे

मूल्य

चार सौ रुपए

मुद्रक

आर–टेक ऑफसेट प्रिंटर्स, दिल्ली

———————— ★ ————————

SHAADI KA LADDOO

novel by Ms. Chaitali Hatiskar

(Hindi translation of SHAADI KA LADDOO)

Published by **PRABHAT PAPERBACKS**

An imprint of Prabhat Prakashan Pvt. Ltd.

4/19 Asaf Ali Road, New Delhi-110002

ISBN 978-93-5521-226-9

₹ 400.00

मेरे माता-पिता
को
समर्पित

आभार

जब लिखना शुरू किया, तब मैंने सोचा नहीं था कि यों ही कुछ-कुछ लिखते रहना एक दिन एक पूरी पुस्तक की शक्ल ले लेगा। इसके लिए मैं कुछ खास लोगों को धन्यवाद देना चाहूँगी।

मैं रेंजिनी नांबियार का शुक्रिया अदा करना चाहूँगी, जिसने हमेशा ही मुझे सही राह दिखाई और मेरा हौसला बढ़ाया।

मैं किन्नरी देसाई की आजन्म आभारी रहूँगी, जिन्होंने हमेशा मेरा साथ दिया और कभी कोई सवाल नहीं किया। इतने वर्षों से उन्होंने हमेशा मेरा उत्साह बढ़ाया, मैंने जो कुछ किया, उसमें बिना शर्त मेरा साथ दिया।

मैं धन्य हूँ कि आलिया और वनीता जैसी दोस्त मुझे मिलीं, जिन्होंने हमेशा ही मुझे खुश और प्रेरित रखा। ईश्वर से मनाती हूँ, हम आनेवाले कई वर्षों तक साथ रहें। दिल को जीत लेनेवाले व्यक्तित्व के लिए इन दोनों का शुक्रिया। आप सभी को मेरा प्यार।

1

"तुमने shaadi.com ध्यान से देखा?"

"हाँ।" गहरी साँस लेते हुए, स्वयं पर नियंत्रण लाते हुए वेद ने संक्षिप्त रूप में हामी भरी।

"जीवनसाथी?" (Jeevansathi?)

"जी" फिर गहरी साँस छोड़ते हुए वेद ने जवाब दिया।

"भारत मैटरीमोनी?" (Bharat Matrimony?) एक और 'हाँ'।

"फिर? कोई पसंद नहीं आई तुम्हें?"

"नहीं मम्मी! नहीं आई", चिल्लाते हुए वेद ने उत्तर दिया। अपना माथा खुजाते हुए वेद अपनी कॉफी को देख रहा था। उसे जीवन में बहुत ही कम चीजें पसंद थीं, जिनमें से 'एस्प्रेसो' कॉफी एक थी। रात वेद की आँखों में कटी थी, इसीलिए सुबह वह व्यापार की ताजा खबरें, कॉफी और सुबह के एकांत के मजे लेना चाहता था। किंतु उसकी माँ ने वेद के ब्याह से संबंधित प्रश्न पूछने की ठान रखी थी। शुरू में तो उन्होंने (माँ ने) आगे बढ़कर शादी की वेबसाइट पर बेटे की शादी की जरूरी जानकारी देते हुए शादी की प्रोफाइल बना ली थी। माँ ने अपने बेटे से पूछना भी जरूरी नहीं समझा। और बिना सोचे-समझे कई लड़कीवालों की तरफ से आए प्रस्तावों पर विचार भी करने की सोची। केवल इतना ही नहीं, मुश्किलें और भी बढ़ गईं, जब वेद का फोन नंबर ही संपर्क के लिए दिया। सभी वेबसाइटों पर वेद का ही फोन नंबर पंजीकृत किया गया। वेद को अनगिनत फोन आते। जाहिर है, बेटियों के माता-पिता अच्छे वर के लिए और किसे संपर्क करते? वेद पूरी तरह हैरान और बौखला गया था।

"क्यों? इसमें क्या गलत है?" पिंकी वेद के पास आकर बोलीं।

"कुछ गलत नहीं है माँ!" वेद ने उत्तर दिया। पिंकी ने गंभीरता से अपने पुत्र की ओर देखते हुए कहा, "मैं बस तुम्हें इतना याद दिलाना चाहती हूँ कि तुम इस वर्ष 30 साल के हो जाओगे। और यदि तुमने शादी के लिए लड़की चुनने में और देर की तो तुम्हारी पसंद की लड़की मिलने की संभावना कम होती जाएगी।"

"हे भगवान्! माँ, तुम कई बार ऐसी बातें करती हो कि बस, आदमी शर्मसार हो जाए।" तकरीबन चिल्लाते हुए वेद ने माँ से कहा।

"शर्मसार?" माँ ने गुस्से में घूरते हुए वेद से कहा। "मैं बताती हूँ तुम्हें कि शर्मनाक बात असल में क्या है? शर्मनाक यह है कि अभी तक तुम खुद के लिए सुशील लड़की ढूँढ़ नहीं पाए।"

वेद ने धीरे से माँ से कहा, "प्लीज माँ! क्या इस बारे में हम शांति से बात कर सकते हैं?"

"नहीं।" माँ ने जिद से नकारते हुए कहा, "आज तुम इस बात से भाग नहीं सकते। तुम कब तक सच्चाई से भागते रहोगे? यह जिंदगी का सच है कि तुम्हें शादी करनी चाहिए और यदि तुम यह सोच रहे हो कि अचानक तुम किसी लड़की से टकरा जाओगे और तुम्हें प्यार हो जाएगा तो तुम गलत समझ रहे हो।"

आज तुम इस बात से भाग नहीं सकते। तुम कब तक सच्चाई से भागते रहोगे? यह जिंदगी का सच है कि तुम्हें शादी करनी चाहिए और यदि तुम यह सोच रहे हो कि अचानक तुम किसी लड़की से टकरा जाओगे और तुम्हें प्यार हो जाएगा तो तुम गलत समझ रहे हो।

वेद थककर सोफे पर बैठते हुए बोला, "लेकिन मुझे यह सब अच्छा नहीं लगता।"

"क्या?" पिंकी ने भौंहें टेढ़ी करते हुए पूछा।

"ये सब" अपने मोबाइल की ओर इशारा करते हुए वेद ने कहा, "ये मेरी इंटरनेट पर खरीदारी।"

"ओह, मैं समझती हूँ" पिंकी ने सहानुभूति से वेद के घुटने पर हाथ रखते हुए समझाते हुए कहा, "मैं समझ रही हूँ कि यह सबकुछ थोड़ा अजीब है, लेकिन हम सब यही चाहते हैं कि तुम जीवन में एक जीवनसाथी का चुनाव करके आराम की जिंदगी बसर करो। कहीं तो ठहरना पड़ेगा।"

अपने स्वभाव के विरुद्ध वेद चुप रहा। पिंकी ने सोचा कि अच्छा मौका है कि वेद के गले कुछ बातें उतारी जाएँ।

"एक दोस्त, अच्छा दोस्त, जो हमेशा साथ रहे, अच्छा खयाल नहीं है क्या?"

पिंकी वेद से बराबरी के जवाब की उम्मीद कर रही थी, लेकिन वेद ने कुछ नहीं कहा। हैरानी से पिंकी ने आँखें ऊपर करते हुए त्यौरियाँ चढ़ाईं। शायद उस समय माँ-बेटे में और नाटक हो सकता था। पिंकी के लिए वैसी स्थिति आम बात थी, लेकिन उसने दुःख से सिर नीचे करते हुए कहा, "कोई और बात है तो बता दे वेद!"

"नहीं। ऐसा कुछ नहीं है, कोई और नहीं है मेरी जिंदगी में।" वेद ने कहा।

"फिर दिक्कत क्या है?" पिंकी बड़बड़ाई और उँगलियों पर एक-एक करके शिकायत गिनाते हुए स्वर में प्रश्न करने लगी। "अभी तक तुमने कोई गर्लफ्रेंड क्यों नहीं बनाई? तुम डेट पर क्यों नहीं जाते? कबीर के अलावा तुम्हारे जीवन में कुछ और है क्या? सामाजिक जीव के नाम पर क्या है तुम्हारे जीवन में? न ही तुम सिगरेट पीते हो, न शराब! न तुमने किसी लड़की को आज तक चूमा। भगवान् के लिए सोचो! यह सबकुछ असाधारण सा है।"

अब शायद वेद के गले बात उतरी। माँ के मुँह पर हाथ रखते हुए वेद ने कहा, "भगवान् के लिए चुप हो जाओ माँ!"

उसकी माँ ने आखिर क्या करने की कोशिश की? जो लड़का रोमांटिक पिक्चर नहीं देखता, उसके लिए माँ का प्रेम-प्रसंगों या प्रेम-विषय पर इतना खुलकर बोलना, मानव हत्या से कम नहीं था। उन्हें कैसे पता कि जीवन में उनके बेटे ने किसी को किस (चूमा) किया कि नहीं? वह सोच के ही शर्म से लाल हो गया।

उसकी माँ ने आखिर क्या करने की कोशिश की? जो लड़का रोमांटिक पिक्चर नहीं देखता, उसके लिए माँ का प्रेम-प्रसंगों या प्रेम-विषय पर इतना खुलकर बोलना, मानव हत्या से कम नहीं था। उन्हें कैसे पता कि जीवन में उनके बेटे ने किसी को किस (चूमा) किया कि नहीं? वह सोच के ही शर्म से लाल हो गया।

वेद रो ही देता अगर उसे परेशान करनेवाली उसकी बहन के आने की आहट नहीं सुनाई देती। अभी वेद कुछ कहता, कमरे में वेदिका ने प्रवेश किया। वेदिका ने वेद के कंघी किए हुए उलझे बालों में हाथ फिराते हुए वेद और पिंकी के बीच हिल-डुल के जगह बनाई और बैठ गई। वेद सिर्फ देखता रह गया। सिर हिलाकर उसने वेदिका की उपेक्षा करनी चाही। एक इनसान एक समय एक ही युद्ध लड़ सकता है।

"माँ, मैं शादी करना चाहता हूँ...पर उसके लिए कोई लड़की तो हो।"...वेद ने अपना तर्क प्रस्तुत किया। और जहाँ तक बाकी प्रेम व अन्य बातों की बात है, मैं बहुत से क्षण उस विशेष व्यक्ति के साथ ही बाँटना चाहूँगा।"

"बुद्धू!" वेदिका ने बीच में ही बात काटते हुए कहा। "लोग आइसक्रीम भी खाते हैं तो हर विशिष्ट स्वाद का पहले रस चखते हैं।"

"वेदिका!" पिंकी ने झिड़की भरी आवाज में वेदिका को फटकार लगाई। "वेदिका! तमीज में रहो।"

"ठीक है, माँ! मैं तुम्हें दूसरा उदाहरण देती हूँ। हम कार खरीदने से पहले कई गाड़ियाँ चलाकर देखते हैं और फिर निश्चित करते हैं कि कौन सी गाड़ी खरीदें! और

जहाँ हमें लगता है कि यह गाड़ी हमारी जरूरतें पूरी कर सकती है, वही गाड़ी खरीदते हैं।"

वेद आँखें बंद करके बैठा रहा। वेदिका के विचार, ब्लैकबोर्ड पर कील चलाने पर जो कर्कशता उत्पन्न होती है, वैसे थे। उसे आश्चर्य हुआ कि उसके माता-पिता वेदिका का अनाड़ीपन चलने कैसे देते हैं?

"कार और लोगों में अंतर होता है वेदिका! कुछ तो लिहाज करो।" वेद ने उसे डाँटते हुए कहा।

"मैं बस इतना कह रहा हूँ कि किसी भी लड़की से थोड़ा सा भी जुड़ने पर मैं उसके साथ घूमने डेट पर जाऊँगा, लेकिन पहले मिले तो!"

"मैं बस इतना कह रहा हूँ कि किसी भी लड़की से थोड़ा सा भी जुड़ने पर मैं उसके साथ घूमने डेट पर जाऊँगा, लेकिन पहले मिले तो!"
"माँ, थोड़ी तो छूट दे दो इसे। यह 40 वर्ष पुरानी भारतीय लड़की ढूँढ़ रहा है और इसीलिए ऐसा है।" वेदिका ने वेद के गाल खींचते हुए कहा।

"माँ, थोड़ी तो छूट दे दो इसे। यह 40 वर्ष पुरानी भारतीय लड़की ढूँढ़ रहा है और इसीलिए ऐसा है।" वेदिका ने वेद के गाल खींचते हुए कहा।

"अपनी बकवास बंद करो।" वेद चिल्लाया।

"क्या?" वेदिका ने वेद को गुस्से से घूरा।

वेद ने लाचारी दिखाते हुए पिंकी को देखा और कहा, "माँ!"

"वेदिका, बस बहुत हुआ।" पिंकी ने थोड़े सख्त मिजाज दिखाने की कोशिश की। हालाँकि पिंकी भाई-बहन की खींचा-तानी के मजे भी ले रही थी, लेकिन वह वेद को परेशान नहीं करना चाहती थी। वह वेद की ओर मुड़ी और कहा, "तुम कुछ कहना चाहते हो?" वेद को इस विषय को जितना हो सके, टालना था। उसने कुछ देर सोचा और मन-ही-मन योजना बना डाली।

एक शिक्षित व गरिमामय व्यापारी की तरह बाँहें मोड़कर वेद सोफे पर बैठा और पिंकी से बोला, "मुझे छह महीने की मोहलत दे दो। यदि इस बीच कुछ नहीं हुआ तो तुम लोग जैसा चाहोगे, मैं वैसा ही करूँगा।"

"एक महीना, उससे ज्यादा नहीं।" पिंकी ने धमकाया।

वेद हक्का-बक्का रह गया। वह आश्चर्यचकित होकर माँ को देख रहा था; उसे न अपने कानों पर विश्वास हो रहा था और न ही आँखों पर। उसका दिमाग काम ही नहीं कर रहा था।

“माँ, मुझे नहीं लगता कि जीवन साथी के लिए और वह भी अच्छी जीवन-संगिनी को ढूँढ़ने के लिए एक महीना काफी है।” उसने (वेद ने) अत्यधिक परेशानी में शब्द चुनते हुए कहा।

“मुझे नहीं पता”, कड़ी आवाज में पिंकी ने कहा। “मैंने तुम्हारी एक शर्त सुनी, तुम्हें भी मेरी शर्तें माननी होंगी।”

“लेकिन…” वेद ने माँ से वाद-विवाद के लिए कुछ कहना चाहा।

पिंकी ने हाथ के इशारे से ही वेद के विरोध को दबाते हुए कहा, “इस बारे में और कोई सौदा तय नहीं हो सकता। एक महीना…।”

वेदिका जोर से हँस पड़ी। वह वेद की शांत दिखाई देनेवाली जिंदगी में हलचल और प्रलय स्पष्ट रूप से देख पा रही थी और मजे भी ले रही थी। वेद का स्वाभिमान! वेद की गरिमा!

वेद ने अपनी झेंप मिटाने को नाक पकड़ी और सोचने लगा, ‘ये सब किस चक्कर में पड़ गए हैं? इतनी जल्दी क्यों है इनको?’

पिंकी ने शांत स्वर में कहा, “तो यही बात पक्की रही।” वेद समझ चुका था कि पिंकी के विरुद्ध जाना अब बेकार होगा। एक बार माँ जब कुछ तय कर लेती थीं तो उसी बात पर अड़ जाती थीं। सो वेद ने चुप रहना ही उचित जाना। वेद खून का घूँट पीकर रह गया, पर कुछ नहीं बोला। “ठीक है, वादा करता हूँ।” वेद ने कहा।

वेदिका जोर से हँस पड़ी। वह वेद की शांत दिखाई देनेवाली जिंदगी में हलचल और प्रलय स्पष्ट रूप से देख पा रही थी और मजे भी ले रही थी। वेद का स्वाभिमान! वेद की गरिमा! वेद ने अपनी झेंप मिटाने को नाक पकड़ी और सोचने लगा, ‘ये सब किस चक्कर में पड़ गए हैं? इतनी जल्दी क्यों है इनको?’

“ये हुई न बात, बिल्कुल ठीक।” पिंकी खुशी से फूली नहीं समा रही थीं।

वेद ने एक नजर अपनी एस्प्रेसो कॉफी की ओर देखा। कोई कैसे इतना पागलपन सहे? परिस्थिति का सामना तो छोड़ो, इस मुश्किल से बाहर कैसे निकले, वह सोच ही नहीं पा रहा था। अपने भाग्य को कोसते हुए उसने अपनी चीजें सँभालते हुए वहाँ से भागने की सोची और कहा, “चलो, अब मुझे ऑफिस जाना है।”

अत्यधिक निराश और बेहाल वेद पैर घसीटते हुए बाहर चला गया। वेदिका अपने भाई को देखकर हँसी। भाई को उसने इतना हताश कभी नहीं देखा था। भाई-बहन के प्यार भरे झगड़े में उसकी जीत हुई थी। उसे पूरी घटना का वीडियो बनाकर आजीवन साथ में रखने की इच्छा थी।

वेदिका ने पिंकी को कंधे से पकड़कर घुमाया और कहा, “माँ, ये जीवन के 29

वर्ष में कोई लड़की नहीं ढूँढ़ सका, तुम्हें ऐसे क्यों लगता है कि वह अब ढूँढ़ लेगा? और वो भी केवल एक महीने में?"

"मेरी प्यारी बिटिया, वो इसलिए कि जब तक हम पीछे नहीं लगेंगे, वो कुछ नहीं करेगा।"

"ओह!"

"हाँ जी।" पिंकी ने आँख मारते हुए चौड़ी सी हँसी दिखाते हुए वेदिका से कहा, "हम भी कच्चे खिलाड़ी नहीं हैं। मैं भी अच्छी-खासी बिजनेस वूमन रह चुकी हूँ। मैं भी जानती हूँ कि ग्राहकों को खुश करने की योजनाएँ कैसे बनाई जाती हैं?"

"मान गए माँ! तुम तो गजब निकली।" अपनी माँ के गाल चूमते हुए वेदिका ने कहा, "मैं तो आगे का तमाशा देखने को उत्सुक हूँ।"

पिंकी ने ठहाका मारते हुए कहा, "मैं भी कहाँ रुक पा रही हूँ?"

□

2

अकीरा ने अपनी मोटरसाइकिल धीमी की। उसकी कराह इतनी ऊँची थी, जो सुनाई पड़ सकती थी। वह 'स्टारबक्स' की लंबी कतार देखकर हताश हो गई थी। उसने सोचा था—चाहे महँगी क्यों न हो, वह फटाफट कॉफी ले लेगी, लेकिन यह क्या, 'स्टारबक्स' के यहाँ तो मानो पूरा शहर ही उमड़ पड़ा था। उसने घड़ी देखी। उसे पहले ही देर हो चुकी थी। उसने अपने बाल धोने, सुखाने, उन्हें चाहे जैसे मोड़ या सीधे करने में नाहक ही समय गँवाया था। उसे खुद को सँवारने में इतना वक्त नहीं लगाना चाहिए था। उसने आह भरी।

उसे अपने दिन की शुरुआत करने के लिए सच में एक कप कॉफी चाहिए थी। अकीरा ने फिर अपनी घड़ी देखी। उसे जल्दी से निर्णय लेना था, इसीलिए सोचना भी गहरा था। अकेले व्यवसाय चलाना आसान नहीं। यदि अगले 10 मिनट भी जाते तो दिन भर की कार्ययोजना शिथिल (ढीली) पड़ जाती।

'जल्दी सोचो अकीरा, जल्दी सोचो!' खुद के कान में फुसफुसाती वह फुटपाथ पर अधीरता से बढ़ती जा रही थी।

अभी वह कॉफी की इच्छा त्यागने ही वाली थी कि उसने देखा, कॉफी शॉप से एक पतला-दुबला किंतु शानदार थ्री-पीस सूट पहने, अच्छे से बनाए बालों में और शाही विमानचालक के धूप के चश्मे चढ़ा रखे थे। उसके आसान व्यवहार से पता चल रहा था कि उसे कहीं जाने की कोई जल्दी नहीं थी और वह ऊँचे पद पर कार्यरत व्यक्ति था। 'यदि उसे देर होने की घबराहट नहीं है तो कॉफी के लिए दुबारा पंक्ति में खड़े होने में भी हर्ज नहीं होगा।' सही सोचा न मैंने! यही करती हूँ, वह खुद की सोच पर गर्व कर रही थी।

इस प्रकार अकीरा ने सोचा कि यदि इस व्यक्ति से कॉफी छीनकर भागा जाए तो गलत नहीं होगा। वैसे भी इस इनसान से वह दुबारा कौन सा मिलनेवाली है! ऐसा भी नहीं कि अकीरा के कॉफी छीनकर भागने के बाद कौन सा वह पीछे आएगा या पुलिस में शिकायत दर्ज करवाएगा और वह भी कॉफी चुराने के जुर्म में?

इसके अलावा, वह चोरी थोड़ी करनेवाली थी। वह कॉफी छीनने के बाद उसे पैसे

पकड़ाएगी न! उस आदमी को यदि कॉफी की उतनी ही तलब लगी होगी, जितनी मुझे थी तो वह दुबारा लाइन में लगकर कॉफी खरीद लेगा। हाँ, लाइन में लगना पड़ेगा, इस बात की सहानुभूति अकीरा को थी।

हो सकता है, खाली पेट अकीरा के सोचने की शक्ति पर भारी पड़ रहा था और वह सही और गलत की पहचान नहीं कर पा रही थी। या फिर वह भूख से पगला रही थी। खैर! अकीरा बेफिक्र हो गई थी।

बिना कुछ सोचे वह उस दुबले-पतले किंतु रुआबदार आदमी के पास गई। वह आदमी अपने फोन में इतना डूबा हुआ था कि ऐसी परिस्थिति अकीरा की योजना में मदद कर सकती थी। एक प्रशिक्षित सैनिक की तरह वह उस आदमी की ओर लपकी और कॉफी छीनकर भागने लगी। छीनने से पहले उसने दो सौ रुपए उसकी ओर फेंके। वह जितनी तेज हो सके, भाग रही थी।

बिना कुछ सोचे वह उस दुबले-पतले किंतु रुआबदार आदमी के पास गई। वह आदमी अपने फोन में इतना डूबा हुआ था कि ऐसी परिस्थिति अकीरा की योजना में मदद कर सकती थी। एक प्रशिक्षित सैनिक की तरह वह उस आदमी की ओर लपकी और कॉफी छीनकर भागने लगी।

वह आदमी इतना हक्का-बक्का रह गया कि केवल 'ओए!' ही बोल सका।

अकीरा की पीछे देखने की हिम्मत नहीं हुई। कुछ ही मिनटों में अकीरा अपनी मोटरसाइकिल पर थी और वहाँ से भाग खड़ी हुई, मानो कोई अपराध करके नौ-दो-ग्यारह होने की सोचता है।

पलायन! वेद भी अपने परिवार के पागलखाने से पलायन करना चाह रहा था। अपना गुस्सा पीते हुए वेद कॉफी के लिए दुबारा लाइन में खड़ा हो गया। वह अपने शोर-शराबा पसंदीदा परिवार से अलग हटकर होता, लेकिन उसने अपने परिवार की इस सच्चाई से समझौता कर लिया था। लेकिन उसका परिवार अब शादी के लिए पीछे लगकर उसे परेशान कर रहा था। वेद ने कॉफी शॉप के मेन्यू कार्ड को उदासी भरी नजरों से देखा। वेद अपने माता-पिता के लिए श्रवण जैसा बेटा था। स्कूल-कॉलेज में भी हमेशा अव्वल आता। वो कभी अपने दोस्तों-यारों के दबाव में आकर शराब या सिगरेट नहीं पीता था। जब कभी उसके दोस्त घूमते-फिरते, पार्टी करते, लड़कियों के साथ रंगरेलियाँ मनाते तो वेद अपनी परीक्षाओं की तैयारियाँ करता। बड़ों का आदर करता। वेदिका चाहे नहीं जाती, परंतु वेद परिवार के सभी उत्सवों और खुशियों में जरूर भाग लेता। वह आदर्श पुत्र था। उसे यह दुःख था कि माता-पिता उसके अच्छे होने की खुशी के बजाय, उसे परेशान करते रहते हैं।

कितने दुःख की बात थी! लेकिन सच्चाई तो यही थी कि एक महीने में वेद को

लड़की ढूँढ़नी थी। वरना उसकी माँ ने उसका जीवन नरक बना देना था। मुश्किल यह थी कि वह समझ नहीं पा रहा था कि कहाँ से शुरू करे? कहाँ से ढूँढ़े लड़कियाँ और बनाए गर्लफ्रेंड्स? यदि कोई सुंदर लड़की दिख भी जाए तो उससे बात कैसे करे? और यदि वह बात करना पसंद न करे तो?

वेद को लग रहा था कि उसके माइग्रेन की स्थिति फिर तैयार हो रही थी। उसका जीवन इतना मुश्किल क्यों? वह तो अभी तक कितना सरल और अच्छा रहा था, फिर जीवन उसके साथ गलत क्यों कर रहा था?

जैसे ही उसने खरीदी हुई कॉफी हाथ में पकड़ी, उसे अच्छा लगा। उसके जीवन में कॉफी का अपना महत्त्व था, जो उसे निराशा से हमेशा बाहर लाने में मदद करती। पर यह भी कैसे कह दे, क्योंकि जैसे ही कॉफी लेकर बाहर आया था, अचानक दो पैरों का विचित्र जीव, जिसके लंबे, भूरे बाल थे, उस पर लपका, कॉफी छीनी और अचानक 200 रुपए अपने चेहरे पर फेंके हुए महसूस हुए। एकदम से वेद की आँखें बंद हुईं और आश्चर्य की प्रतिक्रिया में वह बस इतना कह पाया, "हैं, ये क्या?"

जैसे ही उसने खरीदी हुई कॉफी हाथ में पकड़ी, उसे अच्छा लगा। उसके जीवन में कॉफी का अपना महत्त्व था, जो उसे निराशा से हमेशा बाहर लाने में मदद करती। पर यह भी कैसे कह दे, क्योंकि जैसे ही कॉफी लेकर बाहर आया था, अचानक दो पैरों का विचित्र जीव, जिसके लंबे, भूरे बाल थे, उस पर लपका, कॉफी छीनी और अचानक 200 रुपए अपने चेहरे पर फेंके हुए महसूस हुए।

जब उसकी आँखें खुलीं तो बस वह भागते हुए पैर और हवा में उड़ते किसी के बाल ही देख पाया था। और जो मनुष्य की तसवीर दिखी थी, वह बाइक (मोटरसाइकिल) पर बैठते हुए दिखी। एक हाथ में कॉफी लिये सरर से बाइक चलाकर वह चली गई।

हैरानी से वेद हक्का-बक्का खड़ा रह गया और बोला, "इसकी ऐसी की तैसी!"

□

3

वह बुरा दिन था। वेद सुबह 3 बजे तक जागकर ऑफिस की मीटिंग के लिए रिपोर्ट तैयार करने में लगा था। उसके नाश्ते के सभी सुखद स्वप्न माँ के 30 दिन की चुनौती के आगे काफूर हो गए थे। उसके बाद जैसे ही बाहर आकर कॉफी खरीदी, किसी सरफिरे ने कॉफी छीनी और गायब! वेद का खून उस लड़की के बारे में सोचने पर ही उबलने लगा। उस 'कॉफी चोर' और उस लड़की की तमीज और हिम्मत देखो, बदतमीजी से पैसे भी मुझपर फेंककर गई! जिंदगी अभी भी मेरे साथ टेढ़ी गेंदबाजी कर रही है। वो इसलिए कि उसने ऑफिस के गोष्ठी कक्ष में देखा कि उसके पिता अपने ग्राहकों से गोल्फ खेल की चर्चा कर रहे थे।

"डैड!" झूठ बोलते हुए पिता व अन्य लोगों की चर्चा के बीच बात काटते हुए कहा, "कबीर की कार खराब हो गई । यदि आप लोगों को एतराज न हो तो क्या मैं अभी जा सकता हूँ?"

अविनाश ने ग्राहकों की ओर देखकर कहा, "सज्जनो!"

उनमें से एक ने जवाब दिया, "श्रीमान वेद! कृपया आप अपने मित्र की मदद के लिए जाइए। उन्हें आपकी आवश्यकता है।"

वेद के पिता ने दबी हँसी में कहा, "ठीक है वेद, तुम जाओ।" वे जानते थे कि वेद झूठ बोल रहा था।

सिर हिलाते हुए वेद ने दरवाजे की कुंडी खोली और बाहर जाते ही कबीर को फोन करके पूछा, "कहाँ हो कबीर?" मन-ही-मन वेद कबीर से मिलने की उम्मीद कर रहा था।

"हम्म"मैं काम कर रहा हूँ।" कबीर ने जवाब दिया। वेद ने सिर हिलाया, लेकिन कबीर के पीछे से संगीत और चम्मचों के खड़कने की आवाज साफ सुनाई दे रही थी। वो समझ गया कि कबीर वेदिका के साथ डेट (मिलने) पर बैठा है और वेद की उपेक्षा कर रहा है।

"ठीक है।" बिना कुछ ज्यादा कहे वेद ने फोन काट दिया। 'मित्र हमेशा साथ देते

हैं, जब तक वे किसी लड़की के चक्कर में न पड़ें।' वेद बुदबुदाया। खासकर जब वह रिश्ता आप ही की परेशान करनेवाली बहन से हो। खिन्न मन से वेद घर की ओर मुड़ा। 'आज की रात भी इसी कमरे में बेकार की चीजें देखते हुए बीतेंगी।' खुद से वेद झुँझलाते हुए बोला। ऐसा ही भाग्य था उसका। इंटरनेट पर बेकार चीजें देखते हुए वेद समय काट रहा था।

घर वापस आने की घटना कुछ खास तो नहीं थी, किंतु वेद की नजर सहसा मोटरसाइकिल पर पड़ी और उसे वह मोटरसाइकिल जानी-पहचानी लगी। वेद को अचानक याद आया कि यह बाइक उसी 'कॉफी चोर' की है। हालाँकि उसने उस कॉफी चोर की शक्ल नहीं देखी थी, लेकिन कपड़ों से पहचान गया था कि निस्संदेह वह कॉफी चोर ही थी। वेद के शरीर में गुस्से की लहर दौड़ गई। वेद ने निश्चय किया कि वह उस लड़की का पीछा कर, उससे सवाल-जवाब करेगा। उस लड़की को पता चलना चाहिए कि उसका व्यवहार इस सभ्य समाज में अयोग्य, जंगली और अस्वीकार्य था। इस पर भी और चिढ़ानेवाली बात यह थी कि वह लड़की एक रेस्तराँ में घुस गई। उसने अपनी मोटरसाइकिल भी ठीक से पार्क नहीं की थी; जहाँ मर्जी आई, वहाँ खड़ी करके चली गई। वेद को और भी चिढ़ महसूस हुई। जो भी लड़की है, उसमें जरा भी शिष्टाचार नहीं है।

घर वापस आने की घटना कुछ खास तो नहीं थी, किंतु वेद की नजर सहसा मोटरसाइकिल पर पड़ी और उसे वह मोटरसाइकिल जानी-पहचानी लगी। वेद को अचानक याद आया कि यह बाइक उसी 'कॉफी चोर' की है। हालाँकि उसने उस कॉफी चोर की शक्ल नहीं देखी थी, लेकिन कपड़ों से पहचान गया था कि निस्संदेह वह कॉफी चोर ही थी। वेद के शरीर में गुस्से की लहर दौड़ गई।

एक बेचैन कर देनेवाली गंध ने वेद को और भी बेचैन कर दिया, जब वह उस साधारण से रेस्तराँ में घुसने लगा। मैनेजर ने पूछा, "हाँ जी! आप कितने लोग साथ हैं?"

"मैं अपने दोस्तों को ढूँढ़ने की कोशिश कर रहा हूँ।" वेद ने दाँत पीसते हुए झूठ कह दिया।

"हो सकता है उन्हें देर हो गई हो। कितने लोग?" कंधे उचकाते हुए मैनेजर ने कहा।

वेद ने साँस भरते हुए जवाब दिया, "चार?"

"जी, यहाँ बैठिए।" मैनेजर ने कोने में एक छोटी सी मेज की ओर इशारा करते हुए कहा।

वेद गालियाँ बुदबुदाते हुए वहाँ बैठ गया। कॉफी चोर शांति से भी तो ढूँढ़ा जा

सकता था। 'कहाँ है वह कॉफी चोर?' वेद ने उसे अंदर आते हुए देखा था। यदि वह कर्मचारी है तो हो सकता है कि बावर्चीखाने में हो या वाशरूम में हो। वेद कुछ क्षण रुका, किंतु उसका धैर्य जवाब दे चुका था। वह लड़की वहीं पर खड़ी लिपस्टिक लगा रही थी।

"तुम!" वेद उस पर गरज पड़ा।

अकीरा झटका खा गई। परिणामस्वरूप पूरी लिपस्टिक अकीरा की ठोड़ी पर फैल गई। वह पलटी तो देखा, एक हलके रंग की आँखोंवाला, तराशे नाक-नक्श वाला, पतली-दुबली कद-काठी का मनुष्य दरवाजे पर खड़ा उसे घूर रहा था।

"ये क्या मजाक है, तुम पागल हो क्या?" अकीरा उस पर पलटकर चिल्लाई।

तभी दूसरे बाथरूम से एक छोटा लड़का बाहर आया और उत्सुकता से दोनों के बीच शुरू होती हुई लड़ाई से आकर्षित हो वहीं खड़ा रहा। लेकिन वेद ने उस पर ध्यान देने के बजाय पहले लड़की पर ध्यान केंद्रित किया।

"अच्छा! हैरान हो अजनबी को देखकर?" वेद धमकी भरे अंदाज में आगे बढ़ा, जिसके कारण अकीरा एक कोने में पीछे हो गई। "मैं तब अजनबी नहीं था, जब तुमने मेरी कॉफी चुराई? तब मैं पागल नहीं था? तुम्मम्म 'कॉफी चोर!!!!"

अकीरा झटका खा गई। परिणामस्वरूप पूरी लिपस्टिक अकीरा की ठोड़ी पर फैल गई। वह पलटी तो देखा, एक हलके रंग की आँखोंवाला, तराशे नाक-नक्श वाला, पतली-दुबली कद-काठी का मनुष्य दरवाजे पर खड़ा उसे घूर रहा था।
"ये क्या मजाक है, तुम पागल हो क्या?" अकीरा उस पर पलटकर चिल्लाई।

जैसे ही अकीरा ने वेद के ये शब्द सुने, उसके मस्तिष्क से मानो गुस्से की चिनगारी निकली। उसने कभी सपने में भी नहीं सोचा था कि वह उस आदमी से दुबारा मिलेगी और एक साधारण से रेस्तराँ के बाथरूम में उससे सवाल-जवाब किए जाएँगे!

"मैं...वह तो...मुझे नहीं..." बड़बड़ाती हुई अकीरा की ओर वेद ने घबराहट में उँगली से इशारा करते हुए संताप से कहा, "मिस! इस बात की सफाई तो तुम्हें देनी पड़ेगी, बनती भी है।"

इतने में वेद को पीछे से किसी ने आवाज दी। अकीरा का मुँह आश्चर्य से खुला-का-खुला रह गया था।

"वेद?" अपने मित्र को वहाँ पाकर कबीर अत्यधिक अचंभित था। अगले ही क्षण वेदिका भी वहाँ आ गई।

वेद ने अपनी नाराजगी और घृणा को स्पष्ट दिखाते हुए ताना कसा, "वाह! क्या

बात है! मेरी बहन को खुश करने के लिए कितने अच्छे प्रयास कर रहे हो न! सही कहा न वेदिका? पहले मुझे यह बताओ कि तुम इतनी घटिया जगह पर क्या कर रहे हो?"

"यह तो उस दलाल की तरह है, जिससे मानो भारी कर्जा लिया हो।" अकीरा खुद से बड़बड़ाई। "फर्क सिर्फ इतना है कि कर्ज देनेवाले पैसे माँगते हैं और यह सफाई माँग रहा है।"

"पहले यह बताओ कि महान् वेद अरोरा इस घटिया रेस्तराँ में क्या कर रहा है और वह भी एक लड़की के साथ? और उस पर भी लड़की की लिपस्टिक फैली हुई है?" वेदिका ने पलटकर वेद से प्रश्न किया।

"मैं अकीरा हूँ।"

"यह 'कॉफी चोर' है।"

वेद और अकीरा, दोनों ने एक ही समय पर जवाब दिया।

अकीरा चिल्लाई, "मैं 'कॉफी चोर' नहीं हूँ।"

"हो। तुम कॉफी चोर हो।" वेद भी कटी आवाज में चिल्लाया।

"क्या बकवास कर रहे हो? ऐसा आज मैंने पहली बार किया है।" अपनी भौंहें सिकोड़ते हुए अकीरा ने कहा।

"पहले यह बताओ कि महान् वेद अरोरा इस घटिया रेस्तराँ में क्या कर रहा है और वह भी एक लड़की के साथ? और उस पर भी लड़की की लिपस्टिक फैली हुई है?" वेदिका ने पलटकर वेद से प्रश्न किया।

"मैं अकीरा हूँ।"

"यह 'कॉफी चोर' है।"

वेद और अकीरा, दोनों ने एक ही समय पर जवाब दिया।

अकीरा चिल्लाई, "मैं 'कॉफी चोर' नहीं हूँ।"

"यहाँ तक कि तुमने मेरे मुँह पर पैसे भी फेंके। बिना कुछ कहे, बिना शर्त के मुझसे माफी माँगो।" वेद चिल्लाया।

जीभ चटकाते हुए अकीरा बोली, "ठीक है, मुझे माफ करो, मुझसे गलती हुई, आय एम सॉरी। इतना बहुत है या अब भीख माँगूँ कि मुझे माफ करो?"

"तुम्हारे तेवर बहुत खराब हैं।" वेद ने कड़े स्वर में अकीरा से कहा।

"वैसे ही जैसे तुम और तुम्हारे अपने प्रति विचार।" बनावटी मुसकान से अकीरा बोली।

"तुम तो…!" वेद ने गुस्से में तो अकीरा का गिरेबान ही पकड़ लिया होता अगर कबीर ने उसे रोका न होता।

कबीर ने एक हाथ से वेद के मुँह पर हाथ रखा और दूसरे हाथ से वेद की कमर पकड़ी। वेद ने कबीर के चंगुल से खुद को छुड़ाने की कोशिश की और अकीरा पर

हमला करना चाहा। वेदिका हैरान किंतु सतर्क थी। उसने वेद को कभी इतना परेशान और आक्रामक रूप में नहीं देखा था और वह भी किसी लड़की के प्रति। अकीरा एक कोने में भिचक गई और हैरत से इस आक्रमणकारी स्थिति को देख रही थी, जो उसकी दृष्टि में पूर्णतः अनावश्यक था।

अगले कुछ क्षणों में जो कुछ हुआ, वह सभी के लिए आजीवन अविस्मरणीय बननेवाला था; डरानेवाला था।

"क्या हो रहा है वहाँ पर ?" बिना किसी भूमिका के मैनेजर ने वाशरूम का दरवाजा खोला और अचानक चिल्लाया। मैनेजर की आवाज सुनकर हड़बड़ाहट में कबीर ने वेद का एक हाथ अचानक छोड़ा, जो अनायास ही कबीर के दो पैरों के बीच, गलत जगह जा पड़ा। कबीर दर्द से चीख उठा; वेद को अचानक छोड़ा तो धक्के से वेद अकीरा की ओर और अकीरा पर ही गिर पड़ा।

"हुश्शा बुश्शा, वी ऑल फॉल डाउन" खेल की पंक्तियाँ बोलता हुआ वह छोटा लड़का जोर-जोर से तालियाँ बजाने लगा और उसने अपने फोन का वीडियो रिकॉर्डिंग का बटन भी बंद कर दिया। उस छोटे लड़के ने इस पूरी घटना की वीडियो रिकॉर्डिंग अपने फोन से की थी।

□

4

"वेदिका! यह क्या है?" अकीरा ने घर की दीवार पर टँगी तसवीर की ओर इशारा करते हुए पूछा।

"ओह ये!" खिसियानी हँसी हँसते हुए वेदिका बोली, "यही एक समय था, जब वेद भैया एक विषय में फेल हुए थे, वरना वे तो हमेशा आदर्श छात्र रहे थे। यही वह प्रमाण-पुस्तक था, इसीलिए उसे फ्रेम करके मैंने यहाँ टाँग दिया, ताकि इस बात को वे जीवन में अच्छे से पढ़कर उचित श्रद्धांजलि दें।"

अकीरा अविश्वसनीय निगाहों से अपनी नई दोस्त वेदिका को देख रही थी।

अकीरा को लगता था कि उसका अपना परिवार ही अजीब और थोड़ा सा हटकर है, लेकिन वेदिका का परिवार उसकी इस धारणा को गलत साबित कर रहा था। फिर उसने तिरछी निगाहों से देख मन से विष खुद के सामने ही उगला, "वह मूर्ख व्यक्ति इन्हीं सब चीजों का हकदार है। पिछली रात की घटना याद आते ही वह कराह उठी कि किस तरह वह आदमी हिंसक तरीके से चिल्लाया और फिर उसी पर गिरा! उसे फिर अपनी गलती याद आई कि किस तरह वेद की नजरों से बचने के लिए उसने अपना सिर दूसरी तरफ किया और इसी कारण उसके लब अकीरा के अकीरा के लबों को छूकर निकले! कैसे वेद के होंठों से अनजाने में ही अकीरा की गरदन पर निशान बन गए। अकीरा आगबबूला हो रही थी। अकीरा उस समय इतनी परेशान हो गई थी कि उस घटना के कारण उसने डेट भी रद्द की और घर भाग गई। उसका बॉयफ्रेंड भी हैरान होगा कि क्या हुआ?

इस पूरी घटना में केवल एक अच्छी बात हुई और वह थी वेदिका। उसमें जीने की ऊर्जा व सकारात्मकता साफ दिखाई देती थी। वे दोनों एक ही शाम में दोस्त बन गई थीं। उस युद्ध को विराम देने का एक प्रयास करती हुई वेदिका ने अकीरा को अगले दिन दोपहर के खाने का निमंत्रण दिया था, जिसे अकीरा वेदिका के सौम्य और प्रिय स्वभाव के कारण मना नहीं कर पाई थी।

"गोगो!" पीछे से किसी ने आवाज लगाई।

अकीरा को पलटकर देखने की जरूरत नहीं थी, किंतु उसने देखा और खीस निकालते हुए मुसकराई। दरवाजे में से थ्री-पीस सूट में शैतान अंदर चला आ रहा था।

"मुझे तुम्हारी…चाहिए।" चलते-चलते वेद अकीरा को देखकर रुकते हुए बोला।

"तुम यहाँ क्या कर रही हो?" वेद चिल्लाया।

उतनी ही तेजी से अकीरा भी उस पर पलटकर चिल्लाई।

"तुम यहाँ क्या कर रहे हो?"

वेद गुस्से से उबल रहा था, "यह मेरा घर है।"

"यह मेरी दोस्त का घर है।" इतराती हुई अकीरा ने जवाब दिया।

"दोस्त? एक्सक्यूज मी। माफ करना, कल ही मिले हो तुम दोनों। उसके चेहरे पर गुस्सा और परेशानी साफ दिखाई दे रही थी। उसके लिए दोस्ती की खबर हैरान और व्याकुल करनेवाली थी।

"दोस्त? एक्सक्यूज मी। माफ करना, कल ही मिले हो तुम दोनों। उसके चेहरे पर गुस्सा और परेशानी साफ दिखाई दे रही थी। उसके लिए दोस्ती की खबर हैरान और व्याकुल करनेवाली थी। "हम तुम्हारी तरह धीमी चालवाले नहीं।" वेदिका ने कंधे उचकाते हुए कहा।

"हम तुम्हारी तरह धीमी चालवाले नहीं।" वेदिका ने कंधे उचकाते हुए कहा।

"वेदिका, तुम उल्लू हो। तुम्हें मालूम नहीं, ये औरत उन सबका खून कर सकती है, जिन्हें हम जानते हैं।"

वेद के आरोपों से बिना प्रभावित हुए वेदिका ने सिर हिलाते हुए उससे कहा, "और हमें पता है कि उसका पहला शिकार कौन होगा!"

इतना कहने की देर थी कि दोनों लड़कियों ने जोर से ठहाका लगाया। वेद के व्यवहार में कभी भी बदसलूकी या उत्पात नहीं दिखाई पड़ता था, पर अकीरा ने मानो उसके अंदर के शैतान को जाग्रत् किया था।

वेद ने अपनी आँखें बंद करते हुए स्वयं को याद दिलाया कि उन दोनों लड़कियों से निबटने के लिए न ही उसके पास समय है और न ही शक्ति। वह वेदिका की ओर मुड़ा और बोला, "इन कागजों पर दस्तखत करो।"

"क्यों?"

वेद अभी वेदिका के 'क्यों' का मुँहतोड़ जवाब देने ही वाला था कि कबीर मैराथन भागता हुआ अंदर आता दिखाई दिया।

"दोस्तो!" हाँफता हुआ बोला।

"कबीर!" अपेक्षा के अनुसार वेदिका उत्साह से चिल्लाई।

"क्या हुआ? तुम चिंता में क्यों लग रहे हो?"

बिना कुछ कहे कबीर ने टी.वी. चला लिया। फिर मोबाइल से तकनीकी तरीके को जोड़ वीडियो गेम खेलने लगा। बोला, "दोस्तो, ये देखो जरा!"

वेद का खून जम-सा गया, जब उसने टी.वी. पर पिछले रात की रेस्तराँ में घटी घटना की हास्यानुकृति (पैरोडी) देखी। किसी ने उस पूरी घटना की रिकॉर्डिंग की थी। हालाँकि वीडियो की गुणवत्ता खास नहीं थी, किंतु चेहरे पहचानने में आ रहे थे। सबसे रद्दी बात थी, जब वेद के होंठ अकीरा के होंठों पर लगे। वेद को उस बात को याद करते ही लगा, मानो किसी ने खाल ही उतार ली हो!

वेद ने अकीरा की ओर उसकी प्रतिक्रिया जानने और पढ़ने की कोशिश करते हुए देखा। वेद को यह देख तसल्ली हुई कि अकीरा भी उतनी ही व्यग्र और शर्मिंदगी से सराबोर दिखाई दे रही थी। 'शुक्र है भगवान्, यह चुप है।' मन-ही-मन वेद ने सोचा।

"किसी ने यह वीडियो यू-ट्यूब पर पोस्ट की। किसी जानकार ने देख ली और तब से वायरल (फैलना) हो गई है।" कबीर ने बताया।

"गर्लफ्रेंड और बॉयफ्रेंड की टॉयलेट में अश्लील झड़प!" अकीरा के मुँह से आवाज निकलनी बंद हो गई।

"किसी ने यह वीडियो यू-ट्यूब पर पोस्ट की। किसी जानकार ने देख ली और तब से वायरल (फैलना) हो गई है।" कबीर ने बताया। "गर्लफ्रेंड और बॉयफ्रेंड की टॉयलेट में अश्लील झड़प!" अकीरा के मुँह से आवाज निकलनी बंद हो गई।

"3.5 लाख लोगों ने देख भी लिया?" वेद चकराया। "लोग अपने आप ऐसे वीडियो तक कैसे पहुँच जाते हैं? और हम दोनों जोड़े के रूप में सोच भी कैसे सकते हैं? मैं हैरान हूँ।"

किसने रिकॉर्ड किया होगा यह? वेदिका अभी सोच ही रही थी और बोल भी पड़ी—"उस बच्चे ने। उसके पास मोबाइल था।" वेद को याद आया। "उस समय की अशांति और हलचल भरे माहौल में मुझे सूझा भी नहीं कि कोई रिकॉर्डिंग कर भी सकता है!" वेद ने कहा।

"3.5 लाख लोगों ने देखा कि मुझे उस हाथापाई और झड़प में कहाँ लगी।" कबीर ने घबराहट भरी आवाज में अपना सदमा प्रकट किया। वेदिका ने शैतानी भरी निगाहों से अपने भाई की ओर देखा और कहा, "3.5 लाख लोगों ने अब वेद अरोरा और उसकी गर्लफ्रेंड (दोस्त) की झड़प को देख लिया।"

'ओह! यह तो गड़बड़ हो गई।' वेद ने अकीरा की ओर गुस्से से देखा। 'अब तो उसके व्यावसायिक लोगों में उसकी हँसी भी उड़ाई जाएगी और उसे तिरस्कृत निगाहों से भी देखा जाएगा कि वेद अरोरा महिलाओं के साथ दुर्व्यवहार करता है और उसे महिलाओं के साथ पेश आने की तमीज नहीं। और इसी कारण कई ग्राहक उससे व्यावसायिक संबंध तोड़ देंगे।' मन-ही-मन वेद सोच में पड़ गया।

घबराहट और गुस्से में वह चिल्लाया। वह गुस्से से काँप रहा था। "यह सब तुम्हारे

कारण है। तुम मुझे दुनिया के सामने इस शर्मिंदगी की स्थिति में लाई हो।" वेद अकीरा से बोला।

"कर दो केस मुझ पर!" अकीरा पलटकर चिल्लाई। उसके हर अक्षर से गुस्सा टपक रहा था। "तुम मेरा पीछा करते हुए 'बिस्तरो' कॉफी शॉप में आए थे। तुम बदहवास और असंतुलित मूर्ख की तरह मुझ पर गिर पड़े। यह सबकुछ तुम्हारी वजह से हुआ। अब मुझे अपने बॉयफ्रेंड को तुम्हारी इन मूर्खतापूर्ण बातों की सफाई देनी पड़ेगी।"

"ओफ्फो! बच्चों की तरह बातें करना बंद करो। समस्या पर ध्यान दो।" वेदिका ने वेद को कमर से पकड़ते हुए दिलासा देना चाहा। "हमें इस वीडियो से छुटकारा पाने के लिए कुछ करना होगा।"

"कर दो केस मुझ पर!" अकीरा पलटकर चिल्लाई। उसके हर अक्षर से गुस्सा टपक रहा था। "तुम मेरा पीछा करते हुए 'बिस्तरो' कॉफी शॉप में आए थे। तुम बदहवास और असंतुलित मूर्ख की तरह मुझ पर गिर पड़े। यह सबकुछ तुम्हारी वजह से हुआ। अब मुझे अपने बॉयफ्रेंड को तुम्हारी इन मूर्खतापूर्ण बातों की सफाई देनी पड़ेगी।"

"हम इसे पूरी तरह कभी भी नहीं मिटा पाएँगे।" अकीरा ने व्यंग्य से कहा।

"चुप रहो।" वेद भड़का। "सब तुम्हारी गलती है। यदि तुमने मुझसे कॉफी न छीनी होती तो मैं भी तुमसे सवाल-जवाब करने वहाँ नहीं आता।"

"और ये भी हो सकता था कि जिस क्षण मैंने तुम्हें सॉरी कहा, तुम मुझे माफ कर सकते थे, सही कहा न, मिस्टर परफेक्ट?" अकीरा ने दलील दी।

अभी वेद उसकी बात का जवाब देने ही वाला था कि उसकी माँ दनदनाती हुई कमरे में आईं और अकड़कर वेद के मुँह में मीठा डालते हुए बोलीं, "वेद! मेरा बेटा, ये खाओ।"

"हम्म्म..." वेद ने मुँह का मीठा चबाते हुए कहा, "अब ये क्या है?"

"प्रसाद है। और क्या? आज मैं मंदिर गई थी। तुम लड़कियाँ देखने को तैयार हो गए हो। मैं बहुत खुश हूँ।"

"खैर, खुशी का तो पता नहीं, लेकिन तुम यह वीडियो देखकर बहुत नाराज होनेवाली हो।" यह कहते हुए वेद ने पिंकी के लिए वीडियो चला दिया।

जैसे ही वीडियो खत्म हुआ, पिंकी कल्पना करते हुए साँस छोड़ते हुए बोली, "वाह, तुम्हारी तो गर्लफ्रेंड है और उसकी वजह से तुम मुसीबत में भी पड़ चुके हो! आज तो मेरी जिंदगी का सबसे खुशी भरा दिन है।"

वेद ने खिसियाहट में आँखें दबोचीं और बंद कर लीं। मैंने सोचा था कि कल का

दिन बुरा था; आज का दिन और भी बुरा है। वह वीडियो, अकीरा, कबीर और अब माँ भी। उफ्फ!

"उसने लड़की का पीछा भी पहली बार किया है।" कबीर ने जता दिया।

"क्या?" पिंकी ने गहरी साँस लेकर अकीरा की ओर ऐसे देखा, मानो उसकी पूजा करेंगी। कहने लगीं, "क्या वेद ने तुम्हारा पीछा किया? मैं बता दूँ कि तुम ऐसी पहली लड़की हो, जिसका वेद ने खुशी से पीछा किया होगा।"

वेद को सबकुछ त्यागकर हिमालय में शरण लेने की इच्छा हुई। 'वहाँ एक छोटी-सी कुटिया खरीदकर, दो गाय पाले, आठ भेड़ें भी रखे, लकड़ियाँ काटे, पनीर बनाए और शांति से जीवन जिए। क्या ऐसा हो सकता है?' वेद ने मन-ही-मन सोचा। "वीडियो की किसी को चिंता नहीं?"

"जानती हूँ, नहीं तो···" वेदिका ने अपनी बात पूरी भी नहीं की थी कि एक मोबाइल जाता रहा। वेद ने गुस्से से मोबाइल को दीवार पर दे मारा।

□

5

एक हाथ की घड़ी, हेयर कंडीशनर, यौन संबंधित वस्तुएँ और कंडोम्स।

वेद ने इन सभी उपहारों को देख नजर दूसरी तरफ कर ली। फिर उसने अपने हाथ में रखा रसना से भरा गिलास देखा और दूसरों के हाथ में वोदका से भरे गिलास। शायद वो अच्छी जिंदगी के इंद्रधनुषी रंगों में सबसे फीके रंग पर था, क्योंकि उसे पार्टी में भी जबरदस्ती आना पड़ा था।

यह सबकुछ कबीर को हैरान और खुश करने की वेदिका की तदबीर थी। वेदिका कबीर के जन्मदिन पर आधी रात को खुशी देना चाहती थी, इसीलिए पार्टी रखी थी। कितना दिखावा! वह हमेशा की तरह मामूली पार्टी थी; सिर्फ एक फर्क था कि इस पार्टी में अकीरा भी थी और वेद के लिए पार्टी छोड़कर जाने का भारी कारण भी।

वेद को अहसास हो रहा था कि अकीरा की नजर उसी पर है। वेद ने गहरी साँस ली। अभी तो अकीरा वेदिका की कुछ सहेलियों के साथ किसी फूहड़ हिंदी गाने पर नाचने में व्यस्त थी। उसके नाच के हर ठुमके के साथ उसकी कामुक कर देनेवाली वेशभूषा हरेक की आँखों को उसी की ओर आकर्षित कर रही थी। उस पार्टी में अकीरा सबके आकर्षण का केंद्र थी। किंतु वह लगातार वेद को ही देखे जा रही थी, क्योंकि वह जानती थी कि वेद को दुबारा उसे वहाँ देखकर बिल्कुल अच्छा नहीं लग रहा था। वह मानो वेद को चुनौती देने की खुशी को बनावटी हँसी में प्रकट कर रही थी।

वेद अंदर-ही-अंदर कराह रहा था, क्योंकि जब भी वह अकीरा को देखता, उसे बीते दिनों की वह शर्मिंदा करनेवाली घटना याद आ जाती। ईश्वर की कृपा से वह जान-पहचान के सहारे यू-ट्यूब से वह वीडियो हटवा चुका था। सिवाय कुछ दोस्तों, परिवार के सदस्यों और 3.5 लाख दर्शकों के अलावा उस वीडियो के बारे में किसी को नहीं मालूम था। वेद की बाईं आँख फड़की। वह किसे बहला रहा था? बहुत सारे लोगों ने वह वीडियो देख लिया था।

"ए भाई!" अपने कंधे पर से कबीर का हाथ हटाया।

"बिल्कुल नहीं।"

"लेकिन मेरे सभी दोस्तों ने पी रखी है।" कबीर ने वेद को समझाने की कोशिश की। "जिसका जन्मदिन है, उसे तुम मना नहीं कर सकते। प्लीज!"

वेद यह जानना चाहता था कि इतना पानी मिलाकर पीने के बाद भी वोदका से उसके दोस्तों को इतना नशा कैसे हुआ?" लेकिन वेद बहस में नहीं पड़ा। उस दिन कबीर का जन्मदिन था; उसका खास दिन! वेद का कोमल हृदय गाड़ी के लिए कबीर को मना नहीं कर सका। उसने जेब से चाबी निकालकर, वेद को पकड़ाते हुए कहा, "क्या याद रखना है, बताओ तो जरूरी बिंदु? जल्दी से।"

कबीर खिसियाया, लेकिन छुपा गया और बोला, "तेज नहीं चलानी। रेड लाइट पर रुकना है, बत्ती हरी होने के बाद जाना है, सीट बेल्ट लगानी हैं; डेशबोर्ड पर पैर नहीं रखने; गाड़ी में नहीं पीनी, उल्टी भी नहीं और किसी लड़की के साथ सेक्स भी नहीं और गाड़ी में तो बिल्कुल भी नहीं।"

कबीर खिसियाया, लेकिन छुपा गया और बोला, "तेज नहीं चलानी। रेड लाइट पर रुकना है, बत्ती हरी होने के बाद जाना है, सीट बेल्ट लगानी हैं; डेशबोर्ड पर पैर नहीं रखने; गाड़ी में नहीं पीनी, उल्टी भी नहीं और किसी लड़की के साथ सेक्स भी नहीं और गाड़ी में तो बिल्कुल भी नहीं।"

"शाबाश!"

"शुक्रिया।" कबीर ने वेद की उदारता को ढीली चूम के साथ सलाम किया। वेद को गाल पर कुछ महसूस हुआ। इससे पहले कि वेद उसे दूर करे, कबीर भाग निकला। टिशू पेपर से वेद ने अपना गाल पोंछा। वेद उम्मीद कर रहा था कि कम-से-कम एक इतने वयस्क आदमी द्वारा उसके गाल चूमे जाने का वीडियो अब उसके परिवार के व्हाट्स एप ग्रुप पर नहीं दिखेगा। भावानात्मक थकान को महसूस करते हुए वेद अपने अपार्टमेंट में घर के बाहर जाकर सीढ़ियों पर बैठ गया। अंदर खुद को किसी-न-किसी कारण से परेशान करने से अच्छा था वो बाहर बैठता।

"मुझे लगा, शायद मुझे तुम वाशरूम में मिलो।" पीछे से आवाज आई। "लेकिन तुम यहाँ हो!" वेद पीछे नहीं पलटा, वह जानता था कि वह किसकी आवाज थी।

"आभार तुम्हारा, जो मैं आजीवन सार्वजनिक वाशरूम से दूर ही रहूँगा।"

अकीरा हँसते हुए वेद के गाल खींचने के लिए झुकी ही थी कि वेद ने खतरे का इशारा देते हुए रोकना चाहा। "नहीं, बिल्कुल नहीं।"

"नाग!" अकीरा ने पलटकर कहा।

"कॉफी चोर!" वेद ने काटने के अंदाज में कहा।

"वही घिसा-पिटा रिकॉर्ड।" गुस्से में अकीरा चिल्लाई।

अभी पलटकर कुछ कहने ही वाला था कि वेद ने देखा, अकीरा अपने पर्स से सिगरेट और लाइटर निकाल रही थी।

"यहाँ सिगरेट मत पिओ।" वेद ने अकीरा के होंठों से लटकती सिगरेट खींचकर दूर करते हुए कहा।

"ओ, बदमाश! (एसहोल) मेरी चीजों को छूने की जरूरत नहीं।" अपशब्दों के साथ अकीरा वेद पर चिल्लाई।

"मैं नहीं छुऊँगा, यदि तुम यहाँ धूम्रपान न करो तो..." वेद ने दोनों हाथ ऊपर करते हुए कहा।

"चलो, घर चलते हैं।" वेदिका टहलती हुई आई और दोनों के बीच की झड़प को काटते हुए बोली।

"कबीर को वापस आने दो, तभी हम अपनी कार में वापस जा सकेंगे।" वेद ने वेदिका से कहा और तीखी नजरों से अकीरा की ओर देखते हुए टिप्पणी की, "वैसे भी मुझे पार्टी की भीड़ पसंद नहीं, बेकार का हुड़दंग मचानेवाले असभ्य लोग, जिनमें सार्वजनिक व्यवहार की सभ्य सोच भी नहीं कि दूसरे लोगों को इनसे क्या परेशानी हो सकती है।"

"कबीर को वापस आने दो, तभी हम अपनी कार में वापस जा सकेंगे।" वेद ने वेदिका से कहा और तीखी नजरों से अकीरा की ओर देखते हुए टिप्पणी की, "वैसे भी मुझे पार्टी की भीड़ पसंद नहीं, बेकार का हुड़दंग मचानेवाले असभ्य लोग, जिनमें सार्वजनिक व्यवहार की सभ्य सोच भी नहीं कि दूसरे लोगों को इनसे क्या परेशानी हो सकती है।"

अकीरा ने चिढ़कर मुँह दूसरी ओर कर लिया।

"ओह, वो मूर्ख अभी वापस नहीं आएगा। किसी के पास और भी शराब है और वे दुबारा मदिरापान कर रहे हैं। हमें अब चलना चाहिए और चलो, अकीरा को भी उसके घर छोड़ दें।"

अचानक वेदिका की बोली आखिरी बात वेद के दिमाग में गई और मानो बत्ती जली। उसने ध्यान से वेदिका को देखा।

"गोगो! मुझे पता है, तुम किस कोशिश में हो! खबरदार!" वेद गुस्से में चिल्लाया। "मैं नहीं जा रहा। मैं पैदल घर चला जाऊँगा, रेंगता हुआ चला जाऊँगा। मैं यह नहीं करूँगा।"

अकीरा वेद की इस अचानक विस्फोटक प्रतिक्रिया से स्तब्ध थी।

"ठीक है। मैं वह वाशरूम वीडियो यू-ट्यूब पर दुबारा डाल दूँगी।"

"बंद करो अपनी यह कुलबुलाहट।" अकीरा वेद पर फुफकारी। वेद ने भी गुस्से

से अकीरा की ओर देखा, पर चुप रहा। वह कैसे कुछ कहता? अपनी शातिर बहन की योजना के सामने चुप रहा। अब वे वेदिका की छोटी, बैटरी से चलनेवाली दो सीट की कार में सवार होकर घर की ओर बढ़ रहे थे। वह गाड़ी चलाना केवल वेदिका के वश की ही बात थी। लाख कोशिश करने पर भी उस बैटरी कार के गियर चलाने वेद को नहीं आए। अब वेदिका गाड़ी चला रही थी और वेद पीछे सवार था और अकीरा उसकी गोद में बैठी थी।

वेद की चुप्पी देख अकीरा ने टिप्पणी की, "अरे, कोई व्यंग्य नहीं, कोई ताना नहीं? ऐसे कैसे?" अकीरा ने भौंहें उचकाते हुए यह बात कही थी।

इतने वर्षों में वेद ने आत्म-नियंत्रण की कला में महारत हासिल कर ली थी, जब तक इस दानवी महिला ने उसके धैर्य की परीक्षा नहीं ली थी और जब तक वह वेद से भिड़ी नहीं थी। वेद की नजरें अकीरा के मद से भरे होंठों से पथभ्रष्ट हो रही थीं और उसकी आँखें अकीरा की छोटे बटन जैसी नाक और टॉफी-सी चमकती आँखों पर ही भ्रमण कर रही थीं। वेद ने पूरी कोशिश से अकीरा के रेशमी बालों को छूने से दूर रखा था। भारी दिल से वह इस बात को छुपा रहा था कि अकीरा एक अत्यंत आकर्षक और खूबसूरत लड़की थी।

"अरे! क्या बात है, इतने शांत क्यों हो आज?" अकीरा ने दुबारा वेद को उचकाते हुए कहा और वेदिका भी खिसियानी-सी हँसी हँसने लगी।

"या इस तरह से बैठना ही तुम्हें किसी और दुनिया का नशा दे रहा है, हुआ क्या?" अकीरा ने नशीली आवाज में कहा।

"अरे! क्या बात है, इतने शांत क्यों हो आज?" अकीरा ने दुबारा वेद को उचकाते हुए कहा और वेदिका भी खिसियानी-सी हँसी हँसने लगी। "या इस तरह से बैठना ही तुम्हें किसी और दुनिया का नशा दे रहा है, हुआ क्या?" अकीरा ने नशीली आवाज में कहा।

अभी वेद कुछ कहने के लिए मुँह खोलता, अंदर तक चीर देनेवाली मोबाइल की रिंगटोन बजी। फोन वेदिका का बजा था। फोन देखते ही वेदिका ने गाड़ी के ब्रेक इतनी जोर से लगाए कि वेद और अकीरा अपनी सीट से उछल पड़े। स्वाभाविक रूप से बचाने के लिए वेद ने अकीरा को कमर से पकड़ लिया, ताकि वह न गिरे। जाहिर है, अकीरा भी एकदम चिल्लाई और वेद को कसकर पकड़ लिया। उसने डर से आँखें भी बंद कर ली थीं।

"यह क्या बदतमीजी है वेदिका?" वेद चीखा।

"कबीर फोन कर रहा है, मुझे फोन सुनना होगा।" वेदिका ने सहजता से कहा।

भाई और दोस्त के चेहरे की दहशत पर ध्यान दिए बिना फोन उठाकर वेदिका गाड़ी से बाहर गई और अपने दोस्त (बॉयफ्रेंड) कबीर से बात करने लगी।

"हे भगवान्! मरते-मरते बचे।" अकीरा डर के भाव का घूँट पीते हुए बोली।

तब उसे अहसास हुआ कि उसने वेद को कितना कसकर पकड़ रखा था। उसने जानबूझकर वेद को ध्यान से देखा। वेद ने सुरक्षा भाव से अकीरा की कमर को थाम रखा था। चाहे गाड़ी में अँधेरा था, पर वेद की आँखों से पता चल रहा था कि समय के अनुसार उसे व्यवहार करना आता है। अकीरा वेद की लंबी पलकें देखती रह गई। उसकी सीधी नुकीली नाक उसके चेहरे पर कितनी सटीक-सी लग रही थी। इस अँधेरे में अकीरा की आँखें वेद के होंठों पर भी गईं, जो अधिकतर बेकार की बातें ही करते हैं, पर उसे अहसास हुआ, "कितना सुंदर है यह लड़का! आह!"

"तुम ठीक हो?" वेद के स्वर में अकीरा के लिए चिंता थी। उसे गाड़ी में एक अनजान लड़के की गोद में इस तरह नहीं बैठना चाहिए था, जिसकी तरफ वह आकर्षित भी होती जा रही थी। फिर उसका तो बॉयफ्रेंड भी था। उसने विषय बदलने की सोची और वेद को शर्मिंदा करने से अच्छा और क्या हो सकता था?

"तुम ठीक हो?" वेद के स्वर में अकीरा के लिए चिंता थी। उसे गाड़ी में एक अनजान लड़के की गोद में इस तरह नहीं बैठना चाहिए था, जिसकी तरफ वह आकर्षित भी होती जा रही थी। फिर उसका तो बॉयफ्रेंड भी था।

गला साफ करते हुए अकीरा ने कहा, "फिर, पत्नी मिली क्या तुम्हें? वेदिका ने बताया कि कल रात को शादियाँ करवानेवाली बहुत सी वेबसाइट्स को देख रहे थे।"

वेद ने गुस्से में मुँह भींच लिया और मन में सोचा, 'यह वेदिका अपना मुँह बंद नहीं रख सकती!'

"साथी···जीवनसाथी।" वेद ने अकीरा को ठीक करते हुए कहा।

"पत्नी नहीं, जीवनसाथी।"

"सही। लेकिन एक बात बताओ, तुम देखने में सुंदर, इतने सफल, तो भी अभी तक अकेले हो? ऐसा क्यों?" अकीरा ने ठिठोली करते हुए कहा।

वेद कंधे उचकाते हुए बोला, "प्यार कॉलेज के पढ़ाकू लोगों को नहीं होता। और मैंने जो प्रेम ऑफिसों में देखे हैं, वे रिश्तेदारी के नाम पर व्यावसायिक सौदा था और मुझे ऐसे लेन-देन में कोई दिलचस्पी नहीं।"

"फिर तुम्हें किसमें दिलचस्पी है?" अकीरा ने जिज्ञासुभाव से पूछा।

"मुझे···बहुत कुछ में दिलचस्पी है। जैसे सुबह की सैर, सैर पर मिलकर मूँगफली

खाना, अचानक पिक्चर देखने जाना और मौज-मस्ती करना, गाड़ी से लंबी सैर पर जाना, घूमना-फिरना; साथ में टैक्स भरना, मिलकर खाना बनाना, तारे देखना, एक-दूसरे की पसंदीदा पुस्तकें व कॉमिक्स पढ़ना; बस एक-दूसरे के साथ इस जीवन की सुंदरता का अनुभव करना, जैसे कि मेरे माता-पिता।" वेद ने कंधे उचकाते हुए जवाब दिया।

"वाऽऽऽऽऽऽ। यह तो 'मिल्स एंड बूंज' है तुम्हारा ('मिल्स एंड बूंज' अंग्रेजी उपन्यास की प्रेम से भरी व रोचक श्रृंखला है)। तुम्हारे विचार तो प्रेमरस से परिपूर्ण हैं, न कि मेरे निकम्मे बॉयफ्रेंड जैसे।" अकीरा के स्वर में अपने बॉयफ्रेंड के प्रति घृणा थी।

"तुम्हारा सचमुच में बॉयफ्रेंड है ?" वेद ने शक के भाव अपनी भौंहों और चेहरे से दरशाते हुए पूछा।

अकीरा ने वेद को चिढ़ाते हुए और नकल उतारते हुए कहा, "जी, मेरा सचमुच में बॉयफ्रेंड है।"

अकीरा ने लाख कोशिश की कि वह न हँसे, लेकिन बनावटी मुसकान से चेहरा दमक उठा था। "हमने पहली बार सभ्य लोगों की तरह संवाद किया।"

"बधाई हो।" वेद ने व्यंग्य भरे स्वर में कहा।

अकीरा मुँह दबाकर हँसी और दोनों अचानक ही असुविधाजनक तरीके से चुप हो गए, फिर अकीरा दबी आवाज में बोली, "सुनो···मुझे इस तरीके से तुम्हारी कॉफी नहीं छीननो चाहिए थी।"

"बधाई हो।" वेद ने व्यंग्य भरे स्वर में कहा। अकीरा मुँह दबाकर हँसी और दोनों अचानक ही असुविधाजनक तरीके से चुप हो गए, फिर अकीरा दबी आवाज में बोली, "सुनो··· मुझे इस तरीके से तुम्हारी कॉफी नहीं छीननी चाहिए थी।"

काफी देर चुप्पी के बाद वेद ने कहा, "ईमानदारी से कहूँ तो मुझे भी इतने गुस्से में तुमसे सवाल-जवाब नहीं करने चाहिए थे।"

"क्या हम एक-दूसरे से माफी माँग रहे हैं ?" भौहें चढ़ाते हुए अकीरा बोली।

"शायद हाँ।" वेद ने कंधे पीछे खींचते हुए हामी भरी। "युद्ध विराम ?" हाथ बढ़ाते हुए आशा से अकीरा बोली। ऐसा कहते हुए अकीरा के चेहरे पर बड़ी सी मुसकान और सौहार्दता स्पष्ट लक्षित हो रही थी।

वेद ने कातरता से अकीरा की बढ़ी हुई हथेली पर एक मुसकान के साथ हाथ रखते हुए कहा, "विराम!"

□

6

वेद को अपने हृदय की धड़कन साफ सुनाई पड़ रही थी। वह नाइट क्लब में बिल्कुल आना नहीं चाहता था। उस जगह पर पसीने, उलटी, शराब, सिगरेट की दुर्गंध व्याप्त थी। वेद उस दुर्गंध से बेचैन हो उठा और उसके मस्तिष्क ने भी उसी का साथ दिया। वेद को उस गंध से उबकाई-सी आ रही थी।

कुछ दिनों पहले तक वह ऐसी जगहों पर आने की कल्पना से पहले शायद खुदकुशी कर लेता, क्योंकि ऐसी जगहें ही STD को जन्म देनेवाली जगहें होती हैं, अर्थात् यौन बीमारियों को। दुर्भाग्य के कारण उसे यहाँ आना पड़ा, क्योंकि यदि वह घर पर रहता तो माँ के मेहमानों की मेहमाननवाजी करनी पड़ती।

उसे पिछली बार वह 'बतरा' नाम की लड़की याद थी। किस तरह उसने शराब का गिलास वेद की पैंट पर गिराया और पूरे समय वेद को, लोगों को अपनी पाकीजगी की सफाई देते हुए पूरी पार्टी में घूमना पड़ा था। इस बार मतलब ही नहीं था कि वह पार्टी में 'बतरा' के साथ समय बिताता। उसके पास एक ही विकल्प था कि वेदिका और कबीर के साथ क्लब में आ जाए।

"आओ वेदिका, शॉट्स लें।" कबीर वेद के कान में चिल्लाया। "नहींऽऽऽऽ।" वेद ने घबराकर कहा।

"अरे! ऐसे मत करो। कबीर के जन्मदिन को खराब करोगे क्या?" वेदिका वहाँ चल रहे संगीत से भी तेज स्वर में चिल्लाई।

"ये कारण नहीं है शॉट्स लेने का" वेद गंभरता से बोला। वेदिका ने उसकी बाँह पर हाथ मारा। बारटेंडर (शराब देनेवाला) ने कबीर और वेदिका को शॉट्स पकड़ाए, जो वे दोनों क्षणों में गटक गए।

"आज मैं तुम्हारे कोई बेकार के बहाने नहीं सुनूँगा।" इतना कहकर कबीर वेद के पास शॉट्स से भरा गिलास लाया।

वेद पीछे झुका और बोला, "खबरदार! बिल्कुल नहीं।"

वेद ने कबीर को धक्का दिया। कबीर के धक्के से गिलास का तरल पदार्थ वेद की

जींस पर फिर गलत जगह पर लुढ़क गया। यह देखते ही वेदिका और कबीर जोर का ठहाका मारकर हँसने लगे।

"बिल्कुल सही हुआ।" कबीर खिलखिलाकर बोला।

वेद ने अपनी जींस पर गीला धब्बा देखा। वह 'बतरा' नामक लड़की से बचने के लिए क्लब आया था और कबीर ने ठीक वैसा ही किया, जैसा कि पिछली बार 'बतरा' नाम की लड़की ने उसके साथ किया था। इतिहास की आदत होती है कि वह खुद को दोहराता है, यहाँ तो सदमा और अभिघात (Trauma) भी स्वयं को दोहरा रहा था।

बिना कुछ कहे वेद उठकर वाशरूम की तरफ गया। जैसे ही दरवाजा खोला, वेद ने वह देखा, जो वह कभी देखना नहीं चाहता था। अकीरा एक लड़के के साथ पुरुषों के वाशरूम के दूसरे सिरे पर खड़ी प्रेम प्रसंग में डूबी हुई थी।

"उफ्फ!" वेद चीखा।

जानी-पहचानी आवाज सुनकर अकीरा ने चूम रहे लड़के को थोड़ा पीछे करके वाशरूम में आनेवाले को देखना चाहा।

"उफ्फ!" वह भी आह भरकर बोली।

इससे पहले कि वेद किसी भावनात्मक खरोंच से आहत होता, वह पीछे मुड़ा और टिशू पेपर लेकर अपनी पैंट के गीले धब्बे को सुखाने में लग गया, फिर भी वेद ने व्यंग्य किया—"तुम्हारे और वाशरूम के बीच कुछ है क्या?"

"उफ्फ!" वह भी आह भरकर बोली। इससे पहले कि वेद किसी भावनात्मक खरोंच से आहत होता, वह पीछे मुड़ा और टिशू पेपर लेकर अपनी पैंट के गीले धब्बे को सुखाने में लग गया, फिर भी वेद ने व्यंग्य किया—"तुम्हारे और वाशरूम के बीच कुछ है क्या?"

"यही बात मैं भी तुम्हें कह सकती हूँ।" यह कहते हुए अकीरा वेद की तरफ आई। उसने पैंट के गीले धब्बे की ओर इशारा करते हुए कहा, "और तुम्हारे साथ क्या है? वाशरूम और असुविधाजनक अजीब हालत?

वेद इससे पहले कि कोई सफाई देता, अकीरा का दोस्त वेद की ओर घृणित दृष्टि से देखते हुए बोला, "यही है वह लड़का, जो तुम्हारे वाशरूम वीडियो में था?"

अकीरा ने हामी में सिर हिलाते हुए कहा, "हाँ।"

वेद ने उस लड़के को सिर से पैर तक ध्यान से देखा। वेद उसके बारे में कोई राय या गलत प्रतिक्रिया नहीं बना रहा था, पर उसकी चमड़े की जैकेट मानो लोखंडवाला के बाजार से खरीदी हुई, जूते, टैटू और सिर पर बाँधी चोटी देख रहा था। वेद की दृष्टि में वह पातीवाली प्याज लग रहा था। संक्षेप में कहें तो वेद को वह लड़का घटिया प्रतीत हुआ।

उस लड़के की ओर इशारा करते हुए वेद ने अकीरा से पूछा, "येऽऽऽ···उफ्फ··· कौन··है?"

अकीरा अभिमान से बोली, "यह मेरा बॉयफ्रेंड (दोस्त) है, मोहित।"

"बॉय-बॉयफ्रेंड? येऽऽऽ?" वेद ने हकलाते हुए पूछा। वह अटक-अटककर बोल रहा था, मानो उसके मुँह में भी थोड़ी सी टकीला चली गई हो। वह अपने स्वभाव के विरुद्ध इस तरह की प्रतिक्रिया दे रहा था। मोहित बौखला उठा और वेद की टीशर्ट पकड़ते हुए चिल्लाया, "ऐ! तुम हँस क्यों रहे हो?" अपने पर अनपेक्षित हमले से अचानक वेद सकपकाया और मानो आत्मसमर्पण करते हुए अपने हाथ ऊपर कर लिये। वेद ने मुँह बनाया, क्योंकि लड़के के मुँह से शराब की दुर्गंध आ रही थी। अकीरा से बोला, "अकीरा, इसने पी रखी है, इसे मुझसे दूर करो।"

"मैं दिखाता हूँ कि मैंने कितनी पी रखी है!" मोहित ने धमकाते हुए कहा, वेद को टीशर्ट से पकड़कर उठाया और दीवार से टिकाते हुए दबाव बनाए रखा। इससे पहले कि वेद कुछ समझ पाता, मोहित का घूँसा वेद के जबड़े पर पड़ चुका था।

"यह क्या बदतमीजी है?" वेद ने खुद को सँभालते हुए कहा।

"मैं दिखाता हूँ कि मैंने कितनी पी रखी है!" मोहित ने धमकाते हुए कहा, वेद को टीशर्ट से पकड़कर उठाया और दीवार से टिकाते हुए दबाव बनाए रखा। इससे पहले कि वेद कुछ समझ पाता, मोहित का घूँसा वेद के जबड़े पर पड़ चुका था।

"यह क्या बदतमीजी है?" वेद ने खुद को सँभालते हुए कहा।

मोहित ने दुबारा उस पर मौखिक वार करते हुए कहा, "तुम्हारी हिम्मत कैसे हुई मुझ पर हँसने की?"

"तुम बदतमीजी···।" वेद चिल्लाया और मोहित के दो पैरों के बीच की पिंडली पर घुटना मारते हुए कहा, "जाने दो मुझे।"

"खुशी से।" ऐसा कहते हुए मोहित ने वेद को छोड़ दिया। खुद को उस स्थिति से हटाने हेतु मोहित ने जैसे ही वेद की टीशर्ट छोड़ी, वेद जमीन पर बाद में फिसला, पहले वाशबेसिन से टकराया।

"आह!" वेद जमीन पर गिरकर दर्द से छटपटा रहा था।

अकीरा झुककर घुटने पर बैठते हुए बोली, "कमअक्ल मोहित, ये क्या किया तुमने?"

"इस बदतमीज को यही भाषा समझ आती होगी।" मोहित ने जमीन पर लेटे हुए वेद की ओर देखा और वाशरूम से बाहर चला गया। अकीरा जानती थी कि मोहित अपना संतुलन जल्दी खो देता है ,लेकिन यह तो सीमा से परे था। वेद की धीमी कराह ने

अकीरा की विचार श्रृंखला तोड़ी। उसका हृदय वेद के मुँह से टपके खून को देख भय से काँप उठा। उसने जल्दी से टिशू पेपर लिये और वेद की नाक पर दबाए।

"ऊऽऽऽ!" वेद चौंका।

"मुझे माफ करना।" अकीरा ने वेद से माफी माँगी। वह वेद की टीशर्ट को खून से रँगता देख डर से काँप रही थी। "मुझे लगता है कि हमें आपातकालीन कमरे में जाना चाहिए। क्या तुम चल सकते हो?" वेद नकचढ़ा नहीं था; वह केवल अपने चेहरे और कपड़ों पर खून देख थोड़ा सा परेशान हो गया था। उसने धीमी अवाज में हामी भरी और बोला, "हाँ, चल सकता हूँ।"

"मैं वेदिका को कॉल लगाती हूँ।" अकीरा बड़बड़ाई।

अकीरा कुछ समझ नहीं पा रही थी, बोली, "पता नहीं कहाँ होंगे वह और कबीर?"

चाहे वेद तकलीफ में था, तो भी उसने आँखें छोटी करते हुए कहा, "तुम्हें कैसे पता कि वेदिका यहीं है?"

"नहीं। मेरा मतलब···" अकीरा लड़खड़ाते हुए, घबराहट में बोली। "मैं मानकर चल रही थी कि वह कहीं आसपास होगी, क्योंकि तुम कभी अकेले ऐसे क्लब में नहीं जाते।

अकीरा कुछ समझ नहीं पा रही थी, बोली, "पता नहीं कहाँ होंगे वह और कबीर?" चाहे वेद तकलीफ में था, तो भी उसने आँखें छोटी करते हुए कहा, "तुम्हें कैसे पता कि वेदिका यहीं है?" "नहीं। मेरा मतलब··" अकीरा लड़खड़ाते हुए, घबराहट में बोली। "मैं मानकर चल रही थी कि वह कहीं आसपास होगी, क्योंकि तुम कभी अकेले ऐसे क्लब में नहीं जाते।

"क्या वह आसपास ही है?"

वेद को इतना दर्द हो रहा था कि उसने अपेक्षित झूठ को सच साबित करने की कोशिश नहीं की और हामी भरी।

"मैं उसे फोन लगाती हूँ।" अकीरा ने वेद को बताया। कुछ मिनट वह रुकी, फिर बोली, "उफ्फ! वह फोन नहीं उठा रही।"

"हो सकता है फोन 'सायलंट मोड' पर हो।" वेद ने थोड़ी तेज आवाज में कहा।

"ठीक है···" अकीरा ने अधीरता से दूर से हाथ हिलाया। उसने वेद को पकड़कर खड़ा करने का प्रयास किया और कहा, "अब हम और समय बरबाद नहीं कर सकते, हमें अस्पताल जाना होगा।"

अकीरा ने एक हाथ से उसे कमर से पकड़ा और दूसरा उसकी छाती पर रखकर उसे सहारा देने की कोशिश की। वेद को उसके छूने से झुरझुरी-सी हुई। उसे लगा, वह

किसी और दुनिया में पहुँच गया हो। उसने कुछ अधूरी-सी अकीरा की आवाज में किसी को चिल्लाते हुए निर्देश देते हुए सुना। उन्हें किसी ने सहारा देते हुए पिछले दरवाजे से निकलने में मदद की। जल्द ही ड्राइवर कार लेकर वहाँ पहुँचा, जहाँ अकीरा और वेद खड़े थे। अकीरा ने वेद को गाड़ी में बैठने में सहायता की और खुद चालक की सीट की ओर भागी।

एक आदमी ने गाड़ी के शीशे पर हाथ मारते हुए कहा, "यह लीजिए।"

"शुक्रिया" अकीरा ने बड़ी सी मुसकान से उस आदमी का धन्यवाद करते हुए उसके हाथ से पैकेट ले लिया।

"हाँ, क्यों नहीं?" वेद ने आइस पैक का वह पैकेट हाथ में ले लिया। वेद को लगा, उसे मतिभ्रम हो गया है। अकीरा उसे अस्पताल ले जा रही थी। ये क्या टोना-टोटका है? या वह पागल हो गया है? वह खुद को यकीन दिलाना चाह रहा था कि आजकल भाग्य उसका साथ दे रहा है। "कुछ फायदा हो रहा है आइस पैक से?" चिंतित अकीरा ने पूछा।

स्तब्ध-सा वेद अकीरा को देख रहा था, तभी अकीरा ने उस पैकेट को वेद के हाथ में थमाते हुए कहा, "तुम यह पकड़ोगे क्या? मुझे गाड़ी चलानी है।"

"हाँ, क्यों नहीं?" वेद ने आइस पैक का वह पैकेट हाथ में ले लिया।

वेद को लगा, उसे मतिभ्रम हो गया है। अकीरा उसे अस्पताल ले जा रही थी। ये क्या टोना-टोटका है? या वह पागल हो गया है? वह खुद को यकीन दिलाना चाह रहा था कि आजकल भाग्य उसका साथ दे रहा है।

"कुछ फायदा हो रहा है आइस पैक से?" चिंतित अकीरा ने पूछा।

वेद ने वह आइस पैक नाक से हटाकर देखा तो पाया कि ब्रेड के खाली पैकेट में बर्फ के छोटे-छोटे टुकड़े थे।

"हाँ! विब्स की इटालियन सैंडविच ब्रेड, जो शुद्ध शाकाहारी है, मुझपर जादू-सा असर कर रही है।" वेद ने व्यंग्य से कहा।

अकीरा ने मजाक बनाते हुए कहा, "चूँकि तुम चुटकुले मार पा रहे हो, इसका मतलब है कि आइस पैक काम कर रहा है।"

स्थिति को समझते हुए और मानकर वेद ने हामी में सिर हिलाया और दुबारा उस पैकेट को नाक पर दबा लिया। वह जो भी था, वेद को आराम दे रहा था।

"वैसे तुम हँसे क्यों?"

वेद ने कहा, "मोहित ने मुझे जिम कैरी के 'वॅरा दी माइलो' की याद दिला दी।"

चूँकि अकीरा उसका अर्थ नहीं समझी, उसने झट मोबाइल खोलकर देखने की और गूगल पर इस बारे में जानकारी ढूँढ़ने की कोशिश की। यदि कोई और दिन होता तो वेद अकीरा को गाड़ी चलाते हुए मोबाइल का इस्तेमाल करने पर लंबा भाषण देता, लेकिन वह खुद ही इतने दर्द में था कि कुछ नहीं बोला।

"उफ्फ! इश्श!" अकीरा को अपने प्रश्न का उत्तर मिल गया था। "अब जब भी मैं मोहित को देखूँगी, मुझे यही याद आएगा।"

"वाह! बढ़िया।" वेद ने किसी तरह मुसकराकर कहा, "हे भगवान्!"

अकीरा की हँसी रुक चुकी थी। उसने अपने निचले होंठ को दबाकर शंकित स्वर में पूछा, "क्या तुम नाराज हो?"

यह प्रश्न अनपेक्षित था। ऐसा था तो भी क्या हुआ? वेद के दिमाग में एक योजना चल रही थी कि क्या हुआ, जो वह वेद के मुक्के और हमले से खुद को बचा नहीं पाया? वह मोहित को ऐसी जगह मात देगा, जिससे उसे सबसे अधिक तकलीफ होगी। और यह बहुत अच्छा अवसर था कि वह अपने परिवार का दिल जीत लेता। यह सही वक्त था, जब वह 'अरोरा' परिवार को साबित कर दे कि वह सच्चे अर्थों में 'अरोरा' परिवार का खून है।

वेद ने अकीरा को एक बड़ी सी मुसकान के साथ जवाब दिया, "नहीं, मैं नाराज नहीं हूँ।"

□

7

कौन एल पचीनो? कौन रॉबर्ट डी-नीरो? कौन मार्लन ब्रेंडो?

इसीलिए, क्योंकि वेद अरोरा से बड़ा अभिनेता कोई हो ही नहीं सकता था, क्योंकि उसने दुनिया में जन्म लेकर ही तो अपने में महान् कार्य किया था। अभी तो वह बिस्तर पर पड़े-पड़े दुनिया का एक सफल अभिनय करने में व्यस्त था; ऐसा अभिनय, जो उसे करना जरूरी था। अपने सिर को पकड़कर वह इतना कराह रहा था, मानो वह दर्द से मर ही जाएगा।

"मेरे बच्चे! ज्यादा दर्द हो रहा है क्या?" पिंकी (माँ) ने प्यार से वेद की बाँह सहलाते हुए पूछा।

"नहीं।" धीरे-धीरे साँस लेते हुए कहा।

हालाँकि वेद को सबको बेकार की चिंता में डालने पर ग्लानि अवश्य हो रही थी, किंतु वह स्वयं को मिलनेवाली खास सेवा और आकर्षण बिंदु बनने पर खुश था।

जैसे ही वेदिका उस कमरे में आई, पिता अविनाश वेदिका पर फुफकारते हुए बोले, "ये सब तुम्हारी गलती से हुआ।"

"मैंने क्या किया?" वेदिका ने एकदम से पलटकर पूछा, लेकिन उसकी आवाज में चहक नहीं थी।

"तुम्हें उसे क्लब में नहीं ले जाना चाहिए था।" वे गुस्से से चिल्लाए।

वेद रोना चाहता था। सिर्फ रोना नहीं, छाती पीट-पीटकर रोना चाहता था, जमीन पर लोटना चाहता था और इतनी तेज चिल्लाना चाहता था कि इस अवस्था से वह लाल हो जाए। पिछली बार कब उसके पिता ने उसका साथ दिया था? पिता उसकी तरफदारी कर रहे हैं, यह सोचकर ही वह कितना खुश था!

"वेदिका, मैं तुम्हारे पापा से सहमत हूँ। जब तुम्हें पता है कि वेद शराब नहीं पीता तो तुम उसे क्लब क्यों ले गई? अब ये सब एक तरह से तुमने ही शुरू किया है।"

"हाँ, शायद! मुझसे गलती हो गई। मुझे नाफ करना।" वेद के बगल में बैठते हुए वेदिका बोली।

अब तक वेद की आँखें नम हो चुकी थीं। उसे इस बात का विश्वास था, जैसे आज वह समानांतर ब्रह्मांड में चला गया है। खुशी के आँसू उसकी आँखों से छलक गए।

"बहुत दर्द हो रहा है ?" वेदिका ने वेद के आँसू पोंछते हुए पूछा।

वेदिका का इतना मधुर लहजा सुनकर वेद का हृदय खुशी से फूला नहीं समा रहा था। यदि वह उस सारे अभिनय में नहीं होता तो अभी तक भाँगड़ा कर रहा होता।

"नहीं गोगो!" अपने होंठ दबाते हुए वेद ने कहा। वह तो अपनी हँसी दबा रहा था, लेकिन वेदिका को लगा, वह अपना दर्द छुपा रहा है और वेदिका ने संवेदना प्रकट की।

माँ की तरफ घूरती हुई वेदिका बोली, "माँ! आप भी उतनी ही जिम्मेदार हैं जितनी मैं। वेद क्लब इसीलिए आया, क्योंकि वह 'बतरा' परिवार से बचना चाहता था।"

"वाकई वेदिका, तुम ठीक कहती हो।" अविनाश ने पिंकी को गुस्से से देखा। "ये तुम्हारे 30 दिवसीय मूर्खतापूर्ण चुनौती का नतीजा है।" आगे अविनाश ने जोड़ा।

पिंकी ने अपनी गलती मानते हुए सिर हिलाया और कहा, "मान लिया। मुझे वेद पर इतना दबाव नहीं डालना चाहिए था।"

"वाकई वेदिका, तुम ठीक कहती हो।" अविनाश ने पिंकी को गुस्से से देखा। "ये तुम्हारे 30 दिवसीय मूर्खतापूर्ण चुनौती का नतीजा है।" आगे अविनाश ने जोड़ा। पिंकी ने अपनी गलती मानते हुए सिर हिलाया और कहा, "मान लिया। मुझे वेद पर इतना दबाव नहीं डालना चाहिए था।"

वेद ने आश्चर्य से पलकें जल्दी-जल्दी झपकाईं। अरे, मेरी नाक की केवल हड्डी टूटने से मेरा विचित्र, उपदेशात्मक, सनकी, बिखरा हुआ-सा एडम परिवार में परिवर्तित हो गया!

"वेद! उस बेकार-सी चुनौती के बारे में चिंता करना छोड़ दो।" पिंकी ने प्यार से वेद की हथेली चूमी। "बस तुम ठीक हो जाओ। मुझे और कुछ नहीं चाहिए। सच में।"

वेद को माँ के प्यार और व्यवहार को देख अत्यंत प्रसन्नता हो रही थी, वरना अगर माँ से दुबारा झिड़की मिलती तो वाकई वह किसी और हताशा की दुनिया में पहुँच जाता। वाकई माँ का प्रेम निस्स्वार्थ और शुद्ध था, जो वेद को पूर्ण सुख दे गया।

आज शायद वो जो कुछ भी माँगता, उसे मिल जाता। शायद गर्लफ्रेंड (दोस्त) भी। सो, वेद ने सोचा कि मन से एक अच्छे जीवनसाथी की कामना करना गलत नहीं होगा। उस समय के लिए गर्लफ्रेंड ही माँग ली जाए।

वेद ने अपनी आँखें बंद कर सभी देवताओं से एक अच्छी गर्लफ्रेंड या जीवन-साथी के लिए प्रार्थना की और कहा कि जो भी देवता इस प्रार्थना को स्वीकार कर ले,

वही ठीक। और ऐसा लगा, मानो उसकी प्रार्थना जल्दी सुन ली गई। उसी समय दरवाजे पर दस्तक हुई।

"अरे। अकीऽऽऽरा!" अविनाश का चेहरा चमक उठा।

"आओ, बैठो।"

वेद की धड़कन तो मानो रुक-सी गई। वह चलता-फिरता दुर्भाग्य, वह अंशकालिक कॉफी चोर, पूर्णकालिक उपहास उस्ताद, एक अपूर्ण मानव उसके लिए भेजा है? यह प्रश्न उसके समक्ष था। इसके लिए उसने इतने वर्ष प्रतीक्षा की थी? उसका गला सूख गया। भगवान् के प्रेम खाते में जरूर कुछ गड़बड़ हुई है। 'यह जरूर संयोग होगा कि मैंने गर्लफ्रेंड की कामना और प्रार्थना की और उसी समय अकीरा अंदर आई।' वेद ने खुद को दिलासा दिया।

वेद की धड़कन तो मानो रुक-सी गई। वह चलता-फिरता दुर्भाग्य, वह अंशकालिक कॉफी चोर, पूर्णकालिक उपहास उस्ताद, एक अपूर्ण मानव उसके लिए भेजा है? यह प्रश्न उसके समक्ष था। इसके लिए उसने इतने वर्ष प्रतीक्षा की थी? उसका गला सूख गया। भगवान् के प्रेम खाते में जरूर कुछ गड़बड़ हुई है।

लेकिन अकीरा तो हवा में उड़ती हुई सीधी वेद के बिस्तर तक पहुँची। उसके खूबसूरत बाल उसकी पीठ पर लहरा रहे थे, उसकी आँखों में अलग ही प्रभा (चमक) थी, गाल गुलाबी गुलाब जैसे और उफ्फ उसके होंठ! वेद अपने बिस्तर पर ही कसमसा गया, बेचैन हो उठा। खुद को ही फटकार लगाते हुए वेद ने स्वयं से कहा, 'ये दवाइयों का असर है, जो गलत प्रभाव दिमाग पर डाल रहा है; और कुछ भी नहीं। वह किसी और के साथ रिश्ते में प्रतिबद्ध है, बँधी हुई है। ऐसा सोचना भी गलत है।'

"हैलो, कैसे हो वेद?" सभी को अभिवादन करते हुए उसने वेद से पूछा।

झेंप हटाती हुई मुसकान देता हुआ वेद बोला, "ठीक हूँ।"

"खाक ठीक हो! अभी तो दर्द से इतना कराह रहे थे!" वेदिका ने कहा।

"तुम डॉक्टर के पास दुबारा गए?" चिंतित स्वर में अकीरा बोली।

"हाँ, गए थे, उन्होंने सी.टी. स्कैन और एक्स-रे (C.T. Scan and X-Ray) किया है। देखते हैं, रिपोर्ट्स में क्या बताते हैं?" पिंकी ने बताया।

"मुझे बहुत बुरा लग रहा है, मुझे माफ करना।" ग्लानि से सिर झुकाते हुए अकीरा बोली।

"तुम्हारी गलती नहीं थी।" अविनाश ने हाथ से इशारा करते हुए कहा।

वेदिका ने याद दिलाया, "तुम्हारे बॉयफ्रेंड की गलती थी।"

"खैर, अब दोषारोपण करने का कोई फायदा नहीं। लड़के की नाक तो कट ही गई।" पिंकी ने व्यंग्य और शोक से वेद की नाक पर धीरे से हाथ फेरते हुए कहा।

"माँ!" वेद अचानक करहाया और सभी हँस पड़े।

"अरे! तुम सभी गप्पें मारो, मैं ऑफिस को निकलता हूँ।" इतना कहकर अविनाश खड़ा हो गया। वेद ने निश्चित ही लार टपकाने, करहाने, दर्द में, बीमार होने का अभिनय जोरदार किया था कि पिताजी ने भी झुककर वेद का माथा चूम लिया। इतने सालों बाद पिता का प्यार! वेद खुश था। "और तुम अपना ध्यान रखो, खाओ और सो जाओ! ठीक है?" अविनाश ने कहा।

"अरे! तुम सभी गप्पें मारो, मैं ऑफिस को निकलता हूँ।" इतना कहकर अविनाश खड़ा हो गया। वेद ने निश्चित ही लार टपकाने, करहाने, दर्द में, बीमार होने का अभिनय जोरदार किया था कि पिताजी ने भी झुककर वेद का माथा चूम लिया। इतने सालों बाद पिता का प्यार! वेद खुश था।

वेद को लगा मानो उसका बचपन लौट आया हो। बस पापा का उसे गोद में लेकर सुलाना ही बाकी रह गया था। "हाँ, पक्का। येऽऽऽह!" वेद बोला।

अविनाश ने प्यार से वेद के गालों पर थपकी दी और कहा, "बाय, चलता हूँ।"

पिंकी भी खड़ी हो गईं। "मैं तुम्हारे लिए खाने को कुछ लाती हूँ। आओ वेदिका!"

अकीरा ने उन दोनों के कमरे से बाहर जाने का इंतजार किया। फिर अकीरा ने वेद की पट्टी बँधी हुई नाक देखी, सूजी हुई आँखें और खरोंच आई त्वचा। "वैसे डॉक्टर ने क्या कहा?" अकीरा ने वेद से सवाल किया।

"रिपोर्ट्स तो नहीं आई अभी, लेकिन मुझे लगता है, हड्डियों तक आघात पहुँचा है, हेयरलाइन फ्रेक्चर होगा।" वेद ने लंबी साँस छोड़ते हुए कहा।

"सच में? लेकिन कल रात को आपातकालीन कमरे के डॉक्टर ने कहा था कि सामान्य चोट है।" अकीरा की आवाज में चिंता थी।

वेद कुछ नहीं बोला। अकीरा की बुद्धिमानी स्पष्ट दिखाई दे रही थी। उसे अकीरा को ऐसा जवाब देना चाहिए था, जो वाकई चिंतित करनेवाला होता। उसका दिमाग चकरा रहा था और वह कुछ सोच नहीं पा रहा था। वेद ने धीरे से कहा, "डॉक्टर मूर्ख था।"

"मूर्ख?" अकीरा की भौंहें आश्चर्य मिश्रित गुस्से से चढ़ गईं। "तुम बेवकूफ बना रहे हो। नहीं?"

वेद के आश्चर्य की सीमा नहीं थी। कोई ऐसे अचानक ऐसे कैसे कह सकता है? उसके पास शब्द ही नहीं बचे थे, गले में मानो अटक गए थे, फिर भी खुद को सँभालते

हुए उसने कहा, “बिल्कुल नहीं। मुझे तुम्हारे बॉयफ्रेंड की वजह से गहरी चोट आई है।”

“क्या मतलब है तुम्हारा?”

“तुम झूठ बोल रहे हो, क्योंकि तुम व्रह 30 दिनोंवाली ‘दुलहन ढूँढ़ो’ चुनौती से बचना चाहते हो। पर चिंता मत करो, वास्तव में तुम्हारे परिवार को नहीं बताऊँगी।” अकीरा ने आँख मारते हुए कहा।

“फिर मानना पड़ेगा, कितने बदतमीज हो तुम।”

“क्या बोली?” वेद दाँत पीसकर बोला। “मैं इससे ज्यादा अपने व्यवहार और भाषा के स्तर में नहीं गिर सकता और इसका मुझे अभिमान है।”

“फिर मानना पड़ेगा, कितने बदतमीज हो तुम।” “क्या बोली?” वेद दाँत पीसकर बोला। “मैं इससे ज्यादा अपने व्यवहार और भाषा के स्तर में नहीं गिर सकता और इसका मुझे अभिमान है।” “हाँ, क्यों नहीं? होगा...अगर तुम कहते हो तो!” हँसी उड़ाते हुए अकीरा बोली और वेद हैरान था।

“हाँ, क्यों नहीं? होगा···अगर तुम कहते हो तो!” हँसी उड़ाते हुए अकीरा बोली और वेद हैरान था।

कुछ क्षणों की शांति के बाद अकीरा ने वेद का हाथ अपने हाथ में लेकर पूछा, “एक बात बताओ, तुमने प्रतिकार क्यों नहीं किया? क्यों चुपचाप मार खाई?”

“क्योंकि मैं लड़ाकू नहीं हूँ और उसने भी अचानक अनपेक्षित हमला किया मुझपर।” वेद ने जवाब दिया।

“तो क्या तुम उससे पहले युद्ध के ऐलान करने की उम्मीद कर रहे थे?”

“नहीं। लेकिन समझदार लोग ऐसे किसी को मारते नहीं हैं। पागल है मोहित। तुम्हारा पुरुषों का चुनाव बेकार है।” वेद ने कहा।

अकीरा भी संभ्रमित-सी (संशययुक्त) बोली, “फिर मुझे किस तरह के पुरुषों का चुनाव करना चाहिए?”

वेद की आवाज में गंभीरता आ गई, “ऐसे पुरुष, जो सुविज्ञ, सदाचारी, स्पष्टवादी, शिष्ट हों और इस तरह से लोखंडवाला गुंडों की तरह लड़नेवाले न हों।”

“संक्षेप में, तुम जैसा कोई?”

गुस्से और थकावट की अभिव्यक्ति से वेद सामनेवाली लड़की को स्तब्ध निगाहों से देख रहा था। अचानक फूट पड़ा “तुम ऐसा मुँह क्यों बना रही हो? मुझमें क्या खराबी है?”

“कुछ नहीं। तुम केवल बोरिंग (उबाऊ) हो।” कंधे उचकाते हुए अकीरा ने जवाब दिया।

"मैं बोरिंग नहीं हूँ, पूरा पैकेज हूँ (जैसा चाहिए वैसा)। तुमने मुझे देखा? मेरा चेहरा? मेरा शारीरिक गठन? मेरे नाक-नक्श?" नीचे की ओर इशारा करते हुए बोला, "मैं और नीचे की बात नहीं करूँगा, वरना तुम बेहोश हो जाओगी। लेकिन मैं बोरिंग नहीं हूँ। यह अच्छे से समझ लो। उबाऊ शब्द से बहुत दूर का संबंध है मेरा।"

अपने बारे में वेद का इतना भावुक एकालाप सुनकर अकीरा ने व्यंग्य कसा, "इसमें आत्ममुग्ध (नार्सिस्टीक) का विशेषण भी जोड़ लें।"

"मैं सिर्फ ईमानदारी से बता रहा हूँ।" वेद ने ढिठाई से कहा।

एक भौंह उचकाते हुए अकीरा ने सवाल फेंका, "फिर अभी तक तुम कुँवारे क्यों हो?"

वेद ने अपने बचाव में कहा, "तुम्हें क्या लगता है, लड़कियाँ मुझसे दोस्ती नहीं करना चाहतीं? मुझे भी आते-जाते कई लड़कियाँ छेड़ती हैं, जैसे लड़कियों को लड़के। और वो भी हर उम्र की लड़कियाँ।"

"तो तुम क्यों नहीं छिड़ जाते किसी के साथ?" अकीरा ने मजाक उड़ाते हुए दबी आवाज में कहा।

इस मजाक से वेद का चेहरा गुस्से से लाल हो गया और टेढ़ा मुँह करके वेद बोला, "चुप रहो।"

वेद ने अपने बचाव में कहा, "तुम्हें क्या लगता है, लड़कियाँ मुझसे दोस्ती नहीं करना चाहतीं? मुझे भी आते-जाते कई लड़कियाँ छेड़ती हैं, जैसे लड़कियों को लड़के। और वो भी हर उम्र की लड़कियाँ।" "तो तुम क्यों नहीं छिड़ जाते किसी के साथ?" अकीरा ने मजाक उड़ाते हुए दबी आवाज में कहा।

'रूम सर्विस' की बुलंद आवाज में वेदिका खाने की ट्रे लेकर कमरे में दाखिल हुई। जैसे ही वह कमरे में आई, वेद चुप हो गया। कंधे ढीले पड़ गए और वह गद्दे में धँस-सा गया। अचानक वह बीमार दिखाई पड़ रहा था। अकीरा उसे सम्मोहन की दृष्टि से देख रही थी। वेद अभिनय में उस्ताद दिखाई पड़ रहा था।

"क्या मजाक चल रहा था?" वेदिका ने अकीरा से पूछा। वेद से नजरें हटाकर और उसके अभिनय को देखते हुए अकीरा बोली, "ओह! कुछ नहीं, बकवास चल रही थी।"

"वाह! इसी की उम्मीद थी। जहाँ वेद भैया होंगे, वहाँ बकवास तो होगी ही।" वेदिका हँसते हुए बोली।

"चुप रहो गोगो!" वेद ने दंडित भाषा में वेदिका से कहा। वेदिका व्यंग्यात्मक हँसी और उपमा की प्लेट निकालकर वेद को खिलाने लगी। अपने लिए समोसा उठाते हुए हलके से उपहास के स्वर में अकीरा बोली, "गोगो! कितना मजेदार नाम है।"

"माँ हमेशा मेरे लिए दो साइज बड़ी वर्दी खरीदती, जो मेरे खुलकर जीने के बीच आती थी, मेरी स्कर्ट, जो बहुत बड़ी होती थी। चाहे चलना हो, दौड़ना हो या कार में बैठना हो। मेरी स्कर्ट, जो बहुत बड़ी होती थी, वह तो सुबह-शाम परेशान करती।" वेदिका ने टेढ़ा मुँह करते हुए कहा।

"वो हम दोनों के बीच का हमेशा का चुटकुला था।" वेद ने वेदिका की पैंट पकड़कर कहा, "जी, आपका घाघरा।"

वेद और वेदिका, दोनों ने एक-दूसरे को देखा और हँस पड़े।

वेदिका ने उसे कंधे से पकड़कर अपनी ओर कसा और बोली, "खैर। अब है न!" "मुझे भी कोई झप्पी दे दो।" कुछ थैलों के साथ अंदर आते हुए कबीर ने कहा। "ओ मेरे शेर! कैसे हो तुम?" खुद को वेद के बाईं ओर, पलंग पर धप्प से बिठाते हुए कबीर बोला, "देखो, मैं तुम्हारे लिए फल लाया हूँ। तुम्हें इसकी जरूरत है। एक मुक्का और तुम बिस्तरे में हो। तुम हार गए।"

"कितना प्यारा! काश, मेरी भी कोई बहन होती!" अकीरा बोली।

वेदिका ने उसे कंधे से पकड़कर अपनी ओर कसा और बोली, "खैर। अब है न!"

"मुझे भी कोई झप्पी दे दो।" कुछ थैलों के साथ अंदर आते हुए कबीर ने कहा।

"ओ मेरे शेर! कैसे हो तुम?" खुद को वेद के बाईं ओर, पलंग पर धप्प से बिठाते हुए कबीर बोला, "देखो, मैं तुम्हारे लिए फल लाया हूँ। तुम्हें इसकी जरूरत है। एक मुक्का और तुम बिस्तरे में हो। तुम हार गए।"

"तुम्हारा मतलब लूजर? मैं नहींऽऽऽ···" वेद ने अपनी सफाई देनी चाही, पर कुछ सोचकर चुप हो गया। उसे अचानक याद आया कि सामने बैठे लोगों की बुद्धिलाब्धि (IQ) मिलाकर भी उतनी नहीं, जिसे कि समझाया जाना चाहिए, क्योंकि उनकी समझ में ही नहीं आएगा, इसलिए समझाना बेकार है। कबीर ने अकीरा की ओर देखकर पूछा, "वैसे अकीरा, किस तरह के लोग बिना उकसाए भी हिंसक और घिनौना व्यवहार करते हैं?"

अजीब सी शक्ल बनाकर वेदिका बोली, "असभ्य, अशिष्ट! और वो कौन हैं?"

"ऐसा है!" अकीरा ने साँस छोड़ते हुए कहा। "मैं मोहित की तरफदारी नहीं कर रही। उसने जो किया, वो गलत था, लेकिन उसके बारे में बार-बार बात करके माहौल और दिमाग क्यों खराब करें? प्लीज! अब और नहीं।"

"पर तुम्हें वह सचमुच अच्छा लगता है, क्यों? हाँ या ना?"

"मुझे नहीं पता" अकीरा ने वेदिका की नजर से बचते हुए जवाब दिया। "बस कभी हाँ और कभी ना!"

"अच्छाऽऽऽ! स्विच की तरह? कभी खोल दिया, कभी बंद कर दिया?" वेद ने गुस्से से कहा।

कबीर मानो पछताते हुए बोला, "बुद्धू। उसका मतलब है कि कभी उनका रिश्ता खत्म-सा हो जाता है और कभी फिर दोनों एक हो जाते हैं।"

"ओह! ऐसा!" वेद ने धीरे-धीरे सिर हिलाते हुए दिखाया कि वो बात समझ रहा है। (व्यंग्यात्मक)

दो दोस्तों के बीच इशारे होते देख अकीरा ने अपनी खिसियाहट छुपाने की कोशिश की। वेद कबीर से कुछ खास अलग नहीं होगा।

उसने उत्सुकता से पूछा, "तुम दोनों कब से दोस्त हो?"

"जब हम दूसरी कक्षा में पढ़ते थे। हम दोनों एक फैंसी ड्रेस प्रतियोगिता में मिले थे। सोच, शिवजी का भेस किसने किया था?"

वेद की तरफ देखते हुए अकीरा ने पूछा, "किसने?"

झेंप से माथा खुजाते हुए कबीर ने कहा, "अपने शक्तिमान ने।"

वेद की तरफ देखते हुए अकीरा ने पूछा, "किसने?"

कबीर, वेदिका और अकीरा ने कुछ क्षणों के लिए एक-दूसरे को देखा और चिल्लाते हुए जोर से ठहाका मारते हुए हँसने लगे।

दो दोस्तों के बीच इशारे होते देख अकीरा ने अपनी खिसियाहट छुपाने की कोशिश की। वेद कबीर से कुछ खास अलग नहीं होगा। उसने उत्सुकता से पूछा, "तुम दोनों कब से दोस्त हो?" "जब हम दूसरी कक्षा में पढ़ते थे। हम दोनों एक फैंसी ड्रेस प्रतियोगिता में मिले थे। सोच, शिवजी का भेस किसने किया था?"

"कितना मजेदार!" वेद ने अपनी झेंप मिटाते हुए कहा। उतने में पिंकी कमरे में आईं। वह कुछ दुविधा में नजर आ रही थीं। उन्होंने पूछा, "वेद, तुमने वकील को फोन किया क्या?"

"ओह, श्रीमान दास यहीं हैं।" वेद शैतानी हँसी हँसकर बोला। उसने धीरे से गरदन अकीरा की ओर घुमाई, मानो उसे चुनौती दे रहा हो। "बढ़िया। मुझे किसी से हिसाब चुकता करना है।"

□

8

'उठो!'

वेद को महसूस हुआ कि कोई उसकी बाजू खींच रहा है। उसने दूसरा हाथ बाजू खींचनेवाले पर डाला। कुछ नरम-सा महसूस हुआ। उसने अपना पूरा शरीर ही उस नरमी पर झोंक दिया। उद्देश्य कुछ भी नहीं था। पर अच्छा लगा। ऐसा अच्छा महसूस किया जा सकता है।

"उफ्फऽऽऽ! वेद!"

किसी ने उसे झकझोरा। किसी के अनपेक्षित रूखे व्यवहार से चिढ़ गया और ऊपर की ओर सिर हड़बड़ी में उठाकर देखा।

"अकीराऽऽ!"

वेद मूकदर्शक-सा अकीरा की ओर देखता रहा, जैसे उसके दिमाग के पहिए थम गए हों और जो दिख रहा था, वो बात मानो अंदर ले ही न पा रहा हो। वहाँ अकीरा क्या कर रही थी? और वह उसी से सट रहा था? अकीरा से? शायद धरती अपनी धुरी पर घूमना बंद हो गई थी, क्योंकि अगर उसके जीवन में यह घटना हो रही थी तो कुछ भी हो सकता था।

हैरान था, लेकिन उसे पकड़ना वेद को अजीब नहीं लगा। वह और उसके मस्तिष्क के निष्क्रिय हार्मोंस! उसका दिमाग जड़ हो गया था।

"तुम्हें मुझे देखने की आदत कभी भी नहीं होती।" अकीरा पर इस गड़बड़ का कोई भी प्रभाव नहीं था। "यही नहीं, तुम हमेशा चिल्लाते नजर आते हो।"

लंबी साँस खींचते हुए वेद ने कहा, "पहले तुम इस बात का स्पष्टीकरण दो कि तुम यहाँ क्या कर रही हो?"

"तुम हमेशा सफाई और स्पष्टीकरण ही माँगते रहते हो। खैर, तुम्हारे माता-पिता और वेदिका को जरूरी समारोह में जाना था; कबीर किसी काम में व्यस्त था तो पिंकी आंटी ने मुझे तुम्हारा खयाल रखने को कहा।" अकीरा मुँह टेढ़ा करके बोली।

"क्या? मेरा खयाल? मैं कोई बच्चा हूँ, क्या? तुम मजाक कर रही हो न!"

खुशी से अकीरा के होंठ काँप रहे थे। "नहीं।"

"छोड़ो भी। ये बेकार की बातें बंद करो।" वेद ने व्यंग्य से कहा।

अकीरा हँसी और उसने वेद की पसलियों में उँगली लगाई।

"खैर! तुम ठीक तो हो? अभी तक तुम ठंडे पड़े थे।"

बिस्तर पर खुद को लिटाते हुए वेद बोला, "हो सकता है दवाइयों का असर हो, मुझे वाकई अंदरूनी चोट लगी है। दोनों-तीनों डॉक्टरों ने भी यही कहा। मुझे अभिनय करने की आवश्यकता नहीं है।"

अकीरा ने आँखें फड़फड़ाईं (अविश्वास में)। वेद का दुर्भाग्य अभी चल रहा था। "खैर! इस समय-तालिका के अनुसार तुम्हें कुछ खाना चाहिए।"

"उफ्फ! यह समय-तालिका!" वेद ने दु:ख से कहा। "इसे तो मुझे जला देने का मन करता है।"

"पिंकी ने तो तुम्हारी दवाइयों, खाने और यहाँ तक कि वाशरूम जाने तक के अलार्म लगाए हैं।" वेद ने गलत सोचा था। पिंकी अरोरा जैसी माँ होने पर बीमार होना तो बिल्कुल आसान नहीं था।

"आओ देखते हैं, आपकी महान् माताश्री ने आपके लिए दोपहर के खाने में क्या बनाया है? जरूर लुधियाने का कुछ होगा। आखिर वहीं की जो हैं।" वेद बिस्तर से खड़ा हो गया। अकीरा हँसती हुई रसोईघर की ओर चल पड़ी और वेद पीछे-पीछे चला।

"तुम पिछले कुछ घंटों से यहीं हो। बोर नहीं हुई?"

"आओ देखते हैं, आपकी महान् माताश्री ने आपके लिए दोपहर के खाने में क्या बनाया है? जरूर लुधियाने का कुछ होगा। आखिर वहीं की जो हैं।" वेद बिस्तर से खड़ा हो गया। अकीरा हँसती हुई रसोईघर की ओर चल पड़ी और वेद पीछे-पीछे चला। "तुम पिछले कुछ घंटों से यहीं हो। बोर नहीं हुई?"

"नहीं। मेरा ख्वाब था कि मैं किसी पुरुष को कई घंटों तक सोते, लार टपकाते, करवटें बदलते, खर्राटे मारते और कराहते देखूँ।" अकीरा के सुर के व्यंग्य समझते हुए वेद ने भी ताना कसा, "हमेशा की तरह चिड़चिड़ी और खिसियानी! यही अपेक्षित था।"

वह दबी हुई हँसी हँस रही थी। वेद ने एक बरतन का ढक्कन खोला। देखकर अकीरा को हैरानी हुई, लेकिन वेद को बिल्कुल भी नहीं। वह माँ की इन बातों का आदी था। बरतन में कागज के एक टुकड़े पर लिखा था, 'बाहर से कुछ मँगवा लेना। बहुत सारा प्यार, माँ।'

वेद ने जोर से बरतन का ढक्कन बंद किया। अकीरा मुसकराकर बोली, "क्या घुमाया तुम्हारी माँ ने! लेकिन तुम्हारा भाग्य अच्छा है, मैंने पिज्जा ऑर्डर कर दिया है।"

वेद कृतज्ञता भाव से बोला, "शुक्र है भगवान् का। मुझे बहुत भूख भी लग रही थी।"

अकीरा भी पलटकर हँसी और वे दुबारा अजब सी चुप्पी में रहे। वे पहली बार साथ में अकेले थे। एक बार ही शायद उन्होंने ठीक से बात की थी, वरना अधिकतर वे बात करते ही नहीं थे।

"चलो, बाहर के कमरे में बैठते हैं···" वेद ने सुझाव दिया और दोनों सोफे पर अलग-अलग कोनों पर जाकर बैठ गए।

"वैसे तुम काम क्या करती हो ?" थोड़ी देर बाद वेद ने पूछा।

अकीरा मुसकराती हुई बोली, "मैं वेडिंग प्लानर हूँ। शादियों के प्रबंध करती हूँ।"

"कोई आश्चर्य नहीं कि वेदिका तुमसे दोस्ती क्यों नहीं करना चाहेगी?" वेद ने व्यंग्य से कहा, जिसे सुनकर अकीरा ने एक बनावटी मुसकान वापस की।

अकीरा मुसकराती हुई बोली, "मैं वेडिंग प्लानर हूँ। शादियों के प्रबंध करती हूँ।" "कोई आश्चर्य नहीं कि वेदिका तुमसे दोस्ती क्यों नहीं करना चाहेगी ?" वेद ने व्यंग्य से कहा, जिसे सुनकर अकीरा ने एक बनावटी मुसकान वापस की।

"खैर! तुम्हें नोटिस पर गुस्सा नहीं आया ?" वेद ने पूछा। जैसे ही वेद को लगा कि अकीरा की नजरें उसी पर हैं, उसने अपने हाथों से बाल ठीक किए और खुद को ज्यादा दर्शनीय बनाना चाहा।

झेंपती हुई अकीरा ने कहा, "मेरे खयाल से मोहित के साथ ठीक ही हुआ।"

"ठीऽऽऽक ?" वेद ने भौंहें चढ़ाते हुए कहा। "उसके साथ वैसा ही होना चाहिए था, वैसे क्या तुमने नोटिस पढ़ा अकीरा ?"

"नहीं, मैं क्यों पढ़ूँगी? और यहाँ कौन कानून के अजीब दाँव-पेच में फँसना चाहेगा ?" अकीरा ने कलाई झटकते हुए कहा।

अकीरा के इतने निश्चिंत अंदाज से वेद स्तब्ध था। उसने जब वकील को घर पर बुलाया था, तब भी अकरा पर कोई असर नहीं था। वेद ने अकीरा से पूछा, "तुम कब से साथ हो ?"

"तकरीबन···एक साल। लेकिन उसमें भी चार बार हमने ब्रेकऑफ किया।"

"मतबल हर तीन महीने बाद ब्रेकऑफ ?" वेद बोला।

"कई बार वह बहुत घटिया हो जाता है। किसी भी हद तक जा सकता है।" अकीरा झेंप मिटाते हुए खिसियाकर बोली।

"फिर तुम उसके साथ क्यों हो ?" अब वेद को वाकई जानने की उत्सुकता हो रही थी।

अकीरा थोड़ी देर सोचती रही, फिर बोली, "कई बार प्यार से ज्यादा आदत की वजह से। आदत हो गई है।"

"लेकिन आदतें तो 21 दिनों में बदली जा सकती हैं।"

अकीरा ने एकदम पलटकर पूछा, "क्या कह रहे हो?"

वेद ने सिर हिलाते हुए कहा, "मैंने एक दिन निश्चय किया कि मैं सुबह 5 बजे उठूँगा और लगातार 21 दिनों तक पाँच बजे उठा। अब तो आदत बन गई।"

"वाह! क्या बात है!" अकीरा ने बिना भावों के तालियाँ बजाते हुए बात जारी रखी। "इसमें कोई शक नहीं कि भारत का राष्ट्रीय कॉलेस्ट्रॉल स्तर निश्चित ही तुम जैसों की वजह से गिरा है। वाकई कोई बहुत ही जोरदार तरीके से कोशिश कर रहा है।"

"वाह! क्या बात है!" अकीरा ने बिना भावों के तालियाँ बजाते हुए बात जारी रखी। "इसमें कोई शक नहीं कि भारत का राष्ट्रीय कॉलेस्ट्रॉल स्तर निश्चित ही तुम जैसों की वजह से गिरा है। वाकई कोई बहुत ही जोरदार तरीके से कोशिश कर रहा है।"

वेद को गुस्सा आया, "हम अपने विषय से भटक रहे हैं।"

अकीरा खीसें निपोरती हुई बोली, "सुनो! आदतों और मनुष्यों में फर्क है।"

"शायद नहीं।" उसके विचारों को समझते हुए वेद बोला। "कई बार लोग हमारी आदत हो जाते हैं।"

अकीरा उसे दरवाजे की ओर जाते देख रही थी। वह सही था। अधिकतर लोग किसी भी संबंध में प्यार की वजह से नहीं, आदत की वजह से रहते हैं और ऐसा होना कोई अच्छी बात नहीं।

अकीरा ने वेद को ध्यान से देखा। वेद ने पिज्जा के बक्से के छोटे-छोटे टुकड़े करके बड़े एहतियात से कूड़े के डब्बे में डाले। उसके बाद, जो कुछ भी पिज्जा खाने के कारण जमीन पर गिरा, उसे इकट्ठा किया।

"वेद"। तुम यह घर की कामवाली के काम क्यों कर रहे हो?" अकीरा ने वेद की ठुड्डी पर हाथ मारते हुए कहा।

"यह गंदा हमने मचाया तो हम ही साफ करेंगे न! घर की सफाईवाली हमारी नौकर तो नहीं है न!" वेद ने कहा।

"अरे वाह! घर में एक मानवाधिकार के प्रति सजग कार्यकर्ता भी है। क्या बात है? अब इसके अलावा और क्या-क्या? शाकाहारी भी हो?" अकीरा ने उपहास से हँसते हुए पूछा।

"हाँ। हूँ न।" वेद ने मुँह खोला और फिर बंद किया।

"हे भगवान्!" अकीरा ने यह कहकर मुँह पर हाथ रख लिया।

"अच्छा इनसान होने की सजा दो मुझे, मार डालो।" वेद चिढ़कर बोला।

"तुम्हें पता है कि यदि सभी इनसानों की आइसक्रीम फ्लेवर (स्वाद) से तुलना की जाए, तो तुम वनीला फ्लेवर होगे।" उसने अपनी सोच पेश की।

'किसने सोचा था कि एक लड़की उसकी तुलना आइसक्रीम फ्लेवर से करेगी? यह कैसा दिन दिखा रहा है ईश्वर।' वेद अपना चेहरा पोंछते हुए व्यंग्य से अकीरा पर ताना कसते हुए बोला, "तुम तो अच्छे इनसान को भी अपराधी जैसा ही सिद्ध करके दम लोगी। तुम मेरे परिवार के लिए बिल्कुल उचित हो।"

"वेद, यह क्या है?" वेद ने अकीरा के आश्चर्य भरे स्वर को समझ लिया था। वह पीछे मुड़ा। अकीरा ने एक किताब पकड़ रखी थी। उसके अंदर पन्ने थे और हर पृष्ठ चार खानों में बँटा हुआ था। एक खाना (स्तंभ) वेद के नाम-कार्य के लिए, उसके अंक और एक वेदिका के नाम-कार्य और उसके अंक।

अकीरा की आँखें एक क्षण के लिए हैरत से बड़ी हो गईं। और वैसे ही अचानक वेद की भी। वेद ने खिसियाते हुए जीभ दाँतों तले रखकर नजर उधर फेर ली।

"मैं बोर हो गई…।" अकीरा ने विषय की गंभीरता को खत्म करने की कोशिश में कहा।

"ठीक है…। दुनिया आजाद है, कुछ भी हो सकता है। होओ।" धीरे से व्यंग्य भरी मुसकान से वेद बोला।

अकीरा ने असहमति के स्वर में वेद से प्रश्न दागा, "तुम्हारे पास बोर्ड गेम हैं क्या?"

"हाँ। अगर होंगे तो बोर्ड गेम स्टोर रूम में होंगे।"

वह मुसकराई, "चलो, फिर वही ढूँढ़ते हैं।"

सिर हिलाते हुए वेद खड़ा हुआ और दोनों स्टोर रूम की ओर निकल पड़े। एक छोटे से कमरे में वेद ने ध्यान से अलमारी खोली और बोला, "बोर्ड गेम अगर होंगे तो यहीं होंगे।"

"वेद, यह क्या है?" वेद ने अकीरा के आश्चर्य भरे स्वर को समझ लिया था। वह पीछे मुड़ा। अकीरा ने एक किताब पकड़ रखी थी। उसके अंदर पन्ने थे और हर पृष्ठ चार खानों में बँटा हुआ था। एक खाना (स्तंभ) वेद के नाम-कार्य के लिए, उसके अंक और एक वेदिका के नाम-कार्य और उसके अंक।

वेद ने झेंपते हुए अकीरा की ओर देखा। "वेदिका और मैं अच्छी चीजों, बातों और कार्यों का हिसाब इस बैलेंस शीट में रखते थे। हर अच्छी बात या कार्य का अंक। पेज समाप्त होने तक जिसके ज्यादा अंक, उसकी स्थिति मजबूत और आदरणीय मानी जाती।"

"क्याऽऽऽ ? तुम लोग पागल हो क्या ?"

वेद ने कड़ाई से जवाब दिया, "हम बच्चे थे।"

"बेवकूफ बच्चे।"

अकीरा ने उसमें दर्ज बातें पढ़नी शुरू कीं। वेद समझ चुका था कि बहुत से राज अब शर्मिंदगी लानेवाले हैं और अब उसकी बारी आएगी मुँह छुपाने की।

"2 जनवरी, 1995 : मैंने आधी च्यूंगम-गम दी…"

अकीरा जोर-जोर से पढ़ने लगी।

"8 अप्रैल, 1995 : गणित की उत्तर-पुस्तिका छुपाने में मदद की।"

"17 मई, 1996 : एक गिलास पानी लाया।"

उसने वेद की ओर देखा। वेद शर्मिंदा दिखाई दे रहा था।

हँसी दबाते हुए अकीरा ने आखिर में लिखी हुई बातें पढ़ने के लिए पन्ने पलटे।

"21 दिसंबर, 2004 : पापा के कंप्यूटर के प्रयोग से पहले जहाँ इंटरनेट देखा, सारा इतिहास (History) मिटा दिया (Delete)।

वो ठहाका मारकर हँस पड़ी। उसके गाल हँस-हँसकर लाल हो गए। "वेदिका ने पॉर्न (कामोद्दीपक) साइट खोजी थी, वोऽऽइसीलिए।" वेद मानो क्रंदन स्वर में बोला।

"वाह ! और बधाई हो। तुम्हारे अंक वेदिका से ज्यादा हैं। तुम जीते।" हँसते हुए अकीरा ने कहा।

वो ठहाका मारकर हँस पड़ी। उसके गाल हँस-हँसकर लाल हो गए। "वेदिका ने पॉर्न (कामोद्दीपक) साइट खोजी थी, वोऽऽइसीलिए।" वेद मानो क्रंदन स्वर में बोला।

"वाह! और बधाई हो। तुम्हारे अंक वेदिका से ज्यादा हैं। तुम जीते।" हँसते हुए अकीरा ने कहा।

वेद ने उन पन्नों पर प्यार से वेदिका के नाम पर हाथ घुमाया और बोला, "मैं अभी आता हूँ…।"

अकीरा को हैरानी हुई, पर उसने हामी में सिर हिलाया। कुछ मिनटों बाद वेद पेन लेकर उस कमरे में आया।

वेद ने उन पन्नों पर प्यार से वेदिका के नाम पर हाथ घुमाया और बोला, "मैं अभी आता हूँ…।"

अकीरा को हैरानी हुई, पर उसने हामी में सिर हिलाया। कुछ मिनटों बाद वेद पेन लेकर उस कमरे में आया।

"चलो, इस तालिका को ठीक करते हैं।" वह मुसकाया और वेदिका के खाने (स्तंभ) में लिखा :

"8 सितंबर, 2020 : वेद के बीमार होने पर उसकी देखभाल की।"

उसने अंक गिने, "अब ठीक है, अब कुल अंक समान हैं। अब हम एक जैसे हो गए।"

अकीरा के हृदय में दर्द उठा। उसका हृदय टोस्ट पर रखे मक्खन की तरह पिघल रहा था। वह मुसकाई और वहाँ का माहौल कोमल भावों से भर-सा गया। अकीरा को खुशी हुई, वेद वाकई कुछ विशेष पुरुष जैसा प्रतीत हो रहा था उसे, लेकिन मूर्ख वेद को इस बात का अंदाजा भी नहीं था।

□

9

"साँप-सीढ़ी?" वेद ने एक छोटा सा, फटे हुए गत्ते का बक्सा निकाला और किसी आशा से अकीरा की ओर देखा।

अकीरा की आँखें चमकीं, "बिल्कुल ठीक।"

उसका उत्साह देख वेद मुसकराया। सच में बिल्कुल ठीक था। अकीरा के बॉयफ्रेंड ने वेद की अवनति करा कंप्यूटर की फाइल्स, मर्जर्स से साँप-सीढ़ी खेलने पर मजबूर किया था, वह भी मैले पाजामे में। ये सही है कि मैले पाजामे के लिए मोहित जिम्मेदार नहीं था।

बक्सा खोलते ही वेद दुःख से बोला, "हम नहीं खेल सकते, इसमें पासा नहीं है।"

"धत् तेरे की।" अकीरा घृणा से बोली। "हम परचियाँ बना सकते हैं।"

बेमन से वेद ने छत की ओर देखते हुए कहा, "मैं ऐसा क्यों कर रहा हूँ?"

"उल्लू। इसे कहते हैं मजे करना।" अकीरा ने उसे स्टोर-रूम के बाहर धकेला। "चलो, चलते हैं।"

वे दोनों वेद के कमरे में जाकर बिस्तर पर बैठे। जब अकीरा परचियाँ बना रही थी, तभी अकीरा के फोन का अलार्म बज उठा।

फोन की तरफ देखते ही अकीरा बोली, "रुको। दवाई लेने का वक्त हो गया है।"

कराहते हुए वेद ने डॉक्टर की परची को तीन बार ध्यान से देखा। वेद समझ रहा था कि उसकी इस हरकत पर अकीरा की नजर है, लेकिन उसने ध्यान नहीं दिया। वह अरोरा परिवार का पहला ऐसा सदस्य नहीं बनना चाहता था, जिसकी जान गलत दवाई खाने से गई हो। संक्षेप में, वह दवाई लेने से पहले डॉक्टर के परचे को ध्यान से देखकर दवाई लेना चाहता था।

वेद ने दवाइयाँ निगलीं और कहा, "मैं जीता तो इयरप्लगस और तुम जीती तो पैसिफायर।"

"चुप रहो। मैं कहती हूँ, जीतनेवाला जो चाहे, हारनेवाले को वही करना पड़ेगा।"

"ठीक है…" वेद ने बिना किसी भाव के उत्तर दिया।

"वाह! उत्साह कितना संक्रामक है न!" अकीरा ने उपहास करते हुए कहा।

वेद ने पासे की जगह बनाई परची उठाई, "चार।"

"मेरी बारी", अकीरा ने परची उठाई, "तीन! बिल्कुल मेरे परिवार की तरह।"

उसकी ओर देखते हुए वेद ने कहा, "कितनी अजीब बात है। मुझे तुम्हारे परिवार के बारे में कुछ भी नहीं मालूम।"

"मेरे परिवार में मैं अकेली लड़की हूँ और जब से मेरे माता-पिता गए हैं, तब से मैं अकेली रहती हूँ। कई बार अकेलापन महसूस होता है, पर गुजारा कर लेती हूँ।" अकीरा ने वेद को उसकी बारी याद दिलाते हुए कहा।

वेद अचानक गंभीर हो गया। "माफ करना, मुझे मालूम नहीं था।" वेद के सुर में संवेदना थी।

"माफी? किस बात की?" अकीरा वेद को हैरानी से देख रही थी। "उनकी 29 को शादी की सालगिरह है, वे छुट्टियाँ मनाने गए हैं। वे जिंदा हैं जी।"

"शुक्र है भगवान् का।" वेद ने राहत की साँस ली और इस बात से अकीरा दबी हँसी हँस रही थी।

"हाँ जी। 28, 29, 30।" कहते हुए साँप-सीढ़ी के खेल में अकीरा ने अपनी गोटी चली। "इससे मुझे तुम्हें दी गई 30 दिवसीय चुनौती की याद आ गई।"

"बेकार बातें। पर ये बोर्ड गेम में नहीं चलतीं।" वेद बोला।

"मैं अपने नियम खुद बनाती हूँ।" अकीरा ने पलकें तेजी से झपकाते हुए कहा।

"माफी? किस बात की?" अकीरा वेद को हैरानी से देख रही थी। "उनकी 29 को शादी की सालगिरह है, वे छुट्टियाँ मनाने गए हैं। वे जिंदा हैं जी।"

"शुक्र है भगवान् का।" वेद ने राहत की साँस ली और इस बात से अकीरा दबी हँसी हँस रही थी।

"हाँ जी। 28, 29, 30।" कहते हुए साँप-सीढ़ी के खेल में अकीरा ने अपनी गोटी चली। "इससे मुझे तुम्हें दी गई 30 दिवसीय चुनौती की याद आ गई।"

"बेकार बातें। पर ये बोर्ड गेम में नहीं चलतीं।" वेद बोला।

"तुम्हारे लिए अच्छा है, लेकिन इस खेल के पुराने नियमों के अनुसार मैं जीत रहा हूँ…" बड़ी अकड़ से यह बात कहकर वेद ने अपनी गोटी 99 के खाने में रख दी।

"तुम्हें असल में जीतने के लिए एक अंक चाहिए।" अपनी भौंहें पास लाकर अकीरा बोली, "68, 69, 70…वाह!" सीढ़ी और सीधे 90 के खाने पर पहुँच गई।

वेद ने परची उठाई। खोली तो देखा '5'। वह चिढ़-सा गया।

"हे भगवान् छह आ जाए।" अकीरा ने प्रार्थना में हाथ जोड़े। एक परची उठाई।

"येऽऽऽ। छह!" खुशी के मारे फूली न समाई। अपनी ही जगह पर उछलती हुई उसने बोर्ड पलट दिया। "मैं जीत गई। ऐतिहासिक जीत!"

"बिल्कुल।" वेद ने व्यंग्य से कहा।

अकीरा ने हथेली आगे करते हुए कहा, "चलो! मेरी इच्छी पूरी करो।"

"ठीक है। बताओ, क्या चाहिए तुम्हें?"

अकीरा हँसी और बोली, "तुम्हें मेरे साथ मेरे परिवार के एक सदस्य की शादी में चलना पड़ेगा।"

वेद सन्न रह गया। उसने कहीं गलत दवाइयाँ तो नहीं खा ली थीं? ये चोट के बाद हुआ है। कहीं पिज्जा में तो कुछ मिला हुआ नहीं था? शायद इसीलिए वह साँप-सीढ़ी का खेल खेलने को तैयार हो गया था। "तुम चाहती हो कि मैं तुम्हारे परिवार के सदस्य की शादी में तुम्हारे साथ जाऊँ?"

"जी हाँ। बिल्कुल सही।" अकीरा ने दंभ भरी हँसी हँसते हुए कहा।

"तुम्हारा दिमाग तो नहीं चल गया? मैं ऐसा कुछ नहीं करनेवाला हूँ।"

"जो तुम्हें करना है, करो। तुम्हारी मर्जी।" बहुत प्यारी आवाज में अकीरा बोली। "लेकिन फिर इसका नतीजा भुगतने को भी तैयार रहना।"

"एक्सक्यूज मी। क्या कहा तुमने? कैसा नतीजा?" वेद ने गुस्से से कहा।

अकीरा ने शांति से पूछा, "वेद! ये मिसेज मसकरेनहस कौन हैं?"

वेद सन्न रह गया। उसने कहीं गलत दवाइयाँ तो नहीं खा ली थीं? ये चोट के बाद हुआ है। कहीं पिज्जा में तो कुछ मिला हुआ नहीं था? शायद इसीलिए वह साँप-सीढ़ी का खेल खेलने को तैयार हो गया था। "तुम चाहती हो कि मैं तुम्हारे परिवार के सदस्य की शादी में तुम्हारे साथ जाऊँ?" "जी हाँ। बिल्कुल सही।" अकीरा ने दंभ भरी हँसी हँसते हुए कहा। "तुम्हारा दिमाग तो नहीं चल गया? मैं ऐसा कुछ नहीं करनेवाला हूँ।"

"ओह!" उसने आँखें झपकाई। "वो मुझे स्कूल में बायोलॉजी (जीव विज्ञान) पढ़ाती थीं। मेरी उस टीचर का इस बात से क्या लेना-देना?"

अकीरा ने बड़े चटपटे तरीके से ठहाका लगाया। उसने हवा में औरत की आकृति बनाई और सीटी बजाई, "लगता है जीव-विज्ञान की मैम बिल्कुल सही विषय पर बात कर रही थीं।"

वेद हैरानी से अपना सिर तकिए पर टिकाते हुए बोला, "तुम किस बारे में बात कर रही हो?"

अकीरा ने मोबाइल उठाया और कहा, "ये देखो!" वेद को हैरानी थी कि उसके

सोते समय अकीरा ने उसका वीडियो बनाया। वह अंदर तक काँप गया, जब उसने देखा कि नींद में वह कुछ बुदबुदा रहा था—

"ओ मिसेज मसकरेनहस···आप मुझे वाकई अच्छी लगती हो···हाँ! सच में। मुझे आपके बाल पसंद हैं···आपकी मुसकान···आपके होंठ।" वह मूर्खों की तरह हँसा। वह नींद में भी अल्हड़ लड़के जैसा व्यवहार कर रहा था, जिसे अभी-अभी किसी के प्रति आकर्षण महसूस हुआ हो। वह नींद में कोमल अहसासों से इधर-उधर भी हो रहा था। जैसे ही वेद ने वीडियो देखा, उसे अपना कमरा आसपास तैरता नजर आ रहा था। उसके शरीर का कण-कण शर्मिंदगी से भर उठा था। उसे लगा, मानो वह भाग्य के वृक्ष से नीचे गिर रहा हो और वह भी हर टहनी से टकराता हुआ।

"पिंकी आंटी और अविनाश अंकल के बारे में सोचो। कैसा लगेगा उनको जब यह पता चलेगा कि उनका बेटा अभी भी अपनी बायोलॉजी मैम को लेकर क्या-क्या सोचता है?" अकीरा ने आँखों से आँसू पोंछने का नाटक करते हुए आगे कहा, "इससे भी बुरा अगर सोचो तो क्या हो, अगर यह यू-ट्यूब पर भी आ जाए?"

"तुम मुझे धमका रही हो (ब्लैकमेल)?"

अकीरा ने मानो विजयी मुसकान फैलाते हुए कहा, "हो सकता है ।"

वेद विलाप करता हुआ-सा चीखा, "ये ठीक नहीं है। तुम ऐसा क्यों कर रही हो? मैंने तुम्हारे साथ क्या गलत किया?"

एक क्षण के लिए अकीरा का दिल काँप उठा, क्योंकि वेद वास्तव में अच्छा लड़का था। उसे बुरा लगा, लेकिन वह जल्दी ही सँभल गई। "सिर्फ शादी में ही तो जाना है। डरपोक मत बनो और सजा मान लो।" पूरी तरह से विस्मित वेद बिस्तर पर गिर गया। उसका सिर चकराया और उसे महसूस हुआ कि किस तरह से उसके आसपास के लोग विचित्र, असंगत मानसिकता रखते हैं और चाहते हैं कि मैं भी उसका हिस्सा बनूँ। अकीरा के पास उसे इस तरह से मुश्किल में डाल देने का कोई कारण नहीं है।

एक क्षण के लिए अकीरा का दिल काँप उठा, क्योंकि वेद वास्तव में अच्छा लड़का था। उसे बुरा लगा, लेकिन वह जल्दी ही सँभल गई। "सिर्फ शादी में ही तो जाना है। डरपोक मत बनो और सजा मान लो।" पूरी तरह से विस्मित वेद बिस्तर पर गिर गया। उसका सिर चकराया और उसे महसूस हुआ कि किस तरह से उसके आसपास के लोग विचित्र, असंगत मानसिकता रखते हैं और चाहते हैं कि मैं भी उसका हिस्सा बनूँ। अकीरा के पास उसे इस तरह से मुश्किल में डाल देने का कोई कारण नहीं है।

वह सही थी। दुनिया का अंत थोड़ी न हो जाता, और वेद की दुनिया का अंत तो इन

धमकियों से होने से रहा, लेकिन अकीरा की दुनिया का अंत तो हो ही सकता है। ज्यादा नाटक तो नहीं, लेकिन वेद ने अपनी सजा को अकीरा की सजा में बदल देने का निश्चय किया। वह चाहती थी कि वेद उसके साथ उसके परिवार के सदस्य की शादी में जाए, वह जाएगा, लेकिन अकीरा को अपने निर्णय पर पछताना पड़ेगा।

"वेद! मैं तुम्हारे उत्तर की राह देख रही हूँ।" अकीरा ने शिकायत भरे स्वर में कहा।

वेद भुनभुनाया और बोला, "ठीक है।"

□

10

"तुम मुसकराकर 'हाँ' कहोगे तो ज्यादा अच्छे दिखोगे।" अकीरा व्यंग्य से बोली।

वेद आधे हताश और आधे विस्मित भाव से अकीरा की ओर देखकर बोला, "मैं जो चाहूँ, वह कर सकता हूँ। हम लोकतंत्रीय राष्ट्र में रहते हैं। हाँ! कृपया अपनी नजर रास्ते पर रखें।"

वह रास्ते पर निगाह कैसे रख सकती थी? वेद कितना खूबसूरत लग रहा था, उस काले कुरते और पाजामे में, जैसे कि सीधा किसी फिल्मी पत्रिका के मुखपृष्ठ से बाहर आ गया हो। अकीरा ने गाड़ी चलाते हुए वेद की बाजू देखी तो दिल झटका खा गया। और वेद की आँखें, बाप रे! आज कितनी सुंदर दिखाई पड़ रही थीं। एकदम नीली!

बहुत मुश्किल से खुद को सँभालकर और वेद से नजरें हटाकर अकीरा ने वेद को करारा जवाब दिया, "मेरी आँखें जहाँ होनी चाहिए, वहीं हैं। आपका बहुत-बहुत शुक्रिया।"

"अच्छी बात है। कम-से-कम तुम्हारी नाक की तरह तो नहीं हैं, जो हमेशा मेरे कामकाज और जीवन में घुसी रहती है।" अकीरा को यह ताना थोड़ा अपमानस्पद लगा।

"तुम अपनी जख्मी नाक की चिंता करो। मेरी नहीं।"

वेद ने धीरे से अपनी नाक को हाथ लगाया। वेदिका ने मेरे नाक के जख्म मेकअप से छुपाने का सफल प्रयास किया था। अकीरा कैसे कर पाई यह सब?

"और हाँ, सबके साथ पार्टी में जरा अच्छे से रहना।" अकीरा ने चेताया।

"बिल्कुल। मैं कोई तुम्हारा बॉयफ्रेंड नहीं हूँ, जो दुर्व्यवहार करूँगा।"

"शुक्र है, भगवान् का।" अकीरा ने पलटकर करारा जवाब दिया।

"बिल्कुल सही। शुक्र है भगवान् का।" वेद गुस्से में बुदबुदाया।

वे शायद और तकरार तथा बहसबाजी करते, अगर वे विवाह-स्थल पर पहुँच नहीं गए होते। शायद लोग ठीक कहते हैं, मनपसंद काम करते हुए वक्त कहाँ बीत जाता है, पता ही नहीं चलता।

"आ गए हम।" अकीरा ने बनावटी उत्साह भरे स्वर में कहा। वेद ने भी उतनी ही

कृत्रिम मुसकान अपने चेहरे पर चिपकाई। वह अपने जीवन का सबसे अच्छा अभिनय कर रहा था; बीमार होने के अभिनय से भी अच्छा।

जैसे ही वे शादी के स्थल में अंदर दाखिल हुए, अकीरा ने किसी का अभिवादन किया। "नमस्ते मासी! नमस्ते मासा!" उस महिला ने अकीरा को गले से लगाया। तभी उसकी नजर वेद पर पड़ी। उसने धीरे से अकीरा को कोहनी मारते हुए कहा, "तुम हमें अपने दोस्त से नहीं मिलवाओगी?"

"अरे हाँ! माफ करना मासी!" अकीरा झेंप मिटाते हुए बोली, "ये मेरी माँ की दूर की बहन और ये उनके पति। यह वेद है। मेरा···"

वेद मुसकराया, जब उसने अकीरा को अपना परिचय देते हुए अटकते पाया। अकीरा ने इस परिचय की तैयारी नहीं की थी। वह बनावटी हँसी हँसा। वेद ने अपना हाथ मिलाने के लिए आगे बढ़ाया और अकीरा का वाक्य मानो पूरा करते हुए बोला, "···अकीरा का बॉयफ्रेंड। आपसे मिलकर खुशी हुई।"

वेद ने अकीरा की ओर देखा। वह हक्की-बक्की थी। वह विश्वास से बिना बेचैन हुए खड़ी रही और वेद को देखती रही। शाम की निश्चय ही अच्छी शुरुआत थी।

"ओ यंग मैन!" अकीरा के मासे ने न्योता देते हुए कहा। "आओ, हमारे साथ बैठो।"

"जी।" वेद ने विनम्रता से कहा।

वेद ने अकीरा की ओर देखा। वह हक्की-बक्की थी। वह विश्वास से बिना बेचैन हुए खड़ी रही और वेद को देखती रही। शाम की निश्चय ही अच्छी शुरुआत थी।

"ओ यंग मैन!" अकीरा के मासे ने न्योता देते हुए कहा। "आओ, हमारे साथ बैठो।"

"जी।" वेद ने विनम्रता से कहा।

वे दोनों अभी मेज के पास पहुँचे ही थे कि और भी औरतों ने उनको घेर लिया। अकीरा दाँत पीसकर रह गई। ऐसा लगा मानो वे वेद के बारे में बहुत कुछ जानना चाहती थीं। हालाँकि 'बॉयफ्रेंड' परिचय के बाद वह इस सबकी उम्मीद कर रही थी। वह जानती थी कि वेद उसे कभी भी शांति से जीने नहीं देगा।

"तुम कर क्या रहे हो? अपने आपको तीस मारखाँ समझते हो?" अकीरा गुस्से में वेद पर बरस पड़ी।

"क्या?" वेद ने बड़ी मासूमियत दिखाते हुए पूछा।

अकीरा ने बाजू पर हाथ मारते हुए कहा, "मैंने तुमसे कहा था कि ठीक से रहना। तुमने अपना परिचय मेरे बॉयफ्रेंड के नाम से क्यों दिया? अब बताओ उनको कि तुम मजाक कर रहे हो।"

"लेकिन मैं तो अच्छा व्यवहार कर रहा हूँ। क्या तुम मुझे इधर-उधर नंगा घूमते,

उपद्रव मचाते या तोड़-फोड़ करते देख रही हो? मैं बिल्कुल सभ्य पुरुष की तरह व्यवहार कर रहा हूँ।" एक शांतिपूर्ण दिव्य मुसकान से वेद ने कहा।

"ज्यादा सीधे बनने की कोशिश मत करो। मैं जानती हूँ, तुम क्या करना चाहते हो!" अकीरा पलटकर बोली।

"ये क्या करना चाहता है?" एक महिला, जिसने गाल चूमकर वेद से दोस्ती दिखानी चाही थी, अकीरा से पूछा।

अकीरा कुछ बोल न पाई और 'हाँ', 'न' में उत्तर दिया। वेद ने बनावटी मुसकराहट बनाते हुए हँसते हुए कहा, "यह (अकीरा) सोचती है कि मैं जानबूझकर उसके सभी रिश्तेदारों से अच्छे से बात कर रहा हूँ, ताकि वे अकीरा से ज्यादा मुझे पसंद करें।" वेद समझ रहा था कि उसके दिमाग में हलचल और गुस्सा दोनों हो रहे हैं।

यह सुनकर सभी हँसने लगे। अकीरा वेद को घूर रही थी। वेद आगे बढ़ा और सभी महिलाओं के लिए कुरसी बाहर खींचते हुए सबसे आखिर में अकीरा की बगल में जा बैठा। सभी औरतें उसे (वेद को) प्यार भरी निगाहों से देख रही थीं। अकीरा वेद की बड़ी सी कृत्रिम मुसकान हटाने के लिए एक जोरदार चपत लगाना चाह रही थी। उसे उम्मीद थी कि वेद का व्यवहार विचित्र होगा, पर ऐसा होगा, इसकी उम्मीद नहीं की थी।

यह सुनकर सभी हँसने लगे। अकीरा वेद को घूर रही थी। वेद आगे बढ़ा और सभी महिलाओं के लिए कुरसी बाहर खींचते हुए सबसे आखिर में अकीरा की बगल में जा बैठा। सभी औरतें उसे (वेद को) प्यार भरी निगाहों से देख रही थीं। अकीरा वेद की बड़ी सी कृत्रिम मुसकान हटाने के लिए एक जोरदार चपत लगाना चाह रही थी।

एक महिला ने वेद को मजाक में कोहनी मारते हुए पूछा, "तुम लोग कैसे मिले? जहाँ तक मुझे याद है, अकीरा किसी और के साथ डेट (घूमने) पर जाती थी।"

अकीरा ने अपनी उँगलियाँ गुस्से से एक चम्मच पर लपेटीं। लपेटीं क्या, गुस्से में चम्मच के दो टुकड़े कर दिए।

वेद इस कल्पना को समझते हुए मुसकरा रहा था कि अकीरा चम्मच की जगह उसकी गरदन होने की कामना और कल्पना कर रही थी। मुसकराहट के साथ उसने (वेद) जवाब दिया, "यह लंबी कहानी है, अकीरा ज्यादा अच्छे से बता पाएगी।"

एक भाई नीचे झुका और अकीरा के कान में बोला, "यह उस चोटीवाले से अच्छा है, जिसके साथ तुम पिछले जश्न में आई थीं।"

"अच्छा?" अकीरा ने व्यंग्य से कहा।

"हाँऽऽऽ।" भाई चिल्लाया।

अकीरा ने उसे मुक्का दिखाया। उसका परिवार वेद को खाने के कोने की ओर ले जा चुका था। वह नीली आँखोंवाले, कुर्ता-पाजामा पहने जुहू में रहनेवाले उस लड़के को तिरस्कार व घृणा से देख रही थी।

अकीरा से एक बूढ़ी महिला ने सवाल किया, "तुम्हें यह कहाँ मिला ?"

अकीरा के मन ने जवाब दिया, "बिग बाजार के भारतीय पुरुषों के खाने (वर्ग) में चौथी रैंक पर।" लेकिन बोली नहीं और बनावटी मुसकराहट के साथ जवाब दिया, "हम अचानक एक-दूसरे से टकराए।"

"तुम कितनी भाग्यशाली हो! देखो, इसने कितनी जल्दी सब पर जादू कर दिया। मन मोह लिया सबका। एक घंटे में ही सबको जीत लिया।" उस बूढ़ी महिला ने कहा।

चाहे अकीरा वेद की हरकतों से चिढ़ रही थी, पर उसे यह बात सच लगी और माननी पड़ी। वेद ने पूरे परिवार पर अपना जादू चलाकर खुश कर दिया था। पूरा समूह वेद के आसपास ही नाच रहा था। वेद ढोल की ताल पर नाच रहा था और कितने ही लोग वेद के आसपास नृत्य कर रहे थे। अकीरा ने छोटी सी वीडियो बनाई और एक गुस्सेवाली 'इमोजी' के साथ वेदिका को भेज दी। "देख लो अपने भाई को, जो मूर्खों जैसा व्यवहार कर रहा है।"

चाहे अकीरा वेद की हरकतों से चिढ़ रही थी, पर उसे यह बात सच लगी और माननी पड़ी। वेद ने पूरे परिवार पर अपना जादू चलाकर खुश कर दिया था। पूरा समूह वेद के आसपास ही नाच रहा था। वेद ढोल की ताल पर नाच रहा था और कितने ही लोग वेद के आसपास नृत्य कर रहे थे। अकीरा ने छोटी सी वीडियो बनाई और एक गुस्सेवाली 'इमोजी' के साथ वेदिका को भेज दी। "देख लो अपने भाई को, जो मूर्खों जैसा व्यवहार कर रहा है।"

फिर वेद का ध्यान अकीरा पर गया। उसने उत्साह से अकीरा को सबके साथ नाच करने बुलाया। अकीरा ने ध्यान नहीं दिया तो वह टेबल की ओर भागता हुआ गया, जहाँ अकीरा बैठी थी।

"अपने परिवार के साथ मजे करो अकीरा! मेरी वजह से, मेरे बदले की वजह से अपना दिन खराब मत करो।" बहुत मासूमियत से वेद ने अकीरा को धीरे से कहा। कितना प्यारा व्यवहार और बात लगती, अगर वह वेद के मुँह से न निकलती!

चूँकि सभी उन्हें देख रहे थे तो वह धीरे से बड़बड़ाई, "ठीक है।"

फिर थोड़ी तेज आवाज में वेद ने अकीरा को प्यार से बुलाया। उस आवाज को लोग सहजता से सुन पा रहे थे। "आओ मेरी चंदा!"

सचमुच एक सज्जन और शिष्ट पुरुष की तरह वेद अकीरा को डांस फ्लोर तक

ले गया। जोर-शोर का संगीत अचानक कोमल रूमानी संगीत में बदल गया और वेद ने अकीरा को 'वॉल्ट्स' नृत्य में खींच लिया।

वॉल्ट्ज नृत्य-तीन गुना समय में एक युगल द्वारा किया जानेवाला नृत्य, जो एक जोड़ी के रूप में डांस फ्लोर के चारों ओर प्रगति करते हुए लयबद्ध रूप से गोल होता जाता है।

"माय! माय! मैं तो समझती थी कि तुम तो शायद नाच ही नहीं सकते।" अकीरा बोली।

"मेरे पास वुडू गुड़िया है। और मैंने पिन तुम्हारे नाक पर घुसा दी है। हम सब जानते हैं, वहाँ क्या हुआ।" वेद ने गंभीरता से सिर हिलाया और बोला, "बस कमर के नीचे मत जाना। प्लीज!" "हँसो मत।" अकीरा अपने मन में बोली, 'पर वाकई यह बदतमीज लड़का आज बहुत ही आकर्षक लग रहा है।' "पर तुमने मुझे चंदा क्यों कहा?" विषय बदलते हुए अकीरा ने कहा।

"पता था। तुम बहुत कुछ केवल कल्पना करके चलती हो, खासकर मेरे बारे में।" उपहासात्मक रूप में वेद बोला। "लेकिन आज रात के बाद तुम्हें मेरे वुडू डॉल (Vodoo Doll) की जरूरत पड़ेगी।"

वुडूडॉल (Vodoo Doll)—यह एक झाड़-फूँक के मंत्र जैसा है, लेकिन इसका प्रयोग धार्मिक वस्तु या अंधविश्वास के रूप में किया जा सकता है। यह इस बात पर निर्भर करता है कि उपयोगकर्ता इससे कैसे व्यवहार करता है? वुडू गुड़िया आमतौर पर एक छोटी गुड़िया होती है, जो मुलायम होती है और किसी व्यक्ति का प्रतिनिधित्व करती है। हालाँकि इसके भौतिक विवरण की सीमा भिन्न हो सकती है।

"मेरे पास वुडू गुड़िया है। और मैंने पिन तुम्हारे नाक पर घुसा दी है। हम सब जानते हैं, वहाँ क्या हुआ।"

वेद ने गंभीरता से सिर हिलाया और बोला, "बस कमर के नीचे मत जाना। प्लीज!"

"हँसो मत।" अकीरा अपने मन में बोली, 'पर वाकई यह बदतमीज लड़का आज बहुत ही आकर्षक लग रहा है।'

"पर तुमने मुझे चंदा क्यों कहा?" विषय बदलते हुए अकीरा ने कहा।

"क्योंकि तुम गोल हो। और···मामूली और घटिया पसंद रखनेवाली।" वेद के स्वर में गंभीरता थी। "···और तुम किसी अन्य पुरुष की भी हो।"

एक बेकार-सी गाली देते हुए अकीरा ने धीरे से वेद के पेट में मुक्का दिया।

"ओह! लगी न।" कहते हुए वेद हँस पड़ा। "पर वाकई तुम आज सुंदर लग रही हो, तभी 'चंदा' कहा।" वेद ने कहा।

"लेकिन मैं ऐसे दिखाऊँगी कि तुमने ऐसा कहा ही नहीं।" अकीरा ने पलटकर जवाब पकड़ाया।

"शशऽऽऽ। बातें नहीं, केवल डांस।" वेद ने अकीरा को कुछ ज्यादा ही अपने पास खींच लिया। मेरी आँखों में देखो।"

अकीरा ने जैसे ही वेद की आँखों में देखा, वह उन नीली आँखों में खो-सी गई और भूल गई कि वह क्या सोच रही थी और वह बहुत अच्छे से वेद से ताल मिलाती हुई नाच रही थी और दोनों ही उम्दा नृत्य कर रहे थे। जैसे ही वेद उसके करीब आया, वह अपने में सकुचा गई। वेद ने अपनी नाक अकीरा की नाक से हलकी सी छुई, आँखें फड़फड़ाती हुई बंद हो गईं और अभी उसके होंठ अकीरा के पास जाने ही वाले थे कि सहसा उसने अकीरा के चिल्लाने की आवाज सुनी।

अकीरा ने जैसे ही वेद की आँखों में देखा, वह उन नीली आँखों में खो-सी गई और भूल गई कि वह क्या सोच रही थी और वह बहुत अच्छे से वेद से ताल मिलाती हुई नाच रही थी और दोनों ही उम्दा नृत्य कर रहे थे। जैसे ही वेद उसके करीब आया, वह अपने में सकुचा गई।

"मोहित!" अकीरा चिल्लाई थी।

"इडियट। मोहित यहीं है।" अकीरा ने जब वेद के पीछे आँखें बड़ी करते हुए काँपते हुए कहा। वह एक तरह से चीखी ही थी।

जिस दिशा में अकीरा ने इशारा किया, उस ओर देखते हुए वेद बोला, "ओह, वाह, आ गए यहाँ। हमेशा की तरह आकर्षक और सुंदर। चलो, मिलकर आते हैं उससे।"

"तुम्हारा दिमाग चल गया है क्या?" अकीरा ने वेद को रोका।

इससे पहले कि वेद मोहित से मिलने पर और जोर देता, अकीरा ने वेद की बाजू पकड़ी और खींचती हुई गाड़ी के पास ले गई। मानो वेद कोई गुम हआ बच्चा हो!

"मुझे लगता है कि गाड़ी मुझे चलानी चाहिए। तुमने 'वाइन' पी रखी है।" वेद ने सुझाव दिया।

"मैं नशे में धुत्त नहीं हूँ।" चिढ़कर अकीरा बोली।

बड़ी मुश्किल से अपनी हँसी रोककर किसी तरह वह यात्री की सीट पर बैठा। अकीरा गाड़ी को दौड़ाती हुई विवाह-स्थल से दूर ले गई। थोड़ी देर की संपूर्ण शांति के बाद अकीरा ने वेद से प्रश्न किया।

"तुमने मोहित को आते देख लिया था। है न? इसीलिए तुम मेरे पास आए और

तुम्हारे साथ डांस करने का न्योता दिया। और यही नहीं, जानबूझकर मुझपर और झुके ताकि···।" उसकी आवाज धीमी हो गई।

वेद चुप-सा हो गया था। "झुका ताकि··· ?" वेद बोला।

अकीरा ने गुस्से से वेद को देखा। "अभिनय के लिए तो तुम्हें पूरे नंबर मिलने चाहिए।"

वेद जोर का हँसा। अकीरा ने वेद को हाथ मारते हुए कहा, "चुप रहो। तुम मेरे इतने करीब इसीलिए आ रहे थे, क्योंकि तुम उस पार्टी में मोहित को देख चुके थे। सच यही है न?"

"हो सकता है।"

"तुम कितने बड़े गधे हो!" दाँत पीसकर अकीरा बोली।

वेद ने हैरानी से उसकी ओर देखते हुए कहा, "अब यह मत कहना कि तुमने सोचा कि मैं वाकई तुम्हें 'किस' करनेवाला था। क्यों?"

"ऐसा नहीं था तो तुम्हारी आँखें इतनी चौड़ी क्यों हो गई थीं, मानो कुछ कह रही हों?" अकीरा ने ताना मारा।

वेद ने हैरानी से उसकी ओर देखते हुए कहा, "अब यह मत कहना कि तुमने सोचा कि मैं वाकई तुम्हें 'किस' करनेवाला था। क्यों?" "ऐसा नहीं था तो तुम्हारी आँखें इतनी चौड़ी क्यों हो गई थीं, मानो कुछ कह रही हों?" अकीरा ने ताना मारा।

वेद झेंपता हुआ बोला, "मैंने तो तुम्हें पहले ही कहा था कि मैं अच्छी एक्टिंग (अभिनय) कर लेता हूँ।"

"नहीं। तुम मनोरोगी साइको हो। पिंकी आंटी को तुम्हें हर तरह से बाँधकर रखना चाहिए। तुम समाज के मासूमों के लिए हानिकारक हो।"

"अच्छा, और तुम ठीक-ठाक हो, नहीं?" आँखें झपकाते हुए वेद बोला। "हैलो, उलटा चोर कोतवाल को डाँटे!"

"उफ्फ, चुप रहो।" अकीरा खाने को दौड़ रही थी। वेद हाथ बाँधकर बैठा और बोला, "मैं यहाँ हूँ, क्योंकि तुम मुझे यहाँ चाहती थीं।"

अकीरा ने गुस्सा दबाते हुए गाड़ी के स्टियरिंग को मजबूती से पकड़ा। वह जानती थी कि वेद ठीक कह रहा है। वेद उसी की इच्छा से वहाँ था।

अकीरा को चुप देखते हुए वेद बोला, "अब मेरा धन्यवाद करो, क्योंकि तुम्हारा पूरा परिवार यह सोच रहा है कि तुमने मेरे लिए उस बदतमीज और घटिया मोहित को छोड़ दिया।"

"मुझे थोड़ी न पता था कि तुम खुद का परिचय मेरे बॉयफ्रेंड के नाम से दोगे!"

गुस्से में हाथ हवा में घुमाते हुए अकीरा बोली।

"बिल्कुल ठीक। जब तुम्हें पता था कि मैं कुछ भी कर सकता हूँ तो तुमने यह खतरा क्यों मोल लिया? और हाँ, इस रास्ते पर मत जाओ। वहाँ पुलिसवाले खड़े होते हैं और तुमने पी रखी है। बेकार की परेशानी में पड़ जाएँगे···।"

"पहली बात तो यह है कि मैंने पी नहीं रखी।"

अकीरा ने अपने पैर से एक्सलरेटर दबाया और बोली, "और मैं तो वही रास्ता लूँगी।"

"ठीक है, पर अच्छा होगा, अगर तुम धीरे चलाओ, क्योंकि अगर कार कहीं टकरा गई तो सिर्फ मैं नहीं मरूँगा; हम दोनों मारे जाएँगे।" दबी आवाज में वेद बोला।

इससे पहले कि अकीरा वेद को जवाब देती, कुछ पुलिसकर्मियों ने उनकी कार रोकी। अकीरा ने चेतावनी भरी निगाहों से वेद को देखा। वह कराह उठा था, क्योंकि आनेवाला खतरा उसे दिखाई पड़ रहा था।

एक अधिकारी (पुलिस) उनके पास आया। पूछा, "पार्टी से आ रहे हैं?"

"शादी से···" अकीरा ने धीरे से कहा।

पुलिस अधिकारी ने उसे कहा, हमें डी.यू.आई. (DUI-Driving under the influence) के तहत आपकी जाँच करनी पड़ेगी कि आप नशे में गाड़ी चला रहे थे या नहीं? कार से बाहर आकर इस मशीन में फूँक मारिए।"

अकीरा ने अपने पैर से एक्सलरेटर दबाया और बोली, "और मैं तो वही रास्ता लूँगी।" "ठीक है, पर अच्छा होगा, अगर तुम धीरे चलाओ, क्योंकि अगर कार कहीं टकरा गई तो सिर्फ मैं नहीं मरूँगा; हम दोनों मारे जाएँगे।" दबी आवाज में वेद बोला।

उसे पता चल रहा था कि वेद बहुत गुस्से में है, मानो उसका गुस्से से घूरना ही अकीरा के सिर के पीछे छेद कर देगा। वह उठकर धीमे कदमों से कार के बाहर निकली। पुलिस अधिकारी के हाथ में नशे की जाँच की मशीन थी। अकीरा ने फूँक मारी। एक छोटी सी सीटी बजी। अकीरा को देख अधिकारी ने बताया—"आपका मद्य स्तर (Alcohol Level) अनुमति प्राप्त स्तर से अधिक है। आपको नशे की हालत में तेज गाड़ी चलाने के इलजाम में गिरफ्तार किया जाता है।"

फिर वह पुलिस अधिकारी वेद की ओर मुड़ा और बोला, "आप इसलिए गिरफ्तार किए जाते हैं, क्योंकि आपने नशे में गाड़ी चलानेवाले का साथ दिया।"

□

11

मुझे माफ कर दो···" अकीरा का निचला होंठ काँप रहा था। वेद और अकीरा पुलिस स्टेशन में अधिकारी के कमरे के बाहर एक छोटी सी बेंच पर बैठे थे। अकीरा की आँखों से आँसू टपक रहे थे।

"प्लीज, अब रोना बंद करो। मुझे नहीं पता कि अब मुझे क्या करना चाहिए?" लाचारी से वेद बोला। उसके पास अकीरा को देने के लिए रुमाल भी नहीं था।

वेद ने उसके सिर पर हौले-हौले थपकी दी, इस उम्मीद से कि शायद वह चुप हो जाए। "वहाँ···वहाँ।"

अकीरा हैरानी और अविश्वसनीय निगाहों से वेद को देख रही थी। उसने वेद का हाथ सिर पर से झटक दिया।

"तुम मुझे ऐसे क्यों थपकियाँ दे रहे हो, जैसे पालतू कुत्ते को दी जाती हैं?"

"क्योंकि मैं चाहता हूँ कि तुम रोना बंद करो।" वेद ने अकीरा को रोना बंद करने को कहा, जैसे कि एक बच्चे को कहते हैं।

"खैर! अगर तुम्हारा मुझे शांत करने का यह तरीका है तो मैं अपने आँसू तुमपर बेकार नहीं करूँगी।" अपने गालों पर के आँसू पोंछते हुए अकीरा बोली।

"बढ़िया। तुम्हें किसी के लिए भी अपने आँसू बरबाद नहीं करने चाहिए।" वेद ने सच्चाई से कहा। न चाहते हुए भी अकीरा मुसकरा पड़ी।

"वेद!" अविनाश ने पुलिस स्टेशन के भीतर आते ही वेद को आवाज दी। वह श्रीदास, पिंकी और वेदिका के साथ आया था।

पिता को देखते ही वह अविनाश के गले लग गया।

"डैड।" उसे इस तरह की कैद या किसी भी तरह की सजा कभी स्कूल में भी नहीं मिली थी, लेकिन वह समझ रहा था कि जब बच्चों को विद्यालय में सजा मिलती है तो कैसा लगता होगा!

अविनाश ने वेद के कान में धीरे से कहा, "तुम इस तरह तहलका मचाना छोड़ोगे, प्लीज?"

"सॉरी···।" वेद ने पिता को हलके से छोड़ा और दूर हुआ और अपनी झेंप मिटाने के लिए पापा के लाए वकील से हाथ मिलाने के लिए आगे बढ़ा।

पिंकी ने कमर पर हाथ रखकर पूछा, "वैसे तुम लोगों ने किया क्या?"

"क्या तुम बताना जरूरी समझोगी?" वेद ने अकीरा को घूरते हुए कहा।

"खैर, मैंने थोड़ी पी रखी थी और मैं अनुमति सीमा से तेज गाड़ी चला रही थी।" थूक गटकते हुए अकीरा ने जवाब दिया।

वेदिका ने सदमे से वेद की ओर देखा। "ओहो! और तुमने चलाने दिया? हिटलर के तेवर बदल गए?"

अकीरा बीच में बोली, "नहीं। इसने मुझे आगाह किया था, पर मैंने सुना नहीं।"

वेद ने हामी भरते हुए कहा, "मैंने बहुत कोशिश की, लेकिन मैं दीवार से बातें कर रहा था।"

वेदिका ने सदमे से वेद की ओर देखा। "ओहो! और तुमने चलाने दिया? हिटलर के तेवर बदल गए?" अकीरा बीच में बोली, "नहीं। इसने मुझे आगाह किया था, पर मैंने सुना नहीं।" वेद ने हामी भरते हुए कहा, "मैंने बहुत कोशिश की, लेकिन मैं दीवार से बातें कर रहा था।"

"ओए, बचत और परोपकार की दुकान। अंदर आओ।" एक पुलिस कांस्टेबल ने केबिन के अंदर आने का हुकुम दिया।

अपने दुर्भाग्य पर रोता हुआ वेद सिर खुजाता हुआ केबिन में दाखिल हुआ और बाकी सब भी उसके पीछे चल पड़े।

"अनिल!" कर्ण कटु ध्वनि में चिल्लाती हुई पिंकी केबिन में दाखिल हुई।

इंस्पेक्टर ने सिर उठाकर देखा और कहा, "पिंकी!"

"अविनाश! मुझे विश्वास नहीं हो रहा। हे भगवान्!" ऐसा कहते हुए पिंकी ने इंस्पेक्टर को गले लगा लिया।

इंस्पेक्टर भी उतने ही उत्साह से पिंकी के गले लगा। उसने जल्दी से अविनाश का भी गले लगाकर अभिवादन किया और पीछे होकर मुसकराने लगा। वेद को न जाने वह सज्जन कैसे याद रहा कि वह पिंकी के बचपन का दोस्त है। वेद जानता था कि उसकी माँ दोस्तों के साथ कई बार शिष्टाचार का पल्लू छोड़ देती है और अजीब व्यवहार करती है। अब तो वेदिका और अकीरा भी थीं तो माँ ने और भी विचित्र व्यवहार करना ही था।

"तुम यहाँ क्या कर हो?" पिंकी बोली।

"मैं यहाँ का वरिष्ठ इंस्पेक्टर हूँ।" अनिल बड़ी सी मुसकराहट के साथ बोला। "लेकिन तुम यहाँ क्या कर रही हो?"

पिंकी ने नाटकीयता से सिर नीचे किया और बोली, "तुमने मेरे बेटे को गिरफ्तार किया है।"

वेद कोसे जा रहा था। "अब तो खून-खराबा होगा ही।"

"रुको। क्याऽऽऽ ? ये नशे की गिरफ्तारी का मामला तुम्हारे बेटे का है ?" कागजात देखते हुए भौंहें चढ़ाते हुए पूछा।

वेद ने विनम्रता से इंस्पेक्टर की गलती ठीक करने की कोशिश करते हुए धीरे से कहा, "गाड़ी मैं नहीं चला रहा था।"

"हाँ। इसे नशे में गाड़ी चलानेवाले का साथ देने के जुर्म में गिरफ्तार किया गया है।" एक दूसरे अधिकारी ने अनिल को बताया। "असल जुर्म इस लड़की का है।" अकीरा की ओर इशारा करते हुए अधिकारी बोला।

"अच्छाऽऽऽ। ऐसा है।" कागजात बाज़ू में रखते हुए अनिल बोला। पहले उसने वेद को देखा, फिर वेदिका की ओर देखकर प्यार भरी मुसकान से बोला, "बच्चे कितने बड़े हो गए हैं!"
"हाँ। सही कहा। हम पिछली बार कब मिले थे ?"
"शायद पूनम की शादी में।"

"अच्छाऽऽऽ। ऐसा है।" कागजात बाजू में रखते हुए अनिल बोला। पहले उसने वेद को देखा, फिर वेदिका की ओर देखकर प्यार भरी मुसकान से बोला, "बच्चे कितने बड़े हो गए हैं!"

"हाँ। सही कहा। हम पिछली बार कब मिले थे ?"

"शायद पूनम की शादी में।"

"हाँ।" पिंकी ने ताली बजाते हुए हामी भरी। "कितने साल हो गए, नहीं ?"

"वाकई। मुझे जो याद है, वो ये है कि ये बच्चे 'दीदी तेरा देवर दीवाना' गाने पर नाचे थे। आखिरी बार इन बच्चों को तभी देखा था।"

वेद कुरसी पर झेंपता हुआ बैठ गया। अगर वो बातें सुनकर बेहोश हो जाता तो ज्यादा ठीक होता। इतनी शर्मिंदगी तो नहीं होती।

"मैं देवर और भैया माधुरी दीक्षित बने थे।" वेदिका मुसकराते हुए बोली।

"क्याऽऽऽ।" अकीरा ने चिढ़ते हुए पूछा। "ऐसा क्यों ?"

"क्योंकि मुझे सलमान जैसी पोशाक पहनने का मन था। खासकर वो सस्पेंडर्स (पतलून बाँधने के फीते) उफ्फ! क्या मस्त थे!" वेदिका ने अकीरा को स्पष्टीकरण दिया।

अनिल ने धीरे से चहककर कहा, "वेद कितना प्यारा लग रहा था न! माधुरी जैसा ?"

पिंकी भी चुप रहने को कहाँ तैयार थी। बोली, "वेद तो माधुरी का दीवाना था ही।

वो कितनी बार माधुरी दीक्षित जैसे कपड़े पहनकर शीशे के सामने नाचता था…”

“मॉम, बस कीजिए, प्लीज!” वेद ने पिंकी का जोर से हाथ दबाकर कहा।

वेद का सदमे भरा चेहरा देखकर अकीरा हलके से हँसी और सोचने लगी, ‘जब अरोरा परिवार है तो वेद को सबक सिखाने की प्रार्थना लेकर ईश्वर को परेशान करने की क्या जरूरत?’

“लेकिन वेद, मैंने तुम्हें कहीं और भी देखा है।” अनिल बोला।

“आपने जरूर इसे बाथरूम की लड़ाई के वीडियो में देखा होगा।” अकीरा ने मौके का फायदा उठाते हुए ताना कसा और वेद उसे द्वेष भरी निगाहों से घूर रहा था।

जो ऑफिसर उन दोनों को पुलिस स्टेशन लाया था, झट से बोला, “सर! वह वीडियो मेरे मोबाइल में है, आपको अभी भेजता हूँ।”

अनिल ने गुस्से में उस अधिकारी को देखा तो वह चुप हो गया।

“खैर! तुम करते क्या हो वेद?”

“मैं बिजनेसमैन (व्यवसायी) हूँ।”

“अच्छा, बिजनेसमैन हो।”…अचानक अनिल का चेहरा खिल उठा। “ओ हाँ, तुम्हें मैंने अखबार में देखा है। तुम ‘इकोनॉमिक टाइम्स’ में साप्ताहिक स्तंभ लिखते हो? है न?”

“जी! मैं निवेश और तात्कालिक बाजार की स्थिति के बारे में लिखता हूँ।” वेद ने बड़ी सी मुसकान के साथ उत्तर दिया।

अनिल ने सिर हिलाते हुए कहा, “तभी मुझे तुम्हारा नाम जाना-पहचाना लगा। मैं तुम्हारा वह स्तंभ हमेशा पढ़ता हूँ। तुम्हारी सलाह अच्छी होती है।”

“लेकिन वेद, मैंने तुम्हें कहीं और भी देखा है।” अनिल बोला। “आपने जरूर इसे बाथरूम की लड़ाई के वीडियो में देखा होगा।” अकीरा ने मौके का फायदा उठाते हुए ताना कसा और वेद उसे द्वेष भरी निगाहों से घूर रहा था। जो ऑफिसर उन दोनों को पुलिस स्टेशन लाया था, झट से बोला, “सर! वह वीडियो मेरे मोबाइल में है, आपको अभी भेजता हूँ।”

वेद ने जोर से कहा, “शुक्रिया।”

यदि आसपास के अनचाहे दर्शक नहीं होते तो वेद अनिल को गले से लगा लेता। शुक्र है, कोई तो समझदार व्यक्ति मिला। ऐसा होना भी चमत्कार है। वह धीरे से पिता की ओर झुककर बोला, “मुझे यह अच्छा लगा।”

लेकिन अविनाश की आँखें पिंकी का पीछा कर रही थीं। बोला, “लगता है तुम्हारी माँ को भी यह बहुत अच्छा लगा।”

हैरानी और दुविधा से वेद ने पिंकी की ओर देखा। वह अनिल को जीतने में व्यस्त

थी। “बूढ़ी घोड़ी लाल लगाम!” अविनाश दाँत पीसते हुए बोला।

“डैड!” वेद की आवाज में सख्ती थी, पर धीरे से वह भी हँसा।

“ठीक है। जरा केस पर पहले चर्चा कर लें।” अकीरा को देखते हुए अनिल ने कहा।

“अनिल···।” पिंकी ने उदास चेहरे से कहा। अकीरा की वकालत करते हुए बोली, “उसने बस थोड़ी सी हो तो पी रखी थी। मैं बेटे की तरफदारी नहीं कर रही, पर यहाँ वेद की कोई गलती नहीं थी। उसने अकीरा को तेज न चलाने की चेतावनी दी थी, लेकिन चूँकि अकीरा गुस्से में थी, क्योंकि उनकी लड़ाई हुई थी, इसीलिए बात इतनी बढ़ गई। वेद के खिलाफ आरोप रद्द कर दो। प्लीज!”

“वेद ने तो आजतक शराब को छुआ तक नहीं।” अविनाश ने पत्नी का साथ दिया।

“बिल्कुल सही। यह तो रसना और रूहअफ्जा में विश्वास करता है। मैं आपको बताऊँ, घर में भी यह समय के अनुसार काम करता है; बिल्कुल अनुशासित व्यक्ति की तरह। इसकी कहानी यही जानता है। आपको यह सब सुनने में अविश्वसनीय लगेगा, लेकिन यही सच है।” वेदिका ने सच्चाई जाहिर की।

“वेद ने तो आजतक शराब को छुआ तक नहीं।” अविनाश ने पत्नी का साथ दिया। “बिल्कुल सही। यह तो रसना और रूहअफ्जा में विश्वास करता है। मैं आपको बताऊँ, घर में भी यह समय के अनुसार काम करता है; बिल्कुल अनुशासित व्यक्ति की तरह। इसकी कहानी यही जानता है। आपको यह सब सुनने में अविश्वसनीय लगेगा, लेकिन यही सच है।” वेदिका ने सच्चाई जाहिर की।

वेद छत को देख रहा था। ‘मेरा परिवार मुझे बचाते समय भी मेरा अपमान करता है। हे भगवान्!’

“एक वार्निंग (चेतावनी) देकर छोड़ दो न!” पिंकी इस बात पर जोर देती रही।

वेद ने माँ के कंधे पर हाथ रखा और अनिल से बोला, “कोई बात नहीं। हम दोनों मानते हैं कि हमसे गलती हुई है और जो भी सजा होगी, वह स्वीकार कर लेंगे।”

अनिल ने हलकी सी मुसकान से वेद की ओर देखा।

“ठीक है! तुम्हें किसी भी परिस्थिति में उसे गाड़ी चलानी ही नहीं देनी चाहिए थी। और अकीरा! ‘लड़ाई’ कोई बहाना नहीं हो सकता गलत काम करने का। जब तुम प्यार में हो तो शांति से बैठकर मसले सुलझाते हैं। ज्यादा नशा करके शहर में तेज गाड़ी चलाते हुए घूमते नहीं हैं।”

जैसा कि अपेक्षित था, अनिल का अनुमान और बातें सुनकर वेद और अकीरा ने हैरानी से एक-दूसरे की ओर देखा।

"अनिल! वे पति-पत्नी नहीं हैं।" पिंकी ने अनिल को बताया, ताकि उसकी गलतफहमी दूर हो।

"हाँ, केवल मूर्ख हैं!" वेदिका ने व्यंग्य से कहा। अनिल भी झेंप गया। अकीरा ने तसल्ली देते हुए कहा, "माफ करना...कोई बात नहीं।"

वेद चुप खड़ा था।

"शुक्रिया।" अनिल ने कहा। "मैं तुम्हें चेतावनी और जुरमाने के साथ जाने दे रहा हूँ। आशा करता हूँ, तुम लोग दुबारा ऐसा नहीं करोगे।"

अकीरा ने हामी भरते हुए जोर-जोर से सिर हिलाया और हाथ जोड़ते हुए कहा, "पक्का। मैं वचन देती हूँ।"

वेद ने इंस्पेक्टर से हाथ मिलाते हुए कहा, "थैंक यू।"

"यू आर वेलकम यंग मैन।" अनिल ने हँसकर कहा।

"यह लो! लेकिन गाड़ी किसी और को चलाने के लिए कहो, ताकि वह तुम्हें तुम्हारे घर छोड़ सके।" अकीरा के हाथ में चाबी देते हुए अनिल ने कहा।

अकीरा ने संदेह से, आशंकित मन से चाबी ली, क्योंकि उसे समझ नहीं आ रहा था कि इतनी रात गए वह किसे पुलिस स्टेशन बुलाए?

"उसकी जरूरत नहीं पड़ेगी, क्योंकि यह हमारे साथ हमारे घर चल रही है।" वेद ने चाबी पकड़ते हुए कहा।

□

12

अरोरा परिवार अकीरा को लेकर पुलिस स्टेशन से जल्दी ही घर पहुँच गया। अकीरा की कार वेद ने चलाई। वे दोनों ही थे कार में। अकीरा को हैरानी थी कि गुस्से में वेद ने उसका खून नहीं किया।

जाहिर है, रात को सोने के लिए अकीरा के पास कपड़े नहीं थे। अकीरा ने वेदिका के कपड़े पहनकर देखे, लेकिन वे बहुत ही तंग थे, सो उसे वेद के कपड़े पहनने पड़े। उसे समझ नहीं आ रहा था कि वह क्या महसूस करे, क्योंकि बहुत अंतरंग होने पर ही लोग एक-दूसरे के कपड़े पहनते हैं। लेकिन वेद को कोई झिझक नहीं हो रही थी। यह देख अकीरा विस्मित उस बात से ध्यान हटाकर वेदिका अरोरा परिवार के साथ बैठक के कमरे में जा बैठी। वेद को ढीले कपड़ों में जमीन पर बैठा देख अकीरा का हृदय अजीब भावों से भर गया। वेद उसे प्रिय लग रहा था या उसने खुद पी रखी थी, इसलिए अजीब मनोभावों का सामना कर रही थी; अकीरा समझ नहीं पा रही थी।

वेदिका ने कबीर को भी बुला लिया था और कबीर हजारों तरह की आइसक्रीम लेकर आया था, जिन्हें सभी अब मजे से खा रहे थे। अकीरा ने आह भरी। वाकई कितना अच्छा लग रहा था। सबकुछ ठीक था। सच में वह सबकुछ की आदी हो सकती थी।

"कई बार मुझे ऐसा लगता है मानो हम किसी धारावाहिक का हिस्सा हैं।" वेदिका ने गंभीरता से कहा।

"मजेदार विचार है, लेकिन मैं सोच रहा हूँ, ऐसे धारावाहिक में वेद कौन सा पात्र है", अकीरा ने वेद की ठोढ़ी पर हाथ मारते हुए कहा।

"सूत्रधार।" आइसक्रीम खाते हुए वेद ने उत्तर दिया। "क्योंकि ये धारावाहिक मूर्ख ही नहीं, सर्वाधिक मूर्खों का कथानक है, जिसमें मुझ जैसे पात्र की कोई जगह नहीं।"

"सही, क्योंकि इस परिवार के लिए जिस योग्यता की आवश्यकता है, तुम उससे कहीं ज्यादा योग्य हो।" मुसकराते हुए अकीरा ने कहा।

सभी जोर से ठहाका मारकर हँसने लगे।

"चुप रहो।" वेद ने अकीरा को व्यंग्य से कहा।

"ओके सूत्रधार!" अकीरा हँसी और उसने अपना मुँह जिप की तरह बंद करने का इशारा दिया।

"वैसे वेद, तुमने शादी में क्या किया?" कबीर बोला। कबीर की बात सुनते ही अकीरा चिल्लाई, "अब फिर नहीं।"

"अरे! बताने दो।" वेद की आँखों में चमक आ गई। वह आलथी-पालथी मारकर बैठा और विवाह के बारे में बताने लगा।

"जैसे ही हमने विवाह स्थल में प्रवेश किया, सब मुझे घूर रहे थे। मैंने आत्म-विश्वास से अपना परिचय इसके बॉयफ्रेंड के रूप में दिया···"

वेदिका चिढ़ के बोली, "याडा, याडा! 'किस' वाले हिस्से के बारे में बताओ न!"

"तुम्हें इसके बारे में कैसे पता?" वेद की आँखें आश्चर्य से चौड़ी हुईं। उसने अकीरा को देखा और समझ गया कि हो-न-हो, इसने वेदिका को बताया होगा। फिर तो पूरे परिवार को पता चलना ही था।

"इससे कोई फर्क नहीं पड़ता। तुम हमें सिर्फ इतना बताओ कि तुमने अकीरा को किस करने (चूमने) की कोशिश की या नहीं?" कबीर ने प्रश्न किया।

"इसके अनुसार, यह मुझपर आरोप है।" वेद बोला।

वेदिका चिढ़ के बोली, "याडा, याडा! 'किस' वाले हिस्से के बारे में बताओ न!" "तुम्हें इसके बारे में कैसे पता?" वेद की आँखें आश्चर्य से चौड़ी हुईं। उसने अकीरा को देखा और समझ गया कि हो-न-हो, इसने वेदिका को बताया होगा। फिर तो पूरे परिवार को पता चलना ही था।

वह अपनी बात पर डटा रहा। "मेरा अभी जवाब है, नहीं।" मैंने मोहित को देख लिया था और मैंने सोचा कि मैं अकीरा को किस करने का अभिनय करके मोहित में ईर्ष्या पैदा करूँ। तमाशा हुआ तो मजा आ जाएगा। मेरा बदला पूरा हो जाएगा। लेकिन उस बेवकूफ ने हमारी ओर देखा तक नहीं और उसके बाद क्या हुआ, ये हम सभी को पता है।"

अकीरा ने अविश्वास दिखाते हुए कहा, "सच में?"

"सच में।"

"ठीक है। समझ गई। तुम जुहू के अल पसीनो।" (खूबसूरत अभिनेता)

अकीरा ने जवाब दिया, लेकिन अकीरा समझ नहीं पाई कि वेद क्यों झूठ बोल रहा है, क्योंकि वह तो सचमुच समझ रही थी कि वेद उसे किस करनेवाला था। और इस बात से क्यों निराश थी कि वेद झूठ बोल रहा था। इसका कारण भी अकीरा को पल्ले नहीं पड़ा। "चलो कुछ और बात करते हैं।"

अकीरा की हालत समझ, पिंकी बोलो, "वेदिका! हमारे पास पूनम की शादी की तसवीरें हैं क्या?"

"हाँ। हम..." वेदिका कुछ और बोलती, इससे पहले वेद ने हाथ रखकर वेदिका का मुँह बंद कर दिया।

"नहीं हैं। हमारे पास ऐसा कुछ नहीं है। और तुम लोगों ने अब जरा भी उस शादी का जिक्र किया तो मैं इस घर में आग लगा दूँगा।" वेद चिल्लाकर बोला।

उसकी धमकी का कोई असर नहीं था, क्योंकि थोड़ी देर बाद न केवल सब शादी की तसवीरें देख रहे थे, बल्कि वेद के बचपन की वीडियो भी देख रहे थे। वेद DVD (डी.वी.डी.) के कवर को देख रहा था, जिस पर लिखा था 'अरोराज : ओवर द ईयर्स' (अरोरा परिवार : इतने वर्षों में) वह उन सभी को कोस रहा था, जिसने उस पुराने वी.एच.एस. टेप से डी.वी.डी. में तकनीकी सहायता से परिवर्तित किया और सभी लोग उसे देख पा रहे थे।

> ***"चुप रहो।" झगड़े के स्वर में वेद बोला। "अब मैं खुद को आग लगाऊँगा, और फिर तुम सबको गले। बस तुम अब देखते जाओ।" "कितने अच्छे विचार हैं!" अकीरा हँसते हुए बोली, "वैसे वी.एच.एस. टेप किसने सी.डी. में बदले?" कबीर ने पूछा।***

"तुम कब घर में आग लगा रहे हो?" अकीरा ने पूछा।

"चुप रहो।" झगड़े के स्वर में वेद बोला। "अब मैं खुद को आग लगाऊँगा, और फिर तुम सबको गले। बस तुम अब देखते जाओ।"

"कितने अच्छे विचार हैं!" अकीरा हँसते हुए बोली, "वैसे वी.एच.एस. टेप किसने सी.डी. में बदले?" कबीर ने पूछा।

"मैंने!" वेदिका बोली और फिर टी.वी. स्क्रीन की तरफ इशारा किया, जिसमें छोटा सा वेद बिस्तरे पर मिकी माउस की छोटी सी अंडरवियर पहनकर कूद रहा था। "यह बढ़िया सामग्री देखी, तो मुझे सी.डी. में बदलना ही पड़ा।"

"बिल्कुल वेदिका! ये करना शैतानी आत्मा वेदिका के लिए जरूरी ही था।" वेदिका ने अपनी तसवीरें और वीडियो, जिसमें उसे शर्मिंदगी होती या अजीब लगता, चतुराई दिखाते हुए डाले ही नहीं थे। यह सबकुछ चिढ़ा देनेवाला था।

फिर वीडियो का वह हिस्सा आया, जो खेल दिवस से लिया गया था। वेदिका ने लगभग हर खेल में हिस्सा लिया था। लंबी दौड़, ऊँची दौड़, हर्डल रेस आदि सबकुछ। कितनी उत्साही लग रही थी वेदिका। फिर कैमरा गया मैदान के एक कोने में बैठे वेद पर, जिसने स्कूल का झंडा पकड़ रखा था, लेकिन इसके अलावा खेल दिवस में उसका कोई योगदान नहीं था।

"मैंने वेद से कहा था, अरे! किसी प्रतियोगिता में भी हिस्सा लो, लेकिन लो।" पिंकी ने अकीरा को बताया। "उसने हिस्सा लिया तो। दिनभर स्कूल का झंडा पकड़कर रखा उसने!" अविनाश बनावटी हँसी में बोला।

"तुम बस माधुरी की तरह नाच लो···" अकीरा बोली और सभी हँस पड़े।

जब चिढ़ की इंतेहा हो गई तो वेद ने रूक्षता से कहा, "कम-से-कम एक बात में तो निपुण हूँ।"

"दुबारा स्वागत है, आपका हमारे कार्यक्रम में।" वेदिका बोली, और वेद, जो उसके पीछे बैठा था, पूरी तरह से चिढ़ गया था। कुछ और नहीं तो भी इसकी (वेद) चिढ़ उस दिन से आज तक सिलसिलेवार है। अकीरा मन में सोच रही थी।

"तुम्हें पता है कि तुमने जो दाढ़ी रखी है, वो बिल्कुल ठीक रखी है, कम-से-कम आधा मुँह छुपा रहता है।"

वेद ने उलटा जवाब दिया, "और कितना दुर्भाग्य कि तुम्हें सुखविलास का यह साधन कभी नहीं मिल सकता।"

उसके इस ताने से गुस्सा होकर अकीरा ने उसकी बाजू पर मारा, वेद मुँह दबाकर हँसा, लेकिन जैसे ही अकीरा ने दुबारा मारने के लिए हाथ उठाया, वह पीछे हो गया।

"हाय! (प्यार से) कितना प्यारा लग रहा है वेद!" पिंकी ने वेद की नृत्य करती हुई वीडियो चलाने पर कहा।

"तुम्हें पता है कि तुमने जो दाढ़ी रखी है, वो बिल्कुल ठीक रखी है, कम-से-कम आधा मुँह छुपा रहता है।" वेद ने उलटा जवाब दिया, "और कितना दुर्भाग्य कि तुम्हें सुखविलास का यह साधन कभी नहीं मिल सकता।"

"ओके गाइज···" लंबी साँस छोड़ते हुए वेद ने कहा। वह खड़ा होकर जाने लगा। जाते-जाते बोला, "आज के लिए इतनी शर्मिंदगी काफी है। शुभ रात्रि।"

"सोने से पहले दाँत साफ करना मत भूलना।" वेदिका ने जाते हुए वेद को चिल्लाते हुए कहा। थोड़ी देर बाद सभी को दरवाजे को तेजी से बंद करने की आवाज आई और सभी ठहाका मारकर हँस पड़े।

□

13

"वेद!"

उसे लगा कोई उसकी बाजू में उँगली दे रहा है।

"अम्ममम···।" उसने कराह के अपनी आँखें थोड़ी सी खोलीं, तो क्या देखता है, अकीरा का चेहरा उसे ताक रहा था। "ये क्या तमीज है?" उसने उठकर बैठने की कोशिश की। उसके पैर चादर में फँसे हुए थे। उसने लिपटी हुई चादर को ठीक करने की कोशिश की, लेकिन फिर छोड़ दिया। उसकी आँखें आग उगल रही थीं। "तुम्हारा दिमाग तो नहीं खराब हो गया?"

अकीरा ने अपनी हथेली से उसका मुँह बंद किया। "चिल्लाओ मत।" वेद ने गुस्से से अकीरा का हाथ दूर किया और बोला, "तुम यहाँ क्या कर रही हो? एक मनोरोगी की तरह व्यवहार क्यों कर रही हो, मुझे क्यों उठा रही हो?"

"मुझे नींद नहीं आ रही···।" अकीरा ने बच्चों की तरह शिकायत की।

"तो मैं क्या करूँ? तुम्हें लोरी सुनाऊँ?"

"तुम कर सकते हो?" आँखें मिचकाते हुए अकीरा बोली।

"उफ्फ, परेशात मत करो। जाओ यहाँ से।" वेद चिल्लाया।

"ठीक है, फिर···" अकीरा खुद वेद के पास ठीक और सुविधाजनक तरीके से बैठी, ताकि वेद को उचका सके।

"मैं यहीं तुम्हारी बगल में सो जाऊँगी। हो सकता है, नींद आ जाए।"

"सुनो! मुझे नहीं पता कि छोटे बच्चे के साथ ऐसे समय में क्या करते हैं···। मेरी कल जरूरी मीटिंग है, इसलिए मुझे सोने दो।" यह कहते हुए वेद ने चादर अपनी ठोढ़ी तक तान ली।

"ठीक है।" अकीरा मुसकराकर बोली।

थोड़ी देर की शांति के बाद उसने वेद से पूछा, "क्या तुम कभी तारों के नीचे सोए हो?"

"अकीरा···"

उसने वेद की आवाज को अनसुना कर दिया और बोली, "सोचो, कितना अच्छा लगेगा न! तुम्हें क्या लगता है?" वेद ने सिर पकड़ लिया। जब तक मैं बताऊँगा नहीं, ये चुप नहीं होगी। वह बोला, "बिल्कुल अच्छा नहीं लगता।"

"तुम्हें कैसे पता?" अकीरा घूर रही थी।

वेद ने दूसरी ओर करवट लेते हुए कहा, "बस, मुझे पता है।"

"लेकिन जब तक तुम किसी बात का अनुभव नहीं करोगे, तब तक उसके बारे में अपनी राय कैसे दे सकते हो?"

आँखें तरेरते हुए वेद बोला, "अब ये बताने के बाद मैं सो रहा हूँ। समझ आया तुम्हें?"

अकीरा उसे ध्यान से देख रही थी।

"कई साल पहले हम अपनी गरमी की छुट्टियाँ बिताने लुधियाना जाते थे। मेरी मम्मी का पूरा परिवार लुधियाना रहता है। लुधियाना में गरमियों में रात को छत पर सोने का रिवाज हैं। हे भगवान्! मुझे उससे ज्यादा बुरा इस दुनिया में कुछ नहीं लगता..." भुनभुनाते हुए वेद बोला।

"कई साल पहले हम अपनी गरमी की छुट्टियाँ बिताने लुधियाना जाते थे। मेरी मम्मी का पूरा परिवार लुधियाना रहता है। लुधियाना में गरमियों में रात को छत पर सोने का रिवाज है। हे भगवान्! मुझे उससे ज्यादा बुरा इस दुनिया में कुछ नहीं लगता..." भुनभुनाते हुए वेद बोला।

"क्यों?"

लंबी साँस लेते हुए वेद ने आगे बताना शुरू किया, "यार! वहाँ सुबह इतनी जल्दी हो जाती है। छत पर जो सोते हैं। वहाँ इतने मच्छर और पक्षी हैं। और वहाँ तो हर सुबह हम पर बंदर भी हमला करते थे। एक बुरे सपने की तरह था वह सबकुछ!"

"बंदर?" आँखें चौड़ी करते हुए अकीरा ने पूछा।

भौंहें चढ़ाकर वेद बोला,"हाँ। वो एक छत से दूसरी छत पर कूदते थे। कभी तकिया और कभी कंबल खींचते थे।"

अचानक युवा वेद का रेखाचित्र अकीरा की आँखों के सामने आया कि किस तरह वेद बंदरों से खींचा-तानी कर रहा है! अकीरा की कल्पना की उड़ान थी, और बड़ी मुश्किल से वह अपनी हँसी रोक पाई।

वेद ने अकीरा को अपनी कहानी सुनाना जारी रखा।

"यहाँ तक भी ठीक था, लेकिन मेरा एक दूर का भाई था, वह बचा-खुचा मामला भी बिगाड़ देता था। मैं और वेदिका उससे बेहद परेशान थे। उसे एक बड़ी अजीब आदत थी। वह बीच रात अचानक हाथ हवा में करता और चिल्लाना शुरू करता, 'जो बोले सो

निहाल...' और वह भी अंत:करण से।"

अकीरा को वो बात बहुत सहज लगी और उसने पूछा, "हाँ तो?"

"अकीरा! वो नींद में ऐसे बोलता था।" हैरानी की पराकाष्ठा दिखाते हुए, आँखें चौड़ी करते हुए वेद बोला।

अकीरा अभी भी शांत थी। वह बोली, "उसे नींद में बड़बड़ाने की आदत होगी।"

"हो सकता है। हो सकता है, उसे नींद में बोलने की आदत हो। लेकिन जो भी वो करता, कुछ लोग उसकी बात का जवाब देते और हमें दूसरे घरों की छतों से 'सत् श्रीअकाल' की आवाजें सुनाई पड़ती थीं। वेद ने अपनी समस्या समझाते हुए कहा, "एक समय वे सब गहरी नींद में होते और दूसरे ही क्षण उतने ही उत्साह से मेरे भाई की बात का जवाब देते।"

"हो सकता है। हो सकता है, उसे नींद में बोलने की आदत हो। लेकिन जो भी वो करता, कुछ लोग उसकी बात का जवाब देते और हमें दूसरे घरों की छतों से 'सत् श्रीअकाल' की आवाजें सुनाई पड़ती थीं। वेद ने अपनी समस्या समझाते हुए कहा, "एक समय वे सब गहरी नींद में होते और दूसरे ही क्षण उतने ही उत्साह से मेरे भाई की बात का जवाब देते।"

उसका (वेद) कमरा अकीरा की हँसी से गूँज उठा। "कई सालों तक मुझे और वेदिका को लगता रहा कि वहाँ के बाकी लोग भी इस मंत्र के लिए पागल हैं तो हम डर के मारे रजाई या चादर में छुप जाते और एक-दूसरे का हाथ पकड़ लेते।" बचपन के डर को याद करते हुए वेद कहानी बता रहा था।

जैसे ही वेद ने अपनी बात खत्म की, अकीरा नए सिरे से, फिर ठहाका मारकर हँस पड़ी। शायद उसके ठहाके में जादू था कि वेद भी हँसने लगा।

"हँसो मत।" अचानक गहरी साँस भरते हुए वेद ने कहा; दोनों एक-दूसरे को देखने लगे और फिर हँस पड़े।

"हे भगवान्! मैं हमेशा सोचती थी कि मेरा परिवार ही विचित्र है, पर तुम्हारा परिवार तो कुछ ज्यादा ही अजीब है।"

वेद ने अकीरा को देखा, लेकिन फिर हँस पड़ा और बोला, "ये तो मानना ही पड़ेगा।"

अकीरा उसे ध्यान से देख रही थी। वेद इतना जोरों के हँस रहा था कि उसे बीच-बीच में रुककर गहरी साँस लेनी पड़ रही थी। वेद को जैसे ही अहसास हुआ कि अकीरा की नजरें उसी पर टिकी हुईं हैं, धीरे-धीरे उसकी हँसी खत्म हो गई। अकीरा अत्यंत स्नेहपूर्वक बोली, "तुम्हें अकसर हँसना चाहिए। अच्छे लगते हो तुम ठहाके लगाते हुए।"

वेद को पता चल रहा था कि उसकी आँखें अकीरा के चेहरे पर टिकी थीं और

उसकी आकृति के छोटे-से-छोटे कोने तक जा रही थीं। उसके साथ वेद ने एक क्षण भी शांति का नहीं बिताया था। अधिकतर समय वह अकीरा से दूर भागना चाहता था, लेकिन ऐसा कुछ तो था, जो अकीरा के भोलेपन की चपेट में आ रहा था, लेकिन उसको बचाना चाहता था। कैसी विडंबना थी!

दोनों एक-दूसरे को देखे जा रहे थे। दोनों एक-दूसरे में खो-से गए थे। गालों में गुलाबी-सी आ गई थी। अचानक वेद का मन किया कि अकीरा के बालों में हाथ फेरे। फिर वह सोचने लगा कि उसके होंठ अगर अकीरा के होंठों को छुएँ तो कैसा लगेगा? वह अपने ही विचारों से हैरान था। उसे कुछ भी निगलना मानो मुश्किल हो रहा था। उसने अपनी जिंदगी में ऐसा कभी महसूस नहीं किया था।

माहौल को हलका करने के लिए अकीरा ने मुसकराहट से ताना कसते हुए कहा, "देखो, तुम्हारी पुतलियाँ फिर चौड़ी हो गई हैं।"

दोनों एक-दूसरे को देखे जा रहे थे। दोनों एक-दूसरे में खो-से गए थे। गालों में गुलाबी-सी आ गई थी। अचानक वेद का मन किया कि अकीरा के बालों में हाथ फेरे। फिर वह सोचने लगा कि उसके होंठ अगर अकीरा के होंठों को छुएँ तो कैसा लगेगा? वह अपने ही विचारों से हैरान था।

"यहाँ तो मोहित नहीं है तो किसे क्या दिखा रहे हो?"

एक क्षण के लिए तो वेद समझ ही नहीं पाया कि क्या हुआ? वह अगले ही क्षण अकीरा की तरफ पीठ करते हुए बोला, "सो जाओ।"

"वेद।" हँसते हुए अकीरा बोली, "मैं तुम्हारी चौड़ी होनेवाली आँखों का मजाक नहीं उड़ाऊँगी। प्लीज।"

वेद अचानक पीछे पलटा, अकीरा की आँखों में देखा और पूछा, "तुम और मोहित कैस मिले?"

"कॉलेज फेस्टीवल (उत्सव) में।" अकीरा कंधे उचकाते हुए बोली।

"सिर्फ तीन शब्दों में? तुम्हारी प्रेम कहानी इतनी अरुचिकर नहीं हो सकती।"

अकीरा ने चुभती हुई हँसी हँसते हुए पूछा, "तुम क्या चाह रहे हो? मैं विस्तार से तुम्हें अपनी प्रेम कहानी का बखान करूँ? तुम्हारे साथ मैं वयस्कोंवाली बातें कहाँ कर पाऊँगी और जितना बच्चों को बताया जा सकता है, उतना ही बताऊँगी।"

"अप्रिय टिप्पणियाँ अच्छी करती हो, लेकिन सच कहो, तुम्हारे पास कोई कहानी बताने लायक भी कुछ है क्या?" अपनी ठंडी आँखों से वेद ने अकीरा को चुनौती दी। "क्योंकि मुझे नहीं लगता कि तुम कुछ बता पाओगी, क्योंकि तुम्हारा व्यवहार प्रतिबद्ध और ईमानदार औरतों जैसा नहीं है।"

अकीरा को मानो झटका लगा, "प्रतिबद्ध या वचनबद्ध या यों कहें ईमानदार औरतें

कैसा व्यवहार करती हैं ? जरा इस बात पर प्रकाश डालेंगे ? समझाइए मुझे।"

"जैसे मेरी माँ है, वेदिका है।" वेद ने कहा।

"मुझे तो तुम्हारी आँखों में मोहित के लिए रत्ती भर भी प्यार नजर नहीं आता। तुम असल में मोहित से भाग रही हो। इसलिए तुमने रात को मोहित को पुलिस स्टेशन नहीं बुलाया।"

चिढ़कर अकीरा बोली, "और तुम्हें वह फिर मारता।"

वेद बनावटी हँसी बनाकर बोला, "और फिर घर जाकर वह तुम्हें मारता।"

अकीरा की आँखों में हैरानी थी, "तुम कहना क्या चाहते हो ?"

"मेरा मतलब है कि मोहित तुम्हें गालियाँ देता है, इस बात का सबूत है मेरे पास।" बहुत अधिक पास आकर वेद ने अकीरा से कहा।

□

14

"बकवास। यह कोरी बकवास है।" अकीरा बेडरूम के दरवाजे तक गुस्से में जाकर बोली।

वेद ने निश्चय किया था कि वह इस विषय पर अकीरा से बाद में बात करेगा, लेकिन बस भावनाओं के बहाव में वे शब्द वेद के मुँह से निकल गए थे।

"तुम जिन सबूतों की बात कर रहे हो, मुझे विश्वास है कि तुम मुझे सबके सामने बुरा साबित करना चाहते हो।" अकीरा ने इल्जाम लगाया।

वेद ने अकीरा को जहर उगलने दिया। उसके चेहरे पर अविश्वास का भाव था, लेकिन वह चुप रहा।

वह गुस्से से वेद की ओर गई और बोली, "जिस बात के बारे में पता न हो, उसके बारे में व्यर्थ बातें करने की कोई जरूरत नहीं है।"

वह स्थिति पर व्यंग्यात्मक हँसी हँसा।

अकीरा चिल्लाई "वेद! तुम पागलों की तरह हँसना बंद करके कुछ बोलोगे? तुम्हारे पास सबूत कैसे हो सकते हैं, जबकि आज तक तुम मुझे और मोहित को साथ में कुल एक ही बार मिले हो?"

वेद ने स्वयं को शांत रखते हुए कहा, "एक बार मिलना ही काफी था।"

"क्या मतलब?"

वेद बिस्तर से उठकर अकीरा की तरफ गया। उसकी बेचैन आँखों में देखता रहा। रुककर बोला, "उस दिन जब मैं क्लब के वाशरूम के अंदर आया तो मुझे लगा कि तुम दोनों वाकई प्रेम के कारण एक-दूसरे को चूमने में लगे हो, तब तक मैंने सी.सी.टी.वी. फुटेज नहीं देखी थी।"

अपेक्षा के अनुसार, अकीरा को हैरानीयुक्त शांत पाया। अकीरा की आँखें आकर्षण से भरपूर थीं और स्वयं के बचाव के सारे अस्त्र छोड़ चुकी थी।

"इससे पहले कि तुम मुझ पर इल्जाम लगाओ...मुझे सी.सी.टी.वी. की फुटेज मोहित के विरुद्ध अपने बचाव के लिए चाहिए थी...मैं तुम्हारी समस्या की जाँच नहीं कर

रहा था।" वेद ने बात साफ कर दी। "तब मैंने देखा कि तुम दोनों में पहले लड़ाई हुई; फिर उसने मोबाइल की तरफ इशारा करते हुए तुम्हें कुछ धमकाया। खैर! उसके बाद मैं अंदर आया, लेकिन उससे यह बात साफ हो जाती है कि वह बेकार ही मुझ पर गुस्सा हुआ और मेरे सामने दिखते ही उसने मुझे मारा।"

अकीरा की आँखों में आँसू थे। वह निराश-सी कुरसी पर बैठ गई। सच्चाई को इस तरह बाहर नहीं आना चाहिए था। यह तो उसका राज था।

"और उस दिन की लड़ाई के बाद जब तुम मेरी देखभाल करने मेरे पास आई तो मैं समझ गया कि तुम उससे भाग रही हो।" वेद ने अकीरा की ओर देखते हुए कहा।

अकीरा को काटो तो खून नहीं। गहरी साँस छोड़ी वेद ने। उसका अपना दिल दर्द से जोर-जोर से धड़क रहा था। अकीरा वेद के सामने कितनी खुश दिखाई देती थी कि उसकी खुशी को देख वेद को चिढ़ हो जाती थी। अकीरा का धीरे से हाथ पकड़कर वेद ने मान लिया, "मॉम ने मुझे सब बताया।"

अकीरा को काटो तो खून नहीं। गहरी साँस छोड़ी वेद ने। उसका अपना दिल दर्द से जोर-जोर से धड़क रहा था। अकीरा वेद के सामने कितनी खुश दिखाई देती थी कि उसकी खुशी को देख वेद को चिढ़ हो जाती थी। अकीरा का धीरे से हाथ पकड़कर वेद ने मान लिया, "मॉम ने मुझे सब बताया।"

ऐसा बोलते ही अकीरा खुद के आँसू नहीं रोक पाई और फूट-फूटकर रोने लगी, जैसे कि गलती करने और पकड़े जाने के बाद बच्चा रोता है।

जिस तरह के संबंध उनके थे, वेद जानता था कि ऐसी किसी भी स्थिति में जहाँ कोई आपातकालीन स्थिति या गरिमा की बात होगी, उसका परिवार अकीरा को कुछ नहीं कहेगा।

उसे वेदिका को माँ से सच निकलवाने के लिए कितनी धमकियाँ देनी पड़ी थीं। "अकीराऽऽऽ···" वेद ने धीरे से उसके सिर पर हाथ रखा। उसे खुद को पत्थर जितना मजबूत दिखाना था, क्योंकि वह रो रही थी। "प्लीज चुप हो जाओ। मैं तुम्हारे लिए हूँ न!"

उसका रोना उसे तोड़ रहा था, लेकिन वेद के सांत्वना के शब्द उसके मन-मस्तिष्क में उतर रहे थे। बड़ी मुश्किल से उसने जोर का रोना बंद किया, लेकिन वैसे ही बैठी रही। लेकिन जैसे ही उसे अहसास हुआ कि वह वेद के सामने कमजोर पड़ गई, वह घबरा गई।

वेद ने अकीरा के चेहरे से बाल पीछे किए और आँसू पोंछे। बेचारगी से उसने अकीरा से सवाल किया, "तुम मुझे बता सकती हो क्या हुआ था?"

मानसिक थकावट के कारण अकीरा कुरसी से जमीन पर सरककर वेद के साथ जा बैठी।

"जब मोहित ने तुम्हें मारा, उसके बाद मैंने उससे सारे रिश्ते तोड़ लिये। उसने सोचा, मैं अजनबी की वकालत कर रही हूँ और उसे नीचा दिखा रही हूँ। इसीलिए वह भी ब्रेकअप के लिए तैयार हो गया। उसके बाद जब तुम्हारे भेजे कानूनी नोटिस उसे मिले, तब तो वह पागल-सा हो गया। उसने सोचा, तुम्हारे लिए मैंने उसे धोखा दिया है और तुम्हारे साथ मिलकर सारे नाटक का इल्जाम मैं उसपर डाल रही हूँ।"

"ऐसा क्या हुआ था?" गुस्से में वेद बोला।

उस दिन मोहित ने मुझे गुस्से में अनगिनत मैसेज भेजे। मैं डर गई और अपने घर से भाग निकली। मुझे पता था कि उसके पास तुम्हारा फोन नंबर नहीं है और न ही वह तुम्हारे घर का पता जानता है। यदि मैं यहाँ आ जाऊँ तो थोड़ी देर के लिए सुरक्षित हो जाऊँगी।" अकीरा ने सिसकते हुए अपनी बात जारी रखी। "तुम्हारे परिवार ने सहृदयता दिखाते हुए मेरी मुश्किल को समझने की कोशिश की। हम सबने मिलकर ऐसी कहानी बनाई, जिसपर तुम्हें विश्वास हो जाए। मैंने तुमसे झूठ बोला था कि तुम्हारा ध्यान रखने के लिए तुम्हारे परिवार ने मुझे यहाँ बुलाया था।"

जब मोहित ने तुम्हें मारा, उसके बाद मैंने उससे सारे रिश्ते तोड़ लिये। उसने सोचा, मैं अजनबी की वकालत कर रही हूँ और उसे नीचा दिखा रही हूँ। इसीलिए वह भी ब्रेकअप के लिए तैयार हो गया। उसके बाद जब तुम्हारे भेजे कानूनी नोटिस उसे मिले, तब तो वह पागल-सा हो गया।

"बेबीसिट (दाई) शब्द का इस्तेमाल गलत था।" वेद ने हलके से जीभ दाँतों के बीच रखते हुए कहा।

"वेद!" हलके से अकीरा ने उसकी छाती पर मारा।

"हाँ! सही कह रही हो। माफ करना मुझे।" वेद ने धीरे से घबराते हुए कहा और उसकी बंद मुट्ठी को अपने हाथ में लेते हुए पूछा, "सही। पहले हम तुम्हारे और मोहित की कहानी पर ध्यान केंद्रित करते हैं। इसलिए तुम चाहती थी कि मैं तुम्हारे साथ शादी में चलूँ?"

"हाँ!" अकीरा की आवाज रोने के कारण टूटी और कर्कश लग रही थी। "मुझे मालूम था कि मोहित वहाँ आएगा और मुझे लगा कि मेरे साथ तुम ज्यादा सुरक्षित रहोगे।"

"शायद हम भूल रहे हैं कि वह मेरी नाक की हड्डी तोड़ चुका है।" वेद गंभीरता से बोला।

"मैं मानसिक सहयोग की बात कर रही थी, शारीरिक नहीं।" ऐसी स्थिति के बावजूद अकीरा मुँह दबाकर हलका सा हँसी।

वेद ने उसकी बात, बिना प्रतिक्रिया दिए, चुपचाप सुन ली। जब अकीरा ने वेद को शादी में चलने को कहा, उसे धमकाया भी तो वेद के मन में संदेह उत्पन्न हुआ था। अचानक वेद के दिमाग में नकारात्मक प्रश्न कौंधा—"क्या कभी उसने अपनी सीमा को लाँघा?" वेद ने पूछा। अकीरा पहले थोड़ा सा झिझकी और फिर स्पष्ट रूप से उसने वेद से पूछ ही लिया, "तुम्हारा मतलब शारीरिक संबंध?"

वेद का मन किया कि वह अकीरा का गला दबा दे। "तुम्हें यह सवाल नहीं करना चाहिए था। तुम्हारे पास थोड़ा सा भी दिमाग है या नहीं?"

अकीरा की आँखें फिर आँसुओं से लबालब भर गईं। उसका व्यवहार कितना मूर्खतापूर्ण, असावधानीयुक्त और गैर-जिम्मेदाराना था। उसने वेद को गुस्से में देखा था, लेकिन यह गुस्सा उस गुस्से से अलग था। उसका यह गुस्सा अकीरा को अच्छा लग रहा था। उसको महफूज-सा महसूस हो रहा था। वेद ने उसका चेहरा हाथ में लिया और बोला, "अगर तुम मोहित से सारे रिश्ते तोड़ चुकी थी तो तुम मोहित की तरफदारी क्यों कर रही थी? क्या वह तुम्हें धमकियाँ दे रहा है?"

अकीरा की आँखें फिर आँसुओं से लबालब भर गईं। उसका व्यवहार कितना मूर्खतापूर्ण, असावधानीयुक्त और गैर-जिम्मेदाराना था। उसने वेद को गुस्से में देखा था, लेकिन यह गुस्सा उस गुस्से से अलग था। उसका यह गुस्सा अकीरा को अच्छा लग रहा था। उसको महफूज-सा महसूस हो रहा था।

अकीरा की आँखें लाल थीं। उसने वेद की आँखों में देखा, लेकिन इस बार वेद को किसी भी प्रश्न का उत्तर नहीं चाहिए था। और उस समय वेद को जिंदगी में पहली बार दिल में धक्क-सा कुछ महसूस हुआ।

बिना कुछ कहे, धीरे से अपने वेग के तहत अकीरा को अपनी ओर खींचा। वह एक पालतू कबूतर की तरह कर रही थी। अकीरा के आँसू उसके चेहरे से ठोढ़ी तक आए और वेद की टी-शर्ट को भिगो गए। वेद को भी इस बात की परवाह नहीं थी। अकीरा के कंधे दु:ख से और सिसकियों से थोड़े से हिले। वेद भी शांत था। वेद को फर्क नहीं पड़ रहा था। वेद ने अकीरा को अपनी बाँहों में तब तक थामे रखा, जब तक वह सारा दर्द वेद के आगोश में खाली न कर गई। वेद के सीने पर सिर रखकर अकीरा ने चैन की साँस ली। पेट में अजीब सा भाव होने के बावजूद उसका हृदय धड़क रहा था। वेद की छुअन कमरे को आत्मीयता से पूरित कर रही थी और वेद का होना उसे डर से मुक्त।

"चलो! अब रोना बंद करो, प्लीज।" वेद ने कहा। अकीरा वेद की बाजुओं से

स्वयं को छुड़ाकर पीछे हुई। जब उसने देखा तो उसके आश्चर्य का ठिकाना नहीं था। वेद के गाल आँसुओं से भीग गए थे।

"हे भगवान्! तुम क्यों रो रहे हो ?" अकीरा ने वेद के चेहरे को हाथ में लेकर कहा।

वेद ने विरोध दरशाते हुए कहा, "मैं नहीं रो रहा।"

हाँ! तुम नहीं रो रहे। तुम्हारे गालों पर बारिश हो रही है।" अकीरा ने प्यार से व्यंग्य करते हुए बात खत्म की।

"हाँ! मुंबई का मौसम मनमौजी है, इसके बारे में कुछ नहीं कहा जा सकता।" वेद अकीरा की ओर देखने की हिम्मत नहीं जुटा पा रहा था।

"ओह वेद! तुम क्यों रो रहे हो ? कुछ भी नहीं हुआ है। सब ठीक है।"

"पता है मुझे···मैं बस यह चाहता था कि तुम रोना बंद करो।" वेद बुदबुदाया।

अकीरा ने जल्दी-जल्दी अपने आँसू पोंछे और कहा, "ठीक है! मैं नहीं रो रही, प्लीज! तुम चुप हो जाओ।"

"नहीं! मैं नहीं रोऊँगा···"

रोती हुई आँखों से अकीरा हँस पड़ी और बोली, "तुम कितने प्यारे हो! सच में!"

वेद ने अपनी नाक से निकलते हुए पानी को हाथ की पिछली तरफ से पोंछा और बोला, "लेकिन पहले बताओ कि क्या उसने तुम्हारे साथ कुछ गलत तो नहीं किया ?"

"हमारे संबंधों की शुरुआत से ही वह कुछ चंचल और रंगीले किस्म का था···हम जब भी मिलते, थोड़े करीब आते, वह रिकॉर्डिंग करनी शुरू कर देता। उसे इस बात की आदत थी। अब वह मुझे धमकी दे रहा है कि वीडियो लीक कर (सबके सामने लाना) देगा।"

"हमारे संबंधों की शुरुआत से ही वह कुछ चंचल और रंगीले किस्म का था···हम जब भी मिलते, थोड़े करीब आते, वह रिकॉर्डिंग करनी शुरू कर देता। उसे इस बात की आदत थी। अब वह मुझे धमकी दे रहा है कि वीडियो लीक कर (सबके सामने लाना) देगा।"

हैरानी से वेद ने अपना सिर पकड़ लिया। "कैसा बड़ा झमेला है अकीरा···!"

"झमेला ? तुम जानते हो, जब हमारी पिछली लड़ाई हुई थी, वह नमक को लेकर हुई थी।"

"क्या ?" वेद सदमे में था। "अगर नमक को लेकर मैंने कभी लड़ाई सुनी है तो वह गांधीजी की नमक सत्याग्रह की लड़ाई के बारे में और वह भी हुई थी—1930 में।"

"उसकी माँ ने खाना भेजा था। मैंने ईमानदारी से केवल इतना कहा कि थोड़ा और नमक चल जाता। वह गुस्से से पागल हो गया और मेज पलट दी।"

वेद ने नाटकीय तरीके से अपने सीने पर हाथ रखते हुए कहा, "मुझे लगता है कि

मुझे तो दिल का दौरा ही पड़ जाएगा। तुमने ऐसे इनसान के साथ रिश्ता ही क्यों रखा अकीरा? क्यों उसके साथ घूमने-फिरने गई? वह तो पूरा मूर्ख है।"

बिना जवाब दिए अकीरा ने उलटा वेद से ही प्रश्न किया "ये बताओ, तुम आज तक डेट पर (लड़की के साथ घूमने-फिरने) क्यों नहीं गए?"

"ओह! अजीब प्रश्न है, पर चलो, बता ही देता हूँ। मुझे डर लगता है कि मैं कहीं गलत इनसान को न चुन लूँ।" वेद ने अकीरा को देखकर सोच-समझकर उत्तर दिया।

"मैं अकेले रहने से डरती थी…। इसीलिए मैं उसके साथ थी।" अकीरा के स्वर में दुःख का आभास था। वेद ने उसे ध्यानपूर्वक देखा। एक घंटे पहले वे उसी स्थिति में थे, लेकिन अभी अकीरा बहुत अलग लग रही थी।

वेद ने उसकी ठोढ़ी धीरे से घुमाई और बोला, "अकीरा! मुझे लगता है, तुम्हें सो जाना चाहिए।"

"तुम्हें भी सो जाना चाहिए। तुम भी थके हुए लग रहे हो।" अकीरा ने वेद से कहा।

अपनी बात कहकर वेद ने अकीरा को बिस्तर पर खींच लिया। वह भी झिझक के साथ लेट गई। वेद ने धीरे से पलंग के पास रखा नाइट लैंप बुझा दिया और कमरे को अँधेरे ने घेर लिया। कमरे को ही नहीं; दोनों को भी। क्या उसने ठीक किया? या अकीरा सही थी? क्या ठीक है, प्यार करके हार जाना या और प्यार के लिए सही इनसान की प्रतीक्षा करना? वह यह सब सोच ही रहा था कि अचानक उसे अकीरा के सिसकने की आवाज आई। "अकीराऽऽऽऽ" वेद ने करवट बदलकर अकीरा के कंधे पर हाथ रखा। "क्या तुम चाहोगी कि मैं तुम्हें अपने में समेट लूँ?"

"नहीं! मैं ठीक हूँ।" अकीरा ने जवाब दिया और अपने को चादर से ढक लिया।

वेद थोड़ा उसके पास सरका; उसको अपनी तरफ मोड़ा और अपने में समेटा। अकीरा ने वेद की आँखें देखीं। उसमें अपनत्व का भाव था। उस भाव ने अकीरा के जख्मों पर मरहम का काम किया।

"जब तुम सो जाओगी, तो मैं चला जाऊँगा, पक्का…।" वेद ने विश्वास दिलाया।

बिना कुछ बोले अकीरा ने सिर हिलाया और आँखें बंद कर लीं। अब उसमें वेद से कोई भी प्रश्न करने की ताकत नहीं बची थी। वह वेद की बाँहों में निश्चिंत सी होकर सोने की कोशिश कर रही थी।

वेद ने भी अपनी आँखें बंद कीं और फुसफुसाया, "गुड नाइट!"

□

15

मुर्गे की बाँग से वेद की नींद टूटी। उसे लगा, मानो किसी ने उसे बिस्तर से जकड़ रखा है। हैरानी से अपनी छाती से वजन दूर करने की कोशिश करते हुए वह बोला, "हमारे घर में मुर्गा आ गया है। कैसे?"

"उफ्फ्! ये मेरी घड़ी का अलार्म बजा है।" हड़बड़ी में उसने फोन में बजता अलार्म बंद किया।

वेद ने उस ओर देखा, जहाँ से आवाज आई। अकीरा वहाँ क्या कर रही है? कौन किसे लाया? उसने अपनी आँखें मलीं। "तुम यहाँ मेरे कमरे में क्या कर रही हो?" तुम भी जब उठते हो तो इतने ही मूर्ख होते हो क्या? कल रात हम साथ सोए थे। याद आया?" अकीरा ने चिढ़कर कहा।

उसकी बातें सुन वेद की सारी स्मृतियाँ ताजा हो गईं। उसका भारी हो रखा दिमाग होश में आ रहा था। किस तरह अकीरा देर रात को उसके कमरे में आई; मोहित की कहानी; उसके आँसू; अकीरा को अपने में समेट लेना। ईश्वर की कृपा से मुर्गे की आवाज में भद्दे रिंग टोन में अलार्म का बजना।

"ओह!" वेद ने समय देखा। "अकीरा। अभी तो केवल 6.30 बजे हैं। तुमने इतनी सुबह का अलार्म क्यों लगाया?"

अकीरा ने पूरे कमरे पर नजर डाली। "ओह! यह अलार्म तो मैंने तुम्हारी दवाइयों के लिए लगाया था, जब मैं देखभाल करने तुम्हारे घर रुकी थी। मैं अलार्म हटाना भूल गई।"

"इस वक्त दवाइयाँ?" आँखें छोटी करते हुए वेद सोचने लगा। उसे पक्का याद था कि सुबह 6.30 बजे वह किसी तरह की कोई दवाइयाँ नहीं लेता। वह थोड़ी देर सोचता रहा, फिर उसे समझ आया। वह अकीरा से बोला, "अब तुम यह मत कहना कि मैं समझ नहीं पाई कि सुबह के 6.30 बजे हैं या शाम के।"

अकीरा का चेहरा शर्म से लाल हो गया। वेद बुदबुदाया। "तुम अपने में अनोखी हो अकीरा!"

सुबह-सुबह वेद की व्यंग्यात्मक हँसी अकीरा को बिल्कुल अच्छी नहीं लग रही थी। उसका ध्यान दूसरी तरफ करने के लिए अकीरा ने उसे घूरकर देखा और बोली, "तुमने कहा, तुम सुबह पाँच बजे उठते हो। उन सब बड़े-बड़े दावों का क्या?"

"हाँ! उठता हूँ, पर तब नहीं, जब मैं पाँच बजे सोता हूँ···" वेद ने अपनी उबासी दबाई।

"बहाने, बहाने!" अकीरा ने शैतानी भरी आवाज में ताना कसा। वेद ने उसके जवाब में कुछ नहीं कहा। अकीरा को महसूस हुआ कि वेद उसको ताक रहा है, उसने वेद की ओर देखा। वेद हलकी सी मुसकान लिये उसे देख रहा था। क्या वेद के चेहरे पर राहत थी? अकीरा सोचने लगी।

"बहाने, बहाने!" अकीरा ने शैतानी भरी आवाज में ताना कसा। वेद ने उसके जवाब में कुछ नहीं कहा। अकीरा को महसूस हुआ कि वेद उसको ताक रहा है, उसने वेद की ओर देखा। वेद हलकी सी मुसकान लिये उसे देख रहा था। क्या वेद के चेहरे पर राहत थी? अकीरा सोचने लगी।

वेद की आँखें शीतल प्रतीत हो रही थीं। "तुम ठीक हो अब?"

अकीरा मानो समाधि में हो, उसने सिर हिलाया, "हाँ···" अकीरा ने अपनी आँखें वेद पर से हटाईं। परिणामस्वरूप उसे अपने और वेद की स्थिति का होश आया। मुचड़ी हुई चादर के नीचे अकीरा का एक पैर अभी भी वेद पर था। वे दोनों इतने करीब थे कि वेद की नीली आँखों में हरे रंग की वस्तु की परछाईं देख सकती थी। झिझकते हुए अकीरा ने अपना पैर हटाया।

अपनी झिझक को दूर करने के लिए उसने अपनी छोटी उँगली से वाशरूम में जाने का इशारा किया, 'कुदरत की आवाज!' (Nature's Call)

वह वाशरूम की ओर भागी और जोर से अपने पीछे दरवाजा बंद किया। इस लड़की के साथ एक भी क्षण शांति का नहीं हो सकता। वेद सोच रहा था। गहरी साँस छोड़ते हुए वेद खड़ा हुआ और सीधा रसोईघर की तरफ गया। उसने सबके लिए अच्छा सा नाश्ता बनाने की सोची।

"तुम कुछ बना भी सकते हो?" अकीरा का प्रश्न वेद के कानों में पड़ा, जब वह प्याज काट रहा था।

वेद मुसकराता हुआ बोला, "अगर तुम्हारी माँ पिंकी अरोरा है तो अच्छा होगा कि तुम्हें खाना बनाना आए।"

"कुछ भी! वह इतनी बुरी नहीं हो सकती।" अकीरा तिपाई (बार स्टूल) पर बैठती हुई बोली।

"वह खाना बुरा नहीं पकाती, बस उन्हें रोज खाना पकाना अच्छा नहीं लगता।"

"ओह! अच्छा!" सिर हिलाते हुए अकीरा बोली। "वैसे तुम क्या बना रहे हो?"

घोल फेंटना रोकते हुए वेद बोला, "मसाला आमलेट क्रीम और स्ट्रॉबेरीवाले चीले (Pancakes), सिंकी ब्रेड, कॉफी और डैड के लिए कुछ पराँठे। ज्यादा कुछ नहीं।"

"ये ज्यादा कुछ नहीं है? ये तो दावत है।" अकीरा जोर से बोली।

वेद तवे पर घोल डालता हुआ हलका सा मुसकराया। अपनी आँखें मलते हुए वेदिका रसोईघर में आई और वेद को कमर से पकड़ते हुए बोली, "गुड मॉर्निंग!"

"गुड मॉर्निंग।" वेद ने धीरे से बहन के माथे को चूमा। "अरे! आज तुम इतनी जल्दी कैसे उठ गई गोगो?"

भाई-बहन की बातें सुनकर अकीरा को अच्छा महसूस हुआ। वेदिका भाग्यवान है कि उसे इतना प्यार मिलता है। वह सोच रही थी कि वेद के करीबी लोगों में होकर वेद का प्यार और अपनापन पाकर कैसा लगता होगा? उसकी आँखों के सामने पिछली रात का संवाद और स्थिति का दृश्य जीवंत हो उठा और उसकी इच्छा हुई कि उसे दुबारा वह प्रेम और अपनापन मिले। "मुझे घी की खुशबू आई। वाह! इसीलिए।"

"आह!" मुँह दबाकर वेद हँसा। उतने में खुद की नींद को कुचलने का प्रयास करते हुए वेद ने रसोईघर की तरफ कबीर को आते देखा। "उफ्फ!"

"क्या?" कहते हुए कबीर ने अकीरा की बगल में तिपाई पर खुद को झोंक दिया।

"आह!" मुँह दबाकर वेद हँसा। उतने में खुद की नींद को कुचलने का प्रयास करते हुए वेद ने रसोईघर की तरफ कबीर को आते देखा। "उफ्फ!" "क्या?" कहते हुए कबीर ने अकीरा की बगल में तिपाई पर खुद को झोंक दिया। वेद मजाक उड़ाते हुए बोला, "वेदिका! अपने बॉयफ्रेंड को मेरी ट्रेकपैंट्स (भ्रमण पर पहनी जानेवाली पतलून) को साफ करने की याद दिला देना।"

वेद मजाक उड़ाते हुए बोला, "वेदिका! अपने बॉयफ्रेंड को मेरी ट्रेकपैंट्स (भ्रमण पर पहनी जानेवाली पतलून) को साफ करने की याद दिला देना।"

अकीरा खी-खी करके हँस पड़ी। कबीर ने टेढ़ी आँखों से वेद को देखा, "इस बात का जवाब देता मैं तुझे, पर अभी बहुत सुबह है, मैं नींद में हूँ और सोचना जरा मुश्किल हो रहा है।"

"हा-हा। जैसे बाकी समय सोच लेते हो!" वेद ने हँसते हुए कहा।

वेदिका भी हँसते हुए रसोईघर के ओटे (किचन काउंटर) पर बैठ गई और बोली, "मेरे लिए भी एक ऑमलेट बनाना।"

मजे लेते हुए वेद खिलखिलाते हुए हँसा। उसने तवे पर तेल लगाने के लिए बोतल उठाई। वेदिका बोली, "तुम्हारी तरह तुम्हारा तेल भी अछूता और पवित्र है।"

उसकी बात सुनकर अकीरा ने अपने मुँह पर हाथ रख लिया, ताकि पानी बाहर न आए और कबीर हँसते-हँसते झुक गया। वह पेट दबाकर हँस रहा था।

"घूरो मत।" वेदिका ने ताना कसा।

कबीर ने भी चुटकी ली, "तुम्हारी आँखें ही तुम्हारे में सबसे बड़ी अच्छाई है, इसे बरबाद मत करो।"

पिंकी व्यंग्यात्मक हँसी और बोलीं, "और मैंने तुम्हें बनाया है, इसीलिए चुप रहो।" सभी फिर हँस पड़े। वेद के लिए कहीं से कोई राहत नहीं थी। वेद ने अविनाश को आते देखा तो बोला, "गुड मॉर्निंग।" अविनाश चलते-चलते खाने के लिए नाश्ते की मेज पर आ रहा था।

वेद ने बनावटी हँसी से कबीर की ओर देखा, "पुराना चुटकुला है।"

"तुम तो हड़प्पा संस्कृति जितने पुराने हो।" वेदिका ने तिरस्कार से व्यंग्य कसा।

"चुप रह!" रसोईघर का कपड़ा उसने वेदिका को फेंककर मारा।

"अरे! सुबह-सुबह चिक-चिक मत करो। चलो, हम सब नाश्ता करते हैं। मुझे भूख लग रही है।" वेदिका की पीठ पर धीरे से हाथ मारते हुए पिंकी रसोईघर में आई।

"जो मैंने बनाया है···" वेद ने कहा।

पिंकी व्यंग्यात्मक हँसी और बोलीं, "और मैंने तुम्हें बनाया है, इसीलिए चुप रहो।" सभी फिर हँस पड़े। वेद के लिए कहीं से कोई राहत नहीं थी। वेद ने अविनाश को आते देखा तो बोला, "गुड मॉर्निंग।" अविनाश चलते-चलते खाने के लिए नाश्ते की मेज पर आ रहा था। उसने वेद की गुड मॉर्निंग का जवाब देना जरूरी नहीं समझा और नाश्ते की शुरुआत कर दी। अकीरा हँसनेवाली थी, पर उसने अपनी हँसी रोक ली। वाकई सभी कितने अजीब हैं, लेकिन ऐसे परिवार का हिस्सा बनना कितना अच्छा लगेगा न! जहाँ सभी खुशी से, समझदारी से रहते हैं। उसे अपने माता-पिता की याद आ रही थी। उतने में उसके फोन में किसी का संदेश (मैसेज) आया और उसकी आँखों में चमक आ गई। उसने बड़ी सी मुसकान के साथ सभी को बताया, "अभी-अभी मुझे पता चला है कि मेरे मम्मी-पापा जल्दी वापस आ रहे हैं। वे छुट्टियाँ मनाने गए थे। वे आज ही दोपहर को आ जाएँगे।"

"शुक्र है, भगवान् का। मैं सोच ही रही थी कि तुम्हें यहाँ रुकने को कहूँ। मुझे उस बदतमीज मोहित का जरा भी विश्वास नहीं।" पिंकी ने हामी में सिर हिलाया, "अब मुझे तुम्हारी कोई चिंता नहीं।"

अकीरा ने ह्रदय से आभार व्यक्त किया, "बहुत-बहुत शुक्रिया।"

"अरे, इसमें हमें धन्यवाद करने जैसा कुछ भी नहीं।" अपने चेहरे पर कड़े भाव लाकर पिंकी बोलीं।

"वाह!" अविनाश ने हँसकर कहा और फिर मुड़कर वेद को देखा और बोला, "तुम यहाँ क्या कर रहे हो? मीटिंग के लिए तैयार हो जाओ।"

"अभी सिर्फ 7.23 बज रहे हैं, मीटिंग 11 बजे है।" वेद ने पलकें झपकाते हुए कहा।

"तो? मैंने फाइल्स नहीं देखी हैं, वो तुम्हें देखनी हैं।" अविनाश ने वेद को आदेश दिया।

वेद ने कराहने जैसा किया। उसने चीले की बड़ी सी गिराई मुँह में डाली और अपने कमरे की तरफ चल पड़ा।

"सुनो।" अकीरा ने वेद को आवाज दी। मुसकराते हुए बोली "मिस्टर वेद अरोरा!···फिर मिलते हैं अदालत में।"

वेद मुसकराकर बोला, "ठीक है, मिस़ अकीरा बजाज! अदालत में मिलते हैं।"

□

16

"यहाँ।" पिंकी ने वेद के मुँह के सामने चम्मच पकड़ी।

चम्मच में रखी वस्तु को देख वेद ने मुँह बनाया और पूछा, "ये क्या है?"

"आज रस्म पूरी करने के लिए दही-चीनी नहीं है।"

कुछ क्षणों के लिए वह पिंकी को देखता रहा और फिर खीजे हुए स्वर में बोला, "इसीलिए वनीला आइसक्रीम?"

"मेरे प्यारे बच्चे! वो इसलिए, क्योंकि इसका दूध पिघलने पर दही जैसा होता है और चीनी तो होती ही है।"

पिंकी ने वेद का मुँह वैसे खोला, जैसे छोटे बच्चे का खोलते हैं। मानो वेद आदमी नहीं, छोटा बच्चा हो और उसके मुँह में चम्मच रखते हुए, गरजते हुए बोली, "इसलिए ले लो।"

"अम्म्म्!" वेद बच्चो-सा रिरियाया। हर बार वह सोचता कि अब उसका परिवार बचकानी या अजीब हरकतें नहीं करेगा, पर हर बार वह गलत ही साबित होता।

पिंकी ने अपनी कान की बाली ठीक की। "अब और कितनी देर ऐसे ही खड़े रहोगे? चलो।"

अपने परिवार को मानो घर से बाहर खदेड़ते हुए वेद ने बात दोहराई, "चलो।"

जैसे ही वे अदालत के प्रांगण में पहुँचे, वे मि. दास और कबीर से मिले। वे (अरोरा परिवार) सीधा अदालत के उस कक्ष में जाकर पीछेवाली बेंच पर बैठ गए। सहसा वेद का ध्यान अकीरा पर गया, जो अपने माता-पिता के साथ बैठी थी। जैसे ही अकीरा ने वेद को देखा, उसका चेहरा खिल उठा और उसके होंठों पर मुसकान आ गई। वेद ने भी धीरे से हाथ हिलाकर उसकी मुसकान का जवाब दिया। "मोहित कहाँ है?" कबीर ने वेद से पूछा। वेद को अपनी नसों में गुस्सा महसूस हुआ और उसने मोहित की ओर इशारा किया।

"वो? सच मेंऽऽऽ?" कबीर के होंठ घृणा के भाव में ऊपर की ओर हुए और वह बोला, "मुझे तो इसे देखते ही मानो दाद की बीमारी महसूस हो रही है।"

वेदिका जितना धीरे हँस सकती थी, हँसी। वेद और कबीर की ओर झुककर वेदिका ने धीरे से कहा, "मानना पड़ेगा कि लड़कों के चयन में अकीरा की पसंद बिल्कुल बेकार है। पहले मोहित और अब वेद भैया की ओर खिंच रही है। कितना भयावह, आऽऽऽ थू!"

कबीर मुसकराया और वेद खीझकर वेदिका से बोला, "चुप रह!"

"अगला केस!" क्लर्क ने घोषणा की।

मि. दास जल्दी से कक्ष के आगे की तरफ गए। न्यायाधीश ने आदेश दिया—"दोनों पक्षों को हाजिर किया जाए।"

मि. दास ने वेद को आगे आने का संकेत किया। वेद खड़ा हुआ और उसने बहुत बड़ी गलती की। उसने अपने परिवार की ओर देखा और उसके देखते ही सभी उसकी ओर जोर-जोर से हाथ हिलाने लगे। वेद ने धीरे से नाक पकड़ी और अजीब सा महसूस करते हुए अपनी आँखें बंद कर लीं।

मि. दास ने वेद को आगे आने का संकेत किया। वेद खड़ा हुआ और उसने बहुत बड़ी गलती की। उसने अपने परिवार की ओर देखा और उसके देखते ही सभी उसकी ओर जोर-जोर से हाथ हिलाने लगे। वेद ने धीरे से नाक पकड़ी और अजीब सा महसूस करते हुए अपनी आँखें बंद कर लीं।

"कृपया इन सज्जन के लिए कुरसी लाएँ। मुझे लग रहा है, कहीं ये बेहोश न हो जाएँ।" न्यायाधीश ने कड़क आवाज में आदेश दिया।

जब तक कि वेद को बात समझ आती, किसी ने उसे पीछे से कुरसी दी। अपनी दशा सोचकर वेद समझ गया कि वह ऐसा क्यों कह रही थी। वेद ने जवाब दिया, "मैं ठीक हूँ, साहिबान!"

न्यायाधीश ने उसे रुक्षता से देखा और कहा, "बैठिए।" उसने देखा, अकीरा और उसका पूरा परिवार अपनी हँसी रोकने की कोशिश कर रहा था। खासकर अकीरा।

"क्या मैं काररवाई शुरू कर सकता हूँ... ?" मि. दास ने प्रार्थना की। न्यायाधीश ने हामी भरी। मि. दास ने बताना शुरू किया, "मेरे मुवक्किल ने श्री मोहित पर अकारण ही हिंसा करने का आरोप लगाया है। यह घटना एक क्लब के वाशरूम में हुई। श्री मोहित ने मेरे मुवक्किल पर हमला किया और उन्हें घायल किया।"

न्यायाधीश ने मोहित के पक्ष की ओर देखा, "अपने बचाव में आप कोई दलील देना चाहेंगे?"

मोहित के वकील ने कहा, "श्री वेद अरोरा ने मोहित को उनकी गर्लफ्रेंड से मसखरी करके उकसाया। अकीरा बजाज मोहित की गर्लफ्रेंड (दोस्त) हैं। उसी का परिणाम था कि दोनों के बीच लड़ाई शुरू हुई। मेरे मुवक्किल ने खुद के बचाव में वेद को मारा।"

यह सुनकर वेद को मोहित के चेहरे पर वही कुरसी दे मारने का मन हुआ, जिस पर वह बैठा था। या फिर वेदिका के हवाले ही कर दिया जाए।

मि. दास ने आत्मविश्वास से कहा, "मैं अदालत से दरख्वास्त करता हूँ कि सी.सी. टी.वी. फुटेज चलाने की इजाजत दी जाए। वो फुटेज, जो हमने क्लब से ली है।"

"मंजूर है।"

अदालत के क्लर्क ने एक पुराने से प्लेयर में सी.डी. डाली और शुरू की। थोड़ी देर बाद छोटे से टी.वी. पर वह फुटेज शुरू हुई।

फिर वेद की ओर इशारा करते हुए मि. दास बोले, "यही कारण है कि श्री वेद सीधे भी खड़े नहीं हो पा रहे और बार-बार लगता है कि बेहोश हो जाएँगे।" न्यायाधीश की आँखें श्री वेद पर गड़ी हुई थीं। शर्मिंदगी से वह नीचे देख रहा था। वैसे भी यदि इस तरह से उस पर (वेद) बातें चलती रहतीं तो निश्चित ही वह बेहोश हो जाता। "ठीक है।" न्यायाधीश ने अपनी फाइल में कुछ लिखा।

"जैसा कि आप देख सकते हैं, मेरे मुवक्किल ने कहीं भी मि. खुराना को नहीं उकसाया, न मौखिक रूप में और न ही शारीरिक रूप से। मैंने सभी चिकित्सा संबंधी कागजात और वेद के सी.टी. स्कैन आपकी सुविधा के लिए दिए हैं।" मि. दास ने इशारा करते हुए कहा।

फिर वेद की ओर इशारा करते हुए मि. दास बोले, "यही कारण है कि श्री वेद सीधे भी खड़े नहीं हो पा रहे और बार-बार लगता है कि बेहोश हो जाएँगे।"

न्यायाधीश की आँखें श्री वेद पर गड़ी हुई थीं। शर्मिंदगी से वह नीचे देख रहा था। वैसे भी यदि इस तरह से उस पर (वेद) बातें चलती रहतीं तो निश्चित ही वह बेहोश हो जाता।

"ठीक है।" न्यायाधीश ने अपनी फाइल में कुछ लिखा।

"आपके मुवक्किल ने यह भी दावा किया है कि मि. खुराना लगातार अपनी पूर्व गर्लफ्रेंड को अपशब्द कहकर अपमानित करता रहा है। उनका नाम मिस अकीरा बजाज है।"

वेद को अदालत में हैरानी की प्रतिक्रिया और आपसी खुसर-पुसर सुनाई दे रही थी। उसे यह अपेक्षित था। वेद ने अपने परिवार को यह नहीं बताया था कि उसने अपने नोटिस में अकीरा के प्रति मोहित के अपशब्दों के बारे में भी लिखा है। यह बात केवल वेद और उसके वकील के बीच की थी।

"यदि हम सी.सी.टी.वी. फुटेज शुरू से देख सकते हैं कि मि. खुराना किस तरह मिस अकीरा को धमका रहे हैं।" यह कहते हुए मि. दास ने न्यायाधीश को कुछ कागजात

दिए। "यह मोबाइल पर हुई बातचीत और एस.एम.एस. की प्रतिलिपि (Transcript) है, जिसमें स्पष्ट रूप से पता चलता है कि मि. खुराना मिस अकीरा बजाज को धमकी दे रहे हैं कि वे शुरू से साथ बिताए गए क्षणों के चित्र और वीडियो लीक कर देंगे।"

यह काम मुश्किल था, पर वेद ने किसी तरह सर्विस प्रोवाइडर (जो मोबाइल की सेवाएँ प्रदान करता है) से कुछ निजी संदेश ले लिये थे, क्योंकि अकीरा ने मोहित को सोशल मीडिया पर ब्लॉक कर दिया था, इसलिए मोहित अकीरा को एस.एम.एस. करता रहा, जिसका फायदा अप्रत्यक्ष रूप से वेद को हुआ।

न्यायाधीश ने कागजों से मुँह बाहर करके पूछा, "मिस अकीरा हैं क्या? लाइए उन्हें।"

खुद को सँभालते हुए अकीरा खड़ी हुई। उसने अपने माता-पिता की ओर देखा। दोनों ने ही उसे आश्वस्त कराया। वैसे ही अरोरा परिवार ने उसे साथ होने का आश्वासन दिया। गहरी साँस लेते हुए अकीरा अदालत के कक्ष में सामने की तरफ आकर खड़ी हुई। उसने आँखें नीचे कर रखी थीं। वह जानती थी कि यदि उसने वेद की ओर एक बार भी देखा तो वह रो पड़ेगी।

खुद को सँभालते हुए अकीरा खड़ी हुई। उसने अपने माता-पिता की ओर देखा। दोनों ने ही उसे आश्वस्त कराया। वैसे ही अरोरा परिवार ने उसे साथ होने का आश्वासन दिया। गहरी साँस लेते हुए अकीरा अदालत के कक्ष में सामने की तरफ आकर खड़ी हुई। उसने आँखें नीचे कर रखी थीं। वह जानती थी कि यदि उसने वेद की ओर एक बार भी देखा तो वह रो पड़ेगी।

"मिस अकीरा! आप मोहित द्वारा गालियों और अपशब्दां का शिकार हुईं या नहीं?" न्यायाधीश ने पूछा।

अकीरा ने हामी भरते हुए सिर हिलाया, "हाँ।"

"विस्तार से बताएँ।"

"मैं यहीं हूँ…डरो मत।" यह कहते हुए वेद ने अकीरा का हाथ पकड़ा।

अकीरा खुश थी कि वह अकेली यह सबकुछ नहीं कर रही थी, उसके साथ कोई था। उसने वेद का हाथ कड़ाई से पकड़ा और बोली, "मोहित ने शारीरिक स्तर पर भी मुझे प्रताड़ित किया, मुझे चाँटा मारा। जब मैंने उससे किसी तरह के भी संबंध रखने से मना किया तो उसने मुझे हमारे सारे फोटो और हमारे वीडियो सबके सामने ले आने की (Leak) धमकी दी।"

"आप कोई दलील पेश करना चाहेंगे?" न्यायाधीश ने मोहित के वकील से पूछा।

मोहित के वकील ने सिर झुकाकर कहा, "नहीं।"

"तुम बदतमीज। मैं तुम्हें मेरे बचाव के लिए पैसे दे रहा हूँ।" मोहित अपने वकील

पर चिल्लाया। "ये लोग मेरी छवि खराब करने के लिए अपनी धोखाधड़ी छिपा रहे हैं।"

"तुम्हारे पास इस दावे को साबित करने के लिए कोई सबूत है?"

"नहीं। लेकिन अकीरा सब गड़बड़ कर रही है।..."

न्यायाधीश ने कहा, "अगर तुम कुछ भी कहोगे तो वह अदालत की तौहीन मानी जाएगी और तुम्हारे विरुद्ध उसका प्रयोग किया जाएगा।"

उस बात ने मोहित को चुप करा दिया। उसके बाद न्यायाधीश ने अपने सारे नोट्स ध्यानपूर्वक देखे। वेद और अकीरा तो जैसे अपनी साँसें थामे बैठे थे। उन्हें जैसे पता था कि फैसला उन्हीं के हक में होगा।

"अच्छा।" न्यायाधीश ने ऊपर देखा और फैसला सुनाया, "सभी सबूतों को मद्देनजर रखते हुए अदालत इस नतीजे पर पहुँची है कि आरोपी मि. मोहित खुराना ने हिंसा को अपनाते हुए (अभियुक्त) श्री वेद पर हमला किया, जबकि वेद ने किसी भी तरह से उसे भड़काया नहीं था। उसने अकीरा बजाज को भी शारीरिक और भावात्मक रूप से प्रताड़ित किया। परिणामस्वरूप अदालत मोहित को 20,000 रुपए का जुरमाना देने का फैसला सुनाती है। साथ ही मोहित को श्री वेद से लिखित माफी माँगनी पड़ेगी और एक प्रसिद्ध अखबार में पत्र को प्रकाशित भी करवाना पड़ेगा। इसके अलावा मोहित को दो वर्ष की कैद की सजा केवल हिंसक मनोवृत्तियों के कारण सुनाई जाती है।" न्यायाधीश ने अपने समक्ष रखे कागज पर हस्ताक्षर किए। "अदालत स्थगित।"

"अच्छा।" न्यायाधीश ने ऊपर देखा और फैसला सुनाया, "सभी सबूतों को मद्देनजर रखते हुए अदालत इस नतीजे पर पहुँची है कि आरोपी मि. मोहित खुराना ने हिंसा को अपनाते हुए (अभियुक्त) श्री वेद पर हमला किया, जबकि वेद ने किसी भी तरह से उसे भड़काया नहीं था।

अभी तक अरोरा खुद को पकड़े बैठे थे। फैसला सुनते ही सभी में खुशी की लहर दौड़ गई।

अचानक अकीरा ने वेद को गले लगा लिया। "बधाई हो।"

अकीरा ने वेद के कान में राहत की साँस लेते हुए कहा।

"तुम्हें भी मुबारक!" उसने भी धीरे से जवाब दिया। उसने (अकीरा) अपनी जकड़ थोड़ी गहरी कर ली। कुछ क्षण तक वे ऐसे ही रहे, जब तक पूरा परिवार उन दोनों पर खुशी से टूट नहीं पड़ा।

पुलिस ने मोहित को हथकड़ियाँ पहनाईं और ले जाने लगे; परिवार भी उनके पीछे चल पड़ा था। पुलिस की गाड़ी में बैठने से पहले मोहित वेद पर चीखा, "वाकई तुम्हें

अकीरा और अकीरा को तुम मिलने चाहिए। दोनों हारे हुए, बेकार-से। मैं खुद ही अकीरा को अपने जीवन से बाहर करता हूँ। हमारे बीच अब कुछ नहीं बचा।"

यह सुन वेद का खून खौला और उसने मोहित की ठोढ़ी पर मारा। उसने मोहित का सिर पकड़कर नीचे किया और अपने घुटने से उसके नाक पर घुटना दे मारा कि उसके (मोहित) के नाक से खून निकलने लगा और फिर एक जोर का मुक्का पेट में मारा कि मोहित जमीन पर बैठ गया।

"अब तुम्हारे और अकीरा के बीच कुछ नहीं रहा।" वेद चिल्लाकर बोला।

पूरा परिवार हर्षित था; अविनाश खुशी जताते हुए बोला, "ये हुई न बात मेरे शेर!"

अकीरा अपने पिता के कान में फुसफुसाई "ये अच्छा है न! सही कहा था न मैंने?"

"सबसे अच्छा है।" अकीरा के पिता ने प्यार से अकीरा को आँख मारते हुए कहा और अकीरा खिल उठी।

जब सबने पुलिस को मोहित को ले जाते हुए देखा तो पिंकी ने ईश्वर की प्रशंसा में हाथ जोड़े और कहा, "शुक्र है भगवान् का, अब सब ठीक है।"

"सबसे अच्छा है।" अकीरा के पिता ने प्यार से अकीरा को आँख मारते हुए कहा और अकीरा खिल उठी। जब सबने पुलिस को मोहित को ले जाते हुए देखा तो पिंकी ने ईश्वर की प्रशंसा में हाथ जोड़े और कहा, "शुक्र है भगवान् का, अब सब ठीक है।"

"हाँ, सही कहा।" अकीरा की माँ बोली।

"शुक्र है ईश्वर का" पिंकी ने हँसकर अकीरा से कहा, "अपने माता-पिता से नहीं मिलवाओगो?"

जीभ दाँतों के बीच रखते हुए अकीरा बोली, "अरे! हाँ, ये पिंकी आंटी हैं, ये अविनाश अंकल; ये वेदिका, उनकी बेटी; ये कबीर; वेदिका का बॉयफ्रेंड (दोस्त) और ये है वेद।"

और फिर बड़ी सी मुसकान के साथ उसने अपने माता-पिता का परिचय दिया, "ये हैं मेरे माता-पिता; अवंतिका और हर्ष बजाज।"

"आपसे मिलकर खुशी हुई।" अविनाश ने हर्ष से हाथ मिलाते हुए कहा।

"हमें भी! बहुत अच्छा परिवार है आपका" हर्ष ने मुसकराते हुए जवाब दिया।

"अकीरा से अच्छा नहीं!" अविनाश ने प्यार से कहा और शर्म से अकीरा ने नजरें दूसरी तरफ कर लीं।

पिंकी ने उत्साह से ताली बजाते हुए कहा, "चलो, जश्न मनाते हुए साथ में खाना खाएँ।"

"हाँ!" वेदिका उत्साह से बोली।

अवंतिका को भी यह पसंद आया और बोली, "हाँ! जश्न तो बनता है।"

"पिंकी आंटी…"अकीरा ने झिझकते हुए गला खराशा। उसे कहने से पहले अपने गालों पर झिझक से ऊष्मा महसूस हो रही थी। उसने धीरे से कहा, "क्या हम दोपहर के बजाय रात को खाना साथ खा सकते हैं? मैं थोड़ी देर के लिए आप सबसे वेद को चुराना चाहती हूँ। मुझे उससे कुछ बात करनी है।"

वेद की हैरानी की सीमा नहीं थी और वेद क्या महसूस कर रहा था, उसकी भी। उसने आँखें चौड़ी करके अकीरा को देखा। अकीरा उससे क्या बात करना चाहती है?

पिंकी हँस पड़ीं। "बिल्कुल, तुम जा सकते हो। जाओ।"

कबीर ने वेद के सामने चाबी की और बोला, "मेरी बाइक ले जाओ।"

"शुक्रिया!" वेद मुसकराकर बोला।

□

17

अकीरा सीमेंट की दीवार पर बैठी थी।

समुद्र को न देखते हुए, उसकी नजरें समुद्र के किनारे के पत्थरों से लहरों की ओर, फिर वहाँ से साथ में बैठे उस व्यक्ति की ओर गईं, जो उसके साथ बैठा था। वह दुबारा कुछ महसूस करने का दिन था, जश्न मनाने का दिन था, दुबारा कोई नई शुरुआत करने का दिन था।

"अकीराऽऽऽ!" वेद की आवाज उसे सपनों की दुनिया से वापस ले आई।

"बोलो।" अकीरा ने वेद को देखा, उसे अपेक्षित था।

"मैं तुमसे हमेशा पूछना भूल जाता हूँ। तुम्हारी कंपनी का नाम क्या है?"

अकीरा ने गर्व की मुसकान से कहा, "शादी का लड्डू!"

"क्या?" वेद ने साँस रोकी और जोर से हँसा।

"अगर तुम्हारी मूर्खोंवाली हरकतें खत्म हो गई हों तो हम बात करें?" अकीरा ने पूछा।

व्यंग्य से हँसकर वेद मुड़ा और आलथी-पालथी मारकर बैठ गया। "हाँ। बोलो।"

वेद की आँखों में सीधे देखते हुए अकीरा ने पूछा, "तुमने मोहित द्वारा मुझे दी गई गालियों और अपशब्दों की बात अपने केस में क्यों डालीं?"

वेद को इस प्रश्न की उम्मीद थी। गहरी साँस लेकर उसने बोलना शुरू किया, "शुरू में जब मैंने सी.सी.टी.वी. की फुटेज देखी तो मुझे लगा कि साधारण सी लड़ाई है और मैंने तुम दोनों को चिढ़ाने के लिए वह बात अपने केस में जोड़ दी।"

वेद हँसा और अकीरा ने उसे घूरा, तब जाकर वेद की आवाज में गंभीरता आई। "जब माँ ने मुझे मोहित के बारे में बताया, तब मुझे अहसास हुआ कि मामला बहुत गंभीर है। उसके बाद मैंने सक्रियता से कार्य किया और सबूत इकट्ठे किए, जिससे मोहित को सजा मिल सके।"

"तुमने इसके बारे में मुझे क्यों नहीं बताया?"

"मैंने कोशिश की थी। तुमसे पूछा था कि तुमने नोटिस पढ़ा तो तुम बोलीं कि

कानून के अजीब दाँव-पेच में कौन फँसना चाहेगा और कानून की विचित्र भाषा में लिखीं इतनी पंक्तियाँ मैं नहीं पढ़ सकती।"

अकीरा माथा खुजाते हुए बोली, "लो! मैं इस तरह पूछती हूँ। तुमने एक साधारण मनुष्य की तरह क्यों नहीं बताया?"

चुहलबाजी करते हुए वेद ने कंधे उचकाते हुए प्रतिक्रिया दी।

"सरप्राइज! सरप्राइज! अदालत में सबके सामने?"

"माफ करना, मैं मूर्खों जैसे कर रहा था।" उसने जीभ को दाँत में दबाते हुए कहा।

"और अगर मैं कहूँ कि मैं ऐसा नहीं चाहती थी तो?"

"असंभव! ऐसा हो ही नहीं सकता। तुम जैसी लड़की मोहित को जेल में ही देखना चाहेगी। मैंने बस उस प्रक्रिया को तेज कर दिया। बहुत सी छोटी-छोटी बातों का विवरण हमेशा ही गुप्त रहेगा।"

"वेद! मुझे पता है। बस किसी की सहमति जरूरी होती है ऐसे में…इतना ही कहना था। और ये बात हम दोनों को सीखनी जरूरी है" धीरे से अकीरा ने अपनी बात जोर देते हुए वेद को पकड़ा दी।

"असंभव! ऐसा हो ही नहीं सकता। तुम जैसी लड़की मोहित को जेल में ही देखना चाहेगी। मैंने बस उस प्रक्रिया को तेज कर दिया। बहुत सी छोटी-छोटी बातों का विवरण हमेशा ही गुप्त रहेगा।"
"वेद! मुझे पता है। बस किसी की सहमति जरूरी होती है ऐसे में…इतना ही कहना था। और ये बात हम दोनों को सीखनी जरूरी है" धीरे से अकीरा ने अपनी बात जोर देते हुए वेद को पकड़ा दी।

उसने सिर हिलाया (सहमति में)—"मेरा मकसद तुम्हें मुश्किल में डालने का बिल्कुल नहीं था। आगे से मैं ऐसा कुछ भी नहीं करूँगा। मुझे माफ कर दो।"

"अरे नहीं।" अकीरा ने वेद का हाथ पकड़ा। "जो कुछ भी हुआ, उसकी वजह से मोहित को उसके किए की सजा तो मिली। सारा श्रेय तुम्हीं को और धन्यवाद भी।"

वेद ने अपनी नाक पर उँगली घुमाते हुए कहा, "मुझे अपनी नाक का बदला लेना था।"

"अच्छा! शूर्पणखा!" हँसते हुए अकीरा बोली, जिसे सुन वेद भी हँस पड़ा।

"खैर! जो हुआ, अच्छा हुआ और बात खत्म।" वेद ने राहत की साँस लेते हुए कहा।

"हाँ।" अकीरा मुसकराई और अपनी तरफ इशारा करते हुए बोली, "अब बताओ, क्या मैं तुम्हें पसंद हूँ?"

ये शब्द वेद पर असर कर गए। उसकी झेंप उसके चेहरे पर स्पष्ट नजर आ रही थी। वह हमेशा उदासीन-सा रहता। कभी खिसियाया हुआ, कभी चिड़चिड़ा; हमेशा गुस्से में ही रहता, जैसे लड़ने को तैयार और बार-बार खुद को समझाता कि उसका व्यवहार व विचार बिल्कुल ठीक हैं। इसलिए उसके गालों का बदला हुआ रंग और झेंप एक अलग ही आश्चर्य था।

"मैंने ऐसे पहले कभी नहीं किया अकीरा; कभी किसी के साथ डेट पर नहीं गया।" अपनी गरदन बेचैनी से हिलाते हुए वेद बोला।

"मैंने तुम्हें मुझे डेट करने के लिए नहीं कहा।" होशियारी से अकीरा को मूर्खता समझ आ गई थी।

"तुम जब ऐसे हकलाते हो तो बहुत प्यारे लगते हो।" वेद के गाल खींचते हुए अकीरा बोली। "लेकिन सच बताओ, क्या तुम्हें मैं अच्छी लगती हूँ?"

"मैंने तुम्हें मुझे डेट करने के लिए नहीं कहा।" होशियारी से अकीरा को मूर्खता समझ आ गई थी। "तुम जब ऐसे हकलाते हो तो बहुत प्यारे लगते हो।" वेद के गाल खींचते हुए अकीरा बोली। "लेकिन सच बताओ, क्या तुम्हें मैं अच्छी लगती हूँ?"

वेद ने अकीरा का धीरे से हाथ हटाया, "मैंने तुम्हें उस दिन देखा था, जब हम वेदिका की गाड़ी में बैठे थे। तुम सुंदर हो।"

"सिर्फ सुंदर?" चिढ़ाते हुए अकीरा ने पूछा।

"नहीं!" सोचकर वेद बुदबुदाया। "ऐसा मुझे शुरू में लगा, लेकिन जो बात अच्छी लगी, वो यह कि तुम हमेशा स्नेही रही और कभी भी डरी नहीं और दबी नहीं। मुझे बताया गया कि मैं हमेशा सबको धमकाता हूँ; अपने व्यवहार और बातों से।"

"इसलिए जब तुमने अपना व्यवहार बिना मुझसे डरे वैसा ही रखा, जैसा तुम चाहती थीं, तो मेरे लिए यह नई बात थी। तुम गुस्सैल हो, पर आकर्षक भी।...कुछ अजीब भावनाएँ हैं; जो मुझे बेचैन भी करती हैं और खुशी भी देती हैं। एक साथ दोनों तरह के भाव हैं।" एक गहरी शांत साँस लेने के बाद वेद ने स्वीकारा, "अगर प्रश्न का उत्तर दूँ तो हाँ, तुम मुझे अच्छी लगती हो। और तुम्हें?"

अकीरा ने गहरी साँस ली और नीचे का होंठ दबाते हुए कहा—

"मैं तुम जैसे लड़के से पहले कभी नहीं मिली। तुम अलग हो वेद!"

"अलग हो कहना मेरे सवाल-जवाब नहीं है।" वेद ने कहा।

"अलग हो मतलब आश्चर्यकारी हो, जो खुशी का आश्चर्य देता ही। कुछ हटकर मतलब तुम!"

वेद की भौहें आश्चर्य से चढ़ीं, "आज तक किसी ने मेरे लिए इन शब्दों का प्रयोग नहीं किया।"

अकीरा ने पलटकर कहा, "इसका मतलब तुम आज तक सही लोगों से मिले ही नहीं। तुम खास हो, मुझे तुम अच्छे लगते हो।"

वेद ने कुछ कहा नहीं। उसे समझ नहीं आ रहा था कि वह क्या कहे? लेकिन अकीरा ने उसकी आँखों का बदलता रंग देखा, लेकिन उसका अर्थ समझ नहीं पाई। वह लाखों में एक था!

"तो? अब क्या?" अपने होंठ सिकोड़ते हुए अकीरा बोली।

वेद ने हामी भरी और प्रयोगात्मक रूप में अकीरा बोली, "तो चलो ऐसा करते हैं कि हम दोनों एक-दूसरे को 21 दिनों तक डेट करते हैं, फिर देखते हैं क्या होता है? मेरा मतलब है, तुम इसे व्यावसायिक निवेश के तौर पर देखो। कैसे तुम व्यापार में खतरा उठाते हुए पैसा निवेश करते हो और इस बात के लिए तैयार रहते हो कि पैसे गँवाने भी पड़ सकते हैं। क्यों? है न?"

"मुझे सच में नहीं पता।" कंधे उचकाते हुए वेद ने कहा।

थोड़ी देर कुछ मनन करने के बाद अकीरा बोली, "तुम्हें याद है, तुमने कहा था कि कोई भी आदत बनाने या छोड़ने में 21 दिन का समय लगता है?"

वेद ने हामी भरी और प्रयोगात्मक रूप में अकीरा बोली, "तो चलो ऐसा करते हैं कि हम दोनों एक-दूसरे को 21 दिनों तक डेट करते हैं, फिर देखते हैं क्या होता है? मेरा मतलब है, तुम इसे व्यावसायिक निवेश के तौर पर देखो। कैसे तुम व्यापार में खतरा उठाते हुए पैसा निवेश करते हो और इस बात के लिए तैयार रहते हो कि पैसे गँवाने भी पड़ सकते हैं। क्यों? है न?"

"हाँ!" वेद अकीरा के शब्द अंदर ले रहा था। वह सही कह रही थी, पर उसे संदेह ने घेरा, "क्या होगा अगर बात नहीं बनी?"

अकीरा ने वेद की दाढ़ी पर हाथ फेरा, "अगर बात नहीं बनी तो और भी अच्छा।"

"यह भी सही" वेद ने अकीरा का हाथ पकड़ा और अपने गालों पर दबाया। एक सुखद मुसकान के साथ कहा, "ठीक है फिर, मेरी तरफ से हाँ।"

अकीरा संपूर्ण आश्चर्य से वेद को ताक रही थी। "वाह! तुम-हम अबसे डेटिंग करेंगे?" वेद ने अनिश्चितता दिखाते हुए कहा।

"हाँऽऽऽऽ।" अकीरा धीरे से कान में बोली। वह अभी विश्वास ही नहीं कर पा रही थी कि उसे डेट करने के लिए वेद राजी हो गया है।

"ये तो आसान था···" वेद विस्मित, निश्चिंत, खुश, फिर भी इतना डरा हुआ दिख

रहा था कि अकीरा को हँसी आ गई। "और फिर भी तुम्हें ये करने में 29 वर्ष लग गए।"

वेद पलटकर बोला, "क्योंकि तुम्हें मुझसे मिलने में 29 वर्ष लगे।"

अकीरा की मानो कुछ क्षणों के लिए धड़कन रुक गई। "कितने प्यारे हो तुम!"

फिर जीत की खुशी मनाते हुए बोला, "मुझे माँ के चेहरे पर खुशी देखनी है, जब उन्हें पता चलेगा कि मैंने जो कहा, वह किया।"

"क्या कहा था?" उसने पूछा।

"दुलहन तो नहीं, हाँ, एक गर्लफ्रेंड जरूर ढूँढ़ ली है मैंने। और वो भी दिए गए समय में। मैं मूर्खोंवाली चुनौती जीत गया।"

"सचमुच तुम जीते?" अकीरा ने शुरू ही किया था कि वेद ने बीच में बात काट दी।

"ऐसे मत बोलो, मैंने चुनौती जीतने के लिए तुम्हें 'हाँ' नहीं कहा। माँ ने तो वाशरूम की घटना के बाद आशा की भी नहीं, लेकिन धन्यवाद उस 'कॉफी चोर' का कि आज मैं यह दिन देख पाया।"

शर्मिंदगी से अकीरा ने मुँह नीचे कर लिया। ये कॉफी चुराने की बात उसे कभी भूलने नहीं देगा। उसे अचानक कुछ याद आया। उसने संदेह से वेद की ओर देखा और पूछा, "तुम मोहित के वकील को देख बनावटी हँसी क्यों हँसे? तुमने ऐसी दलील दी कि वह चुप हो गया था, नहीं?"

शर्मिंदगी से अकीरा ने मुँह नीचे कर लिया। ये कॉफी चुराने की बात उसे कभी भूलने नहीं देगा। उसे अचानक कुछ याद आया। उसने संदेह से वेद की ओर देखा और पूछा, "तुम मोहित के वकील को देख बनावटी हँसी क्यों हँसे? तुमने ऐसी दलील दी कि वह चुप हो गया था, नहीं?" "ओह! इसका मतलब यह समझूँ कि तुम मुझे ही घूर रही थी?" वेद ने मजाक उड़ाया।

"ओह! इसका मतलब यह समझूँ कि तुम मुझे ही घूर रही थी?" वेद ने मजाक उड़ाया।

"हो सकता है" अकीरा मुसकराकर बोली।

"जैसे अभी देख रही हो।"

कुछ क्षणों के लिए दोनों एक-दूसरे को दुनिया से बेखबर ताकते रहे। अकीरा को लग रहा था कि तेज धड़कनों के कारण उसका सीना कहीं फट न जाए! धीरे से दोनों पास आए। अकीरा के होंठ बहुत ही तन्मयता और भावों सहित वेद के होंठों पर थे। उस क्षण का मजा लेने में दोनों की आँखें बंद थीं। होंठ एक-दूसरे से सिल गए थे। अकीरा के स्थूल और वेद के पतले होंठ मिले थे कि सहसा अकीरा ने खुद को पीछे किया और जोर-जोर से हँसने लगी।

वेद दुविधा और हैरानी से उसे देख रहा था। एक क्षण पहले वे प्रेम ज्ञापन में थे और

अगले ही क्षण अकीरा हँस रही थी।" वेद बोला, "क्या तुम्हें याद है मैंने एक बार कहा था कि तुम वनिला फ्लेवर इनसान हो? वाकई तुम्हारा स्वाद वैसा ही है।" अकीरा ने कहा।

वेद ने अपना सिर पकड़ लिया। उफ्फ! मेरी माँ और उसकी वनिला आइसक्रीम ने कितने भावुक और अच्छे क्षण खराब कर दिए थे। कितनी मुश्किल से इतना अच्छा समय आया था कि भाग्य ने साथ दिया था।

"अकीरा! ये मेरा पहला 'किस' था।" वेद की प्रतिक्रिया से अकीरा को और भी हँसी आ गई। वेद ने शेखी बघारते हुए कहा, "कल्पना करो, मैं अपने पोते-पोतियों को क्या बताऊँगा कि जब मैंने पहली बार 'किस' किया तो मेरी गर्लफ्रेंड ने कहा कि मेरा स्वाद वनिला आइसक्रीम जैसा है?"

"अकीरा! ये मेरा पहला 'किस' था।" वेद की प्रतिक्रिया से अकीरा को और भी हँसी आ गई। वेद ने शेखी बघारते हुए कहा, "कल्पना करो, मैं अपने पोते-पोतियों को क्या बताऊँगा कि जब मैंने पहली बार 'किस' किया तो मेरी गर्लफ्रेंड ने कहा कि मेरा स्वाद वनिला आइसक्रीम जैसा है?"

अकीरा मुँह दबाकर हँसी और उसने वेद को अपनी ओर खींचा। वह थोड़ा सा शांत हुआ।

अकीरा मुँह दबाकर हँसी और उसने वेद को अपनी ओर खींचा। वह थोड़ा सा शांत हुआ।

"नहीं।" उसने रुखाई से कहा और वेद के माथे पर अपने होंठ रख दिए। "तुम अपने पोते-पोतियों को बताना कि किस प्रकार तुम्हारी गर्लफ्रेंड ने सबसे पहले तुम्हारा माथा चूमा!"

जैसे ही अकीरा के कोमल होंठ उसकी आँखों की तरफ आ रहे थे, वेद की साँसें रुक-सी गईं। अकीरा ने अपने होंठ वेद की आँखों पर रखे और धीरे से चूमा। "तुम उन्हें बताना कि उसने किस तरह से आँखें चूमीं।"

वेद की नसों में लहर दौड़ गई। फिर अकीरा ने वेद के होंठों पर अपने होंठ रख दिए। "और फिर बताना कि कैसे उसने तुम्हारे होंठों पर कब्जा किया।"

"ओऽऽऽह!" वेद चीखा। अकीरा को उसकी चीख एक काँच पर पत्थर के रगड़ खाने जैसी लगी। फिर उसके दिल की धड़कनें बढ़ गईं और वह सोचने लगी कि क्या उसका प्रेम व चुंबन इतना बुरा था कि वेद को चीखना पड़ा? उसने देखा, वेद ने अपनी सीधे हाथ की कलाई पकड़ी और उसे बहुत दर्द हो रहा है।

"ये क्या बदतमीजी है?" वह झगड़े के स्वर में वेद से बोली, लेकिन वेद मानो हाँफते हुए किसी को देख रहा था। जैसे ही अकीरा ने अपना सिर ऊपर किया तो देखा, एक पुलिसवाला चमकीली, लेकिन गुस्से भरी आँखों से उन्हें देख रहा था।

"सार्वजनिक जगह पर 'चूम-वूम'?" पुलिसवाला चिल्लाया और जोर से डंडा सीमेंट की पुलिया पर दे मारा। "बदतमीज! ठहरो! मैं तुम्हें दिखाता हूँ कि मैं क्या कर सकता हूँ। सारी लैला-मजनूगीरी नहीं निकाल दी तो मेरा नाम बदल देना।"

अकीरा ने सिर पकड़ लिया। वेद ने अपना हाथ पकड़ा और दोनों ने एक-दूसरे को देखा और फिर चिल्लाए, "नहीं, अब दुबारा नहीं।"

□

18

वेदिका चिढ़ी हुई-सी वेद का कमरा खोलकर अंदर गई। अकीरा पीछे-पीछे आई। जाहिर है, दोनों की रुचि का विषय एक ही था, जो बिस्तर पर बैठकर, दरवाजे की तरफ पीठ करके पैरों के बीच कुछ कर रहा था। जब से अकीरा को लुधियाना से फोन आया था, तब से वह वेद से मिलना चाह रही थी। अब, जब वह कमरे में आई तो वेद को ऐसे देखने की उम्मीद नहीं की थी।

अकीरा सदमे में आ गई, "वेद क्याऽऽऽऽऽऽऽऽऽऽ कर रहा है?" (आश्चर्य से)

"क्या वह वही कर रहा है, जो मैं सोच रही हूँ?" हैरानी से वेदिका बोली।

दरवाजा खुला, टी.वी. पर 'बिजनेस न्यूज' ही उससे ये सब करवाती है? हैरानी से।

अकीरा ने झटके से वेदिका से कहा, "चुप रहो।" और दोनों दबे पाँव, झुकी हुईं, धीरे-धीरे से गईं और चैन की साँस ली, जब उन्होंने देखा कि वेद असल में कर क्या रहा है?

वेदिका ने साँस छोड़ते हुए कहा, "तुम पैर के नाखून काट रहे हो?"

वेद ने झटके से ऊपर देखा तो अकीरा को देख हैरान और खुश हुआ।

"ओह! हेऽऽऽऽऽअकीराऽऽऽ।" बड़ी सी हँसी और खुशी से वेद बोला। वेदिका की ओर देखकर वेद बोला, "स्वच्छता जरूरी है, इसलिए जरूरी है कि समय से नाखून काटे जाएँ, वेदिका!" स्वर गंभीर था।

वेदिका उचककर बिस्तर पर बैठी और बोली, "मानती हूँ, लेकिन अगली बार जब तुम यह करो तो दरवाजे की तरफ मुँह करके बैठना। प्लीज!"

"क्यों?"

"ऐसे ही! अब चूँकि तुम्हारी गर्लफ्रेंड आई है तो प्यार से उससे मिलोगे नहीं?" वेदिका ने मुसकराकर कहा।

उसने चिढ़कर वेदिका की ओर देखा, लेकिन उसे अहसास था कि उसका परिवार जैसा भी है, उसका अच्छा ही चाहता है और उसका भाग्य अच्छा है कि अकीरा मिली। यह सब सोचते हुए वह अकीरा की ओर मुड़ा और उसे पास आने का इशारा किया।

उसने वेद की उँगलियाँ पकड़ीं और बाजुओं में समाते हुए धीरे से कान में बोली, "हैलो! मुझे तुम्हें कुछ जरूरी बात बतानी है, अकेले में।"

"ठीक है ब्यूटीफुल!" और अकीरा को अपनी बाँहों में समेट लिया।

ऐसा सुनकर शरमाते हुए वेद के गले के पास झुक गई और बोली, "तुम भी न!" ये अकीरा नहीं थी। कुछ अलग-सा व्यवहार था।

धीरे से हँसते हुए वेद ने अकीरा को छोड़ दिया और वेदिका की ओर गरदन करते हुए बोला, "वेदिका, मेरी प्यारी बहन, क्या तुम बाहर के कमरे में सभी को बुला सकती हो? मैं और अकीरा बस अभी आते हैं।"

भौहें चढ़ाते हुए वेदिका बोली, "क्यों?"

"चूँकि हमारी डेटिंग का समय आज से औपचारिक रूप से शुरू होनेवाला है तो मैं कुछ नियम पहले ही सबको बता देना चाहता हूँ।"

"ठीक है, अगर तुम कहते हो तो..." ऐसा कहते हुए वेदिका ने अपनी जींस की जेब से फोन निकाला। पिंकी को फोन लगाया..."मॉम! कृपया डैड के साथ बाहर के कमरे में आ जाइए। श्री वेद अरोरा मासिक सभा के लिए अभी सबसे मिलना चाहते हैं, बस, इतना ही। ओवर एंड आउट।"

"ठीक है, अगर तुम कहते हो तो..." ऐसा कहते हुए वेदिका ने अपनी जींस की जेब से फोन निकाला। पिंकी को फोन लगाया..."मॉम! कृपया डैड के साथ बाहर के कमरे में आ जाइए। श्री वेद अरोरा मासिक सभा के लिए अभी सबसे मिलना चाहते हैं, बस, इतना ही। ओवर एंड आउट।" अत्यंत आत्मसंतुष्टि से वेदिका हँसकर बोली, "लो हो गया तुम्हारा काम।"

अत्यंत आत्मसंतुष्टि से वेदिका हँसकर बोली, "लो हो गया तुम्हारा काम।"

त्यौरियाँ चढ़ाकर वेद बोला, "मुझे एकांत चाहिए। इशारा समझो।"

"ठीक है।" वेद की दाढ़ी पर हाथ रखकर उसे शांत करते हुए अकीरा बोली। "कोई बात नहीं, क्या हम तुम्हारी इस पारिवारिक सभा के बाद बात कर सकते हैं?"

"बिल्कुल।" यह कहते हुए वेद दोनों को कमरे से बाहर ले गया। माता-पिता दोनों पहले से ही बाहर के कमरे में इंतजार कर रहे थे। अकीरा ने गले लगकर उनका अभिवादन किया। वेदिका ने कबीर को वीडियो कॉल किया, ताकि वह भी परिवार का हिस्सा बन सके और मजे के क्षण छूट न जाएँ।

वेद बीच में खड़े होकर बोलने लगा, "जैसा कि हम सब जानते हैं कि मैं और अकीरा दोस्त बन गए हैं और साथ घूमने-फिरने जाते हैं (डेट पर)।"

"वूहूऽऽऽऽऽ!" (प्रसन्नता से) वेदिका चिल्लाई और पिंकी ने तालियाँ बजाईं। इससे अकीरा को हँसी आ गई। माहौल प्यारा-सा हो गया था। वेद ने भी दोनों हाथ

उठाकर खुशी जाहिर की। “येऽऽऽवूऽऽहूऽऽऽऽ।” फिर उसके स्वर में गंभीरता आ गई। “लेकिन जैसा कि हम सब मानते हैं कि अरोरा परिवार में विचित्र, दखलअंदाजी करने के लिए एकांत की कोई परवाह और इज्जत नहीं है…”

“बिल्कुल सही।” अविनाश ने वेद के अरोरा परिवार के विरुद्ध राग अलापने का विरोध करते हुए कहा। “वैसे ही जैसे तुमने अपनी इस सदी की सभा के लिए मेरी और तुम्हारी माँ के एकांतवास की इज्जत करना जरूरी नहीं समझा।”

“अविनाश!” पिंकी ने एक मुक्का अविनाश की बाजू पर मारा। अकीरा और वेदिका ने अपनी हँसी दबाई और एक-दूसरे की ओर देखा।

“और हमारे परिवार में सोच-समझकर बोलनेवालों की भी कमी है, क्योंकि हम जो चाहें, जहाँ चाहें बोल देते हैं।” वेद त्यौरियाँ चढ़ाकर बोलता रहा। “इसलिए भविष्य में हमारे डेटिंग काल के दौरान शर्मिंदगी और भावी आपदाओं से बचाव के लिए मैंने कुछ मूलभूत नियम बनाए हैं, जो हरेक पर लागू होंगे और हरेक को उनका पालन करना है।”

“और हमारे परिवार में सोच-समझकर बोलनेवालों की भी कमी है, क्योंकि हम जो चाहें, जहाँ चाहें बोल देते हैं।” वेद त्यौरियाँ चढ़ाकर बोलता रहा। “इसलिए भविष्य में हमारे डेटिंग काल के दौरान शर्मिंदगी और भावी आपदाओं से बचाव के लिए मैंने कुछ मूलभूत नियम बनाए हैं, जो हरेक पर लागू होंगे और हरेक को उनका पालन करना है।”

वेदिका ने प्रतिकार करते हुए कहा, “और तुमने कैसे सोच लिया कि हम उन नियमों का पालन करेंगे?”

“क्योंकि वेदिका, यदि नहीं करेंगे तो मैं शायद कबीर की बाँहों में कुँवारा ही मर जाऊँगा और तुम मुझे गंगाजल पीने को कहोगी।”

“वेद! क्या बेकार की बात कर रहे हो?” वेदिका ने गुस्से में टोककर कहा।

वेदिका ने एक छोटा तकिया वेद की ओर फेंका और बोली, “बकवास करोगे तो मार ही खाओगे।”

“ठीक है।” वेद हँसते हुए बोला, “नियम कुछ इस प्रकार हैं…”

“वेद!” अकीरा ने परेशान होकर बीच में टोकते हुए कहा, “इससे पहले कि तुम बोलना शुरू करो, मैं एक खबर सुना दूँ आप सबको।”

“वाऽऽऽऽऽऽह! बताओ?” वेद सोफे पर बैठ गया।

“पिंकी आंटी!” अकीरा पिंकी की तरफ मुड़कर बोली, “क्या आपने किसी को मेरे बारे में बताया या किसी को पता है कि मैं वेडिंग प्लानर (शादियों की प्रबंधक) हूँ?”

पिंकी ने धीरे से कंधे उचकाते हुए कहा, “सिर्फ मेरी सहेलियों को। क्यों?”

मुश्किल से निगलते हुए अकीरा बोली, "कल रात कोई नीलू आहलूवालिया ने मुझे फोन किया। उनके बेटे की शादी होनेवाली है।"

"क्याऽऽऽ! अभय की शादी होनेवाली है? कमीनी! नीलू ने मुझे कभी नहीं कहा। उसके पास यह बताने के लिए समय है कि दिन में कितनी बार चीनी खाई, पर यह बताने के लिए समय नहीं है।"

वेदिका ने मजाक उड़ाते हुए कहा, "वो इसलिए, क्योंकि आपके प्यारे बेटे की अभी शादी नहीं हुई है और उन्हें लगता है कि आपको ईर्ष्या होगी।"

पिंकी ने भी मजाक का जवाब उसी स्वर में देते हुए कहा, "इसीलिए मैंने, यही वजह थी कि मैंने अकीरा और वेद की फोटो हर ग्रुप पर डाल दी।"

वेदिका ने मजाक उड़ाते हुए कहा, "वो इसलिए, क्योंकि आपके प्यारे बेटे की अभी शादी नहीं हुई है और उन्हें लगता है कि आपको ईर्ष्या होगी।"

पिंकी ने भी मजाक का जवाब उसी स्वर में देते हुए कहा, "इसीलिए मैंने, यही वजह थी कि मैंने अकीरा और वेद की फोटो हर ग्रुप पर डाल दी।"

यह कहकर पिंकी ने अपने मोबाइल पर एक फोटो निकाली। "यह फोटो मैंने कल रात के खाने पर खींची थी। कितने प्यारे और आकर्षक लग रहे हैं दोनों!"

वेद ने घुरघुराते हुए कहा, "आपने ऐसा क्यों किया?"

अकीरा ने ध्यान आकर्षित करने के लिए खराश की, "प्लीज, ध्यान इधर दो, एक समस्या है।"

"माफ करना, पर धोखेबाज नीलू ने तुम्हें क्या बताया?" पिंकी ने दाँतों के बीच जीभ रखते हुए कहा।

अकीरा मुँह का पानी गटकते हुए बोली, "वो चाहती है, उसके बेटे की शादी का सारा इंतजाम मैं करूँ!"

"वाह! ये तो बहुत अच्छी बात है अकीरा!" वेद उत्साह से बोला। "इसमें दिक्कत क्या है?"

माथा खुजाते हुए अकीरा बोली, "शादी लुधियाना में है।"

□

19

"क्याऽऽऽऽ?" अविश्वसनीय स्वर में वेद बोला। पहले तो वेद को लगा कि यह अकीरा और उसके परिवार की मिलीभगत है और मजाक है, लेकिन अकीरा गंभीर थी। वेद का दिल ही बैठ गया, वो भी मानो पेट तक जाकर। उसका दिल डूबा जा रहा था, मानो पैरों तले नरक की यातनाएँ हों! उसे समझ नहीं आ रहा था।

'कहने से पहले सोचो।' वेद के मन ने उसे याद दिलाया और वेद अपने कमरे की ओर चल पड़ा।

पिंकी ने रोनी सूरत बनाकर कहा, "मेरा बेटा भी कैसा है, उफ्फ!" कुछ समय बाद वेद कमरे में वापस आया और कुछ चीजों से लैस था। वेदिका हँसने लगी, "ये क्या है?"

"एक कागज का थैला और स्ट्रैस बॉल (चिंता मिटाने के लिए पकड़ी जानेवाली गेंद, जो नसों के लिए अच्छी होती है), जिससे कि मुझे कोई दौरा न पड़े, क्योंकि अकीरा कुछ और भी बतानेवाली होगी।

"मैं दुबारा कहती हूँ! हे भगवान्। कैसा बेटा है मेरा?" पिंकी उदासी से धीरे-धीरे बुदबुदाईं।

अविनाश मुँह दबाकर हँसा और बोला, "ड्रामेबाज! मानो चाहे न मानो, पर तुम लुधियाना के लोगों में बिल्कुल फिट (जँचोगे) बैठोगे।"

"अकीरा!" वेद गुस्से में आ गया। "प्लीज बताओ।"

उसने बहुत कोशिश की कि वह न हँसे। "लुधियाना में 20 दिन बाद शादी है। उन्होंने मुझसे इसलिए संपर्क किया, क्योंकि उन्होंने जो पहले प्रबंधक रखा था, वह भाग गया।"

"तो तुमने 'हाँ' कह दिया?" 'हाँ' उत्तर की उम्मीद के डर में वेद ने आँखें चौड़ी करके अकीरा से पूछा।

कमरे में चुप्पी छा गई। अकीरा को वेद की गुस्से भरी आँखें खुद पर महसूस हो रही थीं। उसकी धड़कन बढ़ गई।

"वे बहुत बड़ी रकम देने को तैयार थे, इसलिए…"

"तुम्हारा दिमाग तो नहीं खराब हो गया है?" वेद गुस्से से उबल पड़ा। वह उठा और परेशान होकर सोफे के आसपास घूमने लगा। "तुमने हाँ कह दिया? तुम ऐसे कैसे कह सकती को? ठीक है, तुम्हारे व्यावसायिक निर्णयों पर मुझे प्रश्न करने का कोई हक नहीं, पर अभी यह समय हमारे लिए अत्यंत महत्त्वपूर्ण है। तुम हाँ कहने से पहले एक बार मुझसे बात तो कर सकती थी?"

अकीरा ने अपने स्वर में शांति रखी और कहा, "मुझे माफ करना, पर अगर मैं तुम्हें बताती तो तुम सीधे मना कर देते।"

"ये सिर्फ तुम्हारा निर्णय नहीं हो सकता था। तुम्हें बात समझ आ रही है क्या?" वेद ने कहा, "तुमने कहा था न, किसी भी विषय पर हम दोनों की सहमति आवश्यक है। क्या हुआ उस बात का?"

अकीरा ने अपने स्वर में शांति रखी और कहा, "मुझे माफ करना, पर अगर मैं तुम्हें बताती तो तुम सीधे मना कर देते।" "ये सिर्फ तुम्हारा निर्णय नहीं हो सकता था। तुम्हें बात समझ आ रही है क्या?" वेद ने कहा, "तुमने कहा था न, किसी भी विषय पर हम दोनों की सहमति आवश्यक है। क्या हुआ उस बात का?"

अकीरा ने अपनी आँखें भींच लीं। "मैं सच बोलूँगी। मोहित के कारण मैं अपने काम पर ध्यान नहीं दे पा रही थी। मैं किसी तरह अपना गुजारा कर रही थी। मैंने आधे से ज्यादा कर्मचारियों को काम पर से निकाल दिया था और मेरी आर्थिक स्थिति भी खराब होती जा रही थी। इसीलिए मुझे शादी का यह काम लेना जरूरी था।"

नाराज होकर वेद ने अकीरा को देखा, "क्या होता अगर तुम्हें यह काम (प्रोजेक्ट) नहीं मिलता?"

"लेकिन अब मुझे मिला है तो मैं उसका उपयोग क्यों न करूँ? क्यों मैं इतने अच्छे अवसर को हाथ से जाने दूँ?" अकीरा ने अपनी दलील दी।

वेद जमीन पर पिंकी के बगल में निराशा से बैठ गया। "मेरे पास एक आइडिया (योजना) है।" उत्साह से वेदिका बोली।

वेद जल्दी से उसके पास गया और बोला, "अब तो तुम्हारा आइडिया भी चलेगा।"

वेदिका ने ऐसे किया, मानो जैसे वेद का गला दबा देगी, पर फिर भी उसने तरकीब बताई। "देखो! अकीरा, तुम ऐसा क्यों नहीं कर लेती कि पहले तुम अपना यह काम (प्रोजेक्ट) पूरा कर लो और फिर वह 21 दिनोंवाली डेट पर जाने की योजना बना लो। नहीं? उसके बाद फिर यह समय-सीमा तय कर लेना।"

पहले तो वेद का चेहरा चमका, फिर उदासी से लटक गया; क्योंकि अविनाश ने वेद को याद दिलाया, "अगले महीने मुझे और वेद को मेलबर्न जाना है, क्योंकि जो काम चल रहा है, उसे देखना है और प्रबंध करना है, ताकि काम निकल पड़े। पर तुम्हारा डेटिंग का कार्यक्रम लगातार 21 दिनों का क्यों है ?"

"क्योंकि कोई भी काम लगातार 21 दिनों तक करने पर आदत बन जाती है और ये सलाह अकीरा की थी, मेरी नहीं।" वेद ने अविनाश को बताया।

"अब क्या ?" कबीर के प्रश्न ने पिंकी को हैरत में डाला। वो तकरीबन भूल चुकी थीं कि कबीर भी बातचीत में हिस्सा ले रहा था।

वेद को इस सलाह पर गुस्सा आ गया, "ओय! मैं तुम्हारे साथ सस्ता बैंड बाजा बारात नहीं करनेवाला। ठीक है न! समझ लो!"
पिंकी जोर से हँस पड़ीं। "ओह वेद! कभी-कभी ही सही, पर तुम अच्छा मजाक कर लेते हो।"
लेकिन यह बात कबीर को भा गई और कबीर बोला, "मैं और वेदिका भी साथ चल पड़ते हैं, क्यों ?"

"मैं सोच रही थी···" झिझक से अकीरा ने बोलना शुरू किया। "चूँकि तुमने छुट्टी ले रखी है और हमें साथ में समय बिताना है तो तुम भी मेरे साथ लुधियाना क्यों नहीं चलते ? मेरी भी मदद हो जाएगी !"

वेद को इस सलाह पर गुस्सा आ गया, "ओय ! मैं तुम्हारे साथ सस्ता बैंड बाजा बारात नहीं करनेवाला। ठीक है न ! समझ लो !"

पिंकी जोर से हँस पड़ीं। "ओह वेद ! कभी-कभी ही सही, पर तुम अच्छा मजाक कर लेते हो।"

लेकिन यह बात कबीर को भा गई और कबीर बोला, "मैं और वेदिका भी साथ चल पड़ते हैं, क्यों ?"

"चलो ! हम सभी चलते हैं।" पिंकी ने सपने लेने के स्वर में कहा। "मुझे कितना याद आता है लुधियाना ! हमारी हवेली। वहाँ का खाना। उस शहर की खुशबू।"

"आपको शहर की खुशबू नहीं, वहाँ के पागलपन की खुशबू की याद आती है और आपके परिवार के पागलपन की गंध का तो कोई जवाब ही नहीं।" वेद ने रुखाई से कहा।

"चुप रह !" पिंकी वेद से पलटकर बोलीं।

"हेऽऽऽऽ ! यह कोई छुट्टियाँ मनाने का समय नहीं है।" वेद ने हाथ हवा में घुमाते हुए कहा। "अकीरा ! तुम बिल्कुल नहीं जानती कि लुधियाना कितना झक्की-सा (Crazy) शहर है। तुम्हें क्या लगता है, पहलेवाला शादी का प्रबंधक क्यों भागा होगा ?"

अकीरा परेशान होकर गिड़गिड़ाने लगी, "सही कह रहे हो, मुझे तुमसे पूछना चाहिए था। पर वेद, मैं यह मौका गँवाना नहीं चाहती। प्लीज!"

"नहीं। लुधियाना ने मुझे जख्म दिए हैं।" सोफे पर बैठते हुए वेद ने कहा।

"ओ नौटंकी! जख्म दिए हैं का क्या मतलब? मेरा परिवार बहुत सही है। हाँ। थोड़े अलग हैं, सनकी-से हैं, पर बहुत अच्छे लोग हैं।" पिंकी ने वेद से कहा।

"थोड़े अलग? शेक्सपीयर की अंग्रेजी में उन्हें पागल कहा जा सकता है।" वेद ने उपहास से कहा।

"यार! लोग प्यार के लिए जंग करते हैं, यह तो फिर भी लुधियाना है। इसमें कौन सी बड़ी बात है?" अविनाश ने सवाल किया।

"अब तुम कोई बच्चे थोड़ी न हो, जो परिवार तुम्हें डरा देगा और सदमे पहुँचाएगा। और अगर ऐसा किया भी तो हम तुम्हें इलाज के लिए भेज देंगे बस!"

"हम सब वहाँ तुम्हारे साथ होंगे।" वेदिका ने पटाने की कोशिश की।

"ये खयाल बिल्कुल अच्छा नहीं है वेदिका..." अपना सिर वेदिका के कंधे पर छोड़ते हुए वेद बोला। "ये तो भड़कती आग के पास पेट्रोल ले जाने जैसा है।"

वेद की नौटंकी को भाव न देते हुए अकीरा गिड़गिड़ाई, "प्लीज न! इसके बारे में अच्छे से सोचो, प्लीज! अगर हमने लुधियाना झेल लिया तो समझो सब झेल लिया।"

"यार! लोग प्यार के लिए जंग करते हैं, यह तो फिर भी लुधियाना है। इसमें कौन सी बड़ी बात है?" अविनाश ने सवाल किया।

"अब तुम कोई बच्चे थोड़ी न हो, जो परिवार तुम्हें डरा देगा और सदमे पहुँचाएगा। और अगर ऐसा किया भी तो हम तुम्हें इलाज के लिए भेज देंगे बस!"

"हम सब वहाँ तुम्हारे साथ होंगे।" वेदिका ने पटाने की कोशिश की।

अविनाश वेद की ओर आकर बोला, "तुम दोनों ध्यान से मेरी बात सुनो। खासकर तुम वेद। समझे?"

वेद और अकीरा ने सिर हिलाया। अविनाश मुसकराते हुए वेद से बोला, "तुम्हें अकीरा की खुशी और भविष्य के लिए बहुत सी शंकाओं से उभरना पड़ेगा। कभी वो भी तुम्हारे लिए ऐसा करेगी। रिश्ते ऐसे ही निभाए जाते हैं। गिव एंड टेक होता है। एक हाथ दो, एक हाथ लो, वरना रिश्ते कैसे निभेंगे?"

वेद ने ध्यान से अपने पिता की बात सुनी, पर चुप रहा। अपने बेटे के दिमाग को पढ़ते हुए अविनाश ने आगे कहा, "मैं समझ रहा हूँ कि अकीरा को निर्णय लेने से पहले तुमसे पूछ लेना चाहिए था, पर तुम दोनों के रिश्ते की यह शुरुआत है, तुम दोनों को धीरे-

धीरे एक-दूसरे की पसंद-नापसंद पता चलेगी। इसलिए अकीरा को गलत मत समझो।"

अविनाश की बातें सुनकर अकीरा की आँखें नम हो गईं और उसने अपना सिर नीचे कर लिया, ताकि आँसू छिपा सके। वह अपने बॉयफ्रेंड के परिवार के सामने रोना नहीं चाहती थी।

वेद को ध्यान से देखते हुए अविनाश ने उसे कोहनी मारी, "हाँ?" वेद ने हामी भरी और अविनाश ने उसके हाथ पर थपकी दी।

"रिश्ते जीवनभर की जिम्मेदारी होते हैं। मुझसे पूछो, मैं लुधियाना के एक हिस्से के साथ रहता हूँ।"

"क्या मतलब?" पिंकी ने तीखे स्वर में पूछा।

अविनाश के चेहरे पर हवाइयाँ उड़ने लगीं—"मेरा मतलब है कि मुझे आज भी तुम्हारे बारे में कितनी नई बातें पता चलती हैं, मैं तो मजाक में कह रहा था।"

"मजाक में बोलो तो ही अच्छा होगा।" उसने त्यौरियाँ चढ़ाते हुए अविनाश को घूरा, लेकिन फिर वेद की तरफ पलटकर कहा, "वेद! अविनाश बिल्कुल सही कह रहे हैं। इस बारे में सोचो। यदि ऐसा हो जाए तो बहुत ही अच्छा।"

वेद ने तनाव दूर करनेवाली गेंद हाथ में पकड़ी और उसे जोर से दबाया, फिर अकीरा की ओर देखा। उसके मन ने कहा—'उसके माँ-बाप सही कह रहे हैं। संबंध निभाना आसान नहीं। ऐसा हर रोज नहीं होता कि अकीरा जैसी लड़की किसी की जिंदगी में आती हो और वह भी वेद जैसे के जीवन में! क्या वाकई अकीरा को अपनी जिद की खातिर छोड़ देना ठीक होगा? शायद नहीं।'

"फिर, क्या तुम लुधियाना आ रहे हो?" वेदिका वेद की तरफ लपककर गई और पूछा।

वेद ने बाजू की मेज पर रखी पानी की बोतल उठाई और एक घूँट में पी गया। हाथ की पिछली तरफ से मुँह पोंछते हुए बोता, "हाँ! आ रहा हूँ।"

□

20

'चलो। शुरुआत हुई।' वेद ने सोचा।

पूरा अरोरा परिवार, अकीरा और कबीर सहित, किराए की कार में लुधियाना की तरफ बढ़ रहा था। वेद अपने हमेशा के चिड़चिड़े मिजाज में था, क्यों? क्योंकि वह इस सच्चाई को मानने को तैयार नहीं था कि प्रेम दर्द देता है। कौन सोच सकता था? उसे दोषदर्शी कहा गया। प्रेम? लेकिन अकीरा के साथ के संबंध को अभी प्रेम की संज्ञा देना ठीक नहीं था। लेकिन एक बात स्पष्ट थी कि उसे अकीरा अच्छी लगती थी। यही सोचते हुए, अपना सिर वेद ने हिलाया और सो गया। अकीरा को अपनी राह खोजनी होगी, जो वह कर रही थी। अकीरा पिछली सीट पर वेद के साथ बैठी थी। सड़क भी अच्छी थी और भाग्य से वेदिका ने गाने भी अच्छे लगा रखे थे। लेकिन शायद वहीं अच्छी बात खत्म हो गई।

जैसे ही यात्रा शुरू हुई, बेहूदे चुटकुले, मजाक अकीरा को परेशान करने लगे। शुरू में मजा आया, पर नींद की कमी और भूख के कारण अकीरा अब मजाक और चुटकुलों में मजे नहीं ले पा रही थी।

एक बोर्ड की तरफ इशारा करके कबीर बोला, "क्या ये भाग्य सचमुच 'कुंडली' कहलाता है?

"हाँ। ये ईश्वर का इशारा है। हमें सचमुच अकीरा और वेद की कुंडलियाँ मिलवानी चाहिए।" पिंकी ने अचानक कहा।

"तुम्हारा मतलब मिल गईं।" हँसते हुए अविनाश बोला।

"शायद!" पिंकी ने धीरे से कहा।

"वरना अकीरा पहली रसोई कैसे बनाएगी?" वेदिका ने बीच में कहा।

सभी हँसे, पर अकीरा ने कुंडली का बोर्ड देखा और अजीब सा महसूस किया और मन में सोचने लगी—'अभी तो हम एक भी डेट पर नहीं गए और ये अभी से कुंडलियों के मिलान और शादी की बातें! ये कुछ ज्यादा जल्दी नहीं है?'

अकीरा का पेट भूख से कुलबुला रहा था। उसने वेद की ओर देखा। वह खर्राटे

ले रहा था और इधर से उधर लुढ़क भी रहा था। पिछली सीट पर पूरी तरह मानो उसी का जन्मसिद्ध अधिकार हो। पहली बार उसे वेद से ईर्ष्या हो रही थी। अब वह वेद के परिवार की दशा समझ रही थी कि वेद को क्यों शिकायत होगी, क्योंकि उनके चुटकुले और भी बेहूदे होते जा रहे थे। वह समझ नहीं पा रही थी कि उसका मन उदास है या उसे भूख लग रही है?

"पिंकी, यह वही ढाबा है न, जहाँ हम रुका करते थे?" अविनाश ने पूछा।

"हाँ! वाकई।" पिंकी की आँखों में उत्साह के कारण चमक आ गई।

"चलो, यहीं रुकते हैं, भूख भी लगी है और मेरी पुरानी यादें भी ताजा हो जाएँगी।"

"हाँ-हाँ! चलो रुकते हैं, उम्मीद है कि इनके बगीचे में अब भी वही झूला होगा।" वेदिका बोली।

"ठीक है।" यह कहकर अविनाश ने उस ढाबे पर गाड़ी लगा दी (पार्क कर दी)।

पीछे देखकर पिंकी अकीरा से बोली, "क्या तुम उसे उठाओगी, वह जो सो रहा है?"

"हाँ-हाँ। क्यों नहीं?" अकीरा मुसकराकर बोली।

जब सभी कार से बाहर उतर गए तो अकीरा ने धीरे से वेद को जगाया, "वेद!"

जब वह हिला नहीं तो अकीरा ने थोड़ा और तेजी से हिलाया। वह उठ गया और विक्षिप्तता से उठकर अपनी जगह बैठ गया। जैसे बिल्ली बर्फ के पानी में उछल पड़े। अजीब सी आवाज में उसने पूछा, "क्या हुआ?"

"हाँ! वाकई।" पिंकी की आँखों में उत्साह के कारण चमक आ गई।
"चलो, यहीं रुकते हैं, भूख भी लगी है और मेरी पुरानी यादें भी ताजा हो जाएँगी।"
"हाँ-हाँ! चलो रुकते हैं, उम्मीद है कि इनके बगीचे में अब भी वही झूला होगा।" वेदिका बोली।
"ठीक है।" यह कहकर अविनाश ने उस ढाबे पर गाड़ी लगा दी (पार्क कर दी)।

अकीरा ने होंठ दबाते हुए सोचा, 'ये हमेशा मूर्खों की तरह हरकतें करते हुए क्यों जागता है?' वेद ने आँखें मिचकाईं, खोलीं, बंद कीं, दुबारा मिचकाईं। थोड़े समय के लिए सूरज की रोशनी की वजह से उसे कुछ नहीं दिखाई दिया। उसने दुबारा आँखें मलीं। "हमने अपने डरपोकों की तरह उठने की प्रथा अब भी जारी रखी है।" हँसी दबाते हुए अकीरा बोली।

वेद ने गरदन के नीचे से तकिया हटाय। "मुझे लुधियाना की भीड़ की सोचकर ही बुरे सपने आने लगे थे।"

"तुम्हें ऐसा कहना बंद करना पड़ेगा।"

"जल्दी चलो, इससे पहले कि तुम्हारी मुंबई की भीड़ की कल्पना के घोड़े दौड़ने लगें।"

"ठीक है। वैसे हम हैं कहाँ?" वेद बुदबुदाया।

"तुम्हारे सुनहरे अतीत के किसी ढाबे पर…।"

"हे भगवान्!" इमारत को देखकर वेद ने गहरी साँस ली।

"क्या? अब ये मत कहना कि इस जगह का भी कोई इतिहास है।"

"सिर्फ इतना ही कि यहाँ पर खाने के बाद वेदिका मुझे इतना तेज झुला देती थी कि मैं बीमार हो जाता था। ज्यादा कुछ नहीं…।"

अकीरा हँसी, "तुम्हारे जीवन में कुछ भी औरों जैसा, साधारण क्यों नहीं है?"

"मैं यह प्रश्न रोज पूछता हूँ।" वेद उदासी से बोला। सिर हिलाते हुए वेद के साथ अकीरा ढाबे की ओर चल पड़ी। उन्होंने देखा कि अरोरा परिवार कोने में बैठा है, जहाँ शांति-सी लग रही थी। वेद ने चुपके से ढाबे पर चारों तरफ नजरें घुमाईं। ऐसा लग रहा था मानो वक्त ने एक समय पर बेहतरीन मानी जानेवाली जगह पर कुठाराघात किया है। दीवारों पर से पलस्तर उतर रहा था, मेज हिल रही थी। खैर! उसके परिवार को किसी बात का कोई फर्क नहीं पड़ रहा था और उन्होंने कई तरह के खाने का ऑर्डर दे दिया था।

"मैं यह प्रश्न रोज पूछता हूँ।" वेद उदासी से बोला। सिर हिलाते हुए वेद के साथ अकीरा ढाबे की ओर चल पड़ी। उन्होंने देखा कि अरोरा परिवार कोने में बैठा है, जहाँ शांति-सी लग रही थी। वेद ने चुपके से ढाबे पर चारों तरफ नजरें घुमाईं। ऐसा लग रहा था मानो वक्त ने एक समय पर बेहतरीन मानी जानेवाली जगह पर कुठाराघात किया है।

अकीरा वेद के कान में फुसफुसाई, "इन्होंने आधे पंजाब के लिए ऑर्डर दिया है क्या?"

"हमेशा की तरह…" वेद मुसकराया और अकीरा को खींचता हुआ मेज की तरफ ले गया।

अभी वेद ने मुँह में एक कौर रखा ही था कि वह समझ गया कि खाने में कुछ गलत है, लेकिन सबके मजाक उड़ाने के डर से वह खाता रहा। वह अधमने मन से खाता रहा। अभी आधी रोटी ही खत्म हुई थी कि उसे जोर से खाँसी आने लगी।

"क्या हुआ? थोड़ा पानी पी लो।" अकीरा ने उसकी पीठ पर थपकियाँ देते हुए कहा।

थोड़ा सा पानी पीकर वह बोला, "खाने में तिल है क्या?"

"मुझे तो नजर नहीं आ रहा।" वेदिका ने उसकी तरफ रुमाल बढ़ाया।

पिंकी ने बैरे की खबर ली, "तुमने खाने में तिल का उपयोग किया है क्या ?"

मासूमियत दिखाते हुए बैरा बोला, "नहीं तो।"

"रुको मॉम, कौन से तेल में खाना बनाया है ?" वेद ने पूछा।

बैरे ने इतने प्रश्नों के जवाब से परेशान होकर बता ही दिया, "तिल के तेल में।"

"अच्छा, ठीक है, तुम···जाओ।" वेद ने बैरे को भेज दिया। उसमें शक्ति ही नहीं थी कि वह किसी और बहस में पड़े।

"ओह !" पिंकी की आँखें चौड़ी हो गईं जैसे कि वह सब समझ गई। "अब पता चला कि यहाँ पर खाना खाने के बाद तुम हमेशा बीमार क्यों होते थे ?"

वेद ने आसमान की तरफ देखा और मन में बोला, 'कमाल है, इस ढाबे को भी दुनिया में तिल का तेल ही मिला था, खाना बनाने के लिए, और हमें भी बाकी सारे ढाबे छोड़कर यहीं खाना खाने आना था, जिसके तिल से एलर्जी (तीव्र प्रतिक्रिया) है।' वेद ने धमकाने के, डाँटने के स्वर में माँ से कहा, "वाह मॉम, आपको यह बात पता चलने में 29 वर्ष लग गए ?"

वेद ने आसमान की तरफ देखा और मन में बोला, 'कमाल है, इस ढाबे को भी दुनिया में तिल का तेल ही मिला था, खाना बनाने के लिए, और हमें भी बाकी सारे ढाबे छोड़कर यहीं खाना खाने आना था, जिसके तिल से एलर्जी (तीव्र प्रतिक्रिया) है।' वेद ने धमकाने के, डाँटने के स्वर में माँ से कहा, "वाह मॉम, आपको यह बात पता चलने में 29 वर्ष लग गए ?"

"सॉरी।" पिंकी ने माफी माँगते हुए कहा, "बताओ तो मुझे कैसे पता चलता ? अभी चार साल पहले ही तो तुम्हारी इस एलर्जी के बारे में पता चला।"

वेदिका ने सहानुभूति से कहा, "तुम्हारा चेहरा लाल हो रहा है।"

"अरे, आप सब लोग इतने शांत कैसे हैं ? मैं एंबुलेंस बुलाऊँ क्या वेद ?" अकीरा घबराते हुए बोली।

"चिंता मत करो। तिल खाते ही यह थोड़ी देर के लिए लाल हो जाता है। एलर्जी हलकी है। थोड़ी देर में ठीक हो जाएगा।"

"हाँ।" कबीर हँसते हुए बोला, "अभी आपने बदमिजाज वेद को पॉकिमॉन की तरह अपने सही रूप में विकसित होते हुए देखा।" उसने अपने परिवार को घूरकर देखा। अकीरा समेत सभी उसे चिढ़ा रहे थे। वह भाग जाना चाहता था। "मेरी दवाई मेरे बैग (थैले) में है···।" यह कहता हुआ वेद ढाबे से बाहर निकला।

"वेद !" अकीरा भी उठ खड़ी हुई, "आप सभी खाना खाइए, मैं वेद के साथ जाकर बैठती हूँ।"

यह समझते हुए कि अकीरा अकेले में वेद के साथ कुछ समय बिताना चाहती है, वे मुसकराए। कबीर ने चुटकी लेते हुए आँख मारी और कहा, "ठीक है! मैं तुम दोनों के लिए कुछ ऐसा भिजवाता हूँ, जिसमें तिल न हो।"

हामी भरते हुए अकीरा गाड़ी के पास चली। वेद ने पूछा, "क्या हुआ ?"

अकीरा ने एक हाथ से उसे करीब लेते हुए कहा, "मैं तुम्हें देखने आई थी और जब तुमने खाना नहीं खाया तो मैं कैसे खा सकती हूँ ?"

वेद को बात कुछ धुँधली-सी और संदेहास्पद-सी लगी। अकीरा को पता था कि क्या कहने पर वेद का दिल पिघल जाएगा। और उसके वो पैंतरे काम भी कर रहे थे, लेकिन सिर्फ थोड़ा सा। अकीरा को इस लुधियाना यात्रा की वजह से बहुत मेहनत करनी पड़नेवाली थी। अर्थात् वेद चूँकि लुधियाना उसके कहने पर गया था तो जाहिर है, अकीरा को बहुत सी बातों का ध्यान रखना जरूरी था। "मेरा खयाल है अंदर बहुत सा मक्खन है...तुम्हारे मुँह से और मक्खन नहीं चाहिए। मैं तुमसे अभी भी नाराज हूँ।" वेद की आवाज में तलखी थी। "मैंने ऐसे ही कहा।"

वेद को बात कुछ धुँधली-सी और संदेहास्पद-सी लगी। अकीरा को पता था कि क्या कहने पर वेद का दिल पिघल जाएगा। और उसके वो पैंतरे काम भी कर रहे थे, लेकिन सिर्फ थोड़ा सा। अकीरा को इस लुधियाना यात्रा की वजह से बहुत मेहनत करनी पड़नेवाली थी। अर्थात् वेद चूँकि लुधियाना उसके कहने पर गया था तो जाहिर है, अकीरा को बहुत सी बातों का ध्यान रखना जरूरी था।

"हाँ, पता है मुझे। इसका सिला मैं तुम्हें अच्छा ही दूँगी।" अकीरा ने वेद की नाक पर प्यार से उँगली मारते हुए कहा। "अब तुम ठीक हो? डॉक्टर तो नहीं चाहिए न अब ?"

"मैं अब ठीक हूँ। एलर्जी ठीक करने की दवा ले ली है मैंने।"

"ठीक है।"

अकीरा ने वेद को कुछ कुकीज (बिस्किट) देते हुए कहा, "कुछ कुकीज लोगे ?"

"शुक्रिया।" एक उठाते हुए वेद बोला। अकीरा ने अपनी भौंहों से पसीना पोंछते हुए कहा, "तुम सही कह रहे थे, मुझे इयरप्लग्स की जरूरत है।"

वेद जोर का ठहाका मारकर हँसते हुए बोला, "मैं बताऊँ ? उन्होंने जरूर कुंडली गाँव के बारे में बात की होगी; वेदिका ने मुरथल के खाने की कल्पना की होगी; और रसोई ? और क्याऽऽऽऽ ? सही न ?"

"हाँ!" अकीरा ने आँखें चौड़ी करके कहा, "तुम्हें कैसे पता ?" वेद शैतानों वाली हँसी हँसते हुए बोला, "अभी रुको!"

"किंगकॉन्ग वाटर पार्क आने दो, फिर देखना वेदिका क्या कहती है, वही जोक कि यह वेद का पार्क है। फिर वह बेहूदे गाने चलाएगी। हमारी लुधियाना को जाने की सैर इद-शिरेन के गानों से हुई, लेकिन अंत बेकार भोजपुरी गानों से होगा।"

"शिट् (बकवास)।"

"तुम्हें पता चलेगा कि यह यात्रा और रास्ता कितना बेकार है और लुधियाना उस पागलपन का गंतव्य स्थान।" वेद ने एक तरह से घोषित कर दिया।

किसी ने कार की खिड़की पर दस्तक दी। वह ढाबे का बैरा था। वह छोटा बच्चा हँसा और एक प्लेट आगे कर दी। "अंदर बैठे लोगों ने सैंडविच भेजा है। आप भाग्यशाली हैं, यह आखिरी सैंडविच था। अब और ब्रेड नहीं है हमारे पास।"

अकीरा उसकी सच्चाई पर हँसी, "शुक्रिया।"

"वाह! कबीर ने अपनी बात पूरी की।" अकीरा बोली। "छोटी-छोटी कृपा।"

"वाकई छोटी-छोटी कृपा। चियर्स", वेद बोला और एक टुकड़ा उठा लिया। जिस तरह से अकीरा भूख के कारण फटाफट सैंडविच खा रही थी, वेद ने उसे रोका नहीं और कुकीज का पैकेट उठाते हुए कहा, "मुझे कुकीज ज्यादा पसंद आई।"

"अच्छा!" अकीरा को लगा कि वेद व्यंग्य से बोला, "ठीक है।" अकीरा मुसकराई। वेद को अच्छा लगा कि वह जो कर रहा है, अकीरा को समझ नहीं आ रहा।

"वाह! कबीर ने अपनी बात पूरी की।" अकीरा बोली। "छोटी-छोटी कृपा।" "वाकई छोटी-छोटी कृपा। चियर्स", वेद बोला और एक टुकड़ा उठा लिया। जिस तरह से अकीरा भूख के कारण फटाफट सैंडविच खा रही थी, वेद ने उसे रोका नहीं और कुकीज का पैकेट उठाते हुए कहा, "मुझे कुकीज ज्यादा पसंद आई।"

"तुम्हें पता कैसा लग रहा है?" मुसकराते हुए अकीरा ने कहा। "जैसे हम डेट पर हों।"

सिर उदासी से झुकाते हुए वेद बोला, "नहीं यार! मैंने इससे भी कई गुना अच्छी डेट की कल्पना की थी।"

"इससे क्या फर्क पड़ता है? हम यहाँ पर साथ हैं, हालाँकि तुम टमाटर जैसे दिख रहे हो, लेकिन हो प्यारे टमाटर!"

अकीरा ने प्यार से वेद के गाल पर हाथ रखकर सांत्वना दी।

"रहने दो।" पीछे होकर, लेकिन हँसते हुए वेद ने प्रतिक्रिया दी।

"तुम हँस रहे हो, मुझसे बात कर रहे हो और क्या चाहिए अभी?" अकीरा ने कहा।

"यह एक नजरिया है देखने का···" वेद चिढ़ाते हुए बोला।

"न! एक यही नजरिया है देखने का।"

अकीरा ने वेद को अपनी ओर खींचते हुए कहा।

"तो! खुश हो अपनी पहली डेट पर?" सिर पर प्यार से अकीरा के बालों में हाथ फेरते हुए वेद ने पूछा।

जैसे ही अकीरा ने लुधियाना की प्रसिद्ध हवेलियों में कदम रखा, वैसे ही हिंदी सिनेमा के प्रति उसका सम्मान बढ़ गया। औरों की तरह वह भी यह समझती थी कि इन हवेलियों की भव्यता के बारे में हिंदी सिनेमा में अतिशयोक्ति होती है, पर अकीरा को अपनी धारणा ठीक करनी पड़ी।

सबसे पहले वेद की दोनों तरफ की दादी और नानी ने उनका स्वागत किया। वे दोनों बहुत ही शानदार तरीके से तैयार हुई थीं, बालों से लेकर जूतियों तक, सबकुछ व्यवस्थित था। उन्होंने पूरे परिवार को पाला-पोसा था। फिर बाकी सदस्य भी आए। प्रेम से मिले, गले मिले, बहुतों को आशीर्वाद के लिए माथे पर चूमा, पैरी पौना आदि। रॉकेट को छोड़ने की शक्ति से भी ज्यादा शक्ति और ऊर्जा वहाँ पर महसूस हो रही थी।

सबसे पहले वेद की दोनों तरफ की दादी और नानी ने उनका स्वागत किया। वे दोनों बहुत ही शानदार तरीके से तैयार हुई थीं, बालों से लेकर जूतियों तक, सबकुछ व्यवस्थित था। उन्होंने पूरे परिवार को पाला-पोसा था। फिर बाकी सदस्य भी आए। प्रेम से मिले, गले मिले, बहुतों को आशीर्वाद के लिए माथे पर चूमा, पैरी पौना आदि।

उन्हें फिर हवेली के अंदर ले जाया गया। वह लोगों से खचाखच भरी हुई थी। अकीरा को लगा कि यदि छत पर लगे झूमर पर जगह होती, तो वहाँ भी लोग होते। खाना, मदिरा और हँसी के ठहाके थे। अकीरा रुक नहीं पाई और चुपके से एक समोसा लिया। वह वेद को देख रही थी। उसकी आँखें चमकीली, किंतु भावशून्य सी लग रही थीं।

"तुम ठीक हो?" तुम ऐसे लग रहे हो मानो पीले पड़ गए हो।" अकीरा ने कहा।

"मैं यह देख रहा हूँ कि मुझ पर सबसे पहले किसका ध्यान जाता है? मुझे लग रहा है दादी होंगी।"

"देखते हैं!" बनावटी हँसी से अकीरा बोली। " कम-से-कम कौन-कौन हैं? ये तो बता दो, क्योंकि ऐसा लग रहा है कि लुधियाना की आधी से ज्यादा जनता इस हवेली में आ गई है।"

वेद थोड़ा सा अकीरा के नजदीक आया, "वो जो नीली कमीज में दिख रहे हैं न, वे प्रणव मामा हैं। वे मॉम के बड़े भाई हैं। उनकी बगल में उनकी पत्नी हैं, रोशनी मामी।

वो सिरदर्द का मनुष्य रूप हैं और लुधियाना की निर्विवाद पंचायती रानी हैं, जो अफवाहें उड़ाने और बेकार की गपशप करने के लिए प्रसिद्ध हैं।"

"अच्छा।" गंभीरता से अकीरा बोली, "फिर?"

"उनका एक बेटा है, राजवीर। वह कनाडा भाग गया। उसने बिल्कुल ठीक किया, ऐसा मेरा मानना है।" वेद ने अकीरा को बताया। अकीरा ने अपनी हँसी दबाई। "और वो जो अलमारी के पास खड़ा दिखाई दे रहा है न! वो इनका दामाद है, निरंजन। और उसे जिस बच्चे ने पकड़ रखा है, वह उनका बेटा है, आदित्य। और वो रही प्रणव मामा की बेटी और आदित्य की माँ। साँस थामे सुनो। उसका नाम है, प्रणवी।"

"उनका एक बेटा है, राजवीर। वह कनाडा भाग गया। उसने बिल्कुल ठीक किया, ऐसा मेरा मानना है।" वेद ने अकीरा को बताया। अकीरा ने अपनी हँसी दबाई। "और वो जो अलमारी के पास खड़ा दिखाई दे रहा है न! वो इनका दामाद है, निरंजन। और उसे जिस बच्चे ने पकड़ रखा है, वह उनका बेटा है, आदित्य।

अकीरा ने अपना मुँह और भी जोर से हाथ से दबाया, वह बिल्कुल हँसना नहीं चाहती थी।

उपहास करते हुए वेद बोला, "वैसे ही जैसे वेद और वेदिका। आलस्य खानदान में चला आ रहा है।"

"ठीक है। आगे बताओ।" अकीरा ने खुद को शांत करने के लिए गहरी साँस ली।

"उनके बगल में हैं, प्रमोद मामा। उन्हें घोड़ों का शौक है।"

"ये क्या बतानेवाली बात हुई वेद?" अकीरा मुँह बनाते हुए बोली।

"मैंने इनको घोड़ों के अलावा किसी और विषय पर कभी बात करते नहीं सुना।" वेद ने सफाई देते हुए कहा।

"उनके बगल में हैं, उनकी बीवी, शालिनी। उन्हें छोले-भटूरे बहुत पसंद हैं।"

"उफ्फ! तुम यह सब जानबूझकर बता रहे हो, ताकि मैं हँसूँ।"

"क्या? ऐसा नहीं है। वे छोले-भटूरे इतना पसंद करती हैं कि उन्होंने एक रेस्तराँ खोला है, जहाँ सिर्फ छोले-भटूरे बिकते हैं।"

"ठीक है।" वेद बोला। "उनकी एक बेटी है, जिसका नाम है, ट्विंकल।"

अकीरा ने भौंहें चढ़ाईं। वेद ने तेवर दिखाते हुए कहा, "नाम सुनकर ये भाव हैं?"

अकीरा ने भी चिढ़कर वेद की ओर देखा "नहीं! मुझे ट्विंकल के बारे में कुछ बताओ वेद!"

"मुझे उसके बारे में कुछ नहीं पता कि वह कहाँ है या कैसी है?"

“उफ्फ! आगे!”

वेद ने धीरे से पिंकी के साथ बैठी दो वृद्ध महिलाओं की ओर संकेत किया, “वो मेरी नानी हैं, अरुणा आहलूवालिया। वे अपने पिता के मदिरा व्यापार की वारिस हैं, जो बहुत ही खुशमिजाज और स्पष्टवक्ता हैं, साहसी हैं। उन्हें दो टूक बात कहने में किसी से डर नहीं लगता। ध्यान रहे!”

“इसे किसी का परिचय कहते हैं?” अकीरा ने आँखें चौड़ी करते हुए कहा।

“हाँ, ऐसे ही हैं। नानी के बगल में बैठी हैं, वो लुधियाना की डॉन (मुखिया) हैं, इंद्राणी अरोरा। वह अरोरा परिवार की पहली ऐसी शख्स हैं, जिन्होंने लव मैरिज की, डिग्री ली, ड्राइविंग लाइसेंस लिया और जिन्हें अपने पिता की जायदाद में भाइयों से अधिक हिस्सा मिला।”

“हाँ, ऐसे ही हैं। नानी के बगल में बैठी हैं, वो लुधियाना की डॉन (मुखिया) हैं, इंद्राणी अरोरा। वह अरोरा परिवार की पहली ऐसी शख्स हैं, जिन्होंने लव मैरिज की, डिग्री ली, ड्राइविंग लाइसेंस लिया और जिन्हें अपने पिता की जायदाद में भाइयों से अधिक हिस्सा मिला।”

“वाह! उत्साह से अकीरा बोली। “गजब की शख्सियत है।”

“बिल्कुल सही।” वेद ने हामी भरी। “लेकिन किसी भी बहस में आखिरी शब्द वे ही बोलना पसंद करती हैं, चाहे नानी जैसे व्यक्तित्व की मालकिन नहीं हैं वो। ये ज्यादा खतरनाक हैं।”

“कितने नौटंकी हो तुम वेद!” अकीरा असहमति प्रकट करते हुए बोली।

गहरी साँस लेते हुए वेद बोला “खैर! मुझे बुआ नहीं दिखाई दे रहीं तो हम उनके बारे में चिंता नहीं करेंगे।”

“तुम्हारा कुछ नहीं हो सकता।” कहते हुए अकीरा हँस पड़ी, जैसा कि सोचा था, इंद्राणी ने आवाज लगाई, “भोलू! बच्चे, इधर आ मेरे पास।”

पहली बार अकीरा ने सुना था कि कोई वेद को उपनाम (निकनेम) से पुकार रहा हो। अजीब भी लगा और अच्छा भी, लेकिन वेद के चेहरे पर ऐसे भाव थे, जैसे नीम की निंबोली खा ली हो। “आया दादी!”

वेद दादी के पैर छूने के लिए नीचे झुका और ईमानदारी से बोला, “बाहर इतनी भीड़ थी कि मैं पैरी पौना भी नहीं कर पाया। पैरी पौना दादी, पैरी पौना नानी!”

अरुणा ने वेद का माथा चूमा। “खुश रह बेटा!” इंद्राणी की आँखों से बड़े और मोटे आँसू छलक पड़े। उन्होंने कहा, “मुझे तुम्हारी सबसे ज्यादा याद आई, लेकिन क्या हुआ, तुम इतने लाल क्यों हो रखे हो?”

पिंकी आई और बोलीं, "इसे एलर्जी का दौरा पड़ा था।"

"तुम किस तरह की माँ हो प्रमिला ?" अरुणा खिसियाकर बोली। कबीर हैरान था। "अब ये प्रमिला कौन है ?"

"तुम्हारी होनेवाली सासूमाँ है, प्रमिला।" गरजते हुए अरुणा बोलीं।

कबीर ने पिंकी को हैरत से देखा, "मुझे लगा था कि आपका असली नाम पिंकी है।"

अरुणा वेदिका की ओर देखकर चिढ़कर बोलीं, "ये क्या आदमी है यार ? तुम्हें ये कहाँ मिला ?"

वेदिका ने कबीर को ऐसे देखा मानो मूर्ख हो, "नानी ! ये बहुत अच्छा इनसान है।"

वेद तो मरता क्या न करता, बोला, "मीठी खाने की गोली की तरह।"

पूरा परिवार जोर से हँस पड़ा। प्रमोद मामा ने वेद को जोर से ताली दी। "बढ़िया वेद !"

"नानी !" वेदिका गरजी।

"स्किन एलर्जी की सोचो अब।"

"हाँ।" पिंकी को ठीक करने के उद्द्देश्य से अरुणा पिंकी से कहने लगीं, "प्रमिला, क्या तुम मूर्ख हो ? देखो तो वेद कितना पतला और कमजोर है। जब मैंने दूर से इसे देखा तो मुझे लगा 'एक्स रे' चलकर आ रहा है।" पूरा कमरा ठहाके से गूँज उठा और वेद का चेहरा फीका पड़ गया।

"स्किन एलर्जी की सोचो अब।" "हाँ।" पिंकी को ठीक करने के उद्द्देश्य से अरुणा पिंकी से कहने लगीं, "प्रमिला, क्या तुम मूर्ख हो ? देखो तो वेद कितना पतला और कमजोर है। जब मैंने दूर से इसे देखा तो मुझे लगा 'एक्स रे' चलकर आ रहा है।" पूरा कमरा ठहाके से गूँज उठा और वेद का चेहरा फीका पड़ गया।

"और क्या ? पता नहीं इस पीढ़ी को क्या हो गया है ? न जाने मर्दों जैसे मर्द कहाँ चले गए ?" तेजी से अपना सिर हिलाते हुए अरुणा नानी बोलीं।

"वेद मेरा बेटा है, लड़का है।" पिंकी ने जोर से हँसते हुए कहा और अरुणा नानी त्यौरियाँ चढ़ाते हुए पिंकी को घूर रही थीं। अविनाश ने परिस्थिति देखते हुए विषय बदला और सबने राहत की साँस ली, "और माँ, तुम यहाँ कैसे ?"

"अरे ! पहले यह मेरी सहेली का घर है और फिर तेरी ससुराल। मैंने सोचा कि यहाँ तुम सबके साथ रहूँगी तो अच्छा रहेगा।"

अचानक अरुणा नानी वेद की तरफ पलटकर बोलीं, "वेद ! तुम्हें पौष्टिक और अच्छा खाना खाना चाहिए। नहीं खाते हो, इसीलिए ऐसे बीमारी के दौरे पड़ते हैं। आज लाल हुए हो; कल हो सकता है नीले पड़ जाओ; परसों हरे। कौन जाने ?"

"माँ, वो कोई दिवाली की लड़ियाँ थोड़े न है, जो रंग बदलेगा। वह एलर्जी के कारण लाल पड़ गया था।" पिंकी ने समझाया। "एलर्जियाँ परदेस की बकवास हैं, यह सबकुछ ठीक से न खाने से होता है।" अरुणा नानी बिगड़कर बोलीं।

"अरे गोविंद! और चिकन मँगवाना प्लीज!"

"देखना जरा, उसके पास मटन है क्या?" इंद्राणी दादी चिल्लाती हुई बोलीं।

वेद ने धीमे स्वर में प्यार से इंद्राणी से कहा, "दादी, मैं शाकाहारी हूँ।"

इंद्राणी ने गहरी साँस लेते हुए कहा, "हे राम!"

"प्रमिला!" अरुणा चिल्लाईं, "न तुम्हारी नलिकाएँ जुड़ गई हैं और न ही अविनाश के सैनिक। नए बच्चे के लिए कोशिश करो।"

सबकी आँखें घोर आश्चर्य में थीं और पिंकी शर्म से लाल हो गई। "माँ!"

"तुम मुझसे और क्या उम्मीद करती हो कहने की?" अरुणा बातों से झपटीं। "वेद पीता नहीं है, ठीक है, मैंने मान लिया। न जाने मेरे मरने के बाद कौन ध्यान रखनेवाला है उसका? फिर भी मैंने मान लिया। प्रणव थोड़ा उत्साह दिखाता है, राजवीर कर सकता है।" अरुणा का संयम टूटता हुआ नजर आ रहा था। "मुंगेरीलाल के हसीन सपने! बड़े आए! मैं उस डरपोक को एक फूटी कौड़ी नहीं देनेवाली। उसे कनाडा के मैकडोनल्ड्स में बर्गर-पैटी ही पलटने दो। मैं क्यों फिक्र करूँ?"

वेद ने धीमे स्वर में प्यार से इंद्राणी से कहा, "दादी, मैं शाकाहारी हूँ।" इंद्राणी ने गहरी साँस लेते हुए कहा, "हे राम!" "प्रमिला!" अरुणा चिल्लाईं, "न तुम्हारी नलिकाएँ जुड़ गई हैं और न ही अविनाश के सैनिक। नए बच्चे के लिए कोशिश करो।" सबकी आँखें घोर आश्चर्य में थीं और पिंकी शर्म से लाल हो गई। "माँ!"

प्रणव की पत्नी निराश-सी दिखी, "ऐसा क्यों कह रही हैं, इतनी बेरुखी?"

"मैं इससे भी ज्यादा कड़ा बोल सकती हूँ।" अरुणा ने चेतावनी दी। "खैर! ऐ रुक वेद? मुझे इस तरह की नकारात्मकता नहीं चाहिए घर में। तुम्हारे दादाजी ने तुम्हें जीवन देने के लिए बँटवारा और गरीबी झेली। तुम्हारी अच्छी जिंदगी के लिए क्या कुछ नहीं किया? तो अन्न का अपमान क्यों करना?"

इंद्राणी ने अपने हाथों में वेद का चेहरा लिया और बोली, "जो हम बनाएँगे, वो तुम खाओगे, ठीक है?"

"जी!" वेद ने खेदपूर्वक साँस छोड़ी।

"और नहीं तो क्या? शादी करनी है कि नहीं? बच्चे पैदा करने हैं कि नहीं? कहाँ से आएगी ताकत?" इंद्राणी ने पूछा।

वेद ने अकीरा की ओर धीरे से होंठ हिलाते हुए कहा, "मैंने तुमसे कहा था।"

अकीरा नहीं रोक पाई और जोर से हँस पड़ी।

उसकी हँसी से अरुणा का ध्यान उसपर गया और उन्होंने पूछा, "कौन है ये?"

"माँ! सबकुछ इतना जल्दी हो गया…"

पिंकी नीचे का होंठ दबाकर बोलीं और अविनाश ने जोरों का सिर हिलाते हुए हामी भरी।

अविनाश ने सभी से अकीरा को मिलवाते हुए कहा, "ये अकीरा है। वेद की दोस्त (गर्लफ्रेंड)।"

पिंकी भी आ गईं, "ये हैं वेद की नानी, अरुणा और वो हैं वेद की दादी, इंद्राणी।"

सभी अकीरा को ध्यान से देख रहे थे। वह चुपचाप अपनी जगह से उठी और उनके पैर छुए।

"सच तो यह है कि हम इसी की वजह से यहाँ हैं। वह अभय की शादी का प्रबंध करेगी। हम सभी इसके साथ लटककर यहाँ आ गए।" वेदिका ने सबको बताया।

"हटना जरा!" अरुणा ने वेद को उसकी जगह से हटाया। उनके चेहरे पर से मुसकान और खुशी हट ही नहीं रही थी और अकीरा की तारीफ करते हुए बोली, "तुम बहुत खूबसूरत हो।"

फिर उन्होंने वेद की हथेली चूमी।

"देर आए, दुरुस्त आए।" वेदिका ने कहा।

"हाँ। और क्या! तुमसे मिलकर मुझे खुशी हुई अकीरा!" गले लगाते हुए अरुणा बोलीं। "भोलू का भाग्य पहली बार खुला है, चलो मजे करें और खुशियाँ मनाएँ।"

"चलो! आज रात को ही जश्न मनाते हैं, पार्टी करते हैं।"

"हम्म्म् नानी! मुझे लग रहा है कि वेद थोड़ा लाल हो रखा है तो क्या आज रात पार्टी करनी ठीक रहेगी?" अकीरा ने थोड़ा झिझकते हुए कहा।

"ओ! मेरी प्यारी बच्ची!" उमंग सहित अरुणा और इंद्राणी ने एक साथ अपनी अभिव्यक्ति दी।

जब थोड़ी हँसी कम हुई तो इंद्राणी बोली, "तुम्हें वाकई लगता है कि सब भोलू से मिलने आएँगे?"

प्यार से अकीरा के सिर पर हाथ फेरते हुए अरुणा बोलीं, "पगली! सब तुझसे मिलने आएँगे। वेद तो सालन पर धनिए की तरह होगा; है तो ठीक, नहीं है तो भी ठीक!"

□

21

अकीरा कई तरह की अजीब पार्टियों में जा चुकी थी। जैसे अपने दसवें जन्मदिन के केक पर ही गिर गई। एक बार तो एक शादी में दुलहन को धोखा देकर भाग जानेवाले प्रेमी ने विवाह स्थल पर आकर किस तरह मशीन से धुँआ-ही-धुँआ छोड़ा था। वह मशीन साथ लेकर आया था। फिर भी कोई पार्टी इसके जैसी नहीं थी। हवेली के खूबसूरत बगीचों पर बहुत सी मेजें सजी हुई थीं। वह किसी चाचा, ताया द्वारा हाल ही में खरीदे गए हार्मोनियम पर गजल गाते सुन रही थी। वे हार्मोनियम साथ लेकर आए थे।

मजे शुरू हुए कपड़ों से। नानी चाहती थी कि वेद टेसेडो सूट पहने (जो महँगा होता है) और अकीरा ईवनिंग गाउन। कारण ? क्योंकि वे हमेशा से चाहती थीं कि उनका पोता जेम्स बॉण्ड जैसा दिखे। कपड़ों के बाद आई, लोगों से मिलने की बारी। वेद और अकीरा को मजबूरन उन सभी से मिलना पड़ा, जिन लोगों को वे जानते भी नहीं थे। और उन सभी मेहमानों ने एक-एक करके उन्हें वेद के बचपन से युवा होने तक की जीवन की अनेक कहानियाँ सुनाईं। असल में कई मेहमानों ने अपनी किशोरावस्था और युवावस्था तक की कहानियाँ सुना डालीं। अकीरा अब जान चुकी थी कि जसप्रीत सोढ़ी जब लुधियाना आया था जो जिंदा रहने के लिए उसकी जेब में केवल 10 रुपए थे। वो बात और है कि अकीरा नहीं जानती थी कि असल में जसप्रीत सोढ़ी है कौन ?

फिर वे दोनों गुड़िया के आकार का केक काटने गए। शालिनी मामी का कहना था कि परिवार की पसंदीदा बेकरी पर इससे शालीन और अच्छा केक कोई और नहीं था। फिर जेम्स बॉण्ड दंपती को गुड़िया के आकार का केक काटना पड़ा। उसके फैले हुए बाल और ऊपर की ओर फैले हुए हाथ ऐसे लग रहे थे मानो गुड़िया की देह के बीच की रेखा पर रखकर केक काटा गया। अभी तक यह भी सब विचित्र नहीं लग रहा था तो मामा ने कसर पूरी कर दी और वह भी सचमुच का छोटा सा घोड़ा भेंट करके। अकीरा को अपने जीवन में कभी इतना आश्चर्य नहीं हुआ, जितना कि उस दिन प्रमोद मामा को देखकर हुआ, जब वे पार्टी में उस छोटे से टट्टू को लेकर दाखिल हुए और उसपर और भी हैरानी, जब सबने उनके लिए तालियाँ बजाईं। ऐसा सबकुछ मानो सामान्य प्रक्रिया हो।

अकीरा ने मन-ही-मन ईश्वर से प्रार्थना की कि उसका और वेद का संबंध टिक जाए, कम-से-कम घोड़ी के लिए, जो केवल विलायती फ्रांसीसी घास खाती है। ऐसा प्रमोद मामा ने बताया था।

बॉयफ्रेंड तो नहीं, लेकिन पंजाबी जेम्स बॉण्ड के लिए और अकीरा के लिए यह पार्टी चार घंटे से ज्यादा की हो चुकी थी और अकीरा अब वाकई उस कगार पर थी, जहाँ वह लोगों को घर से बाहर धक्का देने लग जाती, ताकि वे अपने घर जाएँ। वे बहुत देर से सबकुछ सहन कर रहे थे।

सौभाग्य से पिंकी उसकी ओर चलकर आईं और अकीरा से पूछा, "तुम अभी तक यहाँ क्या कर रही हो ? कोई नहीं देख रहा। निकल भागो यहाँ से।"

"ठीक है, शुक्रिया!" कहते हुए अकीरा वहाँ से भाग निकली।
वह पार्टी के शोर-शराबे से दूर घूमती हुई शानदार हवेली की छत पर जा पहुँची। वह ध्यान से बाईं तरफ गई, कोना ढूँढ़ा। वेद वहीं था; मोबाइल हाथ में लिये वेद आलथी-पालथी मारकर जमीन पर बैठा था।

"वेद कहाँ है ?" अकीरा ने पूछा।

"वह पनाहगाह (Hideout) में होगा···। छत पर जाओ और बाईं ओर देखना। एक छोटा सा कोना होगा। जब उससे परिवार का पागलपन असह्य हो जाता है तो वह अधिकतर वहीं जाकर बैठ जाता है।"

"ठीक है, शुक्रिया!" कहते हुए अकीरा वहाँ से भाग निकली।

वह पार्टी के शोर-शराबे से दूर घूमती हुई शानदार हवेली की छत पर जा पहुँची। वह ध्यान से बाईं तरफ गई, कोना ढूँढ़ा। वेद वहीं था; मोबाइल हाथ में लिये वेद आलथी-पालथी मारकर जमीन पर बैठा था।

अकीरा ने बंद मुट्ठी से वेद के सिर पर धीरे-धीरे दस्तक देते हुए कहा, "कोई है ?"

अकीरा की ओर हक्की-बक्की निगाहों से देखते हुए मानो सारा गुस्सा निकालते हुए वेद चीखा, "अब तुम मुझे ऐसे डराना छोड़ोगी ?"

"नहीं!" अकीरा हँसते हुए वेद के बगल में जाकर बैठ गई।

वेद हँसा, "तुम अभी तक यहाँ कैसे ? अगर मैं तुम्हारी जगह होता तो या तो वहाँ के ओवन में पक रहे मुर्गों के साथ अपना भी सिर दे देता या फिर भाग जाता।"

"मैं तुम्हारी वजह से नहीं भागी। तुम इतने 'हॉट' हो कि तुम लाल पड़ गए हो।" उमस की भावनाओं से वेद के चेहरे पर उँगली फिराते हुए अकीरा बोली।

वेद मुँह बनाते हुए बोला, "वेदिका के साथ घूमना छोड़ दो।"

"ठीक है!" मुँह दबाकर अकीरा बोली और इतने में वेद ने उसे अपनी बाजुओं में भर लिया।

"लेकिन सच में यहाँ बैठकर तुम इतनी अच्छी पार्टी का मजा खो रहे हो।" अकीरा बोली।

"बेकार की बात है। अभी चार अंकल मुझे गालों पर चूम चुके हैं और दो होंठों तक भी आ गए थे। इन लोगों को 'पर्सनल स्पेस' (व्यक्तिगत पसंद) की संकल्पना ही नहीं है।"

"हम उन्हें दोष नहीं दे सकते। आधों ने तो हद से ज्यादा पी रखी है—अकीरा"

"क्या बात है! तुम्हें अचानक किसी आंटी ने शादी के बारे में नहीं पूछा? मेरा मतलब है, जब तक ऐसा न हो, ऐसी पार्टी खत्म नहीं होती।"

"करेक्शन (ठीक करता हूँ), आंटियों ने।" वेद ने कहा।

*"हम उन्हें दोष नहीं दे सकते। आधों ने तो हद से ज्यादा पी रखी है—अकीरा"
"क्या बात है! तुम्हें अचानक किसी आंटी ने शादी के बारे में नहीं पूछा? मेरा मतलब है, जब तक ऐसा न हो, ऐसी पार्टी खत्म नहीं होती।"
"करेक्शन (ठीक करता हूँ), आंटियों ने।" वेद ने कहा।*

अपना सिर हामी में हिलाते हुए अपने भाव अभिव्यक्त किए, "सच कहता हूँ आंटियाँ, मेरा मतलब है, इन आंटियों की खूबसूरत बेटियों के दस मीटर के घेरे के बीच रहने से अच्छा है, मैं नपुंसक होकर प्रेम देवता पर कुरबान हो जाऊँ।"

"शुक्रिया।"

अकीरा हतप्रभ-सी वेद को देखकर बोली, "तुम कई बार कितनी अंट-शंट बकवास करते हो वेद!"

"यही सच है।" वेद ने गंभीरता से कहा।

अकीरा ने वेद के कंधे से सिर ऊपर करते हुए कहा, "वैसे हमें घोड़े के बच्चे या हाथी को तो कुछ नहीं कहना न? वो भी भरी सभा में?"

वेद यह सुनकर हँस पड़ा।

"प्रमोद मामा, मैंने कहा था तुमसे। वे घोड़ों के आगे कुछ सोच नहीं पाते।"

"मुझे नहीं पता था कि घोड़ों के लिए उनका पागलपन इस हद तक है?"

वेद अचानक हँसा, "वैसा ही, जैसा न्यारा केक।"

"मैं तो उस सदमे को मानो अनदेखा कर दूँगी।"

"अकीरा! सोचो! यह तो सिर्फ अभी एक दिन था।"

"बार-बार ऐसे कहकर मुझे अपने फैसले पर पछतावे के लिए मजबूर मत करो वेद!"

वेद ने धीरे से नाक दबाते हुए कहा, "चिंता मत करो, मैं तो करवाऊँगा।"

अकीरा ने प्यार से वेद को पीछे किया और वेद ने उसे रोकने के लिए हाथ आगे किया। अकीरा ने उसके गालों पर उँगली लगाते हुए कहा, "अब तुम्हारे चेहरे का लाल रंग कम हो गया है।"

अकीरा की गुलाबी-नारंगी वेशभूषा को देख वेद बोला, "तुम्हारी वेशभूषा के रंग से मिलता-जुलता है न!" वेद ने अकीरा की ओर इशारा करके कहा।

"यही नानी ने भी मुझसे कहा।" अकीरा ने बताया।

"मैं बताता हूँ। 'अकीरा! पुत्तर, ये रंग तो बिल्कुल वेद के रंग से मिलता-जुलता है।' यही शब्द होंगे।" वेद बोला।

वेद ने गहरी साँस छोड़ी और बोला, "किसी दिन अखबार के मुख्य समाचारों में यह खबर होगी कि बार-बार परेशान किए जाने पर एक आदमी ने अपने पूरे खानदान की हत्या कर दी।" अकीरा चिल्लाई, "चुप रहो। मुझे नानी अच्छी लगी। कहाँ मिलेंगी ऐसी नानी, जो एक लड़की को कामुक और नई तरह की पोशाक पहनने को कहेंगी? लेकिन मेरा दुर्भाग्य मेरे बॉयफ्रेंड ने तारीफ तक न की।"

वेद ने गहरी साँस छोड़ी और बोला, "किसी दिन अखबार के मुख्य समाचारों में यह खबर होगी कि बार-बार परेशान किए जाने पर एक आदमी ने अपने पूरे खानदान की हत्या कर दी।" अकीरा चिल्लाई, "चुप रहो। मुझे नानी अच्छी लगी। कहाँ मिलेंगी ऐसी नानी, जो एक लड़की को कामुक और नई तरह की पोशाक पहनने को कहेंगी? लेकिन मेरा दुर्भाग्य मेरे बॉयफ्रेंड ने तारीफ तक न की।"

खैर, वेद ज्यादा कुछ बोल नहीं पाया। उसे क्या कहना चाहिए था कि वह बहुत खूबसूरत दिख रही है? न! वो तो सभी बोलते हैं। 'सेक्सी दिख रही हो' कहना भी मूर्खता होती। हो सकता है वो सच कह दे कि उसे देखने के बाद उसके शरीर में अलग-अलग जगह से न जाने कैसी भावनाएँ उठ रही हैं? किसे पता था कि प्रशंसा करना इतना बड़ा काम हो जाएगा।

"खैर!" बड़ी उम्मीदों से अकीरा वेद को देख रही थी। वेद ने विकलता से कहा, "अच्छी लग रही हो।"

अकीरा ने ऐसे देखा, मानो भगवान् को याद कर रही हो।

"अच्छी!"

वह थोड़ा पीछे हुआ और बोला, "वाकई अच्छी लग रही हो।" वह गुस्से से बोली, "मैंने तुम्हारे लिए तैयार होने में तीन घंटे लगाए, ताकि तुम मुझसे सिर्फ इतना बोलो कि अच्छी लग रही हूँ?"

वेद परेशानी से हँसता हुआ बोला, "मैं वादा करता हूँ डार्लिंग, मैं सीख लूँगा।"

अकीरा का मन इतने प्यार भरे लफ्ज वेद के मुँह से सुनकर फूला न समाया और उसने बात वहीं छोड़ दी। वेद की आँखों में देखती हुई बोली, "तो इस दिन को उस कारवाले दिन का नतीजा समझूँ?"

वेद ने आसमान की ओर देखते हुए कहा, "यह दिन पक्का ही उस दिन से अच्छा है।"

अकीरा ने सिर 'हाँ' में हिलाया। फिर थोड़ी देर बाद पूछा, "वेद, तुम इतने सालों तक अकेले कैसे रहे? अच्छी लड़कियों की कोई कमी थोड़े न है।"

"हाँ, वो अच्छी हैं, लेकिन जैसी चाहिए, वैसी नहीं हैं।" धीरे से वेद ने कहा।

अकीरा के लब खुशी से थिरक रहे थे। "मुझे नहीं पता भविष्य में क्या होगा, लेकिन तुम्हें पता है कि तुम मुझे कैसा महसूस करवाते हो?"

वेद को लगा, मानो उसका चेहरा गरमी से जल रहा हो; वेद बोला, "कैसा?"

अकीरा झुकी, उसने अपना हाथ वेद की छाती पर रखा। उसकी आँखों में चमक थी, जब वह वेद के कान में फुसफुसाई, "जैसे क्रिसमस की सुबह।"

□

22

"तुम वहाँ क्यों बैठे हो?" अकीरा ने वेद से अगले दिन सुबह पूछा, जब वह रसोईघर में गई, क्योंकि वेद रसोईघर की मेज के सबसे कोनेवाली कुरसी पर बैठा था। उसके सामने शुद्ध घी के पराँठों से भरी थाली रखी थी; जैसा कि उसकी दादी ने कहा था।

वेद ने अकीरा की बात का कोई जवाब नहीं दिया। उसने पराँठे का एक टुकड़ा तोड़ा और खिड़की से बाहर फेंक दिया।

"ये क्या है?" अकीरा ने तीखे स्वर में कहा।

"शऽऽऽऽऽ" वेद ने अपनी आँखें चौड़ी करके अकीरा को चुप रहने का इशारा किया।

अकीरा ने वेद को डाँटा, "पर तुम ऐसा क्यों कर रहे हो?"

"क्योंकि तुम्हारी उस घोड़ी को भी नाश्ता चाहिए।" ऐसा कहते हुए वेद बिगड़ैल बच्चे की तरह हँसा। अकीरा ने गरदन ऊँची करके खिड़की के बाहर झाँका तो वह घोड़ी बाहर खड़ी नजर आई। और वह खुशी से पराँठे के टुकड़े खा रही थी, जो वेद बाहर फेंक रहा था। "विलायती घास खानेवाली के लिए यह बहुत ज्यादा है।" चेहरा लटकाते हुए अकीरा बोली।

"और ये पराँठा फेंको मत प्लीज! दादी ने तुम्हारे लिए बनाए हैं, घोड़ी के लिए नहीं। ये दादी का अपमान होगा।" अकीरा ने डाँटते हुए कहा।

"अगर मैं दादी के अनुसार 21 दिनों तक खाना खाता रहूँगा तो निश्चित ही इतना विशाल हो जाऊँगा कि वेद नहीं कहलाऊँगा।"

अकीरा हँसी दबाते हुए होंठ गोल करके बोली, "मेरे खयाल से तुम थोड़ा सा वजन बढ़ जाने से बुरे नहीं दिखोगे।"

"बिल्कुल सही। थोड़ा सा वजन! न कि हैलो! मैं वेद अंशकालिक (Part Time) व्यापारी और पूर्णकालिक विशाऽऽऽऽल वेद! व्हेल जैसा।"

अकीरा हँसी। उसकी हँसी से अरुणा और इंद्राणी का ध्यान उन दोनों पर गया। अरुणा ने कहा, "अरे अकीरा! तुम कब आई?"

"अभी-अभी आई दादी!" अकीरा ने बहुत ही उत्साह से उन दोनों का प्रातः अभिवादन किया, "गुड मॉर्निंग दादी! गुड मॉर्निंग नानी!"

"गुड मॉर्निंग बेटा!" इंद्राणी बोली।

"वेद! देखो तो यह कितनी खुश और उत्साह से भरी है, तुमने तो मानो मरा चूहा सूँघ लिया हो।" अरुणा ने बेकार-सा मुँह बनाते हुए अपने पोते को टोका।

"वो इसलिए कि सुबह-सुबह अकीरा को कोई हवेली दिखाने नहीं ले गया।...और मुझे मेरी कॉफी चाहिए। उसके बिना मेरा दिन शुरू नहीं होता।"

इंद्राणी ने आँखें घुमाते हुए कहा, "यहीं से लत की शुरुआत होती है।"

"मैं आप सबको याद दिला दूँ कि इस पूरे कमरे में अकेला मैं ही हूँ, जिसे कोई लत नहीं है।" वेद ने चिल्लाते हुए कहा।

"मुझसे मेरी प्यारी चीज भी अब मत छीनो, जो मेरे अपने जीवन में वाकई बहुत अच्छी है। ऐसा करना धौंसियाना है और मुझे बिल्कुल मंजूर नहीं है।"

"मैं आप सबको याद दिला दूँ कि इस पूरे कमरे में अकेला मैं ही हूँ, जिसे कोई लत नहीं है।" वेद ने चिल्लाते हुए कहा। "मुझसे मेरी प्यारी चीज भी अब मत छीनो, जो मेरे अपने जीवन में वाकई बहुत अच्छी है। ऐसा करना धौंसियाना है और मुझे बिल्कुल मंजूर नहीं है।"

"अच्छा ठीक है। लेकिन पहले यह बादाम दूध पिओ।" अरुणा बोलीं।

वेद ने अकीरा की ओर देखा। अकीरा ने अपने होंठ दबाए और दूसरी तरफ देखने लगी। लेकिन उसके कंधे अभी भी आनंद से मानो उचक रहे थे।

"तुम्हें मेरी स्थिति पर हँसी आ रही है और तुम मजे ले रही हो न?" वेद बोला।

"झूठ नहीं बोलूँगी; हाँ!" अकीरा ने जवाब दिया।

वेद अभी कुछ कहने ही वाला था, पर कह नहीं पाया, क्योंकि उतने में वेदिका और कबीर रसोईघर में झूमते हुए-से, टूटे हुए-से दाखिल हुए।

"नानी! मुझे 'कॉर्नफ्लेक्स' मिलेंगे?" वेदिका ने बड़े मासूम भावों से अनुरोध किया। "मुझ पर अभी भी रात की पार्टी का असर है।"

अरुणा ने कहा, "हाँ! हाँ, क्यों नहीं?"

वेद चिढ़ते हुए बोला, "वेदिका को उसकी पसंद का खाना और मुझे क्यों नहीं? इसे बच्चे नहीं पैदा करने क्या?"

अरुणा वेद की गरदन को अपने हाथों में प्यार से समेटकर, उसका माथा चूमकर बोलीं, "वेदिका को जो चाहे वो करने दो, मुझे कोई मतलब नहीं, क्योंकि जो भी होगा,

वो कबीर के पास ही जाएगा।"

वेदिका की जैसे अचानक आँखें खुल गई हों और वह किटकिट करती हुई बोली, "नानी! ये तो गलत है।"

"सॉरी बेटा!" अरुणा वेद के साथ हँस रही थीं।

"मेरा खयाल है, यहाँ आने का फैसला गलत था।" दु:ख से कबीर बोला।

"डैड के साथ वापस चले जाओ। वे दो दिन बाद जानेवाले हैं।"

"मुझे जाना चाहिए।" अपनी प्लेट की तरफ देखते हुए गहरी सोच में डूबा हुआ कबीर बोला।

"रेड मामा!" आदित्य भागता हुआ रसोईघर में आया और उसके पीछे-पीछे प्रणवी आई।

वेद ने आदित्य को गोद में उठा लिया और बच्चे के मोटे गब्बू गालों को चूमते हुए प्रणवी से शिकायत की। "प्रणवी? तुम्हारा बेटा ठीक से नाम क्यों नहीं बोल सकता?"

प्रणवी ने वेद को देखा और कहा, "वेद! वो सिर्फ अभी दो साल का है, उसे बख्श दो।"

अपनी भोली और आकर्षक मुसकान से वेदिका को देखते हुए आदित्य बोला, "गुड मॉर्निंग वेदिका मासी।"

बहुत प्यार से शहद भरी आवाज में, "गुड मॉर्निंग मेरे बच्चे।"

"रेड मामा!" आदित्य भागता हुआ रसोईघर में आया और उसके पीछे-पीछे प्रणवी आई।
वेद ने आदित्य को गोद में उठा लिया और बच्चे के मोटे गब्बू गालों को चूमते हुए प्रणवी से शिकायत की। "प्रणवी? तुम्हारा बेटा ठीक से नाम क्यों नहीं बोल सकता?"

वेद ने प्रणवी को देखा और मानो पकड़े जाने पर बेचैनी की हँसी हँसते हुए बोली, "ये बच्चे भी न!"

"ऐसा भी नहीं कह सकते कि 'अरोरा परिवार के बच्चे'। इनका तो डी.एन.ए. ढाँचा ही अलग है।" उदासी भरे स्वर में वेद बोला।

"फिर भी तुम दोनों में मेरा डी.एन.ए. है। उन्होंने तुम्हें स्कूल में क्या सिखाया?" अरुणा ने पूछा।

वेदिका ने चिढ़ाते हुए कहा, "नानी, वेद विज्ञान में हमेशा से कमजोर रहा है।"

"खासकर जीव विज्ञान में।" कबीर चुटकी लेते हुए बोला।

"सामाजिक विज्ञान में भी।" अकीरा ने दाँतों के बीच जीभ दबाते हुए कहा।

यह सुन सभी हँस पड़े, सिवाय वेद के।

वेद ने जानबूझकर आदित्य की ओर देखा। उसका चेहरा अपने हाथ में लेते हुए,

उसे प्यार से समझाते हुए कहा, "मेरा नाम वेद है, 'वेद' कहोऽऽऽऽऽ!"

बच्चा बोला, "रेड…"

वेद ने बच्चे को जाने दिया और बोला, "मुझे बच्चों से नफरत है।" इंद्राणी ने वेद को घूरते हुए कहा, "खोतेया! बचपन में तू भी बहुत तुतलाता था, पर बाद में ठीक हो गया।"

वेद अरुणा को देख मुसकरा दिया, "ओ प्यारी दादी माँ! यहाँ सिर्फ पागलपन ही खानदानी नहीं है।"

अकीरा वेद की ओर झुककर बोली, "अरे! तुम अचानक कैसे मजाक करने लगे?"

"ये लुधियाना की हवा का असर है।" वेद बोला।

"अच्छा! अब हम चलें, पहले ही देर हो गई। अभय का परिवार राह देख रहा होगा।" अकीरा बोली।

अपनी घड़ी देखकर वेद बोला, "हाँ, चलो।"

वो खड़ा हुआ और बोला, "ठीक है, अब हम अभय के घर जा रहे हैं।"

इंद्राणी ने हिदायतें दीं, "छोटी कार ले जाना, दोपहर के खाने तक वापस आ जाना, गाड़ी ध्यान से चलाना।"

"दादी, चिंता मत कीजिए!" अकीरा आश्वासन देते हुए बोली। "वेद कभी भी 40 की गति से ऊपर गाड़ी नहीं चलाता। हो सकता है, हम गाड़ी ज्यादा धीरे चलाने की वजह से मुश्किल में आ जाएँ।"

इंद्राणी हँसी और बोलीं, "ओ सॉरी! मैं भूल गई थी कि मैं किसे हिदायतें दे रही हूँ।"

वेद ने जवाब में बस अपनी आँखें ऊपर की ओर घुमाईं।

"अच्छा वेद! नीलू के घर कुछ मत खाना।" अरुणा बोलीं।

परेशान होकर सिर हिलाते हुए वेद बोला, "हे भगवान्!"

"और तुम भी अकीरा! प्यार से हर चीज के लिए मना कर देना।" अरुणा ने चेतावनी दी।

"ठीक है!" अकीरा को हैरानी हुई, लेकिन उसने ज्यादा नहीं सोचा और मान लिया कि अरोरा परिवार के अजीबोगरीब सोच का हिस्सा होगा। सबसे विदा लेकर वह 'आहलूवालिया परिवार कैसा होगा' सोचती हुई चल पड़ी।

□

23

"परेशान मत हो।" अकीरा ने वेद को डाँटा।

"मेरी बेचैनी खत्म हो जाएगी। अगर तुम उनकी ओर घूरना बंद करो।" वेद ने कमरे में चारों तरफ अपनी नजरें घुमाते हुए धीरे से अकीरा से कहा।

अकीरा ने वेद को गुस्से से देखा, "मैं बात करने आई हूँ; उधर ही तो देखूँगी।"

"मैं भी अपने आप को रोक नहीं पा रहा।" वेद ने जवाब दिया।

अजीब तरीके से सिर हिलाती हुई अकीरा अपने सामनेवाले सोफे पर बैठी हुई महिला को देख रही थी। उसने गहरी साँस छोड़ी। जैसी कल्पना की थी, नीलू आहलूवालिया वैसी बिल्कुल नहीं थी। उसके बाल लंबे, भूरे और घुँघराले थे। उनकी वजह से नीलू की त्वचा हलकी सफेद दिखाई दे रही थी। वह बीच-बीच में कजरारी आँखों की पलकें झपकाती तो लगता तितली के पंख हैं। वह डिजाइनर कपड़े पहने हुए थी, जो बेशकीमती थे। वे अकीरा के घर में रखे सभी कपड़ों की कीमत से भी ज्यादा महँगे थे। वह बॉलीवुड की हीरोइन जैसी पतली-दुबली थी। अकीरा हैरानी से उसकी ओर देख रही थी।

अगर ये कम लगा रहा था तो घर पर आते हैं। अकीरा को उनका घर देखकर लगा, मानो वह 'विक्टोरिया की सदी' में आ गई हो। सुरुचिपूर्ण तरीके से लकड़ी के पैनल लगे थे। महँगे और शोभनीय झूमर छत से लटक रहे थे। और सबसे अच्छी बात! नीलू ने महँगे और अत्यंत सुंदर चीनी मिट्टी के कपों में चाय पेश की थी और साथ में स्वादिष्ट दिखाई देनेवाली पेस्ट्रीज भी थीं। यदि वेद हैरानी से उसे घूर नहीं रहा होता तो अभी तक अकीरा पेस्ट्रीज खा चुकी होती।

एक अनोखी सी मुसकान देते हुए नीलू ने कहा, "मैं तुम्हारे डिजाइनों से काफी प्रभावित हुई, अकीरा!"

"बहुत-बहुत शुक्रिया। ये तो आपकी जर्रानवाजी है।" अकीरा ने बहुत ही शालीनता से जवाब दिया।

"ओ बच्ची! मुझे नीलू मासी कहो।"

अकीरा को मानो झटका लगा, "मासी?"

नीलू मुसकाई, "मुझे मालूम था कि पिंकी तुम्हें कभी नहीं बताएगी कि मैं वेद की मासी हूँ।"

अकीरा वेद की ओर देखने लगी। वेद ने होंठ दबाते हुए मुसकराकर प्रतिक्रिया दी। "वेद। तुमने मुझे कभी नहीं बताया?"

नीलू हँसी, "असल में मैं अरोरा परिवार के पसंदीदा लोगों में से नहीं हूँ।"

"ऐसा कुछ नहीं है मासी!" वेद ने परिस्थिति को सँभालने के उद्देश्य से कहा। "मेरे पास अकीरा को वंश-वृक्ष समझाने का समय नहीं था।"

"वृक्ष? हमारा कोई वंश वृक्ष नहीं है। हमारा घर पागलखाना है, जहाँ अलग-अलग तरह के मानसिक रोगी रहते हैं, जो असल में एक-दूसरे से संबंधित हैं और जिनका पागलपन अलग-अलग स्तरों का है।" नीलू ने कहा।

"वृक्ष? हमारा कोई वंश वृक्ष नहीं है। हमारा घर पागलखाना है, जहाँ अलग-अलग तरह के मानसिक रोगी रहते हैं, जो असल में एक-दूसरे से संबंधित हैं और जिनका पागलपन अलग-अलग स्तरों का है।" नीलू ने कहा।

"ये तो काफी हद तक सही है…।" वेद थोड़ा सा हँसकर बोला। "और ये उन सभी मानसिक रोगियों में 'ताज' के स्थान पर हैं।" धीरे से वेद ने कहा।

अकीरा ने वेद का धीरे से हाथ दबाया, ताकि वह ऐसी नकारात्मक टिप्पणियाँ और न दे। नीलू ने समझाया, "असल में मेरी माँ और वेद की नानी दूर की बहनें हैं। इसकी वजह से मैं और पिंकी बहनें हुईं। शादी के बाद भी मैंने अपना उपनाम नहीं बदला। वैसे मुझे नीलू कपूर कहलाना चाहिए था, लेकिन मुझे अपना नाम नीलू आहलूवालिया कहलाना ही पसंद है।"

"बेशक बहुत अच्छा नाम है आपका।" अकीरा ने तारीफ करते हुए कहा।

"कुछ भी हो, मेरे कानों को तो नकली नाम लगता है, जैसे यह कपड़े को रँगनेवाले किसी रंग का नाम हो।" वेद बोला। अकीरा ने वेद की बाँह में चिकोटी काटी।

"अकीरा! मुझे ये रंग पसंद आया।" नीलू ने एक कपड़े की ओर इशारा करते हुए कहा। ये गुलाबी फूलों और सुनहरे क्रॉकरी (बर्तन) के साथ अच्छा दिखेगा। नहीं?"

"वाकई! मेरा खयाल है कि आप मुझे मेरे द्वारा दिए गए विकल्पों में से जो आपको अच्छा लगे, उसकी सूची दे दें, मैं उसी हिसाब से डिजाइन तैयार कर दूँगी।"

नीलू मुसकराई। "ये बढ़िया रहेगा। मैं आज ही रात अभय और उसकी मँगेतर के साथ बैठकर चुनाव करके सूची बनाती हूँ।"

"ठीक है।" अकीरा मुसकराई। "एक विनती है कि आज ही रात को यह काम कर

लें, क्योंकि हमारे पास वक्त थोड़ा कम है।"

नीलू ने हामी भरते हुए सिर हिलाया, "चिंता न करो, मेरी कोशिश रहेगी कि आज रात नौ बजे तक अपनी पसंद की सूची तुम्हें दे दूँ।"

"शुक्रिया।" अकीरा ने अपना बैग उठाया।

"अब हम चलें?" अकीरा ने पूछा।

"जा रहे हो? तुमने तो कुछ लिया ही नहीं?" नाटकीय तरीके से नीलू ने पूछा।

वेद ने गला साफ करते हुए बात सँभाली, "मासी! असल में दादी और नानी हमारा इंतजार कर रहे हैं। उन्हें हमारे साथ खाना खाना है और आपको तो पता है, नानी कैसी हैं!"

"ओह! लेकिन अगली बार तुम्हें हमारे साथ खाना खाना पड़ेगा वेद!" नीलू मासी ने सिर हिलाते हुए कहा।

"हाँ! पक्का!"

"ठीक है, फिर हम चलते हैं! मासी! बाय!" अकीरा पैरों पर हिलते हुए बोली।

"बाय! अपना ध्यान रखना।" नीलू ने हाथ हिलाते हुए कहा।

दोनों ने हाथ हिलाते हुए अलविदा कहा और आकर कार में बैठे। जैसे ही वे कार में बैठे, अकीरा वेद की ओर मुड़ी और बोली, "तुम वहाँ इतना अजीब व्यवहार क्यों कर रहे थे?"

वेद ने मुँह बनाया। "कुछ भी कहने से पहले, आओ पहले कुछ खा लें। मैंने गूगल पर ढूँढ़ा है। पास ही में एक कैफे है। मैं खाली पेट कोई जवाब नहीं दे सकता और न ही सोच सकता हूँ।"

"ठीक है, फिर हम चलते हैं! मासी! बाय!" अकीरा पैरों पर हिलते हुए बोली। "बाय! अपना ध्यान रखना।" नीलू ने हाथ हिलाते हुए कहा। दोनों ने हाथ हिलाते हुए अलविदा कहा और आकर कार में बैठे। जैसे ही वे कार में बैठे, अकीरा वेद की ओर मुड़ी और बोली, "तुम वहाँ इतना अजीब व्यवहार क्यों कर रहे थे?"

अकीरा ने अपने पेट पर थपकी देते हुए कहा, "मैं भी नहीं।" वेद ने फोन में रास्ता खोजने के लिए जी.पी.एस. शुरू किया और पलभर में वे कैफे के पास पहुँच गए।

"छोटे शहरों के भी अपने फायदे हैं। कितनी जल्दी पहुँच गए।" वेद के साथ कैफे के अंदर जाकर उन्होंने एक सुविधाजनक कोना ढूँढ़ा और बैठ गए। खाने का ऑर्डर देते ही अकीरा ने वेद की आँखों में देखकर पूछा, "हाँ जी। आप लोगों और नीलू मासी के बीच मसला क्या है?"

वेद ने एक उँगली अपनी कनपटी पर रखी और बच्चों जैसे मोड़ी और बोला, "अरे! कुछ नहीं! बस वो पागल हैं।"

"मुझे तो लगा वे अत्यंत शालीन और प्यारी सी हैं।"

"वो इसलिए कि चेहरा धोखा दे सकता है। मैं उन्हें तुमसे ज्यादा लंबे समय से जानता हूँ। इसलिए तुम्हारी राय कोई मायने नहीं रखती।"

"उफ्फ! बताओ फिर!"

"ठीक है।" अपने बचाव के लिए मानो हाथ खड़े करते हुए बोला, "तो फिर सुनो कि किस घटना ने सारे बाँध तोड़ दिए।"

अकीरा झुककर बोली, "हाँ बताओ।"

वेद ने बताना शुरू किया। "इनका बेटा अभय और मैं मेरे लुधियाना आने पर बहुत वक्त साथ बिताते; घूमने जाते। एक दिन मैं और वेदिका रात को उनके घर सोने आए। खेलते समय अचानक मैंने एक चूहा देखा, जिसके हाथ में या पैरों में आलू था। अब मुझे ठीक से याद भी नहीं। लेकिन चूहे के हाथ में कुछ था।"

"फिर!" अकीरा ने प्रतिक्रिया दी। 'वेद की कहानी है तो अजीब तो होगी ही।' मन-ही-मन अकीरा सोच रही थी।

"फिर?"

"फिर क्या? एक साधारण मनुष्य की तरह मैंने मासी को बताया, लेकिन उन्होंने मेरा विश्वास नहीं किया।" वेद बोला।

अकीरा झुककर बोली, "हाँ बताओ।" वेद ने बताना शुरू किया। "इनका बेटा अभय और मैं मेरे लुधियाना आने पर बहुत वक्त साथ बिताते; घूमने जाते। एक दिन मैं और वेदिका रात को उनके घर सोने आए। खेलते समय अचानक मैंने एक चूहा देखा, जिसके हाथ में या पैरों में आलू था। अब मुझे ठीक से याद भी नहीं। लेकिन चूहे के हाथ में कुछ था।"

"ओह, उसके बाद? लेकिन क्यों नहीं विश्वास किया?" अकीरा ने जिज्ञासा दिखाई।

"वो मुझे नहीं मालूम। लेकिन जब मैं और वेदिका वापस घर गए तो मैंने पूरी बात परिवारवालों को बताई, लेकिन उन सभी ने मेरी बात यह सोचकर अनसुनी कर दी कि बच्चे हैं, हो सकता है, झूठ बोला हो। लेकिन एक दिन…" वेद की आवाज में चुभन की तकलीफ जान पड़ी।

इतने में बैरे ने वेद का ऑर्डर मेज पर रखा। दोनों ने उसका धन्यवाद किया और वेद ने दुबारा कहानी बतानी शुरू की। "वो दिवाली के दिन थे। नीलू मासी ने सभी को पत्ते (ताश) खेलने और मजे करने के लिए अपने घर न्योता दिया था। संक्षेप में बताऊँ तो उस रात सभी को विषाक्त भोजन (Food Poisoning) से ग्रस्त होने के कारण अस्पताल में भरती होना पड़ा।"

अकीरा हैरान थी, "क्या हुआ था ?"

वेद मुसकराया, "मुझे ज्यादा तो कुछ नहीं मालूम, लेकिन उस घटना का चूहे से जरूर कुछ संबंध था।" (Tillpglly)

"ईऽऽऽऽश! अब इसके बारे में कभी कुछ मत बताना।" अकीरा बोली।

वेद हँस पड़ा, "ठीक है, नहीं बताऊँगा।" ऐसा कहते हुए वह अपनी एस्प्रेसो कॉफी के मजे लेने लगा।

"क्या तुम भी भरती हुए थे ?"

"नहीं। मैंने और वेदिका ने चतुराई दिखाई और हमने कुछ भी नहीं खाया।"

"हे भगवान्! क्या पागलपन है। फिर क्या हुआ ?" अकीरा ने पूछा।

"खैर! बाद में हमें पता चला कि चूँकि अभय को मिकी माउस का कार्टून चरित्र अच्छा लगता था, इसीलिए नीलू मासी ने चूहे को नहीं मारा था। इसलिए सबको वहम होता है और उनके घर में कुछ भी खाने से बचते हैं।"

"मेरे साथ ऐसा बहुत कम होता है कि शब्द ही न बचे हों, लेकिन सच में मुझे समझ नहीं आ रहा कि क्या कहूँ ?" अकीरा अविश्वसनीय भाव से बोली।

"तुम्हारे परिवार ने तो डिज्नी से ज्यादा अपनी ही पंजाबी खिचड़ी बना रखी है।"

वेद जोर से हँसा। "मैंने कहा था, लुधियाना पागलपन का अड्डा है।"

"हे भगवान्! क्या पागलपन है। फिर क्या हुआ ?" अकीरा ने पूछा। "खैर! बाद में हमें पता चला कि चूँकि अभय को मिकी माउस का कार्टून चरित्र अच्छा लगता था, इसीलिए नीलू मासी ने चूहे को नहीं मारा था। इसलिए सबको वहम होता है और उनके घर में कुछ भी खाने से बचते हैं।"

अकीरा के माथे पर शिकन थी, "मैंने कहाँ खुद को फँसा लिया ?"

"जिंदगी भर के दर्द में।" वेद ने चिढ़ाते हुए कहा।

"शायद जिंदगी भर के ठहाकों में..." अकीरा ने मुसकराकर दिल की बात कह दी।

"अच्छा लगा! तुम्हारा सकारात्मक विचार सुनकर। अच्छा बताओ, अब क्या प्लान है ? इस अविस्मरणीय विवाह के लिए क्या योजना बनाई है ?" वेद ने अपनी उँगलियाँ अकीरा की उँगलियों में लपेटते हुए पूछा।

एक मुसकान अकीरा के होंठों पर बिखर गई। "मैं खुश हूँ कि बहुत से काम पहलेवाले विवाह प्रबंधक करके गए हैं। अब जैसे हमें निमंत्रण पत्र, विवाह स्थल, अतिथियों की सूची आदि की चिंता नहीं करनी पड़ेगी ? बचा हुआ काम देखना है।"

वेद ने व्यंग्य से कहा, "सिर्फ बचा हुआ ? आसान है।"

अकीरा हँसी दबाते हुए बोली, "हाँ! आसान है, यही कुछ सौ काम हैं।"

"प्लीज, अपने नए असिस्टेंट (सहायक) को मत डराओ।" वेद ने कहा।

"मुझे डराना पड़ेगा।" बड़ी सी मुसकराहट से अकीरा बोली। "अभी तो यह योजना है कि नीलू मासी मुझे चुनिंदा डिजाइन की सूची देंगी तो मैं बैठकर सबकुछ डिजाइन करूँगी।"

"खैर! रात बहुत लंबी रहेगी।"

वेद ने हाथ पकड़कर कहा, "मैं कोशिश करूँगा कि तुम्हें रात लंबी न लगे।"

□

24

“ये लो तुम्हारी कॉफी।” वेद ने ऊर्जा व उत्साह से अकीरा के अस्थायी कार्य स्थल पर रखी।

अकीरा का चेहरा खिल उठा, “शुक्रिया। मुझे इसकी जरूरत थी।”

आलीशान और शाही भोज के बाद अकीरा अपने कमरे में शादी के डिजाइन पर काम कर रही थी।

“लगता है नीलू मासी ने सूची भेज दी। और इस कॉफी के लिए मेरा शुक्रिया अदा करो। मुझे पता है कि मैं ये दो कप कॉफी रसोईघर से कैसे लाया हूँ!” वेद ने बिस्तर पर बैठते हुए कहा।

अकीरा ने वेद के कॉफी के साहसिक कार्य की ओर ध्यान न देते हुए कहा, “हाँ! मासी ने सूची भेज दी है।”

“जैसा कि उन्होंने कहा था, सूची तो समय पर भेज दी, पर सिर दर्द भी भेजा है, इसीलिए कॉफी चाहिए थी।”

वेद छोटे बच्चे की तरह हँसा, “जैसा कि अंदेशा था।”

अकीरा चिल्लाई, “वेद ने जो सारी अस्पष्ट बातें नीलू मासी के बारे में बताई थीं, वे कितनी सच थीं। नीलू मासी वाकई मुश्किल में आनेवाली हैं।”

वेद ने मासी द्वारा भेजा कागज उठाया और पढ़ने लगा। थोड़ी देर बाद हँसी में उसके मुँह से कॉफी बाहर आनेवाली थी। अकीरा भविष्यवक्ता नहीं थी, लेकिन उसे वेद से इसी प्रतिक्रिया की उम्मीद थी। उस प्रतिक्रिया को देख कागज के टिशू वेद की ओर फेंके।

“चुप रहो!” अकीरा ने गुस्से से वेद को देखा। वो समझ चुकी थी कि वेद की हँसी संक्रामक है और वह भी हँस पड़ेगी। वह बिस्तरे पर लेटती हुई बोली, “उनकी पसंद में कितना विरोधाभास है! मैं समझ नहीं पा रही कि अलग-अलग डिजाइन (नमूनों) में सुसंबद्धता कैसे लाऊँ?”

जैसे ही वेद ने सुना, वह थोड़ा गंभीर हुआ। वेद ने अकीरा को धीरज बँधाया, “कोई

बात नहीं, मुझे बताओ, मैं क्या कर सकता हूँ?"

अकीरा ठोढ़ी पर हाथ रखकर गहरी सोच में थी, बोली, "गुलाबी रंग के फूलों की व्यवस्था के नमूने इंटरनेट पर देखो और वहीं किसी फोल्डर में सेव करके रखो।"

वेद को अकीरा का बॉसी अवतार अच्छा लगा। "जी बॉस! मैं यह कर सकता हूँ।"

'शुक्रिया' कहकर अकीरा ने अतिरिक्त लैपटॉप वेद को दिया।

किसने सोचा था कि इतना बड़ा व्यापारी, जिसने वर्कशीट्स और आर्थिक कार्यों, अनुसंधान और विकास के कार्यों के अलावा कुछ नहीं सोचा, उसे फूलों की व्यवस्था के नमूने शादी के काम के लिए एकत्रित करने पड़ेंगे? वो भी गुलाबी रंग के; वो भी नीलू मासी के बेटे के लिए! जब तक यह सोचे कि अपने जीवन पर क्या रोना, दरवाजे पर किसी ने दस्तक दी।

किसने सोचा था कि इतना बड़ा व्यापारी, जिसने वर्कशीट्स और आर्थिक कार्यों, अनुसंधान और विकास के कार्यों के अलावा कुछ नहीं सोचा, उसे फूलों की व्यवस्था के नमूने शादी के काम के लिए एकत्रित करने पड़ेंगे? वो भी गुलाबी रंग के; वो भी नीलू मासी के बेटे के लिए! जब तक यह सोचे कि अपने जीवन पर क्या रोना, दरवाजे पर किसी ने दस्तक दी।

वेदिका कबीर के साथ सैर करती हुई कमरे में दाखिल हुई। मतलब वेद को शर्मिंदा करनेवाली एक्सप्रेस गाड़ी आ गई। "किसने भेजी होगी?"

"अब मैं यह गाड़ी अरुणा आहलूवालिय को भेजूँगा। फिर देखते हैं कि कौन किसे शर्मिंदा करता है?" वेद ने धमकाया।

वेदिका मुसकराई; वेद के कप से एक बड़ा घूँट कॉफी का पिया और उसकी बगल में बैठ गई। बोली, "किसने कहा धमकियों का जमाना बीत गया? मेरा भाई तो इस खेल का चैंपियन है।"

"अकीरा, तुम्हारे कारीगर आ गए हैं। उन्हें उनके काम समझा दो।" वेद ने अकीरा से कहा।

मुसकराकर अकीरा ने एक लिस्ट (सूची) वेदिका को पकड़ाई।

"ये लो, इसे पढ़ो पहले।" वेदिका ने सूची पढ़नी शुरू की और हर शब्द के साथ उसकी आँखें चौड़ी होती जातीं। कबीर की प्रतिक्रिया भी कुछ अलग नहीं थी। पूरी सूची पढ़ने के बाद दोनों ने एक-दूसरे को देखा और जोरों से हँस पड़े।

"ये क्या बकवास है?" वेदिका बड़बड़ाई।

"अकीरा! ये शैतान की सूची है।" कबीर बोला और हँस पड़ा। अकीरा दुःख से बोली, "हाँ! क्या नीलू मासी हमेशा से ही इतनी विचित्र रही हैं?"

"बिल्कुल! वे इतनी विचित्र हैं कि एक बार तो वेद भैया की शादी कर दी थी।" वेदिका ने कहा।

"क्या?"

"हाँ! वेद भैया शादीशुदा हैं, ठीक है।" दबी हँसी में वेदिका बोली।

"हम तो ऐसे ही मजाक उड़ाते रहते हैं।"

अकीरा ने वेद की ओर देखा, वह अपने काम में मग्न था। उसने इस बात-चीत में हिस्सा लेना तो दूर, उनकी ओर देखा तक नहीं।

"विस्तार से तो बताओ।" अकीरा ने घटना बताने पर जोर देते हुए कहा। 'फिर एक नई कहानी!' मन में सोचते हुए अकीरा पैर मोड़कर बैठ गई।

"एक बार की बात है, नीलू मासी किसी धर्मगुरु की शिष्या बन गईं। हालाँकि उनके पति नहीं चाहते थे कि वह किसी धर्मगुरु के आश्रम में जाएँ। नीलू मासी को टोकने पर उन्होंने झूठ बोलकर उन बाबा के आश्रम में जाना शुरू किया।"

"क्या?"

"हाँ!" वेदिका ने उत्साह से बताना शुरू किया। "नीलू मासी ने कहा कि वह सब बच्चों को वाटर पार्क लेकर जाना चाहती हैं। हम सब कितने खुश थे, लेकिन मासी हमें वाटर पार्क की जगह बाबाजी के आश्रम में ले गईं।"

"यही होना था, फिरऽऽऽऽऽऽ?" अकीरा बोली।

"हाँ!" वेदिका ने उत्साह से बताना शुरू किया। "नीलू मासी ने कहा कि वह सब बच्चों को वाटर पार्क लेकर जाना चाहती हैं। हम सब कितने खुश थे, लेकिन मासी हमें वाटर पार्क की जगह बाबाजी के आश्रम में ले गईं।"

"यही होना था, फिरऽऽऽऽऽऽ?" अकीरा बोली।

"आश्रम में कोई अजीब सा कार्यक्रम चल रहा था। भैया की नजर पड़ी और कुछ लोगों की भैया पर नजर पड़ी।" उदास आवाज में वेदिका घटना बता रही थी। "फिर क्या था, सबने वेद भैया को जबरदस्ती कृष्ण के कपड़े पहना दिए और उसके बाद तुलसी के पौधे के साथ उनका विवाह कर दिया।"

"क्या?" कर्कश-सी आवाज में अकीरा ने पूछा, "तुम तुलसी से ब्याहे गए हो?"

वेद ने बेदिली से साँस छोड़ते हुए कहा, "हाँ।"

अकीरा ने मुँह बनाते हुए प्रतिक्रिया दी, "मेरे पास शब्द नहीं हैं।"

"होंगे भी कैसे?" लैपटॉप बंद करते हुए वेद ने कहा। उसकी आँखों में चमक थी। "वैसे ही जैसे एक बार वेदिका ने एक बार मासी का घर जलाने की कोशिश की।"

कबीर बीच में बोला, "आगे की कहानी, वेदिका की जुबानी।"

"मैं छोटा नहीं था क्या?" वेद की आवाज से व्यंग्य छलक रहा था। "खैर! हम नीलू मासी के घर खाना खाने गए थे। उन्होंने मेज बहुत ही खूबसूरत तरीके से सजाई थी।

पेरिस से मँगवाया हुआ टेबलक्लॉथ था; मेज फूलों और मोमबत्तियों से सजाई थी। बेहद सुंदर लग रही थी मेज की सजावट। अब चूँकि वेदिका, वेदिका है, बोर हो गई थी। उसने देखा कि कुरसी पर बैठने पर और एक तरफ होने पर कितनी दूर तक बैठे-बैठे जाया जा सकता है। उसने ऐसा ही किया और वह तब तक झुकती रही, जब तक वह गिर नहीं गईं। गिरते समय वह मेजपोश (Table Cover) भी साथ खींचकर ले गई। जली हुई मोमबत्तियों के कारण मेजपोश ने फटाक से आग पकड़ ली।"

कबीर हैरानी से सोच रहा था, "हे भगवान्!"

वेद बताता रहा, "उसी समय वेदिका की कुरसी सीधे वहाँ रखी अलमारी पर गिरी, वह अलमारी सीधी वहाँ गिरी, जहाँ मेजपोश गिरकर इकट्ठा हो गया था। अलमारी का काँच टूटा और कुछ किताबें भी उस मेजपोश पर गिरीं और उन्होंने आग पकड़ ली। कुछ ही क्षणों में आधी से ज्याद चीजों ने आग पकड़ ली। इसलिए इसमें कोई दो राय नहीं है कि नीलू मासी वेदिका से कितना प्रेम करती हैं!"

वेद बताता रहा, "उसी समय वेदिका की कुरसी सीधे वहाँ रखी अलमारी पर गिरी, वह अलमारी सीधी वहाँ गिरी, जहाँ मेजपोश गिरकर इकट्ठा हो गया था। अलमारी का काँच टूटा और कुछ किताबें भी उस मेजपोश पर गिरीं और उन्होंने आग पकड़ ली। कुछ ही क्षणों में आधी से ज्यादा चीजों ने आग पकड़ ली। इसलिए इसमें कोई दो राय नहीं है कि नीलू मासी वेदिका से कितना प्रेम करती हैं!"

अभी तक कबीर हँस-हँसकर लोट-पोट हो चुका था। अकीरा को कहानी अपने अंदर लेने में कुछ समय लगा। "तुम्हें पता है, मुझे सबसे ज्यादा हैरानी किस बात पर होती है? तुम लोगों की सारी कहानियाँ एक से बढ़कर एक हैं। सारी 'विचित्र किंतु सत्य' के रेडियो कार्यक्रम जैसी।"

कबीर साँस लेते हुए बोला, "अकीरा, तुम भी ऐसी ही कहनियाँ बनानेवाली हो।"

"क्यों?"

कबीर ने नीलू मासी द्वारा दी गई सूची में एक पंक्ति की ओर इशारा किया, "एक सफेद रंग का घोड़ा, जिसका वजन लगभग 280 किलो, 16 हाथ नाप, जिसकी मांसपेशियाँ अच्छी हों, पूँछ भी लंबी और सुंदर हो और जिसके खुर भी साफ हों। कोष्ठक में था—मादा हो, जिसका शोषण न किया गया हो। एक ओर कोष्ठक में था—शुद्ध नस्ल का।"

वेद हँसा, "इसके लिए प्रमोद मामा सही आदमी हैं।"

"और ये सबकुछ अभय के लिए? छी: !" वेदिका के स्वर में घृणा थी।

"वाकई!" वेद ने वेदिका के सुर–में–सुर मिलाकर कहा। "पहली बार घोड़ी पर गधा बैठेगा।"

अकीरा कुछ सोचकर बोली, "इसीलिए पहलेवाला प्रबंधक भाग गया।"

"छोड़ यार! चिंता मत कर। कल मामा के अस्तबल पर चलते हैं।" कबीर ने सुझाव दिया।

"कितना सही आइडिया है! डबल डेट हो जाएँगी।" वेदिका ने उत्साह दिखाया। "मजा आएगा।"

"अकीरा?" वेद ने अकीरा से उसकी राय पूछी।

"हाँ, क्यों नहीं? कल चलते हैं प्रमोद मामा के फार्म पर।" अकीरा ने हामी भरी।

□

25

"ये लो आ गए।" अरुणा ने कहा, जैसे ही अकीरा और वेद सीढ़ियों से नीचे आए।

हालाँकि अकीरा नीलू मासी की सूची देखकर अंदर-ही-अंदर परेशान थी। फिर भी मिजाज उसका अच्छा ही था। वेद ने झूठ नहीं बोला था, जब उसने अकीरा से कहा था कि वह कोशिश करेगा कि अकीरा को रात लंबी न लगे। दोनों ने मिलकर वे सारे डिजाइन बना लिये थे, जो नीलू मासी को कहे थे। उसने कुछ चुनिंदा नमूने अपने लोगों की टीम को भेज दिए थे, जो 'एनिमेशन' का काम करते थे और उन्होंने वादा किया था कि वीडियो दिन के आखिर तक मिल जाएँगे। कबीर और वेदिका तो एक घंटे में ही सो गए, पर वेद अपने कहे अनुसार रातभर जागकर अकीरा की मदद करता रहा।

"गुड मॉर्निंग नानी, दादी, आंटी!" चहककर अकीरा बोली।

सुबह की चाय के समय अरुणा, इंद्राणी और पिंकी गप्पें मार रही थीं। चाहे वेद को चाय इतनी पसंद नहीं है, पर वेद बड़े ध्यान से उनके चाय के कप को देख रहा था। वह अपने वो दिन याद कर रहा था, जब उसे एस्प्रेसो कॉफी का कप बिना अत्यधिक मेहनत किए आसानी से मिल जाता था।

"हाय-हाय, वेद का चेहरा तो देखो। सुबह-सुबह कितना परेशानी से भरा दिख रहा है, प्रमिला!" वेद की नाक मोड़कर अरुणा बोलीं।

"क्या यार नानी? ऐसा क्यों है कि जब भी आप कुछ बोलने के लिए मुँह खोलती हैं, तब मेरे बारे में कुछ बुरा ही बोलती हैं?

"फिर तुम भी अच्छे से क्यों नहीं रहते?" अरुणा ने त्यौरियाँ चढ़ाकर पूछा।

"अपने विचारों का पुनर्मूल्यांकन कीजिए नानी माँ! मेरा व्यवहार हमेशा से भी और अच्छा रहा है।" पलटकर नानी को जवाब देते हुए वेद ने अपना सिर पिंकी के कंधे पर रख दिया। "मुझे बहुत नींद आ रही है आज। अकीरा ने मुझे रात को सोने ही नहीं दिया।"

"वेदऽऽऽऽऽऽ!" अकीरा किकियाते हुए बोली। वेद अपने शब्दों और वाक्यों से अजीब सी परिस्थिति में डाल देनेवाला अविवादित बादशाह कहा जा सकता था।

"सच में?" पिंकी ने उत्साह से पूछा।

"इतना खुश होने की कोई जरूरत नहीं है। तुम्हारा बेटा उस तरह का नहीं है।" अरुणा ने नाक से आवाज निकालते हुए कहा।

"हाँ, जानती हूँ।" शिकायती स्वर था इंद्राणी का "वेद ही है, जिसके पास अच्छा चेहरा, अच्छा भविष्य, अच्छा परिवार है, लेकिन उस बात का वह कोई फायदा नहीं उठाएगा। सारी बातें बेकार हैं। उफ्फ!"

"भैया!"

पूरा कमरा किसी के जोर से चिल्लाने से भर गया। वेद को पता था कौन होगा! उसने लाचारी से अपना चेहरा ढक लिया।

"रीशी।" पिंकी खुश हो गईं।

"पिंकी मामी! आपने मुझे बताया क्यों नहीं कि आप लोग आनेवाले हैं, ये ठीक नहीं किया।" रीशी छोटे बच्चे की तरह शिकायत कर रहा था। वेद ने धीरे से सिर उठाकर देखा। वाकई वह ऋषि-मुनियोंवाली महिमा और शोभा उसके चेहरे पर थी। उसे रीशी वैसे ही याद था। उसपर और भी डरावना मंजर था—चोंचले करते हुए बनावटी हँसी हँसना! वह मुसकान और हँसी अपनत्व की न होते हुए वेदिका जैसी मुसकान थी—व्यंग्यात्मक। वेद हवेली से बाहर अभी जाने ही वाला था कि 'भैया।' कहकर रीशी ने उसे जकड़ लिया। और जब तक वेद को कुछ समझ आए, उसे सिर्फ अस्पष्ट रंग दिखे, क्योंकि रीशी ने उसे उठाकर कई बार गोल-गोल घुमाया।

"पिंकी मामी! आपने मुझे बताया क्यों नहीं कि आप लोग आनेवाले हैं, ये ठीक नहीं किया।" रीशी छोटे बच्चे की तरह शिकायत कर रहा था। वेद ने धीरे से सिर उठाकर देखा। वाकई वह ऋषि-मुनियोंवाली महिमा और शोभा उसके चेहरे पर थी।

'भैया-भैया' कहकर मानो रीशी ने वेद को व्यक्तिगत मैरी-गो-राउंड (चक्कर देनेवाला हिंडोला) का अनुभव दिया था। "मैंने आपको कितना मिस किया, याद किया।"

"रीशी! तुम उसे कहीं गिरा न दो।" यह कहकर पिंकी ने उसे रोकने की कोशिश की थी। उन्हें डर था कि उत्साह और खुशी के खुमार में उनके बेटे का सिर कहीं लग न जाए!

अकीरा निःशब्द होकर सिर्फ देख रही थी। जैसे अचानक रीशी ने वेद को घुमाना शुरू किया था, वैसे ही रुक भी गया। "मैं वेद भैया को कभी नहीं गिरा सकता।"

वेद अपनी जगह पर कुछ क्षण सिर पकड़कर खड़ा रहा और खुद को सँभाल रहा था। अकीरा तत्क्षण उसके पास पहुँची। उसने पूछा, "तुम ठीक हो?"

"हाँ।" गहरी आवाज में वेद बोला।

जैसे ही रीशी को अहसास हुआ कि वहाँ अकीरा है, उसके चेहरे पर आश्चर्य था। वह अकीरा को ऐसे देख रहा था, मानो अजायबघर में रखी कोई वस्तु देख रहा हो!

"तुम कौन हो?" रीशी ने हाँफते हुए गाने के स्वर में पूछा और वह भी ऐसा स्वर जो सामान्य मनुष्य जैसा नहीं था।

"अकीरा, ये रीशी है; वेद की बुआ का लड़का, मतलब वेद का भाई है। अविनाश की एक छोटी बहन है। ये उसी का बेटा है।"

अकीरा उसे देख मुसकराई, पर रीशी के चेहरे के भाव वैसे ही थे। फिर पिंकी ने गर्व के स्वर में रीशी को बताया, "ये अकीरा है, वेद की गर्लफ्रेंड!"

"हे भगवान्!" हैरानी से रीशी जमीन पर अपने आप बैठ गया। ऐसा लग रहा था मानो उसका दिमाग चल गया हो। अकीरा हतप्रभ होकर रीशी को देख रही थी। अरोरा परिवार के विदूषकों (जोकर) में एक और भरती।

अकीरा उसे देख मुसकराई, पर रीशी के चेहरे के भाव वैसे ही थे। फिर पिंकी ने गर्व के स्वर में रीशी को बताया, "ये अकीरा है, वेद की गर्लफ्रेंड!" "हे भगवान्!" हैरानी से रीशी जमीन पर अपने आप बैठ गया। ऐसा लग रहा था मानो उसका दिमाग चल गया हो। अकीरा हतप्रभ होकर रीशी को देख रही थी। अरोरा परिवार के विदूषकों (जोकर) में एक और भरती।

वेद के पेट में प्रमोद मामा के फार्म हाउस तक पहुँचने के रास्ते में ही हलचल सी, बेचैनी सी थी, क्योंकि रीशी ने आकर अचानक डबलडेट की ऐसी-तैसी कर दी थी। रीशी वेद और अकीरा के बीच बिना आमंत्रण के ही बैठ गया था, ताकि वेद और अकीरा दोनों के हाथों को पकड़ सके। रीशी के जोर से हाथ पकड़ने की वजह से वेद के सीधे हाथ की हथेली पर पसीना आने लगा था और वेद की बेचैनी भी बढ़ रही थी। अगर रीशी जल्दी से उसका हाथ नहीं छोड़ता तो मुमकिन है, वेद उसके हाथ को झटक देता।

"तुम मेरा नाम अजीब तरीके से क्यों लेते हो?" अकीरा ने पूछा।

"भाभी! चूँकि मैं कुछ दिन कनाडा में रहा, इसलिए मेरे बोलने का लहजा थोड़ा अलग है।"

वेद टेढ़ा मुँह करके बोला, "13 दिन।"

"क्या?" वेदिका खिलखिलाकर हँस पड़ी और साथ में कबीर भी। "रीशी कनाडा में सिर्फ 13 दिनों तक रहा।"

अकीरा रीशी के मुँह पर हँसना नहीं चाहती थी तो गहरी साँस लेते हुए अकीरा

बोली, “हम्म्म! काफी लंबा समय है।”

“मैं समझता हूँ, ठीक है न!” व्यंग्यात्मक हँसी से रीशी बोला। वेद ने सिर पकड़ लिया। पहले ही कम मूर्ख साथ में थे, जो रीशी भी आ गया! रीशी का अजीब तरह का बेवकूफ होना आनुवंशिक था। लेकिन रीर्शी की जो आदत सबसे ज्यादा परेशान करती थी, वह थी उसका वेद के साथ चिपके रहना। बचपन में सारे कजिंस (भाई–बहन) उसे वेद की पूँछ बुलाते थे। उस समय चाहे वह बात प्यार लगती हो, लेकिन अब नहीं थी।

“ओकीरा भाभी! तुम कितनी अच्छी हो!” रीशी चहककर बोला। ‘भाभी’ शब्द सुनकर अकीरा की आँखें झटके से चौड़ी हो गईं। साथ ही नाम के गलत उच्चारण का सदमा भी था।

वेद का माथा ठनका। वेद ने त्यौरियाँ चढ़ाकर पूछा, “स्टड फार्म (अस्तबल) और कितनी दूर है?”

“कुछ मिनट और···” कबीर ने जवाब दिया।

कुछ शांति और बिना घटना के क्षण बीतने के बाद वे सभी स्टड फार्म पर पहुँचे। जैसे ही वे कार से उतरे, रीशी ने मानो दया दिखाते हुए अकीरा और वेद का हाथ छोड़ दिया। वेद और अकीरा जानबूझकर औरों से थोड़ा पीछे चल रहे थे। अपने हाथ को खोलते, बंद करते हुए वेद ने कुछ पंजाबी (अपशब्द) शब्द कहे और अकीरा हँस पड़ी। अकीरा ने वेद की बाजू में हाथ डाला और दोनों स्टड फार्म के अंदर जाने लगे। अकीरा फिर कल्पना कर रही थी कि यहाँ न जाने क्या होगा?

□

26

"हैलो बच्चो!" प्रमोद मामा ने हरेक को हाथ हिलाते हुए कहा। वेद को याद नहीं आ रहा था कि पिछली बार वह उस फार्म पर कब आया था, लेकिन जैसे ही घोड़ों और अस्तबल की गंध उसकी नाक में गई, उसे याद आने लगा। प्रमोद मामा सभी बच्चों को फॉर्म पर ले आते और छोटे-छोटे घोड़ों के बच्चों के साथ मजे करने देते।

"मामा! क्या आपको घोड़ी मिली?" अकीरा ने सीधा प्रश्न किया।

"हाँ! मेरे मित्र ने एक खालिस जाति की घोड़ी ढूँढ़ने में मदद की। आओ, मैं तुम्हें दिखाऊँ..." प्रमोद ने जवाब दिया और सब उनके पीछे चल पड़े।

उन्होंने बॉक्स स्टॉल का गेट खोला। (बॉक्स स्टॉल—एक खलिहान या अस्तबल, जिसके भीतर एक व्यक्तिगत बाड़ा, जिसमें एक जानवर, बिना किसी निरोधक उपकरण के स्वतंत्र रूप से घूम सकता है।)

घोड़े की खाल चमकदार और सफेद कोट जैसी थी; पैर लंबे और मजबूत, सुंदर पूँछ और भूरी आँखें थीं।

प्रमोद ने मुसकराकर कहा, "आइए, हमारी लैला से मिलिए।"

"वाऽऽऽह! कितनी सुंदर!" अकीरा ने हैरानी से कहा।

"तुम भाग्यवान हो! ऐसे घोड़े इतनी आसानी से नहीं मिलते। या तो उन्हें बचपन से पालना पड़ता है या लाखों रुपए देकर नीलामी में खरीदना पड़ता है।"

"शुक्रिया मामाजी! आपका मुझपर कर्ज रहा...।" अकीरा ने आभार जताते हुए कहा।

प्रमोद ने हाथ के इशारे से कहा, "अरे ऐसा कुछ नहीं। बात सिर्फ यह है कि यह डरबी का घोड़ा है और आज तक किसी विवाह प्रदर्शन का हिस्सा नहीं बना है।"

"मामाजी, फिर शायद दिक्कत आए।" कबीर बोला।

"ओह! मुझे नहीं लगता, वह शादी का हिस्सा बनने को तैयार है।" वेद ने जानबूझकर ऐसा कहा।

"वेद! यह देख मुझे अच्छा लगा कि जो मैंने तुम्हें सिखाया, वो तुम भूले नहीं हो।"

"क्या मामाजी ?" वेदिका ने उत्सुकता से पूछा। "क्या हुआ ?"

"ऐसा कुछ नहीं। लेकिन अब समय है···" चुटकियाँ लेते हुए प्रमोद मामा ने घोड़ी की पूँछ उठाई और मल निकाला। सभी ने नाक सिकोड़ी और वेद ठहाका मारकर हँस पड़ा।

"ईऽऽऽश! उम्मीद है, ऐसा यह बारात के समय नहीं करेगी।" अकीरा टेढ़ी शक्ल करके बोली।

लैला की गरदन सहलाते हुए प्रमोद धीरे से बोले, "माफ करना, पर इस बारे में मैं कोई मदद नहीं कर सकता। यह जितना चाहे, जब चाहे···कर सकती है।"

"बिल्कुल वेदिका जैसी।" वेद हँसी दबाते हुए बोला।

कबीर और अकीरा दूसरी तरफ छुपाकर हँसने चले गए। प्रमोद और रीशी को कोई मतलब नहीं था, इसलिए वे वहीं हँस पड़े। वेदिका ने मजाक को मजाक के रूप में लेते हुए वेद से कहा, "चुप रहो!"

हँसते-हँसते अकीरा ने घोड़े की तसवीर ली और नीलू को भेज दी। सबकुछ होने के बाद जब अकीरा ने आसपास देखा तो वेद को एक काले घोड़े के पास खड़ा पाया। वह घोड़ा भी सुंदर था।

"तुम यहाँ क्या कर रहे हो?" अकीरा ने प्रश्न किया।

जब अकीरा ने देखा तो वेद घोड़े की गीली नाक और गरदन को सहला रहा था। पीछे मुड़कर कहा, "मैं इसको अपनी खुशबू से अवगत करा रहा हूँ।"

"अच्छा! वे इस तरह इनसानों की पहचान करते हैं?"

"हाँ। आवाज और खुशबू से। और इन्हें इस बात के लिए भी प्रशिक्षित किया जाता है कि अलग-अलग तरह के लोग उनपर सवारी करें।"

"ओह! क्या तुम्हें घुड़सवारी आती है?"

"हाँ! मैं कर सकता हूँ। चलोगी मेरे साथ?"

वेद की विनीत आँखें देखकर अकीरा का हृदय धक-सा रह गया। उन दोनों को साथ रहने का और समय मिल जाएगा। प्रस्ताव काफी आकर्षक था। अकीरा ने नरम

कबीर और अकीरा दूसरी तरफ छुपाकर हँसने चले गए। प्रमोद और रीशी को कोई मतलब नहीं था, इसलिए वे वहीं हँस पड़े। वेदिका ने मजाक को मजाक के रूप में लेते हुए वेद से कहा, "चुप रहो!" हँसते-हँसते अकीरा ने घोड़े की तसवीर ली और नीलू को भेज दी। सबकुछ होने के बाद जब अकीरा ने आसपास देखा तो वेद को एक काले घोड़े के पास खड़ा पाया। वह घोड़ा भी सुंदर था।

भाषा में कहा, "ठीक है, लेकिन अगर मैं गिर गई तो तुम्हारा खून कर दूँगी।"

"इसकी गारंटी वेद अरोरा लेता है कि तुम नहीं गिरोगी।"

उसने अपनी ट्रेडमार्क (व्यापार-चिह्न) मुस्कान के साथ कहा।

वेद ने हेडगियर (सिर को सुरक्षित रखने का शिरस्त्राण) उठाया और अकीरा के सिर पर रखा। उसकी उँगलियाँ अकीरा के हेडगियर को पक्का करने के लिए गरदन पर हलकी सी छू गईं। अचानक कसने के कारण अकीरा की सहज ही कराह निकल गई। अभी अकीरा अपने खयालों में ही खोई हुई थी कि किस तरह उसे गरदन में गुदगुदी हुई, कि तभी वेद ने अकीरा को कमर से पकड़कर घोड़े की पीठ (जीन) पर बिठा दिया। सहज भाव से अकीरा की चीख निकल गई।

"वेद!" वह हाँफते हुए बोली, "अरे! चेतावनी तो दे दिया करो।"

"नाऽऽऽ!" हँसते हुए वेद बोला और घोड़े की जीन कसने लगा और अकीरा के पैर रकाब (घोड़े पर बैठने पर जिसपर पैर रखे जाते हैं) में रखते हुए पूछा, "ठीक से तो हो?"

अकीरा ने वेद की आँखों में अपने लिए चिंता देखी। वेद की आँखें सुंदर दिखाई दे रही थीं।

"हाँ, मैं ठीक हूँ।" अकीरा ने जवाब दिया।

अपनी हँसी बरकरार रखते हुए वेद बगल में बने चबूतरे पर चढ़ा और वहाँ से घोड़े पर अकीरा के पीछे जाकर बैठ गया। घोड़े की जीन धीरे से पकड़कर अपनी एड़ी से घोड़े को चलने का आदेश दिया।

अकीरा ने वेद की आँखों में अपने लिए चिंता देखी। वेद की आँखें सुंदर दिखाई दे रही थीं।

"हाँ, मैं ठीक हूँ।" अकीरा ने ज़वाब दिया।

अपनी हँसी बरकरार रखते हुए वेद बगल में बने चबूतरे पर चढ़ा और वहाँ से घोड़े पर अकीरा के पीछे जाकर बैठ गया। घोड़े की जीन धीरे से पकड़कर अपनी एड़ी से घोड़े को चलने का आदेश दिया।

घोड़ा धीरे-धीरे चल पड़ा। अकीरा को अपनी गरदन पर वेद का गरम श्वास महसूस हो रहा था और वह कमजोर सी पड़ रही थी। वह निश्चिंतता का अहसास था, खुशी की कमजोरी, उसे समझ नहीं आ रहा था। जो भी था, उसे बहुत अच्छा लग रहा था। बहुत अच्छा सा। वेद ने आगे की तरफ से अकीरा को थामा और अपना चेहरा अकीरा की गरदन से सटा लिया। "खुश अब?"

उनके आसपास सुंदर हरे खेत, घोड़े की धीमी टाप, ठंडी धीमी हवा और वेद की बाजुओं में खुद मूर्ख होती अगर अकीरा खुश नहीं होती! अकीरा ने धीरे से अपनी गरदन मोड़ी और छोटा सा चुंबन वेद के होंठों पर रख दिया।

वेद को एक सुखद झटका लगा। "किसने सोचा था कि यह घुड़सवारी वेद का मन इतना खुश कर देगी?"

"ये नीली आँखोंवाले राक्षस ने मेरा मूड सुहावना कर दिया।" अकीरा बोली।

"राक्षस? मैं दिखाऊँ यह राक्षस क्या कर सकता है?" वेद ने धमकी दी।

"चलो दिखा ही दो कि कितना दम है तुममें?" चुनौती भरे स्वर में अकीरा ने कहा।

वेद ने अकीरा को आगे से कसा, अपनी एड़ियाँ घोड़े के बाजुओं में दबाते हुए घोड़े को तेजी से चलने का आदेश दिया और देखते-ही-देखते घोड़े ने हिनहिनाते हुए मिट्टी के रास्ते पर हवा की गति से भागना शुरू किया। घोड़े की गति का पता उसके खुरों से पीछे की ओर उड़ते हुए धूल के बादलों से चल रहा था। अकीरा जम-सी गई थी। उसे घोड़े के भागने से डर नहीं लग रहा था, बल्कि वेद के शरीर के साथ जुड़कर, जो वह महसूस कर रही थी, वह उसने कभी किसी और लड़के के साथ महसूस नहीं किया था। डेट पर तो वह और लड़कों के साथ भी गई थी।

वेद ने अकीरा को आगे से कसा, अपनी एड़ियाँ घोड़े के बाजुओं में दबाते हुए घोड़े को तेजी से चलने का आदेश दिया और देखते-ही-देखते घोड़े ने हिनहिनाते हुए मिट्टी के रास्ते पर हवा की गति से भागना शुरू किया। घोड़े की गति का पता उसके खुरों से पीछे की ओर उड़ते हुए धूल के बादलों से चल रहा था।

अकीरा को जो महसूस हो रहा था, उसको सँभाल पाना उसके लिए मुश्किल हो रहा था। सहसा वह बोली, "रुको!"

"फिर मुझे कभी राक्षस कहोगी? "अकीरा को कानों में वेद का प्रश्न सुनाई दिया।

"नहीं! वह चीखकर बोली, "भगवान् कसम नहीं!"

"गुड गर्ल! (अच्छी लड़की)" यह कहकर वेद ने घोड़े की लगाम खींची और घोड़ा घू-घू करता हुआ रुक गया। अकीरा बोली, "तुम पागल हो क्या?"

"हाँ, थोड़ा सा।" यह कहकर वह घोड़े से उतर गया।

वह घोड़े को हरे वृक्ष की तरफ ले जाने लगा। जीन की बगल से एक रस्सी निकाली और घोड़े को पेड़ से बाँध दिया। वेद ने अकीरा को कमर से पकड़ा और ऊपर की तरफ करके घोड़े से उतारने की कोशिश की। अकीरा तो थी हलकी-फुलकी! वह भी छोटी बच्ची की तरह पकड़े जाने को तैयार थी।

"आ जाओ!" एक प्यारी सी मुसकान के साथ जब वेद ने अकीरा को इशारा किया तो मानो वह अंदर तक पिघल गई। दूसरा पैर भी एक तरफ करते हुए वह आगे की तरफ झुकी, वेद ने उसे नीचे उतारा और अकीरा का चेहरा शर्म से लाल हो चुका था।

वेद के छूने में कुछ तो अलग था! वेद का व्यवहार उसके प्रति इतना कोमल था कि वह मानो बेहोश-सी ही हो गई थी।

वेद का हाथ अकीरा की कमर पर ही था, जब तक वे पेड़ के नीचे बैठे। अकीरा ने आसपास देखा। नीला आसमान, फसलों की पीली चादर, हरे पेड़ मानो रंगों का उत्सव था। वह सम्मोहित-सी हो गई।

अकीरा ने गहरी साँस लेते हुए कहा, "कितनी खूबसूरत जगह है!"

"हाँऽऽऽऽ!" वेद ने हामी भरी। कुछ शांत क्षणों के बाद वेद ने अचानक अकीरा का हाथ पकड़ा और प्रश्न किया, "अभी तक तुम कितनी डेट्स पर जा चुकी हो?"

अकीरा ने संक्षिप्त उत्तर देना ही उचित समझा, वरना वेद डर जाता।

"कई।"

"और फिर तुमने उन डेट्स पर क्या-क्या किया?"

"वही, जो अकसर होता है। खाना-पीना, कभी डिस्को क्लब, फिल्म देखना आदि। जैसा कि आम है…" अकीरा बोली।

"और बाकीऽऽऽ?" खाँसते हुए वेद ने इशारा दिया। "मुझे गलत मत समझो, पर मेरा मतलब किसिंग या शारीरिक आनंद आदि?"

"मैं मोहित के साथ काफी लंबे समय के लिए थी; कुछ तो होना ही था।" अकीरा ने रूखे स्वर में जवाब दिया और वेद ने सिर हिलाकर हामी भरी। मानो वह समझ रहा हो। "मैंने पहली बार तब किस किया था, जब मैं नवीं कक्षा में थी। खाने के समय के दौरान।"

"और बाकीऽऽऽ?" खाँसते हुए वेद ने इशारा दिया। "मुझे गलत मत समझो, पर मेरा मतलब किसिंग या शारीरिक आनंद आदि?" "मैं मोहित के साथ काफी लंबे समय के लिए थी; कुछ तो होना ही था।" अकीरा ने रूखे स्वर में जवाब दिया और वेद ने सिर हिलाकर हामी भरी। मानो वह समझ रहा हो। "मैंने पहली बार तब किस किया था, जब मैं नवीं कक्षा में थी। खाने के समय के दौरान।"

"तुम्हारे पास खाना खाने के समय इतना वक्त होता था?" वेद की भौंहें मानो आश्चर्य से बालों तक पहुँच गई थीं। "मेरे लिए तो रिसेस (खाने का समय) या तो ठंडी मैगी या फिर समोसे लेने के लिए कैंटीन की लाइन होती थी।"

"हे भगवान्!" अकीरा ने खिलखिलाते हुए कहा।

वेद ने अकीरा की आँखों में देखकर प्रश्न किया, "पर क्या तुम मेरे लिए भी वैसा ही महसूस करती हो, जैसा कि उन लड़कों के लिए करती थी? इस मामले में मेरी क्या जगह है?"

"इससे क्या फर्क पड़ता है?" अकीरा ने वेद की उँगलियों में अपनी उँगलियाँ लपेटते हुए कहा। "किसी ने मुझे ऐसे ही तो जाने नहीं दिया होगा न!"

वेद धीरे से मुसकराकर बोला, "तुम्हें पता था?"

"बिल्कुल!" अकीरा मुसकाई, "तुम्हें लगता है कि तुम बहुत अच्छा अभिनय कर लेते हो, पर ऐसा कुछ नहीं है और मैं तुम्हें यह भी बता दूँ कि तुम बहुत अच्छे हो! औरों से बहुत अच्छे। ये तो मेरी बदकिस्मती है कि मैंने तुमसे पहले बहुत से मेढकों को किस (Kiss) किया।"

वेद ने आँखें छोटी करते हुए कहा, "और अगर मैं भी मेढक निकला तो?"

"देखते हैं!" अकीरा ने आँखें मटकाते हुए कहा। अकीरा ने वेद का चेहरा ध्यान से देखा। अपने हाथ उसके चेहरे पर रखते हुए वेद का सिर नीचे की ओर करके अपने होंठ वेद के होंठों पर फिराकर पीछे हो गई। अब वेद और कितना धैर्य धरता! दोनों प्रेम में खो चुके थे। वह प्रेम का अहसास चुंबन के द्वारा था, जो अत्यधिक मृदु, आत्मीय और प्रेमयुक्त था। अकीरा को उम्मीद नहीं थी कि यह प्रेम अभिव्यक्ति इतनी आसानी से हो जाएगी। उसने अपना माथा वेद के माथे पर रख दिया। वेद ने प्रश्न किया, "कैसा लगा?"

वे दोनों एक-दूसरे में खो चुके थे, जो खुशी और संतोष से परिपूर्ण थे। अकीरा एकदम मुकराकर बोली, "एक राजकुमार, इतने वर्षों के मेढकों के बाद।"

"उफ्फ!" इतना कहकर वेद ने अकीरा के होंठों पर अपने होंठ फिर रख दिए।

□

27

"भैया! आप कुछ खा क्यों नहीं रहे?" रीशी ने मटन का बड़ा सा टुकड़ा मुँह में भरते हुए वेद से पूछा। "पता नहीं लोग खाते हुए बात क्यों करते हैं? वैसे भी वह मटन खानेवालों में नहीं था। वह अपनी भिंडी की सब्जी से खुश था। शुक्र है, पिंकी ने इतने खाने के विविध पकवानों में उसकी पसंद का ध्यान रखा था। उसने धीरे से अपनी प्लेट के कुछ मीट के टुकड़े रीशी की प्लेट में खिसका दिए। बाकी में कबीर उसकी मदद कर रहा था। इसीलिए वेद ने उन दोनों को अपने आसपास बैठने दिया था। इस बात का ध्यान रखने के लिए वेद ने सावधानी से फूलदान और बड़ा कटोरा अपने सामने रख लिया था। अकीरा की तो नहीं, लेकिन वेद की पहली 'किस' थी।

विचारधारा थोड़ी अलग होने के कारण उसे 'किस' करने की अवधारणा हमेशा अजीब और अस्वास्थ्यकर लगी। 'किसी के मुँह में अपनी जीभ डालना' में क्या प्रेम है? और बुरी साँसें और बुरा मुँह का स्वास्थ्य हो तो और भी रोगी। पर अब वेद का विचार थोड़ा सा बदल रहा था। अगर जीवनसाथी मिल जाए, तो 'किस करना' भी बुरा नहीं। वेद मन-ही-मन खुश हो रहा था। उसके होंठ मानो अभी भी लालायित थे। सहज ही उसकी नजरें अकीरा को ढूँढ़ती हुई खिड़की तक पहुँचीं। वहाँ अकीरा किसी से फोन पर बात कर रही थी। उसकी आँखें कितनी सुंदर दिखाई दे रही थीं। अभी तक अकीरा की आँखें उसने इतने ध्यान से देखी ही नहीं थीं। आँखें हों या होंठ, सबकुछ मेरे साथ कितना अच्छा लग रहा था! उसके जज्बात बहुत तेजी से उस पर हावी होने की कोशिश कर रहे थे। उसे अहसास हुआ कि वह पहली बार किसी के ख्वाबों में डूबा-सा जा रहा था। उसने अपनी भावनाओं, विचारों को दिमाग में ठहरने के लिए छोड़ दिया। उसके मन में डरावने विचार आने लगे। अगर 21 दिनों के बाद अकीरा ने इस रिश्ते को आगे ले जाने से इनकार कर दिया तो वह तो टूट जाएगा। इस बात से वेद को लगा कि यह रिश्ता तो लंबा चलना चाहिए।

"तुम्हारा यह हाल देखकर लग रहा है कि एक बिब (एक छोटा कपड़ा, जो बच्चों की छाती पर कपड़ों को गंदा होने से बचाने के लिए लगाया जाता है।) लगा देना चाहिए, कितनी लार टपक रही है।"

"चुप रहो।" वेद ने कहा। "अगर यहाँ कोई बेताब है तो वह है रीशी, जो मृत जानवर पर टूट पड़ा है, जो मसालों से तर है।"

"झूठ! हाय! एक उस किस पर ही मैं मर गया।"

कबीर ने नाटकीय तरीके से अपना हाथ दिल पर रखते हुए कहा।

"ठीक है। मैं मुंबई का गरीब 'शेक्सपीयर' और तुम्हें कैसे मालूम कि मैंने और अकीरा ने 'किस' किया?" दाँत पीसते हुए वेद ने कहा।

"जब तुम स्टड फार्म से वापस आए, तब तुम्हारे चेहरे पर अंग्रेजी मि. बीन के किरदार प्रेम में पड़े भाव थे; हम समझ गए।" वेदिका ने जवाब दिया।

"प्रेम!" झटका-सा लगा वेद को। "सच में?"

"और क्या डंबो (मूर्ख), क्या वाकई तुम अकीरा के प्रेम में नहीं पड़े हो?" वेदिका ने घूरते हुए संदेह की दृष्टि से वेद से कहा, "जाहिर है, तुम पहली बार अपने व्यवसाय के अलावा किसी और वस्तु को इतने ध्यान से देख रहे हो।"

रीशी बीच में खुद को कहने से नहीं रोक पाया, "भैया! मेरे बारे में ऐसा कहना गलत है।"

"और क्या डंबो (मूर्ख), क्या वाकई तुम अकीरा के प्रेम में नहीं पड़े हो?" वेदिका ने घूरते हुए संदेह की दृष्टि से वेद से कहा, "जाहिर है, तुम पहली बार अपने व्यवसाय के अलावा किसी और वस्तु को इतने ध्यान से देख रहे हो।" रीशी बीच में खुद को कहने से नहीं रोक पाया, "भैया! मेरे बारे में ऐसा कहना गलत है।"

वेद के मन में विचार उठने लगे, "चाहे अकीरा के प्यार में हूँ या नहीं, लेकिन वह दिन दूर नहीं, जब बी.बी.सी. में भी यह ऐलान हो जाएगा कि मैं अकीरा के प्रेम में अथाह डूबा हुआ हूँ। कुछ नहीं तो मम्मी कुतुबमीनार पर ढोल-ताशे के साथ जाएँगी और दुनिया को बता देंगी कि मैं अकीरा से प्रेम करता हूँ।"

वेद ने गहरी साँस छोड़ी। उसने अकीरा को देखा तो वह फोन पर बातचीत में डूबी हुई थी। हो सकता है, नीलू आहलूवालिया से बात हो रही हो। अपना फोन बंद करके अकीरा अभी अपनी कुरसी पर बैठी ही थी कि वेद ने पूछा, "नीलू मासी थी न?"

"हाँ।"

परिवार को इसी 'हाँ' की उम्मीद थी। अरुणा ने पूछा, "अब क्या अजीब सी नई माँग है?"

"नीलू मासी चाहती हैं कि सबको वीडियो निमंत्रण भेजा जाए।"

वेद ने त्यौरियाँ चढ़ाईं, "क्या मतलब?"

"इसका मतलब है, वह छोटी सी वीडियो बनाना चाहती हैं, जिसमें वे सभी को अपने बेटे के विवाह पर आमंत्रित करेंगी। ई-मेल या व्हाट्सएप पर याद नहीं दिलाएँगी, वरन् शादी पर आना है, यह वीडियो से बताएँगी।" उसने काँटे-चम्मच में से काँटा उठाया और मटन पीस में घुसा दिया।

"मैं तो अभी से प्रणाम कर रही हूँ।"

"उफ्फ! मैंने तो पहले ही कहा था कि नीलू मासी थोड़ी सी खिसकी हुई हैं।" गहरी साँस लेते हुए वेद ने कहा।

"थोऽऽऽऽऽड़ी?" अरुणा ने व्यंग्य से कहा और सभी हँस पड़े। अकीरा भी हँसते हुए बोली, "मैंने बहुत से वीडियोग्राफर्स से बात की, लेकिन इतने कम समय में कोई यह काम करने को तैयार नहीं है।"

"अरे! तुम्हें ऐसा क्या रिकॉर्ड करना है? उस नीलू की ही रिकॉर्डिंग करनी है न? वो कौन सी इंग्लैंड की महारानी है, जिसे प्रोफेशनल फोटोग्राफर्स चाहिए?"

"बिल्कुल सही।" इंद्राणी ने कहा। ज्यादा-से-ज्यादा वह एक कुरसी पर बैठेगी, अपने हीरों के हार दिखाना चाहेगी। मैं निरंजन से उसका कैमरा भेजने को कह दूँगी। उसके पास अच्छा कैमरा है। कबीर कैमरा पकड़ लेगा, रिकॉर्डिंग वेद कर लेगा। क्यों कबीर? दोनों हाथों का अच्छे से उपयोग हो सकता है न?"

"थोऽऽऽऽऽड़ी?" अरुणा ने व्यंग्य से कहा और सभी हँस पड़े। अकीरा भी हँसते हुए बोली, "मैंने बहुत से वीडियोग्राफर्स से बात की, लेकिन इतने कम समय में कोई यह काम करने को तैयार नहीं है।" "अरे! तुम्हें ऐसा क्या रिकॉर्ड करना है? उस नीलू की ही रिकॉर्डिंग करनी है न? वो कौन सी इंग्लैंड की महारानी है, जिसे प्रोफेशनल फोटोग्राफर्स चाहिए?"

अरुणा भी कृत्रिमता से हँसते हुए बोलीं, "कितना अच्छा हैं न! आलसी मांसपेशियों की कसरत हो जाएगी।"

कबीर और अरुणा की व्यंग्यात्मक बहस पर ध्यान न देते हुए अकीरा ने अपनी बात समझाई, "नानी! ये उतना आसान नहीं है। वीडियो का स्तर अच्छा होना चाहिए। वह वीडियो जब इतने लोग देखनेवाले हैं तो नीलू मासी को सौंदर्य की दृष्टि से वह वीडियो बहुत अच्छी चाहिए होगी।"

"तुम चिंता मत करो। वेद अच्छे से सब काम कर देगा।" इंद्राणी ने दिलासा देते हुए कहा।

"क्या मैं इसमें कुछ कह सकता हूँ?" चिढ़े हुए वेद ने परिवार से प्रश्न किया।

"माफ कीजिएगा। पर आप इस स्थिति में नहीं हैं कि आप अपनी माँगें रख सकें। हमारे पास कोई और विकल्प नहीं है।"

सिर हिलाते हुए वेदिका ने कहा, "मजदूरो! काम पर लग जाओ। नीलू मासी को तुम्हारा खून-पसीना चाहिए।"

वेद ने अकीरा को देखा, "कोई शक नहीं कि उनके काम में बहुत सा खून, बहुत सा पसीना और बहुत से मूर्ख भी शामिल होंगे।"

□

28

वेद को लगा मानो उसकी आँखों में किसी ने बहुत सा पेट्रोल डाल दिया है और आँखों में आग भी लगा दी हैं। इतनी तरफ से इतनी रोशनी मानो उसकी आँखों की पुतलियों में छेद-से कर रही थी। वेद को लगा मानो वह कपड़े के साबुन के विज्ञापन की शूटिंग के लिए वहाँ खड़ा है। निरंजन के पास वन्यजीवों के चित्र खींचने का कैमरा था। निरंजन को वन्यजीव व उनका जीवन अत्यंत भाता था। यह बात दादी बताना भूल गईं थीं, जब वह निरंजन के बारे में बता रही थीं।

वेद ने देखा कि नीलू मासी के आसपास एक हेयर ड्रेसर (बाल बनानेवाला) और दो मेकअप आर्टिस्ट थे। वे सब वन्यजीवों-से अजीब लग रहे थे। उनके बारे में मानो अभी कोई कुछ खोज न पाया हो। वेद को पता था कि किसी के बारे में यूँ राय बनाना ठीक नहीं, लेकिन वह कुछ नहीं कर पा रहा था।

"ये क्या! शादी का निमंत्रण भड़कीला और रंगों से युक्त होना चाहिए। ये तो शव-यात्रा लग रही है।" कबीर धीरे से वेद के कान में फुसफुसाया।

"हाँ! मुझे नहीं पता था कि सफेद रंग के भी इतने अलग-अलग रंग हो सकते हैं।" वेद बोला।

"मुझे भी। वह टेबल हाथीदाँत जैसी सफेद, कुरसी हलके क्रीम रंग जैसी और कपड़े बिल्कुल सफेद।" कबीर ने व्यंग्य करते हुए कहा।

"मैं तो इसी में खुश हूँ कि मासी ने मजमून को देखते हुए अपने बाल सफेद 'डाई' नहीं करवाए।" कबीर और वेद का संवाद सुनकर अकीरा हँसते हुए बोली। उसने ध्यान से कुछ कप केक्स मेज पर रखे।

"एक्सक्यूज मी!" कबीर ने नीलू मासी जैसी त्यौरियाँ चढ़ाकर नकल करने की कोशिश की, "बाल व्हाइट डाई? डार्लिंग, उसे व्हाइट्स नहीं, ग्रे कहते हैं और दूसरी बात, मुझे बालों को डाई करने की क्या जरूरत, मैं तो फॉर एवर यंग हूँ। हैलो!"

अकीरा बोली, "मुझे सिखाने का शुक्रिया कबीर मासी!"

कबीर ने नाटकीयता से अपना एक बाल कानों के पीछे किया और, "यू आर वेलकम!"

"मेरा एक सवाल है, असल में वो कैसी दिखना चाहती हैं?" रीशी ने पूछा।

"हर तरह से लुधियाना की सिम्मी ग्रेवाल···" वेद ने कहा।

अकीरा ने वेद के घुटने पर थाप मारते हुए कहा, "चुप रहो!"

नीलू ने मेज की शोभा का जायजा लेते हुए वेद से पूछा, "वेद, हम कप केक्स पर चेरीज सजा दें तो कैसा लगेगा?"

"नहीं! लाल रंग के कारण लोगों का ध्यान आप से हट जाएगा।" वेद ने इस जवाब के साथ मुँह बंद कर लिया।

"ओह! सही कहते हो।" यह कहते हुए वह सारी व्यवस्था को अलग-अलग नजरिए से देखने लगी। "अब नीलू मासी को चेरीज क्यों चाहिए? लोगों का ध्यान हटाने के लिए लाल लिपस्टिक है न!"

भावशून्य चेहरे से वेद बोला, "मैं तो कहनेवाला था पानी की पीक से लाल होंठ, लेकिन ठीक है···"

अपवाद के रूप में वेदिका इस बार भाई से सहमत थी।

"ऐसा कहना नहीं चाहिए, लेकिन वाकई ऐसा लग रहा है कि अभी मुजरा शुरू कर देंगी।"

"दोस्तो! प्लीज अब हँसना छोड़ो और जल्दी से यह रिकॉर्ड करो। जल्दी से यह काम खत्म करना है।" अकीरा ने याद दिलाया। "मैं करूँगा न। पहले मासी के वाहियात नाटक तो खत्म हों।" वेद ने परेशान स्वर में उत्तर दिया।

"ऐसा कहना नहीं चाहिए, लेकिन वाकई ऐसा लग रहा है कि अभी मुजरा शुरू कर देंगी।"
"दोस्तो! प्लीज अब हँसना छोड़ो और जल्दी से यह रिकॉर्ड करो। जल्दी से यह काम खत्म करना है।" अकीरा ने याद दिलाया। "मैं करूँगा न। पहले मासी के वाहियात नाटक तो खत्म हों।" वेद ने परेशान स्वर में उत्तर दिया।
"आओ! मैं तैयार हूँ।" नीलू मासी ने एक ताली बजाकर घोषणा-सी की।

"आओ! मैं तैयार हूँ।" नीलू मासी ने एक ताली बजाकर घोषणा-सी की।

वेद कैमरे के पीछे गया और मासी को निर्देश देने लगा, "मासी! मैं पहले आपके और आपकी सुंदरता की फोटो लूँगा। आपको कुछ बोलना नहीं है। आप यहाँ बैठिए और फोटो एलबम को उलटते-पलटते रहिए। ऐसा लगने दीजिए मानो आप अभय और आपके पिछले कई वर्षों के अच्छे क्षण याद कर रही हों।"

नीलू मासी ने एलबम उठाई, "ठीक है, ये मैं कर सकती हूँ। शुरू करो।"

ईश्वर और अच्छी आत्माओं की दयादृष्टि से नीलू ने एलबम के पृष्ठ उलटने-पलटने शुरू कर दिए। वेद ने कुछ तसवीरें सामने से, कुछ कंधों के ऊपर से और कुछ

तसवीरें सामने से खींचने की कोशिश की। और इस तरह बार-बार बहुत सी तसवीरें खींची गईं। वेद निरंजन के इतने बड़े कैमरे को सँभालकर और संघर्ष से तसवीरें खींच रहा था।

यह क्रम तब तक चलता रहा, जब तक नीलू को संतोष नहीं हुआ। सातवें टेक में मासी को संतुष्टि हुई, जब वह एलबम की तसवीरों में अपने बेटे के चेहरे को प्यार से देख भी रही थी और हाथ भी फेर रही थी। जैसे ही उसने वह तसवीर देखी तो खुशी से उछल पड़ी। "ठीक है, बिल्कुल सही।"

"इसके बाद अब क्या?"

"अब मुख्य बात, जो आपने कहनी है।" वेदिका ने प्रतिपादन/निमंत्रण के शब्दों का लिखा परचा पकड़ाया।

अकीरा और वेद कैमरे के सामने खड़े थे, जब नीलू मासी अत्यंत भावुकता से अपनी बातें कह रही थीं।

"आत्माएँ कभी भी अचानक एक-दूसरे से नहीं मिलतीं। जब दो लोग एक-दूसरे से अत्यधिक प्रेम करते हैं, इसका मतलब दोनों आत्माएँ एक-दूसरे के लिए तड़प रही हैं।"

वेद ने चुपके से अकीरा का हाथ पकड़ा। हालाँकि जो नीलू ने कहा, वह अतिशयोक्ति था, पर सही था। हम कभी भी किसी से बिना कारण नहीं मिलते। जो दो लोग एक-दूसरे को जानते हैं, वे आत्माएँ एक-दूसरे से कभी-न-कभी मिल ही जाती हैं।

"अब मुख्य बात, जो आपने कहनी है।" वेदिका ने प्रतिपादन/निमंत्रण के शब्दों का लिखा परचा पकड़ाया। अकीरा और वेद कैमरे के सामने खड़े थे, जब नीलू मासी अत्यंत भावुकता से अपनी बातें कह रही थीं। "आत्माएँ कभी भी अचानक एक-दूसरे से नहीं मिलतीं। जब दो लोग एक-दूसरे से अत्यधिक प्रेम करते हैं, इसका मतलब दोनों आत्माएँ एक-दूसरे के लिए तड़प रही हैं।"

"मॉम!" दरवाजे से आवाज आई।

"हे! ये सभी यहीं हैं।" नीलू ने कहा।

सभी की गरदनें मुड़ीं, सिवाय वेद के। उसकी नजरें लैपटॉप पर थीं।

थोड़ी देर बाद आँखों के कोने से वेद ने देखा। वह एक सफेद गोला कमरे में आता देख पा रहा था। अब तो घर के कोनों को देखने की जरूरत ही नहीं थी। वह अभय था।

□

29

“मॉम! कितनी सुंदर लग रही हो आप।”

वेद को उसके प्रति कोई भाव महसूस हो ही नहीं रहा था, क्योंकि उसने देखा, अभय के मन में अभी भी बदला लेने का भाव मौजूद था। वेद ने देखा, अभय के साथ उसकी होनेवाली पत्नी तान्या भी थी।

“इतना मोटा मिकी माउस अपनी वेशभूषा में नहीं है। हैरानी की बात है!” वेदिका ने ताना कसा और वेद केवल मुसकराया।

वेद को याद आया कि बचपन में किस तरह अभय सुपर हीरो की वेशभूषा अकसर पहना करता और वेद को हमेशा उसकी इस आदत पर हँसी आती। अभय ने अपना ध्यान वहाँ खड़े समूह पर लगाया। वेद को देख बाँहें पसार दीं। मानो वह खुद अरोरा परिवार का राजकुमार न हो। वेद को अभय के मन का द्वेष साफ पता चल रहा था।

“हे अभय!” वेद ने खुद के स्वर में अच्छाई लाते हुए कहा। जब वे बड़े हो रहे थे, तो आपस में दोनों की अच्छी बनती थी, लेकिन तब सबकुछ बदल गया, जब वेद को कैंब्रिज विश्वविद्यालय में दाखिला मिला। बिना किसी कारण के अभय का दृष्टिकोण वेद के प्रति बदलकर घृणा में परिवर्तित हो गया।

“वाह! तुम्हें देखो। तुम अभी भी वैसे ही दिखते हो, वेद! मानो अभी पुरुषता छूकर ही नहीं गई हो।” अभय के स्वर में व्यंग्य था।

वेद ने पलटकर जवाब दिया, “मुझे तुम्हें बधाई देनी चाहिए, क्योंकि तुम अभी भी वैसे ही हो, चुटकुले मारने में बुरे। बहुत काम होगा न तुम्हें?”

आँखें घुमाते हुए अभय ने वेदिका की ओर देखा और पूछा, “कैसी हो तुम?”

हाथों को मोड़ती हुई वेदिका बोली, “ठीक हूँ! अच्छा लगा तुम्हें देखकर।”

अभय ने फिर आँखें घुमाईं और बनावटी हँसी से सबका अभिवादन किया। कबीर और रीशी से हाथ मिलाया।

“और तुम शायद प्रबंधक हो···” धूर्तता से बोला। अभी अकीरा उसकी बात का अभिवादन से जवाब देती, अभय आगे बढ़ गया। उसने तान्या को अपनी ओर खींचा और

सबसे उसकी पहचान करवाने लगा। वेद को अचानक गुस्सा आया। खुद का अपमान और बात थी और अकीरा या उसके परिवार के किसी सदस्य का अपमान दूसरी बात। वेद अचानक बोला, "तान्या! ये मेरी सुंदर गर्लफ्रेंड अकीरा है, बहुत ही प्रतिभावान है, जो शादी की प्रबंधक भी है। उसने इतने कम दिनों के होने के बावजूद शादी का प्रबंध करने के लिए खुद को तैयार कर लिया। कितनी बड़ी मदद की। तुम सबको इसका आभारी होना चाहिए। है न बेब!"

अकीरा ने वेद की टकटकी और शब्दों की ओर ध्यान न देते हुए तान्या से हाथ मिलाने के लिए हाथ आगे किया। "आखिरकार तुमसे मिल ही लिये। अच्छा लग रहा है।"

"आ-हा!" अभय मुसकराता हुआ बोला, "पता चल रहा है कि तुम कैमरामैन क्यों बने? प्रेम सारी अजीब चीजें करवाता है।"

अकीरा ने साँसें रोक रखी थीं। अगर अभय टेढ़ी बातें करने से बाज नहीं आया तो वेद निश्चित ही इसे एक घूँसा जड़ देगा, लेकिन वेद केवल मुसकराया।

"बच्चो! मुझे लगता है तुम्हें अभय और तान्या के साथ की कुछ तसवीरें भी उस वीडियो में डालनी चाहिए। है न!" नीलू मासी ने कहा।

कबीर और रीशी ने डरी-सहमी आँखों से वेद को देखा।

वेद उस समय अधिक रोशनी के बीच घिरा हिरन जैसा लग रहा था। उस समय आहलूवालिया परिवार अकीरा के ग्राहक थे। चाहे उनकी माँगें कितनी भी नाजायज क्यों न हों, पूरी करनी ही पड़तीं। वेद वे कहा, "ठीक है।"

"आ-हा!" अभय मुसकराता हुआ बोला, "पता चल रहा है कि तुम कैमरामैन क्यों बने? प्रेम सारी अजीब चीजें करवाता है।"

अकीरा ने साँसें रोक रखी थीं। अगर अभय टेढ़ी बातें करने से बाज नहीं आया तो वेद निश्चित ही इसे एक घूँसा जड़ देगा, लेकिन वेद केवल मुसकराया।

"बच्चो! मुझे लगता है तुम्हें अभय और तान्या के साथ की कुछ तसवीरें भी उस वीडियो में डालनी चाहिए। है न!" नीलू मासी ने कहा।

"वाऽऽऽऽह!" अभय खुश हुआ। उसे यह आइडिया पसंद आया। "ओए वेद, मैं बगीचे में हूँ। सब समेटकर जल्दी वहीं आ जाओ।" अभय बोला, जैसे ही अभय को वहाँ से जाते देखा, रीशी उबल पड़ा, "मुझे अभय अच्छा नहीं लगता, हमेशा तुम्हें नीचा दिखाने में लगा रहता है।"

"तुम्हें यह सबकुछ कैसे चलता है वेद?" कबीर ने कहा।

"अब जो है, वो है।" वेद ने साँस छोड़ते हुए कहा।

बिना कुछ कहे सभी बगीचे की ओर चल पड़े। अभय ने पहले ही अच्छा सा कोना चुन लिया था। मेकअप आर्टिस्ट और हेयर ड्रेसर ने भी मदद कर ही दी थी। "कहो वेद, क्या करना है?"

वेद को वाकई नहीं मालूम था कि अब उन्हें क्या बताए। प्रेम व ऐसी कोमल भावनाएँ व प्रस्तुतीकरण उसका क्षेत्र नहीं था। "अब क्या बोलूँ? एक-दूसरे को देखकर हँस लो।"

अभय को गुस्सा आ गया, "क्या वाकई ये तसवीरों के लिए तुम्हारा निर्देशक है?" तसवीरें खिंचवाने के लिए अकीरा ने मामला शांत करने के लिए उन्हें कुछ मुद्राएँ बताईं। तान्या और अभय ने वैसे ही किया। वेद ने उन्हें 5 बार उस मुद्रा को बार-बार ठीक करने को कहा। "उफ्फ! मजा नहीं आ रहा। दूर से लग रहा है मानो तुम दोनों एक-दूसरे में इतने घुल-मिल गए हो, जैसे मिलकर एक बड़ी सी मूली जैसे हो। और वह भी बगीचे के बीच।"

वेदिका भी कहाँ चुप रहती! "एक बड़ा सा सफेद आवरण जैसा!"

कबीर भी, "दो चॉक के टुकड़ों जैसा" रीशी भी, "अब्बास मस्तान।"

"क्या बकवास है। तुम सबको यह मजाक लग रहा है?"

अभय की बात पर ध्यान न देते हुए कबीर, वेदिका ने और भी ताने कसे। रीशी भी साथ हो लिया। वेदिका की ये बात सुनकर कि "आपकी मुद्रा ऐसी लग रही है मानो छोटे-छोटे बच्चों को सेक्स शिक्षा दे रहे हों" अभय वेदिका पर धमकाने के लिए जैसे ही आगे बढ़ा तो बीच में वेद आ गया। "ठंडे हो जाओ, वो मजाक कर रही है।"

अभय की बात पर ध्यान न देते हुए कबीर, वेदिका ने और भी ताने कसे। रीशी भी साथ हो लिया। वेदिका की ये बात सुनकर कि "आपकी मुद्रा ऐसी लग रही है मानो छोटे-छोटे बच्चों को सेक्स शिक्षा दे रहे हों" अभय वेदिका पर धमकाने के लिए जैसे ही आगे बढ़ा तो बीच में वेद आ गया। "ठंडे हो जाओ, वो मजाक कर रही है।"

"इसमें मजाक जैसा कुछ नहीं है। अगर ये आसान है तो तुम क्यों नहीं करते?"

अभय की आँखों के सामने हाथ हिलाते हुए वेदिका बोली, "वो करेंगे न। वेद भैया, दिखाओ इन्हें कि कैसे करना है!"

अकीरा हक्की-बक्की थी। अधिकतर ऐसी माँग के बाद हड्डी टूटने जैसे हालात हो जाते; जहाँ तक वह वेद का इतिहास और उसके बारे में जानती थी।

हैरानी की बात है, वेद ने मना नहीं किया, "ठीक है।"

"तुम्हें क्या हुआ?" अकीरा ने प्रश्न किया। जैसे ही वेद ने अपनी बाजुओं में

अकीरा को समेट लिया। कबीर पहले से ही दूर से उनकी रिकॉर्डिंग कर रहा था।

"तुम क्या सोचती हो?" भारी आवाज में वेद ने पूछा।

"क्या इतने दर्शकों के सामने तुम नहीं कर पाओगे?" दबी हँसी में अकीरा ने पूछा। वेद ने अपने हाथ पीछे किए। शैतानी हँसी के साथ वेद दो कदम पीछे भी हो गया।

अकीरा बोली, "क्या कर रहे हो तुम?" वेद की शैतानी हँसी बड़ी सी मुसकान में बदल गई, जब वेद ने कुछ शुरू किया। अचानक पानी की फुहारें पड़ने से अकीरा चिल्लाई। हँसते हुए वेद ने अकीरा को कमर से पकड़कर ऊपर की तरफ उठा लिया और तब तक उसे घुमाता रहा, जब तक पैर लड़खड़ा नहीं गए। वेद पीठ के बल जमीन पर जा गिरा और अकीरा उसपर। वेद को अपना 'किस' याद आया। जिस तरह से अकीरा के कपड़े उसकी शोभा बढ़ा रहे थे, वेद को फिर उसके होंठों पर किस करने की उत्कट लालसा हुई। वह कर ही लेता, अगर कबीर बीच में न टोकता, "बहुत अच्छे! बढ़िया शॉट दोस्तो!"

अकीरा बोली, "क्या कर रहे हो तुम?" वेद की शैतानी हँसी बड़ी सी मुसकान में बदल गई, जब वेद ने कुछ शुरू किया। अचानक पानी की फुहारें पड़ने से अकीरा चिल्लाई। हँसते हुए वेद ने अकीरा को कमर से पकड़कर ऊपर की तरफ उठा लिया और तब तक उसे घुमाता रहा, जब तक पैर लड़खड़ा नहीं गए। वेद पीठ के बल जमीन पर जा गिरा और अकीरा उसपर।

रीशी ने आँखों में प्रेम भरकर कहा, "वाह, कैमरा भी खुश है।"

"हाँ! सो हॉट! बहुत खूब!" वेदिका ने मानो अपने हाथ से खुद को हवा करते हुए।

अभय आत्मविश्वास से बोला, "जो भी है, हम ज्यादा अच्छा कर सकते हैं।"

अकीरा खड़ी हुई और बोली, "हाँ! क्यों नहीं?"

अगले दो घंटों तक सबने तान्या और अभय का हर प्रकार का प्रेम-प्रसंग (Romance) देखा। वे दोनों हँस रहे थे, नाच रहे थे आदि-आदि।

वेद ने सबकी किस्मत को कोसा। "चीनी लोग द्वारा दी जानेवाली यातनाएँ इससे कम होंगी। ये तो मूर्खों का सिनेमा लग रहा है। कब खत्म होगा यह?" रीशी बोला।

वेदिका ने यह दिखावा किया कि वह लैपटॉप देख रही है और अचानक चिल्लाई, "डन! हो गया। बढ़िया शॉट।"

वह अचानक ऐसे चिल्लाई कि अभय को भी हैरानी हुई, "हो गया?"

"यस! हाँ!" वेदिका ने इतने उत्साह से कहा कि वेद भी हक्का-बक्का रह गया। अकीरा ने भी तालियाँ बजाईं। "तुम लोगों ने तो हमसे कई गुना अच्छा किया।"

यह वाक्य काम कर गया। अपने बालों को ठीक करते हुए अभय बोला, "देखा! कहा था न मैंने!"

"बहुत खूब!" अकीरा ने प्रशंसा की। "आप लोग कपड़े बदल लीजिए। हम तब तक कैमरा वगैरह समेट लेते हैं।"

"ठीक है!" तान्या अभय को घर के अंदर ले गई।

जैसे ही दोनों घर के अंदर गए, वेद ने दोनों मूर्खों के प्रेम-प्रसंग को लैपटॉप पर देखा और गहरी साँस छोड़ते हुए कहा, "आज सभी को आईड्रॉप्स (आँखों में डालनेवाली दवा) की जरूरत पड़ेगी।"

□

30

जैसे ही दवाई डालने के बाद आँखें बंद कीं, कुछ ही क्षणों में उसे लगा मानो कोई उसकी गरदन पर हाथ घुमा रहा हो। डर के मारे वेद उछल पड़ा और आँखों में डाली गई दवा आँखों से बहने लगी। ऐसा लग रहा था मानो रो रहा हो। वह चिल्लाया, "अकीरा!"

अकीरा ठहाका मारते हुए बोली, "तुम रो रहे हो, क्योंकि मैं तुमसे लिपट गई?"

"मैं रो नहीं रहा; ये आईड्रॉप्स है" उसने अपनी आँखें पोंछीं और चिढ़ते हुए बोला, "कौन ऐसे गरदन दबाता है?"

अकीरा हैरान हुई, "मैं तुम्हारी गरदन नहीं दबा रही थी। मुझे तुम बहुत प्यारे लग रहे थे, इसीलिए मैंने पीछे से तुम्हारे गले में बाँहें डाल दीं।"

"पीछे से गले में बाँहें डाल दीं?" वेद बच्चों की-सी आवाज में बोला। "एक क्षण के लिए मुझे लगा कि वेदिका मेरा खून करने आ गई है।"

"चुप रहो। चलो फिर शुरू करते हैं।"

"शुरू करते हैं?" वेद बोला।

"बिल्कुल चुप हो जाओ।" अकीरा ने वेद के मुँह पर अपना हाथ रख दिया और चुप करा दिया। उसने धीरे से उसके कान को चूमा। "अब बताओ तुम क्या कर रहे हो?"

अकीरा को पता चल रहा था कि उसके हाथ के नीचे वेद मुसकरा रहा है। महसूस करते ही उसका चेहरा भी दमक उठा। वेद ने धीरे से उसका हाथ पकड़ा, उसे घुमाया और अपनी गोद में खींच लिया। उसने यह सब इतनी जल्दी किया कि अकीरा की चीख निकल गई।

"तुम्हें सचमुच मुझे ऐसे खींचना बंद करना होगा।" उसने बनावटी स्वर में धमकाते हुए कहा और दूसरा हाथ अनायास ही वेद के गले में डाल दिया और वेद का हाथ अकीरा की कमर पर था।

"क्यों?" ऐसा कहते हुए वेद ने अकीरा की ठोढ़ी पर धीरे से चूम लिया।

"बुद्धू!" दबी हँसी में अकीरा बोली।

"सॉरी! कुछ नहीं कर सकता। ये मेरे खून में है।" एक मुसकान के साथ वेद बोला।

अकीरा ने भी धीमे से वेद के माथे को चूमा। वेद खुश हुआ और हैरान था कि आज तक वह अकीरा के बिना कैसे जिया?

"वैसे तुम कर क्या रहे हो?" अकीरा ने दुबारा पूछा।

"आज की रिकॉर्डिंग देख रहा हूँ। इनमें से कुछ इतनी बुरी हैं कि हम वीडियो एडिटर को नहीं भेज सकते। अजीब सी हैं¨बाकी जो फोटो ठीक नहीं आए, उन्हें अलग करना¨जो धुँधली तसवीरें हैं, उन्हें निकाल देना, अभय का भावशून्य चेहरा, जहाँ पर तसवीरों का मजा कम कर रहा है, उन्हें हटाना आदि।"

अकीरा ने चुटकी लेते हुए पूछा, "क्या अभय इतना बुरा है?"

"मेरे खयाल से नीलू मासी के कीमती फर्नीचर का सबसे महँगावाला हिस्सा है।"

मुँह दबाकर हँसती हुई अकीरा ने बाद में माफी माँगी। "इस सबके लिए माफी, लेकिन मुझे अजीब सा लग रहा है।'

"तुम चाहो तो मुझे शुक्रिया कह सकती हो।" अकीरा समझ गई कि वेद का ध्यान उसके होंठों पर है। वेद की भौंहें सीधी करते हुए अकीरा बोली, "तुम कुछ ज्यादा रोमांटिक नहीं हो रहे?"

एक हलकी सी मुसकान वेद के होंठों पर दौड़ गई। "ये मेरा स्वाभाविक मिजाज है।"

"वाह! इतना स्वाभाविक है कि अभी तक कुल मिलाकर तुमने केवल एक को डेट किया है!"

मुँह दबाकर हँसती हुई अकीरा ने बाद में माफी माँगी। "इस सबके लिए माफी, लेकिन मुझे अजीब सा लग रहा है।'
"तुम चाहो तो मुझे शुक्रिया कह सकती हो।" अकीरा समझ गई कि वेद का ध्यान उसके होंठों पर है। वेद की भौंहें सीधी करते हुए अकीरा बोली, "तुम कुछ ज्यादा रोमांटिक नहीं हो रहे?" एक हलकी सी मुसकान वेद के होंठों पर दौड़ गई। "ये मेरा स्वाभाविक मिजाज है।"

"भैया।" उतने में रीशी अंदर आया। इससे पहले कि रीशी कुछ कहे, वेद एकदम से बोला, "रुको, हम लोग पाँच मिनट में नीचे आ रहे हैं, जाओ यहाँ से।"

"ठीक है!" रीशी हँसता हुआ कमरे से बाहर चला गया।

"ये क्या था?" अकीरा ने पूछा।

वेद ने लैपटॉप बंद किया, "मैं अभी रीशी से बात नहीं करना चाहता था। नानी हमें नए कपड़े खरीदवाना चाहती हैं।"

"हे भगवान्!" अकीरा बोली।

"हाँ! और क्या? चलो चलकर देखते हैं कि अब क्या नया तमाशा है?" साँस

छोड़ते हुए वेद बोला और अकीरा खिलखिलाकर हँस पड़ी।

हाथों में हाथ लिये वे घर के केंद्र बाहरी बैठक में दाखिल हुए। कहें तो सारी मूर्खता का केंद्र! जैसे ही वे कमरे में दाखिल हुए, उनकी सारी इंद्रियों पर मानो भड़कीले रंगों, चमक-दमक के भावों ने आक्रमण कर दिया हो! जहाँ देखो चमक-दमक! उनकी आँखों को आराम ही नहीं था।

"हे भगवान्! उफ्फ! ये क्या?" वेद चिल्लाया। पूरा कमरा अलग-अलग तरह के कपड़ों से भरा हुआ था और दुकान पर से आए विक्रेता परिवार के सदस्यों को दिखाने और रिझाने में लगे हुए थे।

"अरे भोलू! इधर आ!" नानी ने इशारे से वेद को बुलाकर एक चमकदार पीला कुरता दिखाकर पूछा, "ये हल्दी के लिए कैसा रहेगा?"

"आपको क्या हो गया है नानी?" डर के मारे चिल्लाकर वेद ने कहा, "मैं यह नहीं पहनूँगा। मुझे वीको टरमरिक क्रीम की ट्यूब नहीं दिखना।"

पिंकी सहित सभी हँस पड़े। लेकिन पिंकी ने समझाने की कोशिश की, "अरे! पीला रंग उस दिन की थीम (विषय) है। तुमपर अच्छा दिखेगा।"

"बिल्कुल अच्छा लगेगा, अगर मैं पीलिया का मरीज या फिर बकरी की उलटी दिखना चाहूँ।"

"इयूऽऽऽऽ!" वेदिका ने घृणास्पद मुँह बनाया।

"अरे भोलू! इधर आ!" नानी ने इशारे से वेद को बुलाकर एक चमकदार पीला कुरता दिखाकर पूछा, "ये हल्दी के लिए कैसा रहेगा?" "आपको क्या हो गया है नानी?" डर के मारे चिल्लाकर वेद ने कहा, "मैं यह नहीं पहनूँगा। मुझे वीको टरमरिक क्रीम की ट्यूब नहीं दिखना।" पिंकी सहित सभी हँस पड़े। लेकिन पिंकी ने समझाने की कोशिश की, "अरे! पीला रंग उस दिन की थीम (विषय) है। तुमपर अच्छा दिखेगा।"

"क्या मैं कोई सलाह दे सकती हूँ?" अकीरा ने बीच में आकर प्रश्न किया।

"बिल्कुल पुत्तर!" अरुणा ने प्रशंसनीय मुसकान से कहा।

"हर उस चीज का जो वेद को बेवकूफ और मूर्ख दिखने से बचाए, इस घर में स्वागत है।"

अपने होंठों को हलका सा दाँतों में दबाते हुए अकीरा ने सादा सा सफेद कुरता उठाया, जिसपर केवल कॉलर (गलपट्टे) के पास पीला रंग था। "ये कैसा रहेगा? शालीन-सा है।"

"यस! ये ठीक है। मैं कम-से-कम हल्दी-दूध से भरा गिलास नहीं दिखूँगा।" वेद ने उत्साह से कहा।

“अरे अकीराऽऽऽऽ! उसे छोड़ो। तुम अपनी पसंद के कपड़े चुन लो।” इंद्राणी ने जोर देकर कहा।

दुकानदार ने भी मौके का फायदा उठाते हुए बीच ही में जाकर एक ड्रेस दिखाई। काफी सारे बक्से छानने के बाद वह चमकीली नीली ड्रेस लेकर आया और बोला, “आप इसमें रानी लगोगी।”

अकीरा ने हकलाते हुए नकारात्मक प्रतिक्रिया दी, “न…नहीं, ये रहने दो।”

“शाइनी डिस्को, डिस्को शाइनी बॉल।” वेद पीछे से गीत गा रहा था। दुकानदार कपड़े दिखाता गया और वेद के व्यंग्य का स्वर तीखा होता गया।

“शाइनी डिस्को, डिस्को शाइनी बॉल।” वेद पीछे से गीत गा रहा था। दुकानदार कपड़े दिखाता गया और वेद के व्यंग्य का स्वर तीखा होता गया।
“फेडेक्स लोगो, फिश स्केल्स, पान पसंद, पैकेजिंग, कसाटा आइसक्रीम।”
आखिरकार इंद्राणी ने दुकानदार पर तरस खाते हुए सलाह दी, “भोलू! मेरे प्यारे (डार्लिंग), तुम अकीरा के लिए कोई ड्रेस क्यों नहीं चुन लेते?”

“फेडेक्स लोगो, फिश स्केल्स, पान पसंद, पैकेजिंग, कसाटा आइसक्रीम।”

आखिरकार इंद्राणी ने दुकानदार पर तरस खाते हुए सलाह दी, “भोलू! मेरे प्यारे (डार्लिंग), तुम अकीरा के लिए कोई ड्रेस क्यों नहीं चुन लेते?”

वेद झट से उठा और अलग-अलग लहँगों, सूट, साड़ियों को एक-एक करके देखने लगा। अकीरा भी हैरानी से उसे देख रही थी। आजतक किसी बॉयफ्रेंड ने उसके लिए ऐसा नहीं किया था। वाकई वेद कुछ अलग था।

“ये चार…” वेद ने चार तरह की पोशाक अकीरा के बाजू में लाकर रख दीं।

“अरे वाह! इतनी जल्दी! अकीरा, पहनकर देखो तो।” अरुणा के स्वर में प्रशंसा थी।

हामी में सिर हिलाते हुए अकीरा ने कपड़े उठाए और एक कमरे में चली गई। पहले उसने हलके धूमिल लाल रंग (आड़ू-पीच—Peach रंग) का लहँगा था, बिना चमक का, उसे वह पहली बार में ही पसंद आ गया था। पहनने के बाद तो और भी अच्छा लगा।

ये सोचकर कि वेद की प्रतिक्रिया क्या होगी, अकीरा को शरारत सूझी। उसने अपनी स्कर्ट थोड़ी और नीचे की, जिससे उसका पेट नजर आ रहा था और सीधे बैठक में चली गई। बजाय कपड़े देखने और चुनने के, पूरा परिवार अभय की वीडियो शूट की चर्चा में लगा था।

"अभय के बाल ऐसे लग रहे हैं मानो बगीचे की घास काटी हो!" अरुणा ने व्यंग्य कसा। रीशी अपने मोबाइल में तसवीरें दिखा रहा था। "तान्या के बाल ऐसे दिख रहे हैं, जैसे एक साथ कई मेढक के बच्चे बाँध दिए हों।"

"ओह! नीलू कितनी सफेद लग रही है। अधिकतर तसवीरों में ऐसी दिख रही है मानो बुखार की गोली हो पैरासीटामोल (Paracetamol)!"

ये परिवार तो आलोचकों को शर्मिंदा कर दे, लेकिन अकीरा ने अपनी इस इच्छा को बाजू में रखकर सीधे ठंडे राजकुमार वेद के पास जाने की सोची।

अकीरा आत्मविश्वास से सीधी वहाँ पहुँची, जहाँ वेद था और अकेला बैठा था और परिवार की धोखाधड़ी की बातें देख रहा था। इतने में अकीरा पहुँचकर बोली, "वेद! मैं कैसी दिख रही हूँ?"

उसे जिस प्रतिक्रिया की उम्मीद थी, वैसा ही हुआ। वेद हैरानी और प्रेम से उसे देख रहा था। वेद की आँखों की तपन उसे महसूस हो रही थी। वह वेद की आँखों में देख रही थी मानो वेद उसे कुछ कहे, इसकी उसे उम्मीद थी। शायद कुछ अच्छा!

वेद की नजरें अकीरा की लंबी गरदन, सुंदर बालों और आँखों पर गईं। उसके कपड़ों ने अकीरा की सुंदरता में चार चाँद लगा दिए थे। अगर ईश्वर सामने प्रकट होते तो वह ईश्वर को स्वयं बताता कि ये उसकी सर्वोत्तम मूर्ति है। अपने परिवार से नजर बचाकर वह अकीरा की ओर झुका और बोला, "तुम मुझे विश्व की सबसे सुंदर स्त्री लग रही हो।"

□

31

"कहाँ हैं सब?" वेद ने अपने जूतों के फीते खोलते हुए पूछा।

"वो सब छत पर हैं।" घर में काम करनेवाली नौकरानी ने कहा।

अभी कुछ कहने ही वाला था कि वेद चुप हो गया। "ठीक है! शुक्रिया।"

कामवाली ने भी हैरानी से वेद को देखा और चली गई। वेद ने खुद के रक्तचाप (Blood Pressure) को नियंत्रण में रखने के लिए अपनी श्वास प्रक्रिया पर ध्यान दिया।

अकीरा हँसते हुए बोली, "मुबारक हो! छत पर खेल चल रहा है।"

"ओह रुको!" कराहते हुए वेद कपड़े बदलने अंदर चला गया। कुल 10 मिनट में वेद ढीले-ढाले पुराने कपड़े पहनकर बाहर निकला। "लगता है किसी ने आज मैले-कुचैले कपड़े पहनने के निर्देश दिए हैं।" अकीरा ने वेद को इस तरह के ढीले कपड़ों में पहले कभी नहीं देखा था।

"क्या मैं आज सिरदर्द का बहाना कर सकता हूँ?" वेद ने पूछा।

"चुप करो और चलो।" कहकर अकीरा वेद को खींचते हुए छत पर ले गई।

छत पर सभी लोग परंपरागत चारपाइयों पर बैठे थे; पॉपकॉर्न खा रहे थे; व्हिस्की पी रहे थे और किसी बेहूदा विषय पर गपशप और कानाफूसी (पंचायत) कर रहे थे। वेद ने देखा कि वहाँ तकिए और कंबल भी हैं। उसने हारकर मानो सिर नीचे कर लिया। वह समझ गया था कि जब तक वे लुधियाना में हैं, तब तक रात को छत पर ही सोएँगे।

"बेड़ा गर्क!" वेद कराहकर बोला और अकीरा हँसने लगी।

"आओ मेरे प्यारे बच्चो!" अरुणा ने हाथ हिलाकर कहा।

"हैलो नानी!" वेद ने अरुणा और इंद्राणी से धीरे से गले लगकर इधर-उधर देखा और पूछा, "दोनों मामा और मामियाँ कहाँ हैं?"

"एक मूर्ख दंपती रेस्टोरेंट गए हैं और मूर्खों का दूसरा जोड़ा टी.वी. देख रहा है।" मुँह बनाते हुए नानी ने बताया। वेद दबी हँसी हँस रहा था। अजीब बात है, नानी के पास किसी भी मामा या मामी के लिए प्रशंसा के शब्द होते ही नहीं थे।

"कैसा रहा तुम्हारा दिन?" पिंकी ने पूछा।

"पूछो मत मॉम!" वेद ने ऐसा किया मानो बेहोश हो रहा हो। "अकीरा अत्यंत मूर्खों को ढूँढ़ चुकी है। नीलू मासी से सेट डिजाइनर तक! सभी।"

"क्या कहा तुमने? तुम्हारी वजह से नीलू मासी मुझे ढूँढ़ सकी, और तो और, सफेद फूलों के लिए उस डिजाइनर से मैं नहीं लड़ रही थी।" अकीरा ने बात बीच में काटते हुए कहा।

"जरा मेरी बात पर गौर करें। अगर तुम नीलू मासी को वह नहीं दोगी, जो उन्हें चाहिए तो वे सफेद फूल मेरी तसवीर पर चढ़ा देंगी, ठीक है न!"

रीशी और इंद्राणी ने वेद के सिर पर दो-दो बार मारा और गुस्से से कहा, "मूर्खया! कुछ भी बोलता है।"

"दादी यार!" वेद ने उस जगह को सहलाते हुए बोला, जहाँ दादी ने मारा था।

"बिल्कुल ठीक। वेद, तुम कई बार बहुत बकवास करते हो।" पिंकी बोलीं।

"क्यों नहीं, आखिर तुम्हारा बेटा हूँ।" वेद ने त्यौरियाँ चढ़ाते हुए पिंकी की ओर देखा और कहा। बदले में एक तेज चाँटा आया, जो तकिए द्वारा बचा लिया गया। "खैर, तुम दोनों ने क्या खाया?"

"हाँ जी, हम जे.एफ.सी. चले गए थे।" अकीरा मुसकराते हुए बोली।

"क्या?" वेदिका ने आँखें छोटी करते हुए पूछा।

"जरा मेरी बात पर गौर करें। अगर तुम नीलू मासी को वह नहीं दोगी, जो उन्हें चाहिए तो वे सफेद फूल मेरी तसवीर पर चढ़ा देंगी, ठीक है न!" रीशी और इंद्राणी ने वेद के सिर पर दो-दो बार मारा और गुस्से से कहा, "मूर्खया! कुछ भी बोलता है।" "दादी यार!" वेद ने उस जगह को सहलाते हुए बोला, जहाँ दादी ने मारा था।

"तुम्हारा मतलब के.एफ.सी.? है न!"

"नहीं!" ठहाका मारते हुए अकीरा बोली, "जे.एफ.सी.? जसप्रीत फ्राइड चिकन।"

"आज का दिन कुछ अजीब और बेतुका-सा है।" कबीर ने कहा।

"वाकई।" वेद बुदबुदाया।

"वह विचित्रता तभी शुरू हो गई थी, जब उन्हें कुल दो घंटे सेट डिजाइनर के ऑफिस में उससे मिलने के लिए रुकना पड़ा। और जब दो घंटे बाद वह नीचे उतरा तो उसे सफेद कार्नेशनस (फूलों की जाति) और सफेद कुमुदों (फूलों की एक जाति) में अंतर ही समझ नहीं आ रहा था। उस मंद बुद्धि व्यक्ति को फूलों के चित्र दिखाकर अंतर समझाना पड़ा। फिर वहाँ से सब केटरर (खाना बनानेवाला) के पास गए। नीलू मासी की

पसंद वैसे ही विचित्र थी, इसलिए जब वेद ने आयरिश मॉस, सलाद, बॅगन बटर में सिंकी ब्रेड पर जैम लगाकर खाना और स्पीनेच पॅनकेक खाकर देखा। ये सबकुछ चखकर देखने के बाद वेद का मन किया कि वह पहाड़ी पर से नीचे कूद जाए। और अब सब छत पर हैं।

"वैसे हर कोई अचानक छत पर क्यों हैं?" वेद ने पूछा।

सभी के सिर हैरानी से कबीर और वेदिका की ओर मुड़े। वेद और अकीरा भी हैरान थे। कबीर अपने हाथों की उँगलियों में घुसकर दबी आवाज में बोला, "ज्यादा कुछ नहीं, बस कल रात नानी ने मुझे वेदिका के कमरे में जाते हुए पकड़ लिया।"

अरुणा ने मुसकराकर बताया, "इसलिए हमने पक्का किया कि हम सब छत पर सोएँगे। ये एहतियात बरतने के लिए है।"

अपनी गुस्से की सारी गरमी आँखों में लाते हुए वेद कबीर से बोला, "शुक्रिया कबीर! मुझे हमेशा खुले में सोना अच्छा लगता है।" वेद के स्वर में तीखा व्यंग्य था।

अरुणा ने मुसकराकर बताया, "इसलिए हमने पक्का किया कि हम सब छत पर सोएँगे। ये एहतियात बरतने के लिए है।" अपनी गुस्से की सारी गरमी आँखों में लाते हुए वेद कबीर से बोला, "शुक्रिया कबीर! मुझे हमेशा खुले में सोना अच्छा लगता है।" वेद के स्वर में तीखा व्यंग्य था।

"मुझे भी।" रीशी ने साथ दिया। "खुले में सबकुछ कितना खुला होता है न!"

"कितनी गंभीर बात और अवलोकन।" अकीरा बोली।

कबीर और वेदिका के पास वापस आकर इंद्राणी बोलीं, "इन दोनों की शादी जल्दी कर दो पिंकी! अब बात हद से बाहर जा रही है।"

"अभी? बात हमेशा से ही हद के बाहर थी। कैंब्रिज की बात भूल गई? ये बंदर को उस्तरा पकड़ाने जैसा है, अब वह गाल काटे या बाल, कोई कह नहीं सकता।"

"बातों में साफ रहना ठीक है। बंदर कौन है?" रीशी ने बीच में ही कहा।

"कबीर! अभी कबीर है!" वेद ने जोर देकर कहा।

"एक सेकंड! कैंब्रिज की क्या कहानी है?" अकीरा भावशून्य-सी बोली।

वेद ने दोनों हाथ रगड़ते हुए खुशी जाहिर की, "मैंने अभी तक तुम्हें वो कहानी नहीं बताई।"

अकीरा ने अधीरता से पूछा, "वो कितनी बुरी है?"

"बहुत ही बुरी है। दुर्भाग्य से।" प्रतिशोध से भरी मुसकान से वेद बोला। "हम मेरा जन्मदिन मनाने कैंब्रिज गए थे। फिर उस क्लब में कबीर और वेदिका ने बहुत शराब पी ली।"

"वाह! फिर क्या हुआ?"

वेद कबीर और वेदिका की स्थिति के पूरे मजे ले रहा था। कुछ क्षण रुका, फिर बोला, "उस क्लब में 'जॉक ऑक्शन' जैसा कुछ था। वह बाकी नीलामी जैसा ही था। बस फर्क केवल इतना कि वहाँ पुरुष भी नीलाम किए जाते थे। लोग 24 घंटे के लिए उन पुरुषों को खरीद सकते थे। जिस पुरुष पर सबसे ज्यादा बोली लगेगी, उसे क्लब की तरफ से भी कमीशन (दलाली) मिलता।"

कुछ रंगीन गालियाँ उसे नानी माँ के मुँह से सुनाई दीं।

"अकीरा!" वेदिका लाचारी भरे स्वर में चिल्लाई।

"क्या तुम वाकई इस धोखेबाज से मेरे बारे में कहानी सुनना चाहोगी?"

अकीरा बड़ी सी मुसकान के साथ बोली, "हाँ।"

वेदिका बोली, "शैतानी दिमाग।"

वेद उसकी बात पर हँसा, लेकिन बोलता रहा, "कल्पना करो, कबीर मंच पर अपने बॉक्सर्स, जूते और मोजे में अपनी ताकत दिखा रहा है, मांसपेशियाँ दिखा रहा है और घटिया गानों पर नाच रहा है और मेरी प्यारी बहन उसका प्रोत्साहन बढ़ा रही है···" वेदिका ने अपना पेट पकड़कर कहा, "मुझे उलटी आ रही है।"

वेद ने उत्साह से कहा, "बिल्कुल यही हुआ, फिर हमारी हिंदुस्तानी जॉकी ने मंच पर उलटी कर दी। बोली में, किसी ने भी कबीर की बोली नहीं लगाई। बिल्कुल शून्य। फिर वेदिका मेज पर चढ़ गई और अपनी हथेली हवा में घुमाते हुए बोली और चिल्लाई, 'पाँच पाउंड।' और कबीर-वेदिका को पाँच पाउंड में बेच दिया गया।

वेद ने उत्साह से कहा, "बिल्कुल यही हुआ, फिर हमारी हिंदुस्तानी जॉकी ने मंच पर उलटी कर दी। बोली में, किसी ने भी कबीर की बोली नहीं लगाई। बिल्कुल शून्य। फिर वेदिका मेज पर चढ़ गई और अपनी हथेली हवा में घुमाते हुए बोली और चिल्लाई, 'पाँच पाउंड।' और कबीर-वेदिका को पाँच पाउंड में बेच दिया गया। अकीरा ने अपनी हँसी रोकने की कोशिश की, पर नहीं कर सकी।

"मैं इस घटना से इतना विचलित हुआ कि मैं वहाँ से चला गया। मुझे नहीं पता कि मेरे क्लब से चले जाने के बाद इन दोनों ने क्या किया, लेकिन जब ये दोनों मुझे अगली बार मिले तो पता चला कि ये दोनों एक-दूसरे को डेट कर रहे हैं।" वेद मुँह बनाता हुआ बोला।

"हमने बहुत ज्यादा पी रखी थी। बहुत ही ज्यादा!" वेदिका ने सफाई देने की कोशिश की।

"नशा करने के लिए मदिरा के लिए पागलपन को दोष दो।" इंद्राणी बोलीं।

"मुझे तो अभी से घबराहट हो रही है''सोचो कबीर और वेदिका का बच्चा। एक इनसान जिसमें दो नशेड़ियों के गुण आएँगे।" इंद्राणी ने अपना डर जाहिर कर दिया।

"चिंता मत कीजिए नानीजी! माइनस, माइनस इज प्लस। लोहा लोहे को काटता है।" अकीरा बोली।

"सही! मॉम और डैड इस बात के उदाहरण हैं। मुझ ही को देख लो, हूँ न मैं प्लस! कहाँ असर आया मुझमें!" वेद खिलखिलाते हुए बोला। पिंकी ने अपना मोबाइल उठाया, "मुझे कैलेंडर देखने दो। मैंने लिखकर रखा है कि 'स्लैप यूअर किड्स डे।' (अपने बच्चों को थप्पड़ मारने का दिन कौन सा है)। उम्मीद है, आज ही होगा। तो मैं अपने दोनों बच्चों के जरा गाल तो लाल कर ही दूँ।"

"सही! मॉम और डैड इस बात के उदाहरण हैं। मुझ ही को देख लो, हूँ न मैं प्लस! कहाँ असर आया मुझमें!" वेद खिलखिलाते हुए बोला। पिंकी ने अपना मोबाइल उठाया, "मुझे कैलेंडर देखने दो। मैंने लिखकर रखा है कि 'स्लैप यूअर किड्स डे।' (अपने बच्चों को थप्पड़ मारने का दिन कौन सा है)। उम्मीद है, आज ही होगा। तो मैं अपने दोनों बच्चों के जरा गाल तो लाल कर ही दूँ।"

"मॉम, तुम मुझे प्यारी हो।" कहते हुए वेद जोर से हँस पड़ा।

"चुप हो जा खैर! अकीरा, यह बताओ कि आज नीलू ने कौन सी अजीब सी माँग की?"

पिंकी ने वेद को चुप कराते हुए अकीरा से सवाल किया।

अकीरा ने नीचे के होंठ दबाते हुए कहा, "हाँ! की तो है।"

"अब क्या?" पिंकी बोलीं।

"मासी को उस दिन के रात के खाने, भोज का पूर्वाभ्यास (Rehearsal) चाहिए।"

"हैं? ये क्या अंग्रेजी चोंचले हैं? उससे जाकर कहो कि हल्दी, ढोलकी, संगीत, मेहँदी, ये सब उस रात के भोज के पूर्वाभ्यास ही हैं।"

अकीरा मानो बहुत घबराई हुई–सी लगी। "मैंने उन्हें सलाह दी कि ढोलकी और संगीत एक ही दिन कर लीजिए, तो भगवान् का शुक्र है कि वह मान गई हैं।"

वेद चिल्लाते हुए बोला, "जब तक यह शादी खत्म होगी, मैं शायद पागल हो चुका होऊँगा।"

"चलो। अब सब सोते हैं। हम सभी को आराम चाहिए।" वेद के सिर पर धीरे से मारते हुए अरुणा ने कहा।

वेदिका और कबीर वेद की चारपाई की बाजूवाली चारपाइयों पर सोने के लिए भागे।

"तुम बदतमीज हो।" वेद ने कबीर और वेदिका से कहा। वेद देख चुका था कि अकीरा बेमन से पिंकी की बाजूवाली चारपाई पर जा लेटी।

वेदिका कौन सा छोड़ देती, "एक बदतमीज ही दूसरे को अच्छे से पहचानता है।"

वेद बोला, "नानी! ये अस्पताल का जनरल वार्ड जैसा लग रहा है।"

"सो जा!" अरुणा पलटकर चिल्लाकर बोलीं। अभी वेद दुबारा कुछ कहनेवाला था कि उसके मोबाइल पर अकीरा का संदेश आया।

"तुम्हारा यह रूप अच्छा लगा, गुड नाइट।" उसने थोड़ा सा ऊपर होकर देखा, अकीरा हलका सा मुसकराई। वेद उसकी आँखों की चमक में खो गया। उसके हृदय में संदेश में लिखा 'अच्छा लगा' शब्द घर कर गया और वह अपने से हँस पड़ा। उस मृदु मुसकान में अपनत्व था। वेद ने जल्दी से टाइप किया, 'गुड नाइट।'

□

32

अगली सुबह अकीरा अपने हमेशा के समय से काफी जल्दी उठी। इतनी रोशनी में वह सो नहीं पा रही थी। कुछ कौओं की काँव-काँव भी उसे सोने नहीं दे रही थी। जल्दी आवारा कुत्ते भी भौंकने लगे। उतने में किसी की गाड़ी का 'रिवर्स हॉर्न' बजा। दूधवाला चिल्ला रहा था। वेद ने सही कहा था कि छत पर सोने जैसा बुरा कुछ नहीं है।

रात भर भी वह ठीक से सो नहीं पाई। मच्छर भी थे और रीशी के खर्राटे भी। बची-खुची कसर नीली आँखोंवाले वेद के खयालों ने पूरी कर दी। अकीरा ने आसपास देखा। खयालों का लड़का वहाँ से गायब था। समय देखा और उठ खड़ी हुई। जल्दी से नहा-धोकर तैयार हुई और नीचेवाले कमरे की ओर चल पड़ी। सभी छज्जे पर बैठे थे। जैसे ही वह वेदिका के गले लगने के लिए झुकी, घबराहट के मारे जोर से चिल्लाई। उसने देखा, बगीचे की घास पर वेद मृत व्यक्ति के समान पड़ा हुआ था।

"ओह माई गॉड।"

वह भागती हुई वेद के पास गई और उसे जोर-जोर से हिलाया। "वेद! तुम ठीक हो? क्या हुआ इसे?"

जब वह थोड़ा सा भी नहीं हिला तो परिवार की ओर देखने लगी। वे सभी शांति से नाश्ता कर रहे थे। वह सुन्न-सी हो गई और जोर से चिल्लाई, "क्या हुआ वेद को?"

"चिंता मत करो! सुबह की सैर से थककर चूर हो रखा है।" अरुणा ने कहा।

अकीरा ने मुँह टेढ़ा किया और मन में सोचने लगी। 'इन लोगों की अजीब हरकतें किसी दिन वेद और उसे पागल कर देंगी।'

लेटे-लेटे ही वेद ने अकीरा को आश्वासन दिया, "अकीरा, मैं ठीक हूँ। मैं योगाभ्यास कर रहा था। शवासन।"

अकीरा का मन किया कि वेद का गला दबा दे। "अगर तुम दो सेकंड में खड़े नहीं हुए तो मैं तुम्हें अकेले ही अभय से निबटने को भेज दूँगी।"

काम हो गया। उसैन बोल्ट मानो स्टीरॉइड्स पर हो, ऐसे दौड़ लगाई वेद ने और नाश्ते की मेज पर अकीरा को भी खींचता हुआ ले गया। प्यार से अकीरा ने वेद के घुटने

पर हाथ रखा। अकीरा के हाथ रखते ही वेद को खाँसी आई और कॉफी बाहर। अकीरा ने टिशू से वेद का मुँह पोंछा। बात सँभालने के लिए बोली, "वेद, तुम्हारी कॉफी कड़वी थी, इसीलिए ऐसा हुआ।"

वेदिका ने किकियाकर गाना गाया, "चीनी कम है, चीनी कम है, थोड़ी-थोड़ी है तुझमें कम, है कम, है कम-कम"

वेद ने टिशू मुचकाकर वेदिका की ओर फेंका। "चुप रहो।"

"अए!" कबीर ने बॉल पकड़ी और वापस वेद की ओर फेंकी। "वो तुझसे बात नहीं कर रही। वह ऐसे ही गाना गा रही है, समझ आया?"

वेद ने फिर वापस बॉल फेंकी। "तुम उसकी तरफ से क्यों बोल रहे हो?"

"जब तक तुम किसी सहमति पर नहीं पहुँच जाते, मैं वेदिका का औपचारिक प्रवक्ता हूँ।" कबीर औपचारिक तरीके से बोला। "कम-से-कम उस वक्त तक, जब तक तुम इस बात की माफी नहीं माँग लेते और नहीं मान लेते कि भेड़ की खाल में भेड़िया हो और हमसे राज छुपा रहे हो। ऐसा करना समझौते के विरुद्ध जाना है।"

"जब तक तुम किसी सहमति पर नहीं पहुँच जाते, मैं वेदिका का औपचारिक प्रवक्ता हूँ।" कबीर औपचारिक तरीके से बोला। "कम-से-कम उस वक्त तक, जब तक तुम इस बात की माफी नहीं माँग लेते और नहीं मान लेते कि भेड़ की खाल में भेड़िया हो और हमसे राज छुपा रहे हो। ऐसा करना समझौते के विरुद्ध जाना है।"

"यह समझदारी और समझौते का उल्लंघन पहली बार तब हुआ था, जब तुम्हारी गर्लफ्रेंड ने अकीरा को मेरे लड़की की पोशाक में हिंदी गाने के बारे में बताया था कि मैंने किस तरह बारात में नृत्य किया। जबकि मैं तब बच्चा था।"

"दीदी तेरा देवर दीवाना।' ये गाना था।" अरुणा चहकती हुई बोलीं।

"ईऽऽऽऽश नानी!" वेद चिढ़ते हुए बोला। अकीरा अंदर-ही-अंदर हँसी। वाकई इस घर में मनोरंजन की कोई कमी नहीं है।

"अरे प्लीज! अब सुबह से तुम लोग लड़ाई शुरू मत करो। दिन के लिए भी तो कुछ बचाओ।" अकीरा बीच में बोली।

"सही!" अपने पराँठे पर वेदिका ने मक्खन डाला। "याद है न, हमें दोपहर के खाने के लिए भी जाना है। जल्दी करो।" पिंकी बोलीं।

"मुफ्त का खाना माँ को इतना उत्साहित कर सकता है।" वेद ने कहा।

"और क्या···एक मेज से दूसरी मेज।" अरुणा बोलीं। "मुँह दी बल्ले-बल्ले दे हाता-पाँवाँ दी हड़ताल।"

पिंकी—"माँ! यार!"

अरुणा हँसीं, "चलो खाओ। ये भी मुफ्त है।"

सभी ठहाका मारकर हँस पड़े। ऐसा वहुत कम होता था कि पिंकी को कोई ताना कसे और वह जवाब सुनने से छूट जाए। भगवान् की कृपा से बाकी का नाश्ता सभी ने एक-दूसरे को बिना नीचा दिखाए कर लिया। अकीरा को अच्छा लगा। बस वेदिका अपने फोर्क (काँटे) से वेद को धमका रही थी। वो कोई बड़ी बात नहीं थी। समय कहाँ चला गया, पता ही नहीं चला और वे सब एक रेस्तराँ में बैठे थे। वे अभय की शादी में खाने के इंतजाम के सिलसिले में खाने का स्वाद चखने आए थे। जितना सोचा था, उससे अगले स्तर का रेस्तराँ था। सभी का अच्छे से स्वागत हुआ, गरम रुमाल और स्वच्छ पानी पेश किया गया। सबकुछ बढ़िया था, जब तक कि अकीरा ने मेन्यू कार्ड नहीं पढ़ा था।

सभी ठहाका मारकर हँस पड़े। ऐसा बहुत कम होता था कि पिंकी को कोई ताना कसे और वह जवाब सुनने से छूट जाए। भगवान् की कृपा से बाकी का नाश्ता सभी ने एक-दूसरे को बिना नीचा दिखाए कर लिया। अकीरा को अच्छा लगा। बस वेदिका अपने फोर्क (काँटे) से वेद को धमका रही थी। वो कोई बड़ी बात नहीं थी।

"पक्का न! ये ही नाम है?" 'कितने अजीब और गर्व से भरे नाम हैं।' मन में अकीरा ने सोचा।

"हाँ।" बैरे ने बड़े उत्साह से कहा, "नीलू मैम ने हमें निर्देश दिए थे कि कुछ अलग होना चाहिए। वे चाहती थीं कि दुनिया भर के स्वादिष्ट पकवान हों, किंतु भारतीय स्वाद हो।"

अपनी आह दबाते हुए अकीरा बोली, "वाह! ठीक है।"

वेद शिकायती स्वर में बोला, "कल काई (मॉस) खाई थी, आज हम लॉकी का सूप पी रहे हैं।"

अभी खाने-पीने और शादी के मेन्यू पर चिंतन-मनन चल ही रहा था कि वेद को वीडियो एडिटर की तरफ से निमंत्रण का निर्णायक वीडियो मिला अर्थात् 'तैयार' वीडियो, जो सभी मित्रों और रिश्तेदारों को आमंत्रित करने के लिए भेजा जा सके। खुशी के मारे वेद अपना संतुलन खो रहा था। एडिटर ने बहुत अच्छा काम करके दिया था। नीलू मासी भी बहुत अच्छी और शालीन दिखाई पड़ रही थीं। बस अभय और तान्या के बेस्वाद, रसहीन प्रेम-प्रसंग ने ही मानो वीडियो खराब-सा किया लग रहा था; सब बनावटी!

"अरे! सब इधर आओ, ये देखो वीडियो!"

वेद ने सबको मोबाइल की ओर आकर्षित करते हुए कहा। सभी उत्साह से मोबाइल में झुककर वीडियो देखने लगे, परंतु जल्द ही सबकी हँसी गायब हो गई।

"अगर इसे 360 पिक्सल में चलाया जाए तो शायद ठीक लगे।" पिंकी चकित थी और अकीरा उदास।

वेदिका ने नाक-भौंह सिकोड़ते हुए कहा, "ये कचरा है।"

"ये देखने के बाद आनेवाले मेहमान भी नहीं आएँगे और शादी में अंटार्कटिका की जनसंख्या से भी कम लोगों की संख्या होगी।" कबीर बोला।

"हे भगवान्" कहते हुए रीशी ने अकीरा का हाथ भी झकझोर दिया।

अकीरा ने अपना हाथ छुड़वाते हुए कहा, "क्याऽऽऽऽ?"

रीशी ने दूर इशारा करते हुए कहा और फिर डर से चिल्लाया, "वोऽऽऽ वोऽऽऽ तान्या है क्या?"

"कहाँ?" कबीर ने पूछा।

रेस्तराँ के दूसरे कोने की तरफ रीशी ने इशारा किया, सभी देख रहे थे और एक साथ चिल्ला पड़े, "हाँ!" (धीरे से) पिंकी साँस लेती हुई बोलीं, "बिल्कुल! तान्या ही है।"

"लेकिन वह लड़का अभय नहीं है।" सदमा अंदर लेने के बाद वेद बोला।

"लेकिन वह लड़का अभय नहीं है।" सदमा अंदर लेने के बाद वेद बोला।

"ओह!" हताशा के स्वर में अकीरा बोली, "देखने में बहुत हैंडसम (सुंदर) है।"

"तान्या रो रही है।" पिंकी ने कहा। टिशू से तान्या आँखें पोंछ रही थी और वह लड़का उसे शांत करने की कोशिश कर रहा था।

"ओह!" हताशा के स्वर में अकीरा बोली, "देखने में बहुत हैंडसम (सुंदर) है।"

"तान्या रो रही है।" पिंकी ने कहा। टिशू से तान्या आँखें पोंछ रही थी और वह लड़का उसे शांत करने की कोशिश कर रहा था।

आँखों के कोने से अकीरा ने देखा कि वेद तसवीरें खींच रहा था। उसने हाथ रखकर पूछा, "ये क्या कर रहे हो तुम?"

"मैं तसवीरें खींच रहा हूँ और वीडियो बना रहा हूँ। मैं इन्हें अभय और नीलू मासी को भेजूँगा। बड़ा होशियार बन रहा था।"

अकीरा दाँत पीस रही थी, "तुम ऐसा कुछ नहीं करोगे।"

"क्यों? अभय को पता नहीं चलना चाहिए?"

वेदिका थोड़ी सी तो भाई के साथ सहमत थी ही।

"कब तक चुप बैठें ,अब तो कुछ है बोलना..."

"ला ला ला लाऽऽऽ।" रीशी ने साथ दिया।

"कुछ हम बोलें, कुछ तुम बोलो ओ ढोलना।" कबीर ने पूरा किया।

अकीरा ने गुस्सा दबाते हुए मेज से चाकू उठाकर वेद की तरफ करते हुए कहा

"किसी को किसी के साथ देखने पर तुम कैसे मान सकते हो कि उनका अफेयर (इश्क) है? हद हो गई।"

वेद ने जीभ से चटक की आवाज निकाली और बोला, "कुछ भी हो, अभय परिवार का हिस्सा है, उसे सतर्क करना जरूरी है।"

अकीरा चिल्लाई, "अब अचानक तुम्हें उसके बचाने का खयाल आया! तुम्हारी गर्लफ्रेंड को डुबो दो हिंद महासागर में।"

वेद का हाल देख वेदिका पूरे मजे ले रही थी। उसने अंग्रेजी गीत गाया, "ओ बेबी वेन यू टॉक लाइक दैट, यू मेक वुमन गो मैड (O baby When you talk that, you make a woman go mad'")

मानो किसी के इशारे पर, तान्या के साथ बैठे लड़के ने देखते-ही-देखते तान्या के होंठों पर अपने होंठ रख दिए। सभी शांत पड़ गए; सन्नाटा छा गया। वेद ने नाटकीय तरीके से अपना सिर झुका लिया, "आइरिश मॉस सलाद, घोड़ा, निमंत्रण का वीडियो, अपनी 21 दिन की डेटिंग योजना छोड़कर मैं...यह सब बकवास देखने आया था।"

"चुप रह वेदिका!" अपना नैपकिन वेदिका की ओर फेंकते हुए वेद बोला।

"अकीरा! वेद सही कह रहा है। अभय को यह पता चलना चाहिए।" पिंकी बोलीं।

थकावट की आवाज में अकीरा बोली, "नैतिक मूल्यों की दृष्टि से हाँ, लेकिन मुझे वाकई पैसों की जरूरत है। हो सकता है वह भाई हो! हमें क्या पता कि यह लड़का कौन है?"

मानो किसी के इशारे पर, तान्या के साथ बैठे लड़के ने देखते-ही-देखते तान्या के होंठों पर अपने होंठ रख दिए। सभी शांत पड़ गए; सन्नाटा छा गया। वेद ने नाटकीय तरीके से अपना सिर झुका लिया, "आइरिश मॉस सलाद, घोड़ा, निमंत्रण का वीडियो, अपनी 21 दिन की डेटिंग योजना छोड़कर मैं...यह सब बकवास देखने आया था।"

"अब क्या? बेचारी नीलू! कसम से हमारे परिवार पर शाप है। कोई शादी आराम से,अच्छे से और आसानी से नहीं होती।" पिंकी साँस छोड़ते हुए बोलीं।

वेद ने अकीरा का हाथ पकड़ते हुए कहा, "हम कोर्ट मैरिज करेंगे।"

अकीरा ने वेद के हाथों से अपना हाथ छुड़ाने की कोशिश करते हुए कहा, "अभी तक मैंने हाँ नहीं कहा, न ही तुमने माना कि तुम मुझसे प्यार करते हो और न ही तुमने प्रस्ताव रखा है। पहले 21 दिन तो पूरे होने दो।"

"तुम वाकई शिकायत की पेटी (Complaint Box) हो।" वेद बोला।

"ठीक है, तो देखो तुम्हें क्या करना है?" अकीरा ने अपना चेहरा दूसरी तरफ कर लिया।

"मेरे खयाल से इस बारे में माँ और मम्मीजी से सलाह करनी चाहिए। बहुत ही नाजुक मामला है यह।" पिंकी ने सलाह दी।

अकीरा बेमन से मान गई। पिंकी सही कह रही थीं। यह किसी के जीवन का मामला था।

"और आप सबको नहीं लगता कि अब हमें यहाँ से चलना चाहिए?···मेरा मतलब है कि अगर हम तान्या को देख सकते है तो वह भी तो हमें देख सकती है!" रीशी धीरे से किकियाते हुए बोला।

"देर से अहसास हुआ, पर तुम सही कह रहे हो।" पिंकी बोली और कुरसी से उठ खड़ी हुईं। वेद ने रेस्तराँ के मालिक से माफी माँगी और घर में कोई अचानक मुश्किल आ जाने का कारण बताया, जो कि गलत था।

रीशी ने कार स्टार्ट करते ही कहा, "वैसे भी वाटर क्रेस्ट सलाद में किसी को दिलचस्पी नहीं थी। तान्या और उसके विश्वासघाती होने का शुक्रिया।"

"देर से अहसास हुआ, पर तुम सही कह रहे हो।" पिंकी बोली और कुरसी से उठ खड़ी हुईं। वेद ने रेस्तराँ के मालिक से माफी माँगी और घर में कोई अचानक मुश्किल आ जाने का कारण बताया, जो कि गलत था। रीशी ने कार स्टार्ट करते ही कहा, "वैसे भी वाटर क्रेस्ट सलाद में किसी को दिलचस्पी नहीं थी। तान्या और उसके विश्वासघाती होने का शुक्रिया।"

"मुझे अभय के लिए दुःख हो रहा है। दिल का टूटना दर्दनाक होता है।" कार की खिड़की से बाहर देखते हुए अकीरा ने कहा।

"अभी भी मोहित को याद कर रही हो?" अपनी तरफ अकीरा को खींचते हुए वेद बोला।

"नहीं। मेरा कभी भी उसपर दिल नहीं आया।" अकीरा सच्चाई से बोली।

"उफ्फ! पर मैं मानता हूँ कि दिल का टूटना दर्दनाक होता हैं। बेचारा अभय!" वेद बोला।

"जो मैं ऐसा जानती कि प्रीत करै दुःख होय, तो नगर ढिंढोरा पीटती के प्रीत न करियो कोई···" हवेली के अंदर जाते हुए वेदिका ये गुनगुना रही थी।

इसे पूरे दिन की थकावट कह लो या बढ़िया सा रात का खाना, लेकिन उस दिन वेद को छत पर वाकई बहुत अच्छा लग रहा था। कबीर, वेदिका, रीशी, अकीरा, सभी उसकी चारपाई के आसपास की चारपाइयों पर लेटे थे और तारों से भरा आसमान अच्छा लग रहा था। ठंडी हवा, टिमटिमाते तारे, हवा में फूलों की खुशबू थी; वेदिका चुप थी

और अकीरा का हाथ उसके सीने पर था; सबकुछ कितना ठीक था।

"दोस्तो!" रीशी ने खामोशी तोड़ी और वेद ने कुछ मूर्खतापूर्ण सुनने का मन बना लिया। "ये सिर्फ मुझे लग रहा है कि तुमको भी लग रहा है कि कुछ चिल्लाया जाए, ऐसे ही जैसे भांडे ले लो, आलू ले लो?"

वेद मानो मन में कहे गए शब्द वापस लेना चाहता था, "वाकई इस परिवार में 'सबकुछ ठीक' जैसा कभी नहीं हो सकता।"

"नहीं रीशी!" अकीरा बोली, "लेकिन कुछ लोग अपने बॉयफ्रेंड को छोड़ने की सोच रहे हैं (ब्रेकअप), दुनिया छोड़ हिमालय में अपनी जिंदगी पनीर खाकर और नशा करते हुए रहने की सोच रहे हैं।"

"क्याऽऽऽ! तुम मेरे साथ ब्रेकअप क्यों करोगी?" वेद उठकर बैठ गया।

"क्योंकि तुम मुझे वाकई चिढ़ा-से रहे हो।" अकीरा ने शिकायत की। "खाना खाने के बाद तुमने अभय को फोन किया। तुम उससे तान्यो के बारे में पूछ रहे थे। मैंने पूरी बात सुनी।" वेदिका और कबीर ने अपने हाथों में अपने मुँह छुपा लिये। "हॉऽऽऽऽ!"

"क्योंकि तुम मुझे वाकई चिढ़ा-से रहे हो।" अकीरा ने शिकायत की। "खाना खाने के बाद तुमने अभय को फोन किया। तुम उससे तान्यो के बारे में पूछ रहे थे। मैंने पूरी बात सुनी।"

वेदिका और कबीर ने अपने हाथों में अपने मुँह छुपा लिये। "हॉऽऽऽऽ!"

"हॉऽऽऽ! तुमने छुपकर भैया की बातें सुनीं।" रीशी स्तब्ध था। वेदिका और कबीर की तरफ मुड़कर बोला, "क्या हॉऽऽऽऽ!"

"और क्या? इसमें हॉऽऽऽ जैसा क्या है? मैंने अभय को निमंत्रण की वीडियो के बारे में पूछने के लिए फोन किया और तान्या के बारे में भी पूछ लिया। मैं तो सिर्फ अच्छा भाई बनने की कोशिश कर रहा था।"

"किस कीमत पर? एक बुरे बॉयफ्रेंड बनकर। ऐसा है, अगर अभय की किस्मत में गलत रिश्ते में फँसना लिखा है तो चलने दो प्लीज।" अकीरा ने कहा।

वेद अपनी शेखी बघारती हुई गर्लफ्रेंड को हैरानी से देख रहा था और उसके एकल संवाद (Monologue) को समझने की कोशिश कर रहा था।

"जोड़ियाँ जग तोड़ियाँ ते नारद भतेरे" इस आवाज के साथ दादी, नानी और परिवार के अन्य सदस्य छत पर आए। वेद ने दादी की बात सुनकर उन्हें अचंभे से देखा। "दादी, मेरे साथ आपको इनसानों की भाषा बोलनी पड़ेगी।

इंद्राणी हँसी और हलके से वेद के सिर के पीछे से मारकर बोलीं, "चुप कर कमले!" मेरा मतलब है कि बहुत कम लोगों का सच्चा प्यार मिलता है। बाकी शादी

करके अपने हिस्से के दर्द सहते हैं।"

"बिल्कुल मानती हूँ।" अरुणा बोलीं। एक तकिया उठाकर बैठ गईं और बोलीं, "चलो! कोई बताओ कि आज असल में रेस्तराँ में हुआ क्या?"

"चलो! ये काम मैं करती हूँ।" वेदिका कूदती हुई आई। वह अरुणा के बगल में बैठ गई और उन्हें पूरी बात बताई।

अरुणा उदास होकर बोलीं, "नौसिखिए! कौन अपने प्रेमी से इतने सार्वजनिक स्थान पर दिन के उजाले में मिलता है?"

"मैं तो तुम्हारे दादाजी से फार्म हाउस पर या कब्रिस्तान में मिलती थी। किसी को कभी पता नहीं चला।" इंद्राणी प्रेम से मुसकाते हुए बोलीं।

"कब्रिस्तान जरा सोच में डाल देता है, पर कोई बात नहीं।" कबीर ने हैरानी जताते हुए कहा।

"हैलो! तुम सब और दादी, क्या अभी के लिए हम हड़प्पा सभ्यता की ये कहानियाँ किसी और दिन के मनोरंजन के लिए रख सकते हैं? पहले तान्या और उसकी रासलीलाओं के मामले पर ध्यान केंद्रित कर लेते हैं, क्यों?"

"कब्रिस्तान जरा सोच में डाल देता है, पर कोई बात नहीं।" कबीर ने हैरानी जताते हुए कहा। "हैलो! तुम सब और दादी, क्या अभी के लिए हम हड़प्पा सभ्यता की ये कहानियाँ किसी और दिन के मनोरंजन के लिए रख सकते हैं? पहले तान्या और उसकी रासलीलाओं के मामले पर ध्यान केंद्रित कर लेते हैं, क्यों?"

पिंकी ने गहरी साँस छोड़ी, "सवाल ये है कि हमें ये बात अभय को बतानी चाहिए या नहीं?"

"प्रमिला! मुझे नहीं लगता, अभय हमारी बात सुनेगा और न ही नीलू सुनेगी।"

"और न ही उसका पति!" अरुणा ने सिर नीचे लटकाते हुए कहा।

"सही कहा!" दुःख जताते हुए पिंकी बोलीं। "साथ ही ये किसी लड़की के चरित्र की बात कर रहे हैं। हम किसी पर ऐसे कीचड़ नहीं उछाल सकते। मुझे लगता है, हमें ये बात यहीं छोड़ देनी चाहिए। बहुत ही नाजुक मामला है। जो होगा, देखा जाएगा, अभय की किस्मत मानकर छोड़ देते हैं।"

वेद फिर भी नहीं माना, "दादी! क्या अगर तान्या सचमुच अभय को धोखा दे रही है और हो सकता है कि उसके परिवार को भी न पता हो? अगर अभय की जगह ऐसा मेरे साथ होता तो क्या आप लोग मुझे भी नहीं बताते?"

"पता नहीं भोलू···मुझे भी नहीं पता, मैं क्या करती?" इंद्राणी बोलीं।

"लड़की का नाम क्या बताया?" मानो चुगली और बातें बनाने का मसाला मिल जाने की खुशी हो, रोशनी ने ये सवाल बीच में ही किया।

"तान्या गेरा।" वेद ने रोशनी को बताया।

"ठीक है!" यह कहते हुए उसने अरुणा को विश्वसनीय निगाहों से देखा।

"चिंता मत कीजिए मम्मीजी! कल तक मैं सारी सच्चाई निकालकर लाऊँगी।"

रोशनी की बातें बनाने और पंचायत की आदतों को जानते हुए अरुणा ने उसे चेताया, "पुत्तर, बातें अभय की बना लेना, लड़की पर कीचड़ न उछालना। बड़ी मेहरबानी होगी।"

"जी मम्मीजी!" धीमी आवाज में रोशनी बोली।

"अकीरा पुत्तर! ज्यादा परेशान मत हो। सब अच्छा ही होगा। चिंता करने का काम भोलू का ही रहने दे।"

"जीऽऽऽ!" अकीरा ने मुसकराते हुए कहा।

"चलो सोते हैं। बहुत बड़ा दिन था। मुझे विश्वास है, कल फिर नया तमाशा होगा। गुडनाइट!"

'गुडनाइट' बोलकर वेदिका भी वेद की बगलवाली चारपाई पर कूदी और सो गई।

इतने चिढ़ने के बावजूद, थके होने के बावजूद, वेद को नींद नहीं आई। वह करवटें बदलता रहा, पर सो नहीं पाया। वह जानता था कि जब तक अकीरा से बात न कर ले, वह सो नहीं पाएगा। वह उठा और बड़े ध्यान से अकीरा की तरफ गया। वेद ने चुपचाप कंबल ऊपर किया और अकीरा की बगल में जा लेटा और कंबल सिर के ऊपर ओढ़ लिया। किसी का हाथ कमर पर महसूस होते ही अकीरा चिल्लानेवाली थी कि वेद ने अपनी हथेली से उसका मुँह बंद किया, "चिल्लाओ मत, मैं हूँ।"

इतने चिढ़ने के बावजूद, थके होने के बावजूद, वेद को नींद नहीं आई। वह करवटें बदलता रहा, पर सो नहीं पाया। वह जानता था कि जब तक अकीरा से बात न कर ले, वह सो नहीं पाएगा। वह उठा और बड़े ध्यान से अकीरा की तरफ गया। वेद ने चुपचाप कंबल ऊपर किया और अकीरा की बगल में जा लेटा और कंबल सिर के ऊपर ओढ़ लिया।

अकीरा फुफकारती हुई बोली, "तुम पागल हो गए हो क्या? किसी ने हमें ऐसे देख लिया तो?"

वेद ने उँगली से उसके गालों में गोले बनाने जैसा किया, "अगर किसी ने नहीं देखा तो?"

उसे अकीरा गहरी साँसें लेती हुई सुनाई दे रही थी, "तुम अभी तक क्यों जगे हुए हो?"

"क्योंकि तुम भी जगी हुई हो?"

"तुम कब से ऐसी घटिया बातें करने लगे? बकवास है।" अकीरा ने पूछा।

वेद ने पलटकर जवाब दिया, "बकवास से याद आया, आज हमारी डेट का आठवाँ दिन है... तारों को देखते रहने का।"

चाहे वेद उसे देख नहीं पा रहा था, पर वह देख पा रहा था कि अकीरा झुँझला रही थी। "तुम हमारी डेट्स को बकवास कह रही हो?"

"हाँ!" अकीरा ने सिर हिलाया। "हमारी डेट्स रीशी और वेदिका की खिझा देनेवाली मौजूदगी और अभय की बेकार बातों से भरी हैं; मेरे दिन बादाम-दूध और रात 'लस्सी' से पीड़ित हैं। मेरा खून भी मानो सफेद हो रहा है। शायद अब पसीने में भी मक्खन निकलने लगे। हर रोज नया नाटक, जिसपर पूरा टी.वी. सीरियल बन सकता है। बुरी हैं हमारी डेट्स।"

"हाँ!" अकीरा ने सिर हिलाया। "हमारी डेट्स रीशी और वेदिका की खिझा देनेवाली मौजूदगी और अभय की बेकार बातों से भरी हैं; मेरे दिन बादाम-दूध और रात 'लस्सी' से पीड़ित हैं। मेरा खून भी मानो सफेद हो रहा है। शायद अब पसीने में भी मक्खन निकलने लगे। हर रोज नया नाटक, जिसपर पूरा टी.वी. सीरियल बन सकता है। बुरी हैं हमारी डेट्स।"

अकीरा उसका मुँह देख पा रही थी। "ठीक है, सुनो! हमारी डेट्स लुधियाना के इतिहास में सबसे अनोखी डेट्स होंगी।" वेद ने कहा।

"लुधियाना के नहीं; मनुष्य जाति के इतिहास में!" वेद के गाल पर थपकी देते हुए अकीरा बोली।

"अच्छा?" यह कहते हुए अपनी नाक से अकीरा की गरदन में गुदगुदी की। वेद की दाढ़ी से गुदगुदी होते ही अकीरा जोर से हँस पड़ी।

"चुप हो जाओ।" अकीरा ने वेद को पीछे करने की कोशिश की, पर वह उसे सताता रहा। आवाज अपने नियंत्रण में करते हुए वह गिड़गिड़ाते हुए बोली, "प्लीज वेद! क्या चाहिए तुम्हें?"

"मुझे तुमसे कुछ जरूरी बातों पर चर्चा करनी है।"

"जैसे?"

"तुमने कहा कि तुम मुझसे प्यार नहीं करती अभी..."

अकीरा ने हलके से वेद के गाल को चूमा। "झूठे! मैंने कहा कि तुमने अभी तक यह नहीं स्वीकारा कि तुम मुझसे प्यार करते हो। मैं तुमसे सुनना चाहती हूँ। कहो! मैं चुनौती देती हूँ कि तुम नहीं कह सकते।"

वेद ने साँस छोड़ते हुए जवाब दिया, "मैंने कब मना किया? मैंने कब मना किया? मैंने तो कहा कि मैं तुम्हें पसंद करता हूँ।"

दबी आवाज में अकीरा चिल्लाई, “कृपया ये समझने की कोशिश कीजिए कि प्रेम और पसंद में अंतर होता है। और अगर तुम मुझे पसंद करते भी हो तो ऐसे बताओगे? रोमांस कहाँ है वेद?”

अकीरा ने महसूस किया कि उसके होंठों पर वेद उँगलियाँ फिरा रहा था। “हम एक चारपाई पर, एक कंबल के नीचे एक-दूसरे के साथ खुसर-पुसर कर रहे हैं। तुम्हारे प्रेम की पुस्तक में इस प्रसंग का क्या स्थान है?”

“उफ्फ!” अकीरा ने मानो हार मान ली। वेद ने धीरे से अकीरा का कंधा चूमा।

“उफ्फ! क्या चाहिए तुम्हें? वेद!” अकीरा के पास शब्द नहीं थे। उसने वेद की गरदन में अपना मुँह छुपा लिया। अकीरा जड़-सी रह गई, जब वेद ने उसके हाथों और गालों पर अपने होंठ घुमाने शुरू किए और फिर गले में नाक से छेड़ा।

“उफ्फ!” अकीरा ने मानो हार मान ली। वेद ने धीरे से अकीरा का कंधा चूमा। “उफ्फ! क्या चाहिए तुम्हें? वेद!” अकीरा के पास शब्द नहीं थे। उसने वेद की गरदन में अपना मुँह छुपा लिया। अकीरा जड़-सी रह गई, जब वेद ने उसके हाथों और गालों पर अपने होंठ घुमाने शुरू किए और फिर गले में नाक से छेड़ा।

“रुको!” अकीरा ने कहा।

“तुम्हें चाहिए कि नहीं?” वेद ने पूछा। अकीरा ने उसकी टीशर्ट पकड़ ली और उस पर चिपक गई। “उफ्फ!” “क्या?” वेद हँसा।

“ये न जवाब है और न ही प्रतिक्रिया।”

अकीरा ने कोई जवाब नहीं दिया मानो उसके बाजुओं में पिघल गई हो। वेद ने उसका माथा चूमा।

“चलो, मैं तुम्हारे लिए आसान किए देता हूँ। मुझे नहीं पता मैं आज तक तुम्हारे बिना कैसे जिया। कितना बोरिंग (उबाऊ) होऊँगा न मैं? तुम्हें यह बात शायद अजीब लगे, पर मेरी ब्लैक एंड व्हाइट (सीधी-सादी) जिंदगी में तुम रंग भर गई हो वो भी टेक्नीकलर। मुझे वाकई, वाकई, वाकई तुम बहुत अच्छी लगती हो। मुझे नहीं पता कि जो मैं तुम्हारे लिए महसूस करता हूँ, उसे तुम प्रेम कहती हो या नहीं, लेकिन हम दोनों मिलकर इस सच्चाई का पता लगा सकते हैं, ठीक?”

अकीरा ने वेद की ठोढ़ी को चूमा।

“फ्लैटरिंग! मक्खन? वैसे तुम जब चाहते हो तो प्यारे बन सकते हो, लेकिन अब हमें सोना चाहिए।”

वेद ने उसके बालों को चूमा, “हम्म।”

जब वेद हिला नहीं तो अकीरा ने भौंहें चढ़ाते हुए पूछा, “तुम अपनी जगह पर वापस नहीं जा रहे क्या?”

वेद ने उसे अपने बाजुओं में कसते हुए कहा, "अपनी जगह पर ही हूँ।"

अकीरा मुसकराई और अपने होंठ वेद के होंठों पर रख दिए। पहले तो नहीं पर बाद में वेद ने होंठों से प्रेम जताया। जोर से! दोनों खुश थे। वह पीछे हुआ और अकीरा के माथे से अपना माथा जोड़ लिया। "तुम बुद्धू हो। इस बार ये सवाल नहीं था, एक स्वीकृति थी।"

अकीरा के पास हँसने के अलावा कोई चारा नहीं था। उसने बस इतना कहा, "बुद्धू! सिर्फ तुम्हारे लिए।"

□

34

वेद को महसूस हुआ मानो किसी ने उसकी कमर पर हाथ रखा है। उसने और अकीरा ने एक ही कंबल के नीचे साथ में रात गुजारी थी। वेद को अपना बचपन याद आया, बस ये रात बचपन की रातों से कई गुना अच्छी थी। उसने अकीरा का गाल सहलाया, लेकिन हाथ को कोमलता की जगह मोटे-से बाल हाथ लगे। वेद कूदकर चारपाई पर उठ बैठा, घबराया हुआ-सा। कबीर विजयी आँखों से शांत भाव से वेद को देख रहा था। "तुम मेरे बगल में कैसे आए? कहीं तुम भी तो नींद में नहीं चलते?" कबीर दबी आवाज में चिल्लाया।

"उफ्फ! और कोशिश करो न! (प्यार से कबीर ने कहा) मुझे अब जहर ऑर्डर करना होगा। उम्मीद है एमेजोन पहुँचाता होगा।"

"प्लीज चुप रहो!" वेद ने कंबल फेंका और उठ खड़ा हुआ।

"मुझे 'स्कीन स्पेशलिस्ट' से मिलना पड़ेगा। देखो छिल गया मेरा गाल। कोई दवा लगानी पड़ेगी, बहुत दिनों तक।"

वेद पैर पटकता हुआ अकीरा के कमरे में गया और चिल्लाया, "अकीरा!"

वह काजल लगा रही थी, इस आवाज को सुनकर हाथ हिला और वह डर गई, "क्या है?"

उसे मेकअप के साथ तैयार देख वेद को हैरत हुई, "तुम तैयार भी हो गई?"

अकीरा ने अपनी चिढ़ पर नियंत्रण किया, "और तुमने मेरा काजल खराब कर दिया।"

"सॉरी!" वेद ने धीरे से कहा, "पर आज तुम इतनी जल्दी तैयार क्यों हो गई?"

"क्योंकि आज मेरी टीम आ रही है।" अकीरा ने बताया।

वह गीला वाइप लेकर आँखों के बाहर निकला काजल पोंछने लगी। "मैं पूछना भूल गई। इतनी सुबह-सुबह क्यों उदासी में डूबे हो?" अकीरा ने शीशे में ही वेद को देखकर पूछा।

वेद ने फट से पूछा, "तुम मेरी बगल से कब उठ गई?"

"तकरीबन पाँच बजे! जाहिर है, मुझे अपनी इज्जत प्यारी है।" लिपस्टिक लगाते हुए अकीरा बोली।

"ठीक!" दबी आवाज में वेद ने माना। "इस तरह तुमने कबीर को मेरी बगल में सोने का मौका दे दिया।"

यह सुनते ही अकीरा के हाथ से लिपस्टिक गिर गई, "क्याऽऽऽऽ? क्या कहा तुमने?" हैरानी से दबी आवाज में अकीरा ने पूछा।

"हाँ! मेरी बगल में कबीर सो रहा था और वह भी मेरी कमर में हाथ डालकर, मुझे लगा, तुम हो। वो तो अच्छा हुआ, उसकी दाढ़ी है, नहीं तो पता नहीं क्या हो जाता। ये सोचकर तो मैं काँप रहा हूँ।"

अकीरा ने जमीन से लिपस्टिक उठाई और बोली, "शुक्र है दाढ़ी का, वरना मैं तो दिखती भी कबीर जैसी हूँ और महसूस भी वैसी ही होती हूँ।"

"तुम नानी के साथ रहना छोड़ दो। तुम भी सबके सामने पोपट करने में लग गई हो।" हँसते हुए वेद ने कहा।

अकीरा ने जमीन से लिपस्टिक उठाई और बोली, "शुक्र है दाढ़ी का, वरना मैं तो दिखती भी कबीर जैसी हूँ और महसूस भी वैसी ही होती हूँ।" "तुम नानी के साथ रहना छोड़ दो। तुम भी सबके सामने पोपट करने में लग गई हो।" हँसते हुए वेद ने कहा।

"मुझे माफ कीजिए हुजूर!" अकीरा ने व्यंग्य से कहा, "जाओ, पहले नहा लो, दुर्गंध आ रही है।"

गुस्सैल निगाहों से वेद ने जवाब दिया, "मुझसे दुर्गंध नहीं आती।"

"जाऽऽऽऽओ!" अकीरा ने उसे बाहर धक्का मारा।

दरवाजे पर खड़े होकर वेद बोला, "ये जरूर चोर बाजारवाला इत्र है, जो मोहित तुम्हारे लिए लाया होगा।"

"अगर अब तुम नहीं गए तो मैं वेदिका से कहलवा दूँगी कि तुम और कबीर सुबह साथ में उठे।"

दरवाजे पर धम-धम एकदम बंद हो गई। अकीरा खिलखिलाकर हँस रही थी। वेद को डराना कितना आसान है!

अकीरा रात भर नहीं सोई थी। वेद के इतने पास होने पर, साँसें गरदन पर महसूस होने पर अकीरा कैसे सोती? उसने अपना बाकी का मेकअप पूरा किया। वह मानो जन्नत में थी।

शादी के स्थल पर कबीर सफेद फूलों की सजावट देखकर बोला, "ऐसा लग रहा

है, मानो हम किसी की कयामत की तैयारी कर रहे हैं।"

"बताओ क्या हुआ?" वेद ने पूछा।

"तुमने अकीरा से बात की?" कबीर ने पूछा।

वेद ने मना करते हुए कहा, "बात करना बेकार है, क्योंकि इस वक्त अकीरा सिर्फ अपने बारे में सोच रही है और यदि हमने उस 'डोरा' को उस लड़के के साथ नहीं देखा होता तो हम भी यही करते।"

रीशी हैरान था, "हैं! ये डोरा कौन?"

"तान्या! क्योंकि अभी भी वह निर्णय नहीं कर पाई है।"

रीशी और कबीर स्कूल के बच्चों की तरह हँसे। फिर कबीर ने वेद के कंधे पर हाथ रखकर कहा, "सुन ना! क्यों न हम अभय को ड्रिंक्स पर ले जाएँ और वहाँ तान्या के बारे में कुछ संकेत (Hints) दें कि किसी उधेड़-बुन में है वह?"

"बिल्कुल ठीक! भाभी तान्या को मेकअप ट्रायल (पूर्वाभ्यास) के लिए ले जा रही हैं। इससे अच्छा समय फिर नहीं मिलेगा।"

वेद भी जानता था कि कबीर और रीशी बिल्कुल ठीक कह रहे हैं। वेद ने ध्यान से सोचा कि ऐसा करने से उसके और अकीरा के संबंध में तनाव आ सकता है, लेकिन वह जानता था कि अकीरा उसकी बात समझ जाएगी। उसे खुद के और अकीरा के संबंधों पर विश्वास था।

वेद भी जानता था कि कबीर और रीशी बिल्कुल ठीक कह रहे हैं। वेद ने ध्यान से सोचा कि ऐसा करने से उसके और अकीरा के संबंध में तनाव आ सकता है, लेकिन वह जानता था कि अकीरा उसकी बात समझ जाएगी। उसे खुद के और अकीरा के संबंधों पर विश्वास था।

"ठीक है, उसे फोन करके बुलाओ।"

"ठीक है, उसे फोन करके बुलाओ।"

रीशी ने अभय को फोन लगाया, स्पीकर चालू किया। कबीर बोला, "हे अभय, मैं कबीर।"

अभय ने अभिवादन का जवाब नहीं दिया और सीधे पूछा, "तुम्हें कुछ चाहिए?"

"नहीं! मेरा मतलब है हाँ···क्या आज रात तुम्हारे पास थोड़ा समय है?" कबीर बोला।

"क्यों?"

कबीर ने बातें बनाईं, "हम सभी के लिए कुछ अलग भी हो जाएगा ब्रेक जैसा और शादी से पहले आपसी रिश्ते मजबूत करने का मौका भी। क्या कहते हो?"

कुछ क्षण की शांति रही, फिर सख्त आवाज में अभय बोला, "ठीक है! 'द 'ब्रू

एस्टेट' पर ठीक रात नौ बजे।"

थोड़ा सा सदमा पहुँचा कबीर को अभय की तीखी आवाज से, पर विजयी आँखों से उसने रीशी और वेद को देखा। हँसते हुए बोला, "कूऽऽऽऽल, ठीक है, फिर मिलते हैं।"

"मैं इंप्रेस हुआ। तुम भी ऐसे बात कर सकते हो।" वेद ने कहा। "लूजर!" कबीर की बात सुनकर वेद हँसा। लेकिन कबीर ने चेतावनी दी, "यह बात सिर्फ हम तीनों के बीच रहेगी। उम्मीद है, ये बात स्पष्ट है।"

"कौन सी बात तुम्हारे बीच रहेगी?" पीछे से आवाज आई। वेदिका थी।

"उफ्फ! वेदिका! मारे गए। तुम और नीलू मासी नरक में भी सबसे अच्छे दोस्त रहोगे और तान्या तुम्हारी सेवा करेगी।"

"मुझे चिल्ड बीयर चलेगी, पर तुम अकीरा से क्या छुपा रहे हो?" भौंहें ऊँची करते हुए वेदिका ने पूछा।

कबीर ने उसे बताया, "हम अभय से मिल रहे हैं, ताकि उसे तान्या के बारे में बता सकें।"

"ओह! अभय के लिए ठीक, लेकिन तान्या के लिए बुरा होगा। और भैया, आपके लिए तो बहुत ही बुरा। आपने सोचा क्या कि ये शादी रोको आंदोलन आपकी शादी के लिए भी हानिकारक हो सकता है?" वेदिका बोली।

"इसीलिए हम इस बात को अकीरा से छुपा रहे हैं।"

कबीर ने उसे बताया, "हम अभय से मिल रहे हैं, ताकि उसे तान्या के बारे में बता सकें।"

"ओह! अभय के लिए ठीक, लेकिन तान्या के लिए बुरा होगा। और भैया, आपके लिए तो बहुत ही बुरा। आपने सोचा क्या कि ये शादी रोको आंदोलन आपकी शादी के लिए भी हानिकारक हो सकता है?" वेदिका बोली।

"चिंता मत करो, मेरा मुँह बंद रहेगा।" वेदिका ने विश्वास दिलाया।

अचानक रीशी उठा। वेद ने पूछा, "तुम कहाँ चले?" उसका जवाब सुनकर तीनों जोर से हँस पड़े।

"'पेपर स्प्रे' लेने।"

वेद बहुत ही अधीर होकर अभय का आत्मसंतुष्ट चेहरा देख रहा था। पिछले एक घंटे से अभय केवल तान्या की बातों में गुम था। वेद को व्यंग्य कसने और अपमानित करने के और मदिरा पीने के अलावा कुछ नहीं कर रहा था। वेद पक चुका था।

"तो वेद, मि. सर्वोत्तम, तुम अकीरा से कैसे मिले? इतनी अच्छी लड़की तुम्हारे साथ क्या कर रही है? तुम तो एक-दूसरे के उलटे दिखाई देते हो?" अचानक अभय ने पूछा।

वेद ने आँखें घुमाते हुए कहा, "किसी भी रिश्ते में यह जरूरी नहीं कि तुम्हें एक जैसा होना चाहिए। एक-दूसरे के प्रति प्रेम, सम्मान और विश्वास, यही जरूरी है।"

"सच में?" हँसकर अभय बोला।

"हाँ, यही सच है।" इतने में वेद का फोन बजा। "मुझे ये फोन उठाना पड़ेगा।" कहकर वह दूसरी तरफ चला गया। फोन उठाया, "क्या हुआ वेदिका?"

वेदिका ने सीधा सवाल किया, "क्या तुम लोगों ने अभय से बात कर ली?"

"नहीं! अभी नहीं।" वेद ने कहा।

"क्यों नहीं?" वेदिका बोली।

"...क्योंकि अभय अपनी ही डींगें मारने में लगा हुआ है। मैं तो हैरान हूँ।"

जब वह वापस मेज पर पहुँचा तो अभय तान्या के पुराने संबंध के बारे में बात कर रहा था। "तान्या किसी 'लाइफ कोच' के साथ संबंध रखती थी। अजीब सा था वो। हमारे मिलने के बाद भी तान्या उस 'लाइफ कोच' से मिलती थी। आखिर मैंने उनका मिलना बंद करवाया।"

वेदिका कल्पना करके हँसने लगी।

"यार, जल्दी बात करो और खत्म करो।"

वेद ने गहरी साँस छोड़ी, "मैं कोशिश कर रहा हूँ, वहाँ सब ठीक है?"

"सब ठीक है। मेकअप पर चर्चा हो रही है।"

वेद—"बाप रे! कितनी मूर्खतापूर्ण चर्चा!"

"हाँ! पर वही काम कर रही है।" वेदिका बोली।

"ठीक है। अकीरा ठीक है?"

"हाँ जी सर!"

"अब मैं रखता हूँ, इतनी जल्दी फोन उठा नहीं पाऊँगा, इसलिए फोन करना भी मत, बाय!"

जब वह वापस मेज पर पहुँचा तो अभय तान्या के पुराने संबंध के बारे में बात कर रहा था। "तान्या किसी 'लाइफ कोच' के साथ संबंध रखती थी। अजीब सा था वो। हमारे मिलने के बाद भी तान्या उस 'लाइफ कोच' से मिलती थी। आखिर मैंने उनका मिलना बंद करवाया।" कबीर ने सुनकर सिर हिलाया और पूछा, "क्या वे दोनों अभी भी मिलते हैं?"

"नहीं! उन्होंने सारे संबंध खत्म कर दिए हैं।" अभय ने बताया। फिर अपने चेहरे के भाव बदलते हुए बोला, "अकीरा की तरह नहीं।"

वेद ने पलटकर पूछा, "अकीरा की तरह? क्या मतलब?" वेद की आँखों में गुस्सा था। "तान्या ने मुझे टेक्सट (Text) किया कि मोहित कितना असभ्य-सा था। हैरानी है कि अकीरा के पास अपने पहले बॉयफ्रेंड के बारे में कहने को इतना कुछ है।

मैं उस बेचारी की स्थिति समझ सकता हूँ; पहले बैड बॉय और अब तुम! कितनी बोर हुई होगी!"

वेद हँसने लगा और बोला, "तान्या भी तुम्हारे साथ बोर महसूस करती है, बताया नहीं उसने?" वेद के चेहरे पर भी व्यंग्य के भाव थे।

"हम इस बारे में अच्छे से भी बात कर सकते हैं भैया!" रीशी चिल्लाया।

वेद की आँखें बड़ी हो गईं और बोला, "नहीं! अभय का सच बता ही दिया जाए।"

"सच! कौन सा सच?" अभय की जीभ लड़खड़ा रही थी।

वेद मेज की दूसरी तरफ चलकर आया। कबीर समय की गंभीरता भाँपते हुए बोला, "वेद, तुम अभय की तरफ किस मंशा से ऐसे चलकर जा रहे हो?"

वेद की आँखें बड़ी हो गईं और बोला, "नहीं! अभय का सच बता ही दिया जाए।" "सच! कौन सा सच?" अभय की जीभ लड़खड़ा रही थी। वेद मेज की दूसरी तरफ चलकर आया। कबीर समय की गंभीरता भाँपते हुए बोला, "वेद, तुम अभय की तरफ किस मंशा से ऐसे चलकर जा रहे हो?"

कबीर की बात अनसुनी करते हुए वेद अभय की कुरसी के पीछे जा खड़ा हुआ; थोड़ा सा झुका और धीरे से अभय के कान में बोला, "कुछ दिनों पहले हमने तान्या को उसके पहलेवाले बॉयफ्रेंड के साथ एक रेस्तराँ में देखा।"

वेद को जिस बात की उम्मीद थी, वही हुआ। अभय भड़का, "क्या कहा! रुक!" वेद ने अपना मोबाइल अभय को दिया, "देख, मेरे पास तसवीरें भी हैं; देख तो कितने प्यारे लग रहे हें दोनों!" अभय ने गुस्से में सारी तसवीरें जल्दी-जल्दी देखीं और मालिकाना भाव से ग्रस्त हो (Obsession) वेद पर गाली देते हुए चिल्ला पड़ा।

"शुक्रिया! मैंने सुना है, बीयर बालों के लिए भी अच्छी होती है।" यह कहते हुए उसने गिलास की बीयर अभय के सिर पर उँडेल दी और विजयी जैसे हँसने लगा।

एक क्षण के लिए अभय शांत बैठा रहा, उसके बालों और चेहरे से बीयर टपक रही थी। और अचानक उठकर उसने वेद को एक घूँसा जड़ दिया। वेद पीठ के बल जमीन पर जा गिरा। आसपास के सभी डर के मारे अभय और वेद को देख रहे थे। इससे पहले कि वेद को कोई गहरी चोट आए, रीशी अभय की तरफ उसके हिंसात्मक रवैए को रोकने के लिए बढ़ा।

"उसे मत मारो!" यह कहते हुए रीशी ने अभय को पीछे खींचा।

वेद गुस्से से उठा और उसने एक घूँसा अभय के पेट में जड़ दिया। अभय ने अचानक वेद को जाने दिया। वह खुद ही जमीन पर लेट गया और अपनी आँखों पर

हाथ रखते हुए बोला, "उफ्फ! मेरी आँखें?" वेद भी जमीन पर लेटकर साँस लेने की कोशिश कर रहा था।

रीशी वेद के बगल में उकड़ूँ बैठ गया, ताकि वह समय आने पर वेद को अभय के वार से बचा सके। रीशी के दाएँ हाथ में खरीदा हुआ 'पेपर स्प्रे' था।

कबीर इस सबसे इतना स्तब्ध था कि वह कुरसी पर अभय से मिलने के निर्णय को गलत समझते हुए अविचल-सा थोड़ी देर बैठा रहा। कबीर की चिंतन शृंखला फोन की आवाज से टूटी और उसने बिना देखे फोन उठा लिया।

"भैया कहाँ हैं?" वेदिका ने प्रश्न किया।

"वेदिका!" कबीर की आवाज कमजोर पड़ गई थी। "अब से हम वेद को कभी भी बार या पब में नहीं ले जाएँगे। उसका परिणाम कभी अच्छा नहीं आता।"

□

35

"सो एड, एड्ड और ऐडी। तुम तीनों में से मुझे पूरी घटना कौन सुनानेवाला है?" सामने के सोफे पर बैठे तीन लोगों से अरुणा ने पूछा।

वेद थोड़ा सा झुका हुआ बैठा था। तीनों अपराधियों की तरह बैठे हुए थे। घायल थे, पर पब से जीवित वापस आए थे, ताकि कहानी सुना सकें। पूरा परिवार उनकी कहानी सुनने को इकट्ठा हो रखा था और जरूरत पड़ने पर उन तीनों को और भी सेंका जा सकता था। वेद ने परेशानी से अपना कान खुजलाते हुए, मासूम सी आवाज में पूछा, "नानी, आप क्या जानना चाहती हो?"

"उफ्फ! इन मूर्खों से निबटने के लिए मुझे स्ट्रॉन्ग ड्रिंक चाहिए।" अरुणा ने पलटकर अपने बेटे की तरफ देखा। "प्रणव, प्लीज मेरे लिए एक स्ट्रॉन्ग ड्रिंक बना दोगे? प्लीज!"

इंद्राणी ने अविश्वसनीय आवाज में वेद से कहा, "वेद, क्या हमने ये नहीं सोचा था कि हम अभय को कुछ नहीं बताएँगे? फिर तुमने ऐसा क्यों किया? अब नीलू मासी को फोन करो।"

पिंकी असहाय-सी बोली, "मैंने नीलू को फोन किया था, पर वह किसी का भी फोन नहीं उठा रही।"

अरुणा ने गहरी साँस लेते हुए कहा, "वेद, तुम्हें पता है कि तुम्हारे किसी भी कृत्य से किसी के जीवन पर कितना गहरा असर पड़ सकता है? तान्या के बारे में अभय को बताने से न केवल तुमने पूरी शादी को खतरे में डाल दिया है, बल्कि पूरे परिवार के नीलू के साथ संबंधों को भी संशय में डाल दिया है। अकीरा के साथ भी।"

वेद अकीरा को देख रहा था, लेकिन अकीरा न कुछ कह रही थी, न वेद की ओर देख रही थी। वेद को चिंता सताने लगी।

अरुणा ने अचानक पूछा, "क्या तुम्हारी इस शतक की सबसे बड़ी योजना में वेदिका भी शामिल थी?"

"नहीं!" (वेदिका)

"हाँ!" (वेद)

वेदिका और वेद ने एक साथ प्रतिक्रिया दी। वेद ने गुस्से से वेदिका की ओर देखकर कहा, "झूठी!"

"मैं झूठ नहीं बोल रही।" वेदिका की आवाज थोड़ी ऊँची हो गई।

"नानी! वेदिका झूठ बोल रही है। वो हमारी मदद कर रही थी। वह तान्या के मेकअप ट्रायल में बातें बना-बनाकर अकीरा को व्यस्त रखे हुए थी।"

कबीर ने सीधा अरुणा की ओर देखकर कहा।

अरुणा ने ताली बजाते हुए कहा, "मतलब मेरे घर का पूरा एनिमल प्लैनेट (प्राणी जगत्) इसमें शामिल था।"

कबीर ने सीधा अरुणा की ओर देखकर कहा। अरुणा ने ताली बजाते हुए कहा, "मतलब मेरे घर का पूरा एनिमल प्लैनेट (प्राणी जगत्) इसमें शामिल था।" इंद्राणी गंभीर स्वर में बोली, "वेद! मैं चाहती हूँ कि तुम अभी नीलू के घर जाओ और उनसे माफी माँगो।" "क्याऽऽऽऽ ?" डर और हैरानी मिश्रित भाव से वेद बोला।

इंद्राणी गंभीर स्वर में बोली, "वेद! मैं चाहती हूँ कि तुम अभी नीलू के घर जाओ और उनसे माफी माँगो।"

"क्याऽऽऽऽ ?" डर और हैरानी मिश्रित भाव से वेद बोला।

"तुम समझदार हो वेद!" अरुणा ने माथा खुजाते हुए कहा।

"अधिकतर समय···" पिंकी ने छौंक लगाते हुए व्यंग्य किया।

"वो तो है, इसलिए मुझे दुबारा कहने पर मजबूर मत करो।"

इससे पहले कि वेद कुछ कहता, प्रणव ने बाइक की चाबियाँ वेद की तरफ फेंकीं, जो सीधी वेद की छाती पर लगकर जमीन पर गिरीं और आवाज हुई।

वेद जमीन पर गिरी चाबी को देख रहा था और अपना भविष्य भी।

अपने शैतान परिवार की ओर एक नजर देखते हुए वेद बेमन से गैराज की तरफ चल पड़ा। भगवान् का शुक्र था कि बाइक में पेट्रोल भी था और साथ में हेलमेट भी रखा हुआ था। वेद ने अपने वॉलेट में ड्राइविंग लाइसेंस देखा कि है या नहीं। अभी वो जाने ही वाला था कि किसी ने उसकी कलाई पर हाथ रखा। वह बहुत डर गया।

"मुझे तुमसे कुछ बात करनी है···" अकीरा ने धीरे से कहा। अकीरा गुस्से में दिख रही थी। लग रहा था, मानो उनकी पहली जबरदस्त लड़ाई हो जाएगी। गहरी साँस छोड़ते हुए वेद ने अपना हेलमेट उतारा और अकीरा के हाथ में दिया। बिना वेद की ओर देखे उसने चुपचाप हेलमेट पहन लिया। वह तब से बहुत दुविधा में थी, जब से उन्होंने तान्या

को उस लाइफ कोच के साथ रेस्तराँ में देखा था। शायद वह अकारण ही स्वार्थी हो रही थी। वह खुद समझ नहीं पा रही थी।

अपने खयालों में गुम वे नीलू मासी के घर पहुँचे, केवल यह देखने के लिए कि वहाँ कोई नहीं था।

अकीरा ने साँस छोड़ी, "अब क्या?"

"तुम्हें बात करनी थी न! आइसक्रीम?" वेद ने आशा भरे स्वर में पूछा।

अकीरा ने धीमे से हामी भरी और वे करीबी आइसक्रीम पार्लर पर पहुँचे। आइसक्रीम लेकर वह इंतजार करती हुई अकीरा की मेज पर पहुँचा। उसके सामने आइसक्रीम कप रखते हुए बोला, "तुम्हारे लिए चॉकलेट और मेरे लिए वनिला।"

किसी प्रतिक्रिया की उम्मीद से वेद ने पब की लड़ाई के बारे में बताना शुरू किया, "अभय ने मुझे मारा। तुम भी सोच रही होगी कि कैसा है मेरा बॉयफ्रेंड, हर जगह से पिट के आ जाता है?"

अकीरा ढिठाई से चुप रही। वेद ने धीरे से अकीरा से माफी माँगी, "आई एम सॉरी अकीरा!"

अपनी आँखों में तूफान छिपाए अकीरा ने वेद की आँखों में देखकर कहा, "मैं सोच रही थी कि क्या तुम मेरे बिना रह सकते हो? वैसे अभी 21 दिन नहीं हुए हैं। मेरा खयाल है कि हम दोनों एक-दूसरे के बिना रह सकते हैं।"

वेद स्तब्ध-सा हो गया। "तुम किस बारे में बात कर रही हो?"

किसी प्रतिक्रिया की उम्मीद से वेद ने पब की लड़ाई के बारे में बताना शुरू किया, "अभय ने मुझे मारा। तुम भी सोच रही होगी कि कैसा है मेरा बॉयफ्रेंड, हर जगह से पिट के आ जाता है?" अकीरा ढिठाई से चुप रही। वेद ने धीरे से अकीरा से माफी माँगी, "आई एम सॉरी अकीरा!"

"तुम्हें ऐसा क्यों लगा कि अभय को सच्चाई बताने की योजना अच्छी रहेगी?"

"नहीं!" वेद सफाई देने लगा, "यह खयाल अच्छा नहीं रहा। मुझे पता था...कबीर को मालूम था, हम सबको मालूम था, फिर भी हमने अभय से बात करने का खतरा उठाया।"

"क्यों और किसलिए?" अकीरा ने जोर देते हुए पूछा।

"हमने इस बारे नें पहले भी बहस की थी अकीरा!"

"बिल्कुल! तो अब तुम जान गए होगे कि यह सब सुनकर मुझे कैसा लग रहा होगा!" अकीरा ने व्यंग्यात्मक मुसकान के साथ कहा।

"मुझे बता दो, हमारा ये संबंध तुम्हारे लिए कोई मायने नहीं रखता?" अकीरा ने पूछा।

"ये तुम्हारे या मेरे बारे में नहीं है। ये उस लड़के और लड़की के बारे में है, जिन्हें केवल एक सच्चाई बताकर बहुत से दु:खों और बहुत सारे दर्द से पहले ही बचाया जा सकता है। बस इतना ही।"

"आह! क्या बात है! तुम उन्हें बचाना चाहते हो? वेद अरोरा खुद का दिल टूटने से नहीं डरता। क्या बात है!"

"वो इसीलिए कि मुझे लगा कि तुम समझ जाओगी। तुम केवल किसी बात को इसलिए अनदेखा नहीं कर सकती, क्योंकि उसी में तुम्हारा फायदा है। और मैं भी तो तुम्हारे व्यवसाय (बिजनेस) में तुम्हारी मदद करूँगा।"

"मुझे तुम्हारा परोपकार नहीं चाहिए। मैं अपने दम पर अपना काम कर लूँगी।" गुस्से से अकीरा बोली। "मैंने अपने मॉम-डैड से वादा किया है कि अपने दम पर मैं यह कंपनी चलाऊँगी। ठीक है न! इसलिए यह अधिकार मैंने किसी को नहीं दिया कि कोई मेरे काम में दखलअंदाजी करे। इसलिए मेरे बिजनेस में नाक घुसेड़ना छोड़ दो।"

इस बात से वेद को काटो तो खून नहीं। कप में पिघली हुई आइसक्रीम को गटकते हुए वेद ने सिर नीचे करते हुए कहा, "आइसक्रीम की डेट्स के इतिहास में यह सबसे बेकार डेट थी।"

"चलो, घर चलते हैं।" अकीरा ने कहा और वेद भी जल्दी से इस बात के लिए तैयार हो गया।

जैसे ही वे हवेली के गेट से अंदर आए, कबीर, रीशी और वेदिका उनकी तरफ दौड़ते हुए आए। "मैं तुम्हें अरसे से फोन कर रहा हूँ, कहाँ है तुम्हारा फोन?" कबीर ने कहा।

वेद ने अपनी जेब से फोन निकाला और जाँचा "ओफ्फो! साइलंट मोड पर था।" वेद ने कहा। "लेकिन हुआ क्या?"

कबीर ने निचला होंठ दबाते हुए कहा, "नीलू मासी यहाँ हैं।"

"हे भगवान्!" वेद डर के मारे जमीन पर बैठ गया।

रीशी ने डरकर पूछा, "भैया, आप ठीक हैं न?"

"रीशी मेरे भाई! यहाँ आसपास कोई दिमाग का अस्पताल है क्या?"

"है, पर क्यों पूछ रहे हैं आप?" रीशी ने कहा।

दर्द भरी कराह से वेद बोला, "क्योंकि मुझे उस अस्पताल में अपने लिए एक बिस्तर चाहिए।"

□

36

वेद को लगा मानो वह जोंबियों के इलाके में आ गया हो। फर्क बस इतना है कि इन जोंबियों को मांस की जगह मेरा दिमाग चाहिए। अभय का एक ओर का हलका जख्मी चेहरा देख वेद सोच रहा था कि कितना मजा आए न, अगर दूसरे गाल पर भी घूँसा जड़ दिया जाए!

उसी समय अजीब तरीके से अपना गला साफ करती हुई और खकारती हुई रोशनी मामी बोलीं, "कोई कुछ कहे, उससे पहले मुझे कुछ कहना है।"

"मामी एक वाक्य में हर तरह के विशेषण (गालियाँ) का प्रयोग कर सकती है।" दबी हँसी में वेद कबीर से बोला।

"उससे पहले मैं नीलू से कुछ पूछना चाहता हूँ।" प्रमोद मामा बीच में बोले।

अरुणा नानी दु:खी दिख रही थीं, "हाँ प्रमोद! तू वी दस दे।"

उन्होंने नीलू से सवाल किया, "घोड़ी रखनी है या कैंसिल करनी है?"

अरुणा नानी भड़कती हुई बोलीं, "हमें यहाँ ये नहीं पता कि दुलहन वही रखनी है या नहीं और तुझे घोड़ी की पड़ी है!"

"माँ, मैं···"

अरुणा ने बात काटते हुए कहा, "मुँह ज्यादा न फाड़ा करो।"

बेमन से प्रमोद मामा वहाँ से चले गए। अभय के पिता भी उनके पीछे चल दिए और दोनों एक कोने में जाकर नशा करने बैठ गए।

अरुणा रोशनी की तरफ मुड़ी और पूछा, "तुम क्या कह रही थी?"

"हाँ!" रोशनी ने हामी भरी। "मैंने तान्या के बारे में पता किया। उसका किसी लाइफ कोच से चक्कर था। अभय से वह बाद में मिली। अभय से मिलने के बाद भी वह अपने पुराने बॉयफ्रेंड से मिलती रही।"

"यह सब मुझे पता है नानी! और यह मैंने इन तीनों मूर्खों को भी बताया, क्यों, बताया था न?" अभय बोला।

तीन में से दो ने गुस्से भरी निगाहों से अभय को देखा। एक ने गलत उँगली भी

अभय को दिखाई, "हाँ! घूँसों और पेपर स्प्रे से पहले सब ठीक था।"

नीलू ने आँखें घुमाते हुए कहा, "सब बोल चुके या किसी को कोई और भी मूर्खतापूर्ण बात अभी कहनी है?"

"मुझे एक छोटा सा सवाल वेद से पूछना है।"

वेद ने पलटकर माँ को देखा और पूछा, "क्या?" पिंकी ने अभय के चोट लगे गाल की ओर इशारा किया और पूछा, "ये तुमने किया?"

वेद ने चिढ़कर पूछा, "हाँ! क्यों?"

वेद ने पलटकर माँ को देखा और पूछा, "क्या?" पिंकी ने अभय के चोट लगे गाल की ओर इशारा किया और पूछा, "ये तुमने किया?"
वेद ने चिढ़कर पूछा, "हाँ! क्यों?"
पिंकी ने वेद के गाल को चूमकर कहा, "बस, मुझे पक्का करना था।"
अरुणा ने मानो चेतावनी के स्वर में कहा, "प्रमिला, अब तुम उस उम्र में नहीं हो कि मैं तुम्हारी पिटाई करूँ, इसलिए जरा सोच-समझकर, प्लीज!"

पिंकी ने वेद के गाल को चूमकर कहा, "बस, मुझे पक्का करना था।"

अरुणा ने मानो चेतावनी के स्वर में कहा, "प्रमिला, अब तुम उस उम्र में नहीं हो कि मैं तुम्हारी पिटाई करूँ, इसलिए जरा सोच-समझकर, प्लीज!"

"ठीक है, सॉरी! पर मेरे बेटे ने किसी को घूँसा मारा···! ये सोचकर ही मैं फूली नहीं समा रही।" पिंकी ने मुसकराते हुए कहा।

"मॉम!" वेद ने माँ को चुप कराने के लिए जोर से हाथ पकड़ा।

अरुणा ने साँस रोककर अपनी बेटी के साथ जश्न मनाना चाहा, पर चुप रह गई। अपने चेहरे के भाव संतुलित रखने जरूरी थे।

अरुणा बोलीं, "नीलू, हमने वेद को माफी माँगने के लिए भेजा था।" उनकी आवाज में ईमानदारी थी।

"हाँ!" नीलू ने वेद को छोटी चमकदार आँखों से देखते हुए कहा, "लेकिन हमें उसकी माफी नहीं चाहिए। मैं किसी को दोष भी नहीं दे रही, क्योंकि यह वेद के कर्म हैं। सच कहती हूँ, ऐसा सोचना मेरे लिए छोटी बात है।"

पिंकी मन-ही-मन सोच रही थीं, 'नीचे तो ये होगी···मेरी जूत्ती के।'

नीलू अपनी बात जारी रखे हुए थी, "मैं यहाँ तुम सबको केवल यह बताने आई हूँ कि हमने तान्या और उसके परिवार से लंबी बात की। तान्या उस दिन अपने बॉयफ्रेंड से आखिरी बार मिलने गई थी और उसी दिन तुम सब लोगों ने देखा था। उनका संबंध-विच्छेद कभी ठीक से हुआ ही नहीं था। वो नहीं चाहती थी कि बुरी ऊर्जा उसके भविषय

में साथ जाए। इसीलिए वह सबकुछ हुआ। वह अभय को धोखा नहीं दे रही थी।"

"बेकार! जब मैंने पिछले बॉयफ्रेंड को छोड़ा था तो गुडबाय कहने को एक जूता फेंककर मारा था।" कबीर बोला।

"मुझे भी वह दिन याद है।" कहकर वेद और वेदिका सभी हँस पड़े।

"चुप रहो तुम सभी! मतलब शादी हो रही है, ठीक?" अरुणा ने कहा।

नीलू बोली, "बिल्कुल।"

कमरे में शांति छा गई। "ये बात तो टेक्सट मैसेज में भी हो सकती थी।" कबीर, रीशी और वेदिका, वेद की यह बात सुनकर हँसी रोकने की कोशिश कर रहे थे।

नीलू ने अकीरा से कहा, "तुम प्लीज योजना के अनुसार अपना काम जारी रखना।"

"जी।" अकीरा धीरे से मुसकराकर बोली। नीलू खड़े होते ही बोली, "वैसे तुम लोगों को बरदाश्त करना बहुत मुश्किल है। मिलते हैं खाने के पुनराभ्यास पर (Rehearsal Dinner)" अरोरा और आहलूवालिया परिवार उसे घर से बाहर भेजने को अत्यंत उत्सुक थे। सभी ने उत्साह से 'गुडनाइट' कहा।

नीलू के पति अचानक कहीं से प्रकट हुए और सभी हवेली से बाहर चल पड़े।

"उफ्फ! क्या बकवास करती है ये!" पिंकी खुद को हाथ से हवा करते हुए बोलीं।

"वाकई! पर अकीरा! तुम तान्या के बारे में और नीलू मासी ने जो सफाई दी, उस बारे में क्या सोचती हो?"

नीलू के पति अचानक कहीं से प्रकट हुए और सभी हवेली से बाहर चल पड़े। "उफ्फ! क्या बकवास करती है ये!" पिंकी खुद को हाथ से हवा करते हुए बोलीं। "वाकई! पर अकीरा! तुम तान्या के बारे में और नीलू मासी ने जो सफाई दी, उस बारे में क्या सोचती हो?" अकीरा कुलबुलाकर बोली, "मैं अरोरा नहीं हूँ, इसीलिए मेरी राय मायने नहीं रखती।"

अकीरा कुलबुलाकर बोली, "मैं अरोरा नहीं हूँ, इसीलिए मेरी राय मायने नहीं रखती।"

उसके जवाब ने अजीब सी शांति कमरे में फैला दी। वह धीरे से उठी और बोली, "मुझे बहुत सा काम पूरा करना है, मैं चलती हूँ, गुडनाइट।"

अकीरा को पीछे होते देख अरुणा ने भौंहें चढ़ाकर वेद से पूछा, "तुमने अकीरा से लड़ाई की?"

वेद ने सिर पकड़कर कहा, "हाँ! उसे हमारा अभय से मिलना अच्छा नहीं लगा।"

"बिल्कुल ठीक! तुम्हें उससे बात करनी चाहिए।" इंद्राणी बोली।

"हम्म! प्रार्थना करो कि वो मेरा खून न करे।" वेद ने हामी भरी।

सभी हँस पड़े। इंद्राणी ने जोर देकर कहा, "जाओ, उसे मनाओ।"

'हाँ' कहते हुए सबको 'गुडनाइट' कह वेद चल दिया।

जैसी कि उसे उम्मीद थी, अकीरा छत पर थी। उसके हाथ की सिगरेट की तरफ इशारा करते हुए उसके बगल में जा बैठा। "तो यह है तुम्हारा बहुत सा काम, चलो। अब छोड़ो! जाने भी दो। हो रही है न अब शादी!"

"सही!" एक उत्तर दिया।

"ऐसा लग रहा है न कि पहले भी हुआ है? याद है, कबीर के जन्मदिन की पार्टी में हम कैसे सीढ़ियों पर लड़े थे?"

"कैसे भूल सकती हूँ।" अकीरा ने धीरे से कहा।

वे थोड़ी देर चुप रहे। वेद के धैर्य ने जवाब दे दिया और उसने पूछा, "अकीरा! क्या हुआ?"

अकीरा ने परेशान होकर अपनी गरदन सहलाई और बोली, "मैं व्यावसायिक स्तर पर गलत हूँ। यहाँ कुछ ठीक नहीं है। लुधियाना बिल्कुल बेकार है।"

वेद को हँसना पड़ा, "चलो, कम-से-कम हम इस बात पर तो सहमत हैं कि लुधियाना बेकार शहर है। पर ये लोग सामान्य नहीं हैं।"

अकीरा भी मुसकाई। वेद ने प्यार से अकीरा के गाल पर हाथ फेरा। "अच्छा लगा तुम्हें हँसता हुआ देखकर। लेकिन हमें अपना मसला हल करना होगा। तुम मुझसे, बिना छोड़कर जाने की धमकी दिए भी, नाराज हो सकती हो।"

बिना वेद को देखे अकीरा धीरे से बोली, "मैं नाराज थी।"

वेद मुसकराया, "गुस्से के नाम पर अपने गलत व्यवहार को सही साबित नहीं कर सकती।"

"हाँ! मानती हूँ।"

"सुनो! क्या हम दुबारा शुरू कर सकते हैं? मुझे तुमसे लड़ना अच्छा नहीं लगता।" वेद ने कहा।

अकीरा ने सिर उठाया और वेद की आँखों में देखा, "मुझे भी अच्छा नहीं लगता।"

वेद का चेहरा खिल गया और चेहरे पर बड़ी सी मुसकान खिल गई। उसने अपना हाथ अकीरा की ओर बढ़ाकर पूछा, "युद्ध विराम?"

अकीरा ने अपना हाथ वेद के हाथ में रखकर कहा, "युद्ध विराम।"

□

37

"अगर हम सारे फल होते तो वेद भैया कौन सा फल होते? आम! क्योंकि उन्हें आम लोग पसंद हैं।" वेदिका बोली। पुनराभ्यास भोज (Rehearsal Dinner) के समय मेज पर बैठे सभी लोग, दादी, नानी समेत, खिलखिलाकर हँस पड़े। नीलू मासी ने बहुत ध्यान से शादी के लिए एक सुंदर सा फार्म हाउस चुना था। अच्छी सी धीमे प्रकाश की लड़ियाँ झाड़ियों पर लटक रही थीं; जैज संगीत चल रहा था। बहुत ही मधुर वातावरण था। पर मानो यहीं पर अच्छी चीजें खत्म थीं!

क्योंकि नीलू मासी की खाने की माँगें इतनी अजीब थीं; चाहे वो मशरूम हो चाहे पास्ता।

वेद ने झाँककर अकीरा को ढूँढ़ा। वेद ने देखा, अकीरा अपनी टीम के साथ थी। किसी कारण से वह मुड़ी तो उनकी नजरें मिलीं और एक बड़ी सी मुसकराहट के साथ वह वेद की ओर आई।

"और क्या चल रहा है?" अकीरा ने वेद की ओर आते हुए पूछा।

"खुद ही देख लो…!"

"ओ! एक और!" अकीरा ने वेद के गिलास में से एक घूँट लेते हुए पूछा, "कोई भी राई (Mustard Seeds) से कुछ भी नहीं पूछता?"

अरुणा सोचने लगीं, फिर चिढ़कर पूछा, "राई? क्यों?"

"क्योंकि राई हमेशा यह गाना गाती है, हम हैं राई (राही) प्यार के हमसे कुछ न पूछिए।"

हवा में हँसी के ठहाकों की गूँज सुनाई दी। वेदिका कबीर की तरफ झुकी, रोटी उठाई और बोली, "तुम जब न्यूयॉर्क गए थे, तुम्हें पता है, मैं तुम्हारे लिए कितना रोती (रोटी) थी?"

इस बार तो अकीरा भी जोर से हँस पड़ी। वेद ने अपना चेहरा लटकाया और बोला, "अकीरा, प्लीज, रहम करो मुझपर!"

धीरे से वेद का गाल थपकाते हुए अकीरा एक कोने की कुरसी मेज की तरफ ले

गई। वेद ने कुरसी खींचते हुए शिकायत की, "चुटकुले एक के बाद एक और भी घटिया होते जा रहे हैं। अरोरा परिवार के स्तर से भी नीचे के चुटकुले चल रहे हैं। अपनी बात को साबित करने के लिए मैं वेदिका के और भी चुटकुले बता सकता हूँ।"

अकीरा ने कहा, "ठीक है। बताओ।"

"एक आदमी को कटहल उगाने के जुर्म में गिरफ्तार किया गया था। क्यों? क्योंकि उस आदमी ने कत्ल किया था।"

"हे भगवान्!" अकीरा बिना हँसे गहरी साँस छोड़ते हुए बोली।

"यही तो!" वेद अकीरा की प्रतिक्रिया पर गर्व कर रहा था।

"ये सभी अतुल्य बोर लोगों का झुंड है, जिन्होंने अब पी भी रखी है और अंट-शंट बोलने की शुरुआत है।"

सिर हिलाते हुए अकीरा बोली, "मेरा खयाल है कि वे भूखे भी हैं।"

"इससे याद आया, तुमने कुछ खाया?" वेद ने आँखें छोटी करते हुए पूछा।

"नहीं! मैं दोपहर से काम में लगी हुई थी और तुमने?"

"ईमानदारी से मैंने खाने की कोशिश की, पर नहीं खा पाया। सच तो ये है कि मैं तुम्हारे बिना खाना नहीं चाहता था।"

"तुम कितने प्यारे हो।" अपने पैरों की उँगलियों को सहलाते हुए अकीरा बोली।

सिर हिलाते हुए अकीरा बोली, "मेरा खयाल है कि वे भूखे भी हैं।"
"इससे याद आया, तुमने कुछ खाया?" वेद ने आँखें छोटी करते हुए पूछा।
"नहीं! मैं दोपहर से काम में लगी हुई थी और तुमने?"
"ईमानदारी से मैंने खाने की कोशिश की, पर नहीं खा पाया। सच तो ये है कि मैं तुम्हारे बिना खाना नहीं चाहता था।"

"पता है!" प्यार से वेद बोला, "मैं दो मिनट में आया।"

"कहाँ जा रहे हो?"

"तुम्हारी दोनों समस्याओं का समाधान लाने।" वेद बोला।

जैसा कि वादा किया था, वह वापस आते हुए एक बैग लाया। धीरे से वह थैला अकीरा के पैरों के पास रखा। अकीरा के पैर उठाकर मेज पर रखे। "ये चप्पल तुम्हारे थके हुए पैरों के लिए और पिज्जा भूखे पेट के लिए।"

अकीरा वेद की समझ पर स्तब्ध-सी रह गई। वेद ने अपने प्यार का इजहार नहीं किया था, पर वह अकीरा को खुश करने के लिए कुछ ज्यादा ही कर जाता था। मोहित जैसे के साथ संबंधों के बाद वेद ठंडी हवा का झोंका था।

उसने अपना हाथ वेद के हाथ पर रखा, "आई एम सॉरी वेद!" "अरे, ऐसे समय

में तो लोग शुक्रिया कहते हैं।"

"हाँ, जानती हूँ, लेकिन मैं पिछले दो-तीन दिनों में बहुत ही सख्त मिजाज दिखा रही थी, इसलिए माफी माँग रही हूँ। हमें बात करनी चाहिए।" अकीरा ने गहरी साँस भरते हुए कहा।

एक क्षण के लिए वेद को गुस्सा आया, पर उसने काबू कर लिया और अकीरा का हाथ पकड़कर बोला, "मैं तुम्हें बताना चाहता था कि मुझे ऐसा लगा कि शादी में एक इनसान दूसरे इनसान को धोखा दे रहा है, और कुछ नहीं। लेकिन पिछले कुछ दिनों की घटनाएँ देखकर लग रहा है कि मैं गलत था। लेकिन मेरा विश्वास करो अकीरा, मेरा उद्देश्य तुम्हारा काम खराब करना बिल्कुल नहीं था।"

अकीरा की आँखें भर आईं। "मुझे पता है, लेकिन मुझे बहुत गुस्सा आता है, जब कोई मुझसे बातें छुपाता है। सारी बातें जुड़ गईं और हालात देखकर मुझे और गुस्सा आया, पर तुमने अभय को घूँसा क्यों मारा?"

"क्योंकि उसने तान्या को कुछ कहने के कारण तुम्हारे, मेरे और मोहित को लेकर बकवास की।"

अकीरा की आँखें भर आईं। "मुझे पता है, लेकिन मुझे बहुत गुस्सा आता है, जब कोई मुझसे बातें छुपाता है। सारी बातें जुड़ गईं और हालात देखकर मुझे और गुस्सा आया, पर तुमने अभय को घूँसा क्यों मारा?" "क्योंकि उसने तान्या को कुछ कहने के कारण तुम्हारे, मेरे और मोहित को लेकर बकवास की।"

अकीरा माथा खुजलाते हुए बोली, "कब?"

"ओ रुको! ओऽऽऽऽ! अकीरा हमारे पिछले बॉयफ्रेंड्स के बारे में सवाल कर रही थी। मैंने मोहित के बारे में बात की, क्योंकि वही बात चल रही थी। मेरा विश्वास करो।"

"यार! तुम मुझे सफाई मत दो। मैं तो तुम्हें सिर्फ इतना बता रहा था कि उस चूहे को मेरा घूँसा क्यों पड़ा।"

"वाह! ऐसा लग रहा है मानो तुम दोनों डेट पर हो।" अभय ने उनकी मेज की ओर आते हुए कहा।

वेद और अकीरा ने आसपास देखा तो लगा कि वाकई वे डेट पर हैं। जिसे कि सच्ची डेट कहते हैं। जबकि ऐसा नहीं था। आखिर वेद ने रुखाई से पूछा, "क्या चाहिए तुम्हें?"

अपनी जगह पर हिलते हुए अभय ने एक गाली पकड़ाते हुए कहा, "मुझे क्या चाहिए? अपनी गर्लफ्रेंड से कहो कि जाकर देखे मेरे मेहमानों को क्या चाहिए? बारटेंडर मेरे मेहमानों को ड्रिंक्स (मदिरा) देने से मना कर रहा है। और अकीरा क्या कर रही है? यहाँ तुम्हारे साथ बैठी है।"

अकीरा ने हाथ ऊपर करके कहा, "अरे चिंता मत करो।" और जल्दी से बार की तरफ जाकर पूछा कि क्या हुआ?

"मैम! हमारे बजट में जितना निर्धारित था, उतना अल्कोहल (मदिरा) हमने दी है···" एक कर्मचारी ने अकीरा को बताया।

वेद ने अपना क्रेडिट कार्ड निकालकर एक कर्मचारी को दिया और कहा, "पास की दुकान से और बोतलें ले आओ।"

"नहीं वेद!" अकीरा ने विरोध किया।

वेद ने उसे देखते हुए कहा, "कोई बात नहीं! मैं अपने परिवार को जानता हूँ। मैं देख लूँगा। तुम चिंता मत करो।"

"मैं तुम्हारे बारे में गलत समीक्षा दूँगा। आलोचना से तुम्हारा सारा काम ठप हो जाएगा। तुम बस देखती जाओ। मैं केवल एक स्टार दूँगा और कहूँगा कि इनकी रोड के बाजूवाले ढाबे जैसी सेवाएँ हैं। और ऐसा कुछ करूँगा कि कोई तुम्हें काम भी न दे।" अभय अपना संतुलन खोकर विक्षिप्त (पागल) मनुष्य जैसा बोले जा रहा था।

"मैं तुम्हारे बारे में गलत समीक्षा दूँगा। आलोचना से तुम्हारा सारा काम ठप हो जाएगा। तुम बस देखती जाओ। मैं केवल एक स्टार दूँगा और कहूँगा कि इनकी रोड के बाजूवाले ढाबे जैसी सेवाएँ हैं। और ऐसा कुछ करूँगा कि कोई तुम्हें काम भी न दे।"

"ओह! हम डर गए।" वेद ने मानो चिढ़ाते हुए कहा।

"भैयाऽऽऽ, मैं आ गई।" वेदिका दौड़ती हुई वेद की तरफ आई।

वेद ने उसे ठीक से खड़े होने की कोशिश करते हुए कहा, "गोगो! तुम कुरसी पर बैठ क्यों नहीं जाती?"

"नहीं।" अकड़कर वेदिका बोली। "मैं समझ गई कि यहाँ कुछ लड़ाई हो रही है और मुझे लड़ाई देखना पसंद है।"

"मुझे भी! मुझे तो लड़ाई करना पसंद है।" हँसी उड़ाते हुए अभय ने कहा।

ईश्वर की कृपा से कर्मचारी अल्कोहल की बोतलें ले आए और अकीरा ने राहत की साँस ली। अभय भी खुश हुआ, "मुझे लगा कि तुम्हारा कर्मचारी कहीं तुम्हारा कार्ड लेकर भाग तो नहीं गया।" वेद गुस्से से पगला रहा था। अभय को वेदिका से तू-तू मैं-मैं करते हुए देख बोला, "वेदिका! अगर ये तुम्हारा दुबारा अपमान करेगा, तो मैं छोड़ूँगा नहीं।"

अकीरा ने अपनी आवाज में गंभीरता और स्थैर्य लाकर कहा, "तुम ऐसा कुछ भी नहीं करोगे? समझ आया तुम्हें?"

"अकीरा, मैं···" वेद ने कुछ कहना चाहा।

"नहीं। मैं तुम्हें बता चुकी हूँ कि यह शादी मेरे व्यवसाय के लिए कितनी जरूरी है। जब से तुम अभय से मिले हो, तुम्हारा दिमाग इतना असंतुलित-सा क्यों हो चला है ? मुझे अपना काम करने दो। ठीक है ?" वेद समझ गया कि अब और बहस करने का कोई फायदा नहीं। "ठीक है ! आगे से मैं बीच में नहीं पड़ूँगा।"

उन दोनों की बहस के बारे में अनभिज्ञ वेदिका उन्हें खींचती हुई परिवार के पास ले गई। वेदिका मेज पर चढ़कर बोली, "सेल्फी टाइम" और अपने मोबाइल से फोटो खींचने की कोशिश करने लगी। फिर अपने भाग्य को कोसते हुए वेदिका की टाँगें पकड़कर वेद बोला, "प्लीज, नीचे आ जाओ।"

पिंकी और पूरे परिवार ने सेल्फी में खुद को दिखाने की कोशिश की। पूरा परिवार वेदिका के आसपास था। वेद का लटका चेहरा देखकर अरुणा ने धीरे से उसके सिर पर मारा और कहा, "रब ने दाँत दिए हैं तो हँस ले थोड़ा। जब देखो तो सड़ा हुआ घूमता रहता है। छी: !"

पिंकी और पूरे परिवार ने सेल्फी में खुद को दिखाने की कोशिश की। पूरा परिवार वेदिका के आसपास था। वेद का लटका चेहरा देखकर अरुणा ने धीरे से उसके सिर पर मारा और कहा, "रब ने दाँत दिए हैं तो हँस ले थोड़ा। जब देखो तो सड़ा हुआ घूमता रहता है। छी: !"

यह सुनकर कबीर और रीशी ने वेद को गुदगुदी की। इससे वेद एकदम से खुद को बचाने के लिए बाजू हुआ। उन दोनों से बचने की कोशिश में वेद का हाथ सीधा वेदिका के घुटनों पर लगा, जिससे वेदिका का संतुलन बिगड़ा। वह गिरते हुए सीधी नीचे आई और मेजपोश, मोमबत्तियाँ और सारी सजावट को खींचती हुई ले आई। कुछ ही क्षणों में सारी कटलरी, फूल और जो कुछ भी मेज पर था, नीचे गिरा। मोमबत्ती से फिर मेजपोश में आग लगी। वेद ने तुरंत उस मेजपोश को पास के तरणताल (Swimming Pool) में डाल दिया। यह सभी आपाधापी देखकर चुप्पी छा गई।

"उफ्फ! ये क्याऽऽऽ!" नीलू मासी दबी आवाज में दुःख व्यक्त करते हुए बोली, जब उन्होंने मेजपोश, उसपर रखे चम्मच, काँटे और कुछ मोबाइल फोन स्वीमिंग पूल की तह में देखे।

अकीरा बालों में हाथ घुमाते हुए सदमे में बोली, "ओ शिट!" (उफ्फ)

"खैर!" वेद ने दुःख भरी नजरों से अकीरा को देखा।

"इतिहास वाकई खुद को दोहराता है। खासकर लुधियाना में।"

□

38

"शिकंजी लाइम सौरवेट! वाकई?" अविनाश ने नीलू का पक्का किया गया मेन्यू पढ़कर कहा। अविनाश ने मुँह बनाया।

"हाँ। ये दो भोज के बीच खुद को हलका महसूस कराने के लिए है।" अकीरा ने कागजात पकड़े हुए थे। तभी ये बात भी कही।

सबने ऐसे देखा, मानो भूत देख लिया हो! वे सभी बगीचे में बैठकर ठंडी हवा का मजा ले रहे थे।

"इसकी जगह दारू खींच लेना, मजा आएगा।" अरुणा आँखें मारते हुए बोलीं।

"येऽऽऽऽ!" वेदिका ने ताली दे, अरुणा को ताली दी।

वेद ने धीरे से अरुणा से कहा, "इन नमूनों को नए-नए तरीके मत बताइए।"

अकीरा वेद की तरफ देखते हुए बोली, "इससे मुझे याद आया, मैंने सुबह दुकान से खरीदी जैकेट तुम्हें पहनाकर देखनी है।"

"हाँ! उम्मीद है, मुझे ठीक आएगी।" वेद ने मुसकराते हुए कहा।

"हाँ! क्योंकि एक इंच का फर्क होता है पूरे सुख और पूरे दुःख में।" वेदिका बोली।

"वेदिका! हद है तुम्हारी।" वेद ने कहा। अभी अकीरा कोई प्रतिक्रिया दे, उससे पहले ही एक युवा उनके पास आया और बोला, "एक्सक्यूज मी! माफ करना कि मैं अचानक आपके बीच आया, पर मुझे आपके पास नीलू मासी ने भेजा है।"

अकीरा ने उससे हाथ मिलाते हुए उसका परिचय दिया, "ये है कुनाल। ये कोरियोग्राफर हैं (नृत्य रचनाकार)। नीलू मासी चाहती हैं कि हम 'संगीत' वाले दिन के लिए नृत्य तैयार करके पेश करें। उन्होंने कुछ गाने भी बताए हैं।"

ऐसा कहते हुए एक कागज इंद्राणी को दिया। अपना चश्मा ठीक करते हुए वो जोरों से पढ़ने लगीं। "हम साथ-साथ हैं? ये मजाक है क्या? इस गाने पर नाचने से अच्छा मैं बाटा चप्पल ही नष्ट कर दूँ।"

वेद झुँझलाकर अपना माथा खुजाने लगा।

"पता नहीं शादी है या ज़ुमानजी का खेल! हर स्तर पर मुश्किल ही होता जाता है।"

इंद्राणी चिल्लाकर बोली, "बस कर नौटंकी।" कोरियोग्राफर अभी से परिवार के सामने मानो घुटने टेक चुका था। उसने पूछा, "तो चलें अभ्यास के लिए?"

"ओए ठंड रख!" कड़ी आवाज में अरुणा बोलीं।

"अगर चाहते हो कि हम नाचें तो गाना भी हम बताएँगे। अपनी पसंद के गाने पर ही हम नाचेंगे।"

वेदिका दौड़ती हुई नानी के पास पहुँची और धीरे-धीरे करते सभी कौन से गानों पर नाचना है, इस प्रक्रिया में गाने चुनने पहुँच गए। हर बार की तरह वेद कोने में बैठा हुआ था और भाग्य को कोस रहा था। पीछे से अकीरा ने वेद के कंधे पर हाथ रखा और कहा, "मेरा कुछ सामान होटल के 'बेचलर्स पार्टी' वेन्यू पर आनेवाला है। क्या तुम मुझे वहाँ ले चलोगे?"

वेदिका दौड़ती हुई नानी के पास पहुँची और धीरे-धीरे करते सभी कौन से गानों पर नाचना है, इस प्रक्रिया में गाने चुनने पहुँच गए। हर बार की तरह वेद कोने में बैठा हुआ था और भाग्य को कोस रहा था। पीछे से अकीरा ने वेद के कंधे पर हाथ रखा और कहा, "मेरा कुछ सामान होटल के 'बेचलर्स पार्टी' वेन्यू पर आनेवाला है। क्या तुम मुझे वहाँ ले चलोगे?"

"हाँ! क्यों नहीं?" वेद ने कहा।

जितनी मासूमियत वह चेहरे पर ला सकती थी, लाकर अकीरा बोली, "क्या हम बाइक पर जा सकते हैं?"

"ठीक है।" वेद जल्दी ही तैयार हो गया।

कुछ ही देर में दोनों बाइक पर थे। वेद ने वादे के अनुसार रिहर्सल डिनर (पुनराभ्यास भोज) के समय से अकीरा से एक दूरी बनाए रखी और जब जरूरत होती, तभी बात करता। अकीरा को ऐसा होना अच्छा नहीं लग रहा था। जब उनकी बाइक हरी बत्ती पर रुकी तो अकीरा ने देखा कि उनके पास ही एक और बाइक खड़ी है और वे दोनों, युवा और युवती एक-दूसरे के साथ बाइक की सवारी के मजे ले रहे हैं, तो उसके मन में भी प्रेम की भावनाएँ उमड़ने लगीं। उसने देखा, वेद का ध्यान उन लोगों पर है, जो यातायात के नियमों का पालन नहीं करते और वेद उन्हें कुछ समझा रहा था। उस समय हृदय से वेद के लिए उसके मन में प्रेम उमड़ा और उसने धीरे से अपना सिर वेद की पीठ पर टिका दिया। उसे महसूस हुआ कि वेद अचानक सँभलकर कठोर सा हो गया। उसे नहीं याद कि नियत स्थल पर वे कब पहुँचे?

"आ गए हम···" वेद ने कहा। व्यग्रता से अकीरा ने वेद को देखा, बाइक से उतरी

और वेद को मोटरबाइक पार्क करने जाने दिया।

वह स्थल एक पंचसितारा होटल के अंदर था।

सुरक्षाकर्मियों की जाँच के बाद वे एक बड़े से हॉल में पहुँचे। वाकई वे दोनों अकेले थे। वह स्पष्ट देख पा रही थी कि वेद कितना चुप था।

“कब आ रहे हैं वे लोग सामान देने?” वेद ने पूछा। अकीरा दृढ़ निश्चय के साथ ही आई थी। मुसकराकर बोली, “ऐसा कुछ नहीं होनेवाला; मुझे थोड़ा समय तुम्हारे साथ बिताने का मन था।”

वेद बार के पास जमीन पर बैठ गया। “तो तुमने झूठ बोला?”

अकीरा भी उसके साथ जा बैठी। बिना वेद को देखे बोली, “क्योंकि मुझे तुम्हारे साथ समय बिताना था और यही कारण था। सारे झूठ गलत कामों के लिए नहीं बोले जाते।”

“पता है मुझे···” यह जवाब अकीरा को तोड़ गया।

“मेरी प्रतिक्रिया उस दिन कुछ ज्यादा ही तीखी थी, जैसे कि तुम मुझे अनदेखा करके आज जवाब दे रहे हो।”

“नहीं तो···तुमने कहा कि मैं तुम्हारे काम और रास्ते में न आऊँ। वही तो मैं कर रहा हूँ··· जैसे तुमने कहा था।” धीमी आवाज में वेद बोला।

अकीरा तैश में आ गई। “मैंने तुम्हें अपने व्यावसायिक जीवन से दूर रहने को कहा था, मुझसे नहीं।”

*अकीरा भी उसके साथ जा बैठी। बिना वेद को देखे बोली, “क्योंकि मुझे तुम्हारे साथ समय बिताना था और यही कारण था। सारे झूठ गलत कामों के लिए नहीं बोले जाते।”
“पता है मुझे···” यह जवाब अकीरा को तोड़ गया।
“मेरी प्रतिक्रिया उस दिन कुछ ज्यादा ही तीखी थी, जैसे कि तुम मुझे अनदेखा करके आज जवाब दे रहे हो।”*

वेद जोर से हँस पड़ा, “अगर तुम समझती हो कि आज के दौर में व्यावसायिक जीवन को निजी जीवन से अलग कर सकती हो, तो तुम किसी भ्रम में जी रही हो। ये बड़ा सा मूर्ख ऑरेंगओटेंगो का गंदा तालाब है।”

यह सुनते ही अकीरा आपा खो बैठी। “क्या मतलब है तुम्हारा?”

वेद ने उसके होंठों पर उँगली रखी। “इससे पहले कि तुम पूछो, ऑरेंगओटेंगो की नई जाति है, जो अधिकतर मुंबई और लुधियाना में पाई जाती है और उसमें भी लुधियाना में ज्यादा।”

अकीरा दबी आवाज में हँसी, “वेद! तुम भी कितने अजीब हो न!”

“मेरा खयाल है, ये सच्चाई तो तुम जान ही चुकी हो और ऐसे कैसे कि कल की

घटना की वजह से तुम परेशान नहीं हो?" वेद ने पूछा।

"शादी अभी चल रही है, इसीलिए।"

"हाँ! लेकिन अगर नीलू मासी तुम पर चिल्लाती तो तुम मुझसे नाराज होती। ठीक कहा न मैंने?"

अकीरा दूसरी तरफ देखने लगी। वह जानती थी कि जो वेद ने कहा है, वह ठीक है।

"तुम इस शादी और इस परिवार से गलत उम्मीदें लगाए बैठी हो। अगर तुम इस शादी में भावुकता को स्थान/जगह दोगी तो मुझे डर है कि हमारा संबंध कहाँ तक चल पाएगा?" खुद की और अकीरा की ओर इशारा करते हुए वेद बोला।

अकीरा सिहर-सी गई। वह बिल्कुल ऐसा नहीं चाहती थी।

"सही कहते हो तुम! लुधियाना सनकियों का शहर है और मैं मूर्खों की तरह सोच रही थी कि मैं यह काम सँभाल पाऊँगी।" अकीरा हारी हुई आवाज में बोली। वेद कटुता से जोर से हँसा। उसके बाद दोनों बहुत देर तक शांत रहे, मानो अपने संबंधों की सच्चाई को स्वीकार रहे थे और समझ रहे थे कि उनका संबंध अनिश्चितता के दौर से गुजर रहा है। उन दोनों को ही अच्छा महसूस नहीं हो रहा था।

"सही कहते हो तुम! लुधियाना सनकियों का शहर है और मैं मूर्खों की तरह सोच रही थी कि मैं यह काम सँभाल पाऊँगी।" अकीरा हारी हुई आवाज में बोली। वेद कटुता से जोर से हँसा। उसके बाद दोनों बहुत देर तक शांत रहे, मानो अपने संबंधों की सच्चाई को स्वीकार रहे थे और समझ रहे थे कि उनका संबंध अनिश्चितता के दौर से गुजर रहा है। उन दोनों को ही अच्छा महसूस नहीं हो रहा था।

अकीरा सिर पकड़कर बैठी थी। बोली, "शायद हम दोनों को साथ में और समय चाहिए। चलो, ऐसा करते हैं कि जो बुरी आइसक्रीम डेट है, उसकी भरपाई करते हैं। मैं आइसक्रीम खिलाऊँगी। क्या कहते हो?"

"पक्का न?"

अकीरा मुसकराते हुए बोली, "हाँ!"

"ठीक है फिर!" वेद खुश हुआ।

बाइक पर बैठने के बाद अकीरा को मस्ती सूझी। उसने धीरे से वेद की टी-शर्ट ऊपर की और अपने हाथ अंदर घुसा दिए। जैसा कि अपेक्षित था, वेद चिल्लाया, "क्या

कर रही हो तुम?" अकीरा ने मासूमियत से जवाब दिया, "अपने हाथों को ठंडे होने से बचा रही हूँ।"

वेद ने हाथ हटाने की कोशिश की और बोला, "घर जाकर गरम शॉवर ले लेना।"

"सच में? गरम शॉवर साथ में?"

वेद ने शीशे में ऐसे कहती हुई अकीरा का चेहरा देखा और दोनों एक-दूसरे को देखकर खुशी और संतोष के साथ हँस पड़े। दोनों में से किसी को भविष्य के बारे में कुछ नहीं मालूम था, लेकिन अभी के लिए सब ठीक था। अकीरा ने मन-ही-मन इस शांति को बरकरार रखने की ईश्वर से प्रार्थना की।

□

39

"ये किसी दंत चिकित्सक (डेंटिस्ट) का पता मालूम होता है।" वेद ने पते की ओर इशारा करते हुए कहा।

अकीरा ने पिछली सीट पर रखे बड़े बैग की ओर इशारा करते हुए कहा, "हाँ! हम यह बैग डेंटिस्ट को देने जा रहे हैं।"

थोड़ा सा पीछे मुड़कर देखा तो एक बहुत बड़ा बैग दिखा।। त्यौरियाँ चढ़ाते हुए वेद बोला, "हम अभय के जूते डेंटिस्ट को देने जा रहे हैं? ये क्या नया पागलपन है?"

अकीरा खिलखिलाकर हँस पड़ी, "खैर, इस बात में तुम आधे सही हो। पागलपनवाले हिस्से में।"

"पता है मुझे···" वेद ने हमेशा के स्वर, मतलब निराशा के स्वर में कहा।

"नहीं! हम डेंटिस्ट के पास जा रहे हैं, ताकि अभय से मिलकर उसके जूते दे सकें। इस वक्त अभय डेंटिस्ट के पास है।"

वेद ने आँखों से प्रतिक्रिया देते हुए कहा, "क्या हम सामान्य मनुष्यों की तरह उसके जूते उसके घर पर नहीं दे सकते?"

"दे सकते हैं, लेकिन अभय चाह रहा था कि उसके जूते उसे ही पकड़ाए जाएँ।"

"अगर मुझे तुम्हारी फिक्र नहीं होती न अकीरा, तो मैं तुम्हें गाड़ी से बाहर जाने को कहता।"

अकीरा को उसके शब्द प्रिय लगे और हँसी भी आ गई। उसे पता था कि वेद का यह प्रेम करने का तरीका है। उसने वेद के हाथ पर मारते हुए कहा, "चुप रहो और गाड़ी चलाओ।"

"और मैं कर भी क्या सकता हूँ? चलो।"

डेंटिस्ट के क्लिनिक पर पहुँचने पर वेद और अकीरा स्वागत स्थल (Reception) पर गए और पूछा, "हम अभय से मिलना चाह रहे थे।"

वहाँ की रिसेप्शनिस्ट (अगवानी करनेवाली) ने बड़ी सी मुसकान के साथ कहा, "हाँ! क्यों नहीं? वह डॉक्टर के पास है। क्या आप अंदर जाना चाहेंगे?"

वेद ने उसकी मेज पर हाथ मारकर कहा, "नहीं, हम यहीं बाहर इंतजार करेंगे, शुक्रिया!"

इस उत्तर की रिसेप्शनिस्ट को उम्मीद नहीं थी। इस प्रतिक्रिया को सँभालती हुई वह छोटी सी हँसी के साथ बोली, "ठीक है, कोई बात नहीं।"

उसने अपनी दराज से एक छोटी सी पुस्तिका (Brochure) निकाली और बोली, "मैं एक मिनट ले सकती हूँ क्या आपका? हम दंपतीयों को एक साथ यहाँ इलाज कराने पर 50% की छूट देते हैं बिल पर।"

"हमें अभी डेंटिस्ट की जरूरत नहीं है।" अकीरा ने कहा।

"सही।" नाटकीयता से वेद बोला। "इस वक्त हमें ईश्वर, पवित्र जल और अपने पूरे खानदान के लिए झाड़-फूँक करनेवाला चाहिए।"

रिसेपशनिस्ट डरी हुई-सी दिख रही थी। अकीरा जोर से हँस पड़ी। यह देख रिसेप्शनिस्ट बोली, "कृपया बैठिए! शुक्रिया।"

"हमें अभी डेंटिस्ट की जरूरत नहीं है।" अकीरा ने कहा।
"सही।" नाटकीयता से वेद बोला। "इस वक्त हमें ईश्वर, पवित्र जल और अपने पूरे खानदान के लिए झाड़-फूँक करनेवाला चाहिए।"
रिसेपशनिस्ट डरी हुई-सी दिख रही थी। अकीरा जोर से हँस पड़ी। यह देख रिसेप्शनिस्ट बोली, "कृपया बैठिए! शुक्रिया।"

झेंप मिटाने के लिए अकीरा और वेद स्वागत स्थल से दूर गए और रिसेप्शनिस्ट की नकल उतारते हुए वेद बोला, "क्या आप अंदर जाना चाहेंगे?"

धीरे से हँसते हुए अकीरा ने वेद को चूमा, "चलो, मॉल चलते हैं, समय अच्छा बीत जाएगा।"

"हाँ। यहाँ बैठने से तो अच्छा है।" वेद बोला।

सड़क के उस पार एक छोटा सा मॉल था, जहाँ पर बहुत बड़े-बड़े ब्रांड के कपड़े नहीं थे, पर अकीरा जानती थी कि क्लीनिक में बैठकर अभय के बाहर आने पर बत्तीसी देखने से अच्छा है कि मॉल में समय काटा जाए। थोड़ा घूमने के बाद एक दुकान में एक पुतले को पहनाई गई ड्रेस को देख अकीरा बोली, "ये ड्रेस अच्छी है न?"

वेद ने खुशी से कहा, "हाँ।"

अकीरा ने जूतों का बैग वेद के हाथ में दिया और खुद ड्रेसेस देखने में जुट गई। और कुछ मिनटों में ही वेद औरतों के ट्रायल रूम (जहाँ कपड़े पहनकर देखते हैं) के बाहर बाकी के थके-पके हुए पुरुषों के साथ बैठा नजर आया। वेद को ज्यादा देर बोर नहीं होना पड़ा, क्योंकि जल्दी ही एक ट्रायल रूम में से अकीरा का प्रफुल्लित चेहरा बाहर निकला और आँखें झपकाती हुई अकीरा वेद से बोली, "वेद! ये ड्रेस निकल ही

नहीं रही, तुम मेरी मदद करोगे प्लीज!"

वेद को तो काटो तो खून नहीं, साँस रुक-सी गई। "ठीक है!"

इससे पहले कि आजू-बाजू बैठे पुरुष उसे और घूरते, वह ट्रायल रूम के अंदर था। जल्दी से उसने दरवाजा जोर से बंद किया। उसके बाद अकीरा को सिर से पाँव तक देख साँसें रुक-सी गईं। अकीरा की इतनी अच्छी बिल्कुल कसी हुई वेशभूषा को देख वेद की आँखें आश्चर्य और प्रेम से बाहर आने को हुईं।

अकीरा ने अपनी वेशभूषा ठीक करते हुए नीचे खींची। अचानक वह मुड़ी। उसके बाल वेद के चेहरे से टकराए। अकीरा ने पूछा, "मैं कैसी लग रही हूँ?"

अकीरा को विश्वास था कि वेद उसकी तारीफ कुछ अच्छे शब्दों में करेगा, पर उसकी हँसी काफूर हो गई, जब वेद ने कहा, "हाँ, पार्टी के लिए तुम्हारी ड्रेस अच्छी है।"

अकीरा को गुस्सा आ गया। इशारा करते हुए बोली, "जाओ यहाँ से।"

"ठीक है! ठीक है! जा रहा हूँ।" वेद ने दरवाजा खोलने की बहुत कोशिश की, पर नहीं खुला। अकीरा वेद की जद्दोजहद देखकर डर गई और पूछा, "क्या हुआ?"

वेद के चेहरे पर हवाइयाँ उड़ने लगीं, फिर भी वह पूरी कोशिश में लगा था। "दरवाजा अटक गया है।"

अकीरा के पैर डर के मारे लड़खड़ाने लगे। अचानक उसे याद आया, "वेद! जूतों का बैग कहाँ है?" बेचैनी में वेद ने दरवाजे के साथ की लड़ाई छोड़ दी, और शब्द ही नहीं मिल रहे थे वेद को।

अकीरा को गुस्सा आ गया। इशारा करते हुए बोली, "जाओ यहाँ से।" "ठीक है! ठीक है! जा रहा हूँ।" वेद ने दरवाजा खोलने की बहुत कोशिश की, पर नहीं खुला। अकीरा वेद की जद्दोजहद देखकर डर गई और पूछा, "क्या हुआ?"

"ओह!"

"तुमने बैग बाहर ही छोड़ दिया था न?" अकीरा ने अपेक्षित प्रश्न पूछा।

"मेरा खयाल है कि दिन खराब होने का समय अभी ही है।" वेद ने मजाक में बात टालने की कोशिश की, पर अकीरा मानने को तैयार नहीं थी।

"अब क्या करोगे तुम?" अकीरा चिल्लाई। वेद खिसककर जमीन पर बैठ गया।

"मुझसे मत पूछो। मेरा दिमाग नहीं चल रहा।" उतने में अकीरा का फोन बजा। स्क्रीन पर नाम देखकर अकीरा के हाथ-पैर ठंडे पड़ गए।

"तुम फोन उठाओ। अभय का है। मुझे नहीं पता कि मैं उसे क्या कहूँ?"

"ठीक है। परेशान मत हो।" वेद ने फोन उठाया। दूसरी तरफ से आवाज आई, "कहाँ हो तुम?"

अभय का अकीरा के फोन पर इतनी रुखाई से बात करना वेद को बिल्कुल अच्छा नहीं लगा। उतने ही जोर से चिल्लाते हुए वेद ने जवाब दिया, "मैं वेद बोल रहा हूँ।"

अभय बिना रुके बोला, "फिर भी मेरा सवाल वही है। तुम लोग कहाँ मर गए? मुझे अभी अपने जूते चाहिए। तुमसे बकवास करने का मेरे पास समय नहीं है।" उसका तरीका देख वेद चिल्लाया, "हम्म, मेरी बात सुनो तुम मूर्ख! हमारे पास भी तुम्हारी बकवास सुनने का समय नहीं है। पर तुमने हमें शिकायत करते देखा? लेकिन अगर अगली बार अकीरा से ऐसे बात की तो तेरा जूता होगा और तेरा ही सर, पर हाथ मेरा होगा।"

"तुम्हारी इतनी हिम्मत!" अभय बोला।

"बकवास बंद करो। तुम्हें पार्टी के समय तक जूते मिल जाएँगे। बाय!" वेद ने कहा।

यह बोलकर वेद ने फोन काट दिया और उसे 'साइलंट मोड' पर कर दिया।

"मुझे तुम्हें अंदर नहीं बुलाना चाहिए था।" खुशी से अकीरा बोली।

"हाँ! इतना ज्यादा प्यार में पागल बनने का समय नहीं था यह।"

"मैं कोई पागल नहीं हो रही थी।" अकीरा पलटकर बोली।

"मैं नहीं हो रहा…!" वेद अभी अकीरा से बहस करता, उतने में रोशनी मामी का संदेश वेद के फोन पर आया।

वेद ने जोर से पढ़ा, "तान्या को उसके 'एक्स' (पिछले बॉयफ्रेंड) के साथ जिम में देखा।"

अकीरा इससे पहले कि कुछ कहती, वेद का फोन बजा। उसने चिढ़कर फोन उठाया, "हैलो!"

"दो प्लेट छोले-भटूरे। A-20 रॉयल पाम्स…" दूसरी तरफ से भी चिढ़े हुए स्वर में ऑर्डर आया।

"गलत नंबर!" वेद बोला।

इतने झमेले से परेशान होकर वेद ने फोन बंद कर दिया और अकीरा से पूछा, "अब क्या?"

अकीरा ने साँस ली। उसने दरवाजे पर मारना शुरू किया। "कोई मदद करो, हम अंदर फँस गए।"

□

40

अभय को ऐसा क्यों लग रहा है, मानो उसका पसंदीदा सलाद किसी ने उससे छीन लिया है ?

भाग्य से स्टोरवालों ने उन्हें जल्दी ही उस ट्रायल रूम से बाहर निकाल लिया। अभी वो राहत की साँस लेते, उन्हें पता चला कि किसी ने अभय के जूतों का बैग चुरा लिया। अगला झमेला! दुकानदार ने उनसे वादा किया कि सी.सी.टी.वी. फुटेज से जैसे ही उन्हें पता चलेगा, वे चोर के बारे में वेद को इत्तला कर देंगे। लेकिन तब तक के लिए अभय के जूतों का इंतजाम करना था। अकीरा ने मन-ही-मन अपने भाग्य और कबीर तथा रीशी का धन्यवाद किया, जो पार्टी की तैयारियों का निरीक्षण कर रहे थे। लेकिन वह समझ नहीं पा रही थी कि अभय को वह कैसे यकीन दिलाएगी कि उसके जूते वाकई ब्रांडेड हैं? अकीरा वेद की किसी बात पर हँसी। "जैसे ही अभय नकली जूते देखेगा, चिल्लाना शुरू कर देगा।"

"देखते हैं।" वेद ने जवाब दिया।

मन-ही-मन ईश्वर से प्रार्थना करते दोनों अभय के पास पहुँचे। "ओ अभय।"

अभय पलटा और त्यौरियाँ चढ़ाकर बोला, "तुम बहुत-बहुत लेट आए, बिल्कुल नहीं चलेगा।"

अकीरा ने तुरंत माफी माँगी, "आई एम सो सॉरी!"

इससे पहले कि अभय कुछ कहे, वेद ने जूते निकालकर अभय के पैरों के पास रख दिए।

"ये रहे तुम्हारे सुंदर लूबेटन के जूते! हमारे खूबसूरत (हैंडसम) दूल्हे के लिए!"

अकीरा ने वेद को कोहनी मारते हुए कहा, "ज्यादा हो रहा है।"

वेद ने दाँतों में हलके से जीभ दबाई, "सॉरी!"

अभय ने जल्दी से जूते पहने और कहा, "शुक्रिया!"

वेद की आँखें आश्चर्य से चौड़ी हो गईं। वेद ही नहीं, अभय ने बिना ध्यान से जाँचे, अकीरा को भी धन्यवाद दिया।

अभय ने अकीरा से कहा, "चूँकि अब तुम मेरे जूते पहुँचाने का असंभव-सा लगनेवाला काम कर चुकी हो तो क्या अब मेरी पार्टी की कमान अपने हाथ में लोगी?"

"हाँ! क्यों नहीं?" अकीरा बोली।

हैरान-परेशान वेद भी अकीरा के पीछे चल पड़ा। "ये तो नरक से भेजा गया शैतान-सा व्यवहार करता है, लेकिन यहाँ तो ठीक रहा।"

"वाकई हैरत है! पर कैसे?" अकीरा ने पूछा।

"पता नहीं, पर हमारे लिए अच्छा रहा।" अपना माथा खुजाते हुए वेद ने कहा।

"पता नहीं, पर हमारे लिए अच्छा रहा।" अपना माथा खुजाते हुए वेद ने कहा। अकीरा ने मुसकराकर कहा, "वेद! अब तुम जाओ और पार्टी के मजे लो।"
"ठीक है! कुछ चाहिए तो मुझे बुला लेना।"
"हाँ, जरूर! जाओ!" अकीरा ने आँख मारते हुए वेद से कहा।

अकीरा ने मुसकराकर कहा, "वेद! अब तुम जाओ और पार्टी के मजे लो।"

"ठीक है! कुछ चाहिए तो मुझे बुला लेना।"

"हाँ, जरूर! जाओ!" अकीरा ने आँख मारते हुए वेद से कहा।

अपने में हँसता हुआ वेद अपने परिवार की ओर चल पड़ा, जो काफी दुःखी दिखाई पड़ रहा था।

"हैलो!" वेद ने सबका हँसकर अभिवादन किया। "मानना पड़ेगा कि इन जैकेट में तुम सब पेंग्विन जैसे लग रहे हो। मानो उनका झुंड बैठा हो।" कबीर के साथ बैठते हुए वेद बोला।

"हाँ! और तुम जेम्स बॉण्ड जैसे।" कबीर ने कहा।

अविनाश की प्रशंसा करते हुए वेद ने कहा, "डैड, क्या लग रहे हैं आप, मजा आ गया!"

"यही पिंकी ने भी कहा, चीयर्स!" अविनाश ने कहा।

"चीयर्स!" वेद हँसा। कबीर ने अचानक जूतों के बारे में पूछा।

"वेदिका ने बताया कि अभय की जूता चोरी रस्म हो गई।" कबीर ने कहा।

"सच में? कसम खाओ! वैसे···" अभी वेद बात पूरी करता कि अचानक अकीरा वेद को पागलों की तरह ढूँढ़ती हुई आई और उसे अपने साथ खींचती हुई ले जाने लगी, "मेरे साथ चलो।"

"अरे! पर तुम मुझे पुरुषों के लू (प्रसाधन) में क्यों ले जा रही हो?" वेद चीखा। "इतिहास गवाह है, जब-जब वाशरूम गए थे, कुछ गड़बड़ ही हुई थी।"

"तुम खुद ही देखोगे, चलो तो।" अकीरा आत्मविश्वास से वेद को वाशरूम में ले गई।

वेद ने जो वहाँ देखा, उसकी वीडियो रिकॉर्डिंग होनी चाहिए थी, जो अनंतकाल तक चलाई जा सके। अभय जमीन पर हाथ-पाँव फैलाकर लेटा हुआ था, उसकी आँखें चीख-चीखकर मानो सूज गई थीं और वह सीधा बोतल से शराब पी रहा था।

"हुआ क्या है ?" हैरत से वेद बोला।

"मुझे नहीं पता। डेविड को यह यहाँ मिला।" अकीरा बोली।

वेद अभय के पास बैठकर बोला, "ओय! हुआ क्या है ?"

कुछ क्षणों के लिए अभय ने वेद को ध्यान से देखा और अचानक वेद के बाजुओं में गिरकर रोने लगा, "मुझे तान्या के पास जाना है।"

अगर अभय के रोने से वेद सदमे में न आया होता तो शायद वेद की सारी इंद्रियाँ शराब की दुर्गंध से जल गई होतीं। अभय के आँसुओं से वेद के कोट की बाजू गीली हो गई थीं ? उसे समझ नहीं आ रहा था कि क्या ज्यादा बुरा है और उसके साथ ऐसा क्यों हो रहा है ? वह लाचारी से अकीरा की ओर ताक रहा था।

अगर अभय के रोने से वेद सदमे में न आया होता तो शायद वेद की सारी इंद्रियाँ शराब की दुर्गंध से जल गई होतीं। अभय के आँसुओं से वेद के कोट की बाजू गीली हो गई थीं ? उसे समझ नहीं आ रहा था कि क्या ज्यादा बुरा है और उसके साथ ऐसा क्यों हो रहा है ?

"मेरी तरफ मत देखो! ऐसे लोगों से निबटने से अच्छा मैं मगरमच्छ पाल लूँगी।" अकीरा ने जवाब दिया।

अभय को सांत्वना देते हुए वेद बोला, "अरे कुछ नहीं, शांत हो। सब ठीक हो जाएगा।"

"नहीं। कुछ भी ठीक नहीं है। मुझे··· चाहिए।" रोते हुए अभय बोला। वह बच्चे की तरह रो रहा था।

अभी अभय ने पूरी बात नहीं कही थी, रो रहा था और अगले ही क्षण अभय ने उलटी कर दी। जमीन के अलावा वेद के भी कपड़े खराब हो गए।

"हे भगवान्!" अकीरा सदमे में थी।

वेद ने देखा कि अभय के नकली जूते उलटी से लथपथ हैं तो जोर से बोला, "मुझे नहीं लगता कि अब हमें जूतों की और चिंता करनी चाहिए।"

"मुझे तान्या चाहिए।" अभय पागलों की तरह रोता जा रहा था; केवल साँस लेने के लिए बीच में रुकता।

अकीरा खुद को ठंडा रखने के लिए अपनी कनपटी पर उँगलियों से मालिश किए जा रही थी। उसके कर्मचारियों ने अभय को थोड़ा साफ किया, ताकि उसे घर ले जाया जा सके। किंतु सुरक्षा कर्मचारियों ने अभय को रोक लिया। अगर अकीरा पार्टी की प्रबंधक न होती तो वह अभय के सारे घटिया और तुच्छ स्तर को रिकॉर्ड करती। खैर,

उसे कोई शिकायत नहीं थी, क्योंकि वेद सभी चीजों का ध्यान रख रहा था।

यह कहना कि अभय की हालत देखकर वेद खुश था, गलत होगा, क्योंकि वह परमानंदित था। वेद भी मानो नशे में चूर था; खुशी के नशे में चूर!

"इसे देखो!" वेद खुशी से बोला। "ये सभी वीडियो मेरे घर के पुस्तकालय की शोभा बनेंगे।"

गार्ड्स ने अभय को कार की पिछली सीट पर बिठाया, अकीरा ने उन्हें उदार मन से टिप दिए। अकीरा के हाथ में फोन देकर वेद ने गाड़ी का अगला दरवाजा अकीरा के लिए खोला। "अभय बिल्कुल टूटनेवाला है, तुम्हें हर क्षण की रिकॉर्डिंग ध्यान से करनी है।"

गार्ड्स ने अभय को कार की पिछली सीट पर बिठाया, अकीरा ने उन्हें उदार मन से टिप दिए। अकीरा के हाथ में फोन देकर वेद ने गाड़ी का अगला दरवाजा अकीरा के लिए खोला। "अभय बिल्कुल टूटनेवाला है, तुम्हें हर क्षण की रिकॉर्डिंग ध्यान से करनी है।"

वेद की उत्सुकता और उत्साह का संचार संक्रामक था। अकीरा पलटकर रिकॉर्डिंग करते हुए बोली, "अभय! अपने भाई के लिए तो कुछ कहो, प्लीज! तुम पर कैमरा है।"

अभय रोते हुए बोला, "तान्या ने मुझे त्याग दिया, रिजेक्ट कर दिया।" कितनी खुशी हुई अकीरा को।

"कितनी होशियार है तान्या!" अकीरा बोली और वेद खिलखिलाकर हँस पड़ा।

"अच्छा! वो होशियार है···खाक होशियार है!" अभय पीने के कारण अस्पष्टता से बोला।

वेद खुश था, मुसकराकर बोला, "मैं खुश हूँ कि हमने यह रिकॉर्डिंग की है। जब मेरा बुरा दिन होगा, मैं कला की इस दुनिया में जाया करूँगा।"

अकीरा ने सिर हिलाया, "मतलब हर दिन।"

वेद हँसा, "बिल्कुल सही।"

अचानक अभय ड्राइवर की सीट के पीछे अपनी ठोढ़ी रखकर बोला, "तुम्हें पता है मैंने क्या किया? मैं तान्या के कमरे में गया। वह फोन पर बात कर रही थी। उसके बाद ही मैंने यह सब किया।"

ऐसा कहते हुए अभय ने अचानक वेद की आँखें ढक लीं; वेद डर के मारे काँप गया और जल्दी से उसने ब्रेक लगाए। अकीरा के हाथ से फोन भी गिर गया। अचानक ब्रेक लगने के कारण जोर से आवाज आई और कार रुकी। वेद ने अपनी आँखों से वेद के हाथ हटाने का भरसक प्रयास किया; वह चिल्लाया, "मुझे छोड़!" उस समय इतनी चिल्लाहाट थी कि अकीरा समझ नहीं पा रही थी कि वह क्या करे? उसने बिना ज्यादा

सोचे एक गाली देते हुए अभय के पेट में घूँसा मारा और वेद को छोड़ने को कहा।

घूँसा जोरदार था। अभय पिछली तरफ फिर जा गिरा। "यही तान्या ने भी कहा, छोड़ो मुझे। पता नहीं जब भी किसी की ऐसे आँखें बंद करता हूँ तो लोग गुस्सा क्यों हो जाते हैं?"

वेद ने खुद को सँभालते हुए अपने दिल पर हाथ रखा, "शुक्र है भगवान् का! बच गए।"

अकीरा ने भी राहत की साँस ली, "वो तो अच्छा हुआ कि रास्ते खाली थे, वरना दुर्घटना भी हो सकती थी।"

वेद ने गुस्से में अपनी सीट बेल्ट निकाली। "बहुत हुआ। इसे मैं बाँध के बिठाता हूँ।"

"क्या मतलब?"

वेद ने अपनी बो टाई निकाली और अभय के हाथ बाँध दिए, फिर कार की डिग्गी में से बहुत कुछ टटोलने पर डक्ट टेप मिली।

"तुम्हें डक्ट टेप कहाँ से मिली?" अकीरा ने हैरत से पूछा।

"यह रीशी की कार है···" उसने बड़ी सी टेप अभय के मुँह पर चिपका दी। "अगर तुम कुछ और ढूँढ़ोगी तो शायद कंडोम भी मिल जाए, जिसकी मेरे परिवार में सबसे ज्यादा जरूरत थी।"

"वाकई तुम वेदिका के भाई हो!" अकीरा ने व्यंग्य किया।

अकीरा ने भी राहत की साँस ली, "वो तो अच्छा हुआ कि रास्ते खाली थे, वरना दुर्घटना भी हो सकती थी।" वेद ने गुस्से में अपनी सीट बेल्ट निकाली। "बहुत हुआ। इसे मैं बाँध के बिठाता हूँ।" "क्या मतलब?" वेद ने अपनी बो टाई निकाली और अभय के हाथ बाँध दिए, फिर कार की डिग्गी में से बहुत कुछ टटोलने पर डक्ट टेप मिली। "तुम्हें डक्ट टेप कहाँ से मिली?" अकीरा ने हैरत से पूछा।

"ही-ही-ही! चलो अब!" हँसते हुए वेद बोला। बिना किसी हमले और चिल्ला-चोट के वे जल्द ही तान्या के घर पहुँच गए।

तान्या ने भौंहें चढ़ाते हुए कहा, "तुम दोनों को बेचलर्स पार्टी में नहीं होना चाहिए था क्या? क्या हुआ?"

अकीरा तान्या को खींचकर बोली, "आओ मेरे साथ।"

"क्याऽऽऽ हुआ?" तान्या ने घबराते हुए पूछा।

वेद ने कार की बैकसीट की तरफ इशारा करते हुए कहा, "येऽऽऽ हुआ है।"

"हे भगवान्! ये ऐसे क्यों बँधा हुआ है? ये सब किसने किया?" बगल में बैठकर तान्या ने पूछा। उसे देख अभय दुबारा जीवन में लौट आया था।

"मैंने किया। ये बेकाबू हो रहा था, हमारा एक्सिडेंट हो जाता। हमारे पास कोई और विकल्प नहीं था।" वेद एक साँस में बोल गया।

तान्या ने ताना कसा, "वेद, तुम्हारी कहानियाँ हमेशा अविश्वसनीय होती हैं।"

"वाकई अभय ने उस समय मेरी आँखें बंद कीं, जब मैं गाड़ी चला रहा था।" वेद ने विश्वास दिलाना चाहा।

"छोड़ो!" इतना कहकर तान्या ने अपना ध्यान अभय की ओर किया और उसके मुँह पर लगी टेप निकाली।

अभय ने तान्या का हाथ पकड़कर माफी माँगी, "आई एम सॉरी!"

अपनी हैरानी को छुपाते हुए अकीरा ने कहा, "ठीक है, मैं याद दिला दूँगी।" "शुक्रिया!" इतना कहकर तान्या चली गई। वेद और अकीरा इस घटना से एक-दूसरे को अनजान और अनभिज्ञ देखते ही रह गए। अभय और तान्या तो उन दोनों से भी अजीब थे। वेद ने साँस छोड़ते हुए कहा, "चलो! इस टूटी रेलगाड़ी को भी छोड़ दें।"

"कितनी बार माफी माँगोगे तुम अभय?"

"प्लीज माफ कर दो।" अभय ने आँखों में आँसू भरकर कहा।

तान्या ने कुछ सोचा, "ठीक है, कल सुबह दस बजे वकील के ऑफिस में आ जाना।"

अभय का चेहरा नाटकीय ढंग से दुःख से सुख में बदल गया। "लेकिन..." इतना कहकर तान्या ने उसके मुँह पर दुबारा टेप चिपका दी और उसके माथे को चूमकर कहा, "गुडनाइट।"

उसके बाद तान्या ने अकीरा से कहा, "कल अभय को सुबह दस बजे वकील के ऑफिस में आने की याद दिला देना। हम एक विवाह पूर्व समझौते पर हस्ताक्षर करेंगे।"

अपनी हैरानी को छुपाते हुए अकीरा ने कहा, "ठीक है, मैं याद दिला दूँगी।"

"शुक्रिया!" इतना कहकर तान्या चली गई। वेद और अकीरा इस घटना से एक-दूसरे को अनजान और अनभिज्ञ देखते ही रह गए। अभय और तान्या तो उन दोनों से भी अजीब थे। वेद ने साँस छोड़ते हुए कहा, "चलो! इस टूटी रेलगाड़ी को भी छोड़ दें।"

"हाँ!" अकीरा मान गई। अभय के घर पहुँचने पर एक और निराशाजनक समाचार सुनने को मिला। अभय के माता-पिता हवेली पर नहीं थे। घर की कामवाली को भी नहीं मालूम था कि वे कब वापस आएँगे? बेमन से दोनों ने रात अभय के घर बिताने की सोची। कोई भी नहीं चाहता था कि किसी भी कारण से आधी रात को अभय तान्या के घर जाए। अभय को चिढ़ाने के लिए वेद ने अभय का महँगा सूट पहना और सोने के कमरे में खिड़की के पास अकीरा के साथ जाकर बैठ गया। उसने एक चादर खींची और वेद

की छाती पर सिर रखकर सो गई। कुछ देर तो दोनों को आराम मिला।

अकीरा के बाल अपनी उँगली पर लपेटते हुए वेद बोला, "ऐसा लग रहा है न कि लुधियाना में हम एक जमाने से आए हुए हैं?"

"हाँ! लग तो रहा है!" अकीरा उसकी उँगलियाँ देख रही थी।

वेद हँसते हुए बोला, "हम बहुत पुराने साथी हैं, जो यादें ताजा कर रहे हैं।"

अकीरा हँस दी, "दंपती के लिए दंतचिकित्सक की छूट का प्रस्ताव अभी भी चालू है।"

वेद ने जीभ काटते हुए कहा, "अजीब लोग, अजीब प्रस्ताव!"

"अजीब से याद आया, तुम्हें मेरी तारीफ करनी सीखनी होगी।"

वेद को अपमान-सा लगा, "मुझे अच्छी तारीफ करनी आती है, ठीक है न!"

"अच्छा? ट्रायल रूम में तो तुम एक अच्छा शब्द मेरी तारीफ में नहीं कह पाए।"

वेद ने चिढ़कर अकीरा को देखकर कहा, "तुम क्या चाहती थी कि मैं क्या कहूँ कि उस गुलाबी ड्रेस में तुम फुलझड़ी लग रही थी और इसी कारण मेरा मुँह सूख गया और मैं बकवास करने लगा?"

"वाऽऽऽऽह! क्या बात है! कभी-कभी मुझे अपने भाग्य पर विश्वास नहीं होता।" खुशी के मारे वेद के होंठ चूम लिये।

"वो इसलिए कि तुम्हारा मेरे जीवन में आना बहुत बड़ी और अच्छी घटना है, ऐसा मुझे लगने लगा है।" ऐसा कहते हुए अकीरा वेद की भौंहों और होंठों पर हाथ घुमा रही थी।

"अभी से? अभी तो हमारे 21 दिनों में से कई दिन बचे हैं।" वेद ने ठिठोली करते हुए कहा।

"हाँ! हम आखिरी चरण में हैं।" अकीरा बोली। "तैयार हो जाओ। अगर तुम चाहते हो कि मैं हाँ कहूँ तो मेहनत करो। समझे!"

"वक्त बताएगा कि कौन किसे हाँ कहता है!"

यह कहते हुए अपना माथा अकीरा के माथे पर रख दिया वेद ने "और तुम्हारा तो नहीं मालूम, लेकिन तुम मेरे जीवन के लिए बहुत अच्छी घटना हो।" अकीरा ने जोर देकर कहा।

□

41

"मेरा वकील अब तुम्हारे लिए शर्तें पढ़ेगा।" तान्या की आवाज में विश्वास था, लेकिन भाव नहीं थे। एक खूबसूरत सी पोशाक में तान्या अपने माता-पिता के साथ बैठी थी।

जो शालीनता और पोशाकों की सजावट तान्या के परिवार में थी, वह अरोरा परिवार और अकीरा की तरफ नजर नहीं आ रही थी। रात के तूफान का असर अभी भी अभय के कपड़ों और चेहरे पर नजर आ रहा था; बल्कि उस तूफान में भूकंप का भी असर स्पष्ट दिखाई दे रहा था।

अभय के घर रात बिताने के बाद अकीरा को वहाँ से निकलने की जल्दी थी। चूँकि अभय के माता-पिता अभी वापस नहीं आए थे, तो अभय चाहता था कि अकीरा और वेद उसके साथ वकील के ऑफिस चलें, गवाहों के रूप में। वह माँग ठीक नहीं थी, लेकिन अकीरा मना न कर सकी। वेद ने विद्रोह किया था, लेकिन अकीरा ने अपनी आँखें बड़ी करके वेद को चुप करा दिया था।

अकीरा को वेद का विरोध करना अच्छा लगा था। वह सपने में भी नहीं सोच सकती थी कि वह किसी पर भी अपना इतना प्रभाव डाल सकती है। उसने अपेक्षा ही नहीं की थी कि वह उसके लिए इतना कुछ कर सकता है। अगर अभय साथ नहीं होता तो वह वेद को कार में ही चूम लेती या फिर वकील की मेज पर चढ़कर ही उसे कई तरह से खुश करने की कोशिश करती। उसे सोचकर ही कितना अच्छा लग रहा था और अंदर-ही-अंदर वेद के प्रति कितना प्रेम महसूस हो रहा था। अकीरा ने अपनी मुसकान छुपाते हुए बाल पीछे किए।

"मेरी मुवक्किल ने ये शर्तें रखी हैं।" तान्या के वकील ने अभय के वकील को फाइल पकड़ाई, "पहली शर्त—मेरी मुवक्किल तान्या केवल एक बच्चे को जन्म देना चाहती है। उसकी अगली शर्त है कि विवाह के बाद वह स्वतंत्र घर में रहेगी और जो कुछ तान्या को विरासत में मिलेगा, वह उसी के नाम पर रहेगा। यदि तलाक हो जाता है तो जो भी संपत्ति अभय की है, वह दोनों में एक जैसी विभाजित होगी। इसके अलावा तान्या को शादी में जो गहने मिलेंगे, सबकी हकदार वही होगी। यदि विवाह के बाद दंपती कोई पशु-पक्षी पालते

हैं तो तलाक के प्रसंग में उसकी जिम्मेदारी अभय की होगी।"

अकीरा को वेद के मोबाइल से संदेश आया। उसने देखा और पछताई भी। 'मेरे हिसाब से सारे पालतू पशुओं को उनके नेता अभय के पास ही रहना चाहिए, जो कि स्वयं ही चूहा है।'

बड़ी मुश्किल से अकीरा ने अपनी हँसी रोकी। "ठीक है! अगली शर्त पढ़िए।" अभय ने कहा।

"ये आखिरी शर्त है। मेरी मुवक्किल साल में कम-से-कम एक बार अकेले घूमने जाया करेंगी।"

अब अभय खुद को रोक नहीं पाया, "क्यों?"

"मुझे लगता है कि कुछ गलत टाइप हो गया है।" वेद ने अकीरा को मैसेज भेजा। 'घूमने की जगह 'तीर्थ यात्रा' होना चाहिए था शायद, मतलब अभय के साथ रहने के बाद साल में तो आत्मा के शुद्धिकरण के लिए तीर्थ यात्रा तो बनती है।'

अकीरा ने गुस्से में टाइप करके भेजा, 'शटअप' (चुप करो)।

अपनी हँसी छुपाते हुए अकीरा और वेद, दोनों ने फोन दूर रख दिए।

अब अभय खुद को रोक नहीं पाया, "क्यों?" "मुझे लगता है कि कुछ गलत टाइप हो गया है।" वेद ने अकीरा को मैसेज भेजा। 'घूमने की जगह 'तीर्थ यात्रा' होना चाहिए था शायद, मतलब अभय के साथ रहने के बाद साल में तो आत्मा के शुद्धिकरण के लिए तीर्थ यात्रा तो बनती है।'

इसी बीच तान्या ने अपनी बात की सफाई दी—"अभय! पगलाने की जरूरत नहीं है। मुझे अकेले घूमना अच्छा लगता है। मैं हमेशा जाती हूँ। शादी के बाद ये क्योंकर बदल जाए, मुझे समझ नहीं आया।"

"लेकिन..." अभय ने बहस करनी चाही, पर वह शब्द नहीं जुटा पाया और हारते हुए बोला, "ठीक है।"

तान्या, उसके माता-पिता, वकील और सभी मुसकराए। वकील ने कहा, "ये सारी शर्तें थीं हमारी! अगर मंजूर हों तो कागजात पर दस्तखत कर लें!"

उस समय अभय के वकील ने फाइल तान्या की ओर बढ़ाते हुए कहा, "मेरे मुवक्किल की भी शर्त है।"

अभय के वकील ने स्पष्ट शब्दों में कहा, "अगर मेरे मुवक्किल के साथ बेवफाई और धोखाधड़ी हुई तो मेरे मुवक्किल तान्या की किसी भी शर्त को स्वीकार करने को बाध्य नहीं होगा।"

"ठीक है।" प्रेम भरे स्वर में कहा।

अभय का वकील सभी को उसकी मेज की तरफ ले गया। "ठीक है, फिर कागजात पर हस्ताक्षर कीजिए।"

इतने में शांति भंग करते हुए वेद का फोन कर्कश आवाज में बजा। अकीरा देख रही थी कि नंबर जाना-पहचाना नहीं है। वेद ने फोन उठाया, "हैलो!"

"तीन प्लेट छोले-भटूरे, पता लिखो..." फोन की दूसरी तरफ से आवाज आई।

वेद का सब्र टूटा, "अरे! मैं छोले-भटूरेवाला नहीं हूँ, तुमने गलत नंबर डायल किया है।"

"उम्मीद है, आपने सारी शर्तें ध्यान से सुनीं, क्योंकि आधा समय तो तुमलोग फोन पर बातचीत कर रहे थे, संदेशों द्वारा, कभी रॉन्ग नंबर की बात सुन रहे थे।" अभय ने रुखाई से कहा। अभय पर ध्यान न देते हुए, वह वकील पर नजर गड़ाए हुए था, "आपके मुवक्किल का अरोरा परिवार को ज्ञान देने का चक्र शुरू है, लेकिन मैं 'अभय दोहे' सुनने के पक्ष में बिल्कुल नहीं हूँ।"

गुस्से से वेद ने अपना फोन जेब में रखा। भुनभुनाते हुए उसने गवाह के रूप में दस्तखत करने के लिए कलम निकाली।

"उम्मीद है, आपने सारी शर्तें ध्यान से सुनीं, क्योंकि आधा समय तो तुमलोग फोन पर बातचीत कर रहे थे, संदेशों द्वारा, कभी रॉन्ग नंबर की बात सुन रहे थे।" अभय ने रुखाई से कहा।

अभय पर ध्यान न देते हुए, वह वकील पर नजर गड़ाए हुए था, "आपके मुवक्किल का अरोरा परिवार को ज्ञान देने का चक्र शुरू है, लेकिन मैं 'अभय दोहे' सुनने के पक्ष में बिल्कुल नहीं हूँ।"

"वेद!" अकीरा ने टोका।

वकील ने हस्ताक्षर देखे, फिर कहा, "हो गया काम हमारा।"

अकीरा ने कहा, "शुक्रिया!"

वह जल्दी से वेद को वकील के ऑफिस से बाहर ले गई। जैसे ही लिफ्ट में पहुँची, उसने वेद से पूछा, "अगर अभय बकवास करता है तो तुम भी गुस्सा हो जाते हो। क्यों? अगर वह उचकाता है तो तुम क्यों उचकते हो?"

"क्योंकि वह बदतमीज आदमी है।" वेद ने लिफ्टमैन के लिए रखे स्टूल को एक लात जड़ते हुए कहा, "मैं उसकी बकवास क्यों सुनूँ?"

अकीरा ने मुँह टेढ़ा किया, लेकिन कुछ कहा नहीं। उसे पता था कि कुछ कहने से गुस्सा ही बढ़ेगा। जैसे ही वे अपनी कार की ओर बढ़े, अकीरा ने पूछा, "कुछ खाना है?"

वेद ने अकीरा की ओर देखकर पूछा, "क्या?"

छोटे बच्चों की तरह दाँतों के बीच जीभ रखकर वह झिझक से हँसी और वेद का हाथ पकड़कर आगे-पीछे झुलाकर बोली, "हम दोनों को ही भूख लगी है। चलो कुछ खाते हैं।"

"ज्यादा प्यारी बनने की कोशिश मत करो।" उसकी नकल उतारते हुए वेद ने अकीरा को धमकाया। उसने दूर से किसी चीज की ओर इशारा करते हुए कहा, "तुम बहुत भाग्यशाली हो, मुझे याद ही नहीं आया कि इसी तरफ शालिनी मामी का रेस्तराँ भी है।"

अकीरा के पेट में और जोरों से चूहे दौड़ने लगे। वेद मुसकराकर बोला, "छोले भटूरे डेट के बारे में क्या विचार है ?"

"इस वक्त तो मैं नीलू मासी का 'केल सलाद' भी खा लूँ। मुझे इतनी भूख लगी है।"

वेद ने अकीरा का हाथ पकड़ा और बोला, "चलो फिर!" वे रेस्तराँ की ओर चल पड़े।

□

42

"सच में! मैं उस रात अभय के हाथों को पायल या घुँघरुओं से बाँधनेवाला था। वह बिल्कुल हद से बाहर जा रहा था।" उस रात की बातें याद करते हुए वेद बोला।

"वाह! मैं तो खुश हूँ कि कोई तो मिला, जो पीने के बाद कबीर से ज्यादा अपना संतुलन खो सकता है। वाह आखिरकार!" कबीर खुशी से चहका।

वकीलों के साथ सुबह बिताने के बाद, इंद्राणी ने वेद और अकीरा को बताया कि तान्या बैचलर्स पार्टी की जगह जगराता करवाना चाहती है और उसमें भी अजीब बात यह थी कि अकीरा और इंद्राणी पास-पास बैठे थे, तो भी बजाय अकीरा को बताने के, तान्या ने यह बात इंद्राणी से कही। फिर भी जगराते का प्रबंध करने में वेद ने अकीरा की पूरी मदद की।

दोपहर को दोनों वापस आ पाए। उन्होंने दोपहर एक छोटी सी नींद ली और अकीरा फिर तान्या के घर भागी। वेद उठकर रीशी और कबीर के साथ बैठक में आराम करते हुए गपशप कर रहा था।

"वेदिका! जल्दी करो, हमें देर हो रही है!" अकीरा कमरे में आकर बोली।

वेदिका ने जल्दी-जल्दी अपनी ऊँची एड़ी की चप्पलें पहनते हुए कहा, "मैं कोशिश कर रही हूँ।"

कबीर ने वेदिका की ओर देखकर सीटी बजाई और बोला, "झुमके कितने सुंदर दिख रहे हैं और तुम खूबसूरत!"

वेद ने व्यंग्य से कहा, "गोगो! अगर तुम्हारे कान के झुमके थोड़े से और बड़े होते तो अकीरा उनसे शादी की सजावट में झूमर का काम ले लेती।"

"हो गया? अगर हो गया हो तो अपने होंठ सिल लो।" वेदिका ने वेद को घूरते हुए जवाब दिया।

हँसते हुए अकीरा ने वेद के गाल पर हाथ रखा और कहा, "चलो! कल मिलते हैं! गुडनाइट!"

जैसे ही ये शब्द वेद के अंदर गए, उसे अहसास हुआ कि अकीरा रात भर बाहर रहेगी और वह भी तान्या के परिवार के साथ। उसे अच्छा नहीं लगा। एकदम से उसने अकीरा को रोका।

"अकीरा, रुको!"

"क्या है?"

"सुनो! अगर जगराता है तो हम सब भी तो आ सकते हैं न। बैचलर्स पार्टी तो अब नहीं।" वेद ने अकीरा को समझाने की कोशिश की।

"हाँ! हम कोई मुश्किल खड़ी नहीं करेंगे, कसम से।" कबीर बोला।

"चलो अकीरा, ले चलते हैं इन्हें, हमें भी मनोरंजन चाहिए। इन जोकरों से अच्छा कौन होगा?" वेदिका सिर हिलाते हुए बोली।

उनके चेहरे देख अकीरा पिघल गई और मान गई। बोली, "बस! अच्छे से रहना वहाँ! ठीक है?"

"ये वो कह रही है, जो वेदिका जैसी को अपना साथी बनाकर ले जा रही है!" वेद ने ताना कसा।

इस कथन के बदले उसे कुछ प्यार भरे मुक्के पड़े, पर अकीरा की हँसी की आवाज सुन वेद को अच्छा लगा।

"हाँ! हम कोई मुश्किल खड़ी नहीं करेंगे, कसम से।" कबीर बोला। "चलो अकीरा, ले चलते हैं इन्हें, हमें भी मनोरंजन चाहिए। इन जोकरों से अच्छा कौन होगा?" वेदिका सिर हिलाते हुए बोली। उनके चेहरे देख अकीरा पिघल गई और मान गई। बोली, "बस! अच्छे से रहना वहाँ! ठीक है?"

जैसा वेद ने सोचा था, जगराता वैसा ही निकला। उसे याद नहीं कब तक वह कोने में बैठकर बूढ़ी औरतों को सिर्फ दिखाने के लिए गाता रहा और तालियाँ बजाता रहा।

उसकी पसंदीदा व्यक्ति इधर से उधर दौड़ रही थी और सभी को अनदेखा कर रही थी। उसे अकीरा के साथ कुछ सुकून के लम्हे चाहिए थे, जो लुधियाना जैसे शहर में मिलने नामुमकिन थे।

"हे भगवान्!" वेद के कानों में अकीरा की धीमे स्वर की चीख सुनाई दी। कबीर के हाथों से नाटकीय तरीके से मँजीरे गिरे और रीशी ने वेद के कंधे पर हाथ रखकर कहा, "ये वही है।"

दोनों की प्रतिक्रिया से असमंजस में पड़े वेद ने भीड़ को चीरते हुए देखा तो पता चला कि तान्या का पुराना बॉयफ्रेंड (दोस्त) भीड़ में बैठा है।

"भई! अब तो पक्का है कि अभय की नाक के नीचे ये दोनों एक-दूसरे से मिल

रहे हैं।" वेद ने अपने हाथ हवा में उछालते हुए कहा।

"कसम से!" कबीर वेद के कान में फुसफुसाया और वेदिका को फोन पर मैसेज (संदेश) भेजा।

कुछ ही मिनटों में वेद ने देखा कि कबीर और वेदिका कमरे के दूसरे कोने से तान्या के पुराने बॉयफ्रेंड को छुपकर देख रहे थे।

दोनों हँसे। फिर कबीर ने उसके कपड़ों के बारे में सवाल किया—"इसकी पतलून इतनी बड़ी क्यों है?" "क्योंकि इसमें कई राज हैं।" भावशून्य चेहरे से वेद ने जवाब दिया। रीशी और कबीर बड़ी देर तक जोर से हँसते रहे। आसपास के लोग हैरत से उन्हें देख रहे थे। सबसे माफी माँगते हुए सजावट के बहाने से सभी तान्या के बेडरूम में पहुँचे।

"इसके बाल इतने लंबे क्यों हैं?" रीशी ने जिज्ञासा से पूछा।

"...क्योंकि उसमें बहुत सारे राज छुपे हुए है।" वेद ने जवाब दिया।

दोनों हँसे। फिर कबीर ने उसके कपड़ों के बारे में सवाल किया—"इसकी पतलून इतनी बड़ी क्यों है?"

"क्योंकि इसमें कई राज हैं।" भावशून्य चेहरे से वेद ने जवाब दिया।

रीशी और कबीर बड़ी देर तक जोर से हँसते रहे। आसपास के लोग हैरत से उन्हें देख रहे थे। सबसे माफी माँगते हुए सजावट के बहाने से सभी तान्या के बेडरूम में पहुँचे।

"हे! हे गाइज (दोस्तों)! प्लीज यहाँ की सजावट खराब मत करना। तान्या को यहाँ अपने दोस्तों के साथ कुछ फोटो खिंचवाने हैं।" अकीरा नाटकीय तरीके से कमरे में घुसते हुए बोली।

रीशी ने उलटी होने जैसा किया, "कौन समझदार अभय की फोटो को हाथ लगाएगा? वैसे अभय की फोटो यहाँ क्या कर रही है?"

अकीरा धम्म से बैठ गई, बोली, "मैंने एक खेल सोचा है।"

वेद चिढ़कर बोला, "कौन से खेल में अभय की असल की तसवीर (Life Size Picture) की जरूरत पड़ेगी?"

"बेहूदा खेल!" कबीर हँसा।

"और क्या? हाँ, ये खेल अच्छा बनेगा, अगर तुम तान्या की आँखों पर पट्टी बाँध दो और अभय की पूँछ बनाने को बोलो।" वेद बोला।

रीशी हँस रहा था। "देखो अकीरा! आज वेद हम सबको बेकार की बातें करके हँसाने का काम कर रहा है।"

अकीरा मुसकराकर बोली, "आँख बंद करनेवाली बात सही पकड़ी तुमने। फर्क बस इतना है कि तान्या को अभय के किसी भाग पर लिपस्टिक रखनी है (आँख बंद करके) और फिर उस जगह चूमना है।"

तीनों हैरान थे और उन्हें अजीब लगा। "ऐसा है, बैचलर्स पार्टी सीमाहीन होनी चाहिए न! कुछ विचित्र-सा, जहाँ बंध न हो। राय बनाने का कोई मतलब नहीं।"

"ठीक है! मजे का खेल है। खुशी हुई।" आँखें घुमाते हुए वेद बोला।

उतने में कमरे का दरवाजा खुला और अभय अंदर आया। उसके पीछे-पीछे तान्या और वेदिका आए। "ये किस तरह की हेन पार्टी (Hen Party-Female Party) है? इसमें हम क्या करेंगे?" अभय ने पूछा।

वेदिका ने वेद के कंधे पर हाथ रखकर कहा, "हेन पार्टी नहीं, बहन पार्टी है।"

तान्या और अभय को छोड़ सभी हँस पड़े। अभय ने घृणा की नजरों से वेदिका को देखकर कहा, "मैं देख रहा हूँ। तुम्हारे बच्चोंवाले चुटकुले अभी खत्म नहीं हुए।"

वेदिका ने वेद के कंधे पर हाथ रखकर कहा, "हेन पार्टी नहीं, बहन पार्टी है।" तान्या और अभय को छोड़ सभी हँस पड़े। अभय ने घृणा की नजरों से वेदिका को देखकर कहा, "मैं देख रहा हूँ। तुम्हारे बच्चोंवाले चुटकुले अभी खत्म नहीं हुए।"

सभी की ओर इशारा करते हुए वेदिका बोली, "मुझे भीड़ का मानसिक स्तर ध्यान में रखना पड़ता है।"

अभय झुँझलाकर बोला, "बेचारी! मैंने सुना ही नहीं!"

अभय वेद से नफरत करता था, इस बात का वेद को फर्क नहीं पड़ता था, पर अगर अभय वेदिका, अकीरा या परिवार के किसी भी सदस्य को कुछ कहता तो वेद की नस तड़क-सी जाती।

और वह अचानक बदला लेनेवाला, हिंसक बन जाता। इससे पहले कि वेद का विवेक उसे रोके, उसके मुँह से निकला, "हाँ, वैसे ही, जैसे तुम यह नहीं देख पा रहे कि तान्या का एक्स (पुराना) बॉयफ्रेंड यहीं आसपास छिपकर बैठा है।"

कमरे का वातावरण ही बदल गया। सभी की साँसें मानो अटक गईं। अभय गुस्से में वेद की ओर बढ़ा, "क्या बकवास की तूने?"

वेद बैठा रहा, "क्या करेगा तू? मुझे मेरे मरने तक घूरता रहेगा?"

रीशी और कबीर लड़ाई के लिए तैयार हो गए। "भाड़ में जाएँ तुम और तुम्हारे चेले।"

"अरे-अरे! देखो तो मेरे प्यारे भाई पर लुधियाना ने क्या असर किया है?" भाई की नजर उतारते हुए वेदिका बोली।

"हे भगवान्, वेदिका!" वेदिका को पीछे करते हुए वेद बोला।

तान्या ने ठंडी नजरों से अकीरा को देखकर कहा, "अब ये खुद अपने लिए मुसीबत बुला रहा है।"

अकीरा वाकई थक चुकी थी। धमकाते हुए उसने वेद को खींचते हुए कहा, "क्या आज पागलपन करने की बारी तुम्हारी है, जो तुम बकवास कर रहे हो?"

वेद बात की गंभीरता समझते हुए बोला, "ओह! सॉरी! वो भी सिर्फ तुम्हारे लिए अकीरा!"

"हो गया? अब इस कमरे से बाहर जाओ।" अभय रुखाई से बोला।

अकीरा को परेशानी न हो, यह सोचते हुए वेद और बाकी भी कमरे से बाहर जाने लगे। चाहे अकीरा को परेशान न करने का उद्देश्य था, पर जाते-जाते वेद फोटोग्राफर के पास रुका और धीरे से उसके कान में फुसफुसाया, "क्या तुम मगशॉट्स (सिर्फ चेहरे की तसवीर) भी लेते हो? मुझे लगता है, जल्दी ही मुझे उनकी जरूरत पड़ेगी, क्योंकि मैं किसी का खून करनेवाला हूँ।"

अकीरा ने उसे कमरे से बाहर धक्का देते हुए कहा, "आज क्या हो गया है तुम्हें? तुम उस बच्चे की तरह हरकतें कर रहे हो, जिसे अकेले नहीं छोड़ा जा सकता।"

अपना संतुलन बनाए रखते हुए भी अकीरा के गाल गुस्से से लाल हो रहे थे। "क्या हो गया है आज तुम्हें?"

वेदिका ने अकीरा की पीठ थपथपाई। "ये उसका औपचारिक अजीब व्यवहार है। ये तब होता है, जब वह किसी बात से हक्का-बक्का और उलझन में होता है। चिंता मत करो। अभी उसे मनोरोग विशेषज्ञ के पास ले जाने की नौबत नहीं आई है।"

"तुम्हें पता है?" ये कहते हुए वेद ने अपने बालों में हाथ घुमाया और फिर दोनों हाथों से अकीरा का चेहरा हाथ में लिया और बोला, "अब मैं दादी और नानी के पास जाकर बैठ रहा हूँ। जाते समय मुझे कहाँ ढूँढ़ना है, तुम्हें पता है।"

अकीरा ने बिना कुछ कहे हामी भरी। अकीरा के सिर पर हलके से पीछे की ओर थपकी देकर वेद कमरे से बाहर निकल गया। अभय को देखकर अकीरा की नसों में गुस्सा दौड़ गया। साथ ही वह सोचने लगी कि उसने जो काम हाथ में लिया है, क्या वाकई उसके और वेद के दिल दुखाए जाने लायक है? क्या उसने सही किया?

□

43

"जब मेहमान जाने लगें तो सभी को उनका उपहार अवश्य देना। सभी उपहार नामों के अक्षर के अनुसार लगे हैं, अंग्रेजी के अक्षरों के अनुसार। उनका नाम पूछना, उपहार देना और दी गई सूची में उनका नाम काट देना। सबको बात स्पष्ट है? "वेद ने अकीरा के स्टाफ (कर्मचारी) को हिदायतें दीं। सभी ने सिर झुकाकर हामी भरी और अपने-अपने काम पर चले गए। एक सजाए हुए झूले पर बैठकर वेद इधर-उधर देख रहा था। उसने साँसें छोड़ते हुए राहत महसूस की।

तान्या की मेहँदी की रात थी। वेद को थोड़ी सी तसल्ली थी। आखिरकार शादी की रस्में शुरू हो गईं। बस थोड़े समय की बात थी, पर अभी शादी हुई नहीं थी। तान्या और अभय के रिश्ते को देखते हुए आनेवाले समय में किसी भी अनपेक्षित घटना की संभावना की जा सकती थी। एक अजीब सी लहर उसके पेट में उठी। वह समझ नहीं पा रहा था कि अगर कुछ गलत हुआ तो अकीरा की प्रतिक्रिया क्या होगी? क्या वाकई वह वेद को छोड़कर चली जाएगी, जैसाकि उसने धमकाया था! उसके मात्र छोड़ जाने की कल्पना से वेद एक छोटे बच्चे की तरह सिहर गया। वह इतनी अजीब लड़की से इतना कैसे जुड़ गया?

वह हमेशा से ही व्यावहारिक था, जो इतनी जल्दी भावुक नहीं होता था। अब वह हर वह काम करने को तैयार था, जो अकीरा चाहती थी। शायद उसके प्रति अपनत्व था, क्योंकि वह चाहता था कि यह संबंध आगे तक चले। शायद अपनत्व के कारण ही मनुष्य कई काम दूसरों के लिए करता है।

"हेऽऽऽ! कैसे चल रहा है सब?" वेद ने बड़ी सी मुसकान के साथ पूछा।

"सब बढ़िया! तान्या वाकई खुश लग रही है। और मैंने देखा कि मेहँदी में भी उसने अभय का नाम लिखा है।" अकीरा ने जवाब दिया।

वेद दबी हँसी में बोला, "जाहिर है! तुम देखोगी।"

अकीरा ने मुसकराकर वेद की बाजू में अपनी बाजू डाल दी। "हो सकता है हम कुछ ज्यादा ही तान्या और अभय के संबंधों के बीच अटकलें लगा रहे हों; हो सकता

है वह लड़का वाकई तान्या का बीता हुआ कल हो और यह शादी बहुत अच्छी चल जाए!" वेद इस विषय से तंग आ चुका था, "मुझे लगता है, तुम बेकार ही इनको लेकर इतनी चिंतित हो।"

"ये मेरी कंपनी का सवाल है; अगर मैं इन सब बातों की चिंता नहीं करूँगी तो कौन करेगा? उम्मीद है तुम कल की तरह अभय से नहीं भिड़ोगे! कल तुमने उससे बहस करके लड़ाई मोल ले ली। यह जानते हुए भी कि वह कितना हिंसक हो जाता है!"

"ओ.के.। बस न, हम किसी और चीज के बारे में भी तो बात कर सकते हैं। इन सभी दिनों में हमने केवल अभय के बारे में बात की। बेकार!" वेद ने चिढ़कर कहा।

"ये मेरी कंपनी का सवाल है; अगर मैं इन सब बातों की चिंता नहीं करूँगी तो कौन करेगा? उम्मीद है तुम कल की तरह अभय से नहीं भिड़ोगे! कल तुमने उससे बहस करके लड़ाई मोल ले ली। यह जानते हुए भी कि वह कितना हिंसक हो जाता है!"

"ठीक है!" धीरे से अकीरा मुसकराकर बोली। "गुड। ये बेकार आदमी हमारी कहानी क्योंकर खराब करे?" अकीरा को अपने पास समेटते हुए वेद बोला।

अकीरा भी वेद की कमर में हाथ डालकर वेद की बाजुओं में समा गई और अपनी आँखें बंद कर लीं। पीछे इतना तेज संगीत चल रहा था, फिर भी उसे वेद की धड़कनें सुनाई पड़ रही थीं। उसके साथ की शांति, विश्वास और उसके अपनत्व की जकड़न; सबकुछ महसूस करने के बाद अकीरा का मन सब काम डब्बे में डालकर वहाँ से वेद के साथ भाग जाने का हुआ।

"वेद! जो कुछ तुमने मुझे अभय के घर कहा, वह सच था न?"

"बिल्कुल! बेवकूफोंवाले सवाल मत करो।" वेद बोला।

वेद की उँगलियों में अपनी उँगलियाँ फँसाते हुए अकीरा बोली, "फिर तुम मान क्यों नहीं लेते कि तुम मुझसे प्यार करते हो?"

वेद को धक्का लगा। "खैर! अगर मैं मान भी लूँ कि मैं तुमसे प्यार करने लगा हूँ, तो भी मैं 21 दिनों की डेट्स से पहले कुछ नहीं कहूँगा।"

"क्यों?"

"क्योंकि यही तय हुआ था। और अगर तुम इतनी जल्दी में हो तो तुम ही पहले क्यों नहीं कह देती?" वेद ने होंठ ऊपर की तरफ घुमाते हुए कहा।

अकीरा ने त्यौरियाँ चढ़ाईं, "अरे! मैं क्यों बोलूँ?"

"क्यों! क्या तुम मुझसे प्यार नहीं करने लगी हो?" वेद ने पूछा।

"अजीब हो तुम! मैं क्या पूछ रही हूँ और तुम कहीं और ही निकले जा रहे हो।"

"बिल्कुल तुम जैसे।" अभय ने कहा। "राम मिलाई जोड़ी, एक अंधा, एक कोढ़ी।" अभय ताना देते हुए बोला।

वेद ने फुसफुसाते हुए कहा, "लंगर देखा नहीं कि भिखारी दौड़े-दौड़े आ गए।"

अकीरा ने हँसी दबाकर आत्मविश्वास से अभय की ओर देखा, गहरी साँस ली और पूछा, "हाँ अभय! क्या हुआ?"

"अकीरा! तुम क्या कहने पर अच्छे से काम करोगी? मुझे भीख माँगनी पड़ेगी? क्या करना पड़ेगा मुझे?" अभय ने गाना गाते हुए स्वर में पूछा।

अकीरा उठ खड़ी हुई, "अभय! क्या हो गया है?"

"औरतें तुम्हारे बारे में पूछ रही हैं। उन्हें पीने के लिए कुछ चाहिए। जाहिर है, आज उनके साथ व्यावहारिक दिक्कत है। वे अपने हाथों का प्रयोग नहीं कर सकतीं, तो प्लीज जरा उनकी मदद करो।"

"जरा कुछ काम कर लो। तुम्हारा रोमांस कुछ समय के लिए रुक सकता है।" वेद को देखते हुए अभय ने व्यंग्य किया।

"औरतें तुम्हारे बारे में पूछ रही हैं। उन्हें पीने के लिए कुछ चाहिए। जाहिर है, आज उनके साथ व्यावहारिक दिक्कत है। वे अपने हाथों का प्रयोग नहीं कर सकतीं, तो प्लीज जरा उनकी मदद करो।" "जरा कुछ काम कर लो। तुम्हारा रोमांस कुछ समय के लिए रुक सकता है।" वेद को देखते हुए अभय ने व्यंग्य किया।

कौन सी लड़ाई कब करनी चाहिए, इस बात का विवेक रखते हुए अकीरा ने माफी माँगी और कहा, "मैं देखती हूँ, तुम चिंता मत करो।"

अभय ने उसके सामने झुककर कहा, "बड़ी मेहरबानी होगी।"

अकीरा बिना कोई शब्द कहे वहाँ से चली गई। अभय की बनावटी मुसकान भी। अभी वह पलटा ही था कि वेद के गुस्से भरे स्वर ने अभय को रोका। "अभय! वहीं रुको।"

भौंहें चढ़ाकर अभय पलटा, "क्या है?"

गुस्से से वेद अभय की ओर बढ़ा और कुछ ही दूरी पर रुक गया। गुस्सा दबाकर बोला, "मैंने तुम्हें अकीरा के लिए क्या कहा था? उससे ठीक से बात करना। वह परिवार का हिस्सा है।"

अभय ने मजाक उड़ाने के स्वर में कहा, "क्या मैं उस पर चिल्लाया? क्या मैंने उसका अपमान किया? नहीं! मैंने उसे कितने आराम से कहा कि वह पहले अपना काम करे। और जहाँ तक मुझे पता है, मैं उसके काम करने के पैसे दे रहा हूँ, इसलिए ठंडे हो जाओ भाई!"

वेद ने अभय को पीछे धकेला। वेद चिल्लाया, "तुम मेरे धीरज की परीक्षा मत लो।

अकीरा तुम्हें सुनने को बाध्य है, मैं नहीं। तुम अगर एक और बार उसका अपमान करोगे तो मैं भूल जाऊँगा कि यहाँ तुम्हारी शादी है। फिर मेरा हाथ, तुम्हारा चेहरा और अस्पताल का बिस्तर होगा।"

अभय जोर से हँसा, "तुम्हें पता है अरुणा नानी इसे क्या कहेंगी? मुंगेरीलाल के हसीन सपने! और तुम्हें देखकर लगता भी है कि तुम्हारी इस बॉडी के साथ तुम काफी सपने लेते हो। भौंकते रहो।"

वेद अभय के स्वर में पागलपन का आभास पा चुका था। वेद जानता था कि अभय पंगे ले रहा है, लेकिन उसने दूसरे मेहँदी रचनेवालों के साथ अकीरा को देख लिया था। बात न बढ़े, इसलिए वेद चुप रहा।

"तुमसे बात करने का कोई फायदा नहीं⋯।" वेद बोला।

वह अपनी कार की तरफ गया। अंदर बैठकर ए.सी. चालू किया और खुद को ठंडा करने की कोशिश की। अपने गुस्से को काबू करने के लिए उसने अपनी आँखें बंद कीं और अपनी भावनाएँ समझने की कोशिश ही कर रहा था कि किसी ने कार की खिड़की पर खटखटाया और वेद की सोच की कड़ी टूटी।

वेद ने अचानक आँखें खोलीं। बाहर अकीरा परेशान भाव से खड़ी थी। उसने पूछा, "क्या हुआ?"

"कुछ नहीं⋯मैं ठीक हूँ।"

अकीरा ने लंबी साँस छोड़ी। वह देख पा रही थी कि वेद को अभय पर गुस्सा आया हुआ था। वह वेद के साथ सटकर बैठ गई और वेद के बाल सहलाते हुए बोली, "जब थोड़ा अच्छा महसूस करो तो आ जाना। ठीक है?"

वेद थोड़ा सा हँसा, कहा, "ठीक है।"

अकीरा भी हँसी। उसके सिर पर हलकी सी थपकी देते हुए वह उठी। अपने हाथों को दुपट्टे में छिपाकर वह बगीचे की ओर चल पड़ी। उसके मन में सवाल था कि पता नहीं यह सब कैसे खत्म होगा?

□

44

वेद ने साउंड टीम से पूछा, "हम संगीत की कानों को चुभनेवाली आवाज को ठीक कर सकते हैं?" तकनीशियन ने हामी भरते हुए वेद को विश्वास दिलाया, "हम यह समस्या ठीक कर देंगे सर!"

वेद ने आशा की कि मंच मजबूत बना हो, ताकि यदि कोई समस्या या खून-खराबे की नौबत आ जाती है तो वह न टूटे। खुद से हँसता हुआ बैठने के प्रबंध की ऊबड़-खाबड़ हालत जाँचता हुआ वह आखिरी सीट तक गया।

एक तरफ तान्या और अभय की मँगनी देख वेद को अच्छा महसूस हो रहा था, लेकिन उसने तान्या के एक्स (पुराने बॉयफ्रेंड) को गेट से धक्के मारकर बाहर भेजते हुए देखा था। उसका मन हुआ कि वह सबसे पहले अकीरा को बताए, लेकिन यह सोचकर कि वह परेशान हो जाएगी, उसने नहीं बताया।

"वेद! तुम ड्यूरोसेल के खरगोश की तरह कुरसियों की पंक्ति में क्यों घूम रहे हो?"

"किसके जैसे?" तुलना सुनकर वेद हैरान था। "मैं तो प्रबंध में यह देख रहा था कि कहीं जमीन ऊबड़-खाबड़ तो नहीं, ताकि सुंदर औरतें लड़खड़ाते हुए कहीं गिर न जाएँ। वैसे ही आज की रात आतंक और भय की रात है।"

"मैं तो वैसे ही अभय के एकल प्रदर्शन की सोचकर हँस रही हूँ। वह 'तेरा हीरो इधर है' गाने पर नाचनेवाला है।"

वेद को बात पचाने में कुछ समय लगा। "मुझे पता है, यह सलाह वेदिका की होगी।"

"सही कहा," अकीरा हँसते हुए बोली। "वह तो यह भी चाह रही थी कि हम सभी 'भूतनी के' गाने पर अचानक नृत्य करके सबको हैरान कर दें, लेकिन मैंने मना कर दिया। इस बात के लिए वह मुझे कभी माफ नहीं करेगी।"

अपनी शर्मिंदगी चेहरे पर आने से छुप जाए, इस बात का भरसक प्रयत्न करते हुए वेद बोला, "माफ करना! मेरा परिवार बहुत ही घटिया सोच रखता है।"

थोड़ा सा झुककर अकीरा बोली, "अरे नहीं!"

वेद मुसकराते हुए अकीरा के पीछे चल पड़ा। खाने का प्रबंध एक बड़े से कमरे में था, जिसकी सजावट अत्यंत सुंदर थी।

तान्या और अभय अपने परिवारों के साथ एक ही मेज पर बैठे थे।

"ऐसा लग रहा है कि शैतान और उसकी होनेवाली पत्नी साथ बैठे हैं..." अपने परिवार के साथ बैठने के लिए आगे बढ़ते हुए वेद अकीरा से बोला।

"सच में! ऐसा ही लग रहा है।" अकीरा ने साथ दिया।

वेद सबसे मिला और पूछा, "खाना खाने में मजा आ रहा है?"

"इससे अच्छा तो मैं रबर चबा लेती।" पिंकी ने दु.ख भरे स्वर में कहा।

वेद ने अपनी हँसी दबाई। अचानक वेदिका ने संवाद के बीच अपनी बात छेड़ दी और सबका ध्यान उसकी ओर गया, "यार कबीर! तुम मुझे अँगूठी कब दोगे?"

कबीर अनपेक्षित प्रश्न से घबरा-सा गया और अपनी झेंप छुपाने के लिए बोला, "चिल्ल! बहुत जल्द।"

अविनाश ने मजे लिये, "बच्चे वेदिका। मेरे खयाल से कबीर तुम्हें रिंग (अँगूठी) नहीं, ओनियन रिंग (प्याज से बना पदार्थ) दे सकता है।" और हँसने लगा।

"हाँऽऽऽ।" वेदिका ने शिकायती स्वर में कहा तो कबीर ने विरोध किया, "हमें मत चिढ़ाइए, आपको पता है कि मैं वेदिका से प्रेम करता हूँ और वह भी मुझसे।"

अपने गिलास में से स्कॉच का एक घूँट पीते हुए अरुणा ने ताना कसा, "इसी बात का तो रोना है, बेटा!"

"इससे अच्छा तो मैं रबर चबा लेती।" पिंकी ने दु.ख भरे स्वर में कहा। वेद ने अपनी हँसी दबाई। अचानक वेदिका ने संवाद के बीच अपनी बात छेड़ दी और सबका ध्यान उसकी ओर गया, "यार कबीर! तुम मुझे अँगूठी कब दोगे?" कबीर अनपेक्षित प्रश्न से घबरा-सा गया और अपनी झेंप छुपाने के लिए बोला, "चिल्ल! बहुत जल्द।"

मेज पर बैठे सभी लोग हँस पड़े और वेदिका झेंपती हुई बोली, "हम्मऽऽऽ, गलत बात!"

इंद्राणी ने वेदिका को गले लगाकर पुचकारा, "अरे! चिंता मत कर, हम सब दिल से तुम्हारी इस गलती को स्वीकार कर चुके हैं।"

"दादीऽऽऽ!" वेदिका के इस संबोधन से दादी हँस रही थीं।

इन सब बातों की उपेक्षा कर वेद का ध्यान उसकी और अकीरा की एक-दूसरे में गुँथी उँगलियों की ओर था। जब दोनों के हाथ एक-दूसरे के हाथ में थे तो मानो एक

इकाई थे। वेद ने अकीरा की हथेली देखी। दो उँगलियों के बीच की धुँधली रेखा देखी। वेद को काटो तो खून नहीं, जब उसने देखा कि अँगूठीवाली उँगली पर मेहँदी से अकीरा ने वेद का नाम लिखवाया था। उसने एकदम अकीरा का हाथ पीछे किया। फिर दुबारा उसका हाथ लेकर अपने नाम पर वेद ने उँगली घुमाई। अकीरा को समझ नहीं आया, पर उसे लगा, वेद बहुत खुश होगा, लेकिन वेद की आँखों से बस आँसू टपकनेवाले थे। अविनाश की आवाज मानो उन्हें वापस ले आई। अविनाश नीलू की तरफ देखकर बोला, "पिंकी, लगता है तुम्हारे पूर्वज बंदर नहीं, साँप थे।"

"साँप???" पिंकी ने अपनी छाती पर हाथ रखते हुए पूछा।

"और क्या? ये तो एनाकॉण्डा है। कब से छाती पर लोट रही है।"

पूरा परिवार मुँह दबाकर हँस रहा था। तभी वेद का फोन बजा। इतनी खुशी के क्षण में रुकावट! उसने माथे पर हाथ मारा।

"अब क्या हुआ?" पिंकी ने पूछा।

वेद ने चेहरा लटकाकर कहा, "मुझे अनजान नंबरों से फोन आ रहे हैं और सभी को खाने का ऑर्डर देना है।"

एक शैतानी हँसी वेदिका के चेहरे पर थी। वेद समझ गया और धमकाकर पूछा, क्योंकि उसने अपने हाव-भाव छुपाने की कोशिश की। लेकिन वेद ने पकड़ लिया। वेदिका ने नाटक बहुत अच्छा किया था। "अब ये मत कहना कि इस बात में तुम्हारा कोई हाथ नहीं। वेदिका! क्या किया तूने? बता, वरना कबीर और तेरी धोखाधड़ी की बातें सबको बता दूँगा।"

एक शैतानी हँसी वेदिका के चेहरे पर थी। वेद समझ गया और धमकाकर पूछा, क्योंकि उसने अपने हाव-भाव छुपाने की कोशिश की। लेकिन वेद ने पकड़ लिया। वेदिका ने नाटक बहुत अच्छा किया था। "अब ये मत कहना कि इस बात में तुम्हारा कोई हाथ नहीं। वेदिका! क्या किया तूने? बता, वरना कबीर और तेरी धोखाधड़ी की बातें सबको बता दूँगा।"

"क्या बकवास है? वेदिका, तुमने क्या किया है? बता दो, वरना ये पागल हमारे सारे राज खोल देगा।" कबीर बोला।

"मुझे अपने मूर्ख बच्चों से बात करने के लिए एक स्ट्रॉन्ग ड्रिंक चाहिए।" अरुणा ने माथे को खुजलाते हुए कहा। घबराई हुई वेदिका हँसकर बोली, "मैंने रेस्तराँ के नए परचे (Pumphlet) शालिनी मामी को भेंट किए, जिसमें वेद भैया का फोन नंबर दिया।"

शालिनी हैरान थी, "तभी मैं सोचूँ कि मेरे ग्राहक यह शिकायत क्यों कर रहे थे कि फोन करो तो कोई बहुत रूखी आवाज में बात करके फोन काट देता है? मैं कामों में इतनी उलझी हुई थी कि पैम्पलेट पर देखा ही नहीं कि फोन नंबर ठीक है या नहीं।"

"ये गलत बात है, वेदिका! मजाक करने की भी कोई हद होती है कि नहीं!" पिंकी ने विरोध जताते हुए और डाँटते हुए कहा।

"मॉम, जाने दो। वेदिका अभय जैसी है—असह्य और घृणास्पद। उसका कोई गुण है तो बस इतना कि वह अरोरा परिवार में जनमी है।" वेद गुस्से से बोला।

इस सारे विवाद के बीच अभय की आवाज कमरे में गूँजी। वह एक शहनशाह की तरह अपनी मेज पर बैठा और इशारे से अकीरा को बुलाया। वेद भी झट पीछे हो लिया।

नीलू मासी ने शिकायत की, "खाना इतना बेस्वाद क्यों है?" अभय चिल्लाना चाहता था, पर धीरे बोला, "माँ ने तुम्हें अच्छा खाना बनाने को कहा और तुमने उसका मजाक बना दिया।"

जिस तरह से अभय के हाव-भाव थे, अकीरा झेंप गई, क्योंकि वह समझ रही थी कि अभय के हाव-भाव देखकर कमरे के सभी लोग उसे देख रहे होंगे। उसने माफी माँगी और प्लेट उठाते हुए बोली, "मैं अभी बावर्ची को खाना दुबारा गरम करने को बोलती हूँ।"

इतना कहकर अकीरा सीधे रसोईघर (किचन) में गई और अभय को गुस्से से देखते हुए वेद भी पीछे गया। वेद ने नीलू मासी की प्लेट दुबारा लगाई और दुबारा गरम करने के लिए माइक्रोवेव में रख दिया। अकीरा थकी हुई थी, इसलिए उसने वेद को काम करने दिया। वेद ने वही प्लेट नीलू मासी के आगे रख दी। अकीरा पीछे खड़ी थी।

"ये लीजिए मासी!" वेद ने मुसकराते हुए कहा।

इतना कहकर अकीरा सीधे रसोईघर (किचन) में गई और अभय को गुस्से से देखते हुए वेद भी पीछे गया। वेद ने नीलू मासी की प्लेट दुबारा लगाई और दुबारा गरम करने के लिए माइक्रोवेव में रख दिया। अकीरा थकी हुई थी, इसलिए उसने वेद को काम करने दिया। वेद ने वही प्लेट नीलू मासी के आगे रख दी। अकीरा पीछे खड़ी थी।

संदेह की दृष्टि से नीलू ने चम्मच से खाना शुरू किया।

"देखो अब कितना स्वादिष्ट लग रहा है। ये पहले करने में क्या दिक्कत थी?"

"माफी चाहता हूँ।" कहकर वेद अकीरा का हाथ पकड़कर वहाँ से चला गया।

"ओ भगवन्!" अकीरा बोली, जब उसे दो क्षण राहत के मिले।

"मैंने तुम्हें कहा था कि अव्वल दर्जे के कमीने हैं। खुद को गार्डन रामसे की औलादें मानते हैं।" बनावटी मुसकान के साथ वेद ने जवाब दिया।

अकीरा वेद की बातें सुन और मासी के नाटक देख हँस पड़ी। "खैर, मैं 'संगीत'

कार्यक्रम के प्रबंध का जायजा ले लूँ।" वेद बोला।

अकीरा इससे पहले कुछ कहने को मुँह खोलती, वेद ने अकीरा का हाथ ऊपर किया और मेहँदी से लिखे अपने नाम पर धीरे से चूम लिया। अकीरा खुशी से भरी स्तब्धता से उसे देखती रह गई, मानो अचानक वेद ने उनके संबंध आगे भी चलाने का वादा किया।

"मेरे पास पूछने के लिए बहुत से प्रश्न हैं..." कबीर हाँफते हुए बोला।

वेद के अलावा संगीत 'कार्यक्रम' में अरोरा परिवार नृत्य का छोटा सा प्रदर्शन कर चुका था। अब वे सभी बैठक की आखिरी कतार में बैठकर अभय और तान्या के परिवारों को नृत्य करने की कोशिश में लगा हुआ देख रहे थे।

वेदिका कबीर की हाँ-में-हाँ मिलाते हुए बोली, "इसीलिए मैं एक ही गाने पर नाची।"

"मैं इनका रिश्तेदार क्यों हूँ?" वेद ने आँखें बंद करते हुए कहा।

अकीरा ने भी साथ दिया, "कितना भयानक है ये!"

"हाँ!" कबीर साथ में आकर खड़ा हो गया और आँखें बंद करके ऐसे दिखाया मानो मातम कर रहा हो। "अब हम दो मृत आत्माओं की शांति के लिए दो मिनट का मौन रखेंगे—नृत्य और ताल।"

वेदिका खिलखिलाई और अकीरा वेद की तरफ प्रश्न भरी निगाहों से देखने लगी।

"मुझे ऐसे मत देखो, न ये मेरी सर्कस है, न मेरे बंदर।" वेद ने कंधे उचकाते हुए जवाब दिया।

वेद के अलावा संगीत 'कार्यक्रम' में अरोरा परिवार नृत्य का छोटा सा प्रदर्शन कर चुका था। अब वे सभी बैठक की आखिरी कतार में बैठकर अभय और तान्या के परिवारों को नृत्य करने की कोशिश में लगा हुआ देख रहे थे। वेदिका कबीर की हाँ-में-हाँ मिलाते हुए बोली, "इसीलिए मैं एक ही गाने पर नाची।"

अकीरा जोर से हँस पड़ी, रुकी, फिर से हँसने के लिए।

अरुणा अभय को देखकर बोलीं, "इसको किसने चाबी भरके छोड़ दिया?"

वेद ने सिर पकड़कर कहा, "प्लीज रुक जाइए, ज्यादा हँसने से मेरा सिरदर्द होने लगा है।"

"मेरा तो सचमुच सिरदर्द हो रहा है।" इंद्राणी बुदबुदाईं, "वेद बेटा, क्या तुम हमें घर छोड़ सकते हो?"

वेद झट से तैयार हो गया। वहाँ से बाहर निकलने का इससे अच्छा मौका कहाँ मिलता? उसने धीरे से अकीरा को अपनी ओर खींचा और कहा, "मैं दादी और नानीजी

को घर छोड़ने जा रहा हूँ। आते ही तुमको ले चलूँगा। यहीं रहना, कहीं मत जाना और किसी और के साथ मत जाना।"

अकीरा प्रेम से वेद को देखकर बोली, "मैं इंतजार करूँगी।"

प्यार से आँख मारते हुए वेद बोला, "सी यू (मिलते हैं)।"

वेद की हरकतों पर हैरान होकर अकीरा ने सिर हिलाया और खुद से कहा, 'ऐसे लोग कम ही मिलते हैं।'

गहरी साँस लेकर वह 'संगीत' कार्यक्रम के प्रबंधन में जुट गई। इतना समय बीत गया कि अकीरा ने देखा नहीं। लेकिन वह सोच रही थी कि अभी तक वेद को वापस आ जाना चाहिए था, वह एक कोने में खड़ी होकर मंच का समेटा जाना देख रही थी।

"हाय!" अचानक किसी ने उसे अपनी बाजुओं में ले लिया। अब वह ये हाथ पहचानने लगी थी। "ये संगीत का कार्यक्रम तो बहुत जल्दी खत्म हो गया। मुझे तो था कि अभय और भी देर तक नाचेगा।" अकीरा ने खुद को पीछे की ओर वेद पर छोड़ दिया। वेद ने अपनी ठुड्डी अकीरा के कंधे पर रखी।

"हाय!" अचानक किसी ने उसे अपनी बाजुओं में ले लिया। अब वह ये हाथ पहचानने लगी थी। "ये संगीत का कार्यक्रम तो बहुत जल्दी खत्म हो गया। मुझे तो था कि अभय और भी देर तक नाचेगा।" अकीरा ने खुद को पीछे की ओर वेद पर छोड़ दिया। वेद ने अपनी ठुड्डी अकीरा के कंधे पर रखी।

"नीलू मासी ने कहा, सबको नींद चाहिए ताकि कल तरोताजा लगें और वे चले गए।"

"वो स्मार्ट हैं…" वेद बुदबुदाया।

"बहुत स्मार्ट!" अकीरा दबी हँसी में बोली।

पीछे मुड़कर अकीरा ने वेद को सोफे की तरफ खींचा, जहाँ पिज्जा उनकी राह देख रहा था।

"ये उसी पिज्जा डेट की आगे की कड़ी है।"

वेद खुश हुआ, "वाह!" अकीरा उसकी संक्रामक हँसी से प्रभावित हो हँस पड़ी।

अचानक दोनों के बीच शांति थी। उसके कर्मचारियों ने बड़ी-बड़ी लाइटें हटा दी थीं। अब बस धीमी रोशनी थी। काफी समय बाद अकीरा को अच्छा महसूस हुआ था। उसे लगा कि जो वह दो रातों से अपने मन में छुपाए हुए है, वह कहने का समय आ गया है।

"वेद! मैं तुम्हें कुछ बताना चाहती हूँ।" अकीरा धीरे से बोली। "पैसों की कमी की वजह से मैंने अपने ऑफिस का तीन महीनों का किराया नहीं दिया है। अगर जल्दी ही पैसों का बंदोबस्त नहीं हुआ तो मेरा ऑफिस चला जाएगा।" उसने फोन आगे करते हुए वेद से कहा, "पढ़ो!"

वेद ने फोन की स्क्रीन पर देखते हुए कहा, "असल में जिस दिन अभय के पीने

का कांड हुआ था, तब मैंने 'नोटिफिकेशन' में पढ़ लिया था। अब क्या करोगी तुम?"

"पता नहीं! मैंने अगले ग्राहक से बात करने की कोशिश की, लेकिन उन्होंने कहा, "पहले हम देखेंगे कि यह शादी कैसी रहती है।"

" लोग क्या कहते हैं, फिर सोचेंगे। मुझे स्वीकारते हुए बुरा लग रहा है, लेकिन सच तो यही है कि अभय जब इस शादी का चेक देगा, तभी कुछ हो सकता है। वही मेरी आखिरी उम्मीद है।"

वेद का दिल डूब गया, दूर क्षितिज में देखते हुए इस समस्या के बारे में, जिसे सिर्फ वही जानता था।

"तुम मुझसे कुछ कहना चाहते हो?"

वेद ने अपना सिर अकीरा की तरफ घुमाया।

"तुम्हें कैसे पता?"

अकीरा मुसकराकर बोली, "इतना तो श्रेय तुम्हें मुझे देना पड़ेगा कि मैं तुम्हें पढ़ सकती हूँ।"

अपना माथा खुजलाते हुए वेद ने सच बोला, "आज सुबह मैंने देखा कि तान्या का दोस्त उस एक्स (पुराने बॉयफ्रेंड) को गेट के बाहर धक्का दे रहा था।"

वेद को और भी हैरानी हुई, जब अकीरा ने हामी भरते हुए बताया, "मैं उस समय तान्या के ही कमरे में थी, जब उसका 'एक्स' कमरे में आया। तान्या के दोस्तों ने मिलकर उसे बाहर खदेड़ा।"

वेद ने अपना सिर अकीरा की तरफ घुमाया। "तुम्हें कैसे पता?" अकीरा मुसकराकर बोली, "इतना तो श्रेय तुम्हें मुझे देना पड़ेगा कि मैं तुम्हें पढ़ सकती हूँ।" अपना माथा खुजलाते हुए वेद ने सच बोला, "आज सुबह मैंने देखा कि तान्या का दोस्त उस एक्स (पुराने बॉयफ्रेंड) को गेट के बाहर धक्का दे रहा था।"

"वाह!" खुशी से वेद चहका। उसे विश्वास नहीं हो रहा था।

"एक बात कहूँ? हमें अभय से सहमत होकर, बिना विरोध के शादी निबटा देनी चाहिए।" अकीरा ने धीरे से कहा।

"हाँऽऽऽ!" वेद ने जवाब दिया।

फिर खुद पर ही ग्लानि करती हुई बोली, "कितनी बड़ी विडंबना है न कि जब खुद के बचाव की बात होती है तो मनुष्य सारे नैतिक मूल्य भूल जाता है।"

वेद फिर चुप रहा। अगर अकीरा मुश्किल में है तो उसकी स्थिति और भी खराब है। उसकी चुप्पी देख अकीरा ने अचानक पूछा, "अगर तुम मेरी जगह होते तो क्या करते?"

वेद के चेहरे पर सौम्यता लौटी। वह धीरे से अकीरा की ओर खिसका, "मैं तुम्हारी जगह होता तो मैं अपने बेहद खूबसूरत, मजाकिया और प्रतिभावान बॉयफ्रेंड के साथ पिज्जा के मजे लेती और...उसे कल रात को लगाई मेहँदी दिखाती।"

अकीरा का चेहरा खिल उठा। उसने पूछा, "तुम्हें अच्छी लगी? मेरा मतलब है, अच्छी लगी ही होगी। मेहँदी देखने के बाद तुम्हारी आँखों में आँसू थे।" अकीरा को लगा, शायद वेद मुकर जाए, पर वेद धीरे से बोला, "तुम्हें पता है, जिनसे तुम्हारा खून का रिश्ता है, उनसे तुम्हारा प्रेम स्वाभाविक है, ईश्वर की देन है। मुझे पता है कि न ही मैं आदर्श पुरुष हूँ और न ही आदर्श बॉयफ्रेंड। लेकिन यह भाव कि तुम्हें कोई पसंद करता है, तुम किसी के हो…बेहद खूबसूरत है।"

भाव-विभोर होकर अकीरा ने वेद के सीने पर अपना सिर रख दिया। उसे पहले भी किसी ने समेटा था, प्रेम किया था, लेकिन ऐसा नहीं था। अकीरा वेद को यह बताना चाहती थी, पर शब्द नहीं जुटा पाई। वह हैरान थी कि वेद किस मिट्टी का बना है! अकीरा वेद के और करीब थी। उसे वेद और चाहिए था, पूरा!

अकीरा वेद की आँखों में देख रही थी, जिसमें शैतानी थी। "मुझे एक ही बात का दुःख है कि तुमने मेरी कॉफी बहुत देर से छीनी।"

अकीरा की मुसकान चौड़ी हो गई। उसने वेद की नाक-से-नाक रगड़ते हुए कहा, "फिर इतने सालों की कसर पूरी कर लो।"

वह भी मुसकराता हुआ बोला, "वो भी पूरी करूँगा, एक बार औपचारिक तौर पर तुम्हें अपना बना लूँ, तो वह भी करूँगा, तब तक के लिए…।"

आग और पानी फिर मिले और वेद के होंठों के पास जाकर चिढ़ाते हुए बोली, "तुम्हें कितना विश्वास है न कि मैं हाँ ही कहूँगी?" हलकी ठंड में अकीरा को वेद में समा जाना अच्छा लग रहा था।

"हाँ! तुम बताओ, क्या तुम मुझे 'न' कह सकती हो?" वेद ने चुनौती दी।

अकीरा हँसते हुए बोली, "इस पर बहस हो सकती है।"

"ठीक है, चलेगा।" आँख मारते हुए वेद बोला।

"वेद…" अकीरा की आवाज और भी धीमी हो गई। "मैं तुम्हें कुछ और भी बताना चाहती हूँ, पर पहले यह शादी निपट जाने दो।"

"मैं इंतजार करूँगा। पेट दर्द होगा, पर कोई बात नहीं, इंतजार करूँगा।" वेद बोला।

□

45

"तुम अंदर क्या कर रहे थे, वो भी रीशी के साथ?" अकीरा ने वेद से सवाल किया, जब उसने वेद और उसके पीछे-पीछे रीशी को वाशरूम से एक के पीछे एक साथ में बाहर आते देखा।

वेद ने रीशी की ओर देखकर कहा, "रीशी के पाजामे का नाड़ा अटक गया था। एक बॉबी पिन माँ से उधार ली, तब काम बना।"

पूरी घटना की कल्पना मात्र से अकीरा को हँसी आ गई। वह दबी हँसी में बोली, "चलो अब, हल्दी रस्म शुरू होनेवाली है।"

"येऽऽऽ कितना मजा आएगा!" व्यंग्य से ताली बजाते हुए वेद ने कहा और सभी सजे हुए बगीचे की ओर चल पड़े।

वेद खड़ा तो परिवार के साथ था, लेकिन उसकी नजरें अकीरा का ही पीछा कर रही थीं। वेद फिदा हो चला था। किस तरह उस विचित्र लड़की ने वेद को अंदर तक पिघला दिया था। वह कितना अच्छा महसूस कर रहा था। बस, अब वेद यह चाहता था कि अकीरा को यदि वह विवाह प्रस्ताव दे, तो वह स्वीकार कर ले।

"इसको क्या हुआ है? इसका चेहरा प्रमोद मामा के घोड़ों से भी ज्यादा लटक रहा है।" वेदिका की यह शिकायत वेद सुन रहा था।

पिंकी ने भी माना। "हाँ, नीलू भी मुझसे उतनी ही अनजान बनी थी, जितना कि मांस खानेवाले पनीर को देख अनजान बनते हैं।"

अविनाश हँसा, "शायद उन्हें पता चल गया है कि कितने ढकोसले किए हैं, उन्होंने शादी में।"

"अकीरा!"

अचानक सभी ने पीछे मुड़कर देखा। नीलू अकीरा पर चिल्ला रही थी। "मैंने तुम्हें खासतौर पर कहा था कि जब हम उसे हल्दी लगाएँ तो उसका चेहरा पूर्व दिशा की तरफ होना चाहिए। मैंने अपने गुरुजी के साथ बैठकर अभय की कुंडली देखी थी और सारी योजना बनाई थी।"

वेद ने परेशान होकर अपने बालों में हाथ घुमाया। "उफ्फ! फिर गड़बड़।"

अकीरा अपने हाथ में हल्दी की हाँडी लिये हुए नीलू और अभय के सामने खड़ी थी। बोली, "ये मैंने थोड़ा सा बदलाव इसलिए किया, क्योंकि पूर्व दिशा से ज्यादा रोशनी आएगी तो तसवीरें अच्छी नहीं आएँगी।"

"ओहो नीलू! इतना रोला क्यों मचा रखा है? पाँच मिनट में अकीरा सब ठीक कर देगी।" अरुणा बीच में बोलीं।

"हाँ! मैं अभी सब दुबारा वैसा ही प्रबंध कर देती हूँ, जैसा आप चाहते हैं।" अकीरा आत्मविश्वास से बोली।

"आई एम सॉरी अभय! विश्वास करो, मैं जल्दी सारा प्रबंध ठीक कर दूँगी।" अकीरा अभय को समझाने की भरसक कोशिशें कर रही थी। लेकिन जैसे ही वह आगे बढ़ी, अकीरा का दुपट्टा उसके पैरों में अटका और वह गिरते-गिरते बची। एक क्षण में वह अभय की तरफ बढ़ रही थी और अगले क्षण, उसने हल्दी की पूरी हाँडी अभय के कुरते पर उड़ेल दी। वह खुद ही बहुत डर गई।

"बात यह नहीं है। बात यह है कि तुम कोई काम ठीक से कर ही नहीं सकती।" अभय बोला।

वेद के शरीर में गुस्से की लहर दौड़ गई, पर अकीरा की वजह से चुप रहा। गुस्सा निगल गया।

अभय अकीरा का अपमान-पर-अपमान किए जा रहा था। "हर दिन कोई-न-कोई दिक्कत आती है और हम वह मुश्किल सुलझा रहे होते हैं। हम इसे पैसे क्यों दे रहे हैं?"

"आई एम सॉरी अभय! विश्वास करो, मैं जल्दी सारा प्रबंध ठीक कर दूँगी।" अकीरा अभय को समझाने की भरसक कोशिशें कर रही थी। लेकिन जैसे ही वह आगे बढ़ी, अकीरा का दुपट्टा उसके पैरों में अटका और वह गिरते-गिरते बची। एक क्षण में वह अभय की तरफ बढ़ रही थी और अगले क्षण, उसने हल्दी की पूरी हाँडी अभय के कुरते पर उड़ेल दी। वह खुद ही बहुत डर गई।

"हे भगवान्!"

अभय ने बुरी-सी गाली से अपना गुस्सा जताया, जब उसने अपने कुरते पर हल्दी गिरी देखी। अभय की आँखें गुस्से से लाल हो गईं। वह चिल्लाया, "गाली...ये क्या किया तुमने?"

इस तरह की गाली अभय के मुँह से सुनते ही चारों तरफ शांति छा गई। सभी सदमे में घटना और अभय को देख रहे थे। वेद खुद को काबू में नहीं कर पाया। उसने बिल्कुल नहीं सोचा कि अकीरा क्या चाहती थी और उस समय क्या करना सही था। उसे बस अभय का सिर तोड़ने का मन किया।

"क्या कहा तूने ?" वेद चिल्लाया और अभय को धक्का मारकर पीछे किया। अकीरा बुरे-से-बुरे की कल्पना से डर गई और बोली, "वेद! नहीं!"

लेकिन तब तक वेद का घूँसा अभय के जबड़े पर पड़ चुका था। अभय लड़खड़ाते हुए पीछे हुआ। वेद ने उसे सँभलने का मौका ही नहीं दिया। वह अभय को पागलों की तरह घूँसे-पर-घूँसे मारे जा रहा था।

घबराते हुए अकीरा ने कबीर के पास जाकर विनती की, "इसे रोको! कुछ करो!"

लेकिन कबीर आराम से वेद को अभय के खून का प्यासा रूप में देखता रहा। और बोला, "नहीं!"

अकीरा का दिल बैठ गया, जब वह लाचारी से वेद को अभय की बच्चे की तरह पिटाई करते हुए देख रही थी। "तुम्हारी हिम्मत कैसे हुई ये (Fucking Bitch) कहने की ?" और एक गाली दी।

बड़े-बड़े दावों के बावजूद अभय वेद के सामने नहीं टिक पाया। लहुलूहान और बेहोशी की अवस्था में वह जमीन पर था। "मैंने तुझे कहा था अपनी औकात में रहना। कहा था न ?"

अकीरा का दिल और बैठ गया। वह जान चुकी थी कि यह लड़ाई अब नहीं रुकेगी और उसका व्यावसायिक भविष्य समाप्त हो चुका है।

बड़े-बड़े दावों के बावजूद अभय वेद के सामने नहीं टिक पाया। लहुलूहान और बेहोशी की अवस्था में वह जमीन पर था। "मैंने तुझे कहा था अपनी औकात में रहना। कहा था न ?" अकीरा का दिल और बैठ गया। वह जान चुकी थी कि यह लड़ाई अब नहीं रुकेगी और उसका व्यावसायिक भविष्य समाप्त हो चुका है।

उसकी तसल्लीभर पिटाई करने के बाद अभय को जमीन पर धक्का देते हुए वेद बोला, "किसी लड़की के अपमान और बदतमीजी की यही सजा है तुम्हारे जैसों के लिए।"

नीलू अभय के पास बैठकर उसका खून उसके चेहरे से साफ करते हुए रोते हुए बोली, "अभय, तुम ठीक कहते थे, अरोरा परिवार हमेशा रंग में भंग ही करता है। मैं बेवकूफ थी, जो यह समझी थी कि यह परिवार सुधर गया है।" फिर मासी अकीरा पर चिल्लाई, "देख तूने ये क्या किया।"

पिंकी को बहुत बुरा लगा, "तुम अपनी जबान सँभालो।"

वेदिका ने माँ के स्वर-में-स्वर मिलाया, "आप बेकार की बातें छोड़िए मासीजी, इतने कम समय में पूरी शादी, आपकी माँगें सबकुछ पहले दिन से ही अनुचित थीं। इंद्राणी ने भी कहा, "अभय को अकीरा का अपमान नहीं करना चाहिए था।"

अरुणा बोलीं, "तुम्हें बहुत अच्छे से मालूम है कि वेद को जल्दी गुस्सा नहीं आता

और अगर आता है तो फिर आता है। अभय ने वेद के सामने कुछ ज्यादा ही भाग्य आजमा लिया।"

नीलू गुस्से में आ चुकी थी, वह चिल्लाई, "इससे पहले मैं पुलिस को बुलाऊँ, चले जाओ यहाँ से। फिर कभी अपनी शक्लें मत दिखाना मुझे।"

आँखें ऊपर की ओर घुमाते हुए पिंकी बोलीं, "हमें भी कौन सा यहाँ रुकने का मन है! इससे अच्छा है कि हम कहीं पेंट सूख रहा हो तो वो देख लें।"

सारी तमीज, सारी समझ, विवेक, बुद्धि नीलू को छोड़ चुकी थीं। बोली, "मैं कहती हूँ निकलो यहाँ से।"

"हम तो खुद ही खुश हैं यहाँ से जाकर।" पिंकी चिल्लाईं। उन्होंने अकीरा का हाथ पकड़ा और विवाह स्थल से बाहर चली गईं।

अकीरा के सामने सबकुछ धुँधला था। वह हवेली तो पहुँच गई थी, पर वह अपने होशो-हवास में नहीं थी। सोचा तो उसका दिमाग भी कह रहा था कि वेद ने कुछ गलत नहीं किया। दूसरी तरफ उसका दिमाग कह रहा था कि वेद ने अपना वादा पूरा नहीं किया। बहस की जा सकती थी। चुप भी रहता तो उसी के लिए। वेद अगर नहीं समझ सका तो कोई फायदा नहीं।

अकीरा के सामने सबकुछ धुँधला था। वह हवेली तो पहुँच गई थी, पर वह अपने होशो-हवास में नहीं थी। सोचा तो उसका दिमाग भी कह रहा था कि वेद ने कुछ गलत नहीं किया। दूसरी तरफ उसका दिमाग कह रहा था कि वेद ने अपना वादा पूरा नहीं किया। बहस की जा सकती थी। चुप भी रहता तो उसी के लिए। वेद अगर नहीं समझ सका तो कोई फायदा नहीं।

वेदिका जब दवाई का बक्सा लेकर वेद की ओर भागी और मरहम लगाने की कोशिश की, तब वेद को अहसास हुआ कि उसकी कोहनी छिल गई है। उसके शरीर के विभिन्न अंग दर्द कर रहे थे। अब जोश कम हो गया था तो असर दिख रहा था। उसने वेदिका को दूर किया।

अकीरा से बात करना ज्यादा जरूरी था। वह घुटनों पर बैठा, धीरे से उसके हाथ पकड़े और बोला, "मैं अपना संतुलन बिल्कुल नहीं खोता···लेकिन जब अभय ने तुम्हें गाली दी···" वह ठीक से कह नहीं पा रहा था। उसने अकीरा को अपनी आँखों में देखने को कहा। "मुझे माफ कर दो···"

अकीरा वेद की आँखों में देख रही थी। वेद की आँखों में अकीरा के लिए चिंता थी तो अकीरा की आँखों में वेद के लिए दोषारोपण "तुमने अपनी बात नहीं रखी न!"

अकीरा के साथ एक जो धैर्य का बाँध वेद ने बाँध रखा था, वह टूट गया। वेद ने अकीरा को हिलाते हुए कहा, "तुम्हें क्या हो गया? अभय ने शादी में सबके सामने गाली

दी ? क्या हो गया है तुम्हारी गरिमा और स्वाभिमान को ?"

"वेद!" अरुणा ने वेद को रोकने की कोशिश की।

"नहीं नानी···ये आज की बात नहीं है। तुम्हें इतना आगाह करने के बाद भी तुमने यह शादी का प्रोजेक्ट लिया। तुम मेरी क्यों सुनोगी!"

अपनी तरफ इशारा करते हुए खुद को गाली देते हुए कहा, "वेद तो···(गाली) है। क्या हो गया, बोलने दो। लेकिन अगर कोई निचले स्तर पर उतरता है तो वेद को ही दोष दो। वाह! क्या बात!"

अकीरा सदमे से ठंडी-सी हो रखी थी। वह व्यंग्यात्मक रूप से हँसते हुए बोली, "बिल्कुल ठीक! मैं ही गलत हूँ। हमेशा की तरह···"

"उसके कहने का यह मतलब नहीं था अकीरा!" कबीर ने बहस की।

"फिर क्या मतलब है, जरा समझाना ? वेद की बातों से साफ जाहिर है कि वो ये कहना चाहता है कि मैंने जिंदगी में कुछ ठीक किया ही नहीं।"

वेद ने अपना चेहरा हाथों में छुपा लिया। अकीरा और व्यंग्यात्मक रूप में हँसकर बोली, "देखा जाए तो वेद ने सही कहा। मैं तो असफल ही हूँ, फेल्यर (असफल) हूँ। मैंने न माता-पिता की सुनी, फिर मोहित जैसे घटिया इनसान से जुड़ी और अब ये शादी में तमाशा···।"

वेदिका ने सांत्वना से अकीरा के कंधे पर हाथ रखा, "तुम्हारी गलती नहीं है अकीरा! अभय है ही घटिया इनसान।"

वेदिका ने सांत्वना से अकीरा के कंधे पर हाथ रखा, "तुम्हारी गलती नहीं है अकीरा! अभय है ही घटिया इनसान।"
"हाँ! छोड़ो न। हम कुछ और सोच लेंगे। मुझ पर विश्वास करो।" वेद ने दुबारा अकीरा का हाथ पकड़कर कहा।
"हाँऽऽऽ।" अरुणा ने साथ दिया।
"भूल-चूक माफ करो, मिट्टी पाओ।"

"हाँ! छोड़ो न। हम कुछ और सोच लेंगे। मुझ पर विश्वास करो।" वेद ने दुबारा अकीरा का हाथ पकड़कर कहा।

"हाँऽऽऽ।" अरुणा ने साथ दिया।

"भूल-चूक माफ करो, मिट्टी पाओ।"

अकीरा ने किसी की भी बात की कोई प्रतिक्रिया नहीं दी। उन सबके लिए वो घटना मामूली होगी, पर अकीरा के लिए नहीं थी।

उसने ऊपर की तरफ देखा तो वेद घुटनों के बल बैठकर गिड़गिड़ाकर माफी माँग रहा था, "अकीरा, प्लीज! माफ कर दो मुझे, सॉरी कह तो रहा हूँ।"

"अकीरा! प्लीज! माफ कर दो न! इस बार।" पिंकी ने विनती की। पिंकी ने

विश्वास दिलाया, "कुछ नहीं होगा तुम्हारी कंपनी को। और अच्छे लोग मिलेंगे तुम्हें।"

वेद ने भी कहा, "मैं वादा करता हूँ, हम कुछ सोच लेंगे।"

"बिल्कुल नहीं। मत करो कोई वादा।" अकीरा रोते हुए बोली और गुस्से से आँसू पोंछे। "अगर अभय बदतमीज है तो तुम भी हो। पहले दिन उनकी सजावट में तुम्हें खामियाँ नजर आईं। दूसरे दिन तुमने अभय पर पानी उड़ाया। हम जब से यहाँ आए हैं, तब से एक मिनट भी शांति का नहीं मिला। कुछ-न-कुछ होता ही रहता है···मैं वाकई थक चुकी। बहुत हो गया बस।"

अकीरा ने वेद की छाती पर उँगली रखते हुए कहा, "तुम और तुम्हारे पूरे परिवार ने मेरा धीरज खत्म कर दिया है। मुझे लगा था कि शायद मैं यह सँभाल लूँगी, लेकिन मैं गलत थी। किसी परिवार के इतने पागलपन को कोई नहीं सँभाल सकता, कोई नहीं।"

वेद ने ऐसे देखा, मानो कोई मर गया हो। कुछ क्षणों के लिए अकीरा को विजयी महसूस हुआ। उसे भी ऐसा ही महसूस हुआ था, जब नीलू मासी ने उसे बाहर कर दिया था, लेकिन अगले ही क्षण उसे वेद को गले लगाकर माफी माँगने का मन हुआ। गुस्से से अकीरा का दिमाग बंद हो रखा था और शरीर के अवयव निष्क्रिय। वह चुपचाप वेद को शब्दों के लिए संघर्ष करते हुए देखते बैठी रही।

वेद ने ऐसे देखा, मानो कोई मर गया हो। कुछ क्षणों के लिए अकीरा को विजयी महसूस हुआ। उसे भी ऐसा ही महसूस हुआ था, जब नीलू मासी ने उसे बाहर कर दिया था, लेकिन अगले ही क्षण उसे वेद को गले लगाकर माफी माँगने का मन हुआ। गुस्से से अकीरा का दिमाग बंद हो रखा था और शरीर के अवयव निष्क्रिय। वह चुपचाप वेद को शब्दों के लिए संघर्ष करते हुए देखते बैठी रही।

"वाह! क्या भाषण था!" वेद फुसफुसाया। अकीरा के पेट में मरोड़ उठी, पर वह हिली नहीं।

"मैं जानकर चल रहा हूँ कि अब हमारे बीच में भी अब कुछ नहीं है।" अकीरा ने वेद के बंद गले से निकली आवाज सुनी। वह भी वेद से दूर होने की कल्पना से सिहर गई, पर गुस्सा उस पर हावी था। अकीरा जानबूझकर उसे नहीं देख रही थी। उसमें भी वेद की तरफ देखने की हिम्मत नहीं बची थी।

"हाँ! सब खत्म···" अकीरा ने वेद को कहते सुना।

आँखों के कोने से अकीरा ने देखा, वेद पिंकी को कह रहा था, "मॉम! मैं बगीचे में हूँ।"

"ठीक है।" पिंकी का सदमा भी कम नहीं था।

दीवार पर गड़ी हुई नजरें जब अकीरा ने पूरे परिवार पर दौड़ाईं तो वह खुद ही हैरान थी। उसने सभी को, हमेशा सभी को खुश देखा था, हँसते-मुसकराते देखा था। ऐसे उदास चेहरे देखकर अकीरा को लगा, मानो वह उन्हें जानती ही नहीं थी।

अकीरा जोर-जोर से रोने लगी। जब कबीर से उसका रोना नहीं देखा गया तो बोला, "मैं जरा वेद को देखता हूँ।"

बाहर जाकर कुछ ही क्षणों में कबीर लौट आया, यह बताने कि वेद वहाँ नहीं है।

इससे पहले कि कोई कुछ कहे, वेदिका ने कहा, "अरे! भैया अपनी पसंदीदा जगह पर होंगे; छत पर। मैं देखती हूँ।"

"हाँ।" रीशी ने हामी भरी और वे छत की ओर चल पड़े। वेदिका थोड़ी देर बाद दौड़ती हुई आई, "भैया छत पर नहीं हैं।"

"अपने कमरे में होगा।" अविनाश बोला।

वेदिका चिल्लाई, "हम पूरा घर ढूँढ़ आए हैं, कहीं नहीं हैं।"

सभी शांत पड़ गए और हैरत से एक-दूसरे को देख रहे थे। अरुणा बोली, "उसे फोन लगाओ।"

"हाँऽऽऽ।" वेदिका ने फोन लगाया, घंटी की आवाज आई, लेकिन फोन बीच मेज पर ही पड़ा था। वेदिका परेशान हो गई, "उफ्फ!"

इंद्राणी ने घर के नौकर को बुलाकर पूछा, "बेटा, आपने किसी को बाहर जाते देखा?"

वेदिका चिल्लाई, "हम पूरा घर ढूँढ़ आए हैं, कहीं नहीं हैं।"
सभी शांत पड़ गए और हैरत से एक-दूसरे को देख रहे थे। अरुणा बोली, "उसे फोन लगाओ।"
"हाँऽऽऽ।" वेदिका ने फोन लगाया, घंटी की आवाज आई, लेकिन फोन बीच मेज पर ही पड़ा था। वेदिका परेशान हो गई, "उफ्फ!"
इंद्राणी ने घर के नौकर को बुलाकर पूछा, "बेटा, आपने किसी को बाहर जाते देखा?"

उसने मना कर दिया, "लेकिन मैंने राजवीर बाबा की बाइक की आवाज सुनी।"

प्रमोद गैराज की तरफ भागता हुआ गया और वापस आकर बोला, "वेद बाइक पर बाहर गया है; बाइक जगह पर नहीं है।"

रीशी खड़ा हुआ, "मुझे लुधियाना की वे सारी जगहें मालूम हैं, जहाँ वेद भैया जा सकते हैं। चलो! उन्हें ढूँढ़ते हैं।"

"हाँ चलो, मैं गाड़ी की चाबी लेकर आता हूँ।" कबीर बोला।

अविनाश ने रोक दिया, "मुझे लगता है, तुम्हें यहीं रहना चाहिए, प्लीज!"

"क्यों?"

अविनाश को, घर की सभी औरतों को सदमे और डर में देखते हुए देखा तो कबीर

समझ गया। वेदिका और पिंकी का माथा चूमते हुए अविनाश और बाकी पुरुष घर से बाहर चले गए।

“कुछ नहीं।” वेदिका और पिंकी को गले लगाते हुए कबीर ने दिलासा दिलाई।

अकीरा अपनी जगह बैठी हुई थी; बिल्कुल नहीं हिली। घर के सभी सदस्यों को अत्यंत परेशान और सहमा हुआ देखकर उसे अहसास हुआ कि उसने क्या कर दिया है! वह और भी डर गई और उसकी आँखों के सामने अँधेरा छाने लगा। उस अँधेरे में उसे ‘पछतावे’ शब्द का असल अर्थ समझ आया।

□

46

ग्लानि? दुःख? दर्द?

अकीरा को समझ ही नहीं आ रहा था कि उसे क्या महसूस हो रहा है। उसे पेट और पूरे शरीर में मानो अजीब सा हो रहा था और अलग ही तरह की लहर उसमें उठ रही थी और मानो आँखों से बाहर बह रही थी। वह निरुद्‌देश्य-सी हवेली के अंदर-बाहर घूम रही थी। उसे अपने आसपास हवा हर तरह ठंडी महसूस हो रही थी। वह हवेली, जो ठहाकों से गूँजती रहती थी, वह अचानक शांत थी। सबकुछ उसकी वजह से।

उसका ध्यान दरवाजे की सीढ़ियों पर बैठी वेदिका की तरफ गया। अभी कुछ ही समय से वेद गायब था, पर लग रहा था कि वेदिका पाँच साल बूढ़ी हो गई हो। अकीरा इस कल्पना से और सहम गई कि उसकी वजह से आज वे सब तकलीफ में हैं।

उससे भी ज्यादा तकलीफ और चिंता वेद की थी। किसी को नहीं मालूम था कि वेद कहाँ है? सभी पुरुषों ने पूरा शहर ढूँढ़ लिया, पर वेद का कहीं पता नहीं चला। वेद अपने किसी रिश्तेदार के घर भी नहीं गया था और न ही वापस मुंबई। पता नहीं वेद कहाँ गायब था? अकीरा के पास वेद का इंतजार करने के सिवाय कोई चारा नहीं था।

अकीरा खुद को हमेशा व्यावहारिक समझती थी। उसे अपने जीवन, हर व्यक्ति के लिए अपनी भावनाएँ स्पष्टतया पता थीं। वह हँसमुख और बेफिक्र लड़की थी, लेकिन हर रिश्ते की सीमा रेखा उसने खींच रखी थी। मोहित के साथ भी उसने नपा-तुला रिश्ता रखा था। खैर, वेद से रिश्ता पागलपन में ही उलझा रहा, और बहुत ही अलग तरह के संबंध में तब्दील हुआ। मोहित से छुटकारा पाने की कोशिश में वेद ने उसे असमंजस में डाल दिया था। लेकिन वेद ने उसकी गरिमा बनाए रखने के लिए एड़ी-चोटी का जोर लगा दिया था।

अगर उस समय वेद अकीरा के स्वाभिमान और गरिमा के लिए लड़ा तो अभी उसका लड़ना जायज था। वेद में अकीरा के लिए बेहद अपनापन था, जिसके कारण वह वेद से कट नहीं पाई और न ही दूर रह पाई। अकीरा जानती थी कि वह वेद से प्रेम करने लगी है। अकीरा घुटने मोड़कर वेदिका के पास बैठ गई। अकीरा खुद से पूछना चाह रही

थी कि उसने अपने प्यार का इजहार वेद से क्यों नहीं किया?

यदि शादी में सबकुछ ठीक रहता तो अकीरा ने तय किया था कि वह वेद को 21वीं डेट पर ले जाएगी। उसने सोच रखा था कि उस दिन वेद से अपने मन की बात कह देगी। वह वेद को बताना चाहती थी कि वह वेद के बिना अपने जीवन की कल्पना नहीं कर सकती। और अपने प्यार को स्वीकार करनेवाली थी। अब यह ख्वाब दूर का लग रहा था। "किसी ने पलटकर फोन किया?" वेदिका ने अचानक पूछा। वह गेट को ऐसे देख रही थी, मानो वेद आने ही वाला है।

इसी बीच वेदिका अचानक अकीरा की ओर मुड़ी और बोली, "जब दादा-दादी से मिलते थे तो वे दादी को नेल पॉलिश का अनोखा रंग उपहार में देते। और उसके लिए वे कई बार दिल्ली तक जाते। क्यों? क्योंकि दादी ने एक बार सहज ही कह दिया था कि उनको अपने नाखून को रंगीन देखना पसंद है। ऐसी स्थिति में भी अकीरा थोड़ा सा मुसकराते हुए बोली, "कितना अलग तरह का प्रेम होगा न!"

"नहीं…।"

वेदिका की आँखों से आँसू बहने लगे। शायद वेदिका का वेद के लिए इतना प्यार अकीरा ने दूसरी बार देखा था। पहली बार तब देखा था, जब वेद ने बीमार होने का नाटक किया था।

"आइ होप (मुझे आशा है) वो ठीक होंगे।"…न जाने वेदिका ने वेद की चिंता करते हुए और रोते हुए कितनी बार कहा होगा।

इसी बीच वेदिका अचानक अकीरा की ओर मुड़ी और बोली, "जब दादा-दादी से मिलते थे तो वे दादी को नेल पॉलिश का अनोखा रंग उपहार में देते। और उसके लिए वे कई बार दिल्ली तक जाते। क्यों? क्योंकि दादी ने एक बार सहज ही कह दिया था कि उनको अपने नाखून को रंगीन देखना पसंद है।

ऐसी स्थिति में भी अकीरा थोड़ा सा मुसकराते हुए बोली, "कितना अलग तरह का प्रेम होगा न!"

"उसके बाद नानाजी…" कहते-कहते वेदिका की आँखें बह निकलीं। "उन दिनों में किसी औरत का मदिरा व्यवसाय करना बहुत बड़ी बात थी। नानाजी एक शब्द नहीं बोलते थे, लेकिन सभी डील्स और व्यापार सभी में बैठते। इसलिए नहीं कि उन्हें नानी पर विश्वास नहीं था; वह इसलिए कि सुरक्षा की दृष्टि से नानी के साथ रहना जरूरी था।"

"मॉम को शादी के बाद कुछ अलग-सा हनीमून चाहिए था, तो पापा उन्हें 80 दिनों में दुनिया घुमाने ले गए। यही उपहार था।"

वेदिका की आँखें और नम हो गईं, "और मेरा प्यारा कबीर! झूठ बोलने से लेकर मेरा काम पूरा करने तक; क्या नहीं किया इसने?" अकीरा की आँखों में देखकर वेदिका

बोली, "बात केवल इतनी है कि यह परिवार पागल दिखता है, लोग अजीब हैं। हर इनसान अपनी मरजी का मालिक है। कुछ भी करते हैं, पर हमने एक चीज हमेशा सही की और वह है कि हमारे परिवार में प्यार सभी ने शिद्दत से किया। या तो गहराई से किया, नहीं तो नहीं किया। बीच का प्यार जैसा कुछ भी नहीं था।" अकीरा चुप रही। वेदिका ने जताया, "वेद भैया भी अलग नहीं हैं। जब वो प्यार करते हैं तो दिल की तहों से। वैसा ही पूर्ण गहरा प्यार! तुम समझ गई मैं क्या कहना चाहती हूँ?"

अकीरा ने धीमी आवाज में हामी भरी। अकीरा के सिर को थपकाकर वेदिका ने समझाया, "अकीरा! भैया करके दिखानेवालों में से हैं। मुझे विश्वास है कि अब तक वो तुमसे काफी खुल के बात कर चुके होंगे। वे ऐसे हैं, जो प्यार शब्दों से नहीं, हरकतों से दिखाएँगे। देख लो, उन्होंने तुम्हारे लिए क्या किया..."

अकीरा के पास कहने लायक कुछ बचा नहीं था।

"वेद भैया बहुत स्वाभिमानी हैं अकीरा! अगर उन्होंने अभय से समझौता किया तो बहुत बड़ी बात थी। उन्होंने ऐसा तुम्हारे लिए किया। आज भी वे तुम्हारे लिए लड़े। अगर तुम उनकी इस बात की इज्जत नहीं करती तो कम-से-कम उन पर सवाल तो न करतीं।" वेदिका रोते-रोते कहे जा रही थी।

"वेद भैया बहुत स्वाभिमानी हैं अकीरा! अगर उन्होंने अभय से समझौता किया तो बहुत बड़ी बात थी। उन्होंने ऐसा तुम्हारे लिए किया। आज भी वे तुम्हारे लिए लड़े। अगर तुम उनकी इस बात की इज्जत नहीं करती तो कम-से-कम उन पर सवाल तो न करतीं।" वेदिका रोते-रोते कहे जा रही थी।

अकीरा के हृदय में दर्द की इतनी टीस उठी कि सहायता के लिए उसने वेदिका का हाथ पकड़ा। वह जोर-जोर से रोने लगी, "मैं समझती हूँ! मैं समझ रही हूँ।"

वेदिका ने अकीरा को थोड़ा सा अपने बाजुओं में लिया और कहने लगी, "मुझे माफ करना, अगर इस समय मेरी बातें तुम्हें बुरी लग रही हों, पर जो प्रोजेक्ट तुम्हें अभी मिला है, वह तुम्हें मिलता ही नहीं, अगर तुम वेद को डेट न कर रही होतीं। तुम किस स्वाभिमान की बात कर रही हो? तुम्हारी कंपनी तो वैसे भी बंद हो जानी थी।"

"आई एम सो सॉरी!" माफी माँगते हुए अकीरा फूट-फूटकर रो रही थी।

वेदिका ने थककर लंबी साँस छोड़ते हुए कहा, "बस भैया घर आ जाएँ।"

खुद के अंदर के शैतानों से जूझते हुए वेदिका और अकीरा चुपचाप बैठे हुए थे। वेदिका अपने मन की भड़ास निकाल चुकी थी। अकीरा के पास कहने जैसा कुछ नहीं था और दोनों ही थक चुकी थीं।

कबीर सांत्वना देने पहुँचा और रीशी सीढ़ियों की सबसे ऊपरवाली सीढ़ी पर जा बैठा। "कबीर! हम गुमशुदा के लिए रिपोर्ट नहीं करवा सकते?" वेदिका ने पूछा।

"मैंने अनिल मामाजी से पूछा, लेकिन उनहोंने कहा कि हम 24 घंटे से पहले रिपोर्ट नहीं लिखवा सकते। क्योंकि वेद कोई बच्चा नहीं है और न ही उसका अपहरण हुआ है। इसीलिए हमें कल तक रुकना ही पड़ेगा।"

"उफ्फ!"

कबीर ने वेदिका की आँखों में देखकर कहा, "सुनो! मैं सोच रहा था कि हम अस्पतालों में जाकर देखें।"

यह सुनकर अकीरा के पैरों तले जमीन खिसक गई। "क्या?" "मैंने यह बात अंदर नहीं कही, क्योंकि यह सुन सभी परेशान हो जाएँगे, लेकिन वेद लेकर भी तो बाइक गया है।" कबीर बोला। पहली बार शायद रीशी कबीर से सहमत था, "हाँ। अगर ऐसा है तो हमें वेद भैया के पास जल्द-से-जल्द पहुँचना चाहिए।"

यह सुनकर अकीरा के पैरों तले जमीन खिसक गई। "क्या?"

"मैंने यह बात अंदर नहीं कही, क्योंकि यह सुन सभी परेशान हो जाएँगे, लेकिन वेद लेकर भी तो बाइक गया है।" कबीर बोला।

पहली बार शायद रीशी कबीर से सहमत था, "हाँ। अगर ऐसा है तो हमें वेद भैया के पास जल्द-से-जल्द पहुँचना चाहिए।"

अकीरा मानो सुन्न थी, शब्द ही नहीं जुटा पा रही थी। उसकी आँखों से आँसू छलक रहे थे। वह कबीर और रीशी की सलाह सुनकर, सोचकर दंग थी। वेदिका लाचारी से बोली, "ऐसे मत कहो यार! वह खुद के गलत गुस्से को ठंडा करने गया है बस।"

कबीर ने वेदिका को अपने में समेटकर सांत्वना देनी चाही। "अब मेरी बात ध्यान से सुनो। अब हमें खुद को किसी भी परिस्थिति के लिए तैयार रखना है। अब ये रोने का समय नहीं। हमें वेद को ढूँढ़ना होगा। हाँ न?"

कबीर की बात समझकर दोनों ने सिर हिलाया और गाड़ी में जाकर बैठ गईं। वे अलग-अलग अस्पतालों में जाने के लिए चल पड़े।

अकीरा के लिए इससे कठिन समय शायद कोई नहीं रहा। उसका दिमाग बुरे खयालों से थक चुका था। और जितना बुरा खयाल आता, उसे साँस लेना उतना ही दूभर हो जाता। 'अगर वाकई कुछ गड़बड़ हो गई होगी तो वह वेद के परिवार को मुँह नहीं दिखा पाएगी। और न जाने वो खुद को क्या समझाएगी।" यह सब सोचते हुए अकीरा सहमी हुई कार में बैठी हुई थी।

वे कई अस्पतालों से क्लीनिकों की ओर, फिर वहाँ से नर्सिंग होम में गए, पर वेद का कहीं पता न चला। जब हर जगह से वेद के न होने की खबर मिलती तो अकीरा राहत की साँस लेती और उम्मीद जगती कि कम-से-कम वेद शारीरिक तौर पर सुरक्षित है। आखिर वेद गया कहाँ? इस प्रश्न के साथ वे आखिर एक अस्पताल में पहुँचे, जहाँ के अतिथि कक्ष (Reception) पर उनसे पूछा गया, "आप किस उम्र के व्यक्ति को ढूँढ़ रहे हैं?"

खून का घूँट पीते हुए मानो वेदिका बोली, "29 वर्ष के।"

"ठीक है..." यह कहते हुए उस आदमी ने कंप्यूटर में कुछ देखा और कहा, "आज शाम को अधिकारियों ने नदी में से एक लाश निकाली है। खुदकुशी का मामला है। लेकिन उसके पास पहचान के लिए कुछ नहीं था। आप बॉडी देख के बता दीजिए।"

अतिथि कक्ष के सामने जो बेंच थी, अकीरा वहीं सुन्न-सी बैठ गई।

"वो शाम को जो नई बॉडी आई है, वो दिखा दो इनको।" अतिथि कक्ष के अधिकारी ने एक व्यक्ति को इशारा करके कहा।

किसी अनहोनी की कल्पना से ही वेदिका चिल्ला पड़ी, "कबीर! ये लोग क्या बकवास कर रहे हैं?"

अतिथि कक्ष के सामने जो बेंच थी, अकीरा वहीं सुन्न-सी बैठ गई। "वो शाम को जो नई बॉडी आई है, वो दिखा दो इनको।" अतिथि कक्ष के अधिकारी ने एक व्यक्ति को इशारा करके कहा। किसी अनहोनी की कल्पना से ही वेदिका चिल्ला पड़ी, "कबीर! ये लोग क्या बकवास कर रहे हैं?"

वेदिका को सँभालते हुए कबीर बोला, "ये वक्त लड़ाई का नहीं है, अभी वेद ज्यादा जरूरी है।"

कबीर ने रीशी को देखकर कहा, "रीशी, तुम इन्हें गाड़ी में ले जाओ, मैं देखकर आता हूँ।"

रीशी ने हामी भरी और वेदिका को अपने में सँभाला। वेदिका रीशी से चिपककर रोने लगी। रीशी रोया नहीं, पर डर तो वह भी गया था। अकीरा ने कबीर को इतना निराश पहले कभी नहीं देखा था। कबीर पीला पड़ चुका था। उस आदमी के साथ अंदर जाते हुए कबीर मानो सूख चुका था। अकीरा और डर गई। उसे अपने आसपास सबकुछ धुँधला महसूस हो रहा था। उसे लगा, मानो दर्द ने उसे घेरकर अँधेरी खाई में पटक दिया हो। और वेद को देखे बिना उसमें जान आएगी भी नहीं।

47

कोई भी इनसान कैसी प्रतिक्रिया करेगा, यदि कोई बताए कि उसका प्रियजन मर चुका है? प्रियजन? अकीरा कार की पिछली सीट पर बैठी ही रह गई। गहन चिंतन और सोच उसे परेशान किए जा रही थी। अकीरा को अहसास हो गया था कि वह वेद के प्यार में बहुत गहरे तक जा चुकी है। जहाँ से वापस आना मुश्किल है।

अकीरा वेद से प्रेम कैसे न करती? अगर नहीं करती तो मूर्ख कहलाती। बस एक बात अकीरा को नहीं पता थी और वह यह कि वह कितना अधिक वेद से प्रेम करती है? अकीरा को उस दिन तक खुद ही नहीं मालूम था कि वह वेद को कितना चाहने लगी थी। उसे तब अहसास हुआ, जब वह अपना सबकुछ खोने की कगार पर थी और दुर्घटना का मानो वह दृश्य सामने देख रही थी।

कार की सामनेवाली सीट पर वेदिका धाड़ें मारकर रोए जा रही थी और काबू में नहीं आ रही थी, लेकिन अकीरा के कान में आवाजें सीसा घोल रही थीं।

"अरेऽऽऽ दी! वो वेद पक्का नहीं होगा। वेद भैया कभी भी नदी में नहीं कूदेंगे और लुधियाना में तो कभी नहीं।" रीशी बोला।

वेदिका और ज्यादा रोने लगी। उसके बालों पर हाथ रखकर रीशी ने बात मजाक पर घुमाने की कोशिश की, "वेद ऐसा इनसान है, जिसे अगर खुदकुशी करनी होगी तो वह सैन फ्रांसिस्को जाकर गोल्डन गेट ब्रिज से कूदेगा।"

"यह तो सच कहा।" वेदिका रीशी भाई से सटी रही। रीशी ने अकीरा को देखा। वह कार के दरवाजे के पास ही खड़ा रहा। बहुत देर तक कुछ नहीं बोला। फिर अकीरा के कंधे पर थपकी देते हुए बोला, "फिक्र मत करो, सब ठीक हो जाएगा।"

अकीरा ने कसकर रीशी का हाथ पकड़ा और बोली, "वह वेद नहीं है न!" रीशी लाचारी से अकीरा के सामने झुका। अकीरा अंदर तक हिली हुई थी सदमे से। सिर्फ कुछ घंटों पहले वेद उसके सामने गिड़गिड़ा रहा था कि एक बार उसकी तरफ देख ले, उससे बात कर ले, पर वह तैयार नहीं थी। ऐसे कैसे वह उनके जीवन में साथ का अंतिम क्षण था? उसे इतनी क्रूर सजा कैसे मिल सकती है?

रीशी ने विश्वास दिलाया, "अकीरा, मेरा भरोसा करो, वह वेद नहीं हो सकता।"

रीशी के इन शब्दों ने अकीरा पर उलटा ही प्रभाव किया। जो आँसू उसने रोक रखे थे, वे बह निकले। वह इतनी जोर से रो रही थी। वेदिका और रीशी, दोनों उसे सँभालने में लगे हुए थे।

वेदिका बोली, "वेद भैया बेवकूफ हैं, पर इतने नहीं हैं।"

"हे सुनो…।"

पीछे से कबीर की गहरी आवाज आई। अकीरा जम गई। पता नहीं क्या सुनने को मिलता है? उसकी रगों में डर की लहर-सी दौड़ गई। उसने सदमे की स्थिति में रही वेदिका को कबीर से पूछते हुए सुना, "क्या हुआ?"

कबीर ने वेदिका का हाथ पकड़कर उसकी आँखों में देखकर राहत की साँस छोड़ते हुए कहा, "वह वेद नहीं है।"

अकीरा थोड़ी सी होश में आई। एक पल में सँभलती तो दूसरी में आपे से बाहर हो जाती। वह खुल कर रो ली; कम-से-कम अभी के लिए दुनिया में सबकुछ ठीक है।

कबीर ने वेदिका का हाथ पकड़कर उसकी आँखों में देखकर राहत की साँस छोड़ते हुए कहा, "वह वेद नहीं है।" अकीरा थोड़ी सी होश में आई। एक पल में सँभलती तो दूसरी में आपे से बाहर हो जाती। वह खुल कर रो ली; कम-से-कम अभी के लिए दुनिया में सबकुछ ठीक है।

इसी राहत के साथ वे सभी घर के लिए वापस निकल पड़े। जैसे ही घर में घुसनेवाले थे, पिंकी उनपर चिल्लाईं, "कहाँ थे तुम?"

वेदिका ने धीरे से जवाब दिया, "मैंने कहा था, आपको मैसेज भी किया था कि हम एक-दो जगह और देखेंगे।"

पिंकी ने आराम से पूछा, "कुछ पता चला?"

"नहीं! पर क्या आपने कुछ खाया?"

"मैं कैसे खाती?" पिंकी गुस्से में पलटकर बोलीं।

"पिंकी, उम्मीद मत छोड़ो। हम उसे ढूँढ़ लेंगे।" शालिनी ने कहा।

अविनाश ने गहरी साँस लेते हुए कहा, "हम केवल प्रार्थना ही कर सकते हैं भाभी!"

अकीरा निराशा से पूरे परिवार की ओर देख रही थी। वह ग्लानि में डूबी जा रही थी। उसने इंद्राणी का हाथ अपने हाथ में लेकर कहा, "मुझे बिल्कुल उम्मीद नहीं थी कि ऐसा कुछ हो जाएगा।"

इंद्राणी ने सिर झुकाकर कहा, "किसी को भी उम्मीद नहीं थी।"

अकीरा ने अपने कान पकड़े और जोर से रो पड़ी, "आई एम सॉरी! मुझे माफ कर दीजिए।"

अरुणा ने एक क्षण देखा, फिर बोलीं, "अकीरा, अब और ज्यादा नाटक करने की जरूरत नहीं है। अब रोने का कोई फायदा नहीं है।"

उनकी बातें सुन अकीरा और भी रोने लगी, "मैं कम-से-कम माफी तो माँग सकती हूँ।"

"कोई जरूरत नहीं है। असल में वेद ने ज्यादा अक्ल दिखाई कि बिना बहस किए या चिल्लाए चला गया। वह तुमसे नाराज था। अब हमारा क्या? इस उमर में यही देखना बच गया था अब।" अरुणा की आवाज में रूखापन था।

"कोई जरूरत नहीं है। असल में वेद ने ज्यादा अक्ल दिखाई कि बिना बहस किए या चिल्लाए चला गया। वह तुमसे नाराज था। अब हमारा क्या? इस उमर में यही देखना बच गया था अब।" अरुणा की आवाज में रूखापन था। इंद्राणी ने अरुणा के हाथ को थपथपाते हुए कहा, "वेद बहुत दिनों से विवेकशीलता दिखा रहा था अरुणा!"

इंद्राणी ने अरुणा के हाथ को थपथपाते हुए कहा, "वेद बहुत दिनों से विवेकशीलता दिखा रहा था अरुणा!"

"सही! अच्छों-अच्छों के भी बुरे दिन आते हैं। शायद उसका वही बुरा दिन आज था।"

"और शायद वेद अकीरा को लेकर बहुत भावुक हो गया है··· मेरा मतलब हो गया था।" अविनाश बोला।

"अकीरा! मुझे समझ आ रहा है कि तुमसे यह सवाल इस समय नहीं पूछा जाना चाहिए, पर क्या तुम वेद को लेकर भविष्य के बारे में गंभीरता से सोचती हो?" इंद्राणी ने सवाल किया।

सभी की आँखें, चाहे दोष देनेवाली या गुस्सेवाली, अकीरा पर ही थीं। लेकिन अकीरा में किसी की आँखों का सामना करने की हिम्मत नहीं थी। लेकिन ऐसे समय में एक बात स्वीकारने की हिम्मत उसमें आ गई थी। हालाँकि उसकी आवाज काँप रही थी, पर उसने इंद्राणी के सवाल के जवाब में कहा, "हाँ!"

अरुणा ने राहत की साँस ली, "मुझे तुम अच्छी लगती हो अकीरा, लेकिन हम जानते हैं कि तुमने बदला लेने के लिए वेद को खरी-खोटी सुनाई। हाँ या न?"

अकीरा की जुबान पर ताला था, अरुणा ने प्यार से अकीरा के सिर पर हाथ फेरा, "ये बूढ़ी आँखें हैं बेटा! चेहरे पढ़ना बखूबी जानती हैं। तुम वेद को सिर्फ ये दिखाना चाहती थी कि कोई प्यारी चीज खोने पर कैसा महसूस होता है, लेकिन क्या वाकई तुमने जो खोया, वो सबसे प्यारा था?"

अकीरा चिल्लाकर यह बताना चाहती थी कि 'नहीं? वो नहीं, वेद सबसे प्यारा है।'

“हम ये नहीं कह रहे कि काम जरूरी नहीं है। लेकिन अकीरा, अगर वह काम तुम्हारी गरिमा और स्वाभिमान की कीमत माँगता है तो करना ठीक है क्या?” अविनाश ने धीमी लेकिन गंभीर आवाज में कहा। “वह हमेशा परिवार की आवाज बनता था और आज भी यही हुआ। तुम कह सकती हो कि वेद ने अभय को क्यों पीटा? सही है। पर क्या तुम उस इनसान को छोड़ सकती हो, जिसने तुम्हारे लिए अपने भाई को पीटा?”

इंद्राणी ने अकीरा के आँसू पोछते हुए कहा, “आदमी ही नहीं रहेगा तो क्या करोगी उसकी गलतियों का पुत्तर?”

रीशी ने तकिए पर घूँसा मारते हुए कहा, “भैया को अभय को पहले ही पीट देना चाहिए था।”

एक क्षण के लिए ही क्यों न हो, सब मुसकराए। “किसी और बात के लिए नहीं, पर कम-से-कम मुझे भोलू इसलिए वापस चाहिए, ताकि बता सकूँ कि वह अभय से कितना अच्छा मुक्केबाज है।” अकीरा ने मन में प्रार्थना की। अगर वेद अच्छा मुक्केबाज है तो आए और मुझसे लड़ाई करे न! ऐसे भागना ठीक थोड़ी है।

“सही कह रहे हो! सोचो, अब अभय को कल कितना मेकअप चाहिए होगा…!” कबीर बोला।

एक क्षण के लिए ही क्यों न हो, सब मुसकराए। “किसी और बात के लिए नहीं, पर कम-से-कम मुझे भोलू इसलिए वापस चाहिए, ताकि बता सकूँ कि वह अभय से कितना अच्छा मुक्केबाज है।”

अकीरा ने मन में प्रार्थना की। अगर वेद अच्छा मुक्केबाज है तो आए और मुझसे लड़ाई करे न! ऐसे भागना ठीक थोड़ी है।

अरुणा ने पलटकर पूछा, “वैसे अभय कैसा है?”

“मैंने भाटियाजी से बात की थी। अभय के जबड़े की हड्डियाँ हिल गई हैं; कलाई में मोच है और दो दाँत टूट गए हैं।”

वेदिका मानो इस खबर से उदास थी, “गलती की! अभय के छोटे-छोटे टुकड़े करके, सिगड़ी पर भून के कौओं को खिलाने चाहिए थे।”

अविनाश वेदिका की ओर देखकर बोला (मुसकराकर), “अब कौओं के प्रति इतनी क्रूर मत हो।”

“अकीरा, अब रोना बंद करो। ऐसे तुम खुद को बीमार कर लोगी।” अरुणा ने प्यार से अकीरा से कहा।

"और क्या···रोने से अच्छा है कि ये सोचो कि जब वेद वापस आए तो क्या करना है ? और कुछ सोचो कि इस झंझट से बाहर कैसे आना है ?" पिंकी ने सुझाया।

जब अकीरा ने कोई जवाब नहीं दिया तो पिंकी ने गहरी साँस लेकर कहा, "प्यार धीरज माँगता है, बेटा! ऐसा कई बार होगा कि तुम्हें अपने साथी की कई बातें बहुत बुरी लगेंगी, लेकिन बात करके हमेशा तुम समस्याएँ सुलझा सकते हो।"

पिंकी की तरफ देखकर इशारा करते हुए अविनाश ने कहा, "मिलकर लड़ो और मुश्किलें दूर करो।"

वेदिका की ओर देखते हुए कबीर बोला, "या फिर साथ में हँस के टाल दो।"

अकीरा दोनों की तरफ (पिंकी-अविनाश, कबीर-वेदिका) हँसकर देखती हुई लेटने चली गई। "अच्छे लोग कभी-कभी आते हैं, अकीरा, और अगर ऐसे लोग जीवन में आएँ तो उन्हें सँभालकर रखना चाहिए।"

"अगर तुम अपने माता-पिता से आर्थिक मदद ले सकती हो तो अपने साथी से क्यों नहीं ? जब काम बन जाए तो पैसे वापस कर दो। इसमें क्या बड़ी बात है ? अगर कल को वेद को आर्थिक सहायता की जरूरत पड़ती है तो तुम भी उसकी सहायता कर सकती हो।"

"जीवनसाथी यही तो करते हैं। एक-दूसरे की मदद करते हैं; एक-दूसरे को बचाते हैं।"

"अगर तुम अपने माता-पिता से आर्थिक मदद ले सकती हो तो अपने साथी से क्यों नहीं ? जब काम बन जाए तो पैसे वापस कर दो। इसमें क्या बड़ी बात है ? अगर कल को वेद को आर्थिक सहायता की जरूरत पड़ती है तो तुम भी उसकी सहायता कर सकती हो।"
"जीवनसाथी यही तो करते हैं। एक-दूसरे की मदद करते हैं; एक-दूसरे को बचाते हैं।"

"जहाँ तक परिवार का संबंध है, वो बदला नहीं जा सकता। अब ये तुम्हें सोचना है कि क्या तुम वेद से इतना प्यार करती हो कि हमें झेल सको या नहीं।" अकीरा के बगल में कंबल रखते हुए अविनाश ने कहा।

पिंकी की आँखों से आँसू झर रहे थे। "पर ये सारे प्रश्न तब के हैं, तब हम अपने लड़के को ढूँढ़ लें।" पूरा कमरा दुबारा शांति और चिंता में डूब गया। सभी लोग जो कुछ कहना चाहते थे, कह चुके थे। पिंकी सही कह रही थीं। अब जो सोचना था, अकीरा को सोचना था।

अकीरा को पता था कि उसमें भी खामियाँ हैं, वह पूर्ण नहीं है और न ही वेद है, फिर भी वेद के प्यार में निस्स्वार्थता है। उन दिनों उसने वेद के साथ जो 20 दिन बिताए,

मानो जिंदगी बिताई थी। शुरू से ही वह समझ चुकी थी कि उसे सबसे ज्यादा क्या चाहिए था? वेद और सिर्फ वेद!

अकीरा ने अपनी आँखें बंद कीं और वेद के लिए प्यार की गरमाहट महसूस की। यह विडंबना थी कि अँधेरे में उसे अपने निर्णय की स्पष्टता दिखाई पड़ रही थी। बस, वेद उस समय वापस आ जाता।

"नानी।" एक मदहोश आवाज अकीरा को सुनाई पड़ी और अकीरा की आँखें अचानक खुलीं। गरदन में दर्द के बावजूद उसने उठकर बैठने की कोशिश की।

"अखबार आ गया क्या?" वही आवाज दुबारा। पता नहीं कब अकीरा को रात में नींद लग गई थी। थक जो गई थी। बदहवासी में अकीरा ने आँखें मसलकर खोलने की कोशिश की। उसे एक बिंदु के रूप में सोने की पोशाक पहने वेद दिखाई दिया। अकीरा की धड़कन बढ़ी।

"नहीं! अखबार ज्यादातर 7:30 बजे के लगभग आता है।" तो उसने देखा, वेद बैठक के कमरे से दूर की तरफ जा रहा था। अकीरा को अपनी आँखों पर विश्वास नहीं हुआ। हाँ! वह वेद ही था। नींद का मारा, पर सुरक्षित। उसी समय अरुणा की भी आँखें खुलीं। उन्होंने अचानक अकीरा को देखा। दोनों को एक साथ अहसास हुआ और दोनों एक साथ चिल्लाईं, "वेद!"

□

48

"वेद!" घर की शांति को चीरती हुई आवाज वेद तक पहुँची। वेद भी अचानक मुड़ा और हैरान था, वह बिना हिले अपनी जगह पर था। वह हैरत भरी निगाहों से अरुणा और अकीरा को देख रहा था और अचानक पूरा परिवार चिल्लाता हुआ नजर आया।

अकीरा की नसों में जिंदगी दौड़ गई, जब वाकई वेद को उसने सामने देखा। वह लड़खड़ाते पैरों से वेद की तरफ दौड़ी और उसपर जा गिरी। खुद को उस पर छोड़ दिया था कि वह वेद की धड़कन भी सुन पा रही थी। मानो पिछले कुछ घंटों की चिंता खत्म होते ही मनुष्य राहत की जिस तरह साँस लेता है, वैसे ही वेद को ठीक देखकर अकीरा को महसूस हो रहा था।

अकीरा की आँखों से आँसू बह रहे थे, जब उसे पता चल गया था, वह कितनी मूर्ख थी और वेद के बिना रह सकती है, ऐसा सोच भी कैसे सकती थी?

अकीरा वेद को देख रही थी। उसे वेद की आँखों में अपने प्रेम की परछाईं नजर आ रही थी। जो दोनों को एक-दूसरे के लिए महसूस हो रहा था, वह सच था, कुछ भी झूठ नहीं था। "ये क्या बेहूदा मजाक था वेद?"

किसी के चिल्लाने की आवाज आई। अकीरा की तंद्रा टूटी। उसने वेद को दुबारा देखा। वेद के चेहरे पर अकीरा के शब्दों का दुःख झलकता दिखाई दे रहा था।

अकीरा ने बेमन से अपने हाथ पीछे कर लिये। क्या वेद उसे इतनी आसानी से माफ कर देता? बिल्कुल नहीं, अकीरा को भी दुःख हुआ। पूरा परिवार वेद पर भेड़ियों के झुंड की तरह टूट पड़ा।

"वेद!" पिंकी उसका नाम लिये जा रही थीं।

"क्या हो रहा है?" वेदिका को गले लगाते हुए वेद ने पूछा।

जब तक वह समझता कि दो औरतें उसके गले लगकर क्यों रो रही हैं, तब तक उसके बहादुर पिता ने आकर उसे गले लगा लिया। फिर दादी, नानी, माँओं, मामाओं, मामियों, कबीर और रीशी ने भी।

वेद चिढ़ गया। शायद मेरे परिवार के लिए पागलखाना ही लेना पड़ेगा या पूरे परिवार का नाम पागलखाने के लिए दर्ज कराना पड़ेगा। इंद्राणी चिल्लाई, "कहाँ थे तुम रात भर ?"

वेद विस्मित था। "क्या मतलब ? मैं सो रहा था।"

"कर लो बात!" प्रमोद ने अपने माथे पर हाथ दे मारा।

"एक सेकंड। ये कहने के बाद कि मैं बगीचे में जा रहा हूँ, तो जाहिर है कि तुम वहीं गए होगे।" अरुणा चिल्लाईं, "हमने तुम्हें सब जगह देखा, पर तुम नहीं मिले।" अरुणा चिल्लाती जा रही थीं।

वेद के स्वर में सच्चाई थी, "तुम सभी की आवाजें मुझे पागल कर रही थीं, इसीलिए मैं छत पर चला गया।"

"तुम छत पर नहीं थे।" वेदिका ने कहा।

वेद ने पलटकर पूछा, "तुमने पानी की टंकी पर देखा ?"

"फिटे मुँह!" अरुणा बोलीं।

"अब इसको धर्मेंद्र बनना है।" यह कहते हुए अरुणा ने अचानक चप्पल निकाली और वेद पर मारने का कोशिश की तो वेद ने रीशी को आगे किया। फिर अरुणा ने दूसरी चप्पल निकाली, जो अविनाश के कंधे पर जा लगी।

वेद हँसते हुए बोला, "वाकई! ये हवाई चप्पलें हैं।"

पिंकी गुस्से से वेद को देख रही थीं, "ये मजाक नहीं है वेद!"

"अब इसको धर्मेंद्र बनना है।" यह कहते हुए अरुणा ने अचानक चप्पल निकाली और वेद पर मारने का कोशिश की तो वेद ने रीशी को आगे किया। फिर अरुणा ने दूसरी चप्पल निकाली, जो अविनाश के कंधे पर जा लगी। वेद हँसते हुए बोला, "वाकई! ये हवाई चप्पलें हैं।"

वेद चुप और गंभीर हो गया। "फिर तुमने क्या किया ?" अविनाश ने पूछा।

"फिर मैं अपने कमरे में गया, नहाया, सोने के कपड़े पहने, सोने की दवाई ली और छत पर जाकर सो गया।" शांत स्वर में वेद ने बताया।

रीशी ऐसे देख रहा था, मानो उसे ट्रक ने मारा हो!

"मतलब तुम आराम से सो रहे थे, जब हम सभी दोस्तों, रिश्तेदारों को फोन कर रहे थे, अस्पताल और मुर्दाघर में तुम्हें पागलों की तरह ढूँढ़ रहे थे।" अविश्वास से वेद की आँखें तेज झपक रही थीं।

"क्याऽऽऽ ?"

"जीऽऽऽ।" रीशी ने कहा।

वेद को अचानक अहसास हुआ कि पिंकी ने उसका हाथ पकड़ा है, जो बर्फ की

तरह ठंडा था। वेद की नजर जब पिंकी के चेहरे पर पड़ी तो उसके चेहरे की थकावट देख मानो धड़कन ही तेज हो गई। सच तो यह था कि उन सभी को देख लग रहा था कि किसी तूफान का सामना करके आए हो। वो चाहता नहीं था, लेकिन उसकी नजर अकीरा पर अटकी हुई थी। वो अभी तक उन्हीं कपड़ों में थी, जो हल्दी की रस्म के समय पहने थे। वह ऐसी लग रही थी मानो उसे मार दिया गया था, लेकिन दुबारा जिंदा की गई हो। बहुत अजीब सा अहसास हुआ वेद को मानो उलटी हो जाएगी।

वेद ने सुना, पिंकी कह रही थीं, "हमने सोचा, तुम कहीं खो गए हो।"

"गुमशुदा! क्यों? कैसे?" वेद ने पूछा।

इंद्राणी फट से बोलीं, "क्योंकि हम तुम्हें वहीं ढूँढ़ नहीं पा रहे थे और मोबाइल तू यहाँ छोड़ गया था। गोविंद ने सुना कि किसी ने राजवीर की मोटरसाइकिल स्टार्ट की। हम ये मानकर चले कि तुम घर छोड़कर गए हो।"

"हमने तुमको कहाँ-कहाँ नहीं ढूँढ़ा! हमने गोविंद को नीलू मासी तक के घर भेजा, ये सोचकर कि तुम वहाँ तो नहीं गए।" सोफे का तकिया उसकी ओर फेंकती हुई वेदिका बोली।

अब वेद को वेदिका और पिंकी के आँसुओं और गुस्से, अकीरा को उसको गले लगाने में अर्थ नजर आ रहा था। कोई और दिन होता तो वह अकीरा की आँखें चूमकर उसे सांत्वना देता, लेकिन कुछ चीजें ही समय के लिए नहीं बनीं।

"गुमशुदा! क्यों? कैसे?" वेद ने पूछा। इंद्राणी फट से बोलीं, "क्योंकि हम तुम्हें वहीं ढूँढ़ नहीं पा रहे थे और मोबाइल तू यहाँ छोड़ गया था। गोविंद ने सुना कि किसी ने राजवीर की मोटरसाइकिल स्टार्ट की। हम ये मानकर चले कि तुम घर छोड़कर गए हो।"

वेदिका जमीन पर बैठ गई।

"ये लुका-छुपी का खेल निर्देशित किया था मार्टिन स्कोरसेस ने और लुधियाना द्वारा संकल्पित था।

"कुछ भी कहो, बहुत ही घटिया रोमांच था फिल्म की कहानी में।" रीशी साँस छोड़ते हुए बोला।

"बिल्कुल! तुम्हें पता है, तुम्हारे चक्कर में हम सरकारी अस्पताल तक गए और मुझे बदकिस्मती से एक लाश भी देखनी पड़ी।" कबीर चिढ़कर बोला।

वेद घबराकर बोला, "ये सब मुझे कैसे पता होगा?"

अविनाश ने पलटकर वेद की बात काटी, "चुप! तुम्हें पता नहीं है, अनिश्चितता की स्थिति में होना क्या होता है, इसलिए ज्यादा मत बोलो।"

"विश्वास कीजिए, मैं समझता हूँ कि कैसा लगा होगा?" वेद ने सफाई देने की

कोशिश की; इतना कहकर वेद ने अपनी आँखें झुका लीं। वह नहीं चाहता था कि अकीरा वेद की आँखों के आँसू देखे।

“मेरी गलती थी। मुझे तुममें से किसी को बता देना चाहिए था। आप सभी के लिए कितनी मुश्किल का समय रहा होगा, मैं समझ सकता हूँ। आई एम सॉरी!” वेद बोला।

इंद्राणी और अरुणा को पास लेकर बोला, “सॉरी नानी, सॉरी दादी!”

अरुणा और इंद्राणी की आँखें भर आईं, “पर ऐसा दुबारा कभी मत करना?”

“क्या? सोऊँ न?” वेद ने पूछा।

अरुणा ने गाल खींचकर कहा, “पेंडू की तरह सोना मत।”

वेद उनसे दूर होते हुए बोला, “अब मुझे उस शब्द का अर्थ भी नहीं समझना।”

वेद ने वेदिका को गले लगाना चाहा, पर उससे दूर होती हुई वेदिका बोली, “मैं तुमसे बदला लूँगी।” हँसते हुए वेदिका को और पास खींचकर वेद बोला, “कब? मैं रुक नहीं पाऊँगा।”

“तुम्हें क्या लग रहा है, मैं मजाक कर रही हूँ? मैं तुम्हें दीवार पर चिपकाकर, क्या करूँगी देखना! मैं ऐसा मजाक करूँगी कि मेरे सारे पुराने मजाक तुम्हें वैष्णो देवी यात्रा जितने गंभीर लगेंगे।” वेदिका बोली।

वेद हँसते हुए बोला, “ठीक है।”

वेदिका आखिर वेद के गले मिली। वेद बोला, “बहुत प्यार करता हूँ पगली तुझसे।”

“मैं भी। वो भी बहुत सारा!” कान में वेदिका फुसफुसाई।

“तुम्हें क्या लग रहा है, मैं मजाक कर रही हूँ? मैं तुम्हें दीवार पर चिपकाकर, क्या करूँगी देखना! मैं ऐसा मजाक करूँगी कि मेरे सारे पुराने मजाक तुम्हें वैष्णो देवी यात्रा जितने गंभीर लगेंगे।” वेदिका बोली। वेद हँसते हुए बोला, “ठीक है।” वेदिका आखिर वेद के गले मिली। वेद बोला, “बहुत प्यार करता हूँ पगली तुझसे।”

उसके बाद वेद ने कमरे में हरेक के पास जाकर माफी माँगी। सबसे ज्यादा नाटकीयता जाहिर है, रीशी के साथ हुई। वेद ने रीशी को टिशू दिया और कहा, “मैं कल से माफी माँग रहा हूँ।”

अकीरा और भी गुमसुम थी। इससे पहले कि कोई कुछ कहता, वेद ने सवाल किया, “मेरा एक प्रश्न है कि अगर मैंने बाइक नहीं चलाई तो बाइक बाहर कौन ले गया?”

किसी के पास जवाब नहीं था। “आप लोग ये कहना चाहते हो कि कोई घर में घुसा और बाइक चुराकर ले गया?”

“और क्या हो सकता है?” पिंकी ने कंधे उचकाते हुए कहा।

वेद ने अरुणा की तरफ देखा “इसीलिए मैं हमेशा कहता हूँ कि सी.सी.टी.वी. कैमरे

लगवा लीजिए। ऐसा होता तो कल ही पता चल जाता कि मैं बाहर गया कि नहीं। और आपके सोने के बाद कबीर और वेदिका क्या करते हैं?"

कबीर ने वेद के पैर पर एक घूँसा जड़ा, "तुम्हारी मजाक करने की हिम्मत कैसे हो रही है?"

कबीर बोलते ही पछताया। वेद ने जो खुद को सँभाल रखा था, तटस्थता के मुखौटे से वह अचानक फिसल गया और वेद के चेहरे का तूफान साफ दिखाई देने लगा। गुस्से में आए रोने का एक आँसू वेद की आँखों से टपक ही गया और घायल जानवर की तरह चिल्लाकर बोला, "वरना क्या करूँ, अपनी लाचारी दिखाऊँ और तुम सब देखो?"

अपने विचारों की धुन में वेद भी अपने कमरे की ओर चल पड़ा। वह बाथरूम में शॉवर के नीचे खड़ा था, मानो पानी के साथ कुछ धुल जाना था, जो अभी धुला नहीं था। उसे पिछले दिन जैसा ही महसूस हो रहा था। अकीरा ने सब इतना मुश्किल क्यों कर दिया? प्यार तो आसान होता है, प्यार सबको खुशियाँ देता है। जख्म नहीं देता।

उसका गुस्सा देखकर अरुणा बीच में बोल पड़ीं, "चलो! नहाकर नाश्ता करते हैं साथ में। सभी को अच्छा लगेगा।"

"हाँ!" इतना कहकर सभी अपने-अपने कमरों में चले गए।

अपने विचारों की धुन में वेद भी अपने कमरे की ओर चल पड़ा। वह बाथरूम में शॉवर के नीचे खड़ा था, मानो पानी के साथ कुछ धुल जाना था, जो अभी धुला नहीं था। उसे पिछले दिन जैसा ही महसूस हो रहा था। अकीरा ने सब इतना मुश्किल क्यों कर दिया? प्यार तो आसान होता है, प्यार सबको खुशियाँ देता है। जख्म नहीं देता।

उसने अकीरा के लिए क्या नहीं किया? बिना शर्त उसका साथ दिया और वह उसी से थक गई? वेद की आँखें आँसुओं से फिर भर गईं। उसने खुद को समझाने की कोशिश की। अब उसके आँसू किसी को नहीं दिखने चाहिए। वैसे ही पिछले कई घंटों में परिवार ने तूफान देखा था। वेद बात बिगाड़ना नहीं चाहता था। कुछ सोचकर वह नाश्ते के लिए मेज की ओर चल पड़ा।

आधा परिवार वहीं था। माहौल ठीक करने के लिए वेद ने पूछा, "इस घटना को मजाक में लेने के लिए कौन सा समय ठीक रहेगा?"

कसाई का चाकू वेद को दिखाते हुए पिंकी बोलीं, "कोई भी नहीं।"

"अरे मॉम! ऐसे कैसे?" वेद ने चिढ़ाया।

बाकी शब्द वेद के मुँह में ही रह गए, जैसे ही अकीरा कमरे में आई। उसने अभी भी कपड़े बदले नहीं थे। सिर्फ मुँह धोया था।

"गरम पराँठे।" इंद्राणी हँसी और सबको परोसने लगीं। "वैसे यह तो वही बात हो गई, कोठीवाले रोएँ और छप्परवाले सोएँ।"

वेद ने इंद्राणी को घूरकर देखा, "आप मुझे छप्परवाला कह रही हो?"

"लेकिन तुम तो उन्हीं की तरह चारपाई पर सोए थे न!"

'अजीब परिवार है!' वेद ने सोचा। 'कुछ भी बोलते रहते हैं।'

इंद्राणी बोलीं, "अब खाओ।"

"लेकिन मैं बात कर रहा हूँ।" वेद ने जवाब दिया।

"तो? तुम बात भी कर सकते हो और खा भी सकते हो।" इंद्राणी बोलीं।

वेद ने गरदन हिलाई, "नहीं, गलत बात। खाते समय नहीं बोलना।"

पिंकी अकीरा को देख रही थीं, जिसने अभी तक खाने को छुआ भी नहीं था। अपने बेटे की ओर मुसकराकर देखते हुए पिंकी पराँठे का एक टुकड़ा तोड़कर अकीरा के मुँह के सामने ले गई और बोलीं, "चलो, मैं खिलाती हूँ।" पिंकी को देखकर अकीरा आभार दिखाते हुए मुसकाई और वह कौर खा लिया। आँखों के कोने से देखा तो पिंकी ने पाया कि वेद खा रहा था, उसे उम्मीद हुई कि शायद दोनों में सब ठीक हो जाए। वेद का फोन बजा। उसने अकीरा की तरफ फोन किया और कहा, "तुम्हारे स्टाफ में से किसी का है।"

पिंकी अकीरा को देख रही थीं, जिसने अभी तक खाने को छुआ भी नहीं था। अपने बेटे की ओर मुसकराकर देखते हुए पिंकी पराँठे का एक टुकड़ा तोड़कर अकीरा के मुँह के सामने ले गई और बोलीं, "चलो, मैं खिलाती हूँ।" पिंकी को देखकर अकीरा आभार दिखाते हुए मुसकाई और वह कौर खा लिया।

अकीरा ने फोन नहीं छुआ, "तुम ही बात करो उनसे।"

"इनको सुबह-सुबह लखनवी बनना है, पहले आप-पहले आप।" वेद ने तेवर से कहा।

यह बात सुन सभी हँस पड़े। वेद ने आराम से फोन पर बात की। फोन रखते ही वेद ने बताया, "अभय कोर्ट मैरिज कर रहा है।"

वेदिका हैरानी से बोली, "इतनी जल्दी तारीख कैसे मिल गई?"

"जान-पहचान से किया होगा।" अरुणा बोलीं।

"और भी है! सजावटवाले ने और पैसे माँगे हैं, क्योंकि हमारी लड़ाई की वजह से उसका काफी नुकसान हुआ है।" वेद ने आगे बताया। "और शालिनी मामी के बावर्ची छोले ट्रक में लेकर विवाह-स्थल पहुँच चुके हैं।"

सभी हैरत में थे। "ईश्वर को मुझपर अभी भी तरस नहीं आ रहा।" वेद बोला।

"वाकई।" कबीर ने सांत्वना भरी नजरों से वेद की ओर देखते हुए कहा। वेद ने

अकीरा को देखा और फिर खुद के मन को समझाया। हालाँकि सजावटवालों से बात करने का काम उसका नहीं था, पर इनसानियत की खातिर आखिरी बार अब वह अकीरा की मदद कर रहा था। वेद कुरसी पीछे की ओर उठाकर बोला, "मैं सजावटवाले के दफ्तर जा रहा हूँ; मेरे पास मोबाइल है और मैं कार ले जा रहा हूँ। इतना सबको जानना काफी है, या मेरे शरीर का तापमान भी लेना है किसी को?"

वेदिका बोली, "दिमाग का तापमान लेने का थर्मामीटर नहीं है हमारे पास।"

सभी हँस पड़े। वेद ने कुछ नहीं कहा। बाहर जाते समय वेद चिल्लाया, "तुम सब लोग थोड़ा आराम कर लो। तब तक मैं वापस आ जाऊँगा। सब कितने बेकार दिख रहे हैं।"

अकीरा देर तक वेद का अजीब सा पीछे होनेवाला व्यवहार देखती रही। अचानक उसके दिमाग में कुछ आया और वह कमरे से बाहर भागी।

"दोनों ही कितने अजीब हैं!" कबीर ने अपनी राय जाहिर की। अरुणा ने नाक खुजाते हुए कहा, "असल में ये राम मिलाई जोड़ी, एक कमला तो दूजी होर वी कमली।"

अकीरा कुछ ही समय में वापस आई। उसने लहँगा बदलकर जींस पहन रखी थी, लेकिन लहँगे की चोली वही पहन रखी थी। उसे देखकर अरुणा हँसी और बोलीं, "देखा! कहा था न मैंने।"

वेदिका ने अकीरा के कपड़े देखकर कहा, "क्या हुआ अकीरा, दिमाग तो ठीक है न?"

"इन सब चीजों के लिए समय नहीं है, ठीक है।"

वह रीशी के कंधे पर झुककर हाथ रखते हुए बोली, "रीशी, अपनी बाइक की चाबी देना जरा।"

रीशी अपनी कुरसी पर ही पीछे होता हुआ बोला, "हाँ-हाँ, पर क्यों?"

अकीरा शैतानी हँसी हँसते हुए बोली, "मैं तुम्हारे भाई की कॉफी दुबारा छीनने वाली हूँ।"

□

49

सड़क के किनारे की पटरी पर अपने बूटों से चलती अकीरा अधीरता से वेद के कैफे से बाहर आने की राह देख रही थी। वेद हमेशा के अपने धूप के चश्मे पहने हुए था। उसकी नजरें अपने मोबाइल पर थीं। अकीरा मुसकराई। ऐसा लगा कि पहले भी हो चुका है। वे वापस वहीं थे, जहाँ से वेद और अकीरा की कहानी शुरू हुई थी। और वेद का भविष्य फिर वही होनेवाला था।

जैसे ही वह कार के पास पहुँचा, वेद ने ऊपर देखा और रुका, "क्या ?"

"क्या, क्या ?"

"तुम यहाँ क्या कर रही हो ?" वेद चिल्लाया।

"ये आजाद देश है। मैं जो चाहे कर सकती हूँ।" अकीरा बोली।

"वैसे भी तुम वही करती हो।" वेद व्यंग्य से बोला।

वेद का ताना बुरा लगा, पर वह अकड़ से बोली, "बिल्कुल ठीक !"

"फिर मुझे कुछ नहीं कहना है।" वेद अपनी कार की ओर बढ़ा।

इस बार अकीरा वेद के कॉफी कप की ओर बढ़ी। "तुम वाकई कॉफी चाहती हो ? सच में ?"

अकीरा की आवाज कोमल हुई, "पहले तुम्हें लेकर सीरियस नहीं थी, अब हूँ।"

उसकी बातें अनसुनी कर, "खबरदार ?"

अटल स्वर में अकीरा बोली, "रोक के देखो।"

ऐसा कहकर अकीरा ने वेद की कॉफी छीन ली, जैसे उस दिन के लिए अकीरा का वही काम था। वेद अपनी जगह जम गया।

"मिलते हैं।" अकीरा जल्दी से बाइक पर चढ़ी और चली गई।

"अब लुधियाना में कॉफी चोर भी आ गए हैं।" एक आदमी ने कहा।

वेद बोला, "ये तो मुंबईवाले चोर है। और सिर्फ कॉफी नहीं, काफी कुछ चुराया हुआ है पहले भी।"

"ओए सच्ची ?" आदमी सदमे में था।

"तो क्या सोच रहे हो भाई साहब? करो पीछा और ले लो वापस अपनी चीज।"

वेद ने उस आदमी को घूरा, "ठीक कहते हो।"

वह कार में बैठा और सोचने लगा कि किस तरह पूरे दिल पर अकीरा ने कब्जा कर लिया है और शायद ही वह कभी अपना दिल वापस ले सकेगा अकीरा से! पर कॉफी तो वापस लेनी है। जिंदगी में पहली बार वेद जान लगाकर लुधियाना की तंग गलियों में भी तेज कार चलाकर अकीरा तक पहुँच गया और अकीरा को रोक ही लिया। "रुक जाओ।"

अकीरा की आँखें हैरानी से बाहर आने को थीं।

वेद झेंप गया। फिर धक्क-सा रह गया उसका दिल, जिसका परिणाम अभय की पिटाई थी।

उसे याद आ रहा था कि किस तरह अकीरा की हिम्मत से वह नफरत करता था! कितना गुस्सा आया था उसे, जब उसने पहली बार वेद से उसकी कॉफी छीनी थी! फिर अकीरा उसकी ऐसी दीवानी हुई, मानो वेद ही उसकी दुनिया है; फिर प्यार का पागलपन शुरू करने को तैयार है। क्या हिम्मत है!

"मेरी कॉफी वापस करो।" गुस्से में वेद ने कहा।

अकीरा ने सहज ही कॉफी कप थोड़ा सा टेढ़ा किया तो गिलास की कॉफी गिर पड़ी।

"कैसी कॉफी, क्या कॉफी?" कहकर अकीरा बाइक को लेकर दौड़ गई।

वेद झेंप गया। फिर धक्क-सा रह गया उसका दिल, जिसका परिणाम अभय की पिटाई थी।

उसे याद आ रहा था कि किस तरह अकीरा की हिम्मत से वह नफरत करता था! कितना गुस्सा आया था उसे, जब उसने पहली बार वेद से उसकी कॉफी छीनी थी! फिर अकीरा उसकी ऐसी दीवानी हुई, मानो वेद ही उसकी दुनिया है; फिर प्यार का पागलपन शुरू करने को तैयार है। क्या हिम्मत है!

"आप अपने गंतव्य पर पहुँच चुके हैं।" इस आवाज से वेद का ध्यान टूटा। वह विवाह कार्य स्थल पर आ चुका था। वेद ने सोच रखा था कि पहले विवाह स्थल का मुआयना करके फिर सजावटवाले के कार्यालय जाएगा। हैरानी की बात यह थी कि वहाँ जो गाड़ियाँ खड़ी थीं, उनमें अकीरा की बाइक भी नजर आई। ये सोचकर कि अब क्या नया नाटक है, वेद भी अंदर गया तो क्या देखता है—पूरा परिवार अति-उत्साह से आगंतुकों (मेहमानों) का स्वागत करने हेतु पंक्तिबद्ध कर्मचारियों की तरह खड़ा था। हैरत से वेद ने पूछा, "तुम लोग यहाँ क्या कर रहे हो?"

"हाँऽऽऽऽ! मेरे बेटे का घर बसने जा रहा है, हमें तो आना ही था।" आँखें घुमाते हुए पिंकी ने कहा।

“क्याऽऽऽ?”

“वो ठीक कह रही हैं, हमें आना ही था।” पर यह आवाज अनजानी-सी थी, जो परिवार की भीड़ के बीच में से आई। वेद ने भीड़ को चीरते हुए देखा तो पाया कि अकीरा के माता-पिता आए हुए थे। वेद ने झट पैर छूने की कोशिश की तो अकीरा के पापा ने रोकना चाहा, लेकिन वेद ने पैर छू ही लिये। “वाह! आप यहाँ कैसे?”

“हाँ! अचानक! सरप्राइज!” अवंतिका ने कहा। “कैसे हो तुम?”

वेद के पास जवाब नहीं था, फिर भी खुद को सँभालते हुए कहा, “मैं ठीक हूँ। आप लोग कैसे हैं? उम्मीद करता हूँ, ठीक ही होंगे।”

“अब ठीक हैं!” अवंतिका ने वेद के गाल पर थपकी देते हुए कहा।

“आप हमें बता देते कि आप आ रहे हैं।” वेद ने शिकायती स्वर में कहा। “हम आपको लेने किसी को भेज देते।”

“इन सब बातों के लिए वक्त ही नहीं था। कल जब तुम गायब हो गए थे तो अकीरा का रोते हुए फोन आया। वह बेतहाशा रो रही थी। पता नहीं कहाँ चले गए थे तुम!”

वेद को विश्वास ही नहीं हो रहा था कि पिछले कुछ घंटों में मैंने इतने लोगों को भावात्मक तूफान दिया था। अवंतिका ने सिर हिलाते हुए कहा, “अकीरा इतनी पागल-सी हो गई थी, मानो अपना संतुलन ही खो बैठी। हमने पहली फ्लाइट पकड़ी और पहुँच गए।”

“इन सब बातों के लिए वक्त ही नहीं था। कल जब तुम गायब हो गए थे तो अकीरा का रोते हुए फोन आया। वह बेतहाशा रो रही थी। पता नहीं कहाँ चले गए थे तुम!” वेद को विश्वास ही नहीं हो रहा था कि पिछले कुछ घंटों में मैंने इतने लोगों को भावात्मक तूफान दिया था। अवंतिका ने सिर हिलाते हुए कहा, “अकीरा इतनी पागल-सी हो गई थी, मानो अपना संतुलन ही खो बैठी। हमने पहली फ्लाइट पकड़ी और पहुँच गए।”

“यंग मैन! तुमने सबको खासा डराया है!” हर्ष ने मुसकराते हुए कहा।

“आई एम सॉरी!” वेद ने झेंपते हुए कहा। वेद ने अपना सिर नीचे कर लिया। “मुझे जरा भी उम्मीद नहीं थी कि मेरा सोने चले जाना इस तरह से आपको परेशान कर देगा।”

हर्ष खुलकर हँसा और बाकी सारे भी। वेद खुश था कि इस भयावह घटना को उसके परिवारवाले हँसी में ले रहे थे।

“जिंदगी के लिए अच्छी कहानी बन गई न!” अकीरा की पीछे से आवाज आई। वह पीछे पलटकर जोर से बोला, “तुम इस तरह, जब चाहे, मेरी कॉफी नहीं छीन सकती।”

अकीरा ने शांति से पूछा, "क्यों नहीं?" अकीरा का दर्द उसकी आँखों में छलक आया था (आँसुओं के रूप में)।

"सिर्फ उन लम्हों के लिए, जो हमने साथ बिताए, मेरे लिए, तुम्हारे लिए। सिर्फ दस मिनट के लिए! मेरी बात सुन लो।"

वेद की आँखें गुस्से, दर्द, अकीरा के प्यार के लिए अधीर थीं। वह किसी पर अपना गुस्सा निकालना चाहता था। पर वह चुप रहा। कुछ क्षणों बाद विनती की आवाज में वेद बोला, "प्लीज जाने दो न! बस करो अब!"

अकीरा सिसकती हुई बोली, "मुझे माफी माँगने का मौका तो दो! फिर चाहो तो तुम मेरी जिंदगी से जा सकते हो। मैं तुम्हें नहीं रोकूँगी।"

"तुम्हारे साथ क्या कोई दिक्कत है अकीरा? एक दिन तुम मेरी शक्ल नहीं देखना चाहती; अगले दिन चाहती हो कि मैं तुम्हारी बात सुनूँ! तुमने मुझे समझा क्या है अकीरा?"

वेद ने रुखाई से कहा।

अकीरा में वेद की आँखें में देखकर बात करने की हिम्मत नहीं बची थी। "ये आखिरी बार है, जब मैं तुम्हें मेरी बात सुनने को कह रही हूँ। सिर्फ एक बार।"

जबरदस्त गुस्से में होने के बावजूद वेद ने कहा, "ठीक है।"

अकीरा ने राहत की साँस ली, "याद है, जब तुमसे मैंने पहली बार कॉफी छीनी थी? क्या बेतुकी हरकत की थी, लेकिन याद करूँ तो लगता है कि वह आजतक की सबसे खूबसूरत गलती थी।" अकीरा ने वेद की गुस्से से भरी, भावशून्य आँखों में देखते हुए बात जारी रखी, "मैं मानती हूँ कि मुझे तुमसे बहुत पहले कॉफी छीननी चाहिए थी, वरना मैं तुमसे कैसे मिलती?"

अकीरा सिसकती हुई बोली, "मुझे माफी माँगने का मौका तो दो! फिर चाहो तो तुम मेरी जिंदगी से जा सकते हो। मैं तुम्हें नहीं रोकूँगी।" "तुम्हारे साथ क्या कोई दिक्कत है अकीरा? एक दिन तुम मेरी शक्ल नहीं देखना चाहती; अगले दिन चाहती हो कि मैं तुम्हारी बात सुनूँ! तुमने मुझे समझा क्या है अकीरा?"

वेद अकीरा की बातों से हैरान था। उसने अपने माथे पर हाथ रख लिया। 'तुम' बस एक शब्द, और मानो वेद की जान-में-जान आ गई थी। "उस दिन अभय के संगीत कार्यक्रम की लड़ाई के बाद जब तुमने कहा था कि तुम परिपूर्ण मनुष्य या बॉयफ्रेंड नहीं हो, मुझे तभी तुम्हें बताना चाहिए था कि तुम ऐसे लड़के हो, जो बहुत मुश्किल से मिलते हैं। तुम्हारी जगह कोई और होता तो छोड़ चुका होता, पर तुमने मेरा साथ नहीं छोड़ा। बने रहे आखिर तक मेरे साथ और फिर भी मैंने ही गड़बड़ की।"

अकीरा की भूरी आँखों ने जब वेद की आँखें देखीं तो मानो भाव वापस-से आ रहे थे।

"लेकिन मैं अब समझ पा रही हूँ कि जब आप किसी को प्यार करते हो तो आप उसे दु:खी होते नहीं देख सकते। आप किसी और को दु:ख देने की इजाजत नहीं देते, उनका ध्यान रखते हो, बचाते हो। उनको सँभालकर रखते हो…और तुमने भी यही किया।"

वेद गुस्से में कुछ कहने ही वाला था कि अकीरा ने वेद के मुँह पर हाथ रख दिया। हैरानी की बात थी कि वेद ने विरोध भी नहीं किया। "वेद, तुम्हें समझना होगा कि तुमसे पहले मेरा जिस व्यक्ति से संबंध था, वह तुमसे बिल्कुल अलग था; उलटा था। तुम अलग हो। मुझे पता है कि महँगे डिनर (रात के खाने) थे, न कार की लंबी सैर; न बड़े-बड़े उपहार…पर मैं जब भी तुम्हारे साथ होती हूँ तो अपने में पूर्ण महसूस करती हूँ; खुद से भी जलती हूँ कि तुम्हारे जैसी क्यों नहीं हूँ? खुद को भाग्यशाली कहती हूँ।"

वेद गुस्से में कुछ कहने ही वाला था कि अकीरा ने वेद के मुँह पर हाथ रख दिया। हैरानी की बात थी कि वेद ने विरोध भी नहीं किया। "वेद, तुम्हें समझना होगा कि तुमसे पहले मेरा जिस व्यक्ति से संबंध था, वह तुमसे बिल्कुल अलग था; उलटा था। तुम अलग हो।

पीछे खड़े परिवार में किसी की हँसी सुनाई दी। वेद ने अपनी घड़ी देखकर कहा, "चार मिनट बीत चुके है।"

"चुप रहो वेद!" अविनाश ने डाँटा। "लड़की को पूरी बात तो करने दो। ये तुम्हारी हमेशा की बेवकूफी दिखाने का समय नहीं है।"

वेद जानता था कि अभी बहस करने का कोई फायदा नहीं, तो वह चुप हो गया। उसने धीरे से अपने गालों से अकीरा के हाथ हटाए। अकीरा थोड़ी सी चौंकी, "वेद! मैंने गलती की है और मैं माफी माँगना चाहती हूँ। आई एम सॉरी! मैं गुस्से में आ गई और…"

बीच में ही वेद ने टोका, "शायद तुम नहीं समझ रही हो। ये न ही गुस्से के बारे में है, न ही अपना गुस्सा निकालने के और न ही अभय के बारे में। जरा सी असुविधा होते ही किसी रिश्ते से छुटकारा पाने की कोशिश के बारे में है। मैं हमेशा इस डर में नहीं जी सकता कि थोड़ी सी लड़ाई होते ही तुम शायद मुझे छोड़कर चली जाओ।"

वेद की आँखों में और भी गुस्सा आ गया। "या तो मैं तुम्हारे लिए सबकुछ हूँ या कुछ भी नहीं।"

"तुम वाकई मेरे लिए सबकुछ हो।" अकीरा रो पड़ी। "मैं तो तुम्हारे बगैर साँस भी ठीक से नहीं ले सकती।"

अकीरा की हालत देख वेद की आँखों में आँसुओं की परत छा गई। आँखें झपकाता हुआ वह पीछे हटा। अब जितना सोचा था, संवाद उससे ज्यादा मुश्किल हो रहा था।

"तुमने कहा था—किसी भी आदत को बनने या टूटने में 21 दिन लगते हैं।"

"बधाई।" ताली बजाते हुए अकीरा बोली। "तुम मेरी आदत बन चुके हो, और यह आदत अब टूट नहीं पाएगी। मेरे लिए तुमसे ज्यादा जरूरी कुछ नहीं है। मुझे माफ कर दो। मैं बेवकूफ थी।"

वेद अकीरा पर विश्वास करना चाहता था, पर साथ ही उसे वह क्षण याद आया, जब अकीरा ने उसे भला-बुरा कहने के बाद कमरे से बाहर जाने दिया था।

"माफी माँगना आसान है, लेकिन उस माफी को जीना मुश्किल। मुझे पता है, ये शब्द मैंने पहले कभी नहीं कहे, लेकिन महसूस हमेशा किए; जब मुझे रोता देख तुम रोए; जब मोहित के समय तुमने मेरी मदद की; और जो भी बुरा समय हमने साथ झेला···मैंने हमेशा तुम्हारा प्यार महसूस किया।"

"माफी माँगना आसान है, लेकिन उस माफी को जीना मुश्किल। मुझे पता है, ये शब्द मैंने पहले कभी नहीं कहे, लेकिन महसूस हमेशा किए; जब मुझे रोता देख तुम रोए; जब मोहित के समय तुमने मेरी मदद की; और जो भी बुरा समय हमने साथ झेला...मैंने हमेशा तुम्हारा प्यार महसूस किया।"

इस बार अकीरा ने वेद का चेहरा अपने हाथ में लिया, मानो अधिकार हो उसका वेद पर।

"मैं तुमसे प्यार करती हूँ वेद! बहुत प्यार करती हूँ और विश्वास दिलाती हूँ कि तब तक प्रेम करूँगी, जब तक जान-में-जान है।"

वेद की आँखों के आँसू अकीरा की हथेली पर टपक गए। अकीरा ने वेद की आँखें पोंछीं।

"मैंने गलतियाँ की हैं, आगे भी करती रहूँगी, बस तुम्हें जाने देने की गलती नहीं करूँगी।"

"प्लीज···" उसे खुद भी नहीं मालूम था कि वह अकीरा से किस बात के लिए विनती कर रहा है। वह अकीरा की बातों से इतना भावुक हो गया था कि उसका संकल्प ढीला पड़ रहा था।

"याद है, जब मैंने तुमसे एक बार पूछा था कि तुम किसी भी करीबी रिश्ते से क्या-क्या उम्मीद रखते हो तो तुमने एक लंबी सूची सुना दी थी। याद है ? हम वेदिका की कार में थे।" वेद की नाक पर अपनी नाक रगड़कर अकीरा बोली।

वेद ने हामी भरी। "मैं तुम्हारे साथ वो सबकुछ करना चाहती हूँ, सिवाय टैक्स भरने या उससे संबंधित कुछ भी। सच तो यह है कि वो सबकुछ मैं नहीं कर सकती।"

सभी हँस पड़े। वेद थोड़ा सा ठंडा होकर मुसकराया। अकीरा को थोड़ा सा धीरज

आया। पूरा खुश नहीं था वेद, पर शुरुआत कही जा सकती थी।

"बात यह है कि मैं तुम्हारे साथ रहना चाहती हूँ; तुम्हारे साथ जीवन जीना चाहती हूँ···तुम्हारे परिवार का साथ चाहती हूँ।"

प्यारी सी मुसकराहट के साथ अकीरा ने आसपास देखा। उसके दिमाग में कुछ नहीं था कि उसे वो लोग पसंद हैं या नहीं। परिवार की ओर देखते हुए वेद ने अकीरा को चिढ़ाते हुए कहा, "पक्का न?"

हँसते हुए बोली, "यह परिवार मेरा है और मैं भी उनसे उतना ही प्यार करती हूँ और करूँगी, जितना कि तुम करते हो।"

"हम तुम्हें भैया से ज्यादा प्यार करते हैं।" वेदिका चहकी। वेद ने आँखें ऊपर की ओर घुमाईं, जिससे अकीरा का संकल्प और भी दृढ़ हो गया। "एक मौका दे दो वेद! मुझे माफ कर दो। शायद तुम्हें ज्यादा लगे, लेकिन मेरे पास जो कुछ है, उन सभी भावों की कसम खाकर कहती हूँ कि मैं तुमसे प्रेम करती हूँ।"

"हम तुम्हें भैया से ज्यादा प्यार करते हैं।" वेदिका चहकी। वेद ने आँखें ऊपर की ओर घुमाईं, जिससे अकीरा का संकल्प और भी दृढ़ हो गया। "एक मौका दे दो वेद! मुझे माफ कर दो। शायद तुम्हें ज्यादा लगे, लेकिन मेरे पास जो कुछ है, उन सभी भावों की कसम खाकर कहती हूँ कि मैं तुमसे प्रेम करती हूँ।"

वेद को समझ नहीं आ रहा था कि वह क्या करे? उसने अपने चेहरे को अपने हाथों में छुपा लिया।

उसे अपेक्षित नहीं था, पर अकीरा ने कहा, "नॉक-नॉक (खटखटाने की आवाज)! कोई है?"

कितना अजीब लगा वेद को, जब उसने देखा कि अकीरा घुटनों के बल उसके सामने बैठी थी। "तुम क्या कर रही हो?" वेद मानो अपना आपा खो-सा रहा था। अकीरा ने वेद की हैरानी और प्रतिक्रिया पर ध्यान न देते हुए कहा, "नॉक-नॉक"

वेद ने हार मान ली और पूछा, "कौन है?"

अकीरा का चेहरा खिल-सा गया। बड़ी सी मुसकान से बोली, "लड्डू!"

वेद दुविधा में था, "लड्डू? कौन लड्डू?" अकीरा की मुसकान शरारत में बदल गई और वेद की साँस कुछ सोचकर रुक गई। जब अकीरा ने अपना हाथ आगे किया, तब वेद को पता चला कि उसके हाथ में मोतीचूर का लड्डू था। अकीरा बोली, "शादी का लड्डू!"

"हे भगवान्!" खुशी के मारे पिंकी रुक नहीं पाई।

"क्या?" वेद ने अपनी माँ की ओर देखा।

"वेद अरोरा! क्या आप मेरे साथ..." अकीरा ने यह कहकर वेद का ध्यान अपनी ओर खींचा।

वेद के पास शब्द ही नहीं थे। उसने अपने परिवार की ओर देखा। उस सभी की आँखों में इतनी उम्मीदें थीं कि वह भाव-विह्वल होकर रो पड़े।

उसे भी अकीरा से प्रेम था, उसमें कोई शक नहीं। वो बस इतना ही कह सकता था। पर क्या वे एक-दूसरे के लिए ठीक हैं? यह सवाल वेद के मन में क्यों चल रहा था। उसने अकीरा की ओर देखा। अकीरा उसे इतने प्रेम, उम्मीद और अपनत्व से देख रही थी कि वेद का दिल पसीज गया। अपने माता-पिता के सामने अकीरा का ऐसे घुटनों के बल बैठना छोटी बात नहीं थी। अगर वो इतना कर सकती है तो मैं भी तो पिछला भूलकर आगे बढ़ सकता हूँ! अकीरा जैसी लड़की के लिए यह खतरा मोल लिया जा सकता है।

उसे भी अकीरा से प्रेम था, उसमें कोई शक नहीं। वो बस इतना ही कह सकता था। पर क्या वे एक-दूसरे के लिए ठीक हैं? यह सवाल वेद के मन में क्यों चल रहा था। उसने अकीरा की ओर देखा। अकीरा उसे इतने प्रेम, उम्मीद और अपनत्व से देख रही थी कि वेद का दिल पसीज गया।

"मैं अभी भी घुटनों पर हूँ वेद...भीख माँग रही हूँ, नॉक-नॉक कह रही हूँ, बेहूदा चुटकुले सुना रही हूँ और बेवकूफ भी दिख रही हूँ... सबकुछ तुम्हारे लिए! हाँ तो कह दो।"

"हाँ वेद! हाँ कह दो!" कबीर ने हिम्मत दिलाई।

"हाँ! वरना तुम्हारा अतीत का दुःख-दर्द का इतना बोझ रहेगा कि हमें उस बोझ के भी पैसे हवाई अड्डे पर देने पड़ेंगे, जो हमारे पास नहीं हैं।"

अरुणा ने वेदिका के मुँह पर हाथ रखा। "सॉरी! हमने गलती से इसको खुला छोड़ दिया है।"

सिर हिलाते हुए वेद की आँखें अकीरा पर टिकीं। उनमें प्यार, दृढ़ता और अपनापन था। आखिरकार हलकी सी धमकी की आवाज में वेद बोला, "सोच लो अकीरा! अगर मैं हाँ कहता हूँ तो वो हमेशा के लिए हाँ होगी। फिर बाद में कुछ नहीं बदलेगा।"

"सोच लिया है। आज तक जीवन में मैं इतनी पक्की किसी बात के लिए कभी नहीं हुई।"

"खैर!" साँस छोड़ते हुए वेद बोला। एक मुसकान वेद के चेहरे पर आ गई, जिससे सबकुछ खिल गया। उसका चेहरा; अकीरा का चेहरा! उनकी जिंदगी! उसके बाद जो कुछ हुआ, उससे अकीरा की आँखों में खुशी की धुंध छा गई। वेद भी घुटनों पर बैठ गया, "मैं अधिकतर लड्डुओं के लिए मना नहीं करता, वह थोड़ा झुका और थोड़ा

सा लड्डू खाया। उसकी आँखों में खुशी थी।

"हाँ!" दोनों के लिए समय रुक-सा गया। उन दोनों के परिवार हर्ष से खुशियाँ मना रहे थे, लेकिन दोनों के दिमाग में कोई आवाज नहीं जा रही थी, सिवाय इसके कि उन दोनों ने एक-दूसरे को पा लिया था।

"येऽऽऽ, शुक्रिया भगवान्।"

यह कहकर उसने खुद को वेद की बाजुओं में डाल दिया। इस तरह कि वेद पीठ के बल जा गिरा। अकीरा के बाल वेद के चेहरे पर थे। वेद सिर्फ एक बड़ी सी मुसकान देख पाया और फुसफुसाहट सुनी—"थैंक यू (शुक्रिया)!"

वेद ने अकीरा को समेट लिया और अकीरा ने वेद की गरदन में अपना सिर छुपाकर कहा, "आई लव यू!"

वेद के खुशी के मारे रोंगटे खड़े हो गए कि अकीरा अब उसकी है। अकीरा वे तीन शब्द उसे जिंदगी भर कहेगी। उसका दिल खुशी के गीत गा रहा था। वेद ने कहा, "हे अजीब और मूर्ख लड़की! आई लव यू टू!" अकीरा के बाल चूमते हुए वेद बोला।

वेद ने अकीरा को समेट लिया और अकीरा ने वेद की गरदन में अपना सिर छुपाकर कहा, "आई लव यू!"

वेद के खुशी के मारे रोंगटे खड़े हो गए कि अकीरा अब उसकी है। अकीरा वे तीन शब्द उसे जिंदगी भर कहेगी। उसका दिल खुशी के गीत गा रहा था। वेद ने कहा, "हे अजीब और मूर्ख लड़की! आई लव यू टू!" अकीरा के बाल चूमते हुए वेद बोला।

वे एक-दूसरे के बाजुओं में जमीन पर पड़े थे कि अकीरा की हँसी सुनाई दी। वे एक-दूसरे के साथ खुशी से झूम रहे थे; हँस रहे थे और पिछले दो दिन की कड़वाहट धुल-सी गई थी। अकीरा का दिल ईश्वर के प्रति आभार में डूबा हुआ था कि उसे वेद जैसा साथी मिला और जीवन में अच्छा मोड़ आया।

वेद को भी अच्छा लग रहा था कि अकीरा उसे मिल गई। अभी तक का सबसे अच्छा उपहार था। उसका भी जीवन बदल गया था।

"गॉश।" रीशी ने उनको अलग किया। वह इतना खुश था कि वेद पर टूट पड़ा और अकीरा और वेद, दोनों ही हँस पड़े। उसने अकीरा का हाथ पकड़कर कहा, "मैं तुम्हें अभी भी भाभी बुला सकता हूँ।"

अगली वेदिका थी। उसने वेद और अकीरा को पास जाकर कस लिया और उनके माता-पिता ने भी। खुशी, मुसकान और ठहाकों के आँसू दिखाई पड़ रहे थे। वेद और अकीरा ने झुककर अरुणा और इंद्राणी के पैर छुए। अरुणा की आँखों से आँसू बह रहे

थे। "भगवान् तुम दोनों मूर्खों को खुश रखे।"

"ऐऽऽऽ अकीरा! कितने प्यार से तुमने शादी का प्रस्ताव रखा। मजा आ गया।" कहते हुए वेदिका ने अकीरा को गले लगाया। "अगर मैं यह वीडियो इंटरनेट पर डालूँ तो लोगों को क्या मसाला मिलेगा! बाथरूम में लड़नेवाले दो लोग···अब विवाह प्रस्ताव! वाह! क्या बात!"

वेद ने धमकाया, "वेदिका! तुमने अगर ऐसा किया तो मैं तुम्हारे हाथ तोड़ दूँगा।"

मुर्गियों की तरह भाई-बहन को लड़ता देख अकीरा हँसी। उसने खुद को विश्वास दिलाने के लिए वेद का हाथ पकड़ा कि वह सपना तो नहीं देख रही। वेद ने अकीरा को देखा और कहा, "हँसो मत! क्या भयानक तरीका था विवाह प्रस्ताव देने का!"

वेद ने धमकाया, "वेदिका! तुमने अगर ऐसा किया तो मैं तुम्हारे हाथ तोड़ दूँगा।" मुर्गियों की तरह भाई-बहन को लड़ता देख अकीरा हँसी। उसने खुद को विश्वास दिलाने के लिए वेद का हाथ पकड़ा कि वह सपना तो नहीं देख रही। वेद ने अकीरा को देखा और कहा, "हँसो मत! क्या भयानक तरीका था विवाह प्रस्ताव देने का!"

"क्याऽऽऽ? क्यों?" अकीरा ने नाक टेढ़ी करते हुए कहा।

"लड्डू के साथ कौन शादी का प्रस्ताव रखता है? सभी कुछ अजीब है तुम्हारा। सिर्फ सजावट अच्छी है।"

अकीरा ने चेतावनी भरी निगाहों से वेद को देखा और वेद की आँखें कोने से छोटी हुईं। यही अकीरा चाहती थी। अकीरा को लगा कि हाँ, अब वह साँस ले सकती है, खुश हो सकती है। तभी कबीर बोला, "बिल्कुल ठीक, सजावट बेहद खूबसूरत है। शर्म की बात है कि यहाँ अभय की शादी नहीं हो रही। कोई बात नहीं। मैं इसका उपयोग अच्छे से कर सकता हूँ।"

वेद ने सिर मोड़ के पूछा, "बार खुला है क्या अभी भी?"

उसकी बात पर ध्यान न देकर वेदिका के सामने खड़े होकर कबीर बोला, "चलो, अकीरा की मदद करते हैं।"

सभी हैरान और परेशान थे, "क्या मतलब?"

"पुत्तर! अगर तुझे नहीं समझ आया तो हमें कैसे आएगा?"

"पॉइंट! सही कहा।" वेदिका बोली।

"हो गया?" सबको चिढ़ाता हुआ कबीर घुटनों के बल बैठ गया।

सबकी खुशी का कारण बनते हुए कबीर ने एक सुंदर सी डिबिया जेब से निकाली और बोला, "हमने कितना कुछ एक-दूसरे के साथ बाँटा है। अब एक ही चीज बचती

है। वेदिका अरोरा क्या मुझसे शादी करके तुम मेरा मान बढ़ा सकती हो?"

वेदिका की आँखें हैरानी से बाहर आने को थीं, "सच में? तुम सच कह रहे हो क्या?"

"ये बहुत पहले हो जाना चाहिए था, नहीं?" कबीर प्रेम भरे स्वर में बोले जा रहा था।

वेदिका बहुत देर तक रुक नहीं पाई। कान के पीछे बाल सरकाते हुए, शरमाते हुए बोली, "हाँ, मैं तैयार हूँ।" यह कहते हुए अपना हाथ अँगूठी पहनने को आगे कर दिया।

परिवार के सभी सदस्य जोर की आवाज में दुबारा चहक उठे। अकीरा की आँखें खुशी से भर गईं। आवाजें खुशी के मारे मानो बहरा कर देंगी, ऐसा लग रहा था।

कल सभी कितने दुःख में थे, मानो उभर ही नहीं पाएँगे और आज इतनी खुशी कि खुद की आवाज भी ठीक से सुनाई नहीं दे रही थी। वेद ने कबीर को गले से लगाते हुए और वेदिका की ओर आँखों से इशारा करते हुए कहा, "बधाई हो मेरे प्यारे दोस्त! इसे मेरे घर से ले जाने के लिए तुमने जो महान् कुरबानी दी है, उसके लिए मैं तुम्हारा शुक्रगुजार हूँ।"

कल सभी कितने दुःख में थे, मानो उभर ही नहीं पाएँगे और आज इतनी खुशी कि खुद की आवाज भी ठीक से सुनाई नहीं दे रही थी। वेद ने कबीर को गले से लगाते हुए और वेदिका की ओर आँखों से इशारा करते हुए कहा, "बधाई हो मेरे प्यारे दोस्त! इसे मेरे घर से ले जाने के लिए तुमने जो महान् कुरबानी दी है, उसके लिए मैं तुम्हारा शुक्रगुजार हूँ।"

वेदिका ने वेद के बाजू पर मुक्का मारते हुए कहा, "सुन लिया मैंने।"

हँसते हुए वेदिका का माथा चूमते हुए वेद बोला, "मैं तुम्हारे लिए बहुत खुश हूँ।"

"बस। एक विनती है।" पिंकी बोलीं।

"हमें थोड़ा समय दो। उभरने के लिए।"

"सही।" वेद ने भी माना। "सबको बहुत सी बातें पचानी हैं। खासकर वेदिका की।"

"बस, बारात में घोड़ी मत माँगना।" प्रमोद मामा की यह बात सुन सभी हँस पड़े।

"मैं तो कार से ही आऊँगा।" कबीर बोला।

"मैं कितना खुश हूँ आज! रीशी दोनों दंपतीयों को पास में लेकर बोला। "कितने अच्छे हो तुम! उफ्फ! मेरे तो खुशी के आँसू नहीं रुक रहे।"

रीशी को टिशू देते हुए वेदिका की ओर गुस्से से देखते हुए कहा, "हाँ, कुछ तो अच्छे हैं ही।"

वेदिका अभी कुछ कहने जा ही रही थी कि शालिनी के कर्मचारी ने कहा, "मैडम, शुरू करें? तल दें क्या भटूरे?"

शालिनी चिल्लाई, "उफ्फ! ठंड रख यार! मैं आती हूँ।"

जैसे ही खाने की बात हुई, अविनाश का पेट मानो चिल्लाया, "पता है, हमें वे भटूरे खा ही लेने चाहिए।"

"हाँ! शादी-शादी करके तो जान ले गए हमारी।" पिंकी शालिनी के पीछे चल पड़ी। अवंतिका भी शिकायती स्वर में बोली, "मेरी सोचो! अकीरा तो तब से इस काम में लगी है, जब वह मोहित से पीछा छुड़ा रही थी।"

अकीरा हँसी, लेकिन जल्द ही उसकी हँसी खत्म हुई और जैसे ही उनकी आँखें मिलीं, शांति छा गई। अकीरा ने वेद के सीने पर अपना सिर रखा और माफी माँगते हुए बोली, "आई एम सॉरी वेद!"

अपनी उँगलियों से अकीरा के बाल ठीक करते हुए वेद ने भी माफी माँगी, "आई एम सॉरी टूऽऽऽ। मुझे अभय को ऐसे पीटना नहीं चाहिए था।"

वेद और अकीरा दोनों ने मुँह बनाया। उनका परिवार किसी बात के लिए कभी नहीं छोड़ेगा। लेकिन आखिर में कम-से-कम वे दोनों एक-दूसरे को मिल गए थे। एक-दूसरे से बात करने को तरसे वेद और अकीरा चुपचाप एक कोने में गए।

एक सजे हुए पेड़ के नीचे रखे सोफे पर दोनों आराम से बैठे। पहली बार वे एक-दूसरे के प्रेम की गरमाहट के साथ इतनी देर साथ में बैठे। वेद बोला, "वाकई! भाषण था, क्या बात थी! पूरी नाटकीयता थी। मानता हूँ तुमको!"

अकीरा हँसी, लेकिन जल्द ही उसकी हँसी खत्म हुई और जैसे ही उनकी आँखें मिलीं, शांति छा गई। अकीरा ने वेद के सीने पर अपना सिर रखा और माफी माँगते हुए बोली, "आई एम सॉरी वेद!"

अपनी उँगलियों से अकीरा के बाल ठीक करते हुए वेद ने भी माफी माँगी, "आई एम सॉरी टूऽऽऽ। मुझे अभय को ऐसे पीटना नहीं चाहिए था।"

प्यारी सी मुसकान से अकीरा बोली, "कुछ घूँसे तो उसे पड़ने ही चाहिए थे।"

वेद हँसा और प्यार से वेद की नाक झकझोरते हुए बोली, "बहुत प्यारे हो तुम।"

अकीरा बहुत देर तक वेद की आँखों में देखती रही। उन आँखों की रुखाई की बर्फ अब पिघल चुकी थी। उनमें प्रेम, सौहार्द और कोमलता की चमक साफ दिखाई दे रही थी, जो अकीरा देखना चाहती थी।

"तुम ठीक कह रहे थे वेद! स्वाभिमान से बढ़कर कुछ नहीं है जीवन में।" अकीरा धीरे से बोली।

"मैं मोहित के समय भी यह बात भूल गई थी और अभी भी। पर मैं यह बात सीखूँगी, वादा करती हूँ। और अगर मैं यह बात भूल गई तो मुझे दुबारा याद दिलाना।"

बड़ी मुश्किल से अकीरा वेद के चेहरे से अपनी नजरें हटा पाई। उसने देखा कि उनके परिवार कितनी खुशी से जश्न मना रहे हैं। "हाँ, सही कहा था तुमने। हम राह निकाल लेंगे। वेदिका और कबीर का शुक्रिया।"

अकीरा और वेद चुपचाप सभी को देख रहे थे। आधे सदस्य, जो अविनाश के साथ थे, छोले-भटूरों का मजा ले रहे थे। बाकी खुशी में नाच रहे थे और तसवीरें खींच रहे थे। जाहिर है, वे सब रीशी के साथ थे। कबीर और वेदिका को देख वेद ने कहा, "कितने महान् मूर्ख हैं, पर एक-दूजे के लिए बने हैं।"

"हाँ! सही में! नजर न लगे।" अकीरा ने हामी भरी।

अभय को गाली देते हुए वेद बोला, "उस कमीने ने भाई को कभी महत्त्व नहीं दिया।" अकीरा जोर से हँसी। वेद के मन का गुस्सा फूट पड़ा था। अभी भी हृदय में क्रोध धधक रहा था। वेद उसे हमेशा ऐसे ही हँसते हुए देखना चाहता था। उसने मन में प्रार्थना की कि अकीरा हमेशा ऐसे ही रहे। स्वार्थी हो गया था वेद, लेकिन वह जानता था कि अगर अकीरा खुश रहेगी तो ही वेद खुश रह पाएगा।

"हाँ! सही में! नजर न लगे।" अकीरा ने हामी भरी। अभय को गाली देते हुए वेद बोला, "उस कमीने ने भाई को कभी महत्त्व नहीं दिया।" अकीरा जोर से हँसी। वेद के मन का गुस्सा फूट पड़ा था। अभी भी हृदय में क्रोध धधक रहा था। वेद उसे हमेशा ऐसे ही हँसते हुए देखना चाहता था। उसने मन में प्रार्थना की कि अकीरा हमेशा ऐसे ही रहे। स्वार्थी हो गया था वेद, लेकिन वह जानता था कि अगर अकीरा खुश रहेगी तो ही वेद खुश रह पाएगा।

वेद के गंभीर भाव देख अकीरा की हँसी थम गई। वेद का चेहरा फिर गुस्से से तमतमा रहा था। "ऐसा दुबारा कभी मत करना।"

"मैंने तुम्हें पहले भी कहा था...मुझसे लड़ लेना, चिल्ला लेना, लेकिन छोड़कर मत जाना।"

अकीरा ने वेद के सिर-से-सिर जोड़कर कहा, "अब मैं कहीं नहीं जा रही, हमेशा यहीं रहूँगी।"

"हाँ। कहीं अगर टॉम क्रूज आ गया तो बात और है।" वेद की खिंचाई करती हुई अकीरा बोली। वेद के होंठों से होंठ मिलाए अकीरा ने।

"जानते हो नानी ने मुझसे क्या कहा? जब तुम्हें कोई खास मिले तो उसे जाने मत देना। और मैं अरुणा आहलूवालिया के सिद्धांतों पर प्रश्नचिह्न लगानेवाली कौन होती

हूँ?" वेद ने अकीरा को अपनी ओर खींचा। अकीरा आधी वेद की गोदी में थी। उसने वेद के गले में हाथ डालते हुए कहा, "अब मैंने तुम्हें कसकर पकड़ लिया है।"

"पकड़ लो। लेकिन हमें कुछ मूलभूत नियम बनाने होंगे हमारे बीच। ठीक है?"

"ठीक है।" अकीरा बोली।

"पहला! तुम कभी भी मेरी कॉफी नहीं छीनोगी। पूरी जिंदगी में कभी नहीं।"

अकीरा ने वेद का कान चूमते हुए कहा, "मान लिया, कभी नहीं छीनूँगी।"

हँसते हुए वेद ने अकीरा का गाल चूमा। फिर दूसरा गाल। "जब मैं अपने परिवार के बारे में तुम्हें कुछ बताऊँ तो मान जाओगी।"

अकीरा ने वेद को ठीक करते हुए बोला, "हमारा परिवार।"

अकीरा ने वेद का कान चूमते हुए कहा, "मान लिया, कभी नहीं छीनूँगी।" हँसते हुए वेद ने अकीरा का गाल चूमा। फिर दूसरा गाल। "जब मैं अपने परिवार के बारे में तुम्हें कुछ बताऊँ तो मान जाओगी।" अकीरा ने वेद को ठीक करते हुए बोला, "हमारा परिवार।"

और अचानक सारी हँसी छोड़कर गंभीर होते हुए गुस्से भरी आवाज में वेद बोला, "और तुम्हारे लिए मेरे प्यार पर कभी और कभी भी सवाल मत करना।"

अकीरा के मन में अपने किए का पछतावा फिर उभरा और उसने ग्लानि भरी नजरों से वेद को देखा।

"अकीरा! जो मैं तुम्हारे लिए महसूस करता हूँ, वह क्षणिक नहीं है।" वेद की आवाज में संकल्प था, सच्चाई थी। "वो केवल आकर्षण नहीं था, जिसके तहत मैंने सबकुछ किया। वाकई मैंने शिद्दत से तुमसे प्रेम किया। मेरे लिए यह जिंदगी भर का संकल्प है। मुझे नहीं पता कि भविष्य ने हमारे लिए क्या रखा है, लेकिन जब तक हूँ, मैं शारीरिक, मानसिक और भावात्मक रूप में जहाँ तक होगा, तुमसे प्रेम करूँगा। तो···करने दो न मुझे। छोटे-छोटे मसलों को हमारी खुशी और शांति क्यों छीनने देती हो? हम जीवन में अच्छा पा सकते हैं और खुश रहने का अधिकार है हमारा।"

"मैं अब तुम्हारी हूँ।" कहते हुए अकीरा का गला रुँध गया। ऐसा कहते हुए दोनों प्रेम में डूब गए। होंठ और भाव एक-दूसरे का साथ दे रहे थे। इसी क्षण की मानो दोनों को कब से तलाश थी! सबकुछ कितना अच्छा था, खुशी से भरपूर!

"एक परी कथा-सा लग रहा है सब, जो पुस्तकों में पढ़ते हैं। मुझे तो विश्वास ही नहीं हो रहा कि हमने तूफान का सामना किया और जी गए। क्या सफर रहा···वाह!" वेद के पास आकर अकीरा बोली।

वेद ने बात स्वीकार की, "बस एक फर्क है! हमारी बहुचर्चित पुस्तक है।"

"बिल्कुल।" अकीरा जोर से हँसी। "पर अब क्या?"

"मेरा खयाल है, नहाने से शुरुआत कर सकती हो तुम।" मजाक करते हुए लेकिन गंभीर मुद्रा में वेद ने कहा।

प्यार से वेद की बाजू में मुक्का मारते हुए अकीरा बोली, "चुप!"

"मैं मजाक नहीं कर रहा। और ये क्या कपड़े हुए। अगर तुम्हारे पास लहँगा बदलने का समय था तो जींस के ऊपर कुछ और भी पहन सकती थी। कितनी भयानक है ये वेशभूषा।" वेद ने हँसते हुए कहा।

"लेकिन...।" इससे आगे अकीरा कुछ कहती, तभी पिंकी चिल्लाईं।

"वेद, अकीरा! इससे पहले कि भटूरे खत्म हो जाएँ, आकर खा लो।" पिंकी ने इशारा करके बुलाया।

वेद मुसकराया। ऐसा कोई समय नहीं होगा, जब उसका परिवार उन्हें बीच में आकर परेशान नहीं करेगा। पर उसे वह बुरा नहीं लगता था, जब तक उसकी पसंद उसके साथ थी।

वेद ने अकीरा को देखा और तुरंत समझ गया कि अकीरा के दिमाग में भी यही बात चल रही है। मन में खुद से वादा करके कि एक-दूसरे से प्रेम करेंगे। एक-दूसरे को प्यार करने को वे झुके। वेद ने अकीरा का हाथ पकड़ा और कोहनी मारते हुए कहा, "चलो।"

वेद ने अकीरा को देखा और तुरंत समझ गया कि अकीरा के दिमाग में भी यही बात चल रही है। मन में खुद से वादा करके कि एक-दूसरे से प्रेम करेंगे। एक-दूसरे को प्यार करने को वे झुके। वेद ने अकीरा का हाथ पकड़ा और कोहनी मारते हुए कहा, "चलो।"

अकीरा मुसकराकर बोली, "चलो।"

एक-दूसरे का हाथ पकड़कर दोनों उत्सव मनाते हुए अपने परिवार की ओर चल पड़े और अपने भविष्य की ओर, जहाँ जीवन भर का प्यार, खुशियाँ और हँसी उनका इंतजार कर रही थीं।

□

उपसंहार

वेद अचानक घबराकर उठा। अकीरा ने हैरानी से पढ़ती हुई पुस्तक से मुँह उठाकर देखा। उसने मन में सोचा, 'कुछ चीजें बिल्कुल नहीं बदलतीं।' वे दोनों मेलबर्न के हवाई अड्डे पर बैठे थे। अकीरा वेद के साथ ऑस्ट्रेलिया व्यवसाय के सिलसिले में गई थी।

असल में यह पहली बार हुआ था कि दोनों को एक-दूसरे के साथ एकांत में समय मिला था। अपने परिवारों से दूर वे एक-दूसरे को और जानने का प्रयास कर रहे थे। लुधियानावाली घटना एक बुरे सपने की तरह थी। उन्होंने कहीं से सुना कि अभय और तान्या की शादी में मुश्किलें चल रही हैं, पर उससे इनकी जिंदगी में कोई फर्क क्यों होता? वह खुश थी कि वेद और उसके संबंध दिन-ब-दिन अच्छे हो रहे थे। पर बुरे दिनों की तरह साथ में अकेले रहने के दिन भी खत्म हो चले थे और वे अपने घर वापस जा रहे थे।

अकीरा ने वेद को देखकर पूछा, "अब क्या हुआ?"

"उफ्फ! मैंने देखा, तुम एक बहुत बड़े से लड्डू पर बैठी हो और पूरे शहर में मेरा पीछा कर रही हो।" अकीरा के कंधे पर अपना सिर रखते हुए वेद ने कहा।

धीरे से अकीरा ने वेद के सिर पर पुस्तक मारते हुए कहा, "चुप रहो, कुछ भी।"

"और इसे दीवार स्वप्न कहते हैं, दुःस्वप्न नहीं। समझे! सोचो, मुझ जैसी खूबसूरत लड़की तुम्हारा पीछा कर रही हो! धन्यवाद कहो मुझे।"

वेद ने प्यार से अकीरा को पास में लिया, "हाँ, तुम्हें पाने के लिए मैं ईश्वर का आभारी तो हूँ। सही कहा।"

अकीरा के चेहरे पर भी आभार के ही भाव थे। अभी तक जितने भी महीने वह वेद के साथ थी, वे खुशियों से भरे थे। जब भी वह वेद को देखती तो उससे कॉफी छीनने के अपने निर्णय पर गर्व महसूस करती। पूरी जिंदगी वेद के साथ बितानी है, यह खयाल

उसके हृदय को हमेशा शांति देता। और उसे विश्वास था कि वेद भी ऐसा ही महसूस करता है। लेकिन भाग्य कहो या दुर्भाग्य, उनके आसपास कई ऐसे लोग थे, जो उनके जीवन की शांति भंग करते थे। और यही सोचते हुए अकीरा ने वेद को बताया, "वैसे जब तुम सो रहे थे, तो खतरनाक लोगों की जगह पर कुछ नया हुआ है।"

अकीरा जानती थी कि यह सुनकर वेद और परेशान और पागल हो जाएगा। वेद के माथे पर सिलवटें आईं, "अब क्या हुआ ?" अकीरा ने मुसकराकर मोबाइल की ओर इशारा करते हुए कहा, "अपना फोन देखो न!"

उसका उत्तर सुनकर वेद ने फोन उठाया। उसने देखा कि रीशी के लगभग 24 मिस्ड कॉल्स थे। वेद गुस्से से बोला, "अब ये बेवकूफ मुझे कॉल क्यों कर रहा है ?"

"खुशखबरी सुनाने के लिए, जो वह कबीर और वेदिका को पहले की सुना चुका है।"

"क्या ?"

"...कि वह भी कबीर और वेदिका के रास्ते पर चल पड़ा है।" हँसी छुपाते हुए अकीरा बोली, वेद को अभी भी बात समझ नहीं आई और उसने पूछा, "वह भी कबीर की तरह सोने में पैसा लगाएगा ?"

वेद की नाक दबाते हुए अकीरा बोली, "तुम जब भी सोकर उठते हो तो हमेशा ही मूर्खों जैसे होते हो!"

"ओ. के. सॉरी।" वेद हँसा। उसने अकीरा के हाथ में हाथ दिया और अपने सीने के पास ले गया। "पर मुझे सच में समझ नहीं आया कि तुम किस बारे में बात कर रही हो ?"

"...कि वह भी कबीर और वेदिका के रास्ते पर चल पड़ा है।" हँसी छुपाते हुए अकीरा बोली, वेद को अभी भी बात समझ नहीं आई और उसने पूछा, "वह भी कबीर की तरह सोने में पैसा लगाएगा ?" वेद की नाक दबाते हुए अकीरा बोली, "तुम जब भी सोकर उठते हो तो हमेशा ही मूर्खों जैसे होते हो!" "ओ. के. सॉरी।" वेद हँसा। उसने अकीरा के हाथ में हाथ दिया और अपने सीने के पास ले गया। "पर मुझे सच में समझ नहीं आया कि तुम किस बारे में बात कर रही हो ?"

"रीशी ने अपनी गर्लफ्रेंड को शादी का प्रस्ताव दिया है और उसने मान भी लिया है। रीशी भी अब शादी का लड्डू खाने की योजना बना रहा है, वेदिका और कबीर की तरह..."

फिर वह जरा रुकी। वेद सुन रहा था कि अकीरा आगे कुछ बताएगी, उसका इंतजार कर रहा था। खैर, वेद के चेहरे का रंग पीला पड़ गया, जब उसने अकीरा की आँखों में शैतानी का भाव देखा।

अपनी ओर इशारा करते हुए अकीरा बोली, "और सोचो, उसने शादी का पूरा प्रबंध किसे करने को कहा है ?"

"फिटे मुँह !" अकीरा की उलझन समझते हुए वेद बोला। वेद के पेट में मरोड़ उठी और आँखें बंद करके वह अकीरा की बाजुओं में गिर पड़ा। वेद के कानों में अकीरा के ठहाके की हँसी गूँज रही थी।